THE PAUL A. BARAN — PAUL M. SWEEZY MEMORIAL AWARD

The Age of Monopoly Capital is the second winner of the Paul A. Baran–Paul M. Sweezy Memorial Award, following *Imperialism in the Twenty-First Century*, by John Smith. This award, established in 2014, honors the contributions of the founders of the *Monthly Review* tradition: Paul M. Sweezy, Paul A. Baran, and Harry Magdoff. It supports the publication in English of distinguished monographs focused on the political economy of imperialism. The aim is to make available in English important work written in the tradition of Paul M. Sweezy, Paul A. Baran, and Harry Magdoff, broadly conceived. It will also apply to writings previously unpublished in English, and will include translations of new work first published in languages other than English.

Paul M. Sweezy co-founded *Monthly Review* in 1949, and, with Paul A. Baran, developed the fundamental analysis of accumulation under monopoly capitalism. Baran's *The Political Economy of Growth*, published in 1957, set the template for understanding imperialism in the latter part of the twentieth century—an argument that was to be further developed in Baran and Sweezy's *Monopoly Capital* (1966). Harry Magdoff, who would become the co-editor of *Monthly Review*, carried this project forward in *The Age of Imperialism* (1969) by investigating the historical trajectory of imperialism and tracing the contours of monopoly capitalism as a world system of exploitation. Their collective effort helped form a current of independent socialist thought of increasing importance on a global scale.

Today, the struggle continues against a global capitalist system that has created conditions of increased exploitation in the countries of the global South, alongside a vast transfer of wealth to imperialist centers of the global North. While untold profits accrue to imperialism's ruling elite—the 1 percent of society at home and abroad—the 99 percent of the world's population experience greater hardship and misery. The imperial system of the twenty-first century is one marked by growing uncertainty, instability, and ecological disaster. The promise of national emancipation through independence has not been fulfilled in general. Capitalist globalization is in fact imperialism without colonies.

Please visit our website for complete details of the award.

The Age of Monopoly Capital

Selected Correspondence of Paul A. Baran
and Paul M. Sweezy, 1949–1964

Edited by NICHOLAS BARAN
and JOHN BELLAMY FOSTER

MONTHLY REVIEW PRESS

New York

Library of Congress Cataloging-in-Publication data:

Names: Baran, Paul A., author. | Sweezy, Paul M. (Paul Marlor), 1910–2004,
  author. | Baran, Nicholas, editor. | Foster, John Bellamy, editor.
Title: The age of monopoly capital : selected correspondence of Paul A. Baran
  and Paul M. Sweezy, 1949–1964 / edited by Nicholas Baran and John Bellamy
  Foster.
Description: New York : Monthly Review Press, [2017] | Includes
  bibliographical references and index.
Identifiers: LCCN 2017018385 (print) | LCCN 2017028759 (ebook) | ISBN
  9781583676530 (trade) | ISBN 9781583676547 (insitutional) | ISBN
  9781583676523 (hardcover)
Subjects: LCSH: Baran, Paul A.—Correspondence. | Baran, Paul A. Monopoly
  capital. | Sweezy, Paul M. (Paul Marlor), 1910–2004—Correspondence. |
  Economists—United States—Correspondence. | Economics—United
  States—History—20th century.
Classification: LCC HB119.B3 (ebook) | LCC HB119.B3 A4 2017 (print) | DDC
  330.092/2—dc23
LC record available at https://lccn.loc.gov/2017018385

MONTHLY REVIEW PRESS, NEW YORK
monthlyreview.org

5 4 3 2 1

Contents

In memory of Paul Alexander Baran and Paul Marlor Sweezy
and their great friendship

Preface

by Nicholas Baran

T HE CORRESPONDENCE OF PAUL BARAN AND PAUL SWEEZY
in the 1950s and early 1960s is one of the great unknown legacies
of Marxian political economy in the United States. This book is the
culmination of over two years of work, converting approximately eight hundred
letters to Microsoft Word so that they could be published. The entire collection
of letters is now available online in PDF format at the Paul A. Baran Archive at
Stanford University.[1] They are also available online at the Baran-Sweezy Archive
at Monthly Review.[2] This book is a collection of selected correspondence, focused
primarily on letters that illuminate Baran and Sweezy's intellectual and theoretical
exchanges, with the more personal and extraneous exchanges omitted.

In discussing the letters between my father and his best friend and colleague
Paul Sweezy, the best place to start is with the first two paragraphs of Sweezy's
"Paul A. Baran: A Personal Memoir," part of the short book published by Monthly
Review Press shortly after Baran's death in March of 1964:

> I first met Paul Baran shortly after he came to this country in the fall of
> 1939. I was teaching at Harvard, and he looked me up in Cambridge,
> bringing with him a letter of introduction from our mutual friend Oskar
> Lange who was then a professor of economics at the University of Chicago.
>
> Paul had a very powerful personality, and one could be attracted to him
> immediately on meeting him, just as one could take an immediate dislike to
> him. He and I were drawn together at once and our intellectual and personal
> friendship became ever closer and more meaningful to both of us during
> the next 25 years. As it happens, however, we never for long lived in the
> same locality, so that much of our discourse was perforce by written word.
> While he was alive I always found this deplorable. But now that he is gone
> I can appreciate its positive side. Up until about 1950, we corresponded

sporadically and did not save our letters. But soon after he went to Stanford in 1949, we began to correspond regularly and soon discovered that it was necessary to save letters for reference and continuity. As a result I have a precious file of hundreds of his letters. He was a good letter writer and liked to "think on the typewriter." We exchanged views on current happenings here and abroad, tried out ideas on each other and developed them through criticism and discussion. Some of his best and most stimulating thought is in these letters, and I hope in good time to publish a volume containing a substantial selection which I am confident will be a most valuable addition to his all too few written works.[3]

Sweezy never got around to publishing that volume, but fortunately he did save the file of letters, which amounts to some 1,000 single-spaced typewritten pages. The Baran-Sweezy letters not only reveal the remarkable personal and intellectual friendship between the two men but also chronicle a crucial period in the history of socialist economic thought and Cold War politics: the Marshall Plan and the division of Germany, Eastern Europe, the Korean War, the Eisenhower-Stevenson election, the McCarthy era and its academic witch hunt, the Soviet invasion of Hungary, the Cuban Revolution and the prospect of other revolutions in Latin America, the Sino-Soviet split, and the rise of China in the socialist world. The letters report these events contemporaneously, from Baran's and Sweezy's perspectives as they were occurring, without the benefit of hindsight. One of the key tenets of Marxism is to apply historical perspective to the analysis of social and economic conditions. These letters provide a remarkable historical perspective on the events of the time. They illuminate the issues that faced supporters of socialism living in the capitalist world, particularly within the American academy and in the United States in general.

The other and perhaps most important thread in the letters is, to paraphrase Sweezy, the trying out of ideas on each other and the development of those ideas through discussion and criticism. These letters quite literally represent the foundation of their book, *Monopoly Capital*, as many passages in it are taken verbatim from the letters. In them, Baran worked out his version of the economic surplus theory, which laid the groundwork for his book *The Political Economy of Growth*.

Converting these letters to Word has been a painstaking process. As Sweezy said, my father liked to think on the typewriter. As a young boy, I got the impression that his "tripe-writer," as I called it, was literally an extension of his person. I spent many hours at my father's house listening to his rat-a-tat-tat. He was a two-finger typist but incredibly fast considering his method, and he basically did not believe in paragraphs. His letters were for the most part single-spaced streams of consciousness, often typed on both sides of the page, and often with a worn ribbon. The upshot of his letter-writing style is that most of his letters did not accurately scan into digital format and had to be retyped. Here is what Leo Huberman, co-editor of *Monthly Review*, had to say in a letter to my father about one of his early submissions (March 1950): "Yours is an interesting provocative piece, which if written on 1 side of the paper, double-spaced, would be even better. However, we're gluttons for punishment and we'll decipher it. Particularly because it contains some excellent Baranisms."

In addition to the typewritten letters, there are a considerable number of handwritten letters, which were primarily composed when Sweezy or Baran was traveling. Both men traveled extensively and often wrote to each other on hotel stationery. Their handwriting reflected their very different personalities. Sweezy wrote neatly and legibly, reflecting a more deliberate and methodical style. Baran's handwriting reflected his impatience, anxiously moving to the next thought, no time to worry about delineating the different vowels, which often ended up looking like a series of small sine waves. I spent quite a bit of time with a magnifying glass trying to decipher key words in a Baran handwritten sentence, and not always successfully.

Just as handwriting reflected the two Pauls' different personalities, so did the letters themselves. It is worth pausing to briefly consider the backgrounds of the two men. Baran was educated in the classical European tradition. He spoke and read Russian, Polish, German, and English fluently. He could deliver a lecture in any of those four languages without a hiccup. He also spoke French very well, and had a good grasp of Latin. He was exceptionally well read in philosophy, history, and literature, and of course in classical economics.

Baran grew up in Russia and Germany, and then lived in Europe until his late twenties, when he emigrated to the United States. Like many European intellectuals who came to the United States around the time of the Second World War, Baran had a hard time adjusting to the "American way of life," particularly as exemplified in the suburban backwater of Palo Alto, California. Baran felt at home in a café in Paris, but was a fish out of water at the Stanford faculty swim club (he did not know how to swim). And while some European immigrants embraced American culture and sought to assimilate into it, my father kept his distance, disdainful and contemptuous of American culture. He absolutely despised the game of baseball. He had similar feelings about chewing gum, potato chips, Coca-Cola, and the abomination of American television, all of which were forbidden in his household. Because my father and mother divorced when I was young, my mother was able to allow me some exposure to these things at home, but on the weekends at my father's house I was exposed to Scrabble, chess, and a regular dose of Paul Robeson records—one of his few concessions to American culture, and a good one indeed.

Sweezy, on the other hand, was an American through and through. He got a "classic" American education at Exeter and Harvard, and also did postgraduate studies at the London School of Economics and in Vienna. He grew up in a venerable old New England family, and was a serious baseball fan, often listening to the Boston Braves and then the Boston Red Sox on the radio. He was also a formidable scholar, with a strong background in philosophy and history, as well as being on the path to a tenured professorship in economics at Harvard, where he had a teaching position as an assistant professor until his Marxist views got in the way. (Sweezy was never, as is sometimes supposed, denied tenure at Harvard but resigned his teaching position with two and a half years still left in his contract when it became clear that his prospects for tenure were dim in the growing Cold War climate.) One only has to read Sweezy's *Theory of Capitalist Development*, which was published when he was thirty-two years old, to appreciate the breadth and depth of his intellect and education.

Unlike Baran, Sweezy understood American culture. He was a great admirer of Thorstein Veblen, the merits of whom Sweezy and Baran debated extensively in their letters. Baran did not share Sweezy's enthusiasm, at least until later when they were working on *Monopoly Capital* and Baran came to recognize Veblen's contribution to understanding business enterprise. Although he and Baran were both critical of their colleagues in the American economics profession, Sweezy, with a more nuanced view of the American way of life, was more willing to give the benefit of the doubt to those who had not yet fully embraced Marxism, but at least were on a sympathetic path. Baran was quicker to dismiss those who didn't see the light as intellectually dishonest or incompetent. Sweezy generally tried to mollify Baran's anger, encouraging him to look at things a little more dialectically. It is ironic that for all his understanding of dialectics and historical materialism, Baran had difficulty applying those analytical tools when it came to U.S. society, which was also reflected in his role as a father of a son growing up in America, whom he in vain tried to shield from the culture around him.

Sweezy was Baran's sounding board for his complaints about life at Stanford, about his colleagues "feeding their rhododendrons" and going off on junkets paid by the RAND Corporation in exchange for their toeing the bourgeois line, and about students more interested in their suntans than in their studies. And though he may have been a bit harsh in his assessment of colleagues and students, Baran's complaints about Stanford were not unjustified. Indeed, as Baran became more outspoken in his support for the Cuban Revolution, he was abandoned by his colleagues as well as by the university administration, which froze his salary and tried to make life for him at Stanford as unpleasant as possible, hoping that he would give up the fight and quietly resign. Ironically, as Baran neared the end of his life, large numbers of Stanford students were rallying to his cause, attending his lectures, and demanding that the university stop its harassment of him.

The Baran-Sweezy letters represent an ongoing quest for common ground between two men coming from different cultural and educational backgrounds. Remarkably, as their friendship and understanding of each other grew, they almost always succeeded in finding that common ground. Although my father was strident and passionate about his views, and therefore expressed them frequently in the harshest terms, he would listen to Sweezy, and try to moderate his tone based on Sweezy's criticisms. And Sweezy clearly benefited from Baran's relentless demand for theoretical clarity, leaving no stone unturned. They were a study in the ability to disagree respectfully and then arrive at a mutually acceptable position, a skill that seems all but lost in today's acrimonious intellectual atmosphere.

It is important to emphasize that these letters comprise a private correspondence between two friends and colleagues who trusted and respected each other. Though they sometimes joked about their letters being published posthumously, some of the thoughts and emotions expressed in them were certainly never intended for public consumption and should be read keeping that perspective in mind. In today's world the concept of privacy is almost an anachronism, but it did indeed mean something fifty years ago. Yet fifty years seems long enough to justify publishing these letters largely uncensored, in order to present as full a picture as possible of these two brilliant economists.

—Nicholas Baran
San Francisco, April 2017

---

1.   Paul A. Baran Archive, Stanford University, http://www.oac.cdlib.org/findaid/ark:/13030/ c8xs5zkx/.
2.   Baran-Sweezy Archive at Monthly Review, https://archive.monthlyreview.org/index.php/ baran-sweezy/.
3.   *Paul Alexander Baran: A Collective Portrait* (New York: Monthly Review Press, 1965).

Introduction

by John Bellamy Foster

PAUL ALEXANDER BARAN AND PAUL MARLOR SWEEZY are legendary critics of twentieth-century U.S. capitalism. Their joint work, *Monopoly Capital: An Essay on the American Economic and Social Order*, published in 1966, is the single-most influential book ever published by Marxian political economists in the United States.[1] Long recognized as a classic, it has transcended the epoch in which it was written, charting a course of critique that subsequent thinkers have extended to the twenty-first century's increasingly globalized monopoly-finance capital. Political economists all over the world have built on Baran and Sweezy's work, which has influenced some of the most important radical and revolutionary movements of our time.[2]

In recent years, knowledge of Baran and Sweezy's corpus has expanded as a result of the discovery of the two missing chapters of *Monopoly Capital*, "Some Theoretical Implications" and "The Quality of Monopoly Capitalist Society: Culture and Communications," which were published, respectively, in the July–August 2012 and July–August 2013 issues of *Monthly Review*.[3] These two chapters had both been drafted by Baran, based on the authors' common ideas, but were not included in the final book, as all the issues had not been resolved between them at the time of Baran's sudden death on March 26, 1964. In addition to these works and a number of co-authored essays, Baran and Sweezy left behind in their joint corpus a voluminous set of letters, dated from 1949 to 1964, which have now been made available, largely unedited, as part of the Baran and Sweezy Letters Project.[4]

The present volume, *The Age of Monopoly Capital: Selected Correspondence, 1949–1964,* is an effort on the part of Nicholas Baran, Paul Baran's son, and myself to make available a carefully edited and annotated selection of many of the most important letters by these two thinkers. Here they address core issues in the Cold War period, as well as the development of their own critique of political economy. This volume provides both an invaluable set of reflections on history in the mid-

twentieth century by Marxist scholars whose range of analysis was quite literally
the entire world and a ground-level view of the writing of *Monopoly Capital*. Many
of Baran and Sweezy's most important ideas, such as Baran's conception of "the
heterogeneity of the historical dimensions," appear only in their letters. Other
ideas to be found here provide a much wider and richer context for analyzing
their published work. No correspondence in Marxian economics, since that of
Karl Marx and Frederick Engels themselves, offers such powerful insights into the
making of a political-economic critique.

The Two Pauls

The "two Pauls," as they are sometimes called, first met in fall 1939 at Harvard.
Sweezy was in the stacks in the library doing research when Baran came up to
him with a letter of introduction from their mutual friend, the great Polish socialist
economist Oskar Lange. Baran had just arrived from England to take up graduate
studies at Harvard, where Sweezy was a member of the economics faculty. They
left the stacks and went off to talk, and, as Sweezy recalled, "hit it off right away.
We got along beautifully, and we were in very close agreement on most theoretical
questions."[5]

The two new friends, both around thirty, came from very different backgrounds.
Baran was born into a Jewish family on December 8, 1910, in Nikolaev, Ukraine, on
the Black Sea, then part of the Tsarist Empire. Baran's passport and other documents
said he was born on August 25, 1909, but he said that was incorrect: his real birthdate
was December 8, 1910, and his birthday was always celebrated on December 8. His
father, Abram Baran, was a native of Vilna, and his mother, Rosaly (Braude) Baran,
of Riga. His father in his youth had been involved in the Menshevik wing of Russian
Social Democracy but gave that up when he began to study medicine. Dismayed by
the October Revolution, Abram Baran took his family to Vilna, which was then part
of Poland, and Baran's parents assumed Polish citizenship, with Paul Baran included
on his mother's passport, giving him Polish nationality (his possession of Polish
citizenship would offer him a certain amount of protection in Germany and the
Soviet Union in ensuing years). In 1921 his parents moved to Dresden in Germany
where Baran was educated in the Gymnasium. In 1925 Baran's father was offered
a position in his specialty in lung tuberculosis in Moscow, and his parents departed
Germany, leaving him behind to complete his secondary education. During that time
in Dresden he became involved in the Communist Youth and student organizations.
In 1926 he rejoined his parents in Moscow and enrolled in the Plekhanov Institute
of Economics at the University of Moscow.

Baran had wanted to return to Germany and thus gladly accepted when,
in 1928, his mentor, Professor S. M. Dubrovsky, director of the International

Agrarian Institute in Moscow, invited Baran to accompany him to Berlin as part of a research project with the International Agrarian Institute. While carrying out his research duties, Baran enrolled at the University of Berlin. When his research assignment expired, instead of returning to Moscow, he took a research assistantship at the Institute for Social Research in Frankfurt, then the center of critical Marxian thought in Germany, working under the economist Friedrich Pollock, the associate director of the Institute at Frankfurt. Pollock was then working on a treatise on the Soviet economy, and Baran relocated to Breslau, which had the main Russian archives in Germany, to carry out this research, while at the same time completing his undergraduate studies. In 1931 he moved to Berlin in order to work on his doctorate under the prominent socialist economist Emil Lederer, who was later to found the well-known "university of exile" at the New School for Social Research in New York. Baran was awarded his Ph.D. for a dissertation in social planning.[6]

In this period in Berlin, Baran was disturbed by the position taken in the USSR in what was known as the Third Period, in which social democracy was characterized as a form of "social fascism." Believing that the chief danger was the growth of fascism itself, Baran left the Communist Party and affiliated with the German Social Democrats. During this time he became well acquainted with the Marxist theorist Rudolf Hilferding, the author of *Finance Capital: A Study of the Latest Phase of Capitalist Development* (1910). Hilferding was then the most renowned economist in German Social Democracy, and served as finance minister in the coalition government of the Weimar Republic. As editor of the official paper of the German Social Democratic Party, he invited Baran to write for it, which Baran did under the pseudonym of Alexander Gabriel in order to protect his parents. Fighting fascism, in a radio broadcast entitled "No Vacation from Politics," Baran declared that "the politicization of the working people is dangerous for the rulers of this world, but it is the hope of our entire culture."[7]

In early February 1933, a few days after Hitler was appointed chancellor and prior to the Reichstag fire, Baran met with Hilferding and discussed the dangers of Hitler's rise to power. Hilferding still thought the constitutional order would hold and downplayed Baran's concerns, seeing him as overall too radical. A few days later Hilfderding was forced to go into hiding and then fled the country. He was to die in prison in 1941 at the hands of the Gestapo after the Vichy police turned him over to them (Baran to Sweezy, February 23, 1949).[8]

Baran fled to France in May 1933, where he did various research jobs and in 1934 obtained a visa to visit his parents in the USSR. The situation had changed there, however, and was no longer safe for him. Most of his friends at the University of Moscow had been implicated in either the Bukharin or Trotsky oppositions. His "friend and protector" Dubrovsky had disappeared (he had fallen victim to the Stalinist terror but lived to see his rehabilitation). Baran was unable to extend his visa and after six months with his parents in Moscow was forced to leave the USSR. That was the last time he saw his mother. He left for Vilna where he worked in his family's timber business. He traveled extensively on the Continent, negotiating with foreign buyers. In the process, he built up ties with anti-Nazi groups in Germany and acted at great personal risk as a liaison for exile groups in various countries. He was good at business and in 1938 was sent to London as the permanent trade representative of the Vilna interests. It was during this time that he learned English and decided to pursue an academic career in the United States. By the time he departed with a visa for the United States, Poland had been occupied by the Nazis.[9]

Sweezy's background was worlds away from that of Baran. He was born April 10, 1910, in New York. His father, Everett B. Sweezy, was vice president of the First National Bank of New York, then headed by George F. Baker, a close associate of J.P. Morgan and Co. His mother, Caroline (Wilson) Sweezy, was in the first graduating class of Goucher College in Baltimore. He had two older brothers, Everett, born in 1901, and Alan, born 1907. All three brothers went to Exeter and then to Harvard. In the early years, Paul followed in the footsteps of his brother Alan. Both Alan and Paul were editors of the *Exonian* and then later presidents of the *Harvard Crimson*. Both studied economics at the undergraduate and graduate levels at Harvard. Paul had all but completed his senior year at Harvard when his father died in 1931, interrupting his studies. Consequently, he did not graduate (magna cum laude) until the following year, in 1932. In 1931–32, having completed his undergraduate studies, he began to take graduate courses in economics at Harvard.[10]

In 1932, Sweezy went to England for a year's study at the London School of Economics (LSE). During school breaks he spent several months in Vienna. These experiences decisively changed his life and outlook. Like many he had been shaken by the onset of the Great Depression. His father lost the greater part of his fortune in the 1929 stock market crash, although enough remained, in his mother's estate in particular, to ensure a comfortable existence. In Britain Sweezy was awakened by the intellectual and political ferment in response to the deepening depression and Hitler's rise to power in Germany. In the heated debates then taking place, particularly among younger scholars, Sweezy found himself increasingly attracted to Marxism. Two things played key roles in his change in perspective: lectures by Harold Laski that he attended at the LSE, and his reading of Leon Trotsky's *History of the Russian Revolution*, which had just been translated into English.

In 1933 Sweezy returned to the United States to continue his graduate studies in economics at Harvard, where the intellectual climate had by then been dramatically transformed. Marxism, which in his prior years at Harvard had played no part in his education, had become an important topic of discussion. A big change was the arrival at Harvard of Joseph A. Schumpeter, one of the foremost economists of the twentieth century. A conservative economist and a former Austrian finance minister, Schumpeter nonetheless had enormous respect for the economics of Karl Marx, even going so far—as Sweezy put it in an interview (part of the Columbia Oral History Project)—as "to build a structure of thought which was to rival Marx. In other words he took Marx as a model in a way." Schumpeter had a small seminar of about a half-dozen students in which Sweezy informally took part. Over the years the two became close friends. Sweezy was for two years Schumpeter's teaching assistant in his graduate course in economics.

After John Maynard Keynes's *General Theory of Employment, Interest and Money* was published in 1936, Sweezy became an active participant in the Harvard discussions surrounding the Keynesian revolution in economic theory. At the same time, he married a young economist, Maxine Yaple, who was to become best known for her analysis of privatization of the German economy under the Nazis, introducing the concept of privatization into English for the first time. Sweezy worked for various New Deal agencies. In 1937 he carried out an important study of "Interest Groups in the American Economy" for the National Resources Committee (NRC), which was published in 1939 as an appendix to the NRC's well-known report *The Structure of the American Economy*. In opposition to Adolf Berle and Gardiner Means's *The Modern Corporation and Private Property* (1932), which claimed that a large number of U.S. firms were management controlled, Sweezy demonstrated that it was possible to discern eight leading "interest groups" consisting of industrial and financial alliances. Sweezy also carried out research for the Securities and Exchange Commission on their study of monopoly in 1939, and for the Temporary National Economic Committee, which was charged with analyzing issues of competition and monopoly in the U.S. economy in 1940. He entered into the debates on economic stagnation in this period. Both he and Maxine Sweezy were among the authors and signatories to a small, influential book, *An Economic Program for American Democracy*, written by a group of Harvard and Tufts economists, published in 1938.

In 1937, Sweezy completed his dissertation, "Monopoly and Competition in the English Coal Industry, 1550–1850," which won the David A. Wells Prize and was published the following year by Harvard University Press. In 1938 he was appointed a member of the Harvard economics faculty under a five-year contract. He was to play a key role in the founding of the Harvard Teachers Union. These were years of enormous intellectual productivity. Beginning in 1934 and over the next six years he wrote some twenty-five articles and reviews on economic topics. His crowning achievement was his article "Demand Under Conditions of Oligopoly," published in the *Journal of Political Economy* in 1939, which introduced the famous kinked-demand curve of oligopolistic pricing. This was to be immensely influential in economics, and later provided the basis of Baran and Sweezy's conception of oligopolistic (monopolistic) pricing in *Monopoly Capital*.[11] As John Kenneth Galbraith was to recall of these days, Sweezy was a "dominant voice" in the debates on economic stagnation, capitalism, and socialism at Harvard. Japanese Marxist economist Shigeto Tsuru later recalled that Sweezy in his "sacred decade of twenties" (as Schumpeter famously referred to this period in the life of a scholar) was "the kingpin in the Golden Era of the Harvard Economics Department in the 1930s."[12]

Hence, when Baran and Sweezy first met in October 1939—both just shy of thirty years of age—each had already played significant roles in the world-historical events of the 1930s. Both had arrived at similar political-economic views of the world. Not much is known about the early years of their friendship. Baran completed his graduate studies at Harvard (he supplemented his doctorate from Berlin with an M.A. in economics from Harvard) and went on to take a research assistantship with the Brookings Institution. Sweezy was occupied in 1939–41 with teaching, helping build the Harvard Teachers Union, working on New Deal committees, and writing his classic text *The Theory of Capitalist Development: Principles of Marxian Political Economy*, based on the lecture notes to his course on the economics of socialism. His acknowledgments to the book included "Mr. Paul A. Baran."

With the U.S. entry in the Second World War, both Baran and Sweezy turned to the war effort. Baran worked in wartime Washington, in the Office of Price Administration (OPA), the Research and Development branch of the Office of Strategic Services, and then the Economic Effects Division of the U.S. Strategic Bombing Survey in Germany, serving as a technical sergeant under John Kenneth Galbraith, whom Baran had known during his work at the OPA. He later served as part of the Economic Effects Division of the Survey's mission to Japan, as deputy chief of the division. Baran was sent to Germany in March 1945 for the Survey to view the economic effects associated with the bombing. In his autobiography, Galbraith provided a memorable account of Baran during the war years, when he was under Galbraith's command in the Strategic Bombing Survey:

A technical sergeant in rank, Baran was one of the most brilliant, and by a wide margin, the most interesting economist I have ever known. He was currently celebrating the end of the war with the Germans by intensifying his ongoing war with the United States Army.... Baran's war with the army was tactically diverse. His uniform attracted immediate attention, for his stomach bulged over his belt, his pants were always being hitched up and his shirt was only episodically inside. His hair, like his uniform, was in a constant state of disorder, and once, he said absent-mindedly, he appeared on parade in carpet slippers. He couldn't or wouldn't remember to call an officer "Sir" or to salute except as he might encounter one before a urinal. Least supportable of all, the average officer could not ordinarily understand what Baran was saying but could guess that the extravagantly convoluted sentences reflected adversely on his intelligence....

In Wiesbaden, Baran uncovered General Franz Halder, the commander in the early campaigns on the eastern front who was fired by Hitler in disagreements over strategy at the time of Stalingrad and arrested after the July 20 attempt on Hitler's life. He had expected on the day of surrender to be taken promptly to see General Eisenhower and maybe then to General Marshall. Instead, not uncharacteristically, he had been left in total neglect for several weeks by American soldiers who had never heard his name. Baran, who had specialized on these matters for the OSS, interrogated him for many hours on the details of German operations on the Russian front. When finally Baran showed signs of being satisfied, Halder begged with great respect to have a turn: "Could I now ask my interrogator a question?"

Baran: "Yes."

Halder: "Has the American Army many intelligence officers like you?"

Baran, in an unprecedented sacrifice of truth to modesty: "I wouldn't know, General."

Halder: "If it has, it explains much about this war. I may tell you that your knowledge of the problems facing the Wehrmacht on the eastern front is markedly greater than was that of the Führer."[13]

Sweezy entered the army as an officer candidate and was soon assigned to the Office of Strategic Services working under his former Harvard professor and colleague Edward Mason. In fall 1943 he was sent to London to join the Research and Analysis program of the OSS there, where his immediate superior was another noted U.S. economist, Chandler Morse. The London branch of the Research and Analysis section had been publishing for some time a newsletter that was a weekly summary of what was happening in the Axis countries, derived mostly from the German press, but also from other occupied areas. The information was collected in neutral Portugal and then channeled into London. Sweezy began working on the newsletter and turned it into a monthly magazine, the *European Political Report,* that drew on an expanded range of sources. The newsletter took an explicitly New Deal–leftist, anti-fascist stance. For example, it adopted a strongly anti-British position on the 1944 British assault on the Greek resistance. Having encountered Sweezy in London in these days, economist Tibor Scitovsky later recalled that Sweezy had mentioned how much he enjoyed the work on the OSS magazine, and had declared his desire to start his own magazine when he returned to the United States after the war.[14] The London branch of the OSS relocated to Paris in the winter of 1944–45 and then to Wiesbaden in the spring. Later some of Sweezy's branch relocated to Berlin, where he witnessed the devastation caused by the Allied bombing. During his time in Germany he had frequent contact with members of the Strategic Bombing Survey team, including Baran. In September 1945 Sweezy was sent home and demobilized. He had reached the rank of second lieutenant and was awarded the Bronze Star in 1946. The citation specified the medal was for his role as editor of the *European Political Report.*

The Cold War and *Monthly Review*

The years following the Second World War were those of the developing Cold War and McCarthyism, which became an increasingly dominant reality in the 1950s. After the war, Baran took a job at the Department of Commerce until the end of 1946, during which he lectured at George Washington University in the fall term. He then accepted a position at the Federal Reserve Bank in New York, where he was in charge of the British desk and also had responsibility for reporting on developments in the Soviet Union. In the spring of 1948 he was invited by the Hoover Institute and the Economics Department of Stanford University to teach a graduate seminar on economic planning. The powerful impression that his teaching made on the students led to his being offered a job as an associate professor of economics at Stanford in 1949, followed by his promotion to full professor with tenure in 1951. Baran resigned from the Bank in the summer of 1949, in time to make a trip to Europe. He tried to obtain a visa to visit the Soviet Union to see his parents but the Soviet Embassy in Washington turned him down. He therefore accepted the invitation of Lange, who was well situated within the Polish government, to come to Poland and try to get a visa there. Again the visa was refused. His mother died in the following year (Baran to Sweezy, March 28, 1950; Sweezy to Baran, March 31, 1950). All attempts to get his father out of the USSR so he could come and live with him in Palo Alto failed. Naturally, this left him with a bitter feeling that never went away.

As Sweezy was to write of Baran's general view of the USSR:

Paul's attitude toward the Soviet Union was complex. It is obvious from the fact that he was expelled in 1935 and refused admission in 1949 that he was *persona non grata* there in the Stalin era; and in private he was outspokenly critical of many aspects of the regime.... Nevertheless, he steadfastly refused to criticize the Soviet Union or its leaders in public, and his attitude on the whole was sympathetic and positive. Some people saw in this evidence that he was really a Stalinist, others that he was at heart a Russian nationalist. Undoubtedly there is a grain of truth in both of these explanations: though he deplored the excesses of Stalinism, he was firmly convinced of the rightness and necessity of Stalin's policies of industrialization and collectivization of agriculture; and there is no doubt that he was proud that his native land was playing so important a role on the stage of world history. But much more important, I think, was his feeling about the class struggle and the Soviet role in it. He saw the class struggle in our time as one gigantic worldwide confrontation, and he had no doubt that the Russian Revolution was the greatest victory for the side he was on; to criticize publicly the regime which emerged from it might bring aid and comfort to its enemies who were also his enemies, and that he was determined not to do.[15]

It was in 1950, soon after he joined the Stanford economics faculty, that Baran married Elena Djatschenko. They had in common that they had both been born in Russia and had spent much of their lives in Germany. On April 16, 1952, they had a son, Nicholas Mark Baran. During his years at Stanford Baran remained in close contact with some of his old friends from the Institute for Social Research in Frankfurt who had settled in the United States, in particular Herbert Marcuse and Leo Lowenthal. Baran and Marcuse had an important correspondence over the years, while Baran frequently visited Lowenthal at Berkeley.[16]

Sweezy received a Social Science Research Council Demobilization grant following the war, allowing scholars who had been in the military to resume their research. During the war, his marriage with Maxine Yaple had ended and he married Nancy Adams, whom he had met in Europe while she too was assigned to the OSS. They settled at his family home in Wilton, New Hampshire, and had three children: Samuel Everett (born 1946), Elizabeth (Lybess) MacDougall (born 1948), and Martha Adams (born 1951).

Despite more than two years left on his contract at Harvard, Sweezy decided to resign his position, recognizing that there was little chance in the rightward political climate of the time that he would receive tenure. Instead, he devoted himself to independent research, churning out a wide array of publications. On

March 27, 1947, he engaged in the famous Sweezy-Schumpeter debate at Harvard, "On the Laws of Capitalism" and the future of socialism.[17] In 1948 he chaired the New Hampshire campaign of the Progressive Party, whose presidential candidate was former U.S. vice president Henry A. Wallace.

Based on a gift of funding (three yearly installments of $5,000 each) from the noted Harvard professor of literature F. O. Matthiessen, Sweezy and the socialist writer and journalist Leo Huberman—author of *We the People* (1932) and *Man's Worldly Goods* (1936)—founded *Monthly Review: An Independent Socialist Magazine* in 1949, with the first issue appearing that May. Albert Einstein wrote his celebrated article, "Why Socialism?," for volume 1, number 1, of the magazine.[18] Sweezy was to take the primary responsibility for drafting a major article—known as the Review of the Month (ROM)—for every issue and helped edit the magazine, while Huberman handled the business affairs, did much of the editing, and contributed to the articles and the ROMs. In 1952 Monthly Review Press was started when the acclaimed left journalist I. F. Stone was unable to find a book publisher for his *The Hidden History of the Korean War*.[19]

From 1949 on Baran and Sweezy were to be thousands of miles apart on opposite coasts of the country, Baran teaching economics at Stanford and Sweezy editing *Monthly Review* in New York. They saw each other only occasionally, when their vacations from their main occupations allowed them to travel, or they phoned. Mostly, however, they communicated by way of letters. It is to this that we owe the existence of the Baran and Sweezy correspondence. Some of their letters related to *Monthly Review*, to which Baran contributed. Later, as Baran began to write *The Political Economy of Growth*, and as he and Sweezy worked together on *Monopoly Capital*, their correspondence became more valuable and more frequent, so that they were careful to keep the letters. However, some were clearly lost, and thus the extant letters do not constitute a complete record of their correspondence. It is from this voluminous correspondence that the present edited volume of selected correspondence was compiled.

The early 1950s were dominated by the Cold War, which had been developing throughout the late 1940s with respect both to the growing U.S. conflict with the Soviet Union and, domestically, in the United States, the repression of dissent. The anti-Communist/anti-left witch hunt of the period came to be known as McCarthyism, after U.S. Senator Joseph McCarthy, the most virulent of the witch hunters. But McCarthyism was arguably first launched not by McCarthy but by Truman's red-baiting of Henry Wallace's Progressive Party in the 1948 election. The early years of *Monthly Review* were thus often dominated in its domestic discussions by issues of how to respond to McCarthyism, including a debate on fascism. Up to 1953 Baran contributed to these debates under the pseudonym of "Historicus," reflecting the fact that the red scare was at the time extended to faculty in the universities with loyalty oaths and the firing of noted left academics. Many were imprisoned. On June 19, 1953, Julius and Ethel Rosenberg were executed on charges of "conspiracy to commit espionage," referred to in the press as treason.

Baran played a leading role in defining *Monthly Review*'s response to these developments. His 1950 essay, "Better Smaller But Better" (the title was adapted from Lenin), which argued for a consistent, reasoned critical stance rather than watering down the analysis and political practice by trying to cooperate with retreating liberals, even if that meant a shrinking audience in the present, came to define the magazine's general position in the political conjuncture of the McCarthy era and afterward. Almost twenty years later Sweezy was to refer to this essay as "among the most perceptive diagnoses of the socioeconomic condition of early Cold War America that I know of."[20]

Later, and far less successfully, Baran was to lead the way in treating the issue of fascism in the United States, writing an essay on this topic for the October 1952 issue of *Monthly Review* and a rejoinder to criticisms soon after. These published analyses were to be less fruitful than Baran and Sweezy's private correspondence on the subject of the "jumping place" that distinguished fascism from normal repression associated with the capitalist state.[21] Here they focused on the suppression of all political opposition and the effective setting aside of the rule of law as the determining elements (Baran to Sweezy, October 25, 1952; Sweezy, October 29, 1952; Baran to Sweezy, November 16, 1952). This analysis was to be developed concretely more than a decade later by Huberman and Sweezy in the article "Goldwaterism" in September 1964.[22]

The McCarthy anti-Communist purge was directed against the left of the New Deal coalition that had emerged under Roosevelt, including militant trade unionists, radical leaders within the African-American movement, media figures, and socialist academics. The goal was to marginalize the institutions and movements of the left. At first, attempts were made to defend dissent based on the First Amendment, but once the Hollywood Ten were sent to prison for refusing to cooperate with congressional inquisitors that defense was considered dead, and it was assumed by everyone that the only conceivable defense was based on the Fifth Amendment's provision against self-incrimination. However, in May 1953, Einstein wrote a letter to a teacher, published the following month in the *New York Times*, proposing a more aggressive First Amendment attack on the very legitimacy of the purge itself. The Einstein strategy was adopted by the editors and writers for *MR*, among others, who were called before the various witch-hunt committees based on trumped-up charges of subversion (Sweezy to Baran, July 24, 1953).[23]

In July 1953, Huberman and writer and frequent *MR* contributor Harvey O'Connor both testified before Senator McCarthy's committee.[24] Huberman and Sweezy together with their lawyer worked out the necessary details of implementing an Einstein-based strategy, which required laying "the foundations for a court fight" (Sweezy to Baran, July 24, 1953). Huberman directly confronted McCarthy, and when asked how his views "deviated" from those of Communist Party members declared, "I want to make it crystal clear that Communism is not an issue . . . [T]he issue [is] my right as an author and editor to pursue my occupation." This was the first time since the Hollywood Ten that anyone had risked contempt of court and prison in defiance of the inquisitors, and was a direct response to the Einstein letter. *Monthly Review* defied the inquisition by printing Huberman's entire testimony before the McCarthy committee in the magazine under the title of "A Challenge to the Book Burners." Huberman and Sweezy followed this up in *Monthly Review* by further flaunting their open opposition to McCarthyism, with the publication of the testimonies before the McCarthy Committee by Harvey O'Connor and Corliss Lamont, a November 1953 Review of the Month on "Defend the First Amendment," and a January 1954 Review of the Month on "The Roots and Prospects of McCarthyism."[25]

In January 1954 Sweezy was subpoenaed by New Hampshire attorney general Louis C. Wyman, who was charged by the state legislature with investigating "subversive activities." Wyman focused on a lecture that Sweezy had delivered at the University of New Hampshire. Sweezy was called upon to answer questions on the content of his lecture, turn over his lecture notes, report on his political views and political activities, and name the names of others with whom he had been associated, including Communists, members of the Progressive Party, and fellow travelers of Communism. Sweezy issued his own statement on freedom of speech that he read to the committee. He refused to turn over his lecture notes, provide information on the contents of his teaching, and name names. He also flatly refused comment on the views of others or to judge people on the basis of how they defended themselves, insisting on the need and right of some individuals to utilize "the Fifth," and supporting all of those who defended their civil liberties. He challenged the right of the inquisitors to persecute those simply pursuing their political freedoms. He was cited with contempt of court. His case was appealed and wound its way through the state and federal courts until *Sweezy v. New Hampshire* was decided in favor of Sweezy by the U.S. Supreme Court under Earl Warren, in June 1957, representing one of a number of key decisions that spelled the end of McCarthyism (Sweezy to Baran, January 10, 1954; Cathy Winston to Baran, March 10, 1957; Baran to Sweezy, June 17, 1957).[26]

The Political Economy of Growth and Cuba

Although McCarthyism and the Red Scare with which it was associated was largely defeated by the late 1950s, anti-Communism, which in the United States meant anti-socialism more generally, continually reemerged. In contrast to Sweezy, Baran was not called up by any of the inquisition committees, though he was under FBI surveillance and, given his biography and views as a Russian-born socialist, was constantly hounded by right-wingers. While he was not persecuted with full force within the university in the early 1950s, his department head was worried and there were signs that the hammer was about to drop, though it did not at this time (Baran to Sweezy, November 16, 1952). The reason undoubtedly was that his publications were mainly professional (his political writings in *MR* were under the pen name of Historicus) and he was not openly playing the role of a public intellectual beyond the university and the academic world. Two things would change that in the late 1950s. One was the publication of *The Political Economy of Growth* in 1957, the other was the Cuban Revolution in 1959, which brought Baran out into the open as an outspoken defender of Cuba. His great work *The Political Economy of Growth* was to take on added significance in the context of the Cuban Revolution, influencing Che Guevara. In his last years, in the 1960s, Baran was constantly under pressure within Stanford, his salary frozen, and attempts were made to force him to resign (Baran to Sweezy, June 30, 1961). This did not have to do with dissatisfaction from colleagues or students, but seems to have emanated entirely from outside forces, including those who provided private funding to the university.[27]

The general attitude at Stanford in the 1950s is reflected in this observation in a letter from Baran to Sweezy, November 28, 1956:

> I ran into the Chairman of our Sociology Dept. The Honorable Professor LaPiere—a personally very friendly individual who brags about—among other things—never reading a newspaper, and learned from him that his Dept. has a $12,000 p.a. [per annum] professorship in Sociology (just freshly endowed by Ford) and is unable to find anyone to take it. I said "why don't you try C.W. Mills, he has a mediocre job in Columbia *College* (not Graduate School), is an interesting fellow and might be tempted . . ." LaPiere looked at me with some astonishment, shrugged his shoulders and said: "But Mills is not a sociologist, he is a Marxist."

Baran's great work *The Political Economy of Growth* arose out of his research in the early 1950s in which he was addressing the problems of economic development in poorer countries and the possibility of national economic planning and growth if these countries could somehow free themselves from imperialism. In 1952, he published his powerful essay on "The Political Economy of Backwardness" in the relatively obscure journal *Manchester School of Economics and Social Studies.* This article had been rejected by one mainstream journal after another. One British reviewer rejected it on the basis that its argument on imperialism and underdevelopment applied to Latin America, but not to the present and former British colonies. In a complete reversal of this, a U.S. reviewer rejected it on the basis that it applied to the rest of the world, but it did not apply to Latin America, where the United States played a dominant role.[28]

That same year saw the publication of Baran's long essay on "National Economic Planning" in *A Survey of Contemporary Economics,* edited by B. F. Haley. In the following year, he wrote his article "Economic Progress and Economic Surplus" for *Science & Society.*[29] Baran was sharply critical of the dominant ideological notion of economic development associated with figures like W. W. Rostow, and also wrote a trenchant review of Rostow's *The Process of Economic Growth* in the *American Economic Review* in 1952. As he stated in a letter to Sweezy, "Have for review Rostow's Theory of Economic Growth where it is established that the degree to which economic growth takes place depends on a nation's propensity to . . . grow. Utterly disarming in its straightforward lunacy" (Baran to Sweezy, May 14, 1952).[30]

Baran was invited to spend the fall (Michaelmas) term in 1953 teaching at Oxford University, where he was to present a series of eight lectures under the title "The Political Economy of Growth." It was out of these lectures that his book *The Political Economy of Growth* arose (Baran to Sweezy, May 15, 1953). While he was at Oxford delivering these lectures, Baran signed a contract with the Oxford publisher Blackwell for *The Political Economy of Growth* and received an advance of £50. In October 1955, he was still struggling with the manuscript and saying "the motto of the thing" should be "The truth is the whole" (from the preface to Hegel's *Phenomenology of Mind;* Baran to Sweezy, October 8, 1955).[31] The book was completed in late 1955, just before he left for several months in India as a guest of the Indian Institute of Statistics, during which he wrote an essay on planning in India.[32] Reading the manuscript on November 10, 1955, just before Baran left, Sweezy wrote to him: "It passes muster—with flying colors. The first work in this growth field that is worthy of the great tradition. My warmest congratulations" (Sweezy to Baran, November 10, 1955).

Baran delivered the manuscript to Blackwell early in 1956. The publisher was alarmed by the content and mobilized editorial readers to suggest sharp changes and cuts. One reader, who had been asked to provide advice on cutting the manuscript, wrote: "You have not asked for my opinion on the book: may I give it nevertheless? The author is a Communist. No doubt the administration of underdeveloped countries by Britain and other colonial Powers has been, and is, by no means perfect. But according to the author everything that Western countries have done has been for their own advantage, and the underdeveloped countries have always been exploited. He puts the worst interpretation on all Western motives. . . . If his book were read by, say, an African student, with little knowledge of history, he might be very seriously misled."[33] Baran adamantly refused to make the changes that the readers and Blackwell demanded and withdrew the manuscript, paying back the advance. He then gave the book to Monthly Review Press, where he could be assured that such censorship would not take place. It was published in 1957 and has remained in print ever since. As Sweezy was to write thirty years later, it was one of "the most important works in the Marxian tradition of the post–World War II period."[34]

The Political Economy of Growth was divided essentially into two parts, one part on monopoly capitalism in the advanced capitalist states, the second part on the political economy of underdevelopment in the periphery. It was the latter part of the book that drew the most attention; the first part was to be reconceptualized and developed further in Baran and Sweezy's *Monopoly Capital*.

The key to Baran's analysis was his threefold treatment of economic surplus.[35] Orthodox economics, according to Baran, usually treats the issue of investment necessary for economic growth as if it were merely a question of the disposal of society's *actual* surplus (or actual savings), defined as "the difference between society's *actual* current output and its *actual* current consumption." Yet a fuller understanding of the mobilization of economic resources was offered by the concept of *potential* surplus, defined as "the difference between the output that *could* be produced in a given natural and technological environment with the help of employable productive resources, and what might be regarded as essential consumption." Potential surplus, therefore, can be seen as including both actual surplus *plus* the following: (1) society's excess consumption; (2) loss of output due to the existence of unproductive workers; (3) loss of output due to the irrational and wasteful organization of production; and (4) loss of output due to open and disguised unemployment and underemployment. Enhancing growth thus critically depends on tapping those elements of potential surplus that are being wasted, and which therefore do not show up in actual surplus, as well as mobilizing resources being siphoned off from abroad.[36]

Baran also included a concept of *planned* surplus, or "the difference between society's 'optimum' output attainable in a historically given natural and technological environment under conditions of planned 'optimal' utilization of all available productive resources, and some planned 'optimal' volume of consumption." In a planned economy, Baran insisted, the maximization of output was not necessarily the goal. In such a planned economy, "certain noxious types of production (coal mining, for example)" might be consciously discarded, even though this would cut into the economic growth prospects of the system. There might be "a shortened labor day" or "an increase in the amount of time devoted to education."[37]

Overall, the value of Baran's conceptual approach was evident in the facility with which he was able to counter three of the most important postulates of mainstream development theory: (1) the notion that underdeveloped economies had always been underdeveloped; (2) the idea that the main obstacle to development was a vicious circle of poverty, requiring a diffusion of capital to poorer countries; and (3) the belief that the problems of underdeveloped economies could be attributed to a dearth of capitalist entrepreneurs embodying Western know-how and initiative.

Rather than following the usual practice of presuming that the poorer economies of the periphery had always been relatively "backward," Baran approached the issue historically. "The question that immediately arises," he wrote, "is why is it that in the backward countries there has been no advance along the lines of capitalist development that are familiar from the history of other capitalist countries, and why is it that forward movement there has been either slow or altogether absent?" The answer, he suggested, was to be found in the way in which capitalism was brought to these regions during the period of what Marx had called "primitive accumulation," characterized by "undisguised looting, enslavement and murder," and in the way in which this very process served to destroy fledgling industries in the colonized societies. It was thus the European conquest and plundering of the rest of the globe that generated the great divide between core and periphery of the capitalist world economy that persists to this day.[38]

In illustrating this, Baran highlighted the differing ways in which India and Japan were incorporated into the world capitalist economy, the first as a dependent social formation carrying the unfortunate legacy of what Andre Gunder Frank was later to call "the development of underdevelopment"; the second representing the exceptional case of a society that was neither colonized nor subject to unequal treaties, and that, retaining control over its own economic surplus, was free to develop along the autocentric lines of the core European powers. The implications of this analysis were clear: incorporation on an unequal basis into the periphery of the capitalist economy was itself the main cause of the plight of the underdeveloped countries; in short, they were caught in an imperialist iron cage.[39]

What blocked the use of the enormous potential surplus for economic growth in underdeveloped countries, Baran argued, was imperialism, plus the related archaic, dependent, comprador class structure of these societies. Reactionary class elements, foreign capital, and a dependent-parasitic state all came together to maximize the misappropriation and wasting of the potential economic surplus, trapping these countries in underdevelopment. Only a revolutionary reconstitution of society by emerging classes from below would allow true social and economic development.

One of Baran's most profound observations, developed in a letter to Sweezy, following a "one-gulp perusal" in November 1956 of his forthcoming book, was what he called the "heterogeneity of the historical dimensions." Here he argued that the political, industrial, cultural, and psychological changes associated with a revolution all occurred, but at different paces. Most important,

> the transformation of the capitalist or even pre-capitalist man into a conscious, understanding, honest citizen of a socialist society may last not generations but centuries. It is actually this unevenness of the developmental processes that creates the entire mess…. But isn't this unevenness part of the essence of matters? Marx himself had clearly an inkling of all of this, his remarks about the socialist society emerging from the womb of the capitalist society and many others are clear indication of it. But didn't he in his general overestimation of the tempo assume a much lesser heterogeneity of dimensions? Didn't he believe that what is at issue are years, while in fact it looks more [like] decades and ages? On this there is much to say and much to think. (Baran to Sweezy, November 28, 1956)

Khrushchev's revelations on Stalin in early 1956, followed later that year by the Soviet invasion of Hungary, led to the rise of the First New Left, particularly in Britain.[40] In the United States, *Monthly Review*, which had always been an independent socialist magazine, came out strongly against the Soviet invasion, with Huberman and Sweezy declaring: "An uprising of classic form and proportions took place in Hungary. It was drowned in blood by the Soviet army. These are simple facts which no amount of arguing and no conceivable new evidence can change. After these events, we do not see how the feelings of any socialist toward the Soviet Union can remain unchanged. Any claim the Soviet Union had to moral leadership of the world socialist movement is now extinguished."[41] Baran agreed (Baran to Sweezy, November 15, 1956).[42]

Baran responded to the fissure in Marxism associated with 1956 by writing a series of articles, primarily for *Monthly Review*, on the nature of Marxism, breaking with some earlier conceptions and introducing a view of Marxism that was at one and the same time more classical, in reaching back to Marx, Engels, Luxemburg, and Lenin, and more contemporary, distilling the essence of a Marxian critique and its relation to the present as history. This was very much in the spirit of the First New Left. It is clear that Baran had in mind doing a book titled *An Essay on Marxism*, but it was never completed (Baran to Sweezy, July 29, 1957, Baran to Beatrice and Harry Magdoff, March 22, 1964).[43]

The first of these essays appeared in the October 1958 issue of *Monthly Review* and was titled "The Crisis of Marxism?" It addressed the question of whether historical changes had made Marxism irrelevant. It answered in the negative, though recognizing the problems involved. For Baran, a rational response lay in the development of historical materialism itself in ways that adequately explored the problems of the monopoly stage of capitalism.[44] In "On the Nature of Marxism," published in *Monthly Review* in November 1958, he presented his famous interpretation of historical materialism:

> Contrary to widespread opinion, Marxism is not and never was intended to be a "positive science," an assortment of statements about past and present facts, or a set of predictions about the shape and timing of future events. It was always an intellectual attitude, or a way of thought, a philosophical position the fundamental principle of which is continuous, systematic, and comprehensive *confrontation of reality with reason*. . . .
>
> The confrontation of reality with reason is by no means an abstract, intellectual undertaking. In every society that is split into classes, i.e., based on the exploitation of man by man, the exploiting class is vitally interested in the preservation of the existing pattern of social relations; and in administering the affairs of society it will seek to admit of only such change as will not endanger this pattern. The point is therefore unavoidably reached when the progress of reason and the expansion of our knowledge of reality are impeded, when existing and maturing possibilities for society's further advancement, for further growth and development of all its members, are sacrificed in favor of the interest of the dominant class in the continuation of the established social order—when, in other words, the particular interests of the ruling class come into conflict with the interests of society as a whole. At such historical junctures the confrontation of reality with reason reveals the irrationality of the existing social order, turns—in the words of Marx— into "ruthless criticism of everything that exists, ruthless in the sense that the criticism will not shrink either from its own conclusions or from conflict with the powers that be," and becomes the intellectual expression of the practical, existential needs of the entire society, and in particular of its overwhelming majority, the oppressed and exploited classes.[45]

Baran's distillation in this way of the historical essence of Marxism provided the basis of a renewed and powerful Marxian critique, rising above the stale dogmas that had come to characterize Soviet ideology. Baran, as his close friend, Harry Magdoff (later co-editor of *Monthly Review*) stated, did not simply quote or interpret Marx, "he adopted Marx's way of thinking: he virtually breathed Marxism." It was this revived historical materialism that Baran, along with Sweezy, who also sought to recapture the classical meaning of Marxism, were to bring to their work on *Monopoly Capital*.[46]

The Cuban Revolution in January 1959 was a turning point for Huberman, Sweezy, and Baran, and for *Monthly Review*. Visiting Cuba shortly after the revolutionary triumph, Huberman and Sweezy got to know Fidel Castro and Che Guevara (Sweezy to Baran, May 7, 1960; May 11, 1960). Huberman and Sweezy co-authored an influential work on the transformation of Cuban economic society, *Cuba: Anatomy of a Revolution* (1960), and were among the first to recognize that Cuba would necessarily evolve in a socialist direction. Baran traveled to Cuba for three weeks in September–October 1960, together with Huberman and Sweezy, and wrote his important "Reflections on the Cuban Revolution," appearing in *Monthly Review* in January 1961. Baran's *The Political Economy of Growth* took on a completely different significance with the Cuban Revolution. After Baran's death, Che Guevara wrote: "I believe it is not necessary to give evidence of the admiration I felt for *Compañero* Baran, as well as for his work on underdevelopment, which was so constructive in our nascent (and still weak) state of knowledge of economics."[47]

Baran spoke out strongly in defense of Cuba in the wake of the Bay of Pigs Invasion and the Cuban Missile Crisis, presenting his views on the radio as well as in articles. This led to Cold War attacks on him and the university pressuring him in various ways. Writing to Sweezy in 1961 on the university's attempts to clamp down on him, he confided: "One *should* be above all of this, one *should* know that one cannot have one's cake and eat it too, one *should* realize that after all this is a class struggle and à *la guerre comme à la guerre*—nevertheless it burns me all up, plays havoc with the nervous system, and the rational comprehension does very little if anything to one's irrational sensations and emotions" (Baran to Sweezy, June 30, 1961).

Baran had suffered his first heart attack in December 1960, shortly after returning from Cuba.[48] The pressure did not let up, and in May 1963 he was writing to Sweezy that due to Stanford's attempts to suppress his views (the president of the university declared his statements "irresponsible") and drive him out of the university, he was expected to carry "a teaching load that is about twice as large as that of my 'peers,' with a pay of about 60% of theirs" (Baran to Sweezy, May 26, 1963). In less than a year he died of a second heart attack.

The Making of *Monopoly Capital*

Baran and Sweezy's *Monopoly Capital: An Essay on the American Economic and Social Order* was to be the most influential work in Marxian political economy ever published in the United States. It was also in a number of respects an unfinished work. The book was published in 1966, two years after Baran's death. In his preface to the book, Sweezy indicated that two additional chapters had been drafted, "but in each case one or the other of us had raised important questions which still remained to be discussed and resolved. Since neither chapter was essential to the theme of the essay as a whole, the best solution seemed to be to omit them altogether. I reached this conclusion the more easily since even without these chapters the book turned out to be longer than I had expected or we had originally intended."[49]

Sweezy was right that the book could be read without these two additional chapters, and in its published form was to prove enormously important in reviving a critical Marxian political economy that dealt with the monopoly stage of capitalism and thus with twentieth-century conditions. Nevertheless, one of the missing chapters, "Some Theoretical Implications" (eventually published in *Monthly Review* in July–August 2012), attempted to deal with some of the larger historical and theoretical questions associated with their concept of economic surplus, and hence was crucial to the deeper and wider understanding of Baran and Sweezy's overall theoretical project. Indeed, some of what appeared to be inconsistencies in their treatment of economic surplus could not easily be resolved without it.[50] The other chapter, "The Quality of Monopoly Capitalist Society II" (eventually published in *Monthly Review* in July–August 2013 under the title "The Quality of Monopoly Capitalist Society: Culture and Communications") included a crucial critique of the culture and communications of capitalist society coupled with an unfinished treatment of mental health and related issues.[51] In this overall context, the authors' correspondence with respect to *Monopoly Capital* takes on added significance. It not only provides unique insights into the thinking that went into the published book, it also gives us a window into the struggles they were having in relation to those chapters that were drafted but remained unpublished and that were crucial to their overall critique.

Baran and Sweezy briefly discussed the general idea of doing a "joint opus" as early as the fall of 1952 (Sweezy to Baran, October 18, 1952). It was a few years later, however, after Baran had written *The Political Economy of Growth*, but before its publication, that they began to work on *Monopoly Capital*, which evolved out of both Sweezy's *The Theory of Capitalist Development* and Baran's *The Political Economy of Growth*. It was while Baran was in India and the typescript of Baran's book was being prepared for Blackwell that Sweezy wrote to Baran (December 19, 1955):

> I think I have started work on a book. I find it a little hard to define the subject and quite impossible to think of a title, but in general the problem is the nature of the giant corporation and what changes it makes in the structure and functioning of capitalism to have the capitalist function itself institutionalized in these huge affairs. All the traditional stuff about the capitalist conceived as a natural individual is out of date, and it is this undoubted fact that gives plausibility to all the fancy new theories of the "managerial revolution" type. But what no one has yet done is to point out the *real* meaning of what has happened: not that capitalism has been transformed or replaced, but that it has reached its streamlined apogee. The big corporation as an engine of accumulation puts to shame Marx's most ascetic accumulator. To bring this out into the light of day and explore its implications will be the theme of the opus.

Sweezy went on in this letter to present some of the ideas that were later to define chapter 1 of *Monopoly Capital* on "The Giant Corporation." He developed this idea and then proposed their doing it together in a letter to Baran on January 6, 1956. A letter that Baran wrote from Calcutta on January 31, 1956, indicated his enthusiasm for the project: "For basically priority number one job should be Monopoly Capitalism—as you say, for the rest of the world as well as for those in the U.S. who might be and become interested. The details we would have to talk over, but *en principe*, I am very much *in* favor of the modus operandi which you suggest.... The principal issue is to include in the basic model what is *essential* to it, and I have the feeling that in contradistinction of the competitive model of Marx the *state* has to be brought into the center of the stage, rather than a secondary factor."

From that point until Baran's death in 1964, Baran and Sweezy's correspondence, while addressing various developments in world history, Marxism, and *Monthly Review*, seldom strayed far from the issues of their joint opus. What is most remarkable about this correspondence is how two great Marxian political economists, each of world-historical stature, collaborated, developing their ideas by means of a written back-and-forth. Baran and Sweezy are often seen as always representing the same viewpoint, but these letters reveal how often and passionately they disagreed, and also how they almost always were able to transcend their disagreements by working out the problems step by step and by means of critical reason, in historical-materialist terms. The lowest point in their working relationship on the book came in September–October 1958 with what looked like a possible falling out due to Baran's reservations about Sweezy's approach to the crisis of Marxism. This did not seem to reflect substantive disagreements so much as the search for a method in response to the very real crisis of Marxism in the period. Their momentary disagreement, went so far as to induce Sweezy, who was despondent at the time over the enormous weight of editing *Monthly Review*, to suggest that the book not be by both of them throughout, but that each of them author parts of it separately. This was soon patched up, however, by means of a phone call and a letter from Baran, who wrote of the uniqueness of their "unalienated" intellectual relationship (Sweezy to Baran, September 30, 1958; Baran to Sweezy, October 3, 1958).

Other rifts that arose during their years working on *Monopoly Capital* were usually more specific and substantive. These disputes and their overcoming were the secret to the deep intellectual penetration and absolute clarity that were to characterize *Monopoly Capital*. Such disagreements were evident in their heated back-and-forth about such topics as: (1) fascism in the United States, (2) Thorstein Veblen, (3) underconsumption, (4) Rosa Luxemburg, (5) imperialism, and (6) the Sino-Soviet split. Sweezy was critical of what he saw as Baran's tendency to jump too quickly to the conclusion that full-fledged fascism was developing in the United States in the early 1950s, something that was soon clarified as the dangers and limitations of McCarthyism became clear (Sweezy to Baran, October 18 and October 29, 1952; Baran to Sweezy, October 25 and November 16, 1952).

The dispute over Veblen occurred in the context of the preparation of a special July–August 1957 issue of *Monthly Review* on the centennial of Veblen's birth. For this issue Sweezy wrote on Veblen's *Theory of Business Enterprise* and his *Absentee Ownership*, as well as a Review of the Month with Huberman on Veblen in general, while Baran wrote on *The Theory of the Leisure Class*.[52] Baran was highly critical of Veblen, even seeing him as tending toward fascism. In contrast, Sweezy saw Veblen as a genuine radical economist and the greatest early twentieth-century theorist of monopoly capitalism (Sweezy to Baran June 8 and June 13, 1957; Baran to Sweezy June 11 and June 17, 1957). In the end, Baran seems to have arrived at a much more favorable view of Veblen, making the latter's conception of the penetration of the sales effort into the production process (or what Baran and Sweezy called "the interpenetration effect") the linchpin in the chapter of *Monopoly Capital* on "The Sales Effort," which Baran drafted.[53]

Baran was also initially skeptical with regard to the concept of economic crises arising from underconsumption, questioning Sweezy's earlier analysis of the concept in *The Theory of Capitalist Development*. But Baran went on to develop his own distinctive radical approach to underconsumption—in his "Reflections on Underconsumption"—arriving at a similar reasoned, critical stance to Sweezy, who had by that time abandoned the term, though retaining some of the insights of the classic underconsumptionist perspective (Baran to Sweezy, May 15, 1952; Sweezy to Baran, October 12, 1952).[54] Related to this was Baran's contention that Sweezy had gone overboard in his criticisms of Luxemburg in *The Theory of Capitalist Development*. Since Sweezy too admired Luxemburg's critique of capitalist accumulation, this dispute was soon patched up. However, Sweezy objected to Baran's tendency to follow Lenin in identifying imperialism exclusively with the monopoly stage of capitalism, not seeing it as extending back to the colonial period. Here the problem was to bring the conceptual structure into line with what they both agreed upon—namely, the historic laws or tendencies of international capitalist exploitation (Sweezy to Baran, March 2 and March 7, 1964; Baran to Sweezy March 3 and March 9, 1964).

With the emergence of the Sino-Soviet split, Baran and Sweezy found themselves at odds, with Baran (perhaps due to his heritage) seeing it more in Soviet terms, and Sweezy more in Chinese terms. Baran's final letter to Harry Magdoff emphasized that he was dissatisfied with *Monthly Review*'s view on this. If he had lived, they would no doubt have reached a point of agreement as they had so often in the past (Baran to Sweezy, April 19, 24, and 27, 1963; Sweezy to Baran, April 22, 26, and 30, 1963; Baran to Magdoff, March 22, 1964).

What is so important today about these disputes, all of which were integral in various ways to their analysis in *Monopoly Capital*, was the careful way in which they laid out their historical and theoretical analysis in each case, giving us a clear window into the development of the Marxian critique of twentieth-century capitalism. As Baran wrote, "Either one sticks to Marxian dialectics or else I don't know what we are talking about" (Baran to Sweezy, March 3, 1964). It was precisely this that they had in common.

In an article on Baran for the *New Palgrave Dictionary of Economics* in 1987, Sweezy succinctly summarized *Monopoly Capital* as follows:

> The economic analysis of *Monopoly Capital* is a development and systematization of ideas already contained in [Paul Baran's] *The Political Economy of Growth* [1957] and Paul Sweezy's *The Theory of Capitalist Development* (1942). The central theme is that in a mature capitalist economy dominated by a handful of giant corporations the potential for accumulation far exceeds the profitable investment opportunities provided by the normal *modus operandi* of the private enterprise system. This results in a deepening tendency to stagnation which, if the system is to survive, must be continuously and increasingly counteracted by internal and

external factors. . . . In the authors' estimation—not always shared, or even
understood by critics—the new and original contributions of *Monopoly
Capital* had to do mainly with these counteracting factors and their far-
reaching consequences for the history, politics and culture of American
society during the period from roughly the 1890s to the 1950s when the
book was written. They intended it, in other words, as much more than a
work of economics in the usual meaning of the term.[55]

The analytical device they used to get at the role of these countervailing factors
was to examine the generation and absorption of economic surplus—a concept
modeled after Marx's surplus value—but freed from the usual association of the
latter exclusively with the notion of profits + rent + interest. The flexibility of the
economic surplus concept, which in its most developed definition meant the
difference between the income that could be generated with existing economic and
technological means and the costs of productive labor, allowed Baran and Sweezy
to "follow the money." That is, they could ascertain the statistical traces of the more
convoluted value relations of a monopoly-capitalist economy in comparison with
its freely competitive predecessor. In a monopoly-capitalist society, characterized
by excess capacity and prone to the stagnation of private accumulation, various
counteracting factors intervened to prop up and perpetuate the system. It therefore
became necessary to explore the ways in which the sales effort, the state, finance,
and other factors, entered in to absorb the excess (in the sense of uninvestible)
surplus, thereby altering all aspects of the economic and social order and creating
a system that was increasingly irrational. This extended to the distortion of
consumption itself. As Baran expressed it, in monopoly capitalism workers "do
not want what they need and do not need what they want."[56]

The first title suggested for the book, as far as their extant letters reveal,
arose more than two years into the project. In March 1958 Baran wrote: "As
a possible title of the *Buechlein* it occurs to me: *Advanced Capitalism: Studies
in the Generation and Utilization of the Economic Surplus in the United States.*
(While keeping the subtitle which would be useful to indicate both the tentative
nature of the operation and its orientation towards the U.S., the main title could
be also *Monopoly Capitalism, The Big Business Society, The Corporate Empire,*
or something else similarly 'catchy')" (Baran to Sweezy, March 5, 1958). Sweezy
spent the next month in Palo Alto and they probably agreed on the title of
Monopoly Capital at that time. In any case, by October 1958 they were referring
to their book "on Monopoly Capital" (Baran to Sweezy, October 3, 1958). In
July 1959 Baran proposed a new chapter outline of the book (there had been
a couple prior to that), which, though still far from the final version, had begun

to take shape in terms of the main thread of the generation and absorption of surplus, as well as some of key chapter designations (Baran to Sweezy, July 9, 1959). It is clear from their correspondence that, by the end of 1959, the chapter outline they were then working with conformed to the one they would publish in a special July-August 1962 issue of *Monthly Review* devoted to a preview of parts of their forthcoming book and titled "Monopoly Capital: Two Chapters on the America Economic and Social Order." The two chapters included in the special issue were "The Giant Corporation" and what they then called "On the Quality of Monopoly Capitalist Society I." (The latter chapter was to be revised and shortened in the final version of the book and the roman numeral dropped from the title.)

The Table of Contents for the book as envisioned in the 1962 special issue was as follows:

This remained the Table of Contents during the remainder of the time they worked on the book together, with the sole exception that a new chapter 9 was added on "Monopoly Capitalism and Race Relations," resulting in a renumbering of the subsequent chapters. But in the published version, as Sweezy explained in his preface, the draft chapters of "Some Implications for Economic Theory" (later entitled "Some Theoretical Implications") and "On the Quality of Monopoly Capitalist II" were dropped from the book, since final versions had not been agreed upon by both of the authors. This resulted in a further renumbering of the chapters, accordingly, with chapter 9 as "Monopoly Capitalism and Race Relations"; chapter 10 as "On the Quality of Monopoly Capitalist Society"; and chapter 11 as "The Irrational System."

For Baran and Sweezy, as Sweezy repeatedly stated, the originality of *Monopoly*

Capital did not lie in the first three chapters, aside from their use of the economic surplus concept. The explanation of the problem of accumulation and stagnation had already been definitively laid out in their view by the Polish economist Michał Kalecki, who had anticipated much of John Maynard Keynes's 1936 *General Theory of Employment, Interest, and Money*, and by the Austrian economist Josef Steindl, who had worked with Kalecki at the Oxford Institute of Statistics during the Second World War. It was Kalecki's and Steindl's work that inspired the chapters on monopoly capitalism in Baran's *The Political Economy of Growth*, and which was later to induce Baran and Sweezy in *Monopoly Capital* to enunciate their famous thesis that "the *normal* state of the monopoly capitalist economy is stagnation."[58]

Where the true originality of *Monopoly Capital* resided rather was in connecting this problem of accumulation under monopoly capitalism, associated with the tendency to generate too much surplus, to the problem of surplus absorption, in line with their Hegelian motto "The truth is the whole." If monopoly capital did not simply stagnate (much less fall into a deep depression) due to the inability of capitalist consumption and investment to absorb the enormous surplus-generating potential of the economy, then this had to be accounted for by examining the ways in which the system managed to absorb surplus outside the normal private accumulation process, and in ways contrary to freely competitive capitalism. Here they focused on how the surplus was absorbed by the expansion of civilian government, militarism and imperialism, and the sales effort (with absorption by finance added to the end of the sales effort chapter).[59]

Much of the analysis was directed at what in classical economics had been called unproductive expenditures, that is, those not directly productive of surplus value and/or not representing use values that would be present in a rational society geared to social needs. In broader terms, these forms of surplus absorption could be considered economic waste. Manifestations of this include military spending, most of the "criminal justice system," advertising, product differentiation, unnecessary model changes, product obsolescence, luxury expenditures, public relations spending, insurance, and financial speculation. In relation to the sales effort, Baran and Sweezy placed heavy emphasis on what they called "the interpenetration effect," through which waste penetrated into the costs of production, such that workers were compelled, in purchasing everything from toothpaste to cars, to pay for costs that were primarily related to the marketing rather than the actual production costs of goods.

By exploring the absorption of surplus in this way, Baran and Sweezy were able to uncover the political-economic relations that distinguished monopoly capitalism, in such areas as civilian government, the military, imperialism, the sales effort, finance, education, poverty, culture, and communications (though the last two of these were left out of the published book). They also went on to describe the wider political-economic history of U.S. monopoly capitalism, monopoly capitalism, and race relations. The concluding chapter on "The Irrational System" explained that monopoly capitalism could not reasonably lay claim even to the limited *quid pro quo* (or equal exchange) rationality of competitive capitalism. Rather, it was characterized by growing irrationalities at every level: sex and love, family life, health (including mental health), culture, education, economic production, the state, and the world system.

The economic surplus was essentially equivalent to society's social accumulation fund at any given point in time, reflecting a social formation's freedom to pursue its ends beyond the costs associated with the value of labor power (the reproduction costs of productive workers and their families).[60] Joseph D. Phillips provided a long appendix to *Monopoly Capital* in which he estimated the actual economic surplus in 1963 to be 56.1 percent of GNP. Michael Dawson and I, building on Phillips's methodology, later estimated the surplus, more conservatively, at 49.9 percent in 1963, and 55 percent in 1988, at the end of Reagan's second term.[61] Although the economic surplus concept raised all sorts of problems of conceptualization and empirical analysis (due largely to the fact that capitalist accounting disguised the surplus in various ways), such difficulties did not prevent it from opening up questions about the utilization of society's surplus, and thus the wider ramifications of an increasingly irrational monopoly-capitalist society, alienated in terms of both class and the monopoly power of firms. It allowed one to understand that society's surplus was being wasted from any rational social standpoint on military spending, marketing, financial speculation, and production of "goods" (often better characterized as "bads") for which demand was insatiable, since not aimed at satisfaction or real social and individual needs. The result was a society that produced needless and even harmful products efficiently, while neglecting many of the most vital needs, including the health, education, and welfare of the population.

For Baran and Sweezy, writing in the mid-1960s, the working class in advanced capitalism had been incorporated into the system partly through imperialism and waste, and partly by being divided by race. The main immediate prospects for revolutionary change therefore lay in the populations of color in the advanced capitalist states and in the third world revolution then erupting, as witnessed by the wars/revolutions in Vietnam, Korea, Cuba, and Algeria. The forces for radical change in the United States at the time they were writing were limited, and the movement for black liberation could be defeated. But looking at the long-term and in global perspective, there was "no reason," they wrote, "to write off permanently the possibility of a real revolutionary movement in the United States. . . . In the meantime what we need in the United States is historical perspective, courage to face the facts, and faith in mankind and its future. Having these, we can recognize our moral obligation to devote ourselves to fighting against an evil and destructive system which maims, oppresses, and dishonors those who live under it, and which threatens devastation and death to millions of others around the globe."[62]

Readers of Baran and Sweezy's correspondence will notice the external as well as internal struggles that they were engaged with in developing their opus. In writing *Monopoly Capital*, Baran and Sweezy were very much concerned with views of left-Keynesian and socialist economists associated with Cambridge University in England, particularly those of Joan Robinson and Nicholas Kaldor. Robinson, in particular, had been influenced by Kalecki, and was open to many of Marx's ideas. Baran and Sweezy were friends with both Robinson and Kaldor (as well as other Cambridge economists, such as Maurice Dobb, an old-style Marxist economist, and Piero Sraffa, who was to become famous for his creation of a neo-Ricardian tradition in economics).

Robinson was one of the key younger figures surrounding Keynes when he was writing *The General Theory*, and one of the foremost developers of imperfect competition theory in economics. She was also the courageous author of *An Essay on Marxian Economics*, which, though not itself Marxian in orientation, had done much to forward Marx's ideas.[63] But Robinson was to lambast Baran's *The Political Economy of Growth* for its argument on inflation. For Robinson, the notion that Keynesian deficit spending, particularly if focused on military expenditures, could, in an economy operating below potential output, generate inflationary spending—as Baran argued in *The Political Economy of Growth*—was all wrong, and was a retreat to pre-Keynesian analysis, even if constructed on a different basis.[64]

Sweezy replied to Robinson's original 1957 review of Baran's *The Political Economy of Growth* in *The Nation*, in which her criticism was first advanced. Robinson, he said, had failed to recognize that, in Baran's view, Keynesian deficit spending could be inflationary even below full employment, precisely because of its artificial creation of demand not through investment but through the promotion of "military supplies and similar 'assets.'" Such artificial means of stimulation continually increased "the ratio of cash or near-cash in the hands of the public to currently produced marketable output"—whereas the financing of this by the state was increasingly carried out, in effect, by printing money. (As Prabhat Patnaik would later point out, Baran was implicitly talking about a society in which the danger of inflation was related to wealth or asset preference within a developed financial system, making price increases more perilous.)

Robinson, however, refused to enter a debate on the subject. She was to repeat the same criticism a few years later in her *Economic Philosophy*—something that

Baran bitterly noted (Baran to Sweezy, October 2, 1962; see also Baran to Sweezy, August 22 and August 30, 1962; Sweezy to Baran, September 22, 1962).[65] This certainly made the issue of inflation doubly serious and difficult for Baran and Sweezy, deterring them from straightforwardly advancing Baran's earlier analysis. All of this helps explain the fact that they failed to deal adequately with inflation in their opus, a shortcoming that was to be highlighted by later thinkers.[66]

In reading Baran and Sweezy's correspondence, we discover that Sweezy, who drafted the chapter on civilian government spending (and also the chapter on militarism and imperialism), was struggling to figure out where inflation best fit into the argument. For some reason he did not think it fit well into the main chapter on government spending, as he had drafted it; no doubt because the analysis in the chapter employed a balanced federal budget, without deficits. In writing to Baran, he suggested that the inflation discussion should go into chapter 8, "On the History of Monopoly Capitalism," but in the end it was not inserted there, and the subject of inflation was missing from the book (Sweezy to Baran, October 4, 1962).[67] This may have been due to Baran's untimely death, and Sweezy's reluctance to insert anything as major as that, and as controversial, since they had not worked it out together.

In 1974, Sweezy sought to make up for this deficiency, at least with respect to Baran himself, in an article for *Monthly Review* on "Baran and the Danger of Inflation," pointing to Baran's prescient contribution to a theory of stagflation. "Apart from conservative fundamentalists," Sweezy wrote, "Paul Baran was perhaps the first economist to warn of the inflationary danger inherent in Keynesian fiscal and monetary policies."[68] Still the lack of a discussion of inflation in *Monopoly Capital* itself remained a weakness of the book (though not of the overall theory), given that stagnation emerged in the late 1970s in the confusing form of stagflation, something that Baran had foreseen a decade earlier.

Of much more direct importance to the argument in *Monopoly Capital* were arguments that Kaldor had directed against Baran's *The Political Economy of Growth*. Kaldor had written a review of Baran's book in March 1958 in the *American Economic Review* that argued that the Marxian theory of exploitation, and hence Baran's notion of a rising surplus, was no longer valid given a fairly stable wage share of output (viewed then as an established law characterizing the modern economy).[69] Baran's long preface to the 1962 printing of *The Political Economy of Growth* was partly devoted to explaining that the surplus generated within the economy was hidden in the growth of waste and unproductive labor, disguising the rising rate of exploitation. Much of the surplus, Baran argued there, was actually concealed in the wages of workers who were forced to purchase out of their wages use values that contained more and more negative elements (specifically capitalist use values), increasing the costs of the products for consumers in ways that were essential for the realization of capitalist profits. In essence, this conformed to what Marx had called "profits by deduction," whereby capitalists made profits by appropriating part of the wages of the workers (Baran to Sweezy, May 2, 1960). In monopoly capitalism, Baran and Sweezy argued, the growing dominance of the "interpenetration effect," whereby sales costs were intermingled with production costs, meant that the commodities produced were geared more and more to the realization of profits rather than the satisfaction of social needs, distorting the entire economy (Baran to Sweezy, March 3, 1964; Sweezy to Baran, March 7, 1964). Only a minuscule part of the price of foods sold in the supermarket, for example, was traceable to the direct cost of production of the farmer; the rest was attributable to finance, food processing, marketing, distribution, monopoly pricing, etc.—all beyond the farm. The cost of bread was not mainly a product of the cost of wheat production or baking but included the cost of the production of various additives put into the bread (preservatives, food coloring, etc.), the cost of the plastic bags in which the bread was sold—including the marketing that went into the making of the bags—and the branding of the bread. All of this was formally rational (but substantively irrational) in a monopoly-capitalist society confronted with a chronic lack of effective demand.[70]

The more complicated aspects of this analysis, involving the whole question of the effects on wages, were to be addressed in the chapter 9 on "Some Theoretical Implications" that Baran had drafted and was redrafting in response to Sweezy's criticisms in March 1964. Their letters from February 25, 1964, to March 9, 1964, represented the most intensive theoretical discussion of their entire correspondence. Baran's last letter to Sweezy, of March 9, was never completed or mailed. Instead it seems clear that the ideas he was developing in it on the switch of capitalism from a progressive to a "retrograde" system inspired much of his rewrite of the "Some Theoretical Implications" chapter. Baran was about halfway into the rewrite of that chapter when he suffered his fatal heart attack on March 26, dying the following day. The subsequent publication of "Some Theoretical Implications" more than half a century later in July–August 2016 integrated the nineteen pages of the new draft that Baran was working on with the original version of the rest of the chapter, together with annotations based on their letters. These final letters of Baran and Sweezy (along with "Some Theoretical Implications") thus represent their last struggles together to question the rationality of production under monopoly capitalism.

The Longer View

What was so extraordinary about Baran and Sweezy's *Monopoly Capital*, and the reason it exerted so much influence on the U.S. left in the 1960s and 1970s, is that it leaped across the barriers that normally separate economics from sociology, bringing both within a single whole. Recognizing this, they made *An Essay on the American Economic and Social Order* the subtitle of their work. The social was thus treated equally with the economic. The emphasis on the utilization or absorption of the economic surplus carried into every aspect of social life, leading to many of their more penetrating observations. Thus we are told in chapter 6 on "Civilian Government" that "except in times of crisis," where more authoritarian structures arise, the political system is "democratic in form and plutocratic in content." And in the final chapter they talk about how the internal malfunctioning of monopoly capitalist society has as its "logical outcome," if left to itself and allowed to triumph, "the spread of increasingly severe psychic disorders leading to the impairment and eventual breakdown of the system's ability to function even on its own terms."[71] This destruction of humanity itself was the greatest tragedy. Hope thus lay, for Baran and Sweezy, in a world revolution that would revitalize from without as well as within the emancipatory hopes of humankind. Critics have often suggested, with good reason, that Baran and Sweezy's *Monopoly Capital* neglected culture and communications.[72] We now know, however, as a result of the publication of the draft chapter of *Monopoly Capital* on "The Quality of Monopoly Capitalist Society: Culture and Communications" (originally designated as "On the Quality of Monopoly Capitalist Society II") how deep their concern regarding what they called "the cultural apparatus of monopoly capitalist society" was—a fact that the present correspondence drives home.[73]

Baran and Sweezy's critique of waste as the primary form of absorption of surplus has had an immense impact on the left's understanding of today's environmental problems, and the possibility of transcending them. This was something that Sweezy was to point to in subsequent essays, including "Cars and Cities" and "Capitalism and the Environment."[74]

Still more significant, Baran and Sweezy's analysis was critical to the understanding of the entire imperialist system in the late twentieth century, and, as Samir Amin argues, has taken on added significance in the analysis of the generalized monopoly order of today. Their discussions of monopoly, multinational corporations, militarism, and imperialism in *Monopoly Capital*, and in their letters collected in this volume, thus provide us with a window onto some of the crucial problems of accumulation on a world scale.[75]

In all these, and other respects, Baran and Sweezy's works and correspondence represent "the longer view," the title that Baran chose for his essay collection (published posthumously). More than a half-century later their letters, along with their major published works are as fresh and as insightful as when they were first written.

In relation to Marx and Engels's own correspondence, Lenin once wrote:

> Its scientific and its political value is tremendous. Not only do Marx and
> Engels stand out before the reader in clear relief in all their greatness, but
> the extremely rich theoretical content of Marxism is graphically revealed,
> because in their letters Marx and Engels return again and again to the most
> diverse aspects of their doctrine, emphasizing and explaining—at times
> discussing and debating—what is newest (in relation to earlier views), most
> important and most difficult. . . .
>
>   If one were to attempt to define in a single word the focus, so to speak,
> of the whole correspondence, the central point at which the whole body of
> ideas expressed and discussed converges—that word would be *dialectics*.
> The application of materialist dialectics to the reshaping of all political
> economy from its foundations up, its application to history, natural science,
> philosophy and to the policy and tactics of the working class.[76]

It is perhaps the highest conceivable compliment to Baran and Sweezy's
correspondence that the things that Lenin said with respect to Marx and Engels's
correspondence are largely applicable to Baran and Sweezy's letters as well,
although written by very different thinkers under very different circumstances.
Baran and Sweezy were, above all, the greatest analysts of *The Age of Monopoly
Capital* in the late twentieth century, extending into a whole new stage of capitalist
development the historical materialist method forged by Marx and Engels. In
the letters selected here they distilled the essence of a critical-materialist and
dialectical mode of inquiry and applied it to what is now known as the "golden
era" of monopoly capital and unrivaled U.S. hegemony: the age directly preceding
and giving rise to our own.

---

1.   Paul A. Baran and Paul M. Sweezy, *Monopoly Capital* (New York: Monthly Review Press, 1966).
2.   On the contemporary influence of Baran and Sweezy's *Monopoly Capital* see the contributions
      by Samir Amin, John Bellamy Foster, Kent Klitgaard, Costas Lapavitsas, David Matthews,
      Michael Meeropol, Ivan Mendieta-Muñoz, Prabhat Patnaik, Intan Suwandi, Jan Toporowski,
      and Mary V. Wrenn in the "*Monopoly Capital*: A Half-Century On" issue of *Monthly Review*
      68/3 (July–August 2016).
3.   Paul A. Baran and Paul M. Sweezy, "Some Theoretical Implications," *Monthly Review* 64/3
      (July–August 2012): 24–59; and "The Quality of Monopoly Capitalist Society: Culture and
      Communications," *Monthly Review* 65/3 (July–August 2013): 43–64.
4.   The complete archived Baran and Sweezy letters can be found in the "Baran and Sweezy
      Archive" at MonthlyReview.org. Their co-authored essays include Paul A. Baran and Paul M.
      Sweezy, "Introduction to 'Monopoly Capital: Two Chapters,'" *Monthly Review* 14/3–4 (July–
      August 1962): 131–34; "Rejoinder [to Anatoly Butenko]," *Monthly Review* 14/12 (April 1963):

669–71, 674–78; "Theses on Advertising," *Science and Society* 28 (Winter 1964): 20–30; "Notes on the Theory of Imperialism," *Monthly Review* 17/10 (March 1966): 15–31; "The Economics of Two Worlds," in Baran, *The Longer View* (New York: Monthly Review, 1969), 68–91.

5. Paul M. Sweezy, "Interview," *Monthly Review* 51/1 (May 1999): 45.

6. Paul M. Sweezy, "Paul Alexander Baran: A Personal Memoir," in *Paul A. Baran (1910–1964): A Collective Portrait*, ed. Paul M. Sweezy and Leo Huberman (New York: Monthly Review Press, 1965), 29–33; "Baran, Paul Alexander (1910–1964)," *The New Palgrave: A Dictionary of Economics*, vol. 1 (London: Macmillan, 1987), 188–89.

7. Paul A. Baran, "No Vacation from Politics," *Monthly Review* 67/8 (January 2016): 51–55; Sweezy, "Paul Alexander Baran," 32–33; Rudolf Hilferding, *Finance Capital: A Study of the Latest Phase of Capitalist Development* (London: Routledge, 1981). Baran's articles and radio broadcasts in Germany in this period have been translated and are available with his papers at Stanford University. They can be accessed at http://www.oac.cdlib.org/findaid/ark:/13030/c8xs5zkx/. In addition to the pen name of Alexander Gabriel in writing for *Die Gesellschaft*, Baran wrote under other pseudonyms (one of which was Bruno Iltis) for other publications.

8. All dates of letters in parentheses in this Introduction reflect those in the volume itself.

9. Sweezy, "Paul Alexander Baran," 33–35; Elaine Winick to Paul M. Sweezy, April 20, 1965, Monthly Review Foundation Archives. Dubrovsky was a victim of the Stalinist purge but lived to be rehabilitated. Roy Medvedev, *Let History Judge* (New York: Columbia University Press, 1989), 437.

10. Much text here and in the next few pages is adapted from two sources: John Bellamy Foster, "The Commitment of an Intellectual: Paul M. Sweezy (1910–2004)," and "Paul Alexander Baran (1910–1964)," in *A Biographical Dictionary of Dissenting Economists*, ed. Philip Arestis and Malcolm Sawyer (Northampton, MA: Edward Elgar, 2000), 36–42. The principal primary source on Sweezy used here is Paul M. Sweezy, "Interview," November 1986–February 1987, Columbia University Oral History Project.

11. Paul M. Sweezy, "Demand under Conditions of Oligopoly," *Journal of Political Economy* 47 (August 1939): 568–73; Foster, "The Commitment of the Intellectual," 7–10, 14.

12. John Kenneth Galbraith and Shigeto Tsuru, tributes to Paul M. Sweezy, *Monthly Review* 11/51 (April 2000): 49, 59–60.

13. John Kenneth Galbraith, *A Life in Our Times* (Boston: Houghton Mifflin, 1981), 219–24.

14. Tibor Scitovsky to Paul M. Sweezy, January 25, 1994, Monthly Review Foundation Archives.

15. Sweezy, "Paul Alexander Baran," 41. Sweezy's explanation here, though clearly correct, overstated the case a bit, since Baran did not refrain from publicly criticizing Stalinism in a number of his writings. Still, his criticisms are more evident in the private letters in this volume.

16. The Baran and Marcuse correspondence is included in Baran's papers at Stanford and is available online through the Monthly Review Foundation at http://monthlyreview.org/commentary/baran-marcuse-correspondence/.

17. Paul M. Sweezy, "The Laws of Capitalism," *Monthly Review* 63/1 (May 2011): 12–16; John Bellamy Foster, "On the Laws of Capitalism: Insights from the Sweezy-Schumpeter Debate," *Monthly Review* 63/1 (May 2011): 1–11; "Notes from the Editors," *Monthly Review* 63/10 (March 2012): inside covers.

18. Albert Einstein, "Why Socialism?," *Monthly Review* 1/1 (May 1949): 9–15.

19. I. F. Stone, *The Hidden History of the Korean War* (New York: Monthly Review Press, 1952).

20. See Paul A. Baran, *The Longer View* (New York: Monthly Review Press, 1969), xi, 203–09.

21. Paul A. Baran, "Fascism in America," *Monthly Review* 4/6 (October 1952): 181–89; Baran, "Rejoinder" (on fascism), *Monthly Review* 4/12 (April 1953): 502–4.

22. Leo Huberman and Paul M. Sweezy, "Goldwaterism," *Monthly Review* 16/5 (September 1964): 273–83.

23. John J. Simon, "*Sweezy v. New Hampshire*: The Radicalism of Principle," *Monthly Review* 51/11 (April 2000): 35–37; Simon, "Albert Einstein, Radical," *Monthly Review* 57/1 (May 2005): 11–12; Otto Nathan and Heinz Norden, eds., *Einstein on Peace* (New York: Schocken Books, 1960), 546–50.

24. McCarthy's own committee was the Senate Committee on Government Operations (known until 1952 as the Senate Committee on Expenditures in the Executive Department). The two other major inquisition committees in Congress were the House Un-American Activities Committee and the Subcommittee on Internal Security of the Senate Judiciary Committee.

25. I. F. Stone, *The I.F. Stone Weekly Reader* (New York: Random House, 1973), 30–33; Leo Huberman and Paul M. Sweezy, "A Challenge to the Book Burners," *Monthly Review* 5/4 (August 1953): 158–73; Simon, "*Sweezy v. New Hampshire*"; Leo Huberman and Paul Sweezy, "Defend the First Amendment," *Monthly Review* 5/7 (November 1953): 289–92.

26. Simon, "*Sweezy v. New Hampshire*"; U.S. Supreme Court, *Sweezy v. New Hampshire*, October Term 1956, *U.S. Reports* 1957 (354 U.S. 234).

27. Sweezy, "Paul Alexander Baran," 38, 44, 57; Russell Jacoby, *The Last Intellectuals* (New York: Basic Books, 1987), 177.

28. Harry Magdoff, "The Achievement of Paul Baran," in Sweezy and Huberman, *Paul A. Baran*, 72.

29. All of these essays are included in Baran, *The Longer View*.

30. The same point was to conclude Baran's review, in which he complained of "ever new 'theoretical' constructs that explain with much pomp and circumstance a nation's economic growth by that nation's propensity to grow." Paul A. Baran, review of W. W. Rostow, *The Process of Economic Growth*, in *American Economic Review* 42/5 (December 1952): 921–23.

31. Sweezy, "Paul Alexander Baran," 45. This became the motto of Baran and Sweezy's *Monopoly Capital*.

32. Baran, *The Longer View*, 308–15. Baran's close study of India's economic history and conditions—see his letters to Sweezy of December 15, 1955, and January 8, 1956—no doubt contributed to the strength of his treatment of India in *The Political Economy of Growth*, with these parts of the manuscript no doubt revised for the final version of the book.

33. Anonymous reviewer for Blackwell, quoted in Sweezy, "Paul Alexander Baran," 45–46. See also R. B. Sutcliffe, "Introduction," in Paul A. Baran, *The Political Economy of Growth* (London: Penguin, 1973), 65–66.

34. Sweezy, "Baran, Paul Alexander (1910–1964)," 188–89.

35. This and the following three paragraphs are adapted from Foster, "Paul Alexander Baran (1910–1964)," 38–40; see also John Bellamy Foster, *The Theory of Monopoly Capitalism* (New York: Monthly Review Press, 2014), 161–78.

36. Paul A. Baran, *The Political Economy of Growth* (New York: Monthly Review Press, 1962), 22–24.

37. Ibid., 41–43.

38. Ibid., 136–44; Karl Marx, *Capital*, vol. 1 (London: Penguin, 1976), 914–26.

39. Baran, *The Political Economy of Growth*, 144–62; Andre Gunder Frank, "The Development of Underdevelopment," *Monthly Review* 18/4 (September 1966): 17–31. On the concept of autocentric accumulation see Samir Amin, *Unequal Development* (New York: Monthly Review Press, 1976), 76–78.

40. See Michael Newman, *Ralph Miliband and the Politics of the New Left* (New York: Monthly Review Press, 2002), 63–65.

41. Leo Huberman and Paul M. Sweezy, "The Hungarian Tragedy," *Monthly Review* 8/8 (December 1956): 259.

42. Sweezy had sent Baran the Review of the Month addressing the Soviet invasion of Hungary prior to its publication the following month.

43. These essays were published in Baran's posthumous *The Longer View*, grouped together under the section title "On Marxism." The two essays, "The Crisis of Marxism" and "The Nature of Marxism," which appeared in the October and November 1958 issues of *Monthly Review*, were combined into a single essay "On the Nature of Marxism" in the book.

44. Baran, *The Longer View*, 19–42, xv. Sweezy also addressed the post-1956 crisis of Marxism in the same issue in which Baran's "Crisis of Marxism" originally appeared. See Paul M. Sweezy, "A Talk to Students," *Monthly Review* 10/6 (October 1958): 219–23.

45. Baran, *The Longer View*, 32–36.

46. Magdoff, "The Achievement of Paul Baran," 63.

47. Ernesto Che Guevara, tribute to Paul Baran, in Huberman and Sweezy, *Paul Alexander Baran*, 107–8; Leo Huberman and Paul M. Sweezy, *Cuba: Anatomy of a Revolution* (New York: Monthly Review Press, 1960); Baran, *The Longer View*, 388–436.

48. Sweezy, "Paul Alexander Baran," 47.

49. Baran and Sweezy, *Monopoly Capital*, ix. See also Paul M. Sweezy, "Monopoly Capitalism," in *The New Palgrave: A Dictionary of Economics,* vol. 3 (London: Macmillan, 1987), 541–44.

50. Paul A. Baran and Paul M. Sweezy, "Some Theoretical Implications," *Monthly Review* 64/3 (July–August 2012): 24–59.

51. Paul A. Baran and Paul M. Sweezy, "The Quality of Monopoly Capitalist Society: Culture and Communications," *Monthly Review* 65/3 (July–August 2013): 43–64.

52. Leo Huberman and Paul M. Sweezy, "Thorstein Bunde Veblen, 1857–1957," 65–75; Paul A. Baran, "The Theory of the Leisure Class," 83–90; and Paul M. Sweezy, "The Theory of Business Enterprise and Absentee Ownership," 105–11—all in *Monthly Review* 3/4 (July–August 1957). See also Paul M. Sweezy, "Veblen on American Capitalism," in *Thorstein Veblen: A Critical Reappraisal*, ed. Douglas Dowd (Ithaca, NY: Cornell University Press, 1958), 177–97.

53. Baran and Sweezy, *Monopoly Capital*, 132–33.

54. See also Baran, *The Longer View*, 185–202; Paul M. Sweezy, *The Present as History* (New York: Monthly Review Press, 1953), 358–60; Foster, *The Theory of Monopoly Capitalism*, 19–21, 75–83.

55. Sweezy, "Baran, Paul Alexander," 1:189; see also Sweezy, "Monopoly Capitalism," 541–44.

56. Baran, *The Longer View*, 30.

57. Paul A. Baran and Paul M. Sweezy, "Monopoly Capital: Two Chapters," special issue, *Monthly Review* 14/3–4 (July–August 1962): 132–33.

58. Baran and Sweezy, *Monopoly Capital*, 108.

59. Baran and Sweezy sent chapters of *Monopoly Capital* to Harry Magdoff for comments as they were writing it. Worried that they would never complete the book at that rate, Magdoff encouraged them to proceed without his comments. One of his criticisms, which he would later raise in a review of their book, was that they had not dealt enough with finance, a criticism to which Sweezy was later to accede. Nevertheless, *Monopoly Capital* was unique in incorporating finance (albeit briefly) into the question of surplus absorption, in a way that was historically prescient and presaged the later pioneering work of Magdoff and Sweezy in this respect. See Harry Magdoff, "Monopoly Capital," *Economic Development and Cultural Change* 16/1 (October 1967): 145–50; Paul M. Sweezy, "*Monopoly Capital* after Twenty-Five Years," *Monthly Review* 43/7 (December 1991): 52–57; John Bellamy Foster and Fred Magdoff, *The Great Financial Crisis* (New York: Monthly Review Press, 2009), 63–76.

60. See Foster, *The Theory of Monopoly Capitalism*, 17, 28, 46, 95.

61.   On the statistical conceptualization of Baran and Sweezy's economic surplus concept see
      Joseph D. Phillips, "Estimating the Economic Surplus," in Baran and Sweezy, *Monopoly
      Capital*, 369–91; Michael Dawson and John Bellamy Foster, "The Tendency of Surplus
      to Rise, 1963–1988," in *The Economic Surplus in Advanced Economies*, ed. John B. Davis
      (Brookfield, VT: Edward Elgar, 1992), 42–70.

62.   Baran and Sweezy, *Monopoly Capital*, 366–67.

63.   Joan Robinson, *An Essay on Marxian Economics* (London: Macmillan, 1942).

64.   Joan Robinson, "The Policy of Backward Nations," *The Nation* (June 1, 1957), 485; and
      Robinson, *Economic Philosophy* (New York: Doubleday, 1962), 97.

65.   Paul M. Sweezy, "Baran and the Danger of Inflation," *Monthly Review* 26/7 (December 1974):
      11–14; Prabhat Patnaik, "*Monopoly Capital* Then and Now," *Monthly Review* 68/3 (July–
      August 2016), 34–35; Baran, *The Political Economy of Growth*, 123–25. Baran admitted in his
      October 2, 1962, letter that Robinson's argument against him was partly justified, showing a
      degree of uncertainty in this respect. Yet Baran's argument proved to be of real importance.

66.   Patnaik, "*Monopoly Capital* Then and Now," 34–35.

67.   It is significant that Sweezy's letter to Baran on where to place the inflation discussion in
      Monopoly Capital was written only weeks after their correspondence on Robinson's criticisms
      in *Economic Philosophy*. Robinson's criticism of Baran's argument on the danger of inflation
      pointed to both the importance of the issue and the difficulties in addressing it. It remained
      one of the issues that got set aside, and unfortunately was not dealt with due to Baran's death.
      History, however, vindicated Baran's approach to the topic in *The Political Economy of
      Growth*. Moreover, Sweezy's famous kinked-demand theory of oligopolistic pricing, which
      had been incorporated into the argument of *Monopoly Capital*, was often employed by radical
      economics to explain the inflationary tendencies inherent in monopoly capital: the fact that
      prices only went one way—up. See Harry Magdoff and Paul M. Sweezy, *The End of Prosperity*
      (New York: Monthly Review Press, 1977), 15–20.

68.   Sweezy, "Baran and the Danger of Inflation," 11.

69.   Nicholas Kaldor, "Review of Paul A. Baran, 'The Political Economy of Growth,'" *American
      Economic Review* (March 1958). See also Nicholas Kaldor, "A Model of Economic Growth,"
      Economic Journal 67 (December 1957): 621; Baran and Sweezy, *Monopoly Capital*, 75.

70.   Baran and Sweezy, "Some Theoretical Implications," 53–56; Baran, *The Political Economy of
      Growth*, viii–xxv; John Bellamy Foster, "A Missing Chapter of Monopoly Capital," *Monthly
      Review* 64/3 (July–August 2012): 13–21.

71.   Baran and Sweezy, 155, 364.

72.   Dan Smythe, "Communications: Blindspot of Western Marxism," *Canadian Journal
      of Political and Social Theory* 1/3 (Fall 1977): 1–27; Dan Schiller, *How to Think About
      Information* (Urbana: University of Illinois Press, 2006), chap. 1.

73.   Baran and Sweezy, "The Quality of Monopoly Capitalist Society: Culture and
      Communications"; John Bellamy Foster and Robert W. McChesney, "The Cultural Apparatus
      of Monopoly Capital," *Monthly Review* 65/3 (July–August 2013): 1–33.

74.   Paul M. Sweezy, "Cars and Cities," *Monthly Review* 24/11 (April 1973): 1–18; Harry Magdoff and
      Paul M. Sweezy, "Capitalism and the Environment," *Monthly Review* 41/2 (June 1989): 1–10.

75.   Samir Amin, "Reading *Capital*, Reading Historical Capitalisms," *Monthly Review* 68/3 (July–
      August 2016): 148–49; and Amin, *The Law of Worldwide Value* (New York: Monthly Review
      Press, 2010), 13, 26–28.

76.   V. I. Lenin, extract in Karl Marx and Frederick Engels, *Selected Correspondence, 1844–1895*
      (Moscow: Progress Publishers, 1975), 13–14.

Editors' Note on the Text

The entire archive of letters is available online at the Paul A. Baran archive at Stanford University: http://www.oac.cdlib.org/findaid/ark:/13030/c8xs5zkx/.

Each letter is preceded by the writer-recipient's initials (e.g. PAB-PMS is a letter written by PAB to PMS). Obviously, it is easy to get confused since both writers are named Paul!

Virtually all items in square brackets [ ] are comments or annotations by the editors.

The Pauls used many abbreviations. Except for the obvious ones, we have tried to spell them out in the text, but in case we have missed some, here are the recurring ones, in no particular order:

- *MR*: *Monthly Review*
- MRP: Monthly Review Press
- RoM (sometimes ROM): *MR*'s Review of the Month (RoM)
- Huby, Hubie or Hoob: Leo Huberman, co-editor
  of *Monthly Review* until his death in 1968
- *PEoG*: PAB's book *Political Economy of Growth*
- *TCD*: PMS's book *Theory of Capitalist Development*
- Cap.: capitalism
- Soc.: socialism
- Mono.: monopoly
- Mono cap or monocap: monopoly capitalism
- u/d: underdevelopment
- Udc or u/d/c: underdeveloped country
- Dvpt.: development
- Eco or Econ: economic
- Bourg.: bourgeois
- Corp.: corporation or corporate

- Mx: Marx
- M&E: Marx and Engels
- QoS: Quality of Society (chapter in their book *Monopoly Capital*)
- IS: Irrational System (chapter in their book *Monopoly Capital*)
- IAA: PAB's notation for "1-double-A" importance or priority
- Spec'y or spessy: special delivery letter
- MS. or ms.: manuscript
- spl: surplus
- udc's: underdeveloped countries
- JKG: John Kenneth Galbraith

While spelled out in the text, the notation for their discussions of the economic surplus, constant and variable capital, income, and so forth, can be found in Paul Sweezy's *Theory of Capitalist Development* p. 59–71 (highly recommended reading as well as *PEoG* for putting their theoretical discussions in context).

The two Pauls were fond of German, French, Italian, and Latin phrases and these are generally translated in the text, but some of the more frequently appearing foreign-language flourishes are are listed below:

- Stimmung: German word for "mood" or "state of mind"
- et tutti quanti: "and all the rest"
- mutatis mutandis: "with necessary changes" or "accounting for present circumstances"
- Gleichschaltung: synchronization or bringing into line
- Aktualitaet (adjective is Aktuell): imminence, immediacy, current relevance
- Hic Rhodus, hic salta! [Here Is Rhodes; Jump Here! (meaning "prove your talk by deeds!")]
- Auseinandersetzen: to confront or come to terms with
- Beziehungsweise (abbreviated Bez.): as the case may be
- m.a.w.: mit anderen Worten or "in other words."
- sub specie aeternitatis: "viewed in relation to the eternal"
- Habeat sibi!: "so be it!" or in modern lingo, "whatever!"
- Dreck: garbage

Inside terminology:

- The "opus," also called in earlier letters the "Buchlein," was the name for what eventually became their book *Monopoly Capital*.

- The two Pauls enjoyed referring to their children's terms for things, in particular, Nicholas Baran's words for the following:
    - typewriter: tripewriter (hence typing is triping)
    - immediately: mammediately
    - amazing: mamazing

Also, Nicholas Baran is often referred to as Nickpick or Picknick, or some derivation thereof.

THE AGE OF

MONOPOLY CAPITAL

1

The Early Postwar Years
1949–1952

[1949]

PMS to PAB

Wilton, N. H.
February 17, 1949

Dear Paul,

Many thanks for the *Modern Review* which I have already returned. It is a stinker, isn't it, and Hilferding's article is amazing for one who had been so clear-headed.[1] Also for the reference to Estrin [Samuel Efimovich]. I have written to him (more than a week ago) but have heard nothing as yet. Meanwhile another friend of mine has written me the following information, based on clippings about the time of H's death. I wish you would check it for accuracy and also add anything you can (including, of course, anything the chap who works at the FRB [Federal Reserve Bank—referring coyly to Paul Baran himself] may know):

"Hilferding was in Berlin from 1919-1933 mainly as a lecturer in a S.D. [*Sozial Demokratisch*] school and writer for SD papers. He had been a doctor and was on the Austro-Italian front during World War I. He left Berlin in 1933 and stayed in Prague until Hitler took over Czechoslovakia in 1938, then to Paris. All this time he was active with the main staff of the German SDP, writing for their *Neue Vorwaerts* and a clandestine paper that was smuggled into Germany. When Hitler took Paris he fled south with Breitscheid [Rudolf]. He survived the period of confusion and is reported to have believed that no French government would violate the traditional French hospitality to political refugees. But Vichy police agents picked them up in Arles, Feb. 1941. They were taken to

---

1. Possibly the *Modern Review* (June 1947), pp. 266–71, reprint of article on "State Capitalism" by Rudolf Hilferding.

Paris and turned over to the Gestapo. The end is not established; there are two versions, one that he committed suicide taking poison which he carried with him, the second, execution by the Nazis. He was born August 1877, and thus met his fate in his 64th year. He was a young man when he did his best work:"

The following specific questions occur to me as being important and unanswered: (1) Where was he born? (2) What was the family background; the father's profession? Where did he go to school and university? Did he study law and economics (if so with whom) or only medicine? How much did he ever practice medicine? How did he happen to get into the socialist movement? What positions did he hold in the Austrian and/or German SPs [Socialist Parties]? in the USPD [Independent Socialist Party Germany]? Is it true that he was the leading architect of the merger between the SPD and the USPD in 1922? Is it true that he was inordinately lazy and fond of good living? Why didn't he do anything significant after *Finanzkapital*? Any light you can throw on these or related questions from your own knowledge of the man would be much appreciated. I have finished the part on Boehm-Bawerk, and found it very interesting to write. Shall start on H as soon as possible, so the sooner I can get the dope, the better.[2]

Hope I shall see you in NY around March 4th.

Yrs,

/s Paul

PAB to PMS

Federal Reserve Bank of New York

February 23, 1949

Dear Paul:

Thanks for returning the issue of the *Modern Review*. I understand from the Turtle Bay Bookshop that you will be here early in March, and I am looking forward to having a good chat with you. There are many things I would like to talk over with you at this time.

---

2. The reference here is to the Austrian marginalist economist and a leading member of the Austrian school of economics, Eugen von Böhm-Bawerk. Sweezy at the time was editing a volume consisting of two works, Böhm-Bawerk's *Karl Marx and the Close of His System* and Rudolf Hilferding's *Böhm-Bawerk's Criticism of Marx*. This was to be published by Augustus Kelley as a single volume with his editorship in 1949, with an introduction by Sweezy. It also included as an appendix a translation by Sweezy of Ladislaus von Bortkiewicz's "On the Correction of Marx's Fundamental Theoretical Construction in the Third Volume of Capital." Sweezy here was seeking information from Baran on Hilferding to aid him in his description of the latter in his introduction to the book.

The information on Hilferding summarized in your letter is incomplete and inaccurate. Let me tell you briefly what I think are the most important benchmarks in his career. What follows is not based on any sources but only on my own recollection and ought to be checked as far as details are concerned:

Hilferding was born in Vienna in 1877. He got his training in medicine but never practiced it. Around 1906 or 1907 he became editor of the *Neue Zeit* and very early thereafter political editor of the *Vorwaerts*. He became a German citizen sometime before the First World War and was elected to the Reichstag, where he was one of the leading members of the Social-Democratic caucus. In 1914 he voted with the Left Wing against war appropriations and was prominent as a pacifist. In general, one might say that he was not so much a left winger in his political views as a pacifist by inclination or moral conviction. It is this pacifism of his, which at some point coincided with the position taken by the Left, which misled many people into booking him and for that matter many other liberal politicians as Leftists. An interesting parallel is this country where "interventionists" or anti-isolationists came to be regarded as "progressives." He actually was always, fundamentally, a Right Wing man and his Leftism, if any, consisted on one hand in pacifism and on the other of certain amounts of Marxian orthodoxy in economic theory. When the pacifist issue became less relevant, and the Marxian orthodoxy in economic matters merged in his mind with economic liberalism, he went back where he all the time belonged, namely, to the Right Wing of the Social Democratic Party.

It was his negative attitude towards the war as well as his reluctance to accept the flat empiricism of the Bernstein-revisionist group, that made him one of the leaders of the USP [Independent Socialist Party]. In that capacity, he was editor-in-chief of their newspaper, "Freiheit." He was bitterly opposed to the twenty-one conditions and after "Halle," he became one of the leading protagonists of the merger of the SP and the USP.[3] Once back in the mother party, he became very soon one of the most outspoken Right Wing theorists strongly supporting the advocates of coalition governments and the Fritz Tarnow wing of the trade union movement. He was Minister of Finance first in 1923; flopped, however, completely in an effort to do something about inflation. He became Minister of Finance again in 1928 and flopped equally badly in trying to do something about the impending depression. In both situations, his economics which in his mind transformed itself by that time into an outright laissez faire theory prevented him from understanding the sort of problems which he had to face in the real world.

3. The twenty-one conditions here refer to the conditions for admission to the Third Communist International.

In his later days, he became more and more addicted to his notions of "economic democracy" which he somehow considered to be an automatic process calling for very little political action.

As far as your specific questions are concerned: As I said before, he was born in Vienna; as to the family background and father's occupation, I do not know anything. He did not study economics in any organized fashion but seems to have been working in that field much more than in the field of his formal training, namely, medicine. In both the Austrian and the German SP, he was a high functionary, being member of the Central Committees of both parties. He *was* inordinately lazy and found it extremely difficult to write and had hardly written anything in the last ten or fifteen years of his life. He did occasionally contribute an article to his own magazine, "Gesellschaft,"[4] wrote also from time to time in newspapers, but fundamentally gave up research and writing since he got into "big" politics. He was fond of good living, enjoyed very much consorting with those in power, but was so far as I know, scrupulously honest and completely immune to any kind of corruption. His corruption, such as it was, was ideological and "social" rather than of the sordid variety of accepting outright briberies.

His political judgment was actually very poor. His basic indolence and fear of "antagonizing the enemy" led him to accept "doing nothing" as the best policy recommendation. I remember distinctly having spoken to him a few days after Hitler was appointed Chancellor and asking him whether he thought the time was ripe for the unions to call a general strike. Even then, in the first days of February 1933, he was sitting in a comfortable easy chair with warm felt slippers on his feet and remarked with a benign smile that I was a young firebrand and that political skill consists of waiting for the right moment. After all, he said, Hindenburg is still the President, the government is a coalition government and while Hitlers come and go, ADGB [*Allgemeine Deutsche Gewerkschafts Bund*] is an organization that should not risk its entire existence for a fleeting political purpose.

It was only a few days later that he was hiding at some friend's house being already sought by the Gestapo.

All the weaknesses of a liberal in politics were accompanied in his case with all the venerable characteristics of a liberal in private life. He was extremely intelligent, tolerant of conflicting views, undogmatic to the point of helping and furthering people who were distinctly his adversaries in political and theoretical

---

4. Rudolf Hilferding edited a publication entitled *Die Gesellschaft*, to which PAB contributed several articles under the pen-name "Alexander Gabriel," while he was a graduate student in Berlin in 1932 [see PAB, German Writings, at the Stanford Archive cited in the Preface].

matters, critical to an extent that held barely any definite views, and at the same time full of understanding and brilliant flashes. He was not a great man in the field which he had chosen because he was mainly a weak man. If by some stroke of fortune, he would have chosen medicine as his main occupation, he would have become most likely a great physician and humanitarian. Instead, he became a political utopian, a cowardly petty bourgeois who through his entire active life most likely has cancelled out all that he had contributed through the very short stretch of his imaginative creative work.

This is about all I can say at this point. I do not know how useful it will be to you. As far as other more specific data are concerned, they can be secured, I imagine, through some library work, and as far as the last phase of his career goes, it will still have to be some eyewitness who could contribute the needed information.

I am looking forward to seeing you. Give my best regards to Nancy.

Yours as always,

/s Paul

[1950]

PAB to PMS and Leo Huberman (PMS's co-editor at Monthly Review*)*

Stanford University

March 28, 1950

Dear Paul and Leo:

[. . .]

I was very anxious to shuttle over to NY for the current inter-quarter vacation (10 days), but no money. My general frame of mind is lousy, and I wonder how long I should hang around here. My mother has died in Moscow — my father remained all by himself, I can't get there, he can't get permission to get out — it is frightfully difficult to control oneself, not to join the "baiters" and to call those butchers the names that they deserve. On what grounds of responsible reasoning could they justify not permitting a 65 year-old sick man to join his only son? On what grounds of responsible attitude to human lives could they refuse to permit me to visit for 10 days my dying mother? This brutality is not even a means to an end. It is a means without any conceivable purpose — sheer contempt for human existence, sheer soullessness of power-drunk *soldatesca* [bands of soldiers], sheer weight of a heavy sergeant's boot. How should one think straight on days like these, how does one not lose one's equilibrium, one's ability to see forests, when one is hit over the head with a tree? It takes all that one has not to become desperate. . . .

So much for today. I shall send that thing before the week is over.
Best regards,
        /s Paul

PMS to PAB

Wilton, N.H.
March 31, 1950

Dear Paul,

I was very sorry to hear of your mother's death, and I can certainly understand
your bitterness. At the same time, I think you have to make a distinction between
their not letting you go to Moscow and their not letting your father come out.
If there is justification for an "iron curtain" at all — and I think there is — then
there is justification for not allowing Americans in, even on compassionate
grounds. The reason, of course, is not in the individual case but in the fact that
there are literally hundreds of thousands of Americans with close relations
behind the curtain. If they were to be admitted on compassionate grounds,
the curtain would be turned into a sieve, and you can be certain that not only
individuals with relatives would take advantage of the fact. I don't see how this
logic can be refuted. The case of your father seems to me different, however. He
is old and unwell enough so that I assume they could not materially benefit from
holding him, and I assume too that he has no special knowledge which would be
advantageous to a potential enemy. The only reason I can think of is that there
are probably hundreds of thousands of Russians who would like to get out of the
country, and their discontent would probably be increased by everyone actually
released. This is certainly not an argument that could be ignored, but it seems to
me much less persuasive than the reason for not allowing Americans in. But, of
course, you are right that they don't consider the problem from the point of view
of simple human relations, and they may be acting simply out of callousness. It is
a terrible thing, and one which I believe the socialist movement must find ways of
fighting against, but God knows it is not hard to explain. They are still in power
at all only because they have learned — ever since the attempt on Lenin's life, I
would say — to be supremely callous, and that sort of thing is bound to extend
far beyond the strict limits of necessity.

I know what you mean by feeling sometimes like joining the baiters. The
reasons are not only in the SU [Soviet Union] either. Communists everywhere
are very difficult to take: fanatics always are, I suppose. But one is always
successfully — and in my case easily — restrained by one look at the baiters. The
only real alternative course seems to me to withdraw completely into as private a
life as possible. That seems to suit some people, but I'm afraid it never would me.

The real index of the world crisis is the way it reaches deeply into the personal life of almost everyone. I have a feeling that it has never been so to quite the same extent in earlier transition periods.

[…]

Nancy joins in sending our sympathy and warmest regards,

As always,

/s Paul

[1951]

PAB to PMS

Stanford University

July 15, 1951

Dear Paul,

[…]

During this interlude left to me by the planning business I am trying to finish a paper that I started [a] long time ago, and that has been occupying me quite a lot. Tentative title: The Concept and the Significance of Economic Surplus.[5] You know what I have in mind: every social structure produces a certain amount of what one might call "economic surplus," (i.e. every more or less modern structure incl. feudalism). The mode of utilization of this surplus essentially decides the economic development of that society. This mode of utilization in its turn depends on who gets it, and on the system of values, drives and desires prevailing among those who get it. Where the recipients are landlords of essentially parasitic nature — the surplus gets frittered away. Where they are Ricardian-Weberian-Marxian businessmen, nothing is consumed (almost nothing) and everything puritanically plowed back into business. Where capitalism and the capitalist spirit begin to rot (monopoly + generation of heirs) — economic royalism — the tendency begins to appear of frittering it away once more — on a higher level. GB was example before the war, U.S. in parts. . . . There are lots of sidelines to the whole thing, and I am enjoying very much playing around with it. I have been reading *Theorien* [Marx's *Theories of Surplus Value*] with this stuff in mind, also John Stuart Mill and Marshall — it is amazing how the entire classical school, not only Marx, took it for granted that

---

5. Baran is referring to his article "Economic Progress and Economic Surplus," eventually published in *Science & Society,* Fall 1953. Reprinted in Paul A. Baran, *The Longer View* (New York: Monthly Review Press, 1969), 271–307.

the capitalist "abstains" and [ac]cumulates. Was clearly adequate for the times and not an ideology, because ideology a bit late![6]

Does anything occur to you in connection with this story? Any bibliographical references that should (could) be consulted? I would like to finish the thing before going to NY.

[…]

I guess the "general line" was correct — there won't be any war, certainly not this summer, i.e. this year. These days — every year gained is a lot.

More next time. Write!

Best regards, Yours,

/s Paul

[*Handwritten*]

P.S. This place here [Stanford] is all but deserted — *tout le monde* is in Santa Monica "working" for Rand. The corruption of the universities that this racket produces is unbelievable. Rand pays $50 per diem — you have to be damned cautious not to have security troubles or else you don't get on this gravy train. Ergo: you *are* cautious! Even if your views don't happen to fully coincide with the ruling opinion, you keep your mouth shut — why endanger such a fat paycheck by picayune utterances? Would be a nice little piece for *MR* — on broadly: meaning of academic freedom these days!

PMS to PAB

Wilton, N. H.

July 21, 1951

Dear Paul,

[…]

The only point I would suggest adding to the "Surplus" study is the way the surplus gets disguised and so to speak dissipated under advanced capitalism. If a proper distinction is made between productive and unproductive workers, the former producing surplus and the latter living off it, it will be seen, I am certain, that the surplus of the American economy is vastly greater than statistics of profit plus rent plus interest would indicate. And the potential surplus available to a planned economy is even greater because the unproductive workers could mostly be transferred to productive lines.

6. Karl Marx's *Theorien über den Mehrwert* (*Theories of Surplus Value*) was first published under the editorship of Karl Kautsky in 1905–1910 and subsequently went through various (improved) editions. Baran is here reading it in the German edition. An English translation appeared in 1963.

[…]
More later,
    /s Paul

PMS to PAB

Wilton, N. H.
August 18, 1951

Dear Paul,
Herewith the surplus paper. I would send it to the AER [American Economic
Review], but I would also expect them to reject it. Touches on too many sensitive
subjects, I'm afraid.

From my point of view, the chief weakness of the paper is that it doesn't
discuss what I think is probably the heart of the surplus problem for an advanced
capitalist country, namely, the problem of unproductive labor. You allude to it
several times (e.g. footnote 17, p. 8), but you do not go into it. My own suspicion
is that the potential output of this country, for example, is enormously greater
than even the present war-induced expansion would lead one to believe. It could
be reached only by cutting out unproductive labor (as well as unproductive
consumers) and putting them all into productive pursuits. But when you try
to analyze this problem closely you get into all sorts of conceptual and other
difficulties. (Incidentally, one reason I expect the USSR to overtake the capitalist
countries much sooner than is commonly supposed possible is precisely the fact
that they do with very little unproductive labor.)

[…]
Yours,
    /s Paul

[1952]

John Kenneth Galbraith to PMS

Harvard
Cambridge, Massachusetts
January 24, 1952

Dear Paul,[7]
I have just read your lecture to me in the last issue of the *Monthly Review*

---

7. Galbraith's letter to Sweezy was on Harvard Graduate School of Public Administration
letterhead.

[January,1952] and I don't know that I am as grateful as I should be for your efforts to put me right.[8] Without opening up a public argument, I would like to ask you some questions.

As you observe in my review of Perloff's book I was posing a question, not answering it. Nonetheless I have puzzled over the answer quite a bit and in my careless non-Marxian way I have thought of the explanation you suggest.[9] There is no question that in the past these islands have been farmed for the benefit of outside interests and this has much to do with their peculiar misfortunes. Moreover such absentee or imperialist exploitation is still a factor in a good number of them. But I can see no escape from the fact that it is a singularly unsatisfactory and incomplete explanation of their woes. Consider in particular the following questions which any such explanation leaves unanswered:

1) Other parts of the world — most other parts in fact — were opened up by what you term imperialist exploitation. A goodly number of those so opened up under European auspices — the majority I would suppose — at some stage escaped from their colonial status and proceeded on to a life of their own. This latter has frequently involved movement on to a tolerable standard of living. Why did the development which was commonplace in Canada, Australia, New Zealand or for that matter the United States itself fail to occur in this part of the world. In other words, assuming for a moment that imperialism is the cause, why has it held its grip so strongly on this area and lost it in other areas of European colonization?

2) However, any answer that runs in terms of imperialist exploitation is unsatisfactory — unless indeed some attenuated or even mystical connotation can be given to that phrase. Take the case of Haiti. This is the most poverty-stricken of the islands that I have seen — the United Nations two or three years ago estimated the average annual per capita income at twenty-five dollars. From visual evidence this would seem to be generous. The Haitians won their independence from Napoleon early in the last century and brought to a fairly abrupt end the system of colonial exploitation that had prevailed up to that time. The plantation system of agriculture which had once been extremely profitable

8. The "lecture" Galbraith was referring to here was the introductory note by *MR* editors Huberman and Sweezy to Harvey O'Connor's article "Jamaica: The Colonial Dilemma," *Monthly Review* 3, no. 9 (January 1952), 268. Huberman and Sweezy in their notes commented critically on a review by Galbraith in the *Economic Journal* (September 1951) that referred to the Caribbean Islands as "pest-holes of wasted humanity" but that did not even attempt to address the reasons for underdevelopment in the region or to suggest that it might have to do with imperialism.
9. Harvey S. Perloff was an urban planning expert and wrote numerous books and articles about planning in underdeveloped areas such as Puerto Rico.

in the island (for the French at least) was abandoned and the land was divided up into small holdings. Apart from one sizeable banana plantation, a smallish sugar company and recently established sisal [hemp] plantations there is no outside exploitation of the island. Nor is there any appreciable amount of agriculture that is dependent on foreign markets — and which might thus be considered subject to indirect exploitation. Nor is there any important foreign debt. There is a not unimportant coffee industry in the hills but it has been declining for many years. Yet, as I say, this is the island of the most extreme poverty of all.

3) You will see where I am going and I now take the final step. There is in the area some positive correlation between standard of living in welfare on the one hand and efficient foreign development or exploitation on the other. This is a hard pill to swallow — it is even hard for me to swallow. Nevertheless, it is a fact that in Cuba and Puerto Rico where the agriculture is subject to efficient, well-capitalized exploitation the standard of living is perceptibly above that of say Jamaica. Again on Haiti the few workers who are employed by Standard Fruit or in the sisal operations are quite definitely a favored class. The sisal plantations which are under a company jointly financed by the Haitian and American governments is perhaps the only enterprise in the Republic that pays the official minimum wage. Many similar bits of evidence could be added. Are the Puerto Ricans wrong in seeking more outside investment?

I am seriously puzzled as to what it is that explains the poverty of this and kindred areas and I am going to put a good deal of time in the next two or three years trying to find out. I must say incidentally that I have an uneasy feeling that location and climate have more to do with this problem than in sophisticated times we like to suppose. If these islands had been a thousand miles farther north would their history have been the same. Do you realize that there are no developed and not very many developing countries in the tropics. I also have the feeling that there must be some base for industry before even agriculture can be very progressive.

Kitty joins me in kindest regards to Nancy, the children and especially to the new arrival. Yours sincerely,

/s J.K. Galbraith

JKG/lc

PMS to John Kenneth Galbraith

Wilton, N.H.
February 2, 1952

J.K. Galbraith, Esq.
Littauer Center 205
Cambridge 38, Mass.

Dear Ken,

Thanks for your letter of the 24th: I specially welcome the evidence that *MR*'s lectures are read, even if not always welcomed, in the quarters to which they are addressed. Here, very briefly, is the way I would try to answer your points, it being understood that to do so properly would require at least a book.

1. You are right that most parts of the world were opened up by imperialist exploitation, but I am rather surprised that you should regard this as a damaging fact from my point of view. I think it is safe to say that in no case where imperialism fastened itself upon a native (mostly colored, as it happens) population did it lead to any good for the countries concerned. It is notable that the only cases you cite are the U.S., Canada, Australia, and New Zealand, all of which were essentially extensions of the exploiting imperialist society (achieved by exterminating or isolating the native peoples) rather than subjugated colonies. Most of Asia, Africa, and South America follows the Jamaica pattern far more closely than the pattern of the U.S. and the all-white Dominions.

2. That Haiti, gaining independence long before the full development of capitalism, to say nothing of the appearance of socialism, should not be able to accomplish much for itself seems to me to prove remarkably little. And how in the world the imperialist countries can escape responsibility for the condition of their completely dependent colonies — so dependent, in fact, that the very populations were picked up and put there as slaves — is beyond my comprehension. I don't think there is anything attenuated or mystical about that.

3. Of course, the employees of the big foreign corporations have higher income than the rest of the peoples. Which does not prevent me saying that the big corporations have never attempted, and never will attempt, to bring about an all-around development of the colonial societies for the benefit of the people who live there. If the director of one of the big corporations were to adopt any such goal, the stockholders could sue him for malfeasance in office; his job is to make money for the corporation. I should have thought that it was pretty well accepted by now that imperialist investment in colonies has never failed to undermine the old societies without building any sort of integrated, viable society in their place. That a few thousand natives get relatively better-paying jobs in the process

is small compensation indeed. (An adequate brief description of the typical impact of imperialism on the colony is presented in Fritz Sternberg's new book, *Capitalism and Socialism on Trial*, Chapter 2.)

So much for the numbered paragraphs of your letter. I would express my own positive position somewhat as follows: Imperialism is clearly responsible for the condition of its colonies. Some of them might be pestholes of humanity if they had never been touched by imperialism, but they would be a different kind of pesthole (for example, in the Caribbean, the humanity involved would be racially entirely different), and this fact, to the extent that it is a fact, can in no sense be used as an excuse for the sins of imperialism. There is no hope whatever for the colonies to develop decent, humane, self-respecting societies until they have got completely free of imperialism. This does not mean, of course, that the mere winning of independence by itself will accomplish miracles; it is only a necessary condition, not a sufficient condition. Nor does it mean that, even under the most favorable conceivable conditions, the transition to a better state of affairs can be quick or easy. But when and if it does come, it will be as the result of a collective effort of the peoples themselves and not as the result of the activities of foreign corporations. In other words, for the colonies even more than for the advanced countries, socialism is the only answer.

One final point which I am sure you will not take as a personal jibe since it is in no way intended as such: it concerns a matter which I am sure we both feel to be important and which I can see no reason for not discussing frankly. If you continue along the path your letter indicates you are now following, you will end up, at least on this issue of colonialism and imperialism, in the company of the extreme reactionaries, people who have fought you hard in the past and whom I know you have enjoyed fighting against. This may be another bitter pill which your scientific convictions force you to swallow. I think, on the other hand, that it is rather an unconscious concession to the trend of the times. Liberals have always been right to fight imperialism; those who continue to fight it are still right; and those who go on fighting it in the future will surely be vindicated in the long run. Let me beg of you to make a thorough study of the *whole* history and record of imperialism before you finally commit yourself to the kind of favorable judgment which your letter adumbrates. I believe you will not be sorry and you may save yourself from what later could appear as a terrible mistake.

Nancy and I are both fine, after a somewhat hectic start. How is Kitty? Isn't she due any day now? Anyway, give her our love and best wishes. And we look forward to seeing you all in the not-too-distant future.

Cordially,

/s Paul

PAB to PMS

Stanford University

February 12th, 1952

Dear Paul,

This letter is very much overdue — I was planning to write to you earlier on a large number of subjects. Yet the pressures of current preoccupations have completely swamped me in the last few weeks, actually ever since I returned from the East. There is a lot of to-do at the University, I have to keep preparing my Economic History course, attend all sorts of superfluous meetings, write for MRS [Model, Roland, Stone] and now organize our impending move to a new place. The latter will take place within a few weeks and then Elena will be soon ready to "go into action" [give birth] — it'll take some time until peace and equilibrium is restored. All this is a collection of nuisances that detract from work, but it just cannot be helped. I wonder how do people who are encumbered with jobs, family, etc. etc. manage to get anything done.

Anyway — (1) Attached is [Lawrence] Dennis with many thanks. He is a smart cookie, although in a sense not fully appreciative of the *real* problem facing American capitalism.[10] After all, as you once said "capitalism cannot live in one country," and to lock the doors and pull down the shades is no longer a solution. This is where Dennis and Hoover and Taft and a number of other "isolationist" ruling class boys are off base, that is off base as far as the objective interests and requirements of their class are concerned. By setting up a fascist system at home, welding the country into one armed camp and saying "to hell with the rest of the world" they obviously meet the short-run problem, but what about the long-run problem? The "tragedy" of the situation as far as American capitalism is concerned is really that there is no *correct* policy to follow — as long as it remains capitalism. To move along the Truman-Acheson-Joint Chiefs of Staff-Redbaiter-line would end in war, and war would spell disaster not only to the rest of the world but to the American capitalists as well. To let things ride, to permit all of Asia (undoubtedly soon incl. India) to go Communist, to let the colonial revolt sweep Africa, and to permit the French and Italian Reds finally to clean up their Aegian [Augean] stables, is an unthinkable prospect for people who partly think

10. Baran is referring here to Lawrence Dennis, who wrote *The Coming American Fascism* in 1936 and was indicted for pro-Nazi views under the Smith Act during the war, but who continued to be influential in conservative, isolationist circles after the war, editing a small newsletter entitled *The Appeal to Reason* (lifting the title of the great American socialist paper of the late nineteenth and early twentieth century). For background on Dennis see Gerald Horne, *The Color of Fascism: Lawrence Dennis, and the Rise of Right-Wing Extremism in the United States* (New York: New York University Press, 2006).

in proper historical terms (like George Kennan) and partly in phony strategic categories like politico's and the generals.

The only "dialectical" alternative would be to embark upon a gigantic international New Deal; come to terms with Moscow, recognize the social revolution where it has taken place and organize a real Point Four program [Truman's 1949 technical assistance program for developing countries] in alliance with everything that is progressive in the world. This would outmaneuver the Commies, cost them a lot of support, crush the domestic reactionary forces all over the place, lift Franco out of the saddle etc. etc. But to talk about such a swing in American policy is o.k. for A.P. Lerner [Abba Lerner, economist] — it is such manifest nonsense that dry water by comparison with it appears to be a real tangible commodity. Mind you, I don't say that this should not and could not be the plan of the American Left — it is educationally and propagandistically most likely the only thing that could (and in time would) impress people — but to believe that there is a chance for such a renaissance to materialize would be nothing short of fatuous in my opinion. But that leaves the question open — whither American capitalism? And this question will not answer itself by default, as it might in the case of the British or some "minor" capitalist center, simply because the American capitalists are unprecedentedly strong, are able and willing to fight, have not the slightest reason to give up . . .

That is why I don't believe that in the longer run the Hoover-Taft-Dennis line will win out. I think that what is much more likely is a continuing attempt to fascisize the world, to create "bastions of strength" and to hope for the best, namely for a successful suppression of the social revolution by sheer application of force. Since the Russians are unable to resist it, much of what goes on today in the world may be successfully crushed. They may be able to suppress everything in Europe, may even be able to "pacify" Africa, and possibly parts of Asia (French Indochina), and put the local fascists into power. I don't think that they'll be able to restore capitalism in China, but maybe they'll be able to threaten the Russians and the Chinese so explicitly that the Politburo and Mao will have to beg the Indians, the French Indochina Reds to lay off. This worked in a way in 1947 in Italy, it may work again. They won't stop history; they can make its march, however, terribly uncomfortable and slow. They may even spoil a great deal in the socialist camp — continuous armament, continuous being on guard, continuous mortal fear improves no regime.

(2) Attached Adelman's article — please return at convenience, I collect the issues.[11] The stuff needs to be seriously attacked in a professional magazine. The fellow is obviously reshuffling the cards under the table. Because there is no more concentration by his criteria — the issue is to be taken off the order of the day. The "liberals" are unduly upset, that is all. What about the "cross-industry" concentration, that is, General Motors invading say the lumber trade and becoming important there? Does not reflect itself in any data concerning GM nor for that matter the automobile industry but clearly represents an expansion of GM's *economic power*. What about the whole "prime-contractor-sub-contractor" relationship where de facto, the large firm holding the prime contract completely controls the activities of dozens of small outfits that are only nominally independent. Would not reflect itself in any legal data, since nothing has happened legally. What about the large firms keeping their VIP's all over the Washington agencies, deciding on what, when and where, to produce, on prices, taxes and allocations, and the small fry permitted to say "Amen?" If this is not agglomeration of *economic power*, then what is economic power? As usual, those professional economists employ their ingenuity long enough to find a definition which permits them to brush aside everything that the man in the street attaches some meaning to. Talk long enough about exploitation, and there ain't any. Get really going on the topic of imperialism, and it turns out to be an invention of some lunatics. Really analyze scientifically the notions of rich and poor and it becomes clear that you are using your words carelessly. Mobilize all the available apparatus on monopoly and it becomes an institution domesticated on the moon. When people talk of increased concentration of business they mean that a decreasing number of people or firms control the fate of the economy, conversely that a larger share of the economy is under the command of a given number of huge corporations. This heart piece of the concentration argument is completely untouched by Adelman's learned disquisitions. Any opinion? If you like, we could write a note on that matter jointly.

(3) Kalecki's manuscript is in parts at least a tough nut to crack.[12] I haven't seen his very last 2 chapters where he deals with development etc. You are right [that] it is an odd performance, and the thing that bothered me about it is the strongly classical air about the whole. Somehow or other to treat the capitalist process as purely endogenous, leaving out the government and all

---

11. Baran is referring here to Morris Adelman, "The Measurement of Industrial Concentration," *Review of Economics and Statistics* 33 (November 1951): 269–96.
12. Baran is probably referring to the draft manuscript of Michał Kalecki, *Theory of Economic Dynamics* (London: George Allen and Unwin, 1954).

that goes with it is a concession to bourgeois economics that one should not make under any circumstances. I think the Russky's rightly yelled at [Eugen] Varga for his having nicely split eco[nomics] from politics.[13] Kalecki with all his undeniable masterfulness and brilliance does it even worse. If he were to try to square his theory with Marx, he would also have to push beyond Marx's classicism and really come to grips with the problem what is it that makes today's capitalism tick?

(4) Just received, barely inspected the new book of Sternberg's *Capitalism + Socialism on Trial*. Looks interesting although British Labor Party line. If you ain't got it, could send it to you on lend-lease.

(5) Would very much like to try my hand on JKG's book [J.K. Galbraith, *American Capitalism: The Concept of Countervailing Power*]. It is not too easy to come to grips with. It is really the theory of the liberal line of American monopoly capitalism and will be successful as such. He skillfully avoids issues, goes around lots of hot potatoes, is politically and otherwise stupid, although very bright in some obiter dicta and apercu's [remarks made in passing and illuminating comments] — needs to be exploded, but it has to be done skillfully. Have you read it? I'll write to you more about it, also about the Feb. issue of the *MR* which I just finished reading. It's too late now (2 AM) and I have an early class tomorrow.

Very soon the second installment.

Love for all of you,

/s Paul

[*Handwritten*]

P.S. Had a note from Lee Benson — reports progress on his enterprise. Wants me to be a "co-editor" — says you are willing to serve. Asked him who are the others.[14]

[…]

---

13. Eugen Varga was a Hungarian economist who later relocated to the Soviet Union. He wrote a number of influential works such as *Two Systems: Socialist Economy and Capitalist Economy* (1939).

14. Lee Benson was a young left historian who was to become famous as a representative of the progressive historical tradition of Charles A. Beard. He apparently was involved at this time, the year he completed his Ph.D. at Cornell, in attempts to establish a radical journal. Benson's most influential book was *The Concept of Jacksonian Democracy* (1961).

PMS to PAB

Wilton, N. H.

March 4, 1952

Dear Paul,

I've been meaning to answer yours of Feb 12 almost since it arrived but have
been bogged down with a thousand things to do. The I.F. Stone book on the
Korean war — a bombshell if it only gets some publicity — has taken a lot of
time, and just as I thought I had got my head above water the galley proofs of
Schumpeter's 2-vol *History of Economic Analysis* began to arrive. I had almost
forgotten that I promised Mrs. S [Elizabeth Boody Schumpeter] about a year ago
that I would read them and report any remaining errors. So far the book is not
epoch-making, but it does have the advantage over every other doctrinal history
I ever read of being *interesting*. No small merit if you have to read it.[15] The Stone
book is now scheduled for publication on April 18, and we have advance orders
already of about 900 (paid for). The experts tell us that this is very encouraging.[16]

In re the Adelman article, I haven't had a chance to read it yet but will in due
course. I'll write you about it then. If you want the mag back in the meantime, let
me know.

My fundamental criticism of Kalecki's ms (as far as I have gone in it (7
chapters)) is not that it leaves the state out but that it fails to make any analytical
connections with classical-Marxian theory. K is contemptuous of value theory, of
course, and argues that his system is entirely at variance with the Ricardo-Marx
system. This seems to me to be a superficial view. R-M theory is in a sense a
special case, but it is a special case which provides the absolutely essential link
between the class structure of capitalism and analytical economic theory. Once
this link has been firmly established, it is safe to go on, much along Kalecki's
lines, to analyze the actual modus operandi of the system. K's theory, by the way,

15. Sweezy and Joseph A. Schumpeter were close friends. Sweezy had been Schumpeter's teaching
assistant and then junior colleague at Harvard. They frequently socialized. He was instrumental in
bringing Schumpeter and his future wife Elizabeth Boody together. Sweezy aided Elizabeth Boody
Schumpeter in the editing of Schumpeter's massive *A History of Economic Analysis* (New York:
Oxford University Press, 1954). In her "Editor's Introduction" Elizabeth Boody Schumpeter
wrote: "Paul M. Sweezy read all of the proofs, made many valuable suggestions, and caught several
errors which had escaped me."
16. I.F. Stone's *Hidden History of the Korean War* (New York: Monthly Review Press, 1952) was
the first book published by Monthly Review Press. Meeting Stone in a walk in the park, *Monthly
Review* editors Huberman and Sweezy were startled to discover that one publisher after another
had turned down his critical history of the origins of the war. They therefore offered to publish it as
a book.

provides all the openings that are needed for integrating economic and political factors, it seems to me. I tried to present this line of reasoning to K when I was last in NY, but I did it badly and he wasn't really listening. He's a lovely guy, but I find it almost impossible to carry on a real *two-way* discussion with him. In this connection, incidentally, Schumpeter sensed the essential point — which again shows how much above the level of the vulgar economists he was — when he wrote (in his obituary on Böhm-Bawerk) that "the picture which the theorist paints of the economic process depends in large part on his conception of the value phenomenon" and again that "nearly all of our insight into, and all of our attitude towards, the nature and meaning of capitalism hangs on our view of the meaning and function of interest and profit." *Daher muessen wir* [Therefore we must] stick resolutely to the theory of value and surplus value. This Kalecki doesn't see at all, in fact brushes it aside as an irrelevancy.

I have the Sternberg book and have read a few chapters. Compared to most of the stuff that is being written it is a work of genius, but by more rational standards it is only fair — as far as I've gone. I have agreed to review it, along with Rosa Luxemburg (in the new English translation) and the gigantic 2-vol work by Hallgarten called *Imperialismus vor 1914* for the *Economic History Journal*.[17] It would be worthwhile to do a really thorough job, but I can't see how I'll ever get the time. Incidentally, what do you know about the Hallgarten? It certainly looks interesting.

In the matter of Galbraith, events have already proved that you were right about its being taken up by the "liberal" monopoly capitalists. Did you see the longish article devoted to it by *Business Week*? BW hardly ever reviews a book. And on the question of where JKG is headed the enclosed correspondence is instructive.[18] Please return for the file. I may need it some day. Frankly, the next-to-last paragraph of my letter was written specifically so that if the occasion ever arises I can say "I told you so." I haven't read the capitalism book and probably won't get to, at least not for quite a while. It certainly would be good to expose it in *MR*, and I hope you will be able to do the job. We don't pay enough attention to the liberal apologetics for capitalism: it can be a crucial front in the fight to win young people to a genuinely socialist position.

17. This was published as Paul M. Sweezy, "Review Article: Three Works on Imperialism," *The Journal of Economic History* 13, no. 2 (Spring 1953): 193–201. Sweezy reviewed the English translation of Rosa Luxemburg, *The Accumulation of Capital*, Fritz Sternberg's *Capitalism and Socialism on Trial*, and G.W.F. Hallgarten's *Imperialismus vor 1914: Die Soziologischen Grundlagen der Aussenpolitik europaischer Grossmachte vor dem ersten Weltkrieg* [Imperialism before 1914: The sociological principles of European foreign policy before the First World War].
18. January 26–February 2, 1952 correspondence between Galbraith and Sweezy. See above.

I talked to Benson about a month ago. I don't believe he is going to get the support he talks about. He is politically very naive and doesn't seem to recognize that a so-called scientific magazine (even if genuinely scientific) has political implications. The people he wants to bring together won't come together or work together. I may be wrong, of course. In the meantime, if I were you I would just keep asking down-to-earth questions about how many people are going to write for him, where the money is coming from, who is going to keep the subscription lists, etc., etc. Leo and I have told him that he has to solve these practical problems before he can get anywhere, but he doesn't seem to believe it. He would like us to do this for him, but we made it perfectly clear that we already have more of that kind of thing with MR than we can properly handle.

Your analysis of the "rational" policy for American capitalism agrees pretty much with my own ideas on that subject — ideas which I began to form into some sort of coherent shape while writing the piece on Hoover for the March issue (which you should be getting soon). It is obvious that the Truman-Acheson program won't work, nor will the Hoover program (I doubt very much, by the way, that Taft is a real Hooverite — he may well turn out to be more of a MacArthurite). Suppose an intelligent capitalist comes to understand this. What policy should he recommend? Clearly, he should be interested in prolonging the life of capitalism as long as possible and in making it possible for the class to dissolve itself peacefully and, from the individual point of view, comfortably into the new oncoming social order. A great international New Deal would be the obvious answer. Since the prolonged co-existence and peaceful growing-over is also in the best interest of socialists, it follows of course that we can go along on this policy: as you say, its educational and propaganda advantages are great. But there is one catch. We must at all costs keep this position from degenerating into support for a Point 4 program which is really nothing but a fig-leaf over the Truman-Acheson genitals. In other words, we must at all times make absolutely clear that we are not going down the road of the ADA [Americans for Democratic Action] and the leaders of the U.S. labor movement today.[19] This is not impossible, in fact I think certain relatively easy tests can be devised which must be applied more or less continuously: no militarization, observe the spirit of the charter of the UN (i.e. settle big-power disputes through negotiation outside the UN); channel all international aid through the UN; stay out of other people's civil wars; and perhaps a few other points.

19. Americans for Democratic Action (ADA) was founded in 1947 as a liberal organization meant to forward the values of the New Deal. Its founders included figures like John Kenneth Galbraith, Reinhold Niebuhr, Eleanor Roosevelt, and Arthur Schlesinger, Jr.

We would start by saying that there can be no compromise on any of these issues: they are the essence of a co-existence policy. And within the framework of a co-existence policy we must of course continue to stress that the only solution is socialism. Co-existence, in fact, makes sense only if it has already been recognized that socialism is inevitable and we want to get there as painlessly as possible. Obviously, the American capitalists are not going to "buy" such a program, but if they ever do lose confidence in their ability to manage the situation, a real popular New-Deal-type movement with FDR-like leadership might conceivably be able to drag them behind along that road. This, at any rate, is what we must work for. The alternative is to give up — or start preparing the ground for the eventual occupation of the U.S. by the armies of international Communism, maybe a hundred years from now.

I haven't yet decided definitely, but I think I'll write the April Review of the Month along these lines.[20] It might be useful and help people to clear their minds on what they are for as distinct from what they are against. The one link in the chain of the argument that I haven't quite thought out yet is the tests to be applied to tell whether a program or movement can be supported or not. If you have any rapid thoughts on this, jot them down and send them back by return mail.

Yours,

/s Paul

P. S. What does "*oeklich* "mean? I ran into it in the *Theorien* and can't find it in any of the dictionaries available here.

PMS to PAB

Wilton N. H.
May 10, 1952

Dear Paul,

It was good to hear from you when you were in NY, and I'm only sorry the visit didn't coincide with one of my monthly trips. Helen Lamb tells me that you made the best speech of the conference.[21] What surprised her most was that it was one of the two talks at the whole affair which was applauded. It is perhaps a compliment to American social scientists — to their intelligence, not

20. The April 1952 Review of the Month in *Monthly Review* was to be entitled "Candidates and Issues."

21. Helen Lamb was an economist and historian and a longtime friend of Sweezy's. Her husband Bob Lamb (a *Monthly Review* author) died in 1952 and she subsequently married Sweezy's lifelong friend Corliss Lamont. Lamb's *Studies in India and Vietnam* was published posthumously by Monthly Review Press in 1976.

their temerity — that they like to hear other people tell a few homely truths. It indicates that if it were permitted and fashionable, we should have a flourishing left-wing social science!

Mr. Adelman is a kind of pain in the ass and I somewhat doubt if he is worth all the time and trouble it would take to do a thorough exposure of what he is up to. But I shall look forward to your reply, assuming that Seymour [E. Harris] decides to publish it. Send me a copy, at least on lend-lease: I don't see that magazine [*Review of Economics and Statistics*] in the normal course of events.

I have just finished writing a Review of the Month on "The Threat of Depression" [appeared in *MR*, June 1952] in which I think I have succeeded in explaining more simply and understandably why capitalism generates excess capacity, and at the same time why socialism does not, than I have ever managed to do before. It runs in terms of the Marxian departmental schema and would I think be entirely acceptable to Kalecki. I believe that an elaboration in more precise terms might go some way toward clearing up confusion in the field of Marxian crisis theory (confusion, by the way, which *The Theory of Capitalist Development* did much to increase with that wrong-headed pseudo-mathematical appendix to Chap. X). I would be grateful if you will go over it carefully — the purely analytical part, I mean — and let me have your reactions and comments. After I get them, I will decide whether it is worthwhile to try something further along the same lines.

I met in Cambridge this last week a Dr. Zakir Hussain, Vice-Chancellor of Aligarh University (not far from Delhi), a member of the Indian Council of state, and said to be one of India's leading educators (he trained as an economist in Berlin — [Werner] Sombart, etc. — but isn't really much of an economist, not that that's anything against him). The guy quite touched (and surprised) me by inviting me to come to Aligarh as head of the economics dept. I told him that as long as one can speak out in the U.S. I have to stay here. He's going to be on the West Coast in the fairly near future, and I gave him your name. He's a liberal of a kind one doesn't meet in this country and therefore quite refreshing. Not at all a red or fellow-traveller but neither is he obsessed by the problem — takes it in the spirit that a real liberal ought to. I told him that you would be an ideal person to head his economics dept., and he may talk to you about it. I don't have any idea whether you would be interested or would be allowed to leave the country if you were — but I figured that to talk about it couldn't do any harm.

Hope all goes well with Elena and Nicholas. Our family is doing okay at the moment.

Yours,

/s Paul

PAB to PMS

Stanford University

May 14, 1952

Dear Paul,

I have been planning to write to you for a number of weeks, but could not manage to accomplish even such a modest undertaking. The last 4 weeks — since the arrival of the *filius* — were hectic to an unprecedented extent. Although the burden of the operation falls on Elena's shoulders, I don't have a free minute, and what is worse, a moment of quiet. There is continuously something to be done around the *menage*, the California plague, the garden has to be maintained in some resemblance of order, I have to shop, to take care of millions of small chores, and to help feeding the offspring. His—the offspring's appetite is nothing short of miraculous, he sucks around the clock with very small breaks for incidental naps. Although the Freudians maintain that he is really after sucking rather than after food — it makes actually very little difference. If not provided with oral satisfaction he yells his lungs out, again regardless of whether it is done for the sake of his or the parents' psychic equilibrium — his wishes have to be respected. Anyway, life is quite different from what it used to be, and it would not be altogether forthright to maintain that it is a net improvement. But then, children are a long-term investment, what comes now — as the Russians say — are the flowers, the berries follow later. . . .

In addition to the familial pressures, the college takes a hell of a lot of time, and I cannot even look forward to the summer, because in the summer I'll have to teach to make up for last fall. Still there will be a break between quarters and there will be some 5-6 weeks at the end of the summer quarter — before next year begins.

[. . .]

What you write about excess capacity etc. interests me a great deal. I have been thinking up a few models for my course (Theory of Economic Development) and spent most of the time in this quarter talking about Marx's departmental schemata. I am using your book [*The Theory of Capitalist Development*], and actually told them to disregard that Appendix to Chapter X. (Incidentally, speaking of your book that I have re-read now for the purpose of this course: your treatment of fascism is in my opinion unsatisfactory, and I'll write to you about it separately). I am very anxious to see your treatment — I have come to the conclusion that the simplest way of showing the tendency toward excess capacity is by analyzing the schemata of expanded reproduction with and without technological progress. I think that without technological progress (i.e. rising organic composition) the thing could work alright; it is technological progress that creates the disturbance — need not to do so under socialism because technological progress can be spread over time and because if need be labor hours can be shortened. But let me wait for your story, and I shall write then more about it.

I shall send you a draft of my comments in re Adelman shortly, also an article on fascism that partly deals with your treatment of the subject. Have for review Rostow's Theory of Economic Growth [W.W. Rostow, *The Process of Economic Growth* (1952)] where it is established that the degree to which economic growth takes place depends on a nation's propensity to . . . grow. Utterly disarming in its straightforward lunacy. On the agenda is also something on Galbraith, but God only knows . . . I wonder how people manage to do as much as you do with 3 kids around the house.

What is the situation with the Surplus value? Are you stopping, going ahead?[22] Did I ever tell you that "oeklich" means disgusting (an imitation of some people's way of pronouncing "*eklig*" which in turn is derived from *Ekel*).

I was very sorry not to have had a chance of seeing you in April, but maybe I'll get East sometime soon again.

Write!

Cordially,

/s yours Paul

[. . .]

PAB to PMS

[Palo Alto]
May 15th, 1952

Dear Paul,

After sending off my letter this morning, I received the May issue of the *MR* and read with great interest the "Structure of a Capitalist War Economy"— I must confess to feel quite unhappy about this article, with the main tenets of which I do not agree.[23] There is no argument about the disproportionality thesis. This is o.k. and granted. I would not place too much stress on it because doing so opens the doors to the Hilferding-Bukharin "organized capitalism" stuff which

22. Baran is enquiring on Sweezy's reading (re-reading as he had used it in his *The Theory of Capitalist Development*) of Marx's *Theories of Surplus Value*.
23. A Marxian Economist, "The Structure of a Capitalist War Economy," *Monthly Review* 4, no. 1 (May 1952): 21–30. The author was described as "one of this country's leading authorities on Marxian economic theory."

is of doubtful validity. Still if the disproportionalities of various kinds, lack of coordination, and synchronization were the main trouble, the trouble could be cured within the capitalist society by further concentration of business, by NRA's [National Regulatory Agencies] of various sorts etc.

Much more important I think is the other part of the argument which essentially places the burden of the crisis argument on underconsumption. This seems to me to be fallacious. The crux of the argument would seem to be in the following sentence on p. 23: "The capacity to produce, *which in the final analysis means the capacity to produce consumers' goods* is inevitably expanded beyond the point where the potential products can find a profitable market." The underlined words are neither right nor wrong, they represent a half-truth and are irrelevant. Surely in the "final analysis" everything issues in the production of consumers' goods, but this "final analysis" is misplaced. Just as in the final analysis the entire national product can be dissolved in labor costs, Marx never got tired to point out that *the time* when the labor costs were incurred is of utmost importance. In other words, the part of national produce needed for the replacement of used up "stored" labor (*c*) can be dissolved in live labor in the "final analysis" but cannot be so dissolved in the analysis of any given period. No more is it permissible to speak of the dissolution of the entire product "in the final analysis" into consumers' goods. A large part of that product is made up of investment goods, and the investment goods are *for that period final products*.

In other words, a capitalist economy can very well function producing investment goods for the sake of investment, by accumulating in order to accumulate, by expanding its plant and equipment, its product facilities of various kinds for the sake of expanding them. . . . There is no need for this investment to result in more consumers' goods until Doom's Day. The prerequisite for that, however, is the continuous desire on the part of the capitalists to invest the bulk of their profits, to accumulate and to behave in the way a capitalist is supposed to behave. This desire may be strong in which case we have prosperity; this desire may be weak in which case we have underemployment and crisis. The all-important problem is what accounts for the changes in the capitalists' willingness to invest. I do not think that the consumers' market is *it*, not even in the final analysis. I think that technological progress, the related movements of the rate of profit, monopolistic possibilities and the previously mentioned disproportionalities have to be considered in an attempt to explain the fluctuations in the urge to accumulate.

When technological progress rapid, obsolescence large — modernization of plant and equipment becomes more urgent. With increasing organic composition, larger capital investments — returns tend to decline. As cost elements rise in price (wages, raw materials, etc.) without a possibility of shifting all those cost increases on to the price of final products, profits get squeezed, expectations of profits on future investments (marginal efficiency of capital) become dim, the willingness to invest declines.

Much could be said about this process, but the foregoing will suffice to indicate the trend of thought. Now, this is fully compatible with a notion that there is underconsumption. Surely if v ["variable capital" represents the costs of reproduction of labor power in Marx's *Capital*] would absorb a larger part of total product, if entrepreneurs were satisfied with less s [surplus value], the investment problem would be smaller, the fluctuations due to changes in their willingness to invest less violent. In that sense, but I would say, only in that sense, is underconsumption entering the argument. In other words, in the situation of a growing, effervescent capitalism the crises are due to different causes than under conditions of decaying capitalism. In the former the crises are partly disproportionately caused (with local disproportionalities affecting the entire system and creating overall gluts and losses), partly temporary (cyclical) occurrences due to fluctuations of the rate of profit. They are aggravated by technological developments causing both "booms" and "busts."

In the advanced, monopolistic phase of the capitalist development the situation is much more complex. The decline of the rate of profit has gone a long way and has resulted in a generally *relatively* (relative to past experience) low rate of returns (in the competitive sector of the economy) — every further decline of the rate produces a violent reaction. Monopolistic restraints while promoting some investment cut out other. The development of large scale enterprise renders much investment impossible — only very big capitals are productively investable. The increase of the capitalist income (mass of s) renders the marginal utility of income to capitalists smaller. Political insecurity, changes in the "capitalist spirit" etc. (notions by no means alien to Marx) strongly reduce the willingness to accumulate and to invest. What develops is a parasitic consumption-oriented, decaying capitalism.

Still there is a hell of a lot of surplus to be used up. All waste, all conspicuous consumption do not reduce the available investable funds to a significant extent. Shifting to a "people's capitalism" drastically increasing "v" and cutting "s" is socially impossible. It would mean liquidating the system, abandoning the positions of control and ownership. The only way out is imperialism + armament. Since fluctuations in investment are all-important, there is naturally over-capacity. When investment is large, the sky is the only limit, when investment declines excess capacity appears not only in Department

I [investment goods] but also in Department II (multiplier effect).[24] The indivisibility of industrial investment projects adds additional fuel to the bonfire. Once investment is brisk, the units that are built are large, very large. They must be large because of technology and cost structure. Therefore excess capacity equally large.

This is obviously terribly "desperately" sketchy, but I do believe that it is a better approach than the one outlined in the article referred to above. Even where it smacks with Keynesian notions, it is o.k. because I think that it is fully in keeping with Marx. In fact I have done quite a lot of Marx reading precisely for this purpose and find that all the elements of this picture are there.

This is only a quick comment on the spur of this exceptionally quiet moment — I am looking forward to hearing your opinion and to seeing the other piece you mentioned in your letter. Who wrote this May piece? Not You?

As ever,
        /s Paul

PMS to PAB

Wilton, N. H.
May 19, 1952

Dear Paul,
[...]

I disagree about the underconsumption business. If it were really possible to "build more mills to build more mills and so on ad infinitum" I see no reason why capitalism should ever have entered a declining phase. Your emphasis on the propensity of capitalists to invest puts the cart before the horse. This is a mere reflection of conditions, not a determinant. But to work the whole thing out is very complicated. I haven't tried yet but will try to get to it in the near future and will send you whatever emerges for criticism and comments. I didn't write the piece and don't agree with it on every point, but on the point you select for criticism I agree entirely. I'll tell you about the author some day but would rather not commit the information to writing.

[...]
More on all this later,
        s/ Paul

---

24. Departments I and II in Marx's reproduction schemes in volume II of *Capital* refer to investment goods (means of production) and consumption goods, respectively.

PAB to PMS

Stanford University

Oct. 12, 1952

Dear Paul,

[...]

I have been looking through the existing literature on fascism (German and Italian) and it is actually amazing how little there is by the way of real theoretical thinking. Most of the writers involved (incidentally, including Fraenzchen [Franz Neumann]) spend their time on lots of descriptive material (not always interesting) without having anything like a theoretical structure into which to fit the stuff in. For the U.S. case there isn't even that much done. I would say that working out the relation between growth and development of monopoly, the need for permanent government intervention, the intensification of international class struggle and decay of democracy in America is something that would be eminently worthwhile — even if one is not in the position to realize the "program maximum." There is a tremendous mass of relatively readily available material that literally "flies in the air" and there are certain aspects of the matter that nobody seems to be looking at. One is for instance the close connection between the development in the realm of (social) science and *fascization* of society; another the really fascinating evolution of the "fascist man" whose picture is supplied by [David] Riesman, [C. Wright] Mills, and in a great deal of less weighty material.[25] To pull this stuff together, to give at least a glimpse of the structure of this "Gestalt" would be, in my opinion, most important. Speaking of the matter even from the standpoint of my very limited and very lopsided teaching experience: to many students of social sciences a volume of the alluded to type would be nothing short of a revelation. It always happens to me that when I talk to graduate students they usually remark that they have "never thought of that" and ask me where they could read it up....

It would seem to me that something on these lines may be distinctly worth doing, and I would be very anxious to know your opinion. I fully understand the frustrated feeling that you refer to. My own sense of frustration assumes however much more the form of (a) an awareness of my own inadequacy for doing something really good; and (b) a gnawing doubt as to whether there is any sense in all these activities. The historical movement in our days appears like a Tiger tank moving along while we are trying to deflect it from its course by shooting at

25. Baran was referring here to David Riesman, Nathan Glazer, and Reuel Denney, *The Lonely Crowd* (New York: Doubleday, 1950) and C. Wright Mills, *White Collar* (Oxford: Oxford University Press, 1951).

it with peanuts. . . . But this is "neither here nor there" — most of what one does, one does presumably because one wants to do it, and would do it regardless of its ultimate usefulness. There may be even some merit in trying to keep the candle lit.

If you have any thoughts on the above, let me know — possibly the best thing to do would be to discuss all this when I get East in December. I should think that it might be worthwhile to give it some consideration.

[. . .]

As ever

/s Yours Paul

PAB to PMS

Stanford University

Oct. 15th, 1952

Dear Paul,

I received today the latest issue of *Voprosy Ekonomiki* (Problems of Economics) from Moscow and discovered therein an article by an old specialist in bourgeois economics — Blumin.[26] He has written an awful lot of nonsense before — the present paper is no exception. He goes to town on a large group of writers (Winslow, F.S. Dunn, Toynbee, Hawtrey, Robbins, Boulding, Emery Reves, Candler and Wallace, S.E. Harris, Mises, Hart, and. . . . your good self). The article is pretty long (14 pp), and I don't have the energy of translating all of it. I did, however, translate (crudely but accurately) the passage devoted to your unfortunate piece in the *MR*.[27] While that piece was undoubtedly in error — Blumin is really an s.o.b. and ignoramus. If I were you I would seriously consider to write a letter to Ostrovitianov (he is the editor in chief of the journal) protesting this sort of treatment. Or do you think that this would be inappropriate from the U.S. standpoint? If that bastard would have looked at *MR* in general he could not have possibly characterized you the way he does or is there some special purpose in attacking *MR*?

26. A scholarly journal of the Institute of Economics of the Academy of Sciences of the USSR, published monthly in Moscow beginning in March 1948. The author referred to is the Soviet economist I. Blumin.

27. Unclear which piece this is, but in the November 1951 issue of *MR*, Sweezy had addressed criticisms from the left of several articles he had written in the first two years of *MR*, in particular criticisms from Alexander Bittelman of the American CP (which, as becomes apparent in the following letters, also seem to cover Blumin's criticisms).

Anyway, I did not think you would enjoy reading the enclosure, but I thought you ought to know about it.

More soon.

/s Paul

[*Handwritten*]

P.S. I have looked up your article again. The fellow is quoting out of context and is *really* a skunk. If he would have paged the whole issue, which he undoubtedly did, he could not have honestly written the way he did.

PMS to PAB

Wilton, N. H.
October 18, 1952

Dear Paul,

The Blumin thing is certainly not too pleasant, but I don't think it would do the slightest good to protest. The literary hatchet-men of the SU are an unfortunate fact, perhaps inevitable at this stage of development, and the only thing we can do about it is to work harder for a rational society here. Things we don't care for in the USSR today will improve in proportion not to our protests but to our success in putting our own house in order.

All of which, of course, does not say that the article which Mr. B [Blumin] attacks is not deserving of attack. I myself, as you know, recanted in the reply to Bittelman [*MR*, November, 1951]. What is annoying about Mr. B is the apparently complete inability to distinguish between a description and an advocacy. And what is disquieting about it is the indication that the "leading circles" of the USSR may be vastly underestimating the strength and stability of the U.S. war economy. Do they really want to deny that the war economy is what creates prosperity here? Or perhaps do they really *believe* that things are rapidly going to pot here (as suggested, for example, by B's fantastic statement that 75 percent of U.S. families are living at less than a beggar's subsistence minimum)? Whatever is the case, such illusions can be dangerous. If anything were to be done about the attack, it should probably be a reply in *MR* warning against such illusions. But I'm not even sure that that would really do any good.

On another level, B's thing is symptomatic of a very real problem faced by the Communist movement as we enter the phase which in the future will doubtless be dated from the XIX Congress. They want now to aggravate and exploit the contradictions *within* the capitalist camp. For this, of course, they need to be able to maneuver freely, to join up with all sorts of short- and long-run allies whose ultimate goals may or may not have anything in common with theirs. My guess is that their best bet in many countries will be actually to join and spark the neutralist movement. But all maneuvers of this kind endanger the ideological integrity of the movement, threaten to undermine the comrades' wholehearted loyalty to the center of the movement. In a very real sense Communist and neutralist are contradictory terms. By nature — i.e. by the nature of Communism as a socio-historical phenomenon — CPs want only allies who are also fellow-travellers, and they tend to put the standards very high. Hence the *"willst-du-nicht-mein-Bruder"* attitude as expressed so brutally in Blumin's ignorant vitriol.[28] But in this phase they must have other kinds of allies — and treat them accordingly — or else completely fail to play the role assigned to them. It is a very grave dilemma, and I suspect that the Marty-Tillon crisis has a lot to do with it and that there will be many more crises in other CPs as well.[29] The only country which is in a very good position to make the transition is Italy where the CP already has a strong and relatively independent ally which can bear the brunt of the adjustment burden. It is no accident, I think, that Nenni has been playing an increasingly important role both internationally and within Italy for the last few months.[30] I tend to conclude that it is our duty in this period to assert the independence of Left Socialism more openly and persistently than we have in the past. By doing so we may be able to help the comrades overcome their sectarianism and contribute somewhat to the regrouping of forces which is so badly needed. I need hardly add that we shall not get any thanks for taking that course; quite the contrary, we can expect the worst kind of abuse. But if we refuse to be provoked and persevere, I believe the time may come when it will appear clearly that we were right. It begins to look as though there won't be a war after all for a long while, and we may even live to see that time.

I would like to have your thoughts on all this. *MR* will have to decide how to adjust to the new period too. . . .

In re joint opus again: I accept your general proposition that there are useful tasks to be performed.[31] The next question is to define them in specific terms so that we can begin to orient our thinking and collect necessary material. I shall be thinking about this, and if I can work up anything definite in the near future I'll send it along in outline form. You do the same?

---

28. German phrase from 1848 regarding excessive party loyalty: *Und Willst du nicht mein Brueder sein, so schlage ich dir dein Schaedel ein*: If you won't be my brother then I'll beat your head in!
29. Charles Tillon-Andre Marty expelled from French CP in 1952.
30. Pietro Nenni, secretary of the Italian Socialist Party.
31. Baran and Sweezy were discussing already at this point a joint work, which would be their opus, but the idea of doing a book on monopoly capital specifically was only to emerge later.

Meanwhile I am not yet satisfied in my own mind about the theory of fascism. The difficulty is more or less defined by comparing your own article in the October issue with your contribution to the How-Shall-We-Vote discussion.[32] In the article you strongly suggest that the U.S. has *already* entered the fascist stage. The U.S. state already performs the essential functions of fascism, the differences being mere matters of form. But in the discussion you clearly indicate that it has *not yet* entered that stage when you say that the election of Eisenhower would be the beginning of the fascist era in the U.S. The problem is not a trivial one, I think. It concerns what aspect of the social system the concept of fascism applies to. Is it a characterization of the system as a whole? Or does it concern the political form of the system? I think the answer has to be the latter. The antonym of fascism is bourgeois democracy, not feudalism or socialism. Fascism is one of the political forms which capitalism may assume in the monopoly-imperialist phase. The question then becomes: what are its *differentia specifica*? Clearly, the idea once prevalent (and once shared by myself) that there was a unique pattern of fascist counter-revolution which would usher in a clearly defined set of political institutions as in Germany and Italy, is wrong. But I do not think your article succeeds in solving the problem satisfactorily. Orderly and continuous management of the state by the top echelons of the ruling class in the interest of the class as a whole, control and manipulation of the underlying population, use of violence where necessary (abroad) — these appear to be the criteria you suggest. But the truth is that Britain from the last quarter of the 19th century to World War II fulfilled these three conditions perfectly — and yet Britain during that period has always been regarded, and in my opinion rightly regarded, as the very model of a bourgeois democracy. (For the facts in the case, cf. an admirable section in Hallgarten, vol. I, pp. 70–72, in which each of the above conditions is either explicitly described (as in the case of violence abroad) or strongly hinted at (e.g. the thorough penetration of the state machine by armaments interests and the manipulation of public opinion by the monopoly press).)[33]

What is it then which differentiates the British situation from cases which we would all agree are clearly fascism? I think the answer must be: in the British case there was a relatively high degree of freedom for political opposition, both within the ruling class and also from outside the ruling class; while in the clearly fascist cases there is no freedom of political opposition at all. This must be taken to be the crucial issue, it seems to me. We could establish a political spectrum in

32. Historicus, "Fascism in America," *Monthly Review*, October 1952, and Special Correspondent (Anon.), "How Shall We Vote?," *Monthly Review*, September, 1952 — both by Paul Baran.
33. George Hallgarten, *Imperialismus vor 1914* (1951).

which Britain at the height of the liberal period when Karl Marx sat unmolested in the British Museum represents 100 percent bourgeois democracy (at the very same time, mind you, that Ireland was being starved and India ravished) and Hitler Germany at the other end represents 100 percent fascism. As we move in either direction the political system becomes more (less) fascist and less (more) democratic. In between the extremes there are an infinite number of possible variants, and historically a good many have actually been observed.

The next question I would raise is this: Can we draw lines through the spectrum at well-defined points where quantity changes into quality — as you can, for example, with the color spectrum, differentiating red from violet, violet from orange, etc.? In some cases, you certainly can. When there *is* well-defined fascist counter-revolution (as there may be), you know what's happened and there's no trouble. But in other cases — and the U.S. is one of them — I'm not sure that there ever *must* be a point at which you can say quantity has turned into quality, though of course here again there *may* be (and the election of Eisenhower might well be it). In other words, I think there may well be cases in which a fascist theory of gradualism à la Fabianism — you know how it went years later, after we've been enjoying the socialist utopia for a long time, we'll look back and still we won't be able to say when the change took place — such a theory may be applicable to some countries as regards fascism. Ten years from now, when the concentration camps are full and all opposition spokesmen are completely silenced, we'll know that the U.S. is a fascist country, but will we know just when it got that way?

You will doubtless feel a certain discomfort about what you may regard as an involved political argument that doesn't touch upon the essential questions of the relation of the ruling class to the state, etc. But I don't want to ignore or underestimate these questions. In fact I consider them to be the crucial ones too. What I do want to do is to put them into their correct relation to the problem of fascism and thus to avoid confusion.

But enough of this for the present. Let us try to hammer out a firm agreement on these issues as a preliminary to further planning.

[…]

Yours,

        /s Paul

PAB to PMS

Stanford University

October 19th, 1952

Dear Paul,

I have received and perused with some care Stalin's opus.[34] It has come out
originally in the *Bolshevik* but is reprinted in the *Pravda* of Oct. 3rd and 4th. I
imagine that foreign language editions will be forthcoming in short order — an
additional Russian edition in the form of a booklet is being printed in 1,500,000
copies. The paper itself represents Stalin's comments on a draft of an economics
textbook that has been submitted to the Politbureau in the fall of 1951. The first
part of his article contains his original comments (marked February 1, 1952); the
second half consists of answers to economists who took issue with his comments.
At least one of them (Yaroshenko) seems to have given Joe hell and was treated
brutally in return. Unfortunately these economists' statements are not published,
nor is the draft of the textbook. The latter will appear — presumably soon — in
a final, agreed upon version. What is eminently interesting is the amount of time
and attention given to this type of business. Mr. Yaroshenko for instance seems
irrepressible. Not only did he object to the original text (which was debated in
some quorum last fall) but wrote a letter to all the members of the Politbureau
complaining bitterly about the disregard of his views in the draft as well as about
Stalin's original comments. The Politbureau seems to have been "seized" with
that matter, and one gets the impression that Stalin's statement is actually a
pronouncement gone over by the Politbureau and fully approved by it. In general
I get more and more the feeling that the letters S T A L I N do not denote a man,
they stand for an institution, just as USSR does not stand for a man but is the name
of a country . . . Stalin refers in his article to "comrade Stalin" having said this and
that, as if he had nothing to do with him. It's just like quoting earlier CC decisions.

Anyway—the contents of the thing are rather complex. Although the first
impression of some parts of it is: "Quibble about words"—a second reading and
some thinking suggest that there is an important core of serious subject matter
behind the occasionally obscure verbiage. In many respects it is a reiteration of
the stuff presented by Leontiev in 1944 and is quite obviously directed against
the "ultra-left" who "cannot wait" for the realization of communism. Even the
Soviet Government is not omnipotent and "cannot abolish economic laws." Nor
can it just "introduce" communism. All this looks to me like sound business.

What is disconcerting is the way the damned "law of value" is treated. It
would seem that what is meant by the "law of value" is rationality, calculation

---

34. Joseph Stalin, *Economic Problems of the USSR* (Moscow: Progress Publishers, 1952).

and crucially: the correspondence of cost and income. In other words, the fact that workers get paid according to their contributions, that commodities are exchanged according to their costs etc. Now, I don't know how to call this sort of a situation but I would have thought that this is not what Marx meant by "law of value." Interestingly enough in concluding his statement on this particular subject Stalin says: "More briefly: there can be no doubt that under our present socialist conditions of production the law of value cannot be a "regulator of proportions" as far as the distribution of labor among different branches of production is concerned." But I always thought that this is precisely what the "law of value" as conceived of by Marx was accomplishing under capitalism — among other things.

In the background of all this lurks a terribly interesting problem to which Stalin alludes a number of times. Namely what sort of a situation would be the accomplished socialist — or rather communist — society. There, presumably, reward would be unrelated to output (from everyone according to his abilities, to everyone according to his needs), exchange of things would become essentially meaningless since people could take of what they need as much as they want — the law of value as Stalin uses the term would become inoperative. Still wouldn't there remain the problem of the most efficient allocation of resources in production? Wouldn't we then get for the first time really the "law of value" of the marginal productivity theory in operation — divorced of its capitalist, market, income-imputation aspects? Stalin does not say this in so many words but there is strong reason to believe that he thinks on some such lines.

Most interesting in the whole thing, I feel, is his discussion of the capitalist world. There the really new and important point is that dealing with the "fundamental law of capitalism." What he is trying to do is to get away from the Marxian notion of a competitive capitalism in formulating his "fundamental law." It is *not* the "law of value" which is fundamental to cap., nor is it the "law of the average rate of profit" but what is "fundamental" is the "law of maximum, monopolistic profit": "securing maximum capitalist profit via exploitation, pauperization and ruin of the majority of people in a given country, via suppression and systematic plundering of peoples of other countries, in particular backward countries, finally via war and militarization of the economy that are used for securing maximum profit." What I think this really comes down to is in a sense disregarding the entire Marxian concept of competitive capitalism and approaching the whole business from the standpoint of monopolistic, imperialistic capitalism. This implies really "new economics" where the labor theory of value, equalization of the rate of profit, value-price transformation etc. etc. recede in importance and where the determination of the monopoly

price, monopoly profit, monopoly-caused income distribution etc. moves into
the foreground. However, since there is not a hell of a lot that can be said about
[it] in terms of economic theory (Marxian or otherwise) — we really face a new
situation.

[...]

As always

/s Paul

PAB to PMS

Stanford University

October 25th, 1952

Dear Paul,

[...]

3. *Ad vocem Blumin*: At the bottom of all this business about pauperization in
the capitalist world (apart from domestic property effects) is one of fundamental
disability, namely to understand that up to a certain point both can be had:
guns *and* butter. It is not very strange that they do not get it through their
heads because actually the U.S. is the *only* country where the development of
productive forces has gone so far that this is actually possible. Do you remember
Stalin's interview some time ago where he said that Atlee does not understand
elementary economics; how else could he say that one can build power stations,
dams, etc., and at the same time arm. "As is well known" no such thing is feasible.
Now this is entirely right for Russia, also right for the whole world except
the U.S. An armament effort must mean pauperization — period. That under
U.S. conditions *no* armament effort under capitalist conditions is much closer
to pauperization is a Keynesian paradox which they don't and don't [can't?]
understand. You may be right that there does not seem to be much point in
answering Bl. — but on the other hand a very nicely, politely written letter to
[Konstatin] Ostrovitianov would be interesting to dispatch and to see how they
react. Although it may be better not to do it for internal reasons.[35]

4. I have been thinking much about the point that you raise in connection
with the Blumin affair, and I may have written to you about it earlier. Isn't the
real crux of the matter the old problem of the political theory of the revolutionary
Marxist party in an objectively non-revolutionary (counter-revolutionary)
situation? Lenin solved the problem by a theory + practice of a party that
consisted of a relatively small group of professional revolutionaries steeling

---

35. Konstatin Ostrovitianov was editor-in-chief of the Soviet economic journal *Voprosy Ekonomiki*
in which I. Blumin's work appeared.

itself, training its members, establishing the contacts, the roots that would bring it on top if and when. . . . It was a sort of a dialectical solution (Aufhebung) of the [dichotomy?] of the broad hours' and wages' — struggle — party of the Mensheviks and the SPD and the romantic spontaneity hopes of Rosa and some Frenchmen and Italians. Organization? Yes! Spontaneity? Yes! Ergo: the combination: a party that will be ready to make use of the spontaneity, will be able to help it along, to mould and direct. But now what does one do, if the party for a great number of weighty historical reasons becomes a real mass party? The French and Italian cases. If the party becomes the heart of the TU's [trade unions]? It cannot stay a Leninian party — its membership is too large, its daily responsibilities too consuming. It cannot become a SP — its ideology is quite different, its members have outgrown the reformist attitude.

What does one do with a revolutionary movement, when the revolutionary situation has lapsed? To the extent that your members are essentially radical, revolutionary, thirsty for action — a swing to a Popular Front cooperation with all and sundry men of goodwill will antagonize, disappoint, embitter the workers, and send them to the fascists. The workers have become communists in the first place because they had enough of [Guiseppe] Saragat, of [Léon] Blum & Co.[36] Do you want to do what *they* had done only under the CP name? That was [Heinrich] Brandler's and [August] Thalheimer's line and they were really, genuinely booted out by the membership.[37] Do you want to stick to an "ultra-left" policy of talking *ad infinitum* about the "sharpening contradictions," about the "impending crisis," about "the revolution that is around the corner?" But this cannot be done because (a) the workers get impatient and incredulous (b) allies to the right are unobtainable under such circumstances, unobtainable for vitally important tasks of defending democracy vs. fascism, of defending peace, etc.

I think this is a genuine dilemma and not *ein Scheinproblem* [imaginary problem], and I don't think that it has ever been solved by the revolutionary movement. Possibly in its insolvability lies the real tragedy of missed objective opportunities. You cannot keep revolutionary energies, revolutionary elan on ice. Not given its outlet, it evaporates — if everything goes well, in the direction of apolitical apathy or reformism, if everything goes badly, into the direction of fascism. I know of no answer to the question, and wonder if there is a good one.

5. *Re: theory of fascism.* If I understand your argument correctly, its central core is that the criteria of fascism that I suggest are unsatisfactory. As you put it: "orderly and continuous management of the state by the top echelons of the

36. Italian and French socialists of the thirties, respectively.
37. German CP leaders in the twenties.

ruling class in the interest of the class as a whole, control and manipulation
of the underlying population, use of violence where necessary (abroad) were
characteristic also of Britain from the last quarter of the XIX-th century to WW
II." I think that you have overlooked one important additional "criterion" that I
suggested in my article ["Fascism in America"], that I placed in fact in the center
of the argument: "Fascism is a political system evolved by capitalist societies in
the age of imperialism, wars and social and national revolutions. It is designed to
strengthen the state as an instrument of capitalist domination *and to adapt it to
the requirements of intensified class struggle on the national and/or international
scene.*" (Italics *now* supplied).

What I object to in your reasoning is *not* that you haven't considered the
relation of the ruling class to the state etc. — I know that you are aware of that
and cannot say everything at the same time. What I do regard as a crucial flaw is
that you treat the matter essentially ahistorically. What is democracy under one
set of conditions is no democracy under another, and what is oppressiveness
and terrorism is oppressiveness and terrorism and still democracy in one setting
and fascism in another. To put it more concretely: the Russian Tsar's bloody
pacification of Poland or of the Caucasus, the Britishers' strangulation of Ireland
or India, their joint *Schweinereien* in China is no more fascism than the original
destruction of the Indians in the U.S. or than the oppression of the Negroes.

The crucial point is that the terrorism, oppressiveness, *Gleichschaltung*
[synchronization], state domination, etc. etc. are introduced in a specific
class struggle constellation. It is the counter-revolutionary, anti-socialist,
anti-proletarian direction of the oppressive mechanism, its employment
against the class enemy at home or the uprising colonial peoples abroad that
makes it fascism. You might say that Thiers's drowning in blood of the Paris
Communards has come closest to fascism in the XIX-th century. It is the
capitalist class's domination of the state *sans blague* ["no joking" or "literally"]
used for the suppression of the class enemy (at home and abroad) that makes this
domination fascist.

Therefore prior to the Russian revolution there were only minor *fascistoid*
"blossoms" — the counterrevolution in France, the rather mildly enforced
Sozialistengesetz of Bismarck and such. It is only after the class struggle was
given its life-and-death intensity through the Russian revolution and later on
through the revolutions in SE-Europe + China that the blossoms began yielding
berries. Minus the revolutionary danger going at the very central nervous system
of the capitalist order, the U.S. might have either become the champion of
colonial liberation so as to take over under that sauce the colonies of the French
or the British, or it might have beaten down the Nicaraguans, the Cubans and

the Filipinos — in neither case being fascist. Once more: one cannot — in my opinion — properly analyze and understand fascism outside of the particular condition of intensified, driven to the apex class struggle characteristic of our "interesting" age.

If you are inclined to accept this, the question as to whether one could call Britain truly bourgeois democratic while the British were doing all they did in Ireland, India and elsewhere answers itself in a satisfactory manner. Not threatened in its very existence the lion was a courteous, friendly animal, only occasionally devouring a small animal hanging around unprotected. But the lion and the eagle change their entire mode of behavior when in real, mortal danger.

But what is the transition point? What is the jumping place from quantity of class domination to the quality of fascism? Terribly difficult to say. In the German-Italian-Polish-Spanish-Japanese cases it was a fairly simple matter. In the case of the U.S. it is more complex — for special U.S. reasons partly and tentatively touched upon in my article. You are right that there may be a certain inconsistency between the October and November pieces — although the inconsistency is purely verbal. What I would and should have said is that the tendencies towards fascism are very strong — for the October article's reasons — that in a great number of respects the *fascization* of the country has gone a long way or is complete, that the speed and violence of the completion would be greatly increased through the election of Eisenhower-Nixon-McCarthy *et tutti quanti.*

Not that Stevenson is a guarantee of a reversal, or of a stoppage. Stevenson may offer a chance to the anti-fascist forces, may offer an opportunity for a different development. There is nothing pre-ordained or fatalistic about it. What the November piece should have added — the election of Stevenson is not the end but the beginning of the matter. Let's elect him in order to fight him and such fascist forces that will be operating under him.

[…]
So much for tonight.
[…]
    /s Yours Paul

P.S. […]

PMS to PAB

Wilton, N. H.
October 29, 1952

Dear Paul,

[…]

I suppose you are right in re Blumin. Not understanding the possibility —
indeed the absolute *necessity* — of guns-and-butter in an advanced capitalist
society, he and his friends think that any argument along these lines *must* be
dishonest apologetics. But that being the case, they would hardly look upon
a letter of explanation in any other light, so it would most likely be a mere
waste of time to compose one. It is a paradox that what has become the most
comprehensive contradiction of capitalism — its continued existence depends
entirely on its preparing for total destruction, including self-destruction —
escapes the most orthodox of Marxists. How could one go about getting them to
see this crucial point?

The dilemma of the mass CP which you stress undoubtedly exists, but I'm
not sure it is the central problem just now. If it were true, as you say, that lack
of revolutionary action "will antagonize, disappoint, embitter the workers and
send them to the fascists," then the problem would indeed be a hopeless one.
But I do not see any signs of this in either France or Italy. In France, the problem
seems to be not a swing toward fascism but growing apathy reflected in a decline
in the party press, a drop in CGT [Confederation of Labor] membership, etc.
In Italy it seems that the CP is doing very well with its popular front policy. A
recent article in *L'Observateur* says that it is expected now that the front would
get over 40 percent of the popular vote, and De Gasperi is desperately trying
to rig the electoral law so that a party or coalition which gets a bare majority of
votes will get a comfortable bonus of parliamentary seats. It is noteworthy that
there has been no crisis in the Italian CP, no expulsions or demotions. And I am
inclined to think that what lies behind the French crisis is less your dilemma than
the difficulty of the French Party's really getting behind a policy of neutralism
which is objectively in the interests of the French people and which could now
form the basis of a real popular front. The whole being of the CP is in the Soviet
camp: how can it sincerely and effectively say to Frenchmen, "The best policy
for all of us who are now under the American thumb is a policy of genuine
independence?" Perhaps it can be done but certainly not easily. That's where I
think the real trouble lies now. (All this, by the way, ties up with the Tito question
which I believe to be at bottom a question of Yugo nationalism vs. the special
brand of internationalism which recognizes the unreserved duty to follow the
USSR regardless of local circumstances.)

Finally on fascism: we approach more closely. I doubt if there is any real difference on the substance of the matter, but we have still to find a mutually satisfactory formulation. It seems to me that the inconsistency which exists between your October and November pieces is more than verbal and in fact that it reappears in a different form in your latest letter (Oct. 25). You say about a quarter of the way down the page that "what is democracy under one set of conditions is no democracy under another, and what is oppressiveness and terrorism is oppressiveness and terrorism and still democracy in one setting and fascism in another." This suggests that literally no political changes need take place within a given country to transform it from a democratic to a fascist system; they can all occur outside the country. But this is a very different position from that enunciated about three-quarters of the way down the page when you say: "Not threatened in its very existence the lion was a courteous, friendly animal, only occasionally devouring a small animal hanging around unprotected. But the lion and the eagle change their entire mode of behavior when in real, mortal danger." Precisely. Under changed historical conditions, they change their *entire mode of behavior*; it is not at all a question of the *same* political setup being democracy today and fascism tomorrow, it is a question of a very real change in the political setup which *transforms* democracy into fascism. I do not deny for a moment that what is responsible for this change is the spread of the world revolution with its attendant sharpening of the class struggle on an international scale (and its mortal threat to the continued existence of capitalism), but what I do hold is that the criteria which we are seeking are not to be found in these historical conditions but in the character of the political systems we are investigating. And in my view, we will find that the decisive criteria relate to the suppression (both forcible and non-forcible) of political opposition to the ruling regime and its policies: this is what is common to all the cases which are generally agreed to be fascist, and it is precisely the central content of what is happening in the U.S. today and of what would be enormously intensified and speeded up by an Eisenhower-Nixon victory.

It might be objected that this way of regarding the matter would oblige us to classify Tsarist Russia (which can stand for a large number of similar cases) as a fascist country. But this, I think, would be really to argue in an un- and even anti-historical fashion. Fascism is by no means the only political system which denies the right of opposition; it is that one which emerges under the specific historical conditions of our age. The true nature of fascism can therefore best be recognized and studied in countries where the right of opposition has been won in the bourgeois-democratic phase of capitalist development and is stamped out as those countries go fascist under changed historical conditions.

The position I have sketched here is, I think, basically what may be called
the "classical" Communist position as stated by, e.g., Dutt in *Fascism and Social
Revolution*, esp. pp. 107-110. Cf. the long quotation from the 1928 program
of the Communist International [CI] which begins: "Under certain special
historical conditions the progress of the bourgeois, imperialist, reactionary
offensive assumes the form of fascism."[38] The weakness of the CI concept of
fascism is clearly that it limits too narrowly the political forms which fascism may
assume ("The fascist system is a system of direct dictatorship, etc.") and does
not envisage the possibility of what may be called "parliamentary fascism" which
preserves and utilizes the forms of democracy, as is now happening in the U.S.
This is a very important weakness, of course, and it is particularly important that
it be corrected precisely in this country where, for example, faith in the courts
as a *bulwark against* fascism prevents people from seeing how they are being
used as *instruments of* fascism. But it is a weakness that can be remedied without
rejecting the underlying theoretical idea of fascism which that "early" literature
expounded.

On the question of the transition point, I think it has to be frankly recognized
that while such a point *may* exist it is not *certain* to exist: the transition can be so
gradual that it will never be possible to say precisely when it started or when it
was completed.

Does all this provide any basis for agreement?

[...]

Yours

/s Paul

[...]

PAB to PMS

Stanford University
November 16th, 1952

Dear Paul,

[...]

In re: fascism I think we are in agreement on all the relevant points.
Re-reading your letter, I feel that the only point that would call for additional
discussion is this: what is the analytical line to be drawn between what one
might call "normal," "old-fashioned," bourgeois reaction and fascism? Clearly

---

38. This sentence from the Communist International is quoted in R. Palme Dutt, *Fascism and
Social Revolution* (New York: International Publishers, 1935), 108.

Russian *Okhrana* or Bismarck's police were not "fascist" instruments. On this
we are both agreed. On the other hand the FBI was not one either before say
the First World War but may readily become one before the III World War.
In other words, it is not necessary that the constitutional, institutional *form* of
the mechanism of government be changed, all that is necessary is that under
changing historical conditions, in the light of the changing functions of the
capitalist state, institutions of this state commence to fulfill new tasks. When does
the quantity of those new tasks switch into the new quality of fascism? And while
I fully agree with you that it is the suppression (both forcible and non-forcible) of
opposition that is important, I would tend to "deviate" insofar, as I would place
more accent on the objective performance of the state under given circumstances.

In other words, a capitalist state leaving a certain freedom of opposition,
permitting the publication of some opposition newspapers and tolerating a few
opposition members in its parliament but member of an Anti-Komintern alliance,
warring actively against the social revolution everywhere, supporting and
fostering counter-revolutionary forces all over the globe *is* a fascist state even if it
is — to use Stalin's favorite phrase — a fascist state "of a special kind."[39] It is an
important and difficult question why in one case the performance of the objective
counter-revolutionary role requires a Hitlerian type of fascism, while in another
case the Pilsudski arrangement is satisfactory (don't forget, under Pilsudski
Poland had a number of SD newspapers, a relatively unhampered Trade-Union
movement, a fairly strong Jewish Bund organization etc.) But this is perhaps
something that we may well leave to oral discussion — I'm sure that we could
find some satisfactory way of expressing it, and I think that it would be eminently
worthwhile to clarify the whole subject.

I do agree with you that in my earlier formulation of the CP problem
in Western Europe I made a mistake by saying that the discouraged and
disappointed workers will go to the fascists. Apathy, as you say, is another, and
as far as France is concerned the nearer alternative. I still feel, however, that
the apathy stage is transient, that the danger is great, that under objectively
unsatisfactory conditions, with depressions and worsening standards of living,
the fascist activists may have a terribly good chance, if the CP is definitely unable
to push ahead.

I do *not* agree with your analysis of the Tito situation as of a conflict of
divergent concepts of nationalism or internationalism. I have the strong feeling
that in the Tito case the problem was really a class problem, in the sense that

---

39. Handwritten note in the margin by Sweezy: No. For the form + tactics of the opposition, there
is a crucial difference.

the Yugo peasant prevented the Bolshevization of Yugoslavia. The nationalist ideology was obviously very handy and natural to play up — at the *bottom* it is nothing but a smokescreen. . . . The Polish corridor was quite important to many Germans — but it was not the Polish corridor that sent Hitler into the armament drive and into war. In fact, one might almost generalize and say that the main danger of all the national problems lies precisely in their ability to create fogs behind which really important matters are settled. Like "warm water ports" of the traditional diplomatic historians. . . .

So much for today. There are meanwhile some developments on the Stanford scene, that may produce an explosion "any minute." Some dignitaries perused my paper in Haley's volume "National Economic Planning," and decided that "someone may easily seize upon it" in order to raise hell.[40] Our Dept. Chairman had a long talk with me, and expressed his strong concern. My impression is, that things will start "any minute now," since Ed Shaw would not have talked the way he did if he did not have some hints from above.[41] The Administration is in general terribly frightened. Stanford is now under a contractual agreement with the Byrnes (formerly Tenney) State Un-American Activities Committee and is committed to report to that Committee whatever undesirable happens on the Campus. Moreover on Nov. 4th a proposition was adopted (#5) according to which the State of California will withdraw tax-exemptions from all institutions that rate such tax-exemptions if they harbor, promote, facilitate, tolerate . . . subversive activities, individuals, etc. This will take care of such outfits as IPR [possibly Institute of Pacific Relations] but will obviously have wider repercussions. A University like Stanford could close up in absence of the tax exemption. It would not only drastically reduce its income from the endowment but also kill its gift raising campaigns. . . So it might not be a bad idea, to have a good look at things in NY, and possibly find something in private business. But this would mean spending most of one's time in doing something that would be killing . . . Well, anyway, it just ain't terribly cheerful.

[. . .]

More later.

As ever,

/s Paul

40. Published in B.F. Haley, ed., *A Survey of Contemporary Economics* (1952). Reprinted in Baran, *The Longer View*, 115–81.

41. This is an indication, arising frequently in these letters, of the constant attempts to silence, penalize, and persecute Baran during the McCarthyite period and after. His tenure and principles of academic freedom provided only limited protection and he was under constant pressure within his own department as well as from the Stanford administration and outside political authorities.

2
The Cold War Years to 1956

[1953]

PAB to PMS

Stanford University
April 21-st, 1953

Dear Paul,

[...]

Trying to finish a bit of work before leaving I have run into the following problem on which I would very much like to get your advice. One could define economic development or economic growth as an "increase of per capita or aggregate output of goods and services." This is the sort of a definition which would be normally suggested by conventional economics. It is however quite deficient because obviously expansion of services need *not* constitute economic growth, moreover may represent almost the opposite — expansion of unproductive activities. E.g. in period I a society was producing with the help of 100 productive workers 100 bushels of wheat. At the same time 100 disguised unemployed were doing nothing and lived off their families' tables. In period II those disguised unemployed accept domestic service jobs with the productive workers who have decided to eat less and to enjoy the comforts that such servants provide. They pay them 25 bushels of wheat. The aggregate (or per capita) output as conventionally measured in GNP statistics is 125 bushels: society has grown economically by 25% from period I to period II.

This is obviously nonsense. It is the old Pigovian problem alright of the gentleman marrying and respectively divorcing his cook. The Soviet way out of measuring essentially "material output" is a way out for the Soviet society where we assume that the composition of the annual product-mix is o.k. In a capitalist society this hardly provides a solution. Assume that those disguised unemployed would be hired in period II *not* as domestic servants but to construct toys for the children of the productive workers and would get also 25 bushels of wheat for that activity.

Again the value of total output would be 125 bushels, it would be all based on "material" output — it would still make little sense to say that the society in question has gone through "economic development" and has expanded its output by 25%.

This is no quibble, most of the official statistics of the so-called underdeveloped countries in the West present a completely distorted picture of the situation precisely by this procedure. Nor would actually the Marxian distinction between productive and unproductive labor help in this matter — it goes away alright from the physical distinction between material and non-material output by defining all labor yielding surplus value, i.e. exchanging itself against capital rather than against revenue as productive — but this does not help in finding a measurement of economic growth. The labor of the toy-makers would be productive, of the domestic servants unproductive — if the toy-makers work for an entrepreneur who *sells* their products in the market rather than make them as servants of the rich.

The whole thing could be probably "licked" by simply saying that economic development or economic growth in a capitalist society cannot be studied in any other way but by accepting the market measurements — but then we're back at the Dept. of Commerce GNP concepts which make no sense (for the purpose at hand in any case!)

I don't know whether I have stated the question clearly enough, but may be something will occur to you. I would be most grateful for a line on the matter.

Apropos: The latest *UN Economic Survey of Europe since the War* states (p.25 n):

"In the Eastern European countries, services not directly connected with the production and transport of goods are not regarded as productive and their value is thus excluded from national income. For a poor country which is trying to develop its industry and to reduce the under-employment common in service-trades, the Marxist definition of national income has some obvious advantages over the more inclusive concept suited to wealthy industrialized economies and now commonly adopted in under-developed countries." This is very good — again, in planned economies only such *goods* are being produced that are socially desirable; in capitalist under-developed countries the adoption of the Soviet concept would still involve a falsification since even under that concept toys or carriages or palaces would be included. . . .

[…]
As always,
        /s Paul

P.S. […]

PMS to PAB

                                                        Wilton, N. H.
                                                        April 24, 1953

Dear Paul,

I don't believe there is any satisfactory solution to the problem you raise. You
have to use whatever figures there are and then make qualitative adjustments
and reservations as best you can. As an index of economic development, I think
I would prefer to total or per capita output (of goods or goods-cum-services)
the proportion of the gainfully employed in industry. Historically, I think you
will find that this is the index which gives you the most significant information
about the relative positions of different countries or of one country at different
times. (Industry, of course, has to be defined to exclude the category that used
to be called "hand and neighborhood industries" in the U.S. Census — in
other words, it must be *la grande industrie* in the sense of Engels' *Principles of
Communism*.)
        […]
        Yours,
            /s Paul

P. S. […]

PAB to PMS

                                                        Stanford University
                                                        April 28, 1953

Dear Paul,
        […]

I agree with you that there is no pat formula for defining economic
development, and the criterion which you suggest (## [numbers] of gainfully
employed in modern industry) is probably as good as any other. ## of HP
[hours of production/productive labor] used in the economy might be another
possibility. But my problem is slightly different: what I am after is *not* a good
index of economic development but a measurement that lends itself to a
breakdown into component parts. In other words, what I would like to be able to

measure (or at least conceptually isolate for measurement) is consumption and
"economic surplus." In doing this an index is no good, I need rather some sort
of a GNP magnitude: the one used in the U.S.S.R. is probably the best. But this
is a relatively minor and not terribly interesting problem — just for the sake of
accuracy it should be clearly stated.

The Brantweinbrenner (Buse-brewer) review in the JPE [*Journal of Political
Economy*] made me kind of mad.[42] First of all what business does he (and
Hamilton) have to talk about "close parallelism to the economic faith of certain
elements currently under persecution as 'subversive'"? Even if his intentions, as
it would seem, are most honorable this is nothing short of an official invitation
to political and academic authorities to "draw administrative conclusions." This
may be thoughtlessness, tactlessness or meanness — I don't know. It certainly
is a hell of a thing to do in a "scientific" magazine. But to hell with that. What
is really stupid is the distinction which he introduces between [the] "political-
economic" and "theoretical-economic" explanation of the unworkability of
the capitalist system. This precisely is what makes for the sterility and decline
of so-called "pure economics," and this precisely is what the Marxian method
excludes and condemns. The capitalist order is a "totality" ("*Das Wahre ist
das Ganze*") ["the truth is the whole" — Hegel] and while for some technical
reasons it may be necessary to study its individual aspects in separation (one
cannot talk about everything at the same time) the crux of the matter is to
continuously relate, continuously interconnect those individual aspects in the
consideration of that totality. Otherwise one gets down to the non-sensicality of
the Lernerian "rationalism" or to the naivety of the Grossmanian mechanism.[43]
In "purely economic" terms the capitalist economy need neither break down
nor need it to have depressions. All that would be required "in purely economic
terms" is to drastically raise wages as soon as investment slackens, or to ship
"Milk to the Hottentots" or any number of equally intelligent measures. "*Wenn
meine Grossmutter Raeder haette and nicht mit Schnaps sondern mit Benzin
angetrieben waere, ware sie nicht meine Grossmutter sondern ein Kraftwagen.*"
["If my grandmother had wheels and was driven by fuel instead of schnaps,
then she wouldn't be my grandmother, but instead a car."] And if the "purely
economic" considerations were the governing ones, it wouldn't be capitalism but

---

42. PAB means "Booze-Brewer," a play on Prof. Martin Bronfenbrenner's name. Baran is referring
to Martin Bronfenbrenner, "Review of *What Do Economists Know* by Benjamin Higgins," *Journal
of Political Economy* 61, no. 1 (February 1953): 80–81.

43. Abba Lerner was a Russian-born British economist and Keynesian who emigrated to the
United States in the late 1930s. Henryk Grossman was a German Marxist who converted Marx's
falling rate of profit theory into a mechanical breakdown theory of economic crisis.

some peculiar outfit ruled by Lerner and the other 6 Eldermen of Zion or. . . .
socialism.

[. . .]

As ever,

/s Paul

PMS to PAB

Wilton, N. H.

May 7, 1953

Dear Paul,

[. . .] Needless to say, we march together on the proposition that *das Wahre ist
das Ganze* ["the truth is the whole" from the Preface to Hegel's *The Philosophy
of Mind*]. I regard it as the most important proposition of dialectical materialism,
and one of the very greatest merits of Engels' exposition in *Anti-Dühring* is that
he makes the point with all the emphasis it deserves. [44]

[. . .]

Best to the family.

Yrs.,

/s Paul

PAB to PMS

[*No provenance*]

[Palo Alto]

May 15th, 1953

Dear Paul,

My travel plans have crystallized by now and look about as follows: I shall sail
from New York on August 12-th and proceed to France. There (and possibly in
Germany) I plan to spend some 4–5 weeks returning afterwards to Oxford where
I would spend the so-called Michaelmas Term. During same I will deliver 8
lectures on a topic that I still have to choose, take part in a seminar and otherwise
be free to devote myself to my own interests. I haven't yet fully decided what to
talk about in these lectures (which they may publish, if so desired) but think that
the general topic will be "The Political Economy of Growth" — dealing with
underdeveloped countries but also with some aspects of the growth problem
in the advanced capitalist countries. I shall be preparing myself for this during
the summer. This "load" will give me an opportunity to look around there and

---

44. Baran and Sweezy were to make "The truth is the whole" the leading epigraph (along with a
quote from Franz Fanon) to *Monopoly Capital*.

elsewhere for possible job openings, and if something should turn up in Oxford
or in any other university, I would be strongly inclined to take it and have then
Elena + Nicky follow me in due course. But this is obviously sheer speculation,
and the chances that I would find nothing there and have to come back to
Stanford are probably very high.

[…]

Your editorial in the latest *MR* issue is superb ["The Peace Offensive and
the Job Ahead," *MR*, May 1953] — a really splendid job on which I wish to
congratulate you most sincerely. I am much less satisfied with the Martinet piece
for which I fail to see the *raison d'etre*. … [Gilles Martinet, "The Future of
Communism," *MR*, May 1953]

A minor "doctrinal" problem that has been occupying me: on p. 205 of your
Theory of Capitalist Development you give hell to Rosa [Luxemburg], for what
is in my humble opinion an inadequate reason. You say: ". . . her non-capitalist
consumers could in no way change the situation. It is not possible to sell to
non-capitalist consumers without also buying from them. So far as the capitalist
circulation process is concerned, the surplus value cannot be disposed of in this
way; it can at best change its form. Who is to buy the commodities 'imported'
from the non-capitalist environment? If there could have been, as a matter of
principle, no demand for the 'exported' commodities there can be just as little
demand for the 'imported' commodities."

I fail to see this. (1) — this is a minor matter — the mere exportation of some
domestic output and net importation of luxury goods — furs or diamonds or
caviar — may raise the consumption of the capitalist class and thus reduce the
problem of realization of the surplus value. As I say, this is minor probably. Not
minor, however is (2) *gold* may be brought back in exchange for the exported
goods, and find its ultimate destination in the vaults of the central bank; (3)
"securities" may be brought back i.e. capital exports may take place. Even if
the "non-capitalist" consumer finds himself in the same country with (1) and
(2) therefore irrelevant, (3) can still take place by "internal capital export" — by
"lending up" the peasants' property, by the industrial capitalists buying up land
or other assets in the "non-capitalist" sphere, etc. While it may well be possible
that other ways of getting rid of excess surplus value are more important —
particularly the expansion of the number and per capita income of Rosa's "third
persons" i.e. unproductive laborers of all kinds — there is no logical impossibility
as you suggest of doing some of it via exportation to "non-capitalist" areas. Or do
I misunderstand you, or am I wrong, or are you too harsh on the poor girl?

Comments on this would be highly appreciated.

[…]

Best regards. As ever,

    /s Paul

PMS to PAB

                                      Wilton, N. H.

                                   May 24, 1953

Dear Paul,

On the Rosa Luxemburg problem, it seems to me that you are getting away from her terms of reference, if I may use the expression. Of course, the import of gold would solve the problem (i.e. in proportion to its magnitude), and obviously investing capital in the non-capitalist areas would enable the consumers there to buy without selling. But all this is equally true of capitalist or non-capitalist areas or strata. Rosa clearly argues that there is some magic about consumers' being non-capitalist (by which she really means outside the reproduction scheme) and she completely neglects the question of how these chaps are to pay for what they buy. My point, perhaps not too well expressed, is that in this whole business there is no virtue about being non-capitalist, and if the system can't accumulate when it is all capitalist then setting it in a non-capitalist environment isn't going to help. The point obviously is a theoretical one and doesn't mean that as a practical matter the opening up of non-capitalist areas is of no importance.

[…]

I'm working on a review (possibly for *MR* but more likely for the book of essays and reviews I have almost finished preparing for the printer) of Galbraith's *American Capitalism* and Lilienthal's *Big Business*.[45] When I get it done I want to send it to you for a check on the economic arguments. That should be before the end of this week, maybe in a couple of days. When it arrives can you give it a quick going over and send it back in a few days? I'd like to get the whole ms. to the printer before the end of June so that the book can be brought out some time in the fall.

[…]

    /s Paul

---

45. This was probably Sweezy's *The Present as History* (New York: Monthly Review Press, 1953). The book included a wide set of essays, but not the contemplated reviews of John Kenneth Galbraith, *American Capitalism* (Boston: Houghton Mifflin. 1952), and David E. Lilienthal, *Big Business: A New Era* (New York: Harper and Brothers, 1952).

PMS to PAB

Wilton, N. H.

June 3, 1953

Dear Paul,

Many thanks for the marginal comments [on PMS's review mentioned in previous letter of May 24, 1953]. They show me that I did not make my basic argument clear and that some pretty drastic revision is called for.

The central issue is the importance of profits, and it was here that I failed to develop my argument properly. What I want to get across is that given a high degree of monopoly (to use a Kaleckian turn of phrase) full employment and enormous profits inevitably go together but at the same time are essentially incompatible. The huge profits require huge investment outlets, which, for a variety of reasons, are not forthcoming: (1) at home because the magnitude of profits itself represses the growth of consumption, so that any attempt to invest in such lines quickly leads to overproduction and excess capacity (such investment being further inhibited by the monopolists' desire to protect their already invested capital); (2) abroad because of uncertainty of a number of descriptions which I need not detail here.

American capitalism's answer to this dilemma, which is created by monopoly, unrecognized by Galbraith, Lilienthal et al, and untouched by either the New Competition or countervailing power, is to tax away a large part of the profits, spend them on armaments and foreign subsidies, thus directly returning that part to the circular flow and creating investment outlets in arms industries, etc., for much of the rest. (This points to why profits *before* taxes are the crucial magnitude when it comes to comparing profits with national income: taxes on corporate profits are the most important way of spending profits. If you reduce taxes, you either have to find some new way or else profits will shrink.)

I realize that you may not agree with this line of argument — at least not wholly — but at any rate you can see that what is at stake is not merely a petty bourgeois prejudice against profits as being exploitative. The biggest difficulty is to develop this argument about profits within a reasonable space and in terms that can be understood by the same kind of people for whom Galbraith's and Lilienthal's books were written.

The other apparent differences indicated by your comments are comparatively minor, and call for only a few notes. I don't think there is any inconsistency between the statement that higher money wages are regularly offset, wholly or partly, by higher prices and the statement that the average household has been better off since the war than in any but the best years before. Sustained high employment, with a larger average number working per household, more working days per annum, more overtime, etc., can easily reconcile the two propositions. You are probably right about the large retailer finding the real demand curve for the producer, but this is a technical refinement which would be out of place in a non-technical paper. Finally, what argument *will* convince the liberal, who is determined not to be convinced, that public works cannot be turned on and off at will to take the place of war spending? Either you see that this is a question of the class-structure of society and the location of political power, or you don't. If you do, the question as I posed it does answer itself. If you don't, then the only way to convince you is to change your whole way of regarding social problems.

Yours,

/s Paul

PMS to PAB

Wilton, N.H.

July 6 [1953]

Glad the comments on the paper ["Economic Progress and Economic Surplus"] were of some use. Leo and I (esp. Leo) are getting our first dose of Senator Joe [McCarthy] (he is called for tomorrow a.m. because some of his books were discovered on the shelves of the overseas library), and getting lawyers, preparing a line, etc., etc. have thrown my whole schedule out of kilter. We'll know more about what's involved soon, whether we have a "case" on our hands, and so on. Meanwhile, I'm up to me ears trying to get the next issue lined up.

More on all this and other topics too later.

Hastily,

/s Paul

[...]

PMS to PAB

Wilton, N.H.

July 24, 1953

Dear Paul,

[...]

As to McCarthy, etc., we are printing the full transcript of Leo's testimony in the August issue [of *MR*], also the statement he read before the committee. I will provide a few clarifications but not try to go into any detail. Our original position was Einstein's, but it soon developed that that is not specific enough.[46] How to implement it? Refuse to appear or be sworn? Then you simply go to jail, and the public probably thinks you're a fool. Better lay the foundations for a court fight. But then you must lay the best foundations you can because the chances of winning are not very good at best, and it would be bad to lose, not only because of going to jail but because then some issues which are still unsettled would be settled in favor of them and against us. All of which led to our deciding to state a positive political position — Marxist, socialist, non-Communist but willing to cooperate with Communists — and then refuse to answer any further questions (1) because they violate the First and (2) are outside the powers of the McCarthy committee. Leo carried this out very well. But, not unnaturally I suppose, McCarthy doesn't like to have his court tests made on the most favorable ground for his opponents, so he simply refused to seek a citation for contempt. So we got away with refusing to answer a lot of questions but at the expense of answering the $64 question [whether a member of the CP?], and we didn't have the pleasure of testing the standing of the First Amendment. It was interesting and on the whole as good an outcome as one could expect, I guess. But it was not wholly satisfactory and indeed couldn't be.

46. In the words of John J. Simon: "In 1953, Albert Einstein (. . . part of the extended MR family— his 'Why Socialism?' appeared in the first issue) proposed a renewed First Amendment attack on the very legitimacy of the [McCarthyite] purge; at the time, it must have seemed quixotic at best. Yet that is what editors and writers for *Monthly Review*, among others, did [instead of relying on the Fifth Amendment]. In July 1953, founding editor Leo Huberman and frequent contributor Harvey O'Connor were called before Senator McCarthy. Both challenged the authority of his Committee, citing the First Amendment's freedom of expression guarantees. Huberman, directly confronting McCarthy, when asked how his views 'deviated' from those of Communists said, "I want to make it crystal clear that communism is not the issue . . . the issue [is] my right as an author and editor to pursue my occupation." The strategy had been to get the McCarthy committee to declare Huberman in contempt of court and to use this to appeal all the way to the U.S. Supreme Court on the basis of the first amendment. As Sweezy indicated in his letter to Baran, McCarthy knew better than to allow this to happen. It was Sweezy himself who was subsequently to succeed in taking the first amendment defense all the way to the U.S. Supreme Court in *Sweezy vs. New Hampshire*—after being declared in contempt of court in New Hampshire for refusing to answer the Attorney General's questions. See John J. Simon, "*Sweezy vs. New Hampshire*: The Radicalism of Principle," *Monthly Review* 51, no. 11 (April 2000): 35-37. For Einstein's letter see Otto Nathan and Heinz Norden, eds., *Einstein on Peace* (New York: Schocken Books, 1960), 545–47. Huberman's testimony before the McCarthy Committee was included in full in Leo Huberman and Paul M. Sweezy, "A Challenge to the Book Burners," *Monthly Review* 5, no. 4 (August 1953): 158-73.

We'd like to see you before you leave and, unless something comes up in the meantime to interfere, we'll come to NY August 11th and plan to spend that evening having a good dinner and lengthy discussion. Okay?

Yours

/s Paul

P. S. […]

[*Editor's Note: PAB spent the fall of 1953 at Oxford University in England, where he delivered a series of lectures that formed the basis of his subsequently published book,* The Political Economy of Growth. *If PAB and PMS corresponded during those months in 1953, those letters are missing.*]

[1954]

PMS to PAB

Wilton, N.H.

Jan. 10, '54

Dear Paul, [*Two names, Arthur and Hi, are crossed out.*]
This is addressed to three people who I guess don't know each other to save me time and because I want to say substantially the same to all of you.

First, many thanks for the encouraging message re the N.H. unpleasantness.[47] It is literally true that nothing is so much needed on the American Left today as genuine solidarity. The basis for it doesn't exist on any large scale: there are too many old bitterness's and too many really important differences, but where the basis does exist let us spare no pains to develop it.

My hearing took place on Friday the 8th at Concord, the state capital. Executive session. Present: me, the Attorney General, a flat-foot helper, a couple

47. Paul Sweezy was under subpoena from the New Hampshire Attorney General to testify about the contents of a speech he delivered at the University of Hampshire, which the authorities deemed to be subversive. Sweezy, who took his stand based on the First Amendment and refused to hand over his lecture notes or name names, was declared to be in contempt of court. The appeal process was eventually to lead to the landmark 1957 *Sweezy vs. New Hampshire* decision of the U.S. Supreme Court under Earl Warren, which became one of the primary decisions defending academic freedom, and marking the end of the McCarthy period. See Simon, "*Sweezy vs. New Hampshire:* The Radicalism of Principle"; Paul M. Sweezy, "Statement to the New Hampshire Attorney General," *Monthly Review* 51, no. 11 (April 2000): 37–41.

of undefined individuals, and the steno typist. Lasted about 2 1/2 hrs. I read a statement into the record at the outset announcing intention to take what may be called the Huberman-Lamont line, answering some questions to establish a record (without conceding right to ask them), but refusing others on grounds of (1) lack of a pertinence and invasion of 1st Amendment rights. Within this framework, I exercised discretion as the hearing developed, actually answering many questions I didn't have to so long as they were about myself or were the kind of questions which, if refused, would have established an implication of sinister things to be hidden. But I decisively refused to answer any questions relating to the development, policies, or personnel of the Progressive Party in New Hampshire while I was actively associated with it. I politely baited the questioners from time to time (they are not stupid necessarily, but their thought patterns are inflexible and they are dreadfully ignorant); delivered lectures (short ones) on a variety of subjects such as socialism, Communism, overthrow of government by force and violence, the evils of these investigations, etc.; showed my contempt for the Un-American Activities Committee junk they kept reading into the record.

On the whole, I had the impression at the end that I had come off about as well as could be expected. The Attorney General at any rate was clearly in a dilemma. He had made a rule at the beginning of the investigation that the transcript of all hearings with uncooperative witnesses (i.e. those who refuse to answer any questions for any reason) would be made public. After I had left his office and was standing outside talking to reporters, he called me back and indicated that he did not want to make the transcript public (I think he had doubts as to who would come off best) and sort of hinted that maybe he would be able to withstand pressures to do so — the implication clearly being that he would like to be reassured that I would not make it public. Naturally, I gave no such assurances, merely saying that I would want to go over it with my lawyer before coming to any decisions.

What next? I am still under subpoena. The Attorney General has publicly stated (as he stated to me privately) that he would not make up his mind whether to seek a court order directing me to answer the unanswered questions until he had had a chance to study the transcript (about the middle of this week). I think myself that he is playing for time; would prefer not to take the matter to court for fear of exposing the weakness of his position (he is, I am sorry to say, much more vulnerable on the pertinency than on the 1st amendment issue, but then one has to use whatever weapons come to hand) but is afraid that if he doesn't he will be accused by the local McCarthyites (quite strong and very vocal) of appeasement, etc.

I have a first-rate lawyer (couldn't be with me at Friday's hearing because of a prior commitment to represent another client at a simultaneous hearing in the same building), a liberal Republican who agreed with my statement and gave me 100 percent carte blanche to refuse to answer questions. If it comes to a court fight, I think he will give a good account of himself. I rather hope it does come to a court fight. If we could win it, it would be a political and psychological defeat for the inquisition and, in some ways more important, it would be a protection to other witnesses who are threatened with loss of jobs (mainly teachers at Dartmouth and the University of N. H.) unless they "cooperate."

Nancy comes up on Tuesday and will be accompanied by the lawyer. She plans to take the same position I did, and her case is probably clearer since they can hardly have any Un-American junk to throw into the record on her (her sole "crime" having been to organize the Progressive Party in the state in its early stages; she had to retire, *causa maternitatis* [due to maternity], in the middle of the 1948 campaign and has been too busy with 3 small ones since to return to the wars). Where I answered a lot of questions and talked for the record, she will probably answer very few and volunteer nothing. This may present the Attorney General with an even more painful dilemma than I did. Maybe she will be the one who makes the court test.

The whole affair has acquired a peculiar aspect from the fact that Nancy's mother is Republican National Committeewoman from N. H. The papers got hold of this and have been giving it quite a bit of play. Internal Republican Party squabbles, of which there seem to be plenty, will probably play a role in the final outcome. Meanwhile, it is educational, if not exactly pleasant, for Nancy's mother to learn something about the mechanics of guilt by relation.

There'll probably be a report on the outcome in *MR* sooner or later. And if the transcript of my testimony reads decently, we may publish it "for the record," so to speak.

Meanwhile all the best,

/s Paul

[. . .]

PMS to PAB

Wilton, N.H.

March 12, 1954

Dear Paul,

Just a hasty note in answer to your latest. I'm off to NY in a day or so and won't have a chance to write again for perhaps a week or ten days.

I think your advice is sound. I have just read the briefs in the case testing the constitutionality of the NH inquisition before the state supreme court, and the implications of the Attorney General's contentions are really appalling. He asserts, *inter alia*, that "there is no sound legal or moral reason why any citizen of New Hampshire should not be required to appear and testify relative to knowledge of subversive activity in New Hampshire, on his part, her part or on the part of other persons to the witness' knowledge." Combined with the doctrine, clearly implied elsewhere in the brief, that anything is subversive if it has been so designated "by responsible legislative and executive agencies of both major parties in the Federal government," this is clearly a recipe for making the Inquisition a permanent and unlimited institution. You can't appease this sort of thing: the time has come to say no (it doesn't matter too much at which point) and then simply to stick to it.

I have recently read an analysis by a Tulane law professor which throws more light on the ancestry of the present inquisition than anything I have seen elsewhere. It is precisely the modern analogy of the Roman-law doctrine of *infamia* which, according to the standard treatise on the subject is defined as ". . . a moral censure pronounced by a competent authority in the state on individual members of the community, as a result of certain actions which they had committed, or certain modes of life which they had pursued, this censure involving disqualification for certain rights both in public and in private law." The author (one Mitchell Franklin by name) argues that *infamia* survived the feudal period and that one of the main purposes of the founding fathers was to abolish it altogether through the first and fifth amendments. In this connection there is a most interesting argument about the origin of the clause in the fifth amendment that no one "shall be held to answer for a capital, or otherwise infamous crime unless on a presentment or indictment of a Grand Jury." He shows pretty clearly that the use of the word "infamous" here derives from the doctrine of *infamia* and means an infaming crime, i.e., one for which the punishment is infamy. All in all a most impressive case that the witch hunt is *toto coelo* in violation of the very first principles of the constitution. The pity is that there is absolutely nothing of this in the brief submitted to the Supreme Court in the Emspak case, which is the closest to a real constitutional attack on the witch hunt we have yet got.[48] I am trying to get some offprints of the article in question and will send you one if I succeed (it seems to have appeared in

---

48. The reference is to *Emspak v. United States* 349 U.S. 190, 1955: The Supreme Court reversed the lower court's conviction (violation of 2 U.S.C. § 192), saying Emspak should have been acquitted based on the protections of the 5th Amendment.

something published in Belgium, but the offprint does not even give the name of the journal).

[…]

More in due course.
      /s Paul

PAB to PMS

Stanford University
October 17, 1954

Dear Paul,
[…]

After moving etc. I got ill, some lousy grippe which kept me *hors de combat* for over a week, and then came opening of the school-year, students, classes, department meetings and all sorts of similar chores. Fortunately, I am hardly teaching this quarter. Upon insistence of the Dean I have announced a course on "Economics and the Social Sciences" — being a survey of the place of economics in the general system of social sciences and their mutual interrelationships — calculated *by him* to contribute to the "direly needed broadening of the training of our graduate students." I have actually done quite a lot of reading for it during the summer — mainly historical or rather historiographical, methodological and such literature — and have worked up a fairly interesting bill of fare with the result, which I have foreseen and predicted, that not one solitary student appeared for the occasion. The course is not "required," its usefulness for exam purposes is presumably zero, so that is that. . . . While providing an additional illustration of the "intellectual life" on this campus, it disturbs me very little, since it simply means that I need not lecture 3 times a week, and have only one course to teach — this time elementary economics. Incidentally, teaching that stuff gets more and more difficult, and the feeling that what I am doing is really terribly dishonest becomes more and more overpowering. What the textbooks have is really not "neutral" — it is for the most part plain wrong, but what does one do about it? The Elementary course has to be taught uniformly by everybody according to the same scheme . . . Anyway, this is all not very much worth bothering with, it probably is still the least of existing troubles.

Otherwise I am struggling with my ms, and have finished now the first half. Since the subsequent chapters are pretty well outlined, I ought to finish the whole thing pretty soon now. I have been studying Steindl and Kalecki again, also your exposition of the underconsumption theory, and am still not happy about the whole business. I shall write to you on this matter separately, and will also dispatch to you the chapters involved for such condemnation as they may deserve.

[…]

PAB to PMS

Stanford University

October 30, 1954

Dear Paul,

[…]

2. The underconsumption thing worries me badly, but I don't seem to be able to come to any definite conclusion on the matter. What would seem to be clear is that if capitalists' consumption increases less than proportionately [to] the increase of profits, an ever larger share of income becomes available for accumulation and has to be offset by investment if full employment is to prevail. Even if consumption of capitalists increases proportionately to the increase of income, matters are serious: an ever larger absolute amount has to be invested. So far so good. However, for the underconsumption argument to stand, it is essential to make the assumption which you make in your book (p.187) "… the rate of growth of means of production … is proportional to the increase in consumption goods output." Surely, if it is *less* than proportional the argument stands *a fortiori*, but what if it is more than proportional? In that case such increments in w and l (your notation) [w = total wage bill, l = surplus consumed by capitalists, k = surplus re-invested] as would be forthcoming may call for growing dK/dt. This does not preclude that there might be fluctuations depending on technology and what not. In other words, dK/dt may be less than proportional or more than proportional at different times; there would be no presumption that it must be always less than proportional. If what Steindl has to say on the matter is correct, the ratio of total gross fixed capital to national income (net or gross) has been increasing (p.190 in his book).[49] That would mean — if consumption represented in the same period a fairly stable proportion of income (net), as asserted by Kuznets — that per unit of consumption there has been employed an increasing amount of fixed capital, or that capital was growing *more* than proportionately. As I just said, this per se does not invalidate the thesis, it only tends to undermine its rigidity and simplicity. Now, to be fair to it, the "counteracting tendencies" take care of this matter (new industries, technological advance etc.) but then it becomes problematical whether much is gained by

---

49. Josef Steindl, *Maturity and Stagnation in American Capitalism* (New York: Monthly Review Press, 1976; originally published Oxford University Institute of Statistics,1952).

using that approach rather than saying something like this: since consumption does not grow as fast as output would grow under full employment conditions one of three things must happen: 1) consumption increase — unlikely under capitalism except tor waste etc. 2) investment increase — monopoly problem etc. or 3) unemployment prevails. Which of the latter two actually takes place and in which proportion depends on the specific conditions for investment. As far as (1) is concerned: government spending etc. This sort of a scheme has the advantage that one need not get tied up with a model that can be easily attacked, retaining at the same time all the strategic positions in the debate.

It still is possible to argue that there should be more consumption if the capitalists do not know what to do with their surplus, if they get the govt. to waste it etc. Moreover it leaves room for the "confidence trick" — if the specific conditions of investment are such that capitalists anticipate growing demand on the part of government or otherwise, they may go on investing for a while although there is no real justification for it in the consumer sector. Except: either their anticipations will come through at some point, or else real bust. What you call in your "Crucial Difference" the "end of industrialization" can be also the "end of a hope."[50] As long as the collective hope lasts Dept. II could keep expanding a la Tugan, although an end there must be as long as no *deus ex machina* is assumed: government or colonies or something absorbing the product.[51]

I don't know whether this adds up to anything, but those are the lines I am thinking along — I would be very anxious to know what your reaction is. Incidentally, I think that Steindl is wrong in his footnote on. p. 243 where he rejects the distinction between investment and accumulation. He may be o.k. in the sense that the periods have to be fully taken account of, but there should be no doubt that there is a difference even from the Keynesian standpoint between high organic composition and low organic composition type of investment. After

50. Daniel Creamer's estimates on excess capacity constituted one of the earliest attempts to develop a historical series. Baran was exploring the early development of this data and its relation to Steindl's theorization on monopoly capitalism and stagnation. See Daniel Creamer, *Capital Expansion and Capacity in Postwar Manufacturing* (New York: National Industrial Conference Board, 1961). John Bellamy Foster, *The Theory of Monopoly Capitalism* (New York: Monthly Review Press, 2014), 113, 118.

51. Baran seems to have made a slip here and meant to refer to Department I (investment goods) rather than Department II (consumption goods) since Tugan-Baranovsky's argument relates specifically to the former. He is referring to Sweezy's "A Crucial Difference Between Capitalism and Socialism" published for the first time in Paul M. Sweezy, *The Present as History* (New York: Monthly Review Press, 1953), 341–51.

all, in talking about public works they know that in one case, you get a small
multiplier effect and in the other a high one. What else is this but distinguishing
between investment and accumulation? For a while I thought that in what
you say on p. 222 in connection with population you were wrong making this
distinction, but I became convinced that this distinction is not only correct
but very important. Would be useful to explain it further by that public works
example.

[...]

Your brother Alan is at Stanford today; I am having dinner with him later in
the evening and am looking forward to it.[52]

All the best and love for the entire family.

Yours,

/s Paul

PAB to PMS

[*No provenance, handwritten.*]

[Palo Alto]
November 2, 1954

Dear Paul,

This is a P.S. to my letter of Oct. 30-th. Since mailing it, I have gone through:
Daniel Creamer, *Capital and Output Trends in Manufacturing Industries,
1880–1948* (NBER, 1954 [National Board of Economic Research]) which
comes to a conclusion very much more favorable to the underconsumption
hypothesis than Steindl's data would suggest.

If I see the problem correctly the whole thing centers around the following
question:

Is $dK/dt = L$ (lambda) $(dw/dt + dl/dt)$ where L is the factor of proportionality
— or is it a *rising* or *declining* function of the right hand expression.[53]

Now Creamer's answer would seem to be as follows: The amount of capital
invested per dollar of output rose steadily from 1880 to 1914. The amount of
capital invested per output dollar began to fall in 1914 and continued to fall until
1948. "... we can say that manufacturing has developed along the following
course: In the earlier decades an increasing fraction of a dollar of capital was

---

52. Paul Sweezy's brother, Alan Sweezy, was professor of economics at Cal Tech. He had played
an important role in the development of the secular stagnation theory along the lines of Harvard
economist Alvin Hansen, in the 1940s. See Alan Sweezy, "Secular Stagnation?" in Seymour E.
Harris, *Postwar Economic Problems* (New York: McGraw Hill, 1943), 67–82.
53. Notation used in Sweezy, *The Theory of Capitalist Development*, 187.

used to produce a dollar of output; in more recent decades a decreasing fraction of a dollar of capital has been sufficient to produce a dollar of output. This is consistent with the interpretation that in the earlier decades capital innovations on balance probably served more to replace other factor inputs than to increase output. More recently the balance has been in the other direction — capital innovations serve more to increase the efficiency of capital, hence to increase output, than to replace other factor inputs."

Incidentally, it makes little difference whether one takes total capital or breaks it down into *fixed* and *working* capital. The interesting thing only is that *wage outlay* is not included in either. I wonder, why? Or is it simply because then the turnover is assumed to be so rapid that it would not matter?

I thought this might interest you.

Best regards, Yours

/s Paul

P.S. By the way: it is generally agreed on the basis of Kuznets' data that the ratio of saving to Y [gross output] has not increased for a long time, in other words that there is no tendency of $(w+l)$ to become a [smaller] proportion of income or conversely for a larger share of revenue to become available for accumulation.[54] I have a hunch that this is a *non-sequitur*. All that Kuznets shows is that investment (capital formation) was a fairly steady %-age of Y. This is, however, an *ex post* observation and says nothing about the supply of saving *if* there were full investment. As is, all we can say is that there seems to be some puzzling constancy about the ratio of l to Y — and that possibly quite a lot of "would-be" accumulation transformed itself into unemployment.

Have you read the utterly incredible book by A.A. Berle Jr *The 20-th Century Capitalist Revolution*? Compared with this hosanna cry for monopoly capitalism — JKG's [John Kenneth Galbraith's] *American Capitalism* is a model of scholarly aloofness.

54. The text at this point is difficult to discern.

[1955]

PAB to PMS

Stanford University
August 31, 1955

Dear Paul,

[...]

I haven't sent you the goddamned manuscript of mine because upon my return from the East I started re-reading some of it, and felt compelled to re-do various parts. At the present time there are so many hand-written inserts and changes that the whole bloody thing has to be put back into properly typed shape before it can be used at all. I am now in the midst of chapter VII, hope to finish it within the next few days, then will try to do during September chapter VIII (the last, at last!) and then . . . the whole mess will be in your hands. Es wird Dir nichts erspart! [You will be spared nothing!] The process is tantalizingly slow, the pain of it is not so much the writing as the reading of what was written yesterday, but rien à faire. The worst part of it is the damned time schedule. I still haven't heard about the passport, except that Fanelli wrote an encouraging letter saying that he has spoken to the Dept. and was told that things move very well. But how long they will be moving, God only knows. In any case, I won't leave, if leave I can at all, until the ms is finished, while at the same time in the light of my Univ. time schedule etc. I should get out not later than end of October. It may be just as well — without such pressure I would not finish the thing at all! As it is, I am getting mildly crazy. I cannot sleep at all even with the help of pills — because I keep thinking of some point in the story, at the same time I am too tired to stay up and work. A number of interesting little things have occurred to me, but being an ignoramus and not having read much of the mushrooming journal literature I discover continually that in one way or in another it has been said by other people. Still, they usually say it in a wrong context or so that nobody ever is able to understand the implications. I am terribly, terribly "gespannt" [anxious] to get your reaction, and have a hunch that you will suggest *das ganze Ding der nagenden Kritik der Mauese zu uberlassen.* . . . ["to leave the whole thing to the gnawing critique of the mice.]⁵⁵

55. Baran is quoting here from a famous statement in Marx's 1859 "Preface to a Critique of Political Economy" where he referred to the fact that, due to problems with finding a publisher, he and Engels had decided to leave their manuscript of *The German Ideology* to the "gnawing criticism of the mice," recognizing that it had contributed to their own "self-clarification." Karl Marx, *A Contribution to a Critique of Political Economy* (Moscow: Progress Publishers, 1970), 22.

[...]

Had a letter from Oscar [Lange], he asks to send you regards.

More soon, meanwhile write and let me know how things are moving.

Love for everybody,

/s Paul

PAB to PMS

Stanford University

October 8, 1955

Dear Paul,

I have delayed answering your letter of September 29th—and telephoned
instead—because of my triply damned manuscript [*The Political Economy of
Growth*]. Little progress as I make, I am completely sucked in by that no-good
enterprise, and cannot do anything else, in particular typing. Anyway, the bitter-
sweet end is now in sight, I am on the last chapter, and another pull will have
done it. The real difficulty in the whole matter is my attempting to stick to what
I would like to make the motto of the thing: "The Truth is the Whole," and this
requires continual weaving of economic and non-economic threads of thought:
a job very much more difficult than spinning the "pure" cobwebs of bourgeois
social science. In general, it has become very clear to me that to attempt *really*
Marxist analysis requires a hell of a lot more than even the most ingenious
Samuelsons & Hickses have to offer. The difference is really that in one case one
has to understand the totality of the process, in the other one has to have the
ability of correct reasoning, that is of manipulating adequately the mechanism
of logical inference. Not that the latter is a minor thing or that everyone is good
at that; it is nevertheless in terms of the development of REASON and the
discovery of TRUTH a lesser function than the former. This is why au fond
Marx is a greater thinker than, say, Einstein, although the latter was probably
more powerful in the command of the process of logical inference. As Hegel says
in his *Phenomenologie*: "The easiest is to have a judgment on what has content
and value; more difficult is to really grasp it; the most difficult is what combines
both to realize its development in its entirety." Anyway, all this is merely à
propos: my life with this whole business is a continual up and down: sometimes I
think it is not too bad, sometimes there is nothing but gloom. Quite possible that
what comes out will be merely a draft to be worked on some more — but anyway,
you'll see ...

[...]

All the best to all of you. Love,

/s Paul

P.S. You know, Nietzsche has been terribly misrepresented and abused by the Nazis of all varieties and nationalities. Re-reading his *Also Sprach Zarathustra* I came across the following passage: "I implore you, my brothers, remain faithful to the earth, and trust those not who speak to you of transcendental hopes! They are poison mongers, whether they know it or not. They are scorners of life, moribund and poisoned themselves. The earth is tired of them, so let them travel into the yonder. Once it was blasphemy of God that was the greatest blasphemy. But God died and with him died those *blasphemists*. To be blasphemous of the earth is now the most abhorrent, and to esteem higher the viscera of the unknowable than the rationale of the earth" (Translated for better or worse by me). This is indeed what needs to be said about the "religious revival," mysticism and agnosticism of imperialist "culture." The Nazis and existentialists gave it a lousy and unwarranted twist by interpreting him as an "*elan vital*" man. If one reads more of him, one can see, that what he meant by the "rationale of the earth" is much nearer to Marx than to the Heideggers, Sartre's, not to speak of Goebbelses.

[. . .]

PMS to PAB

Wilton, N. H.
Nov. 10, 1955

Dear Paul,

It passes muster — and with flying colors.[56] The first work in this growth field that is worthy of the great tradition. My warmest congratulations.

As to *practicalia*, I make the following suggestions hurriedly so that they will reach you before you leave and give you some time for pondering prior to our meeting in NY.

(1) Chapter 2 is by far the weakest in the book. I would prefer to see it cut out entirely, with what is essential for the argument in Chs. 3 ff. being put into a new introduction to Ch. 3 (which would become 2, of course, or would remain 3 if, as would seem to me wise, you were to give the Introduction a number).

(2) Chapter 1 is not weak in and of itself, but much of it is really irrelevant to the theme of the book. For this reason, it holds up the flow of the argument and tends to create a false impression of what the book is about. For your purposes, "economic surplus" is an organizing concept, an aid to the marshaling of your material — it does not occupy a strategic analytical place in the structure. It is therefore a mistake to spend so much space on it at the outset. What needs to be said can be very much compressed and added onto the Introduction.

---

56. Baran's draft of *The Political Economy of Growth*.

(3) I would like you to give very serious thought to the desirability of modifying the harshness of the polemics. I wouldn't have you take *any* of the sting out of the content, but the jibes, irony, name-calling will, I am afraid, alienate many who ought to be most attracted (among students, for example). This is a tactical question, not one of principle, and should be decided as such. Among other considerations is that the book in any case is going to make you extremely unpopular with the profession and the academic authorities generally. I think it much wiser not to give them obvious — and superficial sticks to beat you with.

(4) The book is too important to be sent to the printer until you are sure it is right — and that means until you have got back and had some further time for unhurried revision. In the meantime, I suggest that (a) you get Jack [Rackliffe] to do a quick copyediting job (I think he has the time in the next few months), with special emphasis on eliminating awkward sentence structures, peculiar use of tenses, and the like; and (b) that Jack and I together or one of us have the ms. typed so that it will be ready for you in several copies when you get back. (A copy could, of course, be sent you in India as soon as it is ready.)

For the rest, I enclose my notes made while reading the ms. I realize that without the original many of them will not mean much to you. But some will be perfectly intelligible. I do not spend $5 or more sending you the ms. by airmail because it seems foolish with so little time available. I will bring it to NY with me and we can decide on next steps there.

Again, congratulations. This is going to stir things up among the scribes and pharisees, and a damn good thing too.

See you Thursday,
    /s Paul

[...]

PAB to PMS

Calcutta,
Dec. 17-th, 1955

Dear Paul,
After 3 days and 3 nights of nearly uninterrupted flying I arrived night before last in Calcutta. The Institute of Statistics[57] in which I am located is a perfectly fabulous undertaking. It employs over 600 people, occupies vast grounds and

---

57. PAB had a three-month appointment at the Indian Statistical Institute in Calcutta from December to March of 1955–56.

contains among other things a guest house in which foreign visitors are lodged, fed and occupied. The nature of the occupation is difficult to describe; it is somehow ephemeral. One is expected to "contribute" — it is by no means clear in what way, by what specific means. The assorted scholars who preceded me in this assignment have left behind them a number of memoranda which I am at the present time perusing. It will be incumbent upon me — I suppose — to compose something suitable before I leave. Meanwhile it is felt that I should acquaint myself with the country, deliver a few lectures here and elsewhere, and decide myself what it is that I wish to do. Pleasant and slightly disturbing at the same time. I went into the city today (the Institute is a feudal estate some 7 miles out of town), bought some tropical clothing + the Baby-Hermes typewriter which I am now using, and looked around for the very first impressions. This city is nothing but one huge slum, crowded to the limit with people sleeping in the streets and cows and goats and buffalos walking placidly across the main thoroughfares while automobiles and buses stop until the way is clear. I shall see more as time goes on, although it is clear already that to get a real notion of what goes on in this country 3 months is not even enough for a beginning. I shall go to Delhi next week, to Poona thereafter (to attend the Indian Economic Convention) and will settle down here for a few weeks in order to read some material, to lecture in the Institute etc.

As my plans stand, I shall stay here until approximately end of March, return from here to Moscow for another few — less frosty — weeks, and proceed to NY end of April. I shall cut out all of Western Europe except for a stop-over in Warsaw.

Upon arrival here, I found a letter from Blackwell's urging me to expedite the delivery of the manuscript.[58] What shape is it in now? Is the type job proceeding according to plan? Incidentally, did the typing outfit get the money

---

58. This was the manuscript to *The Political Economy of Growth*. As Sweezy later explained, "Baran when delivering the lectures at Oxford in 1953 that were to be the basis of *The Political Economy of Growth* signed a contract to publish the book and received an advance of £50 from Blackwell's, the Oxford bookseller and publisher. This had an interesting sequel. The manuscript was finally completed and sent off to Blackwell's late in 1955 or early in 1956. From the correspondence that followed, it is apparent that the prospective publisher did not know what he was going to get. Readers were mobilized to provide opinions and suggest cuts and changes. The upshot was that Paul angrily refused to make drastic revisions as requested, withdrew the manuscript, refunded the advance, and handed the book over to Monthly Review Press — much, I may add, to Leo Huberman's and my delight. What the quarrel was all about is charmingly revealed in a report to Blackwell's from a reader who had been asked to advise on cutting the length of the manuscript. I quote: 'You have not asked for my opinion on the book: may I give it nevertheless? The author is a Communist. . . .'" "Paul M. Sweezy, 'Paul Alexander Baran: A Personal Memoir,'" in Paul M. Sweezy and Leo Huberman, eds., *Paul A. Baran (1910–1964): A Collective Portrait* (New York: Monthly Review Press, 1965), 45.

from Stanford? I would be most grateful to you if you could send me whatever chapters have become available.

I shall study the psycho books[59] in the evenings, and prepare the main outline of a comprehensive article on the subject. I am at the present time not thinking much about such subjects, but shall go into the matter as soon as this is over. It will be most helpful to have read those things carefully.

So much for today. I shall write more extensively after having seen more. At this stage I am rather bewildered. Ditto with regard to the S.U. There ought to be some articles, but as yet I would not even know how to begin. The digesting process just barely began.

Love for the entire family —

As ever,

     Yours /s Paul

Write!

PMS to PAB

    [*Aerogramme addressed to PAB in Inst. of Statistics in Calcutta, forwarded to Poona Hotel*]

Wilton, N.H., USA,
December 19, 1955

Dear Paul,

[...]

I think I have started work on a book.[60] I find it a little hard to define the subject and quite impossible to think of a title, but in general the problem is the nature of the giant corporation and what changes it makes in the structure and functioning of capitalism to have the capitalist function itself institutionalized in these huge affairs. All the traditional stuff about the capitalist conceived as a natural individual is out of date, and it is this undoubted fact that gives plausibility to all the fancy new theories of the "managerial revolution" type. But what no one has yet done is to point out the *real* meaning of what has happened: not that capitalism has been transformed or replaced, but that it has reached its streamlined apogee. The big corporation as an engine of accumulation puts to shame Marx's most ascetic accumulator. To bring this out into the light of day and explore its implications will be the theme of the opus.

---

59. Baran was preparing to write an essay on "Marxism and Psychoanalysis" (*Monthly Review*, October 1959), and was studying "psycho" books by Herbert Marcuse, Erich Fromm, Lewis Feuer, Freud, and others.

60. First mention of the project that was to become *Monopoly Capital*.

One source I want to exploit is business fiction which I suspect has more raw material for a valid business sociology than all the economic texts and articles. I ran across this a.m. a wonderful piece in *Business Week* dealing with a new novel by Cameron Hawley, the author of *Executive Suite,* which made quite a stir a couple of years ago. The new one is called *Cash McCall* and is about a high-powered operator of the Louis Wolfson type whose main concern is making millions out of the tax laws. BW [*Business Week*] asked a panel of businessmen and advisers of various kinds to comment on it, and the responses elicited from Frank Abrams, retired Chairman of the Board of Standard Oil (N.J.), are absolutely wonderful. Abrams contrasts the "individualist" with the "company man," greatly to the credit of the latter. The individualist (of whom Cash McCall is a prototype) "is apt to be a self-seeker . . . he will switch allegiance from company to company, and seems mainly concerned with personal power and the trappings of wealth." Further: "My business experience has been . . . relatively free of the tax manipulations and promotional shenanigans that seemed the principal concern of the chief characters of the book. Perhaps I have been insulated from some of the facts of smaller business life, and if so I can now, in retirement, appreciate how fortunate I have been." There speaks the aristocrat of U.S. business, the functionary of really big capital, the true "company man." And what scorn for the "individualist" with his lust for "personal power and the trappings of wealth!" What contempt for the sordid details of "smaller" — but still multi-million dollar!—business life. The robber barons used to be the real bosses — now they are little more than incidental excrescences. The real bosses are the big companies with their largely anonymous managers and boards of directors, institutionalized capitalists in the fullest sense of the term. Without an understanding of this, the whole system is seen out of focus. I am really quite excited about the project, and it is a wonderful feeling to have something big that one wants to tackle au fond. I only hope the mood proves to be a lasting one. I have long known that the only "solution" for personal misery is to sublimate the emotions and feelings giving rise to it in work, but I have not been able to get interested in work — a *circolo vicioso*. Maybe this is the break-out. (I'm probably very rash to commit this thought to paper, but I take the chance, keeping my fingers firmly crossed.)

No room to start a new subject, so I'll sign off for now. By the way, any suggestions you have in re the above (bibliography, ideas, criticisms, etc.) will be most welcome.

Yrs.,

/s Paul

[1956]

PMS to PAB

Wilton, N. H.
January 6, 1956

Dear Paul,

[...]

We went to NY for several days last week, bringing the kiddies along for a little urban interlude. I spent part of two days at the annual meetings of the Am Econ Assn at the Commodore — needless to say, *not* listening to papers being read. I got a rather interesting impression from talking to younger economists that there is something of an underground in the profession — chaps who hold jobs and appear as harmless liberals in their professional and social life but who are quite willing to show me, presumably as a person who can be trusted and whose position is definitely known, that they know the score and have very little use for most of the crap that American economists are turning out these days. I am not clear what good they can do, but I suppose that if they can hold out until they get "permanent" appointments they will then be able to afford a somewhat more outspoken position. In any case, you and I have more of an audience, and are more looked to for intellectual guidance, in the profession than would appear on the surface. I made heavy advance propaganda for your book, telling all the development boys (and they're all over the place, as you know) that it is the first really good job in the whole field and by implication challenging them to answer it when it comes out. Chandler Morse, who is one of the more *sympatico* of the middle generation and of course very friendly personally, expressed special interest and asked me if he could see an advance copy.[61] I told him I would ask you. I should think it might be a good idea for me to send him one of the copies that otherwise would simply be sitting around awaiting your return. If you authorize it, I will do so and will tell him that you would like his comments in view of possible amendments and emendments, said comments to be in my hands by the time of your return.

I am most enthusiastic about the prospect of our cooperating in the big business project. For many reasons, it is not good to be isolated in such matters,

---

61. Chandler Morse was then a professor of economics at Cornell. He was to be best known for his work in natural resource economics, particularly for the influential book by Harold J. Barnett and Chandler Morse, *Scarcity and Growth: The Economy of Natural Resource Availability* (Baltimore: Johns Hopkins Press, 1962). He later wrote an important article for *Monthly Review*. See Chandler Morse, "Environment, Economics and Socialism," 30, no. 11 (April 1979): 10–19.

and our small experience with the MRS [Model, Roland, and Stone] study
of foreign investment leads me to believe that effective forms and methods of
cooperation can be worked out despite the normal 3000 miles between us.
Offhand, I am inclined to think that the best way to proceed on such a vast
subject as this is to divide it into closely related but conceptually divisible
projects so that work can go ahead on parallel lines, as it were, without being
held up by the necessity for the kind of agreement on detail and formulation that
joint authorship requires. The result might be a number of essays by both of us
that could be published between the same covers, or it might be several volumes
to be published in a series, perhaps under a common overall title.

But all that is secondary to content, of course, and it is here that a good deal
of work and thought needs to be applied first. One thing that I am becoming
increasingly convinced of is that a thorough investigation of profits *from
our point of view* is essential: none of the material I have seen provides the
information and clues one needs. If you should feel inclined, this might be a good
project for you, since I feel poorly equipped to cope with the statistics involved
and proximity to a good library would be most important. In any case, I am
beginning to collect bibliographical material of a relevant nature. At the same
time, I am beginning to look into recent stuff on the big corporation — *Fortune*,
Peter Drucker, etc. — and to probe the field of business fiction which, as I think
I mentioned in my last letter, seems likely to offer fresh sociological material of a
kind which is completely absent from the professional economic literature.

All this should gradually lead to the formulation of certain hypotheses for
further investigation and testing. In the meantime, there are certain things that I
am becoming convinced one should stay away from. There is no good whatever
in getting into the whole question of whether there has been a measurable
trend toward concentration or monopoly and for the most part any rigid
ordering of data by traditional industry classifications is futile. Adhering to
these two principles will be enough to bypass a large amount of the professional
"monopoly" literature. Positively, my present preference is to proceed by way
of setting up an economy of ideal types and then analyzing the inner nature of
idealized (abstract) units and individuals, much as Marx does in *Capital*. You
will recall the passage in the Preface to the first edition: "I paint the capitalist
and landlord in no sense *couleur de rose*. But here individuals are dealt with only
insofar as they are the personifications of economic categories, embodiments
of particular class-relations and class-interests. My stand-point . . . can less
than any other make the individual responsible for relations whose creation he
socially remains, however much he may subjectively raise himself above them."
Well, Marx's capitalist and landlord don't exist in the form in which he knew

them except as fringe phenomena in the U.S. economy of today. The capitalist par excellence is the billion-dollar corporation, and I think we have to start with an economy in which that is the *only* kind of capitalist. Later, we can introduce smaller capitalists and show how and why they are in the process of being transformed into the dominant type. But before we can do that we have to subject the dominant type itself to a searching analysis — and by that I don't mean a mere statistical analysis of some sample of big corporations: one of the great weaknesses of bourgeois social science is over-reliance on statistics which often deal only with superficial aspects and miss precisely what is essential.

But I ramble — enough of that for now. I received the news of your determination to liquidate the backward-countries commitment with satisfaction. As economists, you and I have a special function to perform and it concerns the analysis and interpretation of the USA for the benefit of the rest of the world as well as of any in this country who happen to be or may become interested. We should get on with that job and not allow ourselves to be turned aside any longer by neuroses, easier tasks, or other interests. Which brings me to one last point before I get back to work: I think you are right that the whole Freudians business has little relevance to India et al. But, damn it, it does have relevance to the U.S. and that's why we have to concern ourselves with it, especially why we have to stand it on its feet again. Herbert's [Marcuse's] book [*Eros and Civilization*], by the way, for all its annoying qualities (and I found there were plenty of them) is most useful in this connection. But more of that another time.

Love

/s Paul

P. S. […]

PAB to PMS

[*Aerogramme from Indian Inst. of Statistics.*]

Delhi

January 8, 1956

Dear Paul,

After attending the Economists' Conference in Poona, and the Indian Science Congress in Agra, I have landed in Delhi where I am supposed to settle down for a few weeks and to study various documents relating to the Second Five-Year Plan. [Oskar] Lange and [Charles] Bettelheim are also here, and we are expected to produce something or other. . . . I am snowed under various memoranda and am only slowly beginning to make something out of them. The whole picture is terribly confusing, and I do not have much confidence in my capacity to say

something worthwhile on it in the course of a few short weeks. Most disturbing
is the sheer lack of relevant information; everything is based on very general
guesswork. Nobody knows e.g. what actually becomes of the gross product
of agriculture. How is it distributed? Opinions range from 15% into rent +
usurers' interest to as much as 50%! It obviously makes quite a bit of difference.
The most important aspect of the matter is what I have in my MS: the ec. spl.
[economic surplus] that is appropriated by rent+interest receivers is eaten by
a vast multitude of men; in other words while constituting spl. in a categorical
sense, it serves to support essential, indeed, minimal consumption of *petty* traders,
petty usurers, *petty* landowners. What do you do about it? Those people have to
be fed somehow unless there are killed as in the case of the Polish Jewry or unless
they emigrate wholesale as in the case of Russia after October. Nor can they really
be shifted to other occupations — it is not merely a matter of the unavailability of
jobs but also of their essential unemployability. To be sure, this may be a problem
for only the current generation — their offspring may be perfectly happy to go
elsewhere — but for the current generation there is no apparent solution. . . . I
shall write a memo on this whole subject, although somehow working in a hotel
room is peculiarly uncomfortable. I wish I could take all the stuff and go . . . home.

Oscar and I spent an afternoon with Kosambi in Bombay.[62] He is quite
brilliant and quite crazy. His theorizing is "ultra-left," all he sees is the
dictatorship of the bourgeoisie; there is somehow no rural problem in his
outlook. He exemplifies the strikingly interesting combination of feudal and
proletarian elements jointly despising the capitalist parvenu . . . what has
happened in Britain of old, in Prussia and elsewhere can be seen now in India.
The *grandseigneurs* and the leftists who want to help the people whose misery
is appalling turn jointly against the traders, merchants and moneybags. I was
thinking that there was actually something of that even in the case of FDR who,
an aristocrat himself, had sympathy for the people and a certain disdain for the
"moneylenders" whom he was prepared to chase out of the temple (at least
verbally) with the help of Sydney Hillman.[63] There is much similarity between
him and Nehru.

I shall remain in Delhi until approximately the end of the month, then return
to Calcutta, go on a lecture tour in February and leave this land in the middle of
March. By that time I shall have definitely enough of the itinerant way of life.

[. . .]

---

62. Damodar Dharmananda Kosambi, Indian mathematician and Marxist.
63. Sydney Hillman, labor leader and key figure in the founding of the CIO.

Give my love to Nancy *et tous les enfants.*

As ever,

> /s Paul

[*Handwritten*]

P.S. I am going to give 3 lectures at the Delhi School *on The Theory of Imperialism Reconsidered.* It should be quite interesting. I wish I had some literature here which is at home.

PMS to PAB

> Wilton, N.H.
>
> Jan. 16, 1956

Dear Paul,

[…]

I was interested in your report on Kosambi. In correspondence with me, he has always insisted that the ruling class in the countryside is bourgeois and not feudal, but he has never given me the impression of denying the existence of a rural problem. It's funny how these seemingly technical terms like "feudal" get mixed up with and are disguises for political positions and emotional impulses. Yes, I think there was something of the Salisbury in FDR, and it's certainly not surprising to find this attitude cropping up in the backward countries.

I took time off last Wednesday to attend a seminar at MIT at which Ed Mason spoke on economic development in Pakistan. As against the formalists, Mason talks a lot of common sense (for example, he has little but derision for the theorists who want to apply equi-marginal-productivity criteria to development planning), but basically he's as cynical as they come. He doesn't really believe in the possibility of developing a place like Pakistan, and of course all the really interesting questions are excluded by a sort of tacit agreement that Soviet and Chinese experience is taboo. The two problems which kept cropping up were those of cadres and of the absence of any sort of machinery and equipment industry which would introduce a degree of flexibility into the Pak economy. But there was no suggestion from Mason or anyone there (a veritably galaxy of stars in the economics firmament) that these problems could be seriously tackled in the foreseeable future. Incompetent personnel and absence of industry are treated as part of the nature of things in that part of the world. The whole affair was a brilliant confirmation of the thesis set forth in your book that the bourgeois developers are merely playing with the problem.

[…]

I hope you write down your lectures on imperialism: I would not like to miss them. In re psycho books: I don't know. If they haven't arrived by the time you leave India, we'll try to get our money back. I did receive the books from Paris, and many thanks — I haven't yet had a chance to more than glance at them. The *Lehrbuch* looks dull, but I suppose such *opera* usually are. Don't know of any other books I need just now, but will let you know if any occur to me.

Yours,

/s Paul

PAB to PMS

Calcutta,
January 31, 1956

Dear Paul,

[...]

For basically priority number one job should be Monopoly Capitalism — as you say, for the rest of the world as well as for those in the U.S. who might be and become interested. The details we would have to talk over, but *en principe*, I am very much in favor of the modus operandi which you suggest. There are a number of essays that one might try at first, or there is a possibility of a larger volume divided into a number of parts. *This*, to be sure, is a mere formality — yet, not unimportant, for it would determine somewhat the way in which the thing should be planned. I wholly agree with you that one should at first get away from the question as to the *extent* to which society is monopolized, suffice it that monopoly capitalism is today the *prevalent* mode of production in the U.S., and the question whether and how large are the competitive (or for that matter even semi-feudal) remnants in the economy as a whole (the semi-feudal in the South) is definitely secondary. This is to be discussed in the second or, for all I know, third approximation. The first task is to work out the model of mono. cap. society as an *ideal type*, and to clearly formulate its laws of motion. The whole futility of economic debates comes from the continual mixing up of the levels of discussion, from the continual confusion concerning the level of abstraction. Only after the model of "pure" monopoly capitalism has been worked out, will it be possible to consider modifications resulting from the existence of the not yet monopolized sphere, from "system-alien" remnants of older formations etc. The principal issue is to include in the basic model what is *essential* to it, and I have the feeling that in contra-distinction to the competitive model of Marx the *state* has to be brought into the center of the stage, rather than as a secondary factor. This is where Keynesiana enter along with many other things, in particular ideological manipulation etc. But all this is for later. . . .

All three psycho books have arrived. I have worked my way through a good part of Marcuse and I must confess that I cannot make out much of most of it.[64] It is written in a swollen high-falutin style which is intolerably exacting, and it is encumbered with "meta"-material which does not appear to me to be necessary to the argument. While in the more lucid pages — particularly those directed vs. Eric Fromm & Co. — he is definitely expressing the correct point of view, in others he is drowning it in a plethora of irrelevancy. Why in hell does he have to drag out the least attractive aspects of Freud such as the death instinct? Why is there nowhere any concrete statement of the psycho problem of capitalism? And why all this beating around the bush about the main features of the oppressive mechanism? With all of his radicalism he still tries to conform to the ruling ideology by fully accepting its despicable lingo, by remaining on its level of debate by being afraid to call a spade a spade. I haven't looked yet at Fromm & Feuer, but I hope to read all of it as time permits.[65] It would be definitely necessary to settle down and write something on all of this — this is centrally related to the monopoly capital project.

So much for the moment. I have to write a few things for the Institute, and hope to leave here having finished a couple of memo's which they expect. At the present time there is a large gathering of economic luminaries. In addition to Oscar, Nicky Kaldor has arrived plus wife plus two daughters, [Charles] Bettelheim is here and [Jan] Tinbergen, and [John Kenneth] Galbraith is due within the next few days. For ours is the age of the racket in which the noblest things become racketized, in which there is no endeavor that is not turned to the profit of some, in which there is no truth that is not converted into a lie. Even the attempt to mobilize talent for the economic development of India is turning into a boondoggling expedition of pleasure-seeking nothing-doers talking in high terms about matters in which they take no real interest. It is difficult to see all this without getting the creeps. And while all the teas are being drunk, all the dinners are being eaten, all the flights to the caves and the memorials are being undertaken, and while all the lies about the "love for the people" are being *ad nauseam* repeated, while all this goes on, nobody, literally, nobody gives a damn about the basic issues of the matter, about saying clearly and openly where the true obstacles lie to any forward movement.

---

64. Herbert Marcuse, *Eros and Civilization* (Boston: Beacon Press, 1955).

65. Erich Fromm had been associated, like PAB, with the Institute for Social Research in Frankfurt before the war and was a leading socialist-humanist proponent of psychoanalysis. PAB is probably referring here to two books: Fromm's *The Sane Society* and Lewis Feuer's *Psychoanalysis and Ethics*, both published in 1955.

I haven't delivered yet the Imperialism lectures. For some mystical (or not very mystical) reasons Rao from the Delhi School withdrew! He probably got cold feet and decided that having various Russkies around is enough; he need not encumber himself with *this* variety of men from the U.S. Those lectures will be delivered in Calcutta. I haven't written them beyond outlines, but hope to write them some time later.

Give my love to Nancy & children.

As ever,

/s Paul

[...]

PMS to PAB

Wilton
Feb. 12, 1956

Dear Paul,

[...]

Now for the *point de theorie*: I agree that the state has to be brought into the model from the outset. The units, or *Wirtschafts-subjekte* [economic entities], are (1) corporations, unions, government, consumers, plus the usual members of the competitive sector which, however, may not enter the picture until a later stage. Each of these units has to be analyzed to discover its essence and implications, and then they have to be fitted together into a working system. Needless to say, they are by no means coordinate or symmetrical, and it is in this connection that many of the most interesting questions regarding the role of the state will arise. As I see it now, the state has a profoundly ambivalent (dialectical?) role to play in the capitalist economy. On the one hand, it is the instrument of the capitalists, the balance wheel without which the system would go smash. On the other hand, it is the enemy which always has to be kept at arms length, defrauded, corrupted, battled.

Most bourgeois writing on the state stresses one or the other of these roles, but hardly any (so far as I know) sees the two sides as indissolubly connected. One could almost make a neat paradox to the effect that the two greatest bourgeois economists of the monopoly capitalist period, Keynes and Schumpeter, split on precisely this question, Keynes seeing the state as the friend and Schumpeter seeing it as the enemy of the existing order. This came to me with particular sharpness recently when I began reading for review the latest volume in the *International Economic Papers* series. The first essay is Schumpeter's "Crisis of the Tax State" which I had never read in the original

German.[66] This develops the theory of the opposition between the state and economy more explicitly and with greater historical detail than any other writing I know. And it makes very good sense *as far as it goes*. What it fails to do is stress the other side, the side that forms the basis of the whole Keynesian construction. It is here, I think, that we have the key to a lot of phenomena which tend to seem contradictory or even mutually exclusive. The state both saves capitalism and distorts and corrupts it. High taxes are *sine qua non*, but some of the very best talent at society's disposal goes into beating the tax collector. In many lines of business, tax considerations even become paramount over production considerations. And so forth. What do you think of this?

More later,

/s Paul

PAB to PMS

927 Mercedes Avenue
Los Altos, California
October 28, 1956

Dear Paul,

[…]

I have been thinking of the weakness of our outline and on somewhat similar lines. What we have not properly allocated in that outline is the entire mechanism of surplus absorption under mono cap. The two most important avenues would seem to me to be technological progress (connected with and resulting from ever growing outlays on research etc.) plus "artificial" obsolescence in such areas as suburbanization etc. I don't think this is fatal to our outline, it has to be reorganized and more sharply focused on these points. I shall write to you about that more. The main trouble with this business is that when it comes to technological matters, it is so damn difficult to know what to say. Does not Schumpy's clustering come in here very importantly?[67] Or putting it differently, isn't there a considerable danger that the bunch of available innovations will run out, with excess capacity stopping further investment? Or should one consider scientific research to be a new factor continually producing and reproducing technological progress? And aren't we then in the lap of Tugan-Baranovsky

---

66. Joseph A. Schumpeter, "The Crisis of the Tax State," *International Economic Papers*, no. 4 (1954): 5–38. This was originally an address delivered in 1918 to the Viennese Sociological Society.

67. The reference here is to Joseph Schumpeter's theory of the clustering of innovations, most famously in his 1939 *Business Cycles* (New York: McGraw Hill, 1939).

with machines producing new machines that produce new machines and so
ad calendas graecas [non-existent day in Greek calendar, i.e. "until hell freezes
over"]? On all of this and number of related problems much additional thought
is needed. Still, it does not, to my mind at least, vitiate the basic structure of the
outline, it merely accentuates the more difficult problems that are included but
not properly underscored.

[…]

So much for today.

Love,

　　/s Paul

PMS to PAB

24 Agassiz Street
Cambridge 40, Mass.
November 1, 1956

Dear Paul,

[…]

　　Yours,

　　/s Paul

P.S. Only one point re outline: you stress, quite rightly, that we are weak "on
the whole mechanism of surplus absorption under mono. cap." We are also, I
am afraid, weak on the whole mechanism of surplus generation. There is a sort
of law of entropy operating in the system tending toward a condition of zero
profits. But the *actual* historical experience is, by and large, exactly the opposite,
indicating the presence of enormously powerful technological and organizational
forces tending to raise the surplus. All this suggests that we might perhaps better
reorganize our outline in some radically new form around two central themes:
the generation of surplus, and the absorption of surplus. I will try playing around
a little with this to see if the main items included in the present outline seem to
fall into place with a better distribution emphasis.

PAB to PMS

927 Mercedes Avenue
Los Altos, California
November 7, 1956

Dear Paul,

[...]

Night before last I gave a talk here (faculty seminar) on Strachey's book and ran primarily into one point which was raised by nearly all of my distinguished colleagues.[68] This point is maddening but one has to deal with it. They all assert that the talk about growing concentration and oligopolization of the economy is so much nonsense. Supposedly all statistical measurements indicate that since 1900 there was no further concentration in American business. Messrs Adelman, Nutter, Stigler et al. have so calculated. I have a very strong feeling that this is not worth a damn, but still one has to deal with it. My main point is that assuming that in 1900 a firm had the same proportion of an industry's output as it has today but has *now* considerable influence in 5 other industries — there is more concentration which none of the concentration indices is taking account of. What is more: if there are, as there are, inter-firm connections that do not appear in their respective balance sheets, those are the ones that matter. Putting all this differently: what the concentration ratios are all designed for is to measure the [Edward] Mason-type of stuff: market structures, price policies etc. They do *not* measure economic *power*. But how does one measure economic power with no information on the *real* connections available? Since your prewar study on the *Interest groups* nothing has been done in this area, how does one get something on it?[69] This is terribly important for the theory of mono cap. and one has to be prepared to deal with it. I have an intuitive hunch that this is all pettifogging and that the real relations are beyond dispute, but ...

[...]

Love,

/s Paul

68. PAB is referring here to John Strachey, *Contemporary Capitalism* (New York: Random House, 1956).
69. PAB is referring to PMS's study "Interest Groups in the American Economy," published as Appendix 13 to Part 1 of the National Resource Committee's *The Structure of the American Economy* (Washington D.C., 1939). It was later reprinted in Sweezy, *The Present as History*, 158–188.

PAB to PMS

Stanford University
November 15, 1956

[...]

It probably is true that the Russian claim to moral leadership of the world socialist movement is extinguished.[70] I do not know, however, whether China, Yugoslavia or Poland can assume that function. What I have in mind is this: the notion world socialist mvt [movement] begins to lose its meaning. To the u/d [underdeveloped] countries (as you state yourself on p.2 a) Russia's position will look different than to the advanced ones; that is to the nationalist socialist movements in those different parts of the world. In the u/d countries Russia and China and Poland and Yugo will probably still continue to exercise an overwhelming influence. In the advanced countries none of them may actually rise at this time to a position of moral leadership. If moral leadership there should be at all (rather than demoralization!) it may be either recaptured in a decade or I don't know when by the socialist bloc as a whole or will have to emerge from the Western mvt. itself. "Polycentrism" would seem to be a more likely situation for the immediate future. . . .

[...]
Love,
        s/ Paul

PMS to PAB

[*Handwritten*]

24 Agassiz Street
Cambridge 40, Mass.
Sun. a.m., Nov 18 [1956]

Dear Paul,
[...]

I have been trying from time to time to re-focus my thinking about the outline of the magnum opus. In the course of it, I tried to think up a good title which would be descriptive of the putative contents. *Monopoly Capitalism* is alright but sufficiently general to cover quite a few variant *opera*. So I devised the following

---

70. PAB was responding to the draft of the December 1956 Review of the Month for *Monthly Review* in which Huberman and PMS (the piece was drafted by the latter) stated: "After these events [the Soviet invasion of Hungary] we do not see how the feelings of any socialist toward the Soviet Union can remain unchanged. Any claim the Soviet Union had to moral leadership of the world socialist movement is now extinguished" ("Assessing the Damage," *Monthly Review*, December 1956).

subtitle: "A Study of the Generation and Absorption of Economic Surplus in Advanced Capitalist Societies." Following this up, one can then divide the mainly economic segment of the book into two parts: Generation of Surplus and Absorption of Surplus, with a certain degree of overlapping in order to indicate the organic interconnection of the two processes. I haven't yet tried working the thing out, but I think it has possibilities.

[. . .]

Yrs.,

/s Paul

P.S. [. . .]

PMS to PAB

[*Handwritten*]

Wilton

November 25 [1956]

Dear Paul,

Just a note after finishing reading Kaldor's lecture at Peking which he thinks of as the outline of a whole theory of economic development. What really astonishes me is the "propensity" of these guys to play around with a few formulas — which are at bottom mere tautologies — and then to draw all sorts of grandiose conclusions from them, conclusions which merely reflect their ideological preferences anyway. Savings = investment and total demand = total supply. Capitalists' spending is not tied to current income, workers' spending is. Total production can't increase faster than technical progress and population growth permit. Capitalists' investment depends on the rate at which they expect the market (= total production) to expand. Throw in a few implicit assumptions about the initial distribution of income between wages and surplus, and believe it or not, you have a theory of economic development. What's more, they want to reduce Marx to their own level. He had some formulas too, and they will show you how his can be transformed into special cases of their own "more general" formulas. So, lo and behold, Marx is a special case of Kaldor and everything is reduced to a level of pure banality.

Let us take a firm resolution to write a whole book without a single formula. Formulas are the opium of the economists, and they acted that way on Marx too. *Vide* the chapter on the falling rate of profit which tries as hard as any of the modern stuff to squeeze knowledge out of tautologies.

The real problems, it seems to me, are:

(1) To get a good working idea of what *is* surplus, and for this the first essential is to understand that it is related only indirectly to ordinary distribution of income data. Lots of wages are paid out of surplus, i.e. whole categories of workers absorb surplus — likewise whole "industries" like advertising and finance. The trouble is that this creates really very tricky problems and paradoxes. One has to go back to classical-Marxian ideas of productive and unproductive labor and adapt them to modern conditions and (if possible) statistics. This is a crucial branch of theory which does not exist for the Keynesian and other neo-classics.

(2) Analysis of the production sector. (The generation of surplus). The institutional capitalist — laws of operation, relation to class structure and behavior, etc. Price policy, wage policy, technological compulsions etc., etc.

(3) Analysis of the unproductive sector (absorption of surplus). The different categories of "absorbers": luxury consumers, unproductive "industries," government, etc., including complex transfer relations.

(4) The interactions of the productive and unproductive sectors — full of unexplored problems. In an underdeveloped capitalist economy, e.g. it might do to assume that wages and profits in the unproductive sector are determined in the (much larger) productive sector. But obviously that won't do in an economy like that of the U.S. today in which the unproductive sector may well be larger than the productive.

(5) The crucial contradiction, i.e., that "working well" for a system of this type means, indeed necessitates, a growing departure from the possible attainments of the system's resources (in human, natural and technological terms) in the line of welfare, abolition of exploitation, freeing civilization from the poison of wealth fetishization, etc. What we have is a progressive *degradation* of civilization instead of its progressive improvement.

Oh hell, these are only some of the problems, but anyway, they are serious. If only one could get the time and environment to work seriously on them. But I see no prospect. Time is chopped up, the intellectual environment is hostile, the world reflects all too accurately the trends of the capitalist system (which unfortunately all too easily infect the socialist societies which are still susceptible because, basically, they are so goddamn poor and will be for a long time to come), and one's personal life is almost inevitably all mixed up.

As you probably inferred at the outset, Nicky [Kaldor] is around Cambridge now, which is how I happened to see his Peking lecture. He is clever enough but incorrigibly superficial. He sits around pontificating about what's been happening to U.S. capitalism, and the sad truth is that it boils down to the

ideological picture which such organs of Big Business and *Fortune* would like to
put across. By contrast, C. Wright Mills is an intellectual giant — and a breath of
fresh air. But if C.W.M. is the best we can point to as a theorist of U.S. capitalism,
what a commentary on present-day social "science"!

[...]

Now that my ink has given out, I guess I'd better sign off.

Love,

   /s Paul

[...]

PAB to PMS

Stanford University
November 28, 1956

Dear Paul,

Before departing to the campus at 1 o'clock, I finished the first reading of the
galley proofs and stepped out to the mailbox to find your letter of November
25th. The hurricane of thoughts and more or less dim emotions provoked
by both, the book and your letter, was blowing through my head during the
entire day filled with a seminar in which a moronic student held forth on a
moronic subject, with office hours in which a dozen or so of representatives
of our *jeunesse doree* [privileged youth, i.e. Stanford students] came to inquire
about the courses which they should or should not take next quarter, and with
a department meeting in which my colleagues debated *ad nauseam* how much
mathematics should be considered a minimum requirement for a Ph.D. In the
corridor, on my way home — or rather to see Nicky, my more or less steady
dinner companion — I ran into the Chairman of our Sociology Dept. The
Honorable Professor LaPiere — a personally very friendly individual who brags
about — among other things — never reading a newspaper, and learned from
him that his Dept. has a $12,000 p.a. professorship in Sociology (just freshly
endowed by Ford) and is unable to find anyone to take it. I said "why don't
you try C.W. Mills, he has a mediocre job in Columbia *College* (not Graduate
School), is an interesting fellow and might be tempted . . ." LaPiere looked at me
with some astonishment, shrugged his shoulders and said: "But Mills is not a
sociologist, he is a Marxist. . . ."

   The one-gulp perusal of my book — I read it in two very long evenings plus
one morning — has made upon me a very complex impact. Having reached now
a certain minimal distance to the thing, I have the feeling that it is not a bad job.
It has faults, and the most important of them is that it covers too much ground

and by so doing deals too sketchily with a number of things. In particular this applies to the first part concerning Monopoly Capital. The basic points are o.k. the accents are properly placed and the crucial problems are at least brought into the open. If it had a chance to be read by a *friendly* audience, it could perform even a function: of stimulating discussion, of steering people to the right kind of questions, of pushing Marxist thought on Mono.Cap. off its dead center and into a deepened consideration of what we both agree is the crux of the matter: the generation and absorption of the eco. spl. [economic surplus] (Incidentally, I like this formulation *very* much!). But in the hands of official economists . . . God only knows what the reaction will be, or perhaps it is only too clear what it will be! There is, furthermore, one trouble with it that is glaring: its vocabulary and its emotive tone! But what in hell does one do about it? As far as the former is concerned, the possibilities of using an Aesopian Language are unfortunately very limited. Should one *not* speak of "bourgeois" economics, not to mention "capitalism," "imperialism," "socialism?" And how does one avoid then sacrificing contents to sticking to an academically sanctioned language? As far as the latter is at issue, matters are more complicated. It is my individual, characterological shortcoming . . . I happen to be too emotive in everything, and therefore in writing, I don't know how to be detached (and to *do* something at the same time!) and I do feel bitter about the superficiality, smugness, opportunism, cowardice or outright stupidity of the so-called profession. And what you call "the hostile intellectual surrounding" is contributing undoubtedly its large share to this pent-up aggression by continually kindling it, by giving it fresh fuel every day, by remarks such as the one above of LaPiere, by the feeling of being surrounded by people with whom one has not even a language in common. And this aggressiveness against all of this does two things at the same time: it chokes one's productivity and channels whatever remains of it into what becomes an angry outcry. — I am making a few — not extensive and not expensive — changes in the proofs, and hope to be done with all of it within the next few days. I understand from the original time-table that the thing is not due back until December 18th; I will have it back no later than end of next week. I have to write a preface, and to go over the text once more. And thereafter *habeant sua fata libelli* . . . [leave its fate with the readers]

I noticed that Fromm formulates an idea which I have had — as you may remember for a long time; the distinction between reason and intelligence, between intellectuals and intellect workers, the phenomenon of what I always thought of as the "High IQ imbecile." ". . . We must differentiate between intelligence and reason. By intelligence I mean the ability to manipulate concepts for the purpose of achieving some practical end. The chimpanzee — who puts the two sticks together in order to get at the banana because one of the two is not long enough to do the job — uses intelligence . . . Intelligence, in this sense is taking things for granted as they are, making combinations which have the purpose of facilitating their manipulation . . . Reason, on the other hand, aims at understanding; it tries to find out what is behind the surface, to recognize the kernel, the essence of the reality which surrounds us." (*The Sane Society*, pp. 169f). And this is precisely where the dog is buried, this is exactly what makes it well nigh impossible to talk to the Kaldors & Co.: they think only in terms of intelligence (of which they usually have a lot): they think *never* in terms of reason. They always take things for granted, always scratch merely the surface, always refuse to look for the essence. And the more sophisticated among them, the "philosophers" of sorts rationalize this attitude by logical maneuvering and by "proving" that there is no "meaning" to the notion essence. Incidentally, this is where the real distinction lies between those who Marx considered to be great economists and the "vulgar" ones. For it is *not* decisive whether those who are devoted to reason necessarily agree with you; what matters is that they are concerned with looking for the *essence* of things, that they are not content to merely manipulate surface phenomena. One can have a meaningful discussion with them; they may see the essence in different processes than one happens to see them oneself — as long as they do not take everything for granted they are intellectuals and not sycophants! The trouble is that all those one has to deal with are precisely the latter: they take everything for granted, and there is nothing to talk to them about, except if — just to maintain some human intercourse — one descends to their own level and talks to them about their stuff. This, I think, applies to what you say about Kaldoriana and the formula game. In the formula game they can display all of the "intelligence" and the less they want to go into the essence of things the more they have to demonstrate their manipulative skills so as to be considered great men. And the greatest manipulator among them will be always held in greatest prestige — a Hicks, a Samuelson *et tutti quanti* — for the more manipulative capacity; the less use of reason, which is precisely what is needed for the education of the young. . . .

All of this fascinating and terribly important, perhaps that is where the nub of bourgeois ideology and culture is located. The thing that is absorbing me now is the question to what extent the same business appears in the East. They want to shift all of their education etc. to technology and such. If (a tremendous "if," to be sure) their society is *en principe* at least *reasonable*, if it is o.k. to take their basic structure for granted, everything is alright. I was for a long time of the opinion that such is the case. Is it? I still am strongly inclined to this view, for I still believe that its *essence* (nationalization, planning, etc.) is rational. The

disturbing feature is really whether the human beast with its psycho structure
is not part of the essence. In other words: I may have written or spoken to you
earlier about the following idea: I call it pompously the "heterogeneity of the
historical dimensions." To wit: the political change (setting up a new regime
via revolution) goes very fast. Industrialization much more slowly. Suitable
reorganization of agriculture even more so. The transformation of the capitalist
or even pre-capitalist man into a conscious, understanding, honest citizen
of a socialist society may last not generations but centuries. It is actually this
unevenness of the developmental processes that creates the entire mess . . .
But isn't this unevenness part of the essence of matters? Marx himself had
clearly an inkling of all of this, his remarks about the socialist society emerging
from the womb of the cap. society and many others are clear indication of it.
But didn't he in his general overestimation of the tempo assume a much lesser
heterogeneity of the dimensions? Didn't he believe that what is at issue are
years, while in fact it looks more [like] decades and ages? On this there is much
to say, and much to think. . . .

All that is in your letter in re: the study of mono cap. is wholly in agreement
with my own notions. And what you say about the prospects or execution is
unfortunately too true also on this end. The miserableness of personal existence
in all of its elements has much to do with this dimness of outlook. I am sure that
even this hick-up of a book that I produced would have never been possible
were it not for the presence of Dorothy here . . . with her around I was at least
moderately able to work.[71] With my little Nicky being my only, repeat only
human contact, I get completely stymied, have no energy for anything and stare
at the desk instead of doing something. It is all phantastic but nevertheless true.
And no prospect whatever to mend matters, certainly not in this rathole! At the
same time a strong feeling that there is so much that could be said, needs to be
said — if for no other reason than to "live oneself out" to let one's energies, one's
thoughts, one's minimal abilities not strangle one. . . .

[. . .]
Love
  /s Paul

[*Handwritten*]

P.S. [. . .]

71. Apparently a female companion of my father's: one whom no one seems to know about, and of
whom I have no memory.

PAB to PMS

Stanford University

Thursday morning [*apparently* November 29, 1956]

Dear Paul,

The "main" letter was composed last night at 2 PM [AM?] [letter of November 28, 1956]. This morning I re-wrote Bill Glazier's statement on the book [*The Political Economy of Growth*], and enclose both his and my own version. Maybe you could try your hand on something that might be better than both.

In connection with the "unevenness" thesis what must be added is that both the laggard echelon of the historical process as well as its *essence* dialectically change in the course of history. In other words, in the transition from feud. to cap. other things were crucial than what is in the center in the transition from capitalism to socialism. What is more, to the extent that the latter transition represents the "end of the prehistory of mankind" the unevenness becomes more pronounced. Finally, the most laggard component of the whole becomes for practical, historical, political purposes to such an extent invariant and parametric that its plasticity can no longer be safely assumed — again, for practical purposes. Thus: it is scientifically, *en principe* beyond doubt that the bloody human nature *does* change with the change in production, social organization etc. But if this change takes *very* much longer than the change in everything else, then does it *really* change within the relevant time dimension? And if such is the case isn't socialism bound to stick itself in the womb of mama's and half outside of same? Which in turn raises the question whether mama, in this case humanity, isn't bound to yell bloody murder *ad calendas graecas* and possibly depart to her maker in the course of such "extraordinary" labor pains?

Have you encountered any information concerning Lukacs? I noticed only that he was member of the six-day Nagy government, then there was no further reference to him. I wonder whether the old man survived all this![72]

Again, *a rividerci*.

Yours,

/s Paul

---

72. The reference is to Marxian philosopher Georg Lukács, who was a member of the anti-USSR. communist revolutionary government, led by Imre Nagy in Hungary, that was brought to an end with the Soviet invasion of Hungary in 1956. PAB is concerned about Lukács's survival (he lived until 1971).

3
A New Left Critique

[1957]

PAB to PMS

Stanford University
January 17th, 1957

Dear Paul,

[...]

    I spent a few truly oppressive days reading the page proofs [*PEoG*]; it goes without saying that at this stage of the game, it all looks to me stale, dull and repulsive. . . . Where I think the chief weakness of the Mono Cap chapters lies is in what is probably an underestimation of the autonomous impact of technological change. I take there the cavalierly (and somewhat undialectical) position of asserting that given the inducements to invest (stemming from the economic structure) there is always plenty of technology to be invested in. This is correct. No less correct, however, is the dialectical counterpart that given plenty of "good" technology (i.e. *really* cost saving devices) there is an extra boost to investment. The former accent is needed against those who would like to detract attention from monopoly cum oligopoly and focus on technology as if same came from God, the latter consideration has to be stressed against the "vulgars" who see nothing but the organizational structure of the economy and ignore completely the technological development as such.

    The real problem arises if one considers that big business enterprise with overflowing eco. spl. [economic surplus] can afford to maintain a research machinery providing for a steady stream of technological improvements breaking thus the Schumpeterian clustering and the Schumpeterian randomness in the occurrence of technological sparks. If in the process of partial rationalization which is an aspect of mono cap, *this* (Schumpeterian) irrationality can be eliminated or at least greatly reduced, does not *this* — all government apart — provide an important stabilizing factor? In my book I sort of vaguely and

reluctantly admit of this possibility; my main accent remains on the proposition
that investment follows its own course with technological stuff being or not being
made use of depending on the nature of the investment climate. I am now afraid
that this may be an "old-fashioned" view capturing only half of the truth with
the other half unduly played down . . . But all this will have to be worked out and
discussed much more thoroughly in the "Big Theme."

[. . .]

Yours,

/s Paul

P.S. [. . .]

PMS to PAB

24 Agassiz Street

Cambridge 40, Mass.

Jan. 19, 1957

Dear Paul,

Got back from NY last night and received your letter in the course of the
evening. Went skating with the kids this a.m. and now, after a bit of a nap, I'm
contemplating getting down to work on the 2nd industrial revolution. It will
put the evil day off a bit more to write a letter, which I'm afraid explains the
promptness of my reply.[73]

[. . .] The essence of the matter is that it is not the statistical concentration
of capital that is decisive but the growth of Big Business to dominance in the
main industries and hence in the economy as a whole. These two processes
are related, of course, but not in any simple fashion. It is possible to have a very
rapid concentration process without any Big Business' developing — e.g. U.S.
agriculture in the last decade; and it is also possible for statistical concentration
to accompany the rise of the most and biggest Big Business in any industry
anywhere — e.g. the oil industry. (Another, and perhaps even clearer, case is
aluminum which started as small business 100 percent concentrated and is now
very Big Business but with four or five firms: statistically, this would look like one
thing, while actually it was something entirely different.)

73. PAB had done research at times for the Wall Street firm Model, Roland and Stone (then at 120
Broadway, New York) as a means of obtaining additional income. He had contracted to do a report
on *The Scientific-Industrial Revolution*. He and PMS had discussed working on it together. In the
end, due to pressures associated primarily with the proofing of *The Political Economy of Growth*,
PMS took over the job completely and wrote the pamphlet, which turned out to be one of the most
prescient discussions of technological change to be written in its time. See [Paul M. Sweezy, writing
anonymously,] *The Scientific-Industrial Revolution* (New York: Model, Roland and Stone, 1957).

The point then is to show that the transition from small to Big Business [BB] is a quantity-to-quality leap and that BB has certain characteristic modes of behavior, esp. with relation to price policy and technology, which are largely independent of specific market situations (i.e. whether there is only one company, or two or three, or what have you). I haven't explored all the implications of this approach yet, but I think it amounts pretty much to chucking the whole formal monopoly-oligopoly theory and substituting what might be called a sociology of Big Business. If anybody wants to know what Big Business is, I say General Motors; and if they want to know what small business is, I tell them the corner grocery store. Then if they want to know just where to draw the line, I send them to hell. Worrying about where you draw lines is the business of bourgeois economics. Explaining the phenomena which indubitably exist on both sides of the line, wherever drawn, is the business of Marxists. On the "sociology of BB" I have a lot of ideas which I think will illuminate recent U.S. history, help to understand the ruling class, and put into the proper light and perspective the whole huge literature of the "managerial revolution" type. I think all this has great possibilities, which makes the inability to get to work seriously on it all the more annoying and frustrating.

[...]
Love from all,
    /s Paul

PAB to PMS

Stanford University
January 22, 1957

Dear Paul,
The same mechanism that induced you to react so rapidly to my earlier letter — the desire to postpone disagreeable chores — makes me respond immediately to yours of January 19th.

(1) I can well understand your distaste for the SIR [*Second-Industrial Revolution*]-job. I am not looking forward to my part in it either. The only consolation in addition to the $$ is that studying that material is important for other purposes. And there is nothing that helps studying as much as the necessity to write something about the subject. Are the two books on Automation that I sent to you of any use? I did not even open them before sending them on.

(2) What you say about concentration is fine. It comes, as so many things do, to the basic question as to what is the *prevalent* type, the essential, the driving factor in a system? This is always the question which bourgeois economics most

carefully avoids or attempts to drown in hair-splitting quibbles, definitions etc. You remember old Usher who did not wish to accept the notion of capitalism because even in this country there are "plenty" of independent artisans, subsistence farmers etc.

There are a few points which I would wish to add to what you have said: (a) I would suggest that all the studies dealing with market structures and the shares in individual markets controlled by BB (Mason-type investigations) can be well left aside — particularly now when it becomes increasingly obvious that individual BB firms keep their fingers in a multitude of different markets. Nevertheless there is one statistical measure which not only may not be ignored, but must be given maximum attention. That is the *distribution* of profits among profit recipients. This can be established with the help of *Statistics of Income* (published by the Bureau of Internal Revenue), and although the data are all but satisfactory, they do show very clearly the process of concentration of *profits*. What matters from our standpoint — I think — is that it can be demonstrated that while under competitive capitalism the economic surplus tended to be broken up into a lot of individual morsels — unequal to be sure, but relatively small — under monopoly capitalism it accrues to a large extent (over one-half) to a handful of enterprises. If the smoke screen of legalities could be dispelled, and if companies under joint control could be treated as such, it would turn out that an even larger part of the total comes under the sway of only a few hundred controlling centers. This, rather than proportions of sales etc. is what really matters! Incidentally, a nice parallelism between this and the individual income situation. If the very unequal distribution of individual income accounts for "underconsumption" — the even more unequal distribution of profits tends to lead — exogenous impulses apart — to "underinvestment."

(b) I do not quite see why the formal monopoly-oligopoly theory has to be entirely discarded. On the contrary, it would seem to me that Marxist economics could be enriched by taking into account some of the better parts of the monopoly-oligopoly theory. M. himself paid little attention to it because he obviously felt — and rightly — that in his days it was *not* monopoly and oligopoly that represented the *prevalent* type of business with competitive enterprise being the rule. At the present time it is exactly the other way around, and as he made full use of Smith-Ricardo in dealing with the competitive structure, we have to make full use of whatever may be the *genuine* achievements of the monopoly and oligopoly theory in bourgeois economics. The accent is clearly on the word genuine. For the greatest danger is always to be attracted by the worm and to swallow in the process the entire hook. . . . Even if and when the bourgeois theory asserts that a market is controlled not by 5 firms but by $5 + n$ and makes

a great amount of noise about that *n* supposedly proving lack of concentration
or what have you, it usually does recognize that the whole operation is run on
the basis of price leadership, trade association deals etc. in other words in a *de
facto* monopolistic fashion. Once this is granted, the logic of monopoly-oligopoly
behavior has to be considered and applied.

(c) What would seem to me crucial is the question as to what exactly that
logic is. Does a monopolistic and oligopolistic enterprise maximize its profits
in the textbook sense, or is their profit policy significantly different? In the
first place, they do not maximize their profits in the short run, but rather their
general profit position in the long run. Secondly for reasons of public policy etc.
they are willing to let a number of side-kicks to travel along without swallowing
them up. Thirdly the "kinked demand curve" business prevents them from
maximizing merely in the light of the market structure (on the demand side).[74]
They have to consider the behavior of fellow-oligopolists and therefore they can
raise their prices only if there is some cost factor that is common to all of them:
wage increases, administrative expenses, taxes etc. This produces an altogether
different form of business behavior, and this is where the sociology of BB comes
in, explaining and exploring the mode of functioning of this new entrepreneur
who is less "anarchic" than the competitive business man, more cautious more
rational (in a partial sense) and more irrational (in the overall, social sense).

(3) Directly related to it is the problem of class distribution of income, or of
what determines the real wage, and conversely, the share of Y [national income]
going into surplus. That the marginal productivity theory has nothing to
contribute to that matter goes without saying. Its own assumptions are such that
it cannot possibly claim to make such a contribution. But I am terribly uneasy
about this cost-of-production-of-labor-power theory because it is so damned
circular. What is that cost of production? The socially necessary wage? And
what is the socially necessary wage? The wage prevailing at any given time! In
India and in similar places this is all simple. There it is the subsistence wage pure
and simple, with subsistence meaning pretty much physiological subsistence
minimum. But in advanced countries? If you try to salvage the thing by saying
the cost-of-production-wage is the wage below which the worker would not
perform, this gets you either nowhere, or into a morass of "psychologism" which

74. The notion of the kinked-demand curve, in which oligopolistic prices trended up but not
down, was introduced by Paul M. Sweezy in his doctoral dissertation and then later on in a famous
article on pricing under oligopoly. See Paul M. Sweezy, *Monopoly and Competition in the English
Coal Trade, 1550–1660* (Cambridge, Massachusetts: Harvard University Press, 1938), "Demand
Under Conditions of Oligopoly," *Journal of Political Economy* 47, no. 4 (August 1939): 568–73.

is worse than nowhere. Why is the worker content to perform for $80 a week permitting him to live the way he does and does not insist on $100 which would allow him to live slightly better and not to go into debt? I got to think about it in approximately such terms: What one has to start with is the rate of accumulation of capital (governed partly by the logic of monopolistic-oligopolistic investment policies and partly by exogenous factors) and the amount of capital needed to equip a worker under prevailing technological conditions. The former divided over the latter gives you the demand for workers (the length of the working day set by the mores of society).

Yet this is not enough. The demand for workers is circumscribed by a crucially important limitation. This is the rate of return on capital which is determined by the riskiness of investment, by alternative earning possibilities (returns on bonds etc.). With this constraint in operation capitalists compete for workers. If the workers are in ample supply, competing with each other for jobs — they'll tend to push the wage below what would have been possible from the standpoint of the capitalist insistence on adequate returns. Profits would increase. This profits increase would not necessarily lead to an expansion of the demand for workers but would more likely lead to a decline in Y — therefore the workers would not benefit by it. If the workers are in short supply, they may manage to push the wage above what is acceptable to the capitalist. This would be, however, a very illusory victory. For the capitalist would immediately get busy introducing labor-saving devices thus reducing the demand for labor, and — more importantly still, particularly under conditions of monopoly — would raise prices so as to wipe out the gain in money wages and restore the right real wage. Trade unions under such circumstances have a larger role to play under conditions of underemployment than under conditions of prosperity. In the former situation they prevent the workers from engaging in cut-throat competition among themselves, and from reducing the wages unduly. In the latter situation by pushing upward money wages they promote technical progress and . . . inflationary development. If this theory is at all worth anything it makes the *central* issue: what *is* the rate of return that is considered by monopolistic and oligopolistic enterprise to be adequate, indispensable, etc.? And this brings us right back into the sociology of BB, into its *modus operandi*, into its profit policies . . . I don't know what you think of it, but this is as far as I have ever got. By the way, the fixed mark-up concept that is generally accepted these days would point in the same direction with the rate of return translated into terms of profits on sales . . .

[. . .]

This is all for the day. [. . .]

Give my love to the family.
Yours,
　　s/ Paul

PAB to PMS

Stanford University
February 3, 1957

Dear Paul,

Being completely unable to do a stitch of work, I spend my time partly thinking about this inability and partly reading and meditating on "subject matter." I have been outlining and organizing in my mind the Psycho business; there is one particular line of thought which has been occupying me most of all and to which I would very much want your reaction. I may have communicated it to you in one form or another before — still tell me what you think of it . . .

In settling his accounts with Hegel, Marx undertook *one* fundamental departure. What Hegel treated as conflicts and contradictions in the realm of ideas, Marx understood and demonstrated to be contradictions and conflicts in *reality*. If in Hegel's universe of ideas those conflicts and contradictions were fought out and *aufgehoben* [resolved] in the area of thought, with the absolute spirit moving onward and forward to the point at which REASON finally prevails, Marx showed that the conflicts and contradictions being *real* conflicts and *real* contradictions can only be *aufgehoben* in the concrete class struggle in society. Why *class* struggle? Because in every societal constellation there is a class which benefits (relatively) from the existing irrationality, while there is another class which experiences the brunt of that irrationality, carries its main burden, pays for it in blood, sweat and tears. The *Aufhebung* [abolition, in this context], the elimination of the irrationality and its replacement by a more rational society becomes then the primary *interest* of that oppressed class, not merely the concern of rational criticism. That oppressed class paying the bill of the irrationality and fetishistic nature of the existing society was under feudalism the bourgeoisie (drawing its support at least from a part of the peasantry). For this proposition to hold, it is essential (not just useful, convenient, desirable, etc.) to postulate the *absolute* pauperization of the working class. *Relative* pauperization wouldn't do. For if the working class experiences a more or less steady improvement of its living and working conditions, it may well consider that it is not rising fast enough (relative pauperization!) — but this kind of a consideration leads to an effort to speed up that rise (reformism!) rather than to *revolutionary* action (and spirit) directed towards the *Aufhebung* of the whole business and towards the establishment of a more rational order. That such a possibility existed in reality, Marx somewhere suspected, and Engels explicitly recognized.

Now comes Lenin who understood fully this basic structure — and this, I think, is the full measure of his genius — and realized that with this structure the entire edifice of Marxian socialism stands and falls. And understanding this he introduced a paramountly important amendment. The popular stratum (class) bearing the brunt of capitalist irrationality is not necessarily the working class of the advanced capitalist countries. Au contraire, that class can become even a partner of the class deriving its benefits from the existing irrationality. Under conditions of imperialism, the sector of society (world society, to be sure) that really pays the bill for the madness of the socio-economic system are the peoples inhabiting the underdeveloped, colonial and dependent world. Socialist criticism of the capitalist system is once more anchored in an existing active, dynamic social *force*, rather than in immanent movements of REASON (towards the latter position not only Bernstein & Co [Eduard Bernstein] but also [Karl] Kautsky undoubtedly tended, for neither of them really grasped the basic issue).

This social force is the complex, infinitely involved and conflict-laden movement of the underdeveloped countries for national and social liberation. A movement which is partly led by the native bourgeoisie's, partly by the native working classes — always requiring support from the native peasantry. With both, the bourgeoisie and the peasantry being inevitably ambivalent (they are against certain aspects of the prevailing irrationality: imperialist exploitation; but wedded to others — even more important ones namely private property!), this movement is bound to be a terribly tough one, slow, conflict-laden and demanding supreme strategic skill. Jumping far ahead it may well be said that this Leninian enrichment of the Marxian "battleground assessment" has proved to be a real vision of genius. Everything that has happened in the last 50 years has demonstrated that this is exactly where the dialectical struggle *in reality* takes place, that he has put his finger precisely on the dynamic social factor that (a) bears the brunt of the prevailing irrationality and (b) struggles for its *Aufhebung*. What is more, this particular social force lifts not merely the entire edifice of the existing society from its foundations in the backward countries, it undermines the capitalist order also in the advanced countries that depend for the relative satisfaction of their working classes on the exploitation of the colonial world. So far so good, and it makes all excellent sense placing at the same time the struggle in the u/d [underdeveloped] countries in its proper historical perspective.

And I am getting (slowly) to what I am driving at. This whole business is perfectly o.k. with regard to both u/d countries *and* those advanced capitalist countries that *really* depend to a considerable extent on imperialist profits for the maintenance of domestic equilibrium, i.e. for the prevention of absolute

pauperization at home. Such advanced countries are indubitably Britain
and to an even more striking extent France. But what about the U.S.? All
the nonsense in Soviet writings notwithstanding it is clear — I think — that
the prevention of absolute pauperization in this country does *not* depend on
imperialism in the strict sense of the word. It can be prevented, indeed a steady
(if less than possible) increase of living standards can be organized with the
help of the internal resources of American capitalism. Given a certain degree
of understanding on the part of the ruling class, a certain ability to eliminate
the worst aspects of irrationality (Keynesiasm!), U.S. capitalism *can* function
without creating at home a class to whom this irrationality becomes increasingly
unbearable. To be sure, it needs for that an imperialism of a "special kind," what
might be called a "social order imperialism." It must maintain a vast military
establishment to protect itself against the fate that may overcome the rest of
the advanced capitalist world. It must go even further, and prevent the other
advanced countries from going down (Capitalism cannot exist in one country!),
but what is crucial to my argument: it does not create in the process a dynamic,
social force *within* the American society that is vitally *interested* in the *Aufhebung*
of the prevailing irrationality. On the contrary, the nation as a whole is faring
better, even *relative* pauperization — which would not matter too much anyway
— does not take place... Therefore the criticism of that irrationality, yours and
mine and that of others, remains an ideational, Hegelian criticism, a criticism
based on the immanent movement of REASON and not on the concrete
movement in society. This is the bottom of what you spoke about in connection
with Starobin's book, of the "emigre status" of the American socialist, etc.[75]

Bear with me on one further step. It is now becoming increasingly fashionable
to say at this point: ah, wait a minute, what you forget is that pauperization is
only one, and one only form in which a class in society can bear the brunt of that
society's irrationality and inability to provide for the development of man. There
is another form: psychic deprivation, sexual repression, cultural misery, general
discontent, boredom, aimlessness ... All this — leading at last to the problem in
hand — is indubitably true. The question, indeed the crucial question, remains:
does this discontent, does this psychic, cultural etc. deprivation represent a basis
for the formation and crystallization of a dynamic social force interested in the
Aufhebung of the existing social order? Indeed, the dissatisfaction, the cultural
misery etc. affect *all* classes of society (a number of psycho's [psychologists] to

75. Joseph Starobin, socialist journalist and later professor; unclear what book, since his book,
American Communism in Crisis, 1953–1957, probably had not yet been published, but could be
referring to either of his already published books: *Paris to Peking* or *Eyewitness in Indo-China*.

whom I spoke all confirm the point: it is *mutatis mutandis* as pronounced in the working class as it is in the bourgeoisie, although the latter suffers from it perhaps more acutely), but does this become the basis for a social movement against the capitalist system? To say this, as is now done with increasing frequency, is not only "psychologism," not only an important, say, departure from Marxism, but — I am afraid — also wrong! For it is the nature of this dissatisfaction that — giving rise as it does to neuroses — it does not become a force against the prevailing irrationality and its mainstay: private property and the rest of the fetishistic ideology. On the contrary it becomes the mainspring of a generally manifested aggressiveness, depression, sense of emptiness and purposelessness of life. This in turn is the basic component of the make-up of the fascist man, rather than of the liberating drive for a more rational social order. . . .

In different words: if the "psycho-struggle" takes the place of the class struggle in the good old sense, what this is likely to lead to is a protracted rotting of society, an extended misery affecting its ruling classes no less than its ruled classes, a general decadence — Rome! — indeed, barbarism in the only meaningful sense of that Rosa Luxemburg alternative![76] And it still is "psychologism" and faith in the immanent movement of REASON to believe — as you occasionally indicated to do — that socialist forces would develop from seeing the *example* elsewhere, in other words from *rationally* comprehending the irrationality of the system in which this society exists . . . Bluntly, unless there is a *class* — a large and important segment of society — that finds itself in its basic, *material* conditions of life in conflict with the organizational principles of that society, all criticism of those organizational principles, all confrontation of them with REASON is bound to remain an *ideational* confrontation, an intellectual operation — interesting, somewhere useful, perhaps even necessary *sub specie aeternitatis* [eternal truth] but still essentially "pre-Marxian," Hegelian! For it is — to repeat it — the "crux of the cruxes" of the Marxian insight, that is the alliance, nay identity of the *material* needs of a *class* with the REASON's criticism of the existing irrationality that is the historically forward driving engine, the motor promoting the entire movement . . .

What we can do (and undoubtedly should do) is to demonstrate the irrationality *per se*. The entire problem of the generation and utilization of the economic surplus is at the heart of this demonstration. It explains — I think — most of what has to be explained. Yet one has to be clear about the other side of

---

76. Baran is referring here to Rosa Luxemburg's famous reference in her *Junius Pamphlet* to "socialism or barbarism" as the only alternative. See Rosa Luxemburg, *The Rosa Luxemburg Reader* (New York: Monthly Review Press, 2004), 321.

the story: it does *not eo ipso* indicate the locus of the social force, of the class that is materially driven to the overthrow of the system providing for this mode of generation and utilization of the economic surplus. And this is the paramountly important gap from the viewpoint of Marxism . . .

You may think offhand that this is all only tenuously related to the psycho-job [essay on Marx and psychoanalysis]. I would not think so. It is my feeling that it is really at the center of the whole matter. But now I would want to hear what you think of all that, for I believe that we have to face it all and to face it squarely.

Love,

/s Paul

P.S. [. . .]

PMS to PAB

Cambridge, Mass.

February 6, 1957

Dear Paul,

[. . .]

A couple of remarks about wages, relative shares, etc., while they are in my mind. I do not advocate adoption of a cost-of-production theory of wages in any literal sense. But I think the *approach* of that theory is right and that cost of production (incl. education and training of course) plays a good deal more of a role than neo-classical theory assigns to it. The most striking fact, to me, is the relative stability of average real wages. I just recently calculated the figure for 1956 (total compensation of wage and salary earners divided by total number of such characters deflated by the consumer price index). It hasn't yet got up to the 1945 figure, and since salaries are included — and so are employer contributions to social security trust funds — it is hard to see how there can have been anything but a fall in the average real wage. I frankly can't quite understand this result — it seems too far out of line with physical figures on sales of consumer goods. To be sure, the 1945 wage included a lot more saving, and much consumption *inzwischen* [in the meantime] has been financed by consumer credit. Also, it is probable that the rich and the *dritte personen* [third parties] have been taking a larger share of consumer goods. But is this enough to explain the discrepancies? Is there something drastically wrong with the statistics? In any case, for what they are worth they indicate that *in the short run* one cannot go far wrong in following Bortkiewicz and treating the real wage as given.[77] The problem then becomes to explain the long-run changes, and there factors like cost of production and the mores of the country can quite properly be brought into the picture without necessarily involving circular reasoning. Damn it all, this whole subject is in a most unsatisfactory state and unfortunately it is crucial to the whole determination of the surplus. (I don't have your letter with me in which you outlined your thinking about the determinants of the wage and so will have to postpone comment on that until later. The carpenters are tearing up my study, and I'm working in the basement of the Millers' house next door so can't get at my files.)

A few very brief comments on your special of Feb. 3rd:

(1) I don't know about the absolute pauperization business. I am inclined to think that as a matter of historical *fact* it would be very difficult to show that revolutionary classes have been moved by a pauperization trend (a crisis is, of course, different). This whole business is very complicated, but I would hesitate to get mixed up in what might easily turn out to be a trap — and basically irrelevant, too.

(2) The real point is that the advanced capitalist systems have been able to domesticate their working classes, and there is no compelling reason to assume that this must come to an end. They are not to be treated as revolutionary or potentially revolutionary material — on that we agree. (I suspect, by the way, that this is true of even so backward an "advanced" country as Italy: its apparently radical working class is a hangover of the past; the trend is toward standard reformism. Eventually the CP may become the big reformist party instead of the SD.)

(3) Lenin saw the point but refused to admit to himself the whole horror of it from the point of view of traditional Marxism. Hence he invented the theory of the corrupted labor aristocracy betraying the "true" instincts of the working masses. This theory has since continuously led to illusions in the western Communist movement. The fact is that there is hardly anything to it; the masses are as reformist as their leaders.

---

77. PMS is referring to the Russian economist Ladislaus Bortkiewicz (1868–1931). Sweezy famously utilized the Bortkiewicz solution to the transformation problem in his account of the labor theory of value in *The Theory of Capitalist Development*. Later Sweezy translated Bortkiewicz's essay on this into English. See Paul M. Sweezy, *The Theory of Capitalist Development* (New York: Oxford University Press, 1942), 120–25; Paul M. Sweezy, ed., "*Karl Marx and the Close of His System" by Eugen von Böhm-Bawerk/Böhm-Bawerk's Criticism of Marx by Rudolf Hilferding* (New York: Augustus M. Kelley, 1949), 199–221 (the page numbers refer to Sweezy's translation of Bortkiewicz, included as an appendix in this volume). Bortkiewicz was a professor at Berlin when PAB was a student there.

(4) Agreed 100 percent that it is the backwards that are the new prime movers — *this* Lenin saw with brilliant clarity — also that the path of advance for them is certain to be extremely rough and long.

(5) Agreed, also, that the U.S. is not fatally dependent on imperialism — or at any rate that so much imperialism as may be essential, in Canada and Latin America, chiefly, can be held in line for a long time to come ("fortress America"). The U.S. *may* also be able to support the other advanceds (esp. Britain) for a long time, but that is less certain and in any case is not crucial.

(6) We don't know enough about how a two-system world will work or what effects the one system will have on the other to say that the U.S. *cannot* do anything but stagnate into barbarism. The experience of Japan, where the ruling class itself carried out a revolution from above to prevent being overwhelmed by the superior system (not because of absolute pauperization!), gives much food for thought here. But the truth is that this is one of those problems which we just don't yet have the facts and experience to solve (this is much the way Lenin treated the problem of the withering away of the state — and I think rightly).

(7) Finally, whatever view one may take of the U.S. road to socialism (if any), our work has much greater meaning than merely in relation to a hypothetical future U.S. socialist movement. The success of the socialist world and of the colonial independence movement depends in large part on dealing correctly with the problem of the United States. And for that, genuine knowledge and understanding are essential. And though it may sound vain or incongruous to say it, we just happen to be the only ones who can provide those commodities. So I would say that at one remove we can play an absolutely crucial role in the *real* movement and are by no means limited to the ideational confrontation of Reason with irrational reality.

(8) This raises a nice question: can the whole U.S. Left play such a role? If not (and I think not), what other role is there for it? Here I think perhaps your dilemma holds full sway. But there is a role for those who are capable of rising above their situation and comprehending the laws of motion of the dying system, for that system happens to be embodied in the USA and only those are able to study it at first hand who live in its body.

More later — I *must* get at the RoM!

Love,

/s Paul

PAB to PMS

Stanford University
March 5, 1957

Dear Paul,

[...]

The more I think about our *magnum opus*, the more I become convinced
that the thing should be organized along the lines suggested by the sub-title: the
generation and absorption of the economic surplus. Part I should deal with the
former problem, part II with the latter. The first part therefore should begin with
the analysis of the profit maximization process under mono cap; the nature of the
maximizing agent (corporation), distribution of the social product as between
the profit sector and the wage sector, wage and price theory, bargaining between
the corporations and unions etc. The second part would address itself to the
mode of utilization of the surplus: state, imperialism and the entire penumbra
of wasteful activities. The last, then undoubtedly crisscrosses with the first part,
in particular with regard to the problem of surplus-shifting (no waste of surplus
without simultaneous increase of surplus) which I consider to be the real nub
of the whole business — but this is inevitable, and does no harm: a book is an
organic whole where matters appear and re-appear in different settings. In the
second part *sub specie* surplus-waste comes the whole cultural, psychological
etc. situation — Russell Lynes' expression "Surfeit of Honey" is excellent.
I don't know what you think of this, but it appears to me to be a simple and
straightforward story. The division of labor does not follow from it automatically,
but in further concretization it will easily emerge. I am now thinking more in
terms of the second part, you apparently more in terms of the first, but again,
there will be criss-crosses. I shall make up an outline, and send it to you within
the next few days.

So much for today.

As ever,

s/ Paul

P.S. [...]

[Excerpt from letter from MR *assistant Cathy Winston to PAB regarding the historic oral argument of Sweezy vs. New Hampshire before the U.S. Supreme Court on March 5, 1957]*[78]

March 10, 1957

The Supreme Court hearing was very exciting. I had never been in the building before and was fascinated with the-almost-intimacy of the court room itself compared with the vast corridors. Paul sat with the rest of the visitors and was ignored by the Justices. They probably didn't even know he was there. Tom Emerson was excellent. He followed his brief fairly closely, but asked to reserve part of his time for the end, when re-answered a point Wyman had raised about Paul's answering the question on believing in communism. (Paul's answer had been, if I remember, that he did not believe in communism as defined by the N.H. legislature, but further than that he refused to answer.) Emerson argued that the questioning violated Paul's rights as protected by the First Amendment, even though the answers might be pertinent in that they would prove if Paul had advocated force and violence. Wyman protested the "First Amendment roadblock" which he said Emerson was trying to use to keep pertinent questions from being asked. Emerson and others felt that there is a possibility that the Court may decide it on the First, but more likely on the pre-emption issue which was the basis of the Nelson decision. There isn't any rule about when a decision will be handed down. No one knows.

At one point Chief Justice Warren asked Wyman if any students in the class had been questioned to find out what Dr. Sweezy said. Wyman replied in a pious tone that he wouldn't think of asking a student to inform on his teacher. Warren said: then you would rather probe a man's mind and beliefs than find out the facts from someone who could tell you? At another point Warren replied to Wyman's implied charge that Paul advocated force and violent change under some circumstances (by reading from the MR piece "On Trials and Purges") by reading from the record the section where Paul had testified that he thought socialism would come to the U.S. but by peaceful means. Our friends all felt that

---

78. In January 1954 Sweezy had been subpoenaed by the Attorney General of New Hampshire. Under oath he was asked to provide notes to lectures he had delivered at the University of New Hampshire, and to name names in relation to his former role as state chair of the Progressive Party during Henry Wallace's presidential campaign. Sweezy refused to cooperate on the basis of his First Amendment rights. He was therefore declared in contempt of court and consigned to jail, though released on bail. This started an appeal process that resulted in the landmark case, *Sweezy vs. New Hampshire*, argued before the U.S. Supreme Court on March 5, 1957, and decided in Sweezy's favor. See John J. Simon, "*Sweezy v. New Hampshire*: The Radicalism of Principle," *Monthly Review* 51, no. 11 (April 2000): 35–41.

the majority of the court was favorably disposed to Paul, and we went out and
had a victory drink to celebrate.

PMS to PAB

Cambridge, Mass.
May 2, 1957

Dear Paul,

[...]

I am re-reading Veblen's *Theory of Business Enterprise [TBE]*, and it is in
many ways an astonishing performance. Almost all the correct conclusions
(about the increasing necessity of waste, the impossibility of corrective
reforms under the existing ruling class, etc., etc.) are there. What is weak is the
supporting theory, though even that has many brilliant insights. But the strange
thing is that one simply doesn't really get all this out of Veblen unless one has
already worked it out for oneself — then, but only then, one can see clearly
enough that it is there. I find this a most interesting phenomenon requiring
careful analysis. Why did Veblen fail to get his really important messages across
and yet succeed so well with some of his secondary ones? It won't do to say that
this is wholly a matter of the receptivity of his audience because the radical left
failed to understand him just as much as the supporters of the status quo did. In
any case, I am now delighted that I have got committed to serious Veblen work;
it will be worthwhile for the opus and it is high time the man should get his due
from someone in a position to understand what he was really trying to say. I shall
be interested to hear whether your reaction to the [*Theory of the*] *Leisure Class
[TLC]* is at all similar.

[...]

Hastily,

/s Paul

P.S. I will make a list of the passages in *Theory of Business Enterprise* which will
give you the meat of the book. He is much too repetitious, and there is no need to
read more than about a fifth to a quarter of the total. You can probably use such a
list and review *TBE* in conjunction with your own consideration of *TLC*.

PMS to PAB

[*Undated; probably May 4, 1957*]

Saturday, a.m.

Dear Paul,

[. . .] By the way, what would you think of asking Shlom [Sol Adler] to do a review of the new Schlesinger book for *MR*?[79] Or do you think it would be better to wait until more volumes are available? And on this subject did you see the really very interesting review of that opus by Bill Williams in the *Nation* of March 23rd.[80] The idea that 1929 *et seq* was the first crisis of the full-fledged corporate order rather than the last of Schlesinger's "old order" really raises important issues, something which ordinarily falls outside the province of American historians. I am not sure about the main point and my re-reading of V[eblen]'s *Theory of Business Enterprise* has increased my doubts. Consider the following (p. 184):

"It might even be a tenable generalization, though perhaps unnecessarily broad, to say that for a couple of decades past the normal condition of industrial business has been a mild but chronic state of depression, and that any marked departure from common-place dull times has attracted attention as a particular case calling for a particular explanation."

And again:

"It may . . . be said . . . that chronic depression, more or less pronounced, is normal to business under the fully developed regime of the machine industry." (p. 234)

Elsewhere (p. 253), he states as a matter of obvious fact that all competent observers would agree that for the last several decades (i.e. before 1904) chronic depression had been the state of U.S. business. All this seems to suggest that all of us, including Steindl especially, have been rather late in dating the arrival of stagnation and maturity. On the other hand, Veblen's own theory suggests an interesting alternative explanation of the whole matter. He explains chronic depression as resulting from competition — never mind the modus operandi at the moment, but it obviously is not nonsense — not from monopoly; and he argues that the trust movement is a reaction to depression-inducing competition, with the implication, and perhaps in places explicit statement, that monopolization is an effective remedy. What he clearly didn't see, or at any rate

79. Arthur Schlesinger Jr., *The Age of Roosevelt*, vol. 1, *The Crisis of the Old Order* (New York: Houghton Mifflin, 1957).

80. William Appleman Williams, "Books, Schlesinger: Right Crisis — Wrong Order," *The Nation*, March 23, 1957.

didn't develop, was that monopoly would *also* induce chronic depression though by a different *modus operandi* (here is where Steindl *et al* come in). Following this line of argument, one could reason that Williams is right, i.e. that 1929 *et seq* was the first onset of chronic depression, monopoly variety, and in this sense the first crisis of a "new" order. It was, of course, delayed until 1929 primarily by World War I. I am inclined to favor this interpretation. One of its great advantages is that it permits a devastating answer to those who would remedy present troubles by a "return to competition" — that would merely be jumping out of the frying pan into the fire.

One requires in this connection a more fully developed theory of chronic depression (competition variety) than Veblen provides. The task should not be too difficult. One needs only to show that if the price system works as the classics assumed it would, it will maintain the equilibrium of the system via progressively raising consumption at the expense of accumulation (and profits). In other words, prices will fall with rising productivity sufficiently to clear the market. This will, however, put a permanent brake on investment and hence the growth of income (for well-known Keynesian reasons, to which can be added the Veblenian argument that the effect is to continuously bankrupt older firms capitalized at higher price levels).

In a nutshell: chronic depression under competition is a matter of too small profits to fuel the capitalist engine, under monopoly of too much profits to find investment outlets. There is no happy medium, and the system only genuinely prospers when exogenous forces are so strong as to overcome depressive tendencies. Curiously, the same kind of exogenous forces work in both kinds of chronic depression — after all, what is wanted is outside stimulation of effective demand. Hence some of Veblen's most brilliant and modern-sounding formulations (see especially pp. 251 at ff — ". . . the absorption of goods and services by . . . expenditures which as seen from the standpoint of industry are pure waste would have to go on increasing in volume. If the wasteful expenditure slackens, the logical outcome should be . . . depression; if the waste on war, colonization, provincial investment, and the like, comes to an abrupt stop, the logical consequence, in the absence of counteracting factors, should be a crisis of some severity." Etc., etc.).

Damn it, what all this suggests to me right now is that the opus needs a hell of a lot more *histoire raisoneé* than we have been planning to include. What's the use of expanding the scope by getting new ideas when one doesn't even get to writing down old ones? What is especially frustrating is that I become more and more convinced that the opus can be *the* work on the last phase of capitalism, and achievement of genuine historic significance.

[...]

Love,

/s Paul

PAB to PMS

Stanford University

May 11-th, 1957

Dear Paul.

Classes, meetings, campus chores of all kinds, rendezvous with Nicky combined with a psycho-state that is very near rock-bottom reduce my capacity to work and output to zero.

This state causes further depressions, and further depressions aggravate this state. The dynamics of misery is as pernicious as it is compelling. For a few days I was meaning to answer your letters of May 2-nd and 4-th, but did not get around to it — partly for the above reasons, and partly because I was engrossed in "deep thought" about some of the problems that they touch upon. And the more deep thought there is, the more I become convinced that what our opus calls for is a theoretical introduction which would clarify "once and for all" the basic theoretical structure to the whole story. Without such a theoretical part all notions like "depression," "stagnation" but also all that one might say about the corporate structure, culture etc. hang in the air or stand on legs so brittle that intelligent pro's can knock them out without too much trouble. The difficulty of getting at a satisfactory theoretical concept is, I think, related to the necessity of departing even further than I originally believed from the conventional economics' apparatus.

What I am trying to get at is the following: It you take a "harmonious" model (Tugan-Baranovski, now Joan Robinson or any variant thereof), you get essentially the following picture: v [value of labor power or wages] (entirely consumed by workers) is a constant ratio of Y [income]; the share of s [surplus] consumed by the capitalists is a constant ratio of Y; the capital/output coefficient does not perceptibly change. In that case the investable share of s can always be re-invested; the resulting increment in output is split into workers' consumption, capitalists' consumption and investment in the old way and the merry-go-round can continue ad inf.

This business can be and has been attacked with reference to each of the assumptions involved. It was argued that v is a declining share of Y; it has been argued that consumption out of v declines with workers saving messing up the situation; it has been argued that capitalists' consumption out of s declines. All this would enter what might be called the family of underconsumption theories. And all this is unprovable within the framework of conventional notions (and statistics!). It has also been argued that the capital/output coefficient becomes increasingly more favorable, that for every additional \$ of investment you get an ever increasing increment of income or output — this, I think is also unprovable. In fact, the opposite may well be true. If this were the end of the story the merry-go-rounders would be unbeatable.

Where the dog is buried is that the concept of v (Marxian as it is but coinciding as it does with the bourgeois notion of wages) is unsatisfactory.[81] For what matters is that the v accruing to the workers engaged in the productive process is a declining share of the total value of output. This is completely obscured by taking all of v paid out in society! Yet this, let us call it "surface v" represents itself as the productive v plus all such v as is paid out of s. If there were no v paid out of s the underconsumption phenomenon would be visible in its entirety. As it is, v spent on wasteful activities added to v spent on productive workers add up to an aggregate v representing a constant share of Y (or thereabout) which overthrows the basic tenet of the underconsumption theory.

It overthrows it, however, only in the superficial sense that it can be shown that C [consumption] (in the misleading and dangerous Keynesian meaning) remains a constant share of Y. The underconsumption theory properly interpreted and developed must demonstrate that this Keynesian C only remains constant (or as large as it is) because of a growing component of Waste in it. Interestingly enough, the underconsumption theory in this framework becomes less of an economic depression theory and more of a cultural degradation theory. Furthermore not seeing this forces the Kuczynsky's & Co into desperate efforts to twist and bend statistics trying to prove that real income of workers etc. does decline where it actually does not, although it is beside the point![82]

But: how come that the mechanism is in the position to continually shift parts of s into wasteful consumption? Under competition it really could not; nor was it then very urgent. Under competition what was wasted instead was a good part of

81. "Where the dog is buried" was a favorite idiom of PAB's and PMS adopted it and utilized it in *MR*. Its origins are unclear, but it seems to have been common in various forms in Polish and Russian. Nikolai Bukharin used the same phrase in his *Philosophical Arabesques* completed in 1937 before his execution by Stalin (a work that would have been unknown to PAB since it was kept in Stalin's secret vault and not discovered for about 50 years). See Bukharin, *Philosophical Arabesques* (New York: Monthly Review Press, 2005), 96.
82. PAB is referring to the economist, statistician, and demographer Robert René Kuczynski (1876–1947).

s that was going into investment (misinvestment). The shifting of large parts of *s* into wasteful consumption is only possible under conditions of monopoly where wasteful consumption becomes elevated to the status of necessary costs. And here comes in the shifting problem: the more wasteful consumption, the more wasteful consumption is needed in the subsequent period because a large part of it "comes back" into *s*.

In *PEoG* this is somehow presented, but actually neither clearly enough nor completely enough. Not that I know exactly, how specifically to go about properly presenting it, but I am persuaded that this must be done, if we are really to make a major theoretic[al] step forward. In a sense we have to go beyond Marx by showing clearly that under advanced capitalism the notions *v* and *s* no longer suffice. The merry-go-rounders can win their point (and the system can keep going) by setting up, so to say, an equation in which

Good C + Bad C + Good I + Bad I = Y at Full Employment. The question that has to be answered: are there any limits to the possibility of expansion of Bad C + Bad I other than their intrinsic irrationality (and the output capacity of Miltowns) [anti-depressant tranquilizer which hit the market in 1955]. This is where I am at my wits' end. The answer to this one I don't know, and the answer to this one is obviously what most readers want badly. On the other hand, a theoretical service of major proportions would be performed, if one would show beyond dispute the essentiality of Bad C + Bad I for the stability of the system. Such a demonstration hinges obviously, on the ability to show that *necessary* (rational!) *v* is a declining portion of Y.

I have the feeling that all this brings the underconsumption theory on a higher level and may actually constitute an important development in the theory of Marxism. Here all Veblenians would fall into their place, but more as hunches and brilliant formulations than as actual theoretic[al] insights. As so frequently: Veblen did not fully understand his own insights!

[...]

Love,

/s Paul

PAB to PMS

[*Undated; probably May 12, 1957*]

Stanford University
Sunday Morning

Dear Paul,

What impresses me most is that if one wants to do anything more than surface theorizing, one cannot accept a solitary bourgeois notion without getting under its skin, without dialectic analysis. Indeed, it would seem, what could be more innocent and unambiguous than the notion "consumption?" Yet in the way in which it is treated in bourgeois writings is implied an entire universe of apologetics. Having looked over my treatment in *PEoG* (Chptr. III) I have come to the conclusion that it is quite inadequate. I am somehow coming out in the right place at the end, but for the wrong reasons. For if one says that mass consumption or wages represent a constant share of Y and leaves it at that, one actually gives the show away. Everything that I go on saying about the difficulty of investment under mono. cap. is o.k. but a Schumpeterian-minded "neo-harmonic" could (and probably will) answer that those are all short-run frictional disturbances, of no major consequence in the long run.

If (Mass Consumption + Capitalist Consumption)/Y is constant, then in the long run it may well be assumed that there will be enough opportunity for investment to satisfy this consumption unless something very awkward should happen to the capital/output coefficient. It has to be clearly shown that the whole thing is a *continual struggle against underconsumption*. In other words, if "left to itself," if only normal, productive, reasonable consumption is considered, then the ratio of consumption to Y tends to fall. For that ratio to stay constant or thereabouts, consumption has to be artificially blown up. All sorts of wasteful forms of it become indispensable (civilian no less than military). It is only together with these wasteful forms of consumption that total consumption is from time to time a sufficiently large share of Y. As soon as the wasteful forms of consumption cease to absorb a sufficient quantity of resources, the underconsumption breaks through. Only in periods in which investment is more than proportional, in other words if there are major industrialization phases (railroads, major new industries or simply large initial spurts of economic development) [handwritten insert: or when the capital/output coefficient worsens badly!], is it possible to dispense with wasteful consumption, to permit underconsumption to take its course.

All this has to be worked out in very precise and detailed terms to make the whole story watertight. I am kind of tempted to write an article criticizing *PEoG*, but maybe it would be preferable to let it go for a while, and to develop the whole thing anew in our opus. In that case what would seem to be indicated would be to do Part I (possibly as a first vol.) "The Theoretical Framework" which would actually lay the foundations for what would come later. What do you think? The fundamental difficulty is how does one demonstrate really well the inherent decline of "Good Consumption?" I have various ideas on that, but they are all kind of hazy. The manpower approach is probably the best!

Whatever comments you may have would be most welcome. If you think that I should try do such a piece of "self-criticism" — where could one print it? It would be kind of too technical and too heavy for MR. S&S [*Science & Society*]?

[...]

Tout a toi,

/s Paul

PMS to PAB

[*Written on* MR *Letterhead*]

May 14, 1957

Dear Paul,

[...]

The enclosed review by Joan, in my considered opinion, is a stinker, and I must say that I am both surprised and disappointed.[83] You seem to have needled her — probably the derogatory attitude toward her world and she is obviously getting back at you. But it is a petty performance on her part. The very best of Cambridge-Keynesian economists — and she is that — simply cannot surmount their environment. Actually, I'm afraid that goes for the whole U. S. and British profession. Oh well, *sub specie aeternitatis* things will look different.

One final point: we still are committed to publish the review of the Moore book, but it's too late for the June issue. Please don't forget it. But the main point is the Veblen. We really must have that or the special issue will be badly mutilated. After all, *The Theory of the Leisure Class is* a key book and it has to be included. So please don't let us down on that. *This should be your first priority task between now and June 1.*[84]

[...]

Love,

/s Paul

PAB to PMS

927 Mercedes Avenue
Los Altos, Cal.
May 20, 1957

Dear Paul.

[...]

The more I think about Chapters III and IV [the two chapters on "Monopoly Capitalism" in *The Political Economy of Growth*], the more I become convinced

83. Joan Robinson, "Policy of Backward Nations" (review of *PEoG*), *The Nation*, June 1957.
84. Special summer issue on Thorstein Veblen, *MR*, July–August 1957.

that they need the kind of a revision of which I wrote to you before. I really think that bourgeois economics not only does not help understanding matters but actually paralyzes one's ability to think. If instead of following the Keynesian procedure one would treat everything that is not productive investment as consumption, one would immediately realize the difference between "natural" consumption generated by the productive process and "makeshift" consumption artificially promoted in order to avoid the underconsumption situation. The economic surplus would become clearly visible as an *increasing share* of national output with the problem of its utilization equally visible as the central problem of the system. The way I treat it — accepting the constancy of the consumption share in Y — is analytically pernicious, because it really leaves the question open why there should be an overflow of surplus. All this must be straightened out in our opus. We have to start with a good, well-considered theoretical part explaining the mechanics of this whole business, and making it clear that bourgeois fetishism reaches so far that even most elementary statistical information cannot be taken at face value. If it is not possible to say anything reasonable about profits on the basis of published profit data, so it is not possible to say anything sensible about consumption on the basis of consumption statistics, or even wage statistics. All this has to be worked out, and I wonder what might be the best procedure for clarifying the whole thing in our minds. Maybe a systematic exchange of memo's would bring us a step further.

[...]

I think that I know now what I want to say about *The Theory of the Leisure Class*, and the problem "reduces" itself to saying it. If nothing catastrophic happens, you'll get the article in time.

Love,

/s Paul

PMS to PAB

[*Undated; probably May 20, 1957*]

Mon. a.m.

Dear Paul,

[...]

I haven't time for a proper answer to your letters re opus theory on May 11 and 12. But a few notes are in order while certain points are in mind.

There is no disagreement on the general substantive arguments, but my reaction to the idea of a preliminary or separate *Auseinandersetzung* [debate] with creators of harmonic models is distinctly negative. I do not believe that our crucial theses can be established by way of disputation with Tugan-Joan & Co.

They can only be established by way of analysis of the essence of the big business system. To put the matter in the smallest nutshell: our first job is to set up our own model which correctly reflects the real relations of the system, demonstrate its contradictions, and show how out of these contradictions there emerge the decisive surface phenomena of capitalist reality: waste, imperialism, armaments, cultural degradation, etc.

After this job has been done, but not until then, the confrontation with the neo-harmonikers can fruitfully take place. Hence I stick to something like the order of indicated in my "Six Lectures on American Capitalism" notes, of which you have the first four lectures:

(1) methodology (Marx brought up to date and made intelligible);

(2) the sociology of big biz (isolating the essential motor of the system);

(3) the interplay of prices, money wages, and technology (how the motor goes if left to itself);

(4) the rock-bottom tendency to rising surplus and chronic depression;

(5) the counteracting forces: (a) selling costs, (b) waste in production, (c) government;

(6) why government role takes the destructive path rather than the constructive (here comes the crucial battle with the "left-wing" Keynesians);

(7) the social, political, and cultural consequences;

(8) how all this compares and contrasts with the received orthodoxies.

Thus you see that what you propose to put first I think must come last. And my feeling is that we ought to start actual operations by your doing (1) and my doing (2) above.

I have just re-read the letters to compare with the foregoing, and I am more convinced than ever that there is perfect agreement on substance (to convince yourself of this, re-read my lecture notes and you will see the innumerable parallels). The difference is of procedure. You say that the "fundamental difficulty is how does one demonstrate really well the inherent decline of 'good consumption.'" The answer, I think, is clear: one shows what happens to a big biz model deprived of selling costs, wasteful methods of production, government orders for armaments, etc. Then one shows how and why these are necessary and how they are generated, not as *dei ex machinis* but out of the actual pressures and compulsions acting on the main classes and groups in the system.

I don't quite understand what you mean when you say that the "manpower approach is probably best" for demonstrating the inherent decline of good C. The inner dynamics have to do with wages, prices, and productivity, not with manpower in any sense that I can readily give to the term. However, if you mean that analyzing occupational trends is the best way of showing how these underlying tendencies leave their traces in the surface statistics, then I agree entirely. But the two problems — elucidating the dynamics and measuring the outward effects — should not be mixed up. Further, it must always be kept in mind that the most important effects are nothing more nor less than "the American way of life" which has statistical dimensions but cannot be forced into a statistical mold to satisfy the philistines of orthodoxy.

Next time you write, react specifically to the above outline and suggested *modus procedendi*. We need a new agreed outline and specific assignments so that the work of excavation and foundation building can get under way. I am taking on nothing beyond the Cole review and the Veblen stuff: as soon all that is attended to, opus comes next.[85] NB that Veblen *must* come first not only for me but also for you.

Love,
        /s Paul

[...]

PMS to PAB

                                                                        May 22, 1957
Dear Paul,
Yesterday's *Christian Science Monitor* contains what ought to become a classic remark in a piece by one Dr. Mischa H. Fayer, Professor of Russian at Middlebury College. Fayer is reporting on a trip to the USSR. He discovers that some university students are devoted to U.S. jazz. Then: "When I ribbed them that after all they were 'building socialism' and should not worry about such trifles as boogy-woogy, one of them replied: 'It is good to build socialism, but oh how wonderful it would be to live somewhere else while it is being built!'" I submit that there in a nutshell is the basic dilemma of the world today!
        Hastily,
            /s Paul

85. This refers to Sweezy's review article on G.D.H. Cole's three-volume *History of Socialist Thought*. See Paul M. Sweezy, "Professor Cole's History of Socialist Thought," *American Economic Review* 47, no. 6 (December 1957): 985–94.

PMS to PAB

Cambridge,
May 29, 1957

Memo:

To: PAB

From: PMS

Subject: Methodological Chapter

Be sure to read Veblen's 4-page introductory chapter to *The Theory of Business Enterprise*. Absolutely first rate and so far above the level of modern orthodox eoonomics that there is simply no comparison.

In fact, this is the only place that I know of where it is explained that big business is what is essential in modern capitalism, why it is essential, and hence why its analysis must be the core of a "theory of the modern economic situation."

What V is really calling for is a rigorous analysis of a stripped-down model of a big business economy. The pity is that he didn't follow up this insight and do the job *rigorously*. Instead, he contents himself with a very loose-jointed analysis which is often too amorphous even to be confidently pinned down. But here, as elsewhere, the insights are incredibly keen and profound.

PMS to PAB

Cambridge
June 8, 1957

Dear Paul,

You make some very good points in the Veblen piece[86] just received, but there are some changes which I hope you will make to protect yourself against justified criticism. (I do not mean criticism from respectable "Veblenites," let alone orthodox social scientists, but from, to be quite specific, people like Sol [Adler] and Arthur Davis who know their Veblen backwards and forward. I should add that I am not trying to use them as a cover: I think myself that the changes need to be made. I will be very brief in order to get this into the mail at once. I do not think the total amount of work involved is large, so that if you agree to make the changes you ought to be able to get them in the return mail a day or so after you get this letter. I return the ms herewith so that you can make sure any cuts or inserts are made at the right places.

1. The piece needs a footnote or insert in the text, probably at the end of the first paragraph, saying that it is based only on a re-reading of [Veblen's] *Leisure*

---

86. This refers to the initial draft of the piece eventually published as Paul A. Baran, "The Theory of the Leisure Class," *Monthly Review* 9, no. 3-4 (July-August 1957): 83–91.

Class and is not intended as an evaluation of Veblen's whole intellectual output. As you know, I have just finished reading *Business Enterprise* [BE] and *Absentee Ownership* [AO], and I found myself saying quite often as I read your ms: "But that isn't the position Veblen takes in BE and/or AO." In particular, I found the idea that Veblen idealizes the simple commodity producer quite incompatible with the line of the later books. There it is the technician and factory workman whom he idealizes, and he has some harsh things to say about the superstitions and values of the pre-capitalist artisan. I'm not saying you're wrong about *Leisure Class* which I haven't looked into since the 30s, but don't lay yourself open by generalizing from LC to all his books.

2. P. 2: Again, I can't say about *Leisure Class*, but I was astonished to read that "there is ample reason to believe . . . that Veblen thought of it [barbarism] as extending to his own days." It is true that he is vague about the matter (your criticism of his "historical" method in general is very sound), and it is also true that be finds many leftovers of barbarism among the determinants of the societal pattern of his own day. But this is something entirely different from what you say.

3. P. 2: I would not say that Veblen "flirted with historicism." The term is mostly known through the writings of such as Hayek and Popper, if I am not mistaken, and I can see no flirtation with what they mean by it in Veblen. You can fix this by just cutting the clause "while most persistently . . . historicism" out.

4. P.3: ". . . robbed him even of the chance to visualize clearly the *real similarities* of consecutive historical periods" is *much* too strong. He saw *many* such similarities very clearly, intuitively perhaps rather than because of his method of analysis, but see them he did. On the other hand, it is true that he didn't see *all* of them. But you should beware of trying to make a case by overstating it in a case like this: it lays you too open to crushing counterattack.

5. Pp. 3-4, your attack on Veblen's "economic determinism" is justified — sometimes. But there are also magnificent examples of a genuine and subtle kind of historical materialism — e.g. in *Imperial Germany and the Industrial Revolution* or in the so-called War Essays. Both are parts of the same man. You cannot attack one without giving credit for the other — unless you are going to insist that a writer must be *interpreted* as though he had been consistent and reduce him to the level of his poorest stuff. (What could be done with chaotic geniuses like Fourier, Owen, St. Simon, etc., on this principle of interpretation!)

6. In general, I think you attach too much importance to Veblen's use of such terms as "instincts" and "race." It was very common in his day (you will find quite a bit of racism, mostly derogatory to Slavs, in Engels, but it would never occur to me to stress it today), and on examination much of it turns out to be expressible in other terms. In this connection, [Joseph] Dorfman quotes an

exchange between Veblen and a real believer in "instincts" which shows quite clearly that he was far from being any sort of dogmatist. But here again, I readily admit that he was worse in LC than in the later books, and perhaps all you need to do is indicate an awareness of this.

7. P. 5: I have already mentioned above the matter of the idealization of the simple commodity producer.

8. P. 6: The cut at the bottom is to save space and because the comparison in the last sentence strikes me as malapropos: monuments, castles, etc., are not to feudalism what slavery is to Athenian society. The comparison should be between social relation and social relation, or between physical relic and physical relic. But it isn't necessary anyway.

9. NB insert near bottom of p. 7. Give the devil his due.

10. P. 9: Since I haven't read LC lately, I may be quite off the mark on this, but I would certainly never associate with Veblen a *general* condemnation of emulation, etc. You make him out to be a small-spirited petty shopkeeper with no appreciation of anything civilized. Actually, it isn't the kind of guy he was at all. However, I don't think any basic change is needed here to make your point, which is a good one. Instead of directly attributing to Veblen the views you want to criticize, you could simply put it in the form that such ideas as conspicuous consumption, waste, etc. readily lend themselves to this kind of misinterpretation or misuse in the hands of the unwary.

11. P. 10: Here you must surely make it explicit that you are not attributing to Veblen the view that "all the paintings, music, literature, architecture created in the course of millennia by the genius of mankind [are] nothing but a series of violations of the principle of frugality and productivity." He was really a very civilized man!

12. Last page: Again as throughout, I can't speak to LC, but the picture of Veblen presented here is cockeyed if judged by the evidence of BE and AO. (When you have time, read the concluding chapters of those two books, and you will quickly see what I mean.) He saw more clearly than any thinker in his generation that the alternative was "back to barbarism or forward to socialism," and he knew perfectly well that socialism (he even used the term sometimes) in the age of the machine had nothing in common with Paradise Lost.

13. Last page: I hope that you will reconsider and decide not to present the theory of increasing alienation in this offhand way. It is *certain* to be misunderstood. And I think that V probably came as close to understanding what you really want to say as anyone ever has. Far from wanting to stop technological progress and go backwards, he wanted to *unleash* it and follow it to its ultimate conclusion in a classless society of production for use.

14. Last page: the statement near the top — "that misery contains in itself the forces of its abolition" — is surely not true of the U.S., and it was of the U.S. that Veblen mostly wrote. You seem now to be going back on what you've been saying all along about the dilemma of the socialist movement in the advanced capitalist countries. Veblen was no great optimist, but who the hell is in this country and why should one be? Finally, the very last sentence sounds much too pat and out of the past to one reader at any rate. Lots of people have taken that "decisive step" without amounting to anything, and lots of people who never took it have contributed to shaping the world. The implications of Veblen — of his best work, which I value over his worst — are plenty revolutionary. It is for us to use them effectively, not to decry his reticence about their implications.

My brevity, I see, leaves something to be desired. Anyway, do what you think required in the light of these suggestions and caveats, and let me have the ms back as soon as possible. My main concern is that you should not lay yourself open to the criticism of your best friends.

If anything specific requiring consultation comes up, call me up collect, and it will go on the MR bill as part of the costs of the issue. Perhaps you'd better do that anyway and tell me as near as possible when I can expect to get the ms back. All the others are in hand now except Sol's and my own introduction, so the sooner the better.

Love,

/s Paul

PMS to PAB

Cambridge
June 9, 1957

Dear Paul,

I send you the enclosed draft of the editors' introduction (simultaneously with sending it for Leo's comments and additions) so that you can see the tone we intend to set for the issue. This does *not* mean that I want you to fall in line with it but only that I would like you to be able to take account of it.

A couple of points I forgot to mention in yesterday's letter:

(1) Somewhere, you call Veblen a "bourgeois thinker." I don't happen to think he was: he not only believed the bourgeois order to be transitory (Schumpeter believed that too), but he also believed it unworthy to survive (in which he was the opposite of Schumpy [Schumpeter]). But whether you are right or I am right needn't be debated, the point is that in the context it is a term of derogation which is out of place, and even more important it will strike many

readers as quite incongruous (like Pravda calling me a bourgeois economist: maybe I am but most people in this country don't know it).

(2) I had a feeling all the way through your paper that there was something wrong about your attribution to Veblen of the ideals of productivity and *frugality or abstemiousness*, but I couldn't think of how to express the matter better. (Productivity is okay, of course.) Frugality and abstemiousness both have a connotation of a desire to economize and save, not to spend something which one has available for spending. I don't think this was Veblen's attitude. What he was moved by, both in his personal life to judge from Dorfman's biography and in his social criticism, was a taste for simplicity, functionalism, and non-ostentation. He didn't care about having a big income out of which to save: he just wanted enough to live on simply. But Dorfman says somewhere that his wardrobe was well stocked and of good quality.

This suggests that there may have been a contradiction in Veblen's ideals: doesn't productivity logically imply bigger incomes and more and more costly consumption? Very possibly there was just such a contradiction, and that's the end of the matter. But I'm not sure and want to check in some of the later essays to see if he didn't have some positive ideas about what should be done with the fruits of greater productivity. I have a feeling that *The Engineers and the Price System* may have something on this matter. (By the way, the streak of technocracy which is specially strong in that book is, in my judgment, Veblen's greatest lapse. I'm glad to say that Arthur Davis takes him sharply to task for it in his essay.)

(3) Finally, one must remember in evaluating Veblen that he was a satirist and one must not take everything at face value. I have as little use as anyone for the view that he was primarily or wholly a satirist: this is the fashionable view nowadays. But the element should not be forgotten.

If possible, will you send back two corrected copies of your ms, one to Cambridge and one to NY? I may be leaving before you can get it back, in which case it would save at least a day to have the two copies sent simultaneously.

Love,

/s Paul

PAB to PMS

Stanford University
June 11, 1957

Dear Paul,
The "fixed" Veblen piece was mailed to you late last night, and this morning I received your letter of the 9th together with the Introduction. Reading both made me even more keenly aware than I was before of the difference in our basic

"feeling tone" about Veblen. To be sure, I have no strong views or emotions on that matter, in fact hate to argue about it since you obviously know and thought about it more than I ever did. The only thing that is clear is that there is not much more that I can do to "adjust" my article; it is quite impossible to change its *tone* piecemeal, and the way it stands now it has either to go or to be thrown away. And believe me, whichever way you decide is entirely agreeable to me.

As to the substance of the matter, we apparently disagree seriously on the general *locus* of Veblen in the history of thought. You consider him a socialist, a man on the Left, a writer whose "vision" was surpassed only by that of Marx. If I were to put my appraisal of him into a comparable nutshell, I would say that he was a radical all right but of the *"wild-gewordener Spiessbuerger"* [petit bourgeois gone wild] variety, with lots of brilliant insights but of the hunch type, in one word that he was in the ideological line of succession nearer to being a forebear of the Nazis than to representing a part of the socialist tradition. Indeed, his productivity cum frugality ideal, his psychology, his biology, his business vs. industry argument, his technocracy — all add up more to an intellectual profile reminiscent of Alfred Rosenberg and Gottfried Feder [both Nazi ideologues] rather than of Marx. The Nazis had all of this in their intellectual arsenal. They also spoke of races, instincts, of *Schaffendes gegen Raffendes Kapital* [productive vs. rapacious capital], they also said *"wenn ich das Wort Kultur hoere, entsichere ich meinen Revolver"* [When I hear the word "culture," I load my revolver]. Nor do I think is this similarity altogether fortuitous: the Nazis at their best were also radicals, were also anti-capitalist in a way, had also notions of socialism, planning, etc.

Please, don't misunderstand me: I am not saying or even suggesting that Veblen was *subjectively* anywhere near the Nazis, I am not saying or even suggesting that he wouldn't have abhorred them were he alive at the time of their advance to power. All I am trying to say is that by judging a man's objective performance, his objective place in the evolution of ideologies one should not judge him by what he thinks of himself, by his radicalism, or even by his intelligence and perspicacity. He must be judged by the kind of scientific-intellectual outlook that he represents, by the *mode* of his argument, by the implications of his philosophy etc. You could ask at this point, why then at all bother with Veblen? And my answer to this would be that one has to bother with Veblen precisely because he *looks* so close to socialism, *looks* so close to Marxism, because he represents the furthest-going position taken by petty-bourgeois protest. I would hold that he has to be analyzed in terms of dialectical materialism, rather than accepted "with reservations." This incidentally, refers also to your remark that he should not be called a "bourgeois" thinker. Needless to say, I do not care about the word. What matters, however, is again the same point: whether a man is or is not a bourgeois or any other kind of thinker does not depend on what he thinks he is, or for that matter on what the general public may think he is. Your example (*Pravda* on yourself) is unfortunate. It so happens that in this particular case the *Pravda* scribe was wrong. But he was wrong *not* because you don't consider yourself to be a bourgeois economist and because I don't think so and all of the country does not. He was wrong only if you are *objectively* not a bourgeois economist but a socialist economist. This is not a matter to be settled by a vote in which the object is permitted to cast his vote too. In fact, if this criterion were accepted, if the opinion of the man of himself or even the opinion of lots of other people of him were decisive, neither Eduard Bernstein nor Proudhon, neither Tugan-Baranovski nor Henri George would qualify as bourgeois thinkers. But they were! Veblen no doubt hated the capitalist system and considered it to be transitory; this still would be wholly compatible with his being a bourgeois thinker if his entire mode of thought, his set of philosophical concepts became part and parcel of a bourgeois ideology. And interestingly enough this is precisely what happened. All such notions as conspicuous consumption, pecuniary emulation etc. corresponding as they do to the innermost feelings of a frustrated petty bourgeois have become integral parts of the "progressive" muck-raking type liberal social science.

To repeat: I do not maintain that my way of looking at the matter is correct, and that yours is wrong. All I submit is that my way of looking at it is a *possible* way, and perhaps even a way more in keeping with the "tradition." But the tradition may be wrong, I may be wrong in interpreting it, and — in any case — pay no attention to all of this if you don't feel like it!

[…]

So much for today.

Love,

    s/ Paul

PMS to PAB

                                                June 13, 1957

Dear Paul,

The Veblen problem raises some very interesting questions which we should not let drop but which I haven't the time to tackle at the moment. Basically, of course, it's a problem where the "total" judgment, as it were, comes first and largely determines the weight to be given to various matters of detail. I suppose it's always that way in interpreting intellectual history, but this just happens to be a very clear case. Anyway, I continue to think my general position is right without in any way wanting to be dogmatic about it. Your revised ms reduces what I considered to be the vulnerability of the first draft, and will add interest to the issue. I never considered leaving it out because it doesn't agree with the editorial line of course.

Do you have any objection to my sending your letter of Tuesday to Sol? His reaction should be interesting and useful: he has been a collector of Vebleniana for many years and has a high regard for the man, but he is of course much brighter (and a better Marxist) than Davis. I have been trying for quite some time to persuade Sol to do the full-length study of V that I think is needed and which I think he is better equipped than anyone else to undertake. The correspondence might spur him into action.

[...]

All for now,
       /s Paul

P.S. I opened up the envelope to jot down two points for later consideration, the points which I consider to be decisive against your theory of an affinity between Veblen on the one hand and Feder et al on the other. (Naturally, there is *some* affinity — between Marxists and Feder too — but I mean *au fond*).

(1) Veblen's hostility to private property was by no means confined to the financial variety: it was to absentee ownership *en generale* which he defined in almost exactly the same way that Marx defined capital. His treatment of the financial element in *Absentee Ownership* is 100% orthodox Hilferding-Lenin.

(2) Veblen's absolutely consistent anti-nationalism, and his profound understanding that whenever the system gets into trouble it has recourse to "national politics." It was on the basis of these insights, or whatever you want to call them, that he saw through the German Social Democrats long before Lenin did, and that he immediately recognized the Bolsheviks as the true bearers of the revolutionary tradition. It is a pretty good and safe principle that the sheep can be separated from the goats by their respective attitudes toward the Russian Revolution. Measure Veblen by this yardstick and you will find that he emerges several heads taller than the vast majority of those belonging to the organized socialist movement (and I include all segments in that generalization)! Think it over!

PAB to PMS

[*No provenance*]

[Palo Alto]
June 17th, 1957

Dear Paul,

The news about the Supreme Court is superb[87] — my most cordial congratulations on a terribly important victory! It should actually turn a new leaf in the whole business of witch-hunting; more people may find strength to invoke the First rather than the Fifth Amdmt. I wish I could raise a glass of something nice and chilly in honor of the occasion, in particular since it is subhumanly hot. . . .

[. . .]

As far as the Veblen issue itself is concerned, I have ever more the feeling that what matters in this — as in many similar instances are *nuances,* one might almost say shades of philosophical doctrine that distinguish one position from another. To overlook those and to concentrate on the more "bulky" parts of the story is frequently most misleading. If you try to think out the differences between Marxism on one side, and positivism and pragmatism on the other — you will also find lots of similarities. The crux of the thing, however, is in the "tiny" differences which when followed through in their implications account for the entire hiatus between bourgeois social sciences and Marxism. Lenin's greatness was perhaps less in the way in which he wrote *Empiriocriticism* but in his grasping the essentiality (because far-reaching implications) of the problem. . .

[. . .]

It's over 90 degrees in my chalet and more outside. California climate . . .

Yours prostrate,

/s Paul

PMS to PAB

Cambridge
June 21, 1957

Dear Paul,

A quickie to bring matters up to date. The Court decision, having made me into something of a celebrity for a few days (showing once again how little one's own efforts have to do with such matters!), has added to the burdens on my time — pleasurably to be sure, but none the less noticeably.

---

87. *Sweezy vs. New Hampshire*, 354 U.S. 234 (1957).

[...]

No time now for more on the Veblen question. I have a feeling that the basic problem in a case of this kind may be more one of strategy than of doctrine. Both positive and negative elements are present (never mind the proportions just now), and the question is can one make use of and absorb the positive without being corrupted and/or overwhelmed by the negative. When a new corpus of ideas is struggling to establish itself, it has to guard its own purity and fight against the similar more energetically than against the obviously hostile. Hence the vigor of Engels' attack on Duehring, of Lenin's polemic against the positivists, etc. You would treat Veblen in this tradition. My argument would be that times change and we should change with them. There is no danger of Veblen corrupting the world socialist movement any longer, and there is much relating to the special and enormously important case of U.S. capitalism that can be got from him. All of which argues for a basically positive attitude combined with a firm exposure of errors and correction of weaknesses. As I think I mentioned in one of my latest letters, I am trying to persuade Sol to undertake a full-dress review of the whole Veblen problem. He obviously has the right combination of qualities to do a good job. His initial reaction is that he would love to but can't afford the time. If you ever have any ideas about how he might be subsidized for the duration please pass them on to me.

[...]

Yrs.,

/s Paul

PAB to PMS

927 Mercedes Avenue
Los Altos, California
July 21st, 1957

Dear Paul,

I have read and re-read a couple of times the attached lecture notes, and have come to the (tentative) conclusion that there seems to be a certain not substantive but procedural disagreement between us. To wit: it is my feeling that what is required is not merely an analysis of the working principles of the American BB [big business] economy, but a study focused on the questions that are in the center of people's interest at the present time. Those questions, if I understand the situation correctly are: (a) what is the quality of performance of American capitalism; to what extent is the system capable of furthering the health and happiness of American people; (b) what are the prospects for American capitalism to provide for full employment, economic growth and development of productive resources; (c) how is the situation in the U.S. linked up with the developments in the outside world (imperialism, etc.).

If this is right, then the proper *modus procedendi* is to start with those questions and to say that in order to answer them such and such knowledge is needed. And faithful to the fundamental tradition of Marxism, the operation has to be conducted throughout critically, that is in continual *Auseinandersetzung* [distinguishing from] with the prevailing doctrine.

If one begins the way the lectures do, one tends to beg the issue, and is liable to be confronted with the question, so what? Assume that all we say about the changing role of BB [big business], about its price policies and output policies and polities with regard to technology, assume that all of this is right — what follows from it? Do not misunderstand me: I do not mean to say that you do not address yourself to the principal question; I have merely the feeling that you do it in an indirect kind of a way, more by implication than by squarely facing it. Thus e.g. the IAA [top-priority] question why there is a tendency in the system to generate more and more surplus is neither properly asked nor anywhere properly answered. The existence of that tendency is merely asserted and then repeatedly referred to. In connection with it a statement is made which, indeed, represents the "nerve center" of the whole thing: "Upshot: a tendency for the producers' share to decline and the surplus (= total product - producers' share) to rise." (Lecture III, point 2. — I do not think that the reasons for this assertion nor its tremendous significance are fully explained: Or rather, are placed in the right perspective: no *full* explanation is obviously expected in these lecture notes.

To put all of this in different terms: I think that the exposition should start with the questions above or something like them. It should proceed with the statement that the defenders of the capitalist system have asserted always in one form or another that capitalism (a) provides for welfare and (b) can generate full employment, growth etc. Harmony models and what they actually assume (and their ideological function!!!). This is all wrong. In actual fact the producers' share *does* decline, but this calls for extensive discussion and qualifications: *truly* productive workers receive a declining share. Therefore surplus has a tendency to grow (as share of income). This tendency counter-acted by various developments, but primarily by expansion of unproductive consumption which becomes *institutionalized*. What could not be done under competition (or at least not in the same measure) becomes natural under monopoly capitalism. Costs need not be minimized if nobody minimizes them. And here comes in on a broad front sociology and morphology of BB, its policies with regard to prices, output and investment etc., etc. By the way, an interesting point: in the Joint Committee study, also in latest BW [Business Week], worry is expressed about the more favorable capital/output ratio; could there be a more manifest proof of the system's craziness than unhappiness about such a development?

Thereafter the resulting imperialist consequences, state and all and after that the entire cultural mess. I would entirely agree with you that we should go out of the way of all cyclical stuff, I share your suspicion that the whole biz-cycle affair may be a huge trap which even KM [Karl Marx] was unable to escape, that in reality there has been through the entire history of capitalism a continual tendency towards depression and stagnation, a tendency from time to time counteracted and frustrated by various "exogenous" forces. Difference between this and Schumpeter & Co: the frustrated tendency was *not* one towards stationary state and slow expansion, but towards depression!

What do you think of all this? What this approach would call for is essentially the adherence to the original Chicago-Outline (copy attached!) except for (a) addition of a longish theoretical chapter in the beginning and (b) some re-ordering of the material. Class distribution of income etc. must be tackled in a preliminary way right at the outset so as to get at the surplus notion. Incidentally, I do not think, one can get a wage theory of any kind without reference to demand for labor i.e. capital accumulation. Cf. your lecture # 2, point 4 — Accumulation etc. must be treated, however, first of all in the surplus context.

I would very much like to have your reaction to this, and then attempt to draw up a new tentative outline. It would seem to me that once the marching orders are clearly formulated we should be able to proceed fairly rapidly with the production of drafts. For at the moment the marching orders are still hazy.

So much for the time being; more upon receipt of your answer.

Love,

/s Paul

PS. […]

PAB to PMS

Stanford University

July 29, 1957

[…]

I wrote to Leo in response to his inquiry that I am at the moment kind of "obsessed" with the idea of doing a little book (30-40 thousand words) on Marx — An Essay on Marx — somewhat on the lines of my April MR-Association talk in N.Y. All sorts of ideas on the subject float through my head, and I have a strong feeling that I have to get the stuff out of my system. If I weren't what I am but a decently functioning individual the whole biz should be feasible within a few months. As it is, it all bothers me no end, I read, make notes, jot down all kinds of ideas that strike me as interesting, but cannot settle down to serious work. This stuff, incidentally, is closely related to the methodology and philosophy of our opus, and for me personally writing it all down and thinking it out in the process would constitute a major step towards *Selbstverstaendigung*. More on that later.[88]

More soon,

/s Paul

PMS to PAB

Tuesday a.m.

[*probably* August 6, 1957]

Dear Paul,

[…]

I have been thinking a bit about all the inflation talk that has been spouting out of all quarters lately. Isn't the most obvious "explanation" that for the first time ever capitalism — thanks mainly to arms and more efficient waste than ever before, backed by a conscious full-employment policy in some countries where the labor movement is politically strong — has maintained a reasonably high level of demand for a reasonable number of years running? (Without the maintenance of demand, neither the corporations nor the unions could exercise all the pushes and pulls people chatter so much about.) But if this is so, isn't the present inflationary atmosphere merely the other side of the chronic depression coin which up to World War II was the normal currency in the capitalist world? And if this is so, doesn't the whole interpretation of recent economic history (say, since the early 19th. century) need to be drastically reinterpreted? And shouldn't the reinterpretation take place around a theory which (a) relegates the so-called business cycle to either a very minor place or else scraps it altogether, and (b) assumes that depression is the equilibrium state of the economy disturbed only by extraneous factors such as major technological discoveries, opening new territories to exploitation, wars, etc.? Goddamn it, I'm afraid we ought to write not only a theory of monopoly capitalism but also a whole new history of capitalism!

More soon,

/s Paul

88. A reference to Marx's 1859 "Preface to a Critique of Political Economy" where he refers to leaving *The German Ideology* to the "gnawing criticism of the mice," and that it had served its purpose in promoting "self-criticism." Karl Marx, *A Contribution to a Critique of Political Economy* (Moscow: Progress Publishers, 1970), 22.

PAB to PMS

> 927 Mercedes Avenue
> Los Altos, California
> August 10th, 1957

Dear Paul,

[...]

(2) I am *tout d'accord* with what you say about inflation. I was also thinking about this stuff lately and wondered about the following points: (a) with gov't spending as important as it is, some inflation is inevitable even if they match spending with revenues — unit multiplier effect of the balanced budget! — (b) with the gov't spending being directed continually towards unproductive purposes — i.e. not leading to the output of marketable goods and services an inflationary effect would seem to be inevitable; but most importantly perhaps (c) does not the inflationary spiral become to some extent a function of the monopolization and oligopolization of the economy? This relates directly to our old problem of *shifting*! Under competitive conditions increased demands for wages or rising raw material prices need not always but tend to be at least partly absorbed by profits; under mono and oligo conditions they are immediately shifted on to the buyer. I haven't fully thought it out, but have a feeling that there is something to it. [handwritten insert: and giant unions with whom mono and oligo biz prefer to maintain "partnership relations."]

[...]

Expect to speak to you early next week ...

Love,

/s Paul

PAB-PMS

[Handwritten]

> Moscow
> August 29th, 1957

Dear Paul,

By the time this will reach you, you will be probably back in Cambridge. I hope you had a pleasant time in the Vineyard with a lot of rest and diversions. When I arrived here my father was in a hospital. He came home a few days later and is now around the house, half bed-ridden, very weak and very old. While hanging around here is thus anything but a pleasure, I am glad that I did not decide to skip the expedition. He does not look very durable to me!

The general *Stimmung* [mood] here is very much "more of the same." There is a noticeable relaxation everywhere and also a marked improvement in living conditions. Supplies in shops are plentiful and matters have undoubtedly gone a step forward even by comparison with last year. I saw a few economists; interestingly enough those working on *domestic* problems are very much more aware, very much more open-minded than those blockheads who deal with international economic problems. The latter are now concentrated in a newly created Institute for World Economics and International Relations; what one hears there could have been equally said 5 or 10 years ago. They do not understand anything, work with completely outdated notions and have absolutely no "feeling" for the capitalist economy. Conversations with them are highly unrewarding — except perhaps for the fact they demonstrate beyond possible doubt that nothing can be expected from here when it comes to the study of monopoly capitalism.

PEoG has had an extremely favorable reception among a number of people and its translation into Russian seems to be assured. They are willing to pay for it 20,000 rubles; currently $5000, but the chances of getting $$ are very slim. . . . I am still "working" in an attempt to induce them to send at least a part of the money in $$, but, as I said, I am not too optimistic. On Sunday Sept 8th I am leaving for Warsaw, on 12th to 15th for Paris, and on Thursday the 19th, I expect to be back in N.Y., to stay there overnight getting to SF on Saturday, 21st.

Looking over my old books sitting here (there are books that I read and cherished when I was in High School) I found a marked up volume of Selections from Goethe. Therein the following two passages thickly underscored:

(1) *"In der jetzigen Zeit soll niemand schweigen oder nachgeben; man muss reden und sich ruehren, nicht um zu ueberwinden, sondern sich auf seinen Posten zu erhalten; ob bei der Majoritaet oder Minoritaet, ist ganz gleichgueltig."*

["In the present time, no one should remain silent or surrender; one must speak and motivate oneself, not to overcome, but to maintain one's position; whether with the majority or the minority, makes no difference."]

(2) *"Man muss sein Glaubensbekenntnis von Zeit zu Zeit wiederholen, aussprechen was man billigt, was man verdammt das Gegenteil laesst's ja auch nicht daran fehlen."*

["One has to review one's belief system from time to time, express what one supports, but at the same time don't neglect what one condemns."]

I cannot think of anything more timely. You could stick it as a space filler in an issue of *MR*.

Will I see you in NY on the 19th, or towards the end of the month at
Stanford? The urgency of our opus becomes doubly clear around here!
   Love,
      /s Paul

P.S. [...]

PAB to PMS

[*Handwritten*]

Warsaw
September 10, 1957

Dear Paul,
Had a number of conversations with local economists and the like — it would
be a major exaggeration to say that one emerges from them particularly elated.
The general temper is somewhere between "revisionism" and "liquidatorism,"
and a Western socialist is looked upon with a certain sense of curiosity. Making
money, working for a stockbroker firm and giving no more than a damn for
social questions would strike them as the very much better part of wisdom.
It ain't encouraging at all! A perfectly phantastic trend towards *buergerliche
Vereinsamung* [bourgeois isolation] with the accent heavily placed on private
affairs in a frantic desire to *live* better, to *have* things. The American way of life
looks awfully [good, well?] at this distance, and the American impact on the
structure of wants may be a larger "secret weapon" than anything else. Lots of
things wander through one's mind, and I am very much looking to seeing you
soon and talking these things over. We become "zoological" phenomena! Is
everyone except Sammy [Samuelson] out of step?
   Am leaving first thing tomorrow morning.
   All the best.
   Love, Yours
      /s Paul

PAB to PMS

[*Handwritten*]
Hotel Lutetia Boulevard Raspail, Paris
September 11th, 1957

Dear Paul,
Re-emerging in the West from "socialism" and "underdevelopment" causes
a sense of relief that is hard to describe and hard to exaggerate. I know, it is
a very "touristy" and very bourgeois approach to [matters?], and the toiling

masses here are in parts at least no better off than there (etc., etc.) — but still
— Compared with the God-awful mess that has overtaken that other world,
even "*der Untergang der Abendlaender*" looks mightily attractive [the decline
of the West]. Interestingly enough the only person who has *not* lost his sense
of proportion, who is *now* at the height of his intellectual and moral power is
Kalecki (my admiration and respect for that embodiment of talent and integrity
has grown immensely during those few days in Warsaw!) — while the Stalinists
present a repulsive picture of a disintegrating morassmus, and while the Lange's
have become completely [unreadable] opportunists and corruptivists. — It is all
upsetting beyond words and disheartening and miserable —

The best thing would be to have money, to stay *sous les tois des Paris ou les
jeunes filles sint jolies*, to drink Courvoisier and to devote oneself to the study of
literature — For I cannot get rid of the feeling that the whole thing is going to pot
not with a bang but with a whimper. —

I shall spend the week-end with the Bettelheims in the country and will leave
for N.Y. (probably) on Wednesday. I'll try to get on a plane going via Boston; if
you will be there, I'll stop, if not I'll go on to N.Y. Could you send me a wire on
that or have you written about it already?

Tout a toi,

/s Paul

PAB to PMS

Los Altos, California
October 7th, 1957

Dear Paul,

[...]

I have been going through stuff on industrial concentration (my course is
on Economics of Industry, as you may remember) and am deeply impressed
with the chaotic state of that literature. Depending on what you read, you get
diametrically opposite views of the state of matters. The disagreements are
not on details, they affect the central theme. Some argue that the economy
is effectively controlled by no more than 200 corporations, others claim that
nothing of the sort is true, that we have now *more* competition than ever before,
etc. I have the feeling that one has to cut through this entire maze, leave alone
the whole hopeless concentration debate, forget about the "market controls"
and such and go right into the question of the *dominant* sector of the economic
system. Otherwise one gets all the time into the situation like this: plenty,
indeed excessive competition in the toilet paper market, minimal competition in
chemicals — workable competition on the average! This is all sheer obfuscation,

but to show it for what it is we have to do a certain amount of debunking work; for this lots of stuff has to be read.

When it comes to increase of waste and unproductive labor, matters are even harder. Occupational statistics are tough to deal with; what is required is continual exercise of "arbitrary" judgment. The same with output "sorting." It is clear that a "Cerulean mink jacket with rhinestone trim ($250 up)" for dogs (*Bus. Week*, September 28th, 1957, p. 170) is hardly to be considered good utilization of resources but how does one get out of the example and illustration stage into more or less precise demonstration? There certainly is no lack of examples and illustrations . . .

[. . .]

The Russki's latest performance in re: satellite [Sputnik] is quite something! Whatever there is to be said about lots of things there — productive forces have been developing at an unprecedented rate! And somehow I don't believe that if it were simply "oriental despotism" this would have been possible! The forces of socialism and planning and rationalism were and are even stronger than Stalin + OGPU — in the final reckoning what will be remembered is the former and not the latter . . .

More later.

Love,

/s Paul

PAB to PMS

Stanford University

October 9th, 1957

Dear Paul,

[. . .]

I have read with great pleasure and profit your very, very nice paper on Veblen.[89] While I obviously cannot pretend to dispute your *interpretation* (and account) of what he said, (you know him so very much better than I do!), I would like to raise a few points which are marginal to the report on Veblen's views.

(1) I think that you go over too lightly the theme of technological progress (pp. 6 & 7). Regarding technological knowledge as an attribute and possession of the community as a whole, and its increase as a social process obeying its own logic and taking place automatically is (a) a terrible weakness of Veblen's

---

89. PAB is referring to PMS's chapter "Veblen on American Capitalism" in Douglas F. Dowd, ed., *Thorstein Veblen; A Critical Reappraisal* (Ithaca, New York: Cornell University Press, 1958), 177-97.

and (b) as un-Marxian as it could be! Indeed, if I understand it right, the entire kernel of Marxian dialectic is contained in the relation between the development of productive forces (technology etc.) and the evolution of productive relations. They interact! The businessman is *not* perennially hampering technological progress, the engineer is *not* perennially advancing it! In certain historical situations precisely the opposite is true! To assign independence and automaticity to the technological process is both idealist and metaphysical; this is what H.B. Acton (*The Illusion of the Epoch*) accuses Marx of, although Marx was never guilty of that kind of "deviation." Accepting this position amounts to espousing some kind of a Hegelian conflict between the *Geist* of technology and the *Geist* of business which is sheer "speculation." And indeed to Veblen it was something of the sort: instinct of workmanship vs. predatory instincts, *Schaffendes Kapital vs. Raffendes Kapital* (Gottfried Feder) — this is as far from Marxism as *Der Untergang des Abendlandes* ["Decline of the West," Oswald Spengler, 1918] from the *Communist Manifesto*. Now, to be clear, I do not quarrel with your exposition of Veblen's views; it is probably entirely accurate. I do think, however, that at least one paragraph or a longish footnote is needed setting off those views against the Marxist concepts!

(2) On p. 13 you say that Marx thought of the conflict of interest between capitalist and worker as turning *exclusively* around the division of the product between wages and surplus value. This is really not true and most unfair to the old man. He in fact never tired to inveigh against the anarchy of capitalist production, against capitalism's inability to make full use of the available productive potentialities, against its keeping output quantitatively and qualitatively below the potential! And by stressing that labor by struggling against capital struggles for the interests of society *as a whole*, he left no room for misunderstanding his position that it was not merely a redistribution of a given output between capital and labor, but a reorganization of the entire social process of production and therefore a change in the size and composition of that output that matters. Your sentence as cited above would really bring Marx down to the Meany's and the Strachey's, and he did not do anything to deserve that fate! Here I really must "insist" on your changing the formulations for coming from *you* they are inadmissible!

(3) The nationalism business leaves me in a state of uneasiness. A minor point first: didn't Hobson have it all very nicely before Veblen? (Your tribute of Veblen on p. 22 notwithstanding!) But more important: the general condemnation of nationalism is a very dangerous business — here lies the reason why, I think, one should be terribly careful in condemning *imperialism* rather than *nationalism*! For aren't all imperialist writers (conscious or unconscious)

up in arms against *nationalism* even where that nationalism is a distinctly
progressive force, a force against national subjugation by an imperialist power?
There is nothing the matter with the nationalism of the weak, there is everything
the matter with the nationalism of the strong! That this thing keeps shifting
all the time, is in a continual dialectical movement is true, but one should not
"throw out the child with the bathwater" and endorse a general anti-nationalist
position. The Czechs in the Austro-Hungarian monarchy were nationalists and
the Indians today, and the Latin Americans vs. the U.S. and so forth and so on
— let's not get into the situation of condemning an u/d [underdeveloped] or a
weak capitalist country because in a "nationalist" spirit it kicks out a British or
an American oil company! You could tell me that Veblen had clearly not u/d c's
in mind but the U.S. or G.B. This is undoubtedly true, but it is precisely for that
reason that imperialism is a better notion than nationalism. Here both Hobson
and Hilferding or even Brailsford are much better, and I think it would be worth
pointing out that difference in a paragraph or footnote.

(4) On p.17 you kind of endorse Veblen's assigning to nationalism the role
of the *crucial* instrument used by the vested interests to control the underlying
population. Do you really want to go that far? Wouldn't it be more accurate to say
that nationalism is an important element in the ideology formation of capitalism
with other elements perhaps no less significant and perhaps at times even more
so? Religion? Property? Law and Order? And incidentally, don't we witness a
process which may actually point in the opposite direction: "cosmopolitanism"
turned *against* nationalism, with the former becoming increasingly the ideology
of the imperialist haves against the nationalist have-nots?

I don't disagree by any means with your generally pessimistic conclusions
(second paragraph of your letter), except again I am worried about too much
"psychologizing." When it comes to capitalist countries including the U.S. the
roots of the trouble are after all not "bad habits of thought and behavior" but the
objective stability of the system. Assume for a minute that the 30's would return
in the 50's and 60's — quite a few habits of thought would begin changing and
changing rapidly. The irony or rather tragedy of history is that the bad habits .
. . have become a real curse to the socialist countries! That is where they must
be assigned an almost autonomous significance in hampering development.
And it is perhaps there where KM was much too optimistic by considering
human nature a hell of a lot more plastic than it actually is, and by believing that
those birth marks of the old society will disappear pdq. Well, all this is for your
consideration, make of it and with it what you please; I *do* believe that those
points are worth clarification in the paper.

I am glad that you'll be off on Nov. 1 — the trip will refresh you and pick you up. Lorie told me that I can get travel money for the Philadelphia meetings which means that I'll probably fly over. When do you expect to be back? But we'll correspond before then. . . .

So much for today.

Love,

s/ Paul

PMS to PAB

Cambridge, Mass.
October 14, 1957

Dear Paul,

[. . .]

I agree that the industrial organization field is in a state of chaos, and unfortunately rather low-level chaos at that. (Vide, e.g., Watkin's review of Mason's latest book in the AER.[90] W has little difficulty in making M look weak, but W makes himself look even weaker. But of one thing I am sure: we cannot allow ourselves to get bogged down in this swamp. We must take *our* stand on this whole set of issues and move resolutely on. Your predilection for proceeding via polemics against established positions is okay *if there are firm positions to polemicize against*. But to enter into, and attempt to settle, disputes among the orthodox priests is an entirely different — and for our enterprise fatal — matter.

In re Veblen I will get to the revising when I return from NY at the end of this week. Meanwhile just a few comments on your points:

1. My paper is not intended as a critique of Veblen but as an exposition, with just enough critique at the end to "explain" how it happens that his theory is so relevant in some ways and yet misses many of the most obvious developments of the last few decades.

2. I agree that Veblen's theory of technological progress is in need of thorough criticism, but one would have to study *The Instinct of Workmanship* carefully before attempting the job, and I haven't looked at it in years. For the purposes of my paper, the matter is not crucial.

3. I will soften the point about Marx having made the class struggle turn exclusively around the division of the product, though I think that for M the other weaknesses of capitalism were at bottom secondary to and derived from this division of the product, and to this extent cannot be treated as independent

---

90. The reference is to Myron Watkins's review of Edward S. Mason's *Economic Concentration and Monopoly* in the *American Economic Review* 47, no. 5 (September 1957): 747–53.

counts of an indictment. However, again the point is of no great moment for this paper, and there is no reason for raising a controversial issue in that context.

4. On nationalism, I have no intention or desire either to praise or blame it in the paper. I am trying to report the position it occupies in Veblen's system. But since you raise the question, I would not agree that V's position implies any necessary condemnation of the force of nationalism *in general*. For him, it is the modern form of the feeling of group solidarity (i.e. the historically predominant form). He not only admits but insists that this sentiment once played a positive role in enabling the group to survive, and there is no reason at all why he couldn't take the same view of the nationalism of the u-d [underdeveloped] peoples. As it happens he was talking about the nationalism of the advanced imperialist countries exclusively, and no one who reads him with any attention can be under any misapprehension on the matter.

5. As to the force of nationalism in the modern world, I can only say that I think he was much nearer right than the old-fashioned Marxists. And I think he was also right that it is what enables the ruling class to manage the workers of the advanced countries so easily. Religion, law, and property all break down quickly enough in the face of prolonged depression* and none can be used to support an effective anti-depression policy [handwritten footnote: *Note that they don't disappear, however. They come back to cause trouble again when conditions of life return more nearly to normal.] Nationalism does *not* break down, and lends itself to the cold war witch hunt maneuvers which (in my judgment) have been the saving of the U.S. ruling class and its world. So far. To be sure, it doesn't take care of the basic and long-run contradictions, but that's another story. (Incidentally, Veblen himself didn't use the word nationalism much, if at all; but there's no good quarreling over terminology.)

6. Your point about cosmopolitanism replacing nationalism in the ideology of the imperialist powers has only a very restricted validity. Cosmopolitanism is for the eggheads, crude nationalism-cum-chauvinism for the masses. The division of clientele and labor is very neatly illustrated throughout post-WW II U.S. history: Vandenberg for the eggheads, McCarthy for the masses, etc., etc.

7. You are right that the stubbornness of habits is a terrible curse to the socialist countries. But it couldn't become such unless it had existed under capitalism and every earlier form of society. In other words, it *is* a trait of human nature (an invariable of human conduct) that people don't change their ways *quickly*, and this is precisely what makes history the cruelest of goddesses, to quote Engels. On this point, Marxists have always (and perhaps necessarily) been overoptimistic. I am afraid Veblen was not too pessimistic.

8. Your objection to the above: "Assume for a minute that the 30s would return in 50s and 60s — quite a few habits of thought would begin changing and changing rapidly!" is beside the point. Habits of course are of very varying stubbornness, and it is only the most deeply rooted that resist change over decades or centuries. But the real point is that the 30s do not return precisely because the national feeling of the U.S. masses can be played upon in such a way as to make them enthusiastic supporters of an obviously suicidal foreign and arms policy. This is what gives the system its "objective stability," and it is in this sense that nationalism is the key to the whole business. If you object that this explanation relies too much on "psychologizing," I would make two replies: (1) so in a sense does the whole Marxian theory of capitalism: the overwhelming force of the urge to make profits is neither more nor less rational, neither more nor less psychologistic than the overwhelming power of national sentiment; and (2) how can you explain the success of cold war and witch hunt without psychologizing? I wouldn't be afraid of the word or the idea — the only question is whether the theory explains better than any other, and whether it is subject to investigation by ordinary scientific methods.

But enough of that for the present. As you can see, I am neither thinking very clearly nor typewriting correctly!

[...]

Love,

    /s Paul

P. S. [...]

4
The Search for a Method

[1958]

PAB to PMS

Los Altos, California
January 28, 1958

Dear Paul,

Haley gave me yesterday the attached proofs of Nicky Kaldor's review of *PEoG*.[91]
It is obviously terribly nice of Haley to invite such a prominent reviewer to
do this job and to give him such a lot of space; it is also most gratifying from
the standpoint of circulation etc. to get such a long and thorough review in
the *AER*.[92] The review itself is the first reaction of a highly qualified pro, and I
must admit that he — being undoubtedly very bright — has put his finger on
the one spot in the book about which I have felt all the time quite uneasy. And
nevertheless I am convinced, having thought about it for 24 hours, that Kaldor
is fundamentally wrong, that the position taken in *PEoG* is fundamentally right
except that the thing is there inadequately handled. I think the whole problem
is most important — whether we like it or not, we have to face up to it in the
Buechlein [the "opus"]. I think, I wrote to you about it earlier — am too lazy
now to try to find a carbon of the relevant letter — but let me try to restate the
problem.

91. Bernard F. Haley was editor of *The American Economic Review*, 1952–1962.
92. Nicholas Kaldor, "The Political Economy of Growth by Paul A. Baran," *American Economic
Review*, 48, no. 1 (1958):164–70. Kaldor's review of *The Political Economy of Growth* was
regarded by Baran (and Sweezy) as the major challenge to Baran's concept of surplus. Kaldor's
criticisms were answered in the second printing of *The Political Economy of Growth* and this
played a major role in the evolution of the surplus concept between the framework offered in *The
Political Economy of Growth* to that of *Monopoly Capital*. See Paul A. Baran, *The Political Economy
of Growth* (New York: Monthly Review Press, 1962), xviii–xxv; John Bellamy Foster, *The Theory of
Monopoly Capitalism* (New York: Monthly Review Press) 14–15, 35.

It has become habit now with the Cambridge economists (and not only with them alone) to go back way behind Keynes and to smuggle through a side door Say's Law into the picture again. This is done in the following manner: given that the share of labor is constant and given that the capital/output coefficient is constant and given that capitalists' consumption is a constant share of profits — why shouldn't there be a perpetual merry-go-round? As productivity increases, income increases and as income increases consumption increases *pari passu* [hand-in-hand] and as consumption increases, investment has to increase *pro tanto* [to the same extent]. Matters would be disagreeable if capitalists' consumption or workers' consumption were *declining* shares of their respective incomes. Then only a worsening of the capital/output coefficient would help. Otherwise trouble even in that model (which, incidentally is essentially Tugan-Baranovsky's scheme).[93] Now, I am of the view that all of this is sheer poppycock. In the first place (this is not the most important argument) labor's share could be constant with surplus at the same time increasing (contrary to what NK [Nicholas Kaldor] says): via squeezing the middle class, the peasants, the white collar workers et al as a result C [Consumption] as a proportion of Y [income] could decline (as it indeed does!) — Much more important, however, for this merry-go-round to function the economy has got to get like the Sputnik into its prescribed (full employment) orbit and continually, uninterruptedly *stay there*. The moment it gets off that orbit for whatever reason (excess capacity in period I when the BB[big business]-boys got exuberant and therefore drop in investment in period II when the BB-boys got despondent) there is no mechanism whatever in action to bring it back into that orbit! This is of paramount importance, indeed this is the sum total of the Keynesian insight!

Now the Tobin's Patinkin's *et tutti quanti* [and all the rest] drag out the famous Pigou effect (or rather an entire family of the Pigou effects) and argue that once the Sputnik is off, prices will fall, liquid assets will appropriately appreciate and spending will therefore increase again bringing the Sputnik back where it belongs . . . on the [Roy] Harrod-Joan Robinson-[Evsey] Domar & Co route![94] The craziness of that thing has been already proven by [Oskar] Lange in his *Price Stability plus Full Employment* where he made clear that if adverse expectations are considered there is no reason whatever to suppose that the

93. The reference is to Michael Tugan-Baranowsky. See Paul M. Sweezy, *The Theory of Capitalist Development* (New York: Oxford University Press, 1942), 156–73.
94. The Pigou effect, related to the contemporary notion of the wealth effect, has to do with the stimulus to consumption when wealth increases. Baran is here referring to models of economic growth that point to relatively stable expansion, countering the Keynesian notion of underemployment equilibrium. The term "Sputnik" is used as a metaphor for economic takeoff.

Pigou effect will go into action at any predictable time. Meanwhile some bird in the Cowles Commission has figured out that unless you assume some out of this worldly elasticity it would take a generation or two before the Pigou effect would actually do the trick in the case of a halfway decent recession. Anyway, it was precisely the contribution of Keynes and the then Keynesians to show that the underemployment equilibrium can last indefinitely unless it is given from the outside an upward kick. It took only 10 years of a postwar boom to have those thinkers forget all about it and to rediscover Say's Law dressed up in mightily dynamic garb. All this is entirely clear to [Michal] Kalecki — the only economist who understood it all, mainly because he did not have to learn from Keynes and the Keynesians. . . .

I have some sympathy, as you know, for Kaldor's contention that the *Verelendung* [immiseration] proposition is terribly important and that it cannot be "shrugged off." But this is a different story which has nothing to do with the above argument.

It is my impression that we have to deal with all of this, whether we like it or not — simply to cover the flanks against this kind of attack. I am coming around to your view that there would be probably no merit in dealing with this stuff in a second preface to a new printing of *PEoG*. Nobody will see it, since nobody who has the book will buy another printing: neither libraries nor individuals. There would be the following possibilities: (a) the most important stuff could be handled in our *Buechlein*; (b) we could publish a pamphlet "*PEoG* & Its Critics"; (c) I might try to write an article for say *AER* taking up the relevant points sort of independently — carrying the critics along in the foot-notes (trouble with that is that most *PEoG* readers would not get it [would not get the article].) Anyway, read the thing and let me know what you think about all of this.

[. . .]
Love,
    Paul

PMS to PAB

Cambridge
February 3, 1958

Dear Paul,
Thanks for sending me the Kaldor review which is returned herewith. It is actually a very weak performance so far as real substance is concerned, but the trouble is that he is able to make out a fairly plausible case (at least it will be so to the readers of the *AER*) because you were struggling in *PEoG* for the right way to formulate basically absolutely correct ideas but never wholly succeeded

in finding it. Actually, I think, there are in *PEoG* too many concessions to the Kaldorian way of going at these problems, so that the argument seems to take place very much more on his grounds than it really ought to.

At the heart of the problem, I think, there is a rock-bottom methodological issue. Can we take global statistics, which portray the final results of extremely diverse and complicated economic forces, and use them to build a revealing model of the economic process? Kaldor et al say yes. Manufacture your sputnik from a constant profits/wages ratio, a constant capital/output ratio, and a constant savings/income ratio, hoist it into its orbit by whatever trick is for the time being preferred, and, presto, the thing goes on and on forever. But is this at all realistic? Why not, say Kaldor et al, since the statistics seem to make all these constant ratios as plausible as any other set of assumptions? My contention is that this is all utterly superficial and completely fails to get at the real underlying forces at work.

Global statistics (leaving aside for the present the questions whether they are reliable or constructed in an appropriate fashion) are always *resultants* of cooperating and counteracting forces — they emerge from a bundle of *tendencies* — they do not in and of themselves express or reveal *any* of the basic characteristics of the system. The real problems of political economy are to identify and abstract from the system the decisive tendencies and to analyze their interactions. Only after this has been done is a confrontation with global statistics meaningful and needless to say, the meaning is then quite other than what the Kaldors assume it to be. The question is whether the theory is adequate to explain the observed results, not to take the results as building blocks from which to construct a theory. Old KM [Karl Marx] saw all this clearly enough, though he did not succeed in expressing it clearly enough. His "laws" (like immiseration, falling rate of profit, rising s.v. [surplus value], etc.) are interpreted by the Kaldors as though they were statements about the behavior of Kaldor-type models: on this basis, it is of course easy to show that the alleged "Marxian model" is full of contradictions. Actually, they are the *tendencies* which operate to bring about the final behavior of the system, and as such they not only may be contradictory but are bound to be so.

If I am right, the problem of answering the Kaldors is not an easy one. The weakness of the answer which you sketch in your letter is that you go much too far in meeting him on his own grounds. I do not say that he isn't vulnerable on his own grounds: indeed I quite agree that even there his argument suffers from the fatal error of failing to supply the forces for putting the sputnik in orbit and keeping it there. But this is not the heart of the matter, and no real understanding is to be gained from engaging in or even winning an argument along these lines.

What is to be done then? In my judgment nothing effective can be done until we have succeeded in giving to our own positive position an adequate formulation. And that is precisely the function of the *Buechlein*. We must *not* let it get cluttered up with polemics vs. Kaldor et al because that will only serve to hide from our readers what we are really trying to do. But *after* we have made our positive presentation, we not only can but should settle accounts — not only with NK but with the whole model-building tribe. What this points to, it now seems clear to me, is an appendix in which reference can be made not only to their *opera* but also to the doctrines elaborated in the body of the text.

How does all this strike you?

Incidentally, you don't speak of the last part of NK's review, but it is very characteristic. Some well-taken debating points (e.g. why should a bourgeois revolution have taken place *everywhere*?) coupled with a total failure to see the important things. The formal political independence of Latin America is interpreted as meaning freedom from domination by the advanced powers; the fact that U.S. imperialism made use from the beginning of anti-colonialism as a weapon against other imperialisms is completely missed; etc., etc. And the final tone of toadyism is utterly repulsive. However, there is one thing that can perhaps be learned from Kaldor's argument. One should try not to give the impression that nothing can be done until capitalism has been overthrown, and instead show that a struggle for rational policies under capitalism is in essence a struggle against capitalism and that it can be most effectively carried on when its full scope and implications are understood. In the meantime, partial victories are not to be scorned and may in fact be very important. Thus, we are not against a policy of generous aid to backward countries; we merely say that the best way of furthering it is not gentle admonitions to the powers-that-be about their own misunderstood interests but a principled fight *for* the interests of the masses.

[…]

Love,

/s Paul

PAB to PMS

Los Altos, CA

February 12, 1958

Dear Paul,

As requested in your letter of February 6th, I did submit to our merciful Creator a number of intense and, I hope, eloquent prayers concerning your "take-off" on the *Buechlein*, and am naturally now most anxious to find out what effects if any my intervention has produced. In addition to praying (and teaching) I have been working a little bit on the same project, and need now some clarification of the nature of my operation. When we discussed the thing rather briefly in NY, matters were left — if I remember correctly — in such a way that I should draft the first chapter "Methodology, etc." and the last part "Surplus Disposal and Its Effects with special reference to the *Kulturscheisse* [cultural mess]." Is this also your recollection or do you have now any different ideas viz. any modifications of that plan? If my understanding is right then your primary concern should be the structure of the corporation (oligopoly, etc.) and the forces making for the growth of the Economic Surplus.

In your MRA [Monthly Review Association] lecture notes, I find lecture I altogether satisfactory; I am using it in composing my first chapter. Where I find myself rather unenthusiastic — and actually in tentative disagreement — is lecture II dealing with the distribution of income i.e. with the phenomenon of large and growing ES [economic surplus]. It hardly needs to be stressed that the problem is of crucial importance for us, for if there is no tendency toward ES being larger and increasing, our argument loses most of its force. I think, we have to show as convincingly as possible, why — *if left to itself* — the system tends to generate less and less "Good Consumption" (GC) as proportion of Y [gross output]. Given some relation between I [investment] and C (in an advanced country different from an underdeveloped country) — the decline in GC leads necessarily to decline in I = decline in Y. Since therefore the decline in GC cannot be made up by an increase in I — only solution is an increase in "Bad Consumption" (BC), and/or capital exports.

The real problem therefore, what makes for the decline of GC? The answer undoubtedly lies somewhere in the area of technology: increasing productivity of labor, i.e. less labor is needed to produce a given volume of output. The increased productivity of labor is at the same time not accompanied by a sufficient "worsening" of the capital/output ratio i.e. the given output can be produced with less labor and with the same or only insignificantly increased amount of capital (in terms of a flow, that is replacement). In fact, the replacement on a higher technical level reduces even the cost in terms of capital per unit of output. At the same time wages are relatively sticky, i.e. do not increase *pari passu* [hand-in-hand] with increasing productivity — ergo $c + v$ [constant capital + variable capital] together tend to decline per unit of output + as a share of Y. *NB* when we speak now of wages we must mean: wages of productive workers, not *total* wages! This is troublesome but inevitable. If this were the end of the story ES would be rising by leaps and bounds and even in terms of the Harrod-Robinson-Kaldor *perpetuum mobile* it would be demonstrable that the system is headed from one Dreck-situation into a deeper Dreck-situation.

What prevents this is (1) the steady increase of *BC* (*le gouvernement y compris*) [including government spending] + capital exports (magnitudinally much less significant.) In connection with the latter most important, incidentally, that U.S. is reaching rapidly the status of a mature creditor nation, i.e. its receipts on account of profits, interest, etc. from abroad begin to catch up with its capital outflow abroad! When it comes to the necessary increase of *BC* the situation is mightily complicated by the damned shifting phenomenon. The more privately organized *BC*, the more *ES* increases — at least when it comes to *BC* organized by business (advertising, sky-rocketing executive salaries, expense accounts etc.). Only *BC* that sticks and uses up effectively *ES* is consumers' *BC* (artificial obsolescence of automobiles and other durables, etc.) and that part of government-provided *BC* that is not shifted (A very large part!). In other words, even madness cannot be properly organized by the free enterprise system privately; it needs the government to provide enough *BC* for the system to jog along.

But to come back to the beginning of the page. We have to try to make this story as convincing as possible because it is the argument that *if left to itself* the system tends to cause *GC* to contract as a share of *Y* that causes incredulity among economists, grad students and such. I know this pretty well because right now I have a pretty good graduate seminar where I have been going over all this business. Everything goes well except for this point! Now a good theory of wages would be obviously mightily helpful, but I am afraid that your version of the distribution theory (in Lecture II) is not altogether convincing. Coontz notwithstanding, I cannot see my way clear to doing something useful with the cost-of-production-of-labor-power concept. It really begs the issue. Granted that the cost of production of a modern, intense factory worker is quite a bit higher than, say, of a manufacturing worker 100 years ago in Manchester. It certainly is not higher in the U.S. than, say, in an equally modern factory in Western Germany or Switzerland. Nevertheless the real wage is here higher than there. Why? I fully agree with you that to explain the thing exclusively in terms of power struggle between capital and labor is most unsatisfactory. Incidentally Karl Marx was by no means altogether adverse to that line of reasoning: "… der Kapitalist versucht staendig, die Loehne auf ihr physisches Mindestmass herabzudruecken und den Arbeitstag auf sein physisches Hoechstmass auszudehnen, waehrend der Arbeiter staendig einen Druck nach der entgegengesetzten Richtung ausuebt. *Die Sache loest sich auf in die Frage nach den verhaeltnismaesigan Kraeften der Kaempfenden.*" (Lohn, Preis und Profit, p. 63 — my italics) — ["The capitalist tries constantly to push down wages as low as possible and to extend the work day as long as possible, while the worker constantly exerts pressure in the opposite direction. *The matter resolves itself in the question of the relative strengths of the combatants.*" [PAB's emphasis]

I still feel, as I wrote to you earlier, that the more promising approach to the matter is to think of the whole business in terms of demand for labor depending on capital accumulation (and value of equipment per man) and supply of labor depending on population, destruction of small business, migration from the countryside and unionization. This by the way does not entirely throw out cost of production but relegates the cost of production concept to where I think it belongs: a very, very broad indicator of the general level. Also I think the unions do possibly play a not unimportant role in forcing technical progress. To the extent that wage increases (money wages) are not immediately passable on to the consumer, they do render labor-saving devices more tempting. They may render them more tempting even if the increase in money wages is used as an excuse for higher prices.

I have done quite a lot of work on the shifting problem which I think is most important from our standpoint, and have now a very strong feeling that the shifting thing is okay. Not that everything is shifting, but a lot is. Ergo, one has to be careful with the profit maximization proposition. Big Business does not maximize profits in the stupid textbook sense. It maximizes it in the long run with all kinds of qualifications. I shall send you material on shifting soon; it has to be typed together.

[...]

Looking forward to hearing from you soon.

Haendedruck,

/s Paul

PMS to PAB

24 Agassiz Street
Cambridge 40, Mass.
February 22, 1958

Dear Paul.

[...]

2. Yes, your recollection of the way we divided up the job checks with mine. But I think it should be revised, at least to a certain extent. Or perhaps what I really mean is that I think we should start working on whatever part interests each of us most and then see how things go. I know that I have to get this business of the big corporation and what kind of animal it is out of my system before I can do anything else. I also know that I am no better satisfied than you with the theory of Lecture II, and I suggest that since you have been

thinking about this you make it your first task — i.e. why the system if left to itself generates insufficient *GC* [Good Consumption] to maintain a moving equilibrium, or m.a.w. [German abbreviation for *mit anderen Worten* or "in other words"] why in a "pure" system (made up solely of corporations employing productive workers) ES [economic surplus] tends to rise right through the ceiling. Once we have this demonstrated we can proceed to the genesis and evolution of the various forms of *BC* [Bad Consumption], including the shifting problem. etc. (incidentally, I have a slight feeling that you may have a tendency to underestimate the amount of *BC* the private sector succeeds in generating, but this bridge can be crossed when we get to it: in the meantime it is absolutely crucial that we must establish the law of increasingly deficient *GC*).

I am perfectly agreeable to proceeding as indicated at top of p. 3 of your letter of Feb. 12. But I confess to a certain amount of pessimism about the chances of working out a theory of real wages, even in a quite simple system, that will satisfy our professional brethren. This doesn't mean that the attempt should not be made, but it seems to me it does mean that we musn't rest our whole case on a theory that is almost certain to be rejected no matter how well satisfied with it we may be ourselves. And I think we can provide a good second line to which to fall back and dig in along when it comes to fighting the doubters. Provided we can show that from any given starting point, *however it may have been reached*, there is a tendency for productivity to *rise faster* than real wages, we shall have made the point that is most essential for our overall thesis. And I think it ought to be possible to show this both theoretically (from an examination of the forces acting on, respectively, prices, money wages, and productivity) and statistically. The statistical part is tricky, I know, but somehow I think it can be done.

[…]
Love,
    /s Paul

P.S. […]

PMS to PAB

[*No provenance*]

February 24, 1958

Dear Paul,
Here is a quotation which should prove valuable to you:

"Management abhors a disturbance of equilibrium. The manager's nirvana would be stable costs, stable prices, loyal customers. He believes that his profits are reasonable and therefore a change of any cost, e.g., the wage, raises the specter of a price change. More cost, more price — this is managerial instinct. How often does a manager say to his board, 'Our profits are unusually good, so let us raise wages, or pay more for our raw materials, fuel, or power, or increase the interest rate on our bond issue?'

"The assumption is that every cost, particularly every increase in cost, must shift. And there is no place for it to shift but to price. Fundamentally, the assumption is correct: business must recover its costs — all of them — plus a profit. No one supposes that business can endure on losses. A wage increase therefore offers a prima facie justification for a price increase." (Leland Hazard, "What Economists Don't Know about Wages," *Harvard Business Review*, January-February 1957, p. 53.)

And again:

"One may say with certainty . . . that management does not make payments for labor in an amount which will preclude a profit, at least not for any sustained period of time. Yet, curiously enough, management, if necessary, will permit a limited invasion of profit by the wage before suffering an interruption in its production schedule.

"Why? The explanation lies in the profit margin in heavy technology. Management may not know how much margin there is, yet may be convinced that a vanishing profit can be restored by adjustments in technology. This conviction is strong even where the ratio of wages and salaries to product sales value is high . . . " (Ibid., p. 53.)

Mr. Hazard is an authentic Big Bus. man, GM's Counsel and V-P of Pittsburgh Plate Glass Co. *N. B.* the number of our favorite themes that are expounded in these passages: the passivity of price policy, the love of quiet and security, the belief that whatever profits may be they are fair, the propensity to shift all cost increases, the flexibility of technology as a weapon against unavoidable (and presumably unhittable) wages increases.

*   *   *   *

On the question of maximizing profit., which you raised in a recent letter: it seems to me that the way to formulate the question is not whether management seeks an absolute maximum in terms of some function which is given and known over its whole range, but whether *from any given starting point* (which may or may not be a maximum: who can possibly know?) it seeks to increase its profit. And on this point it seems to me the evidence is overwhelming. The studies of Jim Early in this connection are very revealing and useful, esp. *American Economic Review Supplement.*, May 1957, pp. 333-335.

I think I finally have got the right outline for my first chapter (it may not be *the* first chapter, of course).[95] After perhaps some stuff about competitive and monopolistic models, it states our intention to start from a monopolistic one. Why? (1) Because this isolates for study the decisive forces. (2) Because it is becoming more and more realistic all the time. Here the concentration stuff is dealt with and shown to be (1) largely irrelevant but (2) supporting our position anyway. Monopoly is then shown to be roughly equivalent to the Big Corporation which *all* authors (I haven't found a single exception) agree is the dominant factor in the economy. How does the big crop change matters from the old-fashioned entrepreneur? Two schools of thought (1) the wicked corporation (Brandeis, Veblen, the era of the trusts, etc.), and (2) the "soulful" corporation (the term is actually Carl Kaiser's, a lovely subject for irony) of Kaiser, Berlet, etc.

I next show that either of these notions raises hell with economic theory. In the wicked corporation, the managers are out for their personal profit and may as well ruin the corporation as build it up (Veblen argued this very strongly and it is implicit in the whole literature): the rational economic behavior of the actual producing units, as distinct from the income-receiving units, is disrupted. In the second, management tries to play the philanthropist and there are absolutely no rules to that game — mind you, it is not only a matter of playing the philanthropist with a maximized net income (that would cause no trouble) but of running the company in such a way that costs and profits are hopelessly confused.

Next comes a critique of both schools, showing that the old tycoon is out of date and that the modern corporation is in fact a rationalized profit-making machine. This is then compared to the old-fashioned entrepreneur, showing that in certain respects they do differ but that the change is by no means fatal to all received economic theory. What it needs is extension and improvement, not rejection.

The only trouble is that there is much more than a chapter here. But never mind, I'll make it into as many chapters as necessary. I will have to compress very severely all the same — and this is going to be one of our great problems throughout. The book is intended to be short, essayistic — we will continuously have to resist the temptation to make it a treatise.

95. Sweezy was drafting what would become Chapter 2 of *Monopoly Capital*, entitled "The Giant Corporation."

I have been thinking about titles. Why not just plain "Capitalism" with a subtitle indicating that the material is drawn from the U.S. case? "American Capitalism" might be better in some ways, but I don't want any jurisdictional or copyright quarrels with JKG. "Capitalism in the United States" is too awkward.

More anon,

/s Paul

PAB to PMS

Los Altos, California

March 5th, 1958

Dear Paul,

I am very sorry to be late in answering your letters of February 22nd and 24th. The delay was partly to pressures of college business (approaching end of the quarter), partly — and more importantly — to a dip in my general *Verfassung* [state of mind] in the course of which any form of writing becomes entirely impossible. If I knew of a psycho who could cure me of that affliction, I would gladly turn over to him all my worldly goods and agree to boot to staying in his *Zinsknechtschaft* [servitude] until the end of my days. But no such specialist exists to my knowledge, and I have to continue carrying my cross. . . .

A large number of points:

[. . .]

As a possible title of the *Buechlein* it occurs to me: *Advanced Capitalism*: Studies in the Generation and Utilization of the Economic Surplus in the United States. (While keeping the subtitle which would be useful to indicate both the tentative nature of the operation and its orientation towards the U.S., the main title could be also *Monopoly Capitalism, The Big Business Society, The Corporate Empire*, or something else similarly "catchy").

[. . .] I fully agree with you that we probably do not have a chance of advancing a wage theory which would satisfy our professional colleagues. I have the strong feeling that something quite sensible could be done on the lines that I suggested earlier, and am even more optimistic on that score having discovered an article by a Polish economist Z.J. Wyrozembski "Accumulation and Employment" where this approach is worked out very nicely. What is more important, however, upon further reflection, I begin to think that a *wage* theory really is not what is primarily needed. Our point is fully made as long as it is shown that the increases in productivity of "good workers" outstrip by far the wage increases of "good workers." In other words, if "good workers" claim an ever declining share of total output — "bad workers" must be multiplied if total C [consumption] is to remain somewhere within the working requirements of the system. Now, even if we do not know for sure what exactly determines the wages of both "good" and "bad" workers — we can show easily that the wage *increases* of the "good" workers do *not* keep *their* share in Y [gross output] constant or anything like it. For this there is plenty of evidence. The whole problem consists in sorting out "good" and "bad" workers — this is needed not so much for the wage story as for the productivity story. The usual productivity analyses stick into the denominator *all* workers with obvious repercussions.

[…]

More later, now I have to go and teach all day. But this will be over next week. Love,

/s Paul

[*PMS spent April 1958 in Palo Alto with PAB working on the outline for the "opus" or "Buechlein," which eventually became* Monopoly Capital. *Therefore there is no correspondence until early May 1958 after PMS's return to Cambridge.*]

PMS to PAB

[*Handwritten on MR letterhead*]

Monday
early May, 1958

Dear Paul,

Just a note to say that I got home without incident, though somewhat shattered for a while by the abruptness of our parting. The stay in Los Altos was very important to me, and I felt terribly badly about not at least being able to try to tell you so and why. Despite my own emotional troubles and weaknesses, those weeks did me a hell of a lot of good. And I came away with enhanced respect for the quality of your mind and the greatest admiration for your moral courage and generosity. In addition, I think we've got a good book started. May the keeper of socialist heaven smile on the venture — which means let us settle down and actually put on paper what we know in our heads!

[…]

My heartfelt thanks and love,

/s Paul

PAB to PMS

Los Altos, CA

June 4, 1958

Dear Paul,

It was wonderful to hear your voice again, and to learn that you are in good
health and "tolerable" spirits.

As I told you, the operation Mexico was — as far as I am concerned — a
great success. I liked the city, and — in particular — the countryside, and found
the people there most friendly, benevolent and hospitable. It was such a relief
to be surrounded for a while by economists who are honest, open-minded and
intelligent who have some enthusiasm for what they are doing, and who do not
consider what we have to say to be merely manifestations of crackpotism or
neurosis. Not that many of them are not confused and on the wrong track —
the important thing is that they are willing and indeed eager to discuss matters
rationally, to correct errors if they can see them, and to express their opinions
freely and without regard to immediate "existential" consequences. Their basic
trouble is the trouble of the whole country: a corrupt, demagogic government
lives still off the great tradition of the Revolution (and Oil Nationalization),
engages continually in what Lenin used to call "centrism" — left phrases and
right deeds — with only very few people seeing through this game and capable of
piercing this ideological fog. The fog is at its thickest at the moment: an election
is coming up and the presidential candidate — Adolfo Lopez Mateos — has
chosen a distinctly left tack; anti-imperialist, anti-foreign domination, etc. The
boys are disturbed: they would *like* to trust him, although they know that this
is all so much electoral eye-wash. What is more important, the masses are taken
in by it, and the fear of antagonizing the northern neighbor serves always as a
powerful argument against any critical view. They know that they are a "semi-
colonial" country — this is the way they refer to themselves all the time — and
feel that impotence strongly. Many remark sadly that the leading role of Mexico's
on the LA continent is gone, that it is now up to Frondisi in Argentina, to the
new regime in Venezuela and perhaps to the Chileans to pick up the banner of
resistance and to carry it forward. Nowhere can the dialectic of the bourgeois
revolution be studied as fruitfully as in Mexico; its *salto mortale* from the
progressiveness to reaction with the glorious spirit of the former covering up the
sordid practice of the latter . . . What develops is a "cultural lag" producing that
strange phenomenon of the main street in the city called *Avenida de Insurgentes*,
of revolutionary peasant leaders being worshipped as the nation's saviors, of
Diego Rivera's sickles and hammers adorning the presidential palace which is
the residence of a president wholly subservient to the most rapacious, most cold-

1. Paul A. Baran (1963)

2. Paul M. Sweezy (1963)

3. Gathering of distinguished economists at the Indian Statistical Institute, Calcutta, 1956. PAB is fourth from left. (Professor Lange, Mrs. Lange, Mrs. Podea, PAB, Mrs. Galbraith, Prof. Mahalanobis, Mrs. Mahalanobis, Dr. Podea, Mrs. Bettelheim, Prof. Bettelheim, Prof. Galbraith, Dr. Tinbergen, Mr. Links, and Mrs. Wiener.)

4. Fidel Castro with Paul Sweezy (right foreground), Leo Huberman, and Paul Baran. (1960)

5. (left to right) Baran, Sweezy, an unidentified Cuban officeal, and Huberman. (1960)

6. Sweezy, Baran, Castro, and Huberman. (1960)

7. PAB with other economists during his 1963 trip to Latin America

8. Sociedad Económica del Amigos de País (SEAP) (Economic Society of Friends of the Country), Cuban economic society founded in 1793 during Spanish rule. PMS (left), Leo Huberman, and PAB (second from right) participating in a panel discussion in Havana, 1960. The speaker, sitting between Huberman and PAB, appears to be Juan Noyola, Mexican-born Cuban economist, who died in a plane crash two years later.

9. PAB with Pablo Neruda during his 1963 trip to Latin America

10. Harry Magdoff (ca. 1950)

blooded ruling class. All fascinating stuff, but unfortunately hardly any qualified observers there to fully develop and describe it. But the intuitive understanding of all of it simmers underneath, and this is the reason why we mean so much to them. They *do* sense that it is in Marxism where they can find a possibility of comprehending their situation.

Your citation from Aristotle terribly interesting.[96] Marx wasn't unaware of this. "Der Kommunismus ist die Position als Negation der Negation, dazu das *wirkliche*, fuer die naechste geschichtliche Entwicklung notwendige Moment der menschlichen Emanzipation und Wiedergewinnung. Der Kommunismus ist die notwendige Gestalt und das energische Prinzip der naechsten Zukunft, *aber der Kommunismus ist nicht als solcher das Ziel der menschlichen Entwicklung*." (MEGA I/3, p. 126, italics added [*Marx-Engels Gesamtausgabe*])

["Communism is the position of negation of the negation, representing for the next historical development, the real and essential moment of human emancipation and renewal. Communism is the essential form and life-giving principle of the near future, *but Communism is not in itself the goal of human development*."]

The true aim of human development is the restoration of man himself, the abolition of alienation, the transformation of human nature. This obviously raises a fundamental problem: is there any reason to share Marx's view that what is at issue is a *return* to a Paradise Lost, a liberation of the *intrinsically good* human nature of the shackles and distortions imposed on it by the thousands of years of exploitation and injustice — or could it be, that what lies ahead is simply a forward movement in which there is a chance of improving, changing the human nature with this change and improvement being altogether new, unprecedented, not a return but a fresh arrival? To be sure, operationally — as is fashionable to speak now — there may be little difference. Still, the notion of a *return* has an optimistic connotation which the notion of the new trip does not have. If there is no return, there is no *Selbstentfremdung*, no alienation! For both *Selbstentfremdung* and alienation imply a *departure* from a "Selbst" that was originally good, integral, un-warped. If there is no return then there is only the hope that in the course of history with changed social relations man will change too and become *better* rather than recapture something that is deeply seated in him. I would tend to the latter interpretation as being the more sober one, as being also more "contingent." There is no fixed goal of return to a point of departure: who knows what that point was anyway? There *is* a goal of changing society so as to create the best possible (or at least best possible from our present

96. Sweezy's citation to Aristotle was either in a missing letter or over the phone.

view point) conditions for human development. All we need to say is that enough
is known about the mouldability of human nature, its plasticity to assume that
a better society can produce a better human being. Period. It also leaves open
the possibility that the whole thing may capsize!!! Marx in keeping with his
time stuck to that notion of the aboriginal "Selbst" and carried it into his entire
reading of history (*Urkommunismus*). Regardless of whether this has a certain
ideological effect or not — there is no need for it. The teleology is superfluous;
all that matters is that there is a possibility for a step forward. . . .

    [. . .]
    Much love,
        s/ Your Paul

PAB to PMS

                                        Los Altos, California
                                          [June 5, 1958]
Dear Paul,
This is a continuation of my yesterday's letter and its purpose is to *fixer les
idees* [to set these ideas down] on a "small" point in theory *zum Zwecke der
Selbstverstaendigung* [for the purpose of self-understanding]. You remember,
when you were here we discussed a number of times the almost generally
prevailing reluctance, nay unwillingness, to accept the proposition that 2 x 2 = 4,
in other words to recognize rationality as a binding principle both of thought and
conduct. I had made this point in *PEoG* (p.297) but have had an uneasy feeling
about this whole business ever since. Having thought about it quite a lot (on
airplanes, in the gardens of Veracruz and on sleepless hotel beds). I have decided
that this relates to a much more fundamental problem than appeared to me
earlier. Viz.: the characteristic feature of capitalist mentality at its present stage of
development (i.e. ever since it has become a conservative, and indeed reactionary
attitude) is the separation of Reason from Practical Intelligence. Reason refusing
to take anything for granted, subjecting the status quo to searching criticism,
examining reality with the view to discovering its correspondence (or lack of
same) with the requirement for a healthy and all-sided development of man —
this reason that has been traditionally the subject matter of all philosophical and
scientific effort has become ostracized as a dangerous tool of social subversion.
    At the same time Practical Intelligence, i.e. the capacity of making the best
of the given status quo, of exploiting fully the opportunities offered within
the framework of what is being taken for granted — this practical intelligence
which is indispensable for the functioning of the capitalist society itself has
been furthered and promoted by bourgeois education, bourgeois science and

bourgeois ideology. What is more, a powerful attempt has been made and is being made continually (positivism in all its forms!) to deny the existence of the above distinction, to blur the boundaries between Reason and Practical Intelligence, to declare the mere making of this distinction to be metaphysical, unscientific and what have you. [Handwritten note in margin: "This is the biggest crime of bourgeois science!"] As a result in the common mode of thinking this differentiation hardly exists, or appears only in the form of short and sharp lightnings in times of crises. For the rest reason and practical intelligence are identified with both appearing in the form of 2 x 2 = 4. Yet, practical intelligence which takes everything for granted is by its very nature an ideological machine defending and perpetuating the status quo, defending and perpetuating the state of injustice, alienation, exploitation of man by man and the overall misery resulting therefrom.[97]

And as this misery increases, as this state of *Unmenschlichkeit* [inhumanity] becomes progressively intolerable — the revulsion against it, the protest against it assumes naturally the form of hostility, indeed bitter aggressiveness against Practical Intelligence. Practical Intelligence, however, is identified in the minds of people — and necessarily so because it is the only thing that they know — with Reason itself. Hence "anti-intellectualism," hence the revolt against both Reason and Practical Intelligence. While revolt against the former o.k. with the ruling class, the revolt against the latter is most dangerous — it undermines the foundations of the capitalist society itself, its ability to produce, to make profits.

In somewhat different terms: the man who refuses to accept the proposition that 2 x 2 = 4 is actually *right*. This proposition *taken by itself* justifies the perpetuation of his misery. But since he is unable to move from this proposition to reason, i.e. to ask himself what is the end which practical intelligence is serving, what is it that it takes for granted, since he identifies practical intelligence with reason — he "throws up" both, expresses his frustration in neuroses, turns to god, to blood, and to soil and becomes a fascist. I think that it is very important to understand this point, namely that irrationality is *not* the refusal to accept the canons and conclusions of practical intelligence. On the contrary that is probably the supreme test of rationality. Irrationality is the refusal to accept practical intelligence in *favor* of religion, mysticism etc. Therefore Marxist efforts

---

97. Baran was here working out the ideas that would appear in his articles "The Crisis of Marxism, Part I" and "The Crisis of Marxism, Part II: On the Nature of Marxism," *Monthly Review* 10, no. 6 and 7 (October and November 1958). Later published together as "On the Nature of Marxism," in Baran, *The Longer View*, 19–42.

which appeal exclusively to practical intelligence are doomed to failure: practical intelligence is very likely to be against them! The elucidation of the profound distinction between reason and practical intelligence is, however, terribly hard both to provide and to accept. Hence the scantiness of real Marxist influence ... Only where reality is so obnoxious that taking it for granted becomes altogether unbearable — in underdeveloped countries — does practical intelligence collapse and yields either to reason or to utter mysticism. . . .

I would like to work it out sometime; what do you think of it? It belongs to the Marx story if and when it should be written. There are lots of interesting radiations from this central point, but on those some other time.

So much for today.

Con amore

/s Paul

PMS to PAB

Cambridge

June 12, 1958

Dear Paul,

I have just read over again your letter of the 5th in re reason vs. practical intelligence and am even more impressed than on first reading. You are right that it belongs to the Marx story, and what is most important it goes beyond Marx himself. The enclosed clipping from last Sunday's *Times Book Review* is an interesting commentary. *N. B.* how the conservative critic of the *status quo* puts his finger on the taking-for-granted disease but poses a mystical (and ultimately, of course, religious) alternative. Reason is, functionally and logically, the exact counterpart of religion. In this connection, it is most significant how in underdeveloped conditions Marxism (reason) merges into a sort of religion, showing again how close the two are in an epistemological sense.

I return herewith the photostat on productivity which Linc sent you. Most interesting. Points very strongly in the creeping stagnation direction: if productivity increases sharply, the rate of investment needed to produce any sort of decent recovery in employment will grow *pro tanto*. I'm not sure whether the distinction between production workers and nonproduction workers employed in these figures has much significance — or rather I'm sure it hasn't got much. The point is not whether a worker actually mans the machine or works in an office, but whether his actions are directed toward the production of goods and services (real utilities, if you like) or whether they are directed toward selling the products in the capitalist market. There is overlap, of course, but it is certainly wrong and misleading to identify nonproduction workers with nonproductive workers.

It would be good if you had time to write up your Mexican impressions, but my own feeling is that the time now should go into the opus. Anyway what you say makes excellent sense. Too bad we don't have more writers in this country (or anywhere else for that matter) who can *get at what is important*. But the left is almost as badly committed to "superficialism" as the Right.

On *Urkommunismus*, I agree wholly. In this matter, Marx was very much the child of his times (and of then prevailing anthropological notions). There is no need for piety in such things, and no need for elaborate disassociation either. As to the actual capacity of the human animal for real improvement, as distinct from changing the forms of expression of his "bad" nature, this is something which I don't believe can possibly be determined except by experience. But the point is that until a centuries-long experiment has been tried and tried seriously, there is no justification for concluding that it is impossible any more than that it is possible. In the meantime, it is by no means a matter of indifference whether evil takes one form or another. That would be like saying there is no difference between Oedipus and Micky Spillane. Some forms of evil are worthy of human beings, others trivial or contemptible.

[...]

More soon.

Love,

/s Paul

PAB to PMS

[*No provenance*]

July 2nd, 1958

Dear Paul,

[...]

After much thought I decided not to waste time on re-writing the surplus story for the Haley volume but to do for that purpose the originally intended article on underconsumption.[98] It has the advantage that writing on this topic helps clarifying issues which are of general importance for our opus. And, indeed, I got stuck right at the beginning. As you correctly state in your letter of

98. Baran appears to be indicating here that he does not intend to rewrite the economic surplus discussion from his essay "National Economic Planning" that appeared in B.F. Haley, ed., *A Survey of Contemporary Economics* (1952) for a book edited by Moses Abramovitz on *The Allocation of Economic Resources* (1959), but instead is choosing for his contribution to follow his earlier idea of addressing underconsumption, as more useful in developing the ideas for the opus (*Monopoly Capital*). See Baran, "Reflections on Underconsumption," *The Longer View*, 115–202, also published in the Abramovitz collection cited above.

June 12 the distinction between production and nonproduction workers is not the one that matters. What *does* matter is the distinction between those workers whose actions are directed toward the production of goods and services (real utilities) and those employees whose actions are directed toward selling the products in the capitalist market. So far so good and so simple.

Assuming that one could statistically sort out those workers, Surplus would be equal Net Output minus the Real Wage of the let us call them Useful workers. What worries me, however, is the following: a goodly number of those Useful workers are engaged in putting chrome on automobiles, on building fins for same, in turning and twisting a product *not* with the view of increasing its *real utility*, but merely in order to promote its sale in the capitalist market. Why should we differentiate between the man who sits in the advertising office designing a new wrapping device (to promote the sale of the product) and the worker who *manufactures* that wrapping device? Both of them are surplus eaters and both of them *counteract* the surplus-overflow! But if this is true, then Surplus is equal to Rationalized Total Output minus (workers needed for the production of the Rationalized Total Output times their per capita real wage). It is *this* potential surplus that has to be continuously "fought off" by the system, and this potential surplus is obviously much larger than the one mentioned first. In a sense, one may say that the distinction that matters is whether an activity "comes natural" i.e. relates to the output of more and better use values, or whether it is dictated by the necessity to *sell*. But how does one say all this without immediately getting into the philosophical problem of what *is* a rationalized output? For what it comes down to is the proposition that we have to distinguish between work actually performed and work that would be performed in a more rational society still producing the same quantity of real utilities. From the standpoint of our underconsumption approach the whole thing is most important — if one wants to be consistent! What are your views on the matter? I am most anxious to get them at this stage of my meditations.

[…]
All the best,
Love,
    /s Paul

PMS to PAB

Wilton, N.H.
July 2, 1958

Dear Paul,

[. . .]

Preparing for Cornell has had the consequence of making me read a lot of stuff and attempt to put a few pieces together for the first time since we were working on the opus together at Los Altos. I'm afraid that the horrible truth, which I have long resisted, is that there is not a scintilla of hope for this country. It will be either bypassed by history and sink into a state of putrefaction or it will infect the whole world with its fatal diseases. The very notion of reform from within is the wildest kind of utopia. And if all this is true, it makes the position of people like us doubly and triply excruciating. To go on writing *MR*-type stuff, which had its origins in very different assumptions, is almost as dishonest as selling out to the American celebration. And yet for me, at any rate, there is no other possibility to make even a pretense at employment and earning power. And it is obvious that *MR* couldn't survive a year purveying the kind of black pessimism (for the U.S.) which I know in my bones to be the truth. All of which adds up to intellectual confusion, moral doubt, and psychic torture . . . Unfortunately, there is even more grief than that. To cope with one's frustrations and neuroses in an environment of activity and hope is at least a possibility. In an atmosphere of unrelieved gloom and despair, they become monsters of supernatural size and power.

Pardon my lucubrations. One ought, I suppose, to keep them to oneself. But somehow it seems to help just to say things sometimes, and you have the misfortune of being about the only one likely to understand what I'm saying.

Yours as ever,
/s Paul

PAB to PMS

Los Altos, California
July 7, 1958

Dear Paul,

In connection with your letter of July 2nd first of all a word of protest: if a relation between people is that of friends (in the German sense of that word rather than in its Anglo-American meaning in which it is only orthographically distinguishable from acquaintance) then intercommunication, solidarity, mutual support and cooperation are not only admissible but constitute in fact the essence of the matter. Your apologies for not keeping to yourself what oppresses you at any particular time are therefore not only redundant but rather insulting; they would suggest that you consider me a cocktail party encounter with whom PM (pleasant moments!) are agreeably shared but with whom nothing that matters ought to be talked about . . . This is not the way I view things, and I may assure you that my being possibly able to understand what you are saying does not strike me as a misfortune. I would prefer to feel that this is a happy constellation, and that I may address myself to you without the thought that your exposure to my communications would expose you to additional suffering . . .

But to turn to the substance of your letter. Let us leave out for a minute the frustrations and neuroses, and address ourselves to the question as to the usefulness and meaning of our present activities. I would be less than candid if I did not say at the outset that I fully share your profound pessimism with regard to the developments in this country. There *are* no seeds of change, nor is there any reason to expect that those seeds will appear in the foreseeable future. In the light of that situation there can be little doubt that what we are engaged in is Quixotic, that the chances of our influencing anyone here are approximately zero, that even if a few undergrounders should feel heartened by what we are doing this heartening hardly matters. On this I never had any illusions but this was also never what actually determined my own attitude. For I am willing to accept the proposition, albeit un-Marxian, that the confrontation of reality with reason is not only a worthwhile but an eminently necessary and meritorious job *in and of itself*, i.e. without regard to its attaining the politically, historically crucially important confluence with some popular movement!

While in the realm of practical intelligence (in the bond market for example) it would be obviously idiotic to say that what matters is reason regardless of what everyone else is thinking and doing — in the sphere of reason it is not only possible but imperative to say that "everyone except Sammy is out of step" *if such is objectively the case*! If all Americans go stark mad, if fascism should take over, if Negroes, Italians, Puerto Ricans, Jews and bicyclists should all be put into concentration camps or get one ear cut off — I still would believe that nothing has changed in what I consider to be my function in life: in the job of confronting the mad reality with reason! If the U.S. & allies would tomorrow subdue the USSR & China and reestablish capitalism there, I still would continue to believe that socialism is a more rational order than capitalism, that reality is departing further from reason but that reason remains what it always was: a distant star, sometimes appearing and sometimes covered up by clouds but always to be concerned with, to be located, to be sought! At the present juncture we have to get away from the notion of "success," of "acclaim," of political effectiveness and go nearer the sense of *L'Art pour L'Art*, of serving reason for reason's sake. When

Marx said that the philosophers have interpreted the world differently while what matters is to change it, he did not really announce that the philosophers were a bunch of do-no-good-ers. What they did was not *sufficient*, but it surely was *necessary*! We certainly cannot do a damned thing to change the prevailing *Scheisse* — but saying this is far from saying that we cannot or should not do something about interpreting it!

More concretely: as you well know I never was an *MR* enthusiast (or for that matter a Left-Observer devotee) in the sense of believing that *MR* could or would greatly increase its circulation, expand its influence, etc. I always thought that *MR* is something of a necessary evil. It provides a bit of income, it forces you to write an article per month (usually a good one) and — last but not least — provides a mechanism for the publication and distribution of books which is not only useful but actually indispensable. It has and can fortify an additional *raison d'etre* by being and increasingly becoming the best if not the only source of intelligent information on and appraisal of developments in the United States, not so much for the U.S. public as for the world at large.

Now, you say that if *MR* should openly and frankly purvey the truth about U.S. prospects — it wouldn't survive one year. I doubt that. Such a hard core of friends as it has will continue to stay with it, and to expect more than hard core is unreasonable anyway. What is required is (1) not to attempt to prophesize, to create illusions, to see silver stripes where there are none, and (2) stick adamantly to uncompromising, unvarnished criticism of the American scene. In the long run this will pay off, in the short run there isn't a hell of a lot to lose. I would reduce to minimum articles on foreign events (except to the extent to which those affect U.S. policy etc.), give as much room as possible to theoretical work, and hope that the mag can survive.

As for the rest: theoretical work, thinking and to use your expression "squeezing problems until they squeak." We won't be M & E alas but we may turn out to have [been] X and Z who have retained their heads on their shoulders at a time when everyone was losing his, who lived up to the function of an intellectual at a time when prostitution became the profession of all! I think — presumptuous as it may be on all counts — that if we manage to fight off to a tolerable extent our frustrations and neuroses, if we manage to do some thinking and some work, if we stick together and don't give in come hell or high water — we'll be able to say at the end that we have lived a meaningful life that was not by any means plain sailing but a purposeful and fruitful journey. And what more does one want from one's existence? And why should one give a damn what "they" say, for success, for influence? I could not care less — nor should you!

This all sounds perhaps very naive, but this is what has been going through my head since I received your letter and even the most beautiful young girl of France cannot give more than she has. . . . [another of PAB's favorite not-exactly politically-correct phrases.—Eds.]

I hope Cornell is bearable. Write!

As ever,

/s Paul

PMS to PAB

[*Reply to PAB letter of July 2, 1958*]

Cornell University

Tuesday [July 8, 1958]

Dear Paul,

A very hasty note in reply to yours which was waiting for me when I got here. (I'm still too busy getting classes started, etc., to attempt anything more .) I agree entirely with your analysis. Useful workers are what we are interested in. I think it was at least part of what Marx meant by "socially necessary," but I haven't checked the relevant passages. And clearly the maker of the fins is not useful. However, it must be stressed that there is no sharp dividing line: this is a case where practical judgment must decide what has real utility and what is a mere adjunct to salesmanship. It is not necessarily only in relation to a more rational society that the judgment can be made however — *vide* wartime simplifications which show that even the bourgeois ideologues, when put to it, can make rough and ready judgments about what is and what is not useful.

Don't overlook other categories of unproductive and useless workers judged by the standard of a more rational society. E. g. the several hundred thousand people employed in life and other kinds of insurance. With insurance socialized, most of these would immediately be seen to be redundant without the public's getting any worse protection against insurable risks. Or the whole financial and real estate apparatus which is engaged in selling titles or otherwise trading in "values." All nonsense by any rational standard.

[. . .]

More soon,

/s Paul

PMS to PAB
    [*On Cornell letterhead, but PMS is back in Cambridge or NY*]
                                                        Sept. 30, 1958
Dear Paul,
    […]
    As to your differing with some of the positions suggested in my piece ["A
Talk to Students," *Monthly Review*, October, 1958] I am not surprised since it
has long been clear to me that on certain "ultimates" (if one may use the term) we
do not always see quite eye to eye. That in itself, though regrettable, i.e. nothing
to get upset about. Or rather it wouldn't be if we could be quite sure that these
differences won't get in the way of our reaching agreement about what should
go into the book. If they do, perhaps we can go back to the plan which I believe
was suggested once before, that each of us assume responsibility only for the
part of the book of which he is the author. What do you think about this whole
problem?
    All of this assumes that there is going to be a book, about which I must
say I feel somewhat less than 100% certain. My output lately is asymptotically
approaching zero: the monthly RoM seems to be about all I can manage, and
unfortunately I can see no hope of early improvement. [omitted]
    Love,
        /s Paul

PAB to PMS
                                                    Los Altos, California
                                                        October 3, 1958

Dear Paul,
To repeat what I have said over the telephone, I did not have the slightest
intention to offend you when writing my hasty note to Leo, and I am terribly
sorry (and apologize) if this has nevertheless happened. I did not care for
this particular piece of yours, and felt that it failed to do justice to both your
standards and your actual position. Not having the article in front of me, I
cannot right now specify the passages to which I took exception. When I get
the October issue of MR [PMS, "Marxism: A Talk to Students," MR, October
1958] I'll write to you about it — just for the sake of theoretical clarity. It may
be silly and Quixotic on my part, but I *do* attach considerable importance
to that theoretical clarity; the neglect of it and indeed contempt for it that is
characteristic of our academic colleagues is one of the many signs of intellectual
decadence which confronts us on all sides. Even if no one should care about it, I
would want to strive for it for [its] own sake.

I said "our," and I mean our. This too may sound silly and sentimental, but
to me our intellectual (and human) solidarity is not just a matter of agreeable
personal relations (those one can cultivate with lots of people!) but a crucially
important aspect of my life and work. Indeed, the mere fact of our being able to
maintain and develop genuine cooperation and community of outlook represents
a "dialectical jump" from the quantity of commonly observable (and vacuous)
conviviality to what might be called an "unalienated" relation. To be sure, this
does not mean that we have to see eye to eye on every damn thing that happens
to turn up; what it does mean, however, that we ought to try to thrash out such
important problems as we encounter, and to try to reach an understanding about
them. Discussion may be pointless and worthless when the basic positions are
so far apart that no amount of talk or correspondence can hope to bridge the
gap. Discussion and effort at a clarification of possible disagreements are most
necessary, if the basic premises are very similar, if in other words the chances of
agreement are very large. Needless to say, this is *my* view of the matter which may
not coincide with yours. I would greatly deplore it if such were the case, but I
thought and still think that you might think similarly.

Most concretely, I am convinced that whatever differences we may have with
regard to what you call the "ultimates" — not that I am too certain as to what
those differences actually amount to — they have *absolutely* nothing to do with
what we have planned to put into our book on Monopoly Capital. In general, I
would suspect, that in everything related to *economics* we would have nothing to
quarrel about; at least I know of no proposition which I would wish to maintain
which would be unacceptable to you. Nor do I know of any statement of yours
that I would not wholeheartedly subscribe to. Such divergences of views as there
may be refer rather to some philosophical aspects of Marxism where I am at the
moment groping for some new ground. Being far from clear on all this myself
(and merely pregnant with some reflections), I obviously don't expect you to
agree with me (agree with what?) or to change your own views on the matter.
What I would want very much would be to have an opportunity to clarify all
those things as soon as possible, to talk it over with you and to arrive at some, if
ever so tentative *common* conclusions! 3000 miles is a long distance . . .

Still more concretely, we must do the book come hell or high water, and I am
terribly sorry to hear that "der huendische Kommerz" [the canine commerce]
detains you from working on it. Still we have to try our best and aim to complete
it by next summer. Such is at least my plan, and I wish I could do something to
help you in realizing the project. But, alas!

So much for today. I hope that you won't regard all of this as immature sissiness not worthy of white-haired men living in a business world. But I am just saying what I have on my mind, and changing that mind is by now beyond me . . .

Love as always,

/s Paul

P.S. [. . .]

PMS to PAB

66 Barrow

Nov. 15 [1958]

Dear Paul,

We had dinner with Harry Magdoff last night, and it seems clear from the ensuing conversation that your articles (especially the second) have already, or soon will, succeed in fluttering the dovecotes of the keepers of Marxist purity.[99] Harry disagrees with just about everything in the articles or at least with just about everything he *thinks* are in the two articles. He is especially dismayed by all suggestions that Marxism is not a positive science, finds your juxtaposition of reason and reality to be a distressing example of relativism, etc., etc. My attempts to defend you — e.g. by insisting that you do not want to deny that Marx was an economist but only that he can be judged simply as an economist; that your emphasis on the changing character of reason in history is not an example of Hegelian idealism; and so on — all such efforts, I am afraid, achieved very minor results, except to put me in the same category of heretic as your heretical self.

All this took place most amiably and without any heat or hard feeling, but the good will hardly served to bridge the ideological gaps. Harry is writing you a letter about all this, and I mention it mainly to forewarn you of the nature of the arguments which will be advanced and to indicate my own guess that his reaction will be fairly widespread among Marxists. (Stanley Moore phoned Leo yesterday and said that he takes issue with some points — unspecified — and is also writing you: we don't know to what extent he covers the same ground as Harry since the two have apparently not talked the matter over, but I would be surprised if there weren't considerable concordance of views between them.) Under the circumstances, the opportunity would seem to be present for a useful discussion in the pages of *MR*, and we invited Harry to put his arguments in

99. Baran, "The Crisis of Marxism, Part I" and "The Crisis of Marxism, Part II" (*MR*, October and November 1958) reprinted as "On the Nature of Marxism," in Baran, *The Longer View*, 19–42.

form for publication and rebuttal by you. He said he would think about it. I
rather hope he and/or Stanley takes us up on this, because I think it would give
you an excellent chance to repeat and expand your arguments, something which
obviously has to be done if the essential ideas are to be got across. Let us know
what you think about the whole matter, esp. after you've got Harry's message.

[...]
Love as always,
        /s Paul

P. S. [...]

PMS to PAB

                                                        Cambridge
                                                December 1, 1958
Dear Paul,
[...]
        I have been once again turning my mind to the problems of the opus, having
actually brought myself recently to re-read all the accumulated outlines and drafts
which have been residing undisturbed in a folder for many months now. Your last
outline is excellent, and even the draft chapters which I wrote in Los Altos have
much that is okay. But I think I can see a weakness or a difficulty in the way my
work was developing: the last two or three chapters are tending to get into too
much detail — too much attempt to justify theoretical generalizations, too much
casual empiricism. The effect is to divert attention from the large, bold theoretical
framework which it is the essential purpose of the opus to put across, and to
give the critics all sorts of small things to dwell on and haggle over. I believe that
it is essential to establish at some length that the corporation is a rationalized
profit-making machine; but, having done that, it is not necessary to attempt to
give arguments satisfactory to the economics profession to the effect that realized
prices and profits tend toward the monopoly solution while competition remains
in the realms of salesmanship and technology. The economics profession is not
going to be convinced of anything it doesn't want to be convinced of, and this
book is not the place for the kind of arguments that properly belong in a treatise
on price theory. These matters can more properly be stated, so to speak, in the
form of theses, with supporting detail (both theoretical and empirical) left to
another occasion or other workers.
        All this leads to the conclusion that what most wants doing on the drafts is
cutting and pruning and streamlining — perhaps even telescoping of chapters. I

hope fairly soon to be able to clean up various chores and to get to work along these lines. When I get into it, I suspect that other problems and difficulties may crop up, but as of now the crucial thing is to make a genuine start toward doing something. In any case, I am more convinced than ever that the opus is important and that if it is done right, it can re-focus the thinking of the whole international Left about the problems of U.S. capitalism (and hence capitalism in general).

We (i.e. *MR*) are publishing an American edition of J. D. Bernal's new book *World Without War* (Routledge is the British publisher). It is a first-rate piece of work, much broader and more socio-politically oriented than [Richard] Meier's *Science and Economic Development*. But his conceptions of the mono cap economy are often rather naive. It ought to be a very useful book for use in economic development courses — i.e. in any such courses where the instructor wants the class to think rather than be obfuscated and confused.

In re Stanley Moore's letter which you asked about over the phone a week ago: I will have to be clearer (from you) as to how correct he is in his interpretations of what you say. He seems to think that you wanted to say that Marxism is *nothing but* an intellectual attitude, has *no* elements of positive science about it, etc. I did not interpret you that way, perhaps because I know that that is not the way you *use* Marxism. I thought that you were trying to emphasize certain aspects of Marxism which have been badly neglected and which, *in our present circumstances in the capitalist world*, are of transcendent importance. If Stanley is correct in his interpretation, then I would accept some of his criticisms. But nothing that he says convinces me that he is correct. In any case, I think there should be some discussion in *MR* to clarify these points.

In thinking about these matters, I have run into a problem. Marxism is on the one hand what Marx said and implied about a lot of subjects and things. On the other hand, it is a living set of principles and doctrines which must in the nature of the case change with time. Since many of the things Marx said or implied are dated and have since been disproved or become irrelevant, does it not follow that Marxism the living set of ideas grows progressively away from Marxism the creation of Marx? If one follows this logic up to its ultimate conclusion, I am inclined to think that one finally comes to the result that Marxism *is* nothing but an intellectual attitude, that this is the only contribution of Marx that can survive all change. Further that this attitude is basically nothing but that of all real science, the search for closer and closer approximations to the truth and for ways of employing knowledge in the interests of humanity. But at the same time, there is as of any given point of time a whole body of knowledge which also has a right to the name of Marxism, even though it may and will change through time. How then can one avoid the conclusion that Marxism is necessarily two different things?

[...]

As always,

/s Paul

PAB to PMS

Los Altos, California
December 5, 1958

Dear Paul,

[...]

In re: opus, I fully share your views. I have also gone over the available material and some additional (unfortunately not very voluminous) scribblings of mine, and have come to the conclusion that the story as it is written down is somewhat out of balance. We should hit at a *theoretical* presentation — advancing *a way of looking* at American Capitalism — rather than try to present an empirical study of the vast penumbra of matters that would be relevant to our theme. For doing the latter well would require a multi-volume operation which is beyond our present possibilities, while doing the latter in a spotty and tentative way would immediately open us to the accusation of using "selected and biased" evidence, "casual empiricism" etc. We would make the same error as was made by Steindl who obscured his important theoretical contribution by loading his book with doubtful (and essentially superfluous) statistics. It is my feeling that our story should be relatively short and snappy, challenging both orthodoxies (the bourgeois and the Marxian) not on the level of facts, but on the level of the theoretical framework within which those facts are examined. This would make our task more fruitful, and — at the same time — in the light of our possibilities more manageable. We can talk it over in NY, and D.V. [God willing] should be able to complete the thing this spring and summer.

As far as Stanley's critique of my *MR* articles is concerned, I must admit that some of it is due (or rather is justified) by excessive brevity and therefore imprecision of my formulations. The way I would put it is the following: as a *matter of principle* Marxism is *nothing but* an intellectual attitude, or better, a philosophical position. In the words of Lukács: "Supposing — if by no means granting — that more recent research had proved beyond all possible doubt that all single statements of Marx are substantively wrong, a serious 'orthodox' Marxist could accept those findings without any difficulties, could reject all the particular Marxian statements — without abandoning for a minute his Marxian orthodoxy." (*Geschichte und Klassenbewusstsein* [*History and Class Consciousness*], p.13). This is obviously a terribly strong, indeed too strong a statement, for if taken literally it would cover the limiting case of rejecting Marx's finding that the capitalist system is an irrational system. If that were true then there is nothing left of Marxism: the confrontation of reality with reason comes to a close with the attainment in the form of capitalism the best of all conceivable worlds.

I would argue that the Lukács statement is o.k. *short* of this point at which the quantity of "wrongness" would switch into the quality of irrelevance. As long as the fundamental finding of the irrationality of capitalism (irrationality not by absolute standards of reason, but by dialectical standards of reason) stands, I would argue that it is immaterial for the validity of Marxism as a philosophical position in what specific form this irrationality appears, how the irrational system works, etc. Marx may be outlived on those concrete details, he remains right on the basic issue. And this leads to the point which you raise at the end of your letter. I would agree with you that *abstractly* speaking there is a tendency for the individual Marxian statements to become irrelevant with the progress of science. *De facto,* however, this tendency is not quite as strong as one might think, simply because *in the realm of social sciences* there has been very much less progress since the days of Marx than one would think on the basis of what has happened in the field of natural sciences. Putting it quite simply, there is still a hell of a lot that is o.k. in Marx — all that has happened since his days notwithstanding. In other words, following the dialectical principle of truth being always concrete the general principle of Marxism being nothing but a philosophical position is fully compatible with the specific statement that much of what Marx has said by the way of positive-scientific assertions is still fully valid. My impression is that Stanley may be "long" on materialism but somewhat "short" on dialectics; he always sees "either-ors'" where there should be "as well as." — We can talk about it more in NY, and then, I suppose, one ought to reformulate and clarify the thing in the course of subsequent discussions.

[...]
Auf baldiges Wiedersehen [See you soon],
Love,
        /s Paul

PMS to PAB

Cambridge
December 8, 1958

[...]
We are completely *d'accord* on the opus problem. Remains only to figure out concretely what is to be done. Also probably we are in step on Marxism, though I

think one has to say that even the irrationality of capitalism is a *result* of applying Marxism, not an axiom or starting point. I think it most unlikely that anyone will succeed in proving the rationality of that system — the possibility causes me not one minute's loss of sleep — but *if* one should produce such a proof it could only be by Marxist methods! *M.a.w* [German: in other words], Marxism *is* science in the realm of social phenomena — the search for truth by appropriate methods. It can also be extended to mean the knowledge thus acquired — but the two meanings must be recognized as quite distinct.

   [...]

Love,

     /s Paul

P.S. [...]

5
The *Magnum Opus* and the Cuban Revolution

[1959]

PMS to PAB

Cambridge
Jan. 7 [1959]

Dear Paul,
Have a look at [Robert] Dorfman's review-article[100] on [Tjaling] Koopmans'
Three Essays on the State of Economic Science [New York, 1957] in *Kyklos*,
XI/4. It is the most devastating commentary on what goes on among these fine
"scientists" that you are likely to find anywhere. Here is the key passage: ". . . as
an answer to the detractors of the mathematical method in economics I almost
wish it [Koopmans' book] had never been written. For it does not contain an
adequate answer to their essential charge — that of sterility. What is the purpose
of building a refined mathematical structure on premises that are a crude first
approximation to the reality we seek to understand? The efforts of some of the
best brains of a whole generation of economists have extirpated Walras' old
slips in logic but how little they have added to his insights. To doubts such as
these Koopmans provides only the inadequate answer that the new methods will
show their power and value in the future. And I doubt that there is any adequate
answer except performance which, as Koopmans concedes, has not been
commensurate up till now with the enormous effort and talent expended."
    After which comes a pitiful collection of arguments as to why Dorfman
thinks these methods will "pay off," including the lovely argument that "it is
intellectually satisfying, at least it is to a large proportion of young recruits
to the profession; they can hardly be prevented from adopting it." (!) The

100. Robert Dorfman, "Economic Science," *Kyklos*, Vol. 11, #4, New York, 1957.

whole thing is a virtual confession of bankruptcy and escapism. I wonder if we shouldn't do something like Mills' "autopsy" job on economics?[101] It is high time someone came out with a really hard-hitting indictment of all this high-sounding crap. Maybe that should be the next piece of work after the opus? The only drawback is that one would have to read and study an awful lot of boring and worthless stuff.

I am trying to do a sort of "Thoughts on China" RoM.[102] The implications of what is going on over there are really staggering. I am inclined to think that the commune may be the crucial institutional form of socialist society, combining agriculture and industry, government and economics, public and private life. The big puzzle is what to do about the city. The Chinese have postponed that problem because even for them it is going to be a very difficult one. But they are lucky compared to the advanced capitalist countries (and also to a lesser extent the USSR) where urbanism has already grown to cancerous proportions. The Chinese are also lucky in that they are starting the building of socialism before the automobile has become a real factor in their economy. They will be able to use it rationally, combining it with a highly developed public transport system.

But I must get to work. Don't forget that you were going to get Chapter 1 copied and send it to me. I hope to be able to do some work on the opus in the not too distant future and need Chapter 1 so as to be able to start Chapter 2 on the right note.

Write!

Love,

/s Paul

PAB to PMS

Los Altos, California
January 11, 1959

Dear Paul,

[…]

1) I'll try to get hold of Dorfman's review. On the basis of my local contacts I have been suspecting for quite some time that the more honest and intelligent

---

101. Sweezy is referring to C. Wright Mills's book *The Sociological Imagination* (New York: Oxford University Press, 1959), which Mills had initially entitled "Autopsy of Social Science"; see Dan Geary, *Radical Ambition: C. Wright Mills, the Left, and American Social Thought*, Berkeley, 2009. Part of Mills's book was pre-published in *Monthly Review*: C. Wright Mills, "Psychology and Social Science," *Monthly Review* 10, no. 6 (October 1958): 204–09.

102. Leo Huberman and Paul M. Sweezy, "The Chinese Communes," *Monthly Review* 10, no. 10 (February 1959): 369–78.

practitioners of mathematical economics are getting increasingly uncomfortable
in their chairs. There is, however, one very important escape clause which
many of them employ, and which is by no means altogether mendacious. This
is the argument that while most if not all of the mathematic maneuvering is
indeed irrelevant to the comprehension of the capitalist economy — it is fully
significant to economics of planning. This line of reasoning permits even some
of the brethren to consider themselves "crypto-socialists" and to think that in
a very sophisticated way *they* are really pushing forward the economics of the
future. And there may be actually something to that. Input-output research,
linear programming and similar things which advance neither the understanding
nor the criticism of the existing conditions (except perhaps for helping some
monopolies to plan better their policies or the Defense Dept. to develop better
M-Day schedules) may very well turn out to be significant tools of scientific
planning under socialism.

The peculiarity of the situation is arresting: diverting people's attention from
political economy, from the comprehension of the irrationality of capitalism
represents a contribution to the stabilization of the capitalist system — the means
by which this diversion is accomplished may lead to the advancement of the
science of socialist planning. This is just as it is with the development of other
forces of production. . . . A thorough critique of all of this, and a clear separation
of what is science and what is ideology in the present social science mill would
be indeed a terribly important task. For there can be no doubt that we all have
lived too long off Marx's critique of bourgeois ideology, adding very little to
it — while a hell of a lot of ideology has piled up unanalyzed, uncomprehended,
uncriticized.

2) You ought to be careful with regard to the Chinese "communes." From
a number of Chinese statements that I saw in the Soviet press one gets the
impression that they are beating a retreat on that front, and consider much of
the communes movement to be premature, a "left" deviation. This is not to say
that your principal notion is wrong and that the communes will not represent
eventually the genuine nucleus of a socialist society — garden settlements
abolishing for all practical purposes the city-village dichotomy — it may be only
too early to assign to them this role now. China will have to go through quite
a lot of dirty industrialization including expansion of old and creation of new
cities before it will have the wherewithal for organizing a plentiful existence
in the countryside. And this undoubtedly raises the whole nasty dialectic
question: do the dialectical negations work? Can you get back to a decent life via
maximization of misery? If one destroys all basis for humanist education as they
do now in Russia in order to obtain more skilled manpower for the advancement

of the economy which is then to provide the basis for humanist education — if one does that, can one still return to humanist education? And if not, how else?

3) I have reached a state of mixed-upedness which is worse than ever before. At this stage I think that going back to economics, to an effort to comprehend as well as possible what in hell goes on in that relatively matter-of-fact realm of human affairs would be a good thing. An attempt to orient oneself in the "larger universe" is too damn frustrating. And better still, perhaps — give it all up, teach 6 hours a week whatever happens to be in the textbook, and for the rest read novels. I do not know!

4) Just received Starobin's piece.[103] He understands nothing, resurrects Eduard Bernstein, sees in the establishment of every new public *pissoir* a step toward socialism — and is at the same time hard to answer! For it all comes back to the basic question: what is the use of talking about the need for socialism, about the irrationality of what is, about the urgency of a transformation if there are no social forces pushing in the direction of a change? I am aware of the fact that my attempt to deal with that in *MR* was inadequate. But how does one deal with it? The dilemma becomes in a way very simple: either one says that one has to ally oneself with such social forces as there are and become their spokesman (in a struggle for better wages, for more public roads and schools, etc.), their ideologist, their Galbraith — or one has to stick to uncompromising criticism of the existing conditions in the light of reason, stick to the truth — even at the risk of remaining completely isolated and politically ineffective. *Tertium non datur* [there is no third option], at least not here and now. Starobin slides into the former position and becomes a social-democrat; the alternative is "dialectical rationalism" a la Adorno which in a sense breaks with Marx because Marx believed that the latter position is only a temporary, fleeting one and that insight and movement will meet very quickly in a revolutionary party.

[...]

More later. Write!

Love as always,

    s/ Paul

103. See Joseph Starobin, in "On Marxism: A Discussion" (in which Stanley Moore also participated, and PAB replied), *Monthly Review* 11, no. 5 (September 1959): 136–48. The discussion concerned PAB's articles "Crisis of Marxism" that appeared in two parts in the October and November 1958 issues of *MR*.

PMS to PAB

>[*No date but appears to be mid-January 1959 (replies to PAB's comments on Chinese communes in PAB's letter January 11, 1959)*]

Cambridge

Dear Paul,

[. . .]

Your theory of the present state and trend of bourgeois economics is neatly paradoxical, and I have no doubt that there is something to it. But let's not exaggerate. What you say *may* apply to a small segment (input-output and linear programming); but I can see no reason whatever to assume that it applies to a very much larger pile of *dreck* [garbage] —econometric model-building, activity analysis, welfare economics, etc. All this seems to me to be not only useless but also completely without prospects of becoming useful. And I am inclined to discount the *importance* of the contribution which Leontief et al are making to the economics of the future. My guess is that the job will be much better done, and independently too, by those who are actively engaged in the *practice* of economic planning. If this hasn't yet happened in the USSR, the reasons are special historical ones which are unlikely to continue operative for much longer. I get mad every time I pick up one of the professional journals these days: how unseriousness, triviality, moral degeneration can be so tied up with intellectual arrogance and an assurance of moral superiority is almost more than the human understanding can encompass. I have half a mind to write a slashing polemical piece on the subject, using the Dorfman article in KYKLOS as a spring board. I wonder if it might not actually find a warm reception in large parts of the profession, people who are deeply suspicious of what is going on but afraid to say anything out loud for fear that they can't back it up with differential equations of the nth degree. What do you think?

You are of course right that one must be careful about what one says on the subject of the communes (which, however, doesn't excuse us from speaking out in their defense when they are attacked as they are being today!). I finally managed to complete an RoM on the subject and confined it mainly to a few points:

(1) The basic driving force behind the movement is nothing more nor less than our old friend "economies of scale."

(2) It is only natural that this should be first sensed and acted upon by the peasants themselves, once they have been liberated from the shackles of individual cultivation; and in fact all the reliable evidence suggests that this was par excellence a movement from below, not (like collectivization in the USSR)

a revolution imposed from above. (This is a terribly important matter, with probably the most far-reaching of implications for the future of Chinese society, but of course I haven't tried to go into that yet.)

(3) It is the *aims* of the Communes rather than their present practice which arouses the fury of bourgeois critics, precisely because these aims — as boldly stated and defended in the Chinese press — are the classical aims of socialism from the utopians onward. Let the bourgeois journalists and academic hacks scream bloody murder: they have every reason to. But socialists should rejoice that the Chinese are really trying to put socialist ideals into practice and wish them all success.

(4) Finally no one should get the idea that everything is hunky-dory in China. There is a long uphill road to be travelled, and all indications are that the present is a period of strict discipline and intellectual regimentation.

[...]

I imagine you will have heard from Leo by now. I was gratified that *MR* is in a position to send you a non-negligible check, even though one could wish that it were much bigger. He will also have told you our feeling about the Starobin piece. I don't think one needs to answer him at the level of the need for socialism, but it would be useful to demolish his apologetics for monopoly capitalism. It is most interesting how these people, once they begin to turn away from the party, can find all kinds of hitherto hidden virtues in capitalism, become addicted to bourgeois democracy (as though Marxists never paid any attention to that subject before!), etc. What it shows, I suppose, is that they never really understood anything and it was only the party line that kept them from ideological capitulation long ago. I suppose one could account this a virtue in the party, though I am inclined to think that it is more than offset by the party's failure to teach them anything about the nature of capitalism, the true meaning of Marxism, etc.

[...]

Love as ever,
　　/s Paul

[*PMS visited PAB for most of April 1959, and then PAB accompanied PMS back to New York in May for the* MR *birthday party.*]

PAB to PMS

[*No provenance*]

July 9, 1959

Dear Paul,

[…]

Attached is the outline [of the opus] which was drawn up in 1958. The only additional outline document is the one which you wrote in longhand, and which reads as follows:

Introduction

1. Nature of the System

2. Microdynamics

3. Macrodynamics

4. Defense Responses: Internal Waste

5. Defense Responses: External Waste

6. Political Repercussions

7. Cultural Repercussions

8. Prognosis

The way matters have jelled in my head at the end of our this year's discussions is something like this:

Introduction: Methodology, etc. — written and to be revised;

Part I: *The Factory of Surplus* or *quelque nom comme ça* [some name like that]

Chapter 1: The physiology of the corporation

Chapter 2: The corporation as surplus maximizing agent

Chapter 3: The "good" uses of the surplus and their limitations: Why not full re-investment for "good" expansion? But also new products, new industries, spilling over into other markets, primarily competitive ones, etc.

Part II: *Brakes and Braces* — The Surplus Absorption mechanism

Chapter 1: The *automatically* functioning absorption mechanism resulting from non-price competition.

Sales promotion

Product variation for artificial obsolescence

[in brackets in margin: Perhaps in 2 chapters?]

Chapter 2: The *automatically* functioning absorption mechanism — capital export — imperialism

Chapter 3: The *deliberately* provided absorption

"Good" absorption and its limitations: welfare spending, etc.

PMS-Nation article[104]

---

104. Paul Sweezy, "Power Blocks to a Peace Economy," *The Nation*, March 28, 1959.

Chapter 4: The *deliberately* provided absorption

"Bad" absorption: military etc. etc.

Part III: Culture etc. To be worried about a bit later!

I am now working on Part II/Chapter 1. If you are done with Part I, the question is whether you want to leap into Part III or whether there are sections in Part II which you want to do. If I remember correctly you said something about wanting to do Part II/Chapter 3. With regard to Chapter 2: we may be able to use some of the MS on Imperialism which we did for MRS some time ago.

More later, I want to send this off right away. It is absolutely subhumanly hot. Regards for Zirel!

Love,

    /s Paul

PAB to PMS

Oregon Ave.
Palo Alto, Calif.
August 3, 1959

Dear Paul,

Thank you very much for fixing the psycho piece.[105] I have adopted nearly all of your suggestions, and made a couple of additions where they seemed to serve a useful purpose. I did not use the — excellent — quote from Gramsci because I have no quotes in the whole thing, and thought that sticking in one would merely underscore the absence of references everywhere else. There would be after all many places at which Marx, Freud but also Fromm et al. could have been appropriately quoted. This all I must leave to a later occasion if such ever occurs.

With regard to your "general" questions I could embark on a longish exposition for which there is no time at the present. The more I have thought about all of it, the less I am impressed with the whole "repression coefficient" problem as treated particularly by Marcuse. If you wish to use Freud's model, there are *three* ways of discharging libidinous energy: 1. sexual activity, 2. sublimation, and 3. repression. The crux of the thing is that (1) is superior to (3) but *not* superior to (2); in fact, if (1) should be the *only* outlet matters would be in lousy shape even from the standpoint of the libidinous household itself. The trouble with capitalist culture is *not* that it provides too little of (1) — of this there is actually a lot — the trouble is that it provides too little of (2). And it is by no means utopian ("badly" utopian, that is) to expect at a relatively early stage of

---

105. Paul A Baran, "Marxism and Psychoanalysis," *Monthly Review* 11, no. 6 (October 1959): 186–200.

socialist development a significant widening of sublimation possibilities. I would say, that even at the present stage of the Soviet development this has already taken place with regard to the young. And only if the sublimation outlets drain off enough from the direct sexual activity outlet can the latter become a genuinely "happyfying" experience. The identification of sublimation with repression which is continually explicitly or implicitly smuggled in in bourgeois writings confuses badly the entire issue. Instead of talking about "human nature" one gets to talking about "highly complex industrial societies," and before you know it you have landed in the so fashionable swamp of monopoly capitalism and socialism being essentially the same because they are both highly industrialized, therefore alienated etc. etc. This is where Mills gets off but also many others.

After everything else is settled, I'll try a tiny book on all of this: an essay on Marx with various Marxiana.

By the way, Gus Kelley sent me a copy of Bernstein's *Voraussetzungen des Socialismus*.[106] It is amazing, how little the modern welfare boys have added to what the old fellow said 60 years ago!!!!

More later! Write! Since you got to Cornell, you stopped writing.

Love,

/s Paul

PAB to PMS

Palo Alto
December 1st, 1959

Dear Paul,

[...]

Have you read [Oskar] Lange's article on Marxism and Bourgeois Economics?[107] It was published in Polish early last year and has appeared in English in some Indian Students' journal in London. There he argues that Marxism has not been keeping up with the *positive* developments in bourgeois economics, while the latter have been leading to a far-reaching "de-apologization" and "scientification" of the discipline. I have the feeling that he touches upon but fails to come to grips with a very important problem. As Stalin put it in his last booklet, we are confronted with the emergence of "two world markets" i.e. two economic systems. It would be silly to believe that the *same* economic theory should be appropriate for both, that those two radically

106. Eduard Bernstein, *The Prerequisites for Socialism*, 1899.
107. Oskar Lange, "Marxism and Bourgeois Economics," *On Political Economy* (Bombay, India, 194), 52–82.

different forms of economic organizations should admit of the *same* system
of generalization. And if this is silly to assume then what reason is there to
think that Marx's *Capital* represents such an all-embracing set of propositions
encompassing not merely all of capitalist development but also the development
of socialist economies?

Now the interesting thing is that in the West economic science is doing
very little indeed to comprehend and to elucidate the working principles of
monopoly capitalism but is driven partly by escapism, partly by the necessities
of the individual monopoly enterprise and partly by the intellectual logic of the
subject matter into developments most significant to the science of economic
planning (programming etc.). Yet, in this very process it develops also its
apologetic, unscientific character as far as monopoly capitalism is concerned
— by washing out the all-important point that what it arrives at scientifically is
relevant to socialism and *not* to capitalism. The fact that it does produce certain
things useful to socialist planning (as it has produced machines, computers and
other productive resources no less useful to socialism) should not obscure the
different role played by all of this under monopoly capitalism. This dialectic is
of IAA importance. It would be a terrible trap to fall into to say that because of
the excellence of General Motor's distribution system it *is* a socialist enterprise. I
think to disentangle that, to show how Marxian economics are of prime necessity
under monopoly capitalism and how bourgeois economics — regardless of its
technical accomplishments possibly useful to socialist planning — remains an
instrument of obfuscation and ideology formation would be a very useful job.
When done with opus, let's write a longish article on Marxism and Economics.
Those things should serve as stimulants to finish quickly the first volume.

More later.

[...]

Love as always,
/s Paul

PAB to PMS

Palo Alto, California
December 2, 1959

Dear Paul.

Just received the MS of my Stresa "hick-up" [transcript from PAB's lecture at
Stresa conference] — much obliged! I'll have it mimeographed and give it to
whoever wishes to look at it. Incidentally, this statement includes a sentence of

which I am proud particularly in the light of the Schultze monograph[108] "... an economy in which a large part of output is accounted for by monopolistic and oligopolistic producers is marked by an asymmetry which may not have been entirely absent under competitive conditions but which grows increasingly pronounced with concentration of capital: while declines of demand (unless assuming major proportions) do not lead to declines of prices but rather to reductions of output (and employment), increases in demand (unless assuming major proportions) tend to cause price increases rather than larger output (and employment). From this follows, however, that such fiscal and monetary policy measures as might be undertaken with a view to raising sagging demand to the level required for the maintenance of full employment do not necessarily lead to full employment but produce inflation instead."

[...]

Last night Nicky Kaldor gave a paper here (he is spending the current academic year in Berkeley) which I thought was really elegant. In particular the part of his talk in which he devastatingly demolished the marginal productivity theory was absolutely superb. I believe that he is on weaker or actually weak ground in his theorizing in re: growth etc. I had a talk with him this morning and it became even more clear to me that the whole dog is buried in the notion of the surplus. It is here where the best bourgeois economists dig in and refuse to yield ground. He says that our position would be o.k. if we could show a rising share of *profits* in Y [income]. To my reply that what matters is not the share of profits alone but the share of (profits + unproductive surplus utilization of all kind) and that one could even have a continual increase of S [surplus] with a stable or declining share of P [profit], his answer is, "this may be right, but who cares?" This means, he admits, less than potential growth, less than potential good consumption, less than potential education etc. etc., but this is somehow outside of the economic domain. We have to stress the S concept, and we have to place very much emphasis on two points: (1) the waste of a large portion of S is not merely a cultural phenomenon: without that waste the system would go to the dogs, and (2) the cultural phenomenon and all that goes with it is nothing to be pushed aside. Either we are social scientists or not; if not then what is all this theoretical fuss about?

More on all of this later.

[...]

As ever,

/s Paul

---

108. Charles Schultze, *Recent Inflation in the United States* (Washington, D.C.: U.S. Government Printing Office, 1959). Schultze put forward a theory of cost-push inflation.

PAB to PMS

[*No provenance*]

December 3, 1959

Dear Paul,

Bombarding you with what must strike you by now as eminently tiresome reading! — I have been pondering one remark made by Kaldor in our yesterday's conversation. His point was that all that we are saying in re: S [surplus] may be well and good, but that our notion of S has "no firm point of anchorage" (his expression). How does one get it a "firm point of anchorage?" Mind you, I have no illusions about our ability to influence the professional brethren, still the thing ought to be formulated as well as possible even by their standards.

In Marx the situation is fairly unambiguous. The difference between Y [income] and $(c+v)$ [constant capital + variable capital] is S, and there you are. Out of this S all sorts of things are covered: profits, rent, interest, mercantile activities (at least a part of them), etc.[109] When it comes to unproductive labor Marx obviously operates with two concepts not always clearly separated. *One* [apparently "standard (a)" as discussed below] is that various labor contributing to the bourgeois-shaped output is unproductive because necessitated by the bourgeois-shaped social order. There the most obvious example: police etc., necessitated by the existence of the bourgeois state but also *Pfaffen, Prinzen und Huren* [priests, princes and whores] who would not exist in a decent society. In other words, in establishing the unproductive nature of that team he uses a criterion of "objective reason" or of a model of another society which would be according to his reasonable judgment a better, more rational outfit. This, however, [being] music of the future, and very anxious not to appear as a Utopian, he continually sidesteps that line of argument. Since the bourgeois society *is* a progressive society as compared with feudalism, no point in raising ahistorical hell about a future, better society.

From this comes the *second* view [apparently "standard (b)"] of what constitutes unproductive labor, namely all labor which does not contribute to bourgeois output, i.e. does not produce surplus value and is paid out [of] the basic income streams: v and s [surplus value]. This latter unproductive labor may be most essential and laudable: doctors, scientists etc. — it still is unproductive *by the standards of the capitalist order.* — Now, as long as the capitalist order was genuinely progressive, and as long as it actually was cleaning out all kinds of feudal modes of existence: courtiers and clowns and ecclesiastic parasites and

109. In the analysis here Baran uses S for the concept of economic surplus and s for surplus value, as in Marx's conception.

knights and butlers, those two standards *tended* to lead to the same results. What did not contribute to bourgeois output was not much good by standard (a) as well as by standard (b). To be sure, the bourgeois output began generating its own "feudal-type" *Dreck* (bankers, stockbrokers, but also bureaucrats, whores *et tutti quanti* [and all the rest]) but this could have been treated as yet as a minor matter, and in any case taken out of the *positive* economic theory, as something to worry about in the general critique of the capitalist order. What is more, since full employment was assumed, all of those birds may have been either eating into consumption of the capitalists — no great loss there — or into accumulation of capital — more serious but still unimportant in absolute terms.

Now we have a different baby altogether. Standards (a) and (b) do *not* tend to lead to similar results *mais au contraire* [but quite the contrary]. What by standard (a) — objective reason, more rational society or however you wish to formulate it — is staggering madness, is by standard (b) ok. The stuff is paid out of the basic income streams allright (both *s* and *v*) but to the extent to which it is paid out of *s* is *indispensable* to the functioning of the system as it has evolved. Therefore when well-meaning liberals kindly agree with us that there is unproductive stuff going on, they actually — without ever officially acknowledging it — use the otherwise despised objective reason criterion. But when it comes to official attitudes they stiffen up and say where is your "point of anchorage?" Surely for this system all the rubbish is indispensable, but what this means is that this system is mad. In other words, Marx's second criterion which he took over from Smith and Ricardo and which historically in the anti-feudal struggle made excellent sense is of no use to us. Then we get back to the formulation which I have in *PEoG* p. 32 as a starting point, and this thing re-worked and re-explained and re-iterated has to be somehow stuck in at the beginning of the opus. Without it the *S* notion hangs in the air. I do not think that the term "utility" which you have been using on and off is too good; it opens you immediately to the asinine attack "how do you know that Jim Bim does *not* derive 'utility' from having his chewing gum nationally advertised?" As you may remember even a Marxist like Marcuse is not above this line of reasoning.

Well, think about it too, and let me know what occurs to you. This is important for *Selbstverstaendigung* [self-understanding].

Love as always,

/s Paul

PMS to PAB

[*Handwritten*]

Ithaca

Dec. 4 [1959]

Dear Paul,

This will be a quickie.

[…]

The Dorfman review certainly shows that he didn't understand anything from your piece in the Haley volume. I suppose the fate of the opus will be the same. But you are right: this doesn't make it any less important for us to try. I'm beginning to understand one thing about intellectual history: not only is it hard to get a new idea accepted, it seems to be even harder to get it recognized as a new idea. There's the real challenge. . . .

What you say about NK [Nicky Kaldor] is most interesting. "Full employment" is all any of the Keynesians have ever worried about. That one offers them an entire economic theory of the sociocultural shape of an historic epoch means absolutely nothing to them. Who cares? My God!

I suppose I should do a piece on Schultze for MR? I find that the professional economists around here tend to find in it nothing but a slightly fancy version of the cost-push inflation story. My guess is that it will get the same sort of silent treatment as Steindl — a result to which Schultze, ironically, probably contributes since it is clear that he doesn't understand any of the deeper implications of the work. Schultze needs to be saved from Schultze. . . .[110]

[…]

Yrs.,

/s Paul

P.S. […]

---

110. In the late 1950s inflation was treated as a baffling phenomenon in neoclassical economics, and was being explained in cost-push terms. Baran meanwhile had offered a theory of inflation in *The Political Economy of Growth* that was being ignored in the profession. See Paul M. Sweezy, "Baran and the Danger of Inflation," *Monthly Review* 26, no. 7 (December 1974): 1–10.

PMS to PAB

[*Replying to PAB's December 3 letter re: Nicky Kaldor*]

Cornell University

Thurs. p.m. [mid-December 1959]

Mon cher Pavel,

Pardon my long non-writing. I am not only one of the world's worst
correspondents but an even worse character. Nor do I see much hope for
improvement . . .

    I have been thinking much about your letter re the need for pinning things
down for the likes of Nicky Kaldor. It would be desirable, of course. But my
trouble is always that what they are asking for is a solution of the problem in
advance. I don't see how the question of what is and what is not productive
(bez. [*beziehungsweise* or "as the case may be"] socially necessary) labor can
be sensibly discussed in a vacuum. After the dimensions of the problem — and
its nature — have been established by an analysis of the system as it really is,
then I think a useful discussion of definitions might be possible. But as a part
of the introduction I can only see it as delay and diversion which would not
convince anyone. Maybe I'm wrong, but that's my reaction to the problem as you
formulate it.

    To put it otherwise, I think that a realistic analytical discussion of the system,
the tendency of profits, the character of costs in the concentrated industries,
etc., will convince anyone who isn't hopeless that there is a very real and in fact
ineluctable problem of waste and unproductivity. But tell them that there is such
a problem before you have shown it to them and I think 90 percent will pay no
attention at all.

    [. . .]

    Love,

        /s Paul

PAB to PMS

Palo Alto

December 17, 1959

Dear Paul,

Our last night's telephone conversation transported me into a state of acute
despondency. It is obviously inappropriate for me to offer you unsolicited advice
on what you should do with your time and on how you should run MR, but
— even having slept over the matter — I feel that I should register dissent in re
Cuba. Not that Cuba is not a very interesting place at this particular moment,
and not that you could not do a very good report on the situation down there

filling in this way the Summer issue. My feeling is only that at this stage of the game the opus deserves IA priority. And this is not only because of our personal commitment to produce it, but because at the present time this is the opportunity that we have to make a lasting contribution to socialist thought. Ours is the time not of articles and reportages but of weighty books that may push Marxism a step further and rescue it from being accused of sterility, obsoleteness etc. What needs to be said about Cuba can be said by Harvey O'Connor and a number of other people who have their heart in the right place and their nose stuck out in the right direction. You should do now more than ever theoretical work of basic nature and not fritter away your energies on running after the latest event. I know that you have to do some of it for the RoM's etc., but doing it more than is absolutely necessary is, in my humble opinion, misinvestment of energies.

Concretely: if after finishing with Cornell you will spend some time reading up on Cuba, then go there (in March) and then spend some time writing it all up, you'll be busy with it until you go back to Cornell for the summer session. This means that as far as work on the opus is concerned, you won't have time for it until autumn 1960! I emphatically protest against such an allocation of resources!!! You can clearly send me to hell, and tell me to not to pester you with my wisdom, but if you choose not to do so, I would submit to you a different scheme: make the Summer issue in something that is (a) of burning interest, and (b) is relevant to the opus: e.g. a somewhat deeper analysis of American education or the "fallacy of the Soviet comparison," explaining that the problem of socialism in the U.S. is fundamentally different from that in the SU or any other poor country). After you are through with Cornell or whenever is convenient come out here and work here solidly for as long as possible on the opus. And let us get it done by the end of this year!! The financial side of that project is surely no more complex than that of going to Cuba!! In the first place, if MR can finance your Cuba expedition, it could equally well give you an advance on the book. Secondly, I am confident that we can get some extra money for the book from the Rabinowitz foundation [Louis Rabinowitz Foundation].

Anyway, think it over! Pity, I won't see you, but I hope to see you here soon!

Don't be mad at me for sticking my nose into your affairs, but in this case I act as the German lawyers used to say "*in Wahrnehmung berechtigter Interessen.*" [in representation of justified interests]

Love always,

/s Paul

[. . . *followed by a quote from Marx*]

PMS to PAB

[*Handwritten*]

Cambridge
December 19, 1959

Dear Paul,

Your "quickie" was waiting when I got back here about midnight last night (10 hours from Ithaca to Cambridge by public conveyance in this richest country in the world!) Please believe that I gave full and careful — even agonizing — consideration to the points you make before agreeing to the Cuba issue. If I finally decided to go along with Leo on it, the reasons I think are very strong ones. I will set them out, not necessarily in order of importance:

(1) A good Cuba issue will be a coup for *MR* both here and abroad. It is true that Harvey [O'Connor] can write about Cuba, but I don't trust him to get to the real heart of the matter (he is a good reporter but even glories in his inability to understand any of the subtleties or complexities of Marxist theory). And I know of *no* others whom I would even ask to write for *MR* on the subject.

(2) I shall *in any case* have to spend quite a lot of time on the double summer issue — I always do. Going to Cuba for a week or so will add to the time, but will by no means imply, as you suggest, that I will have no time for opus between Cornell first semester and Cornell summer school. I expect to spend *most* of that period on opus.

(3) *MR* can finance the Cuba trip, and both Leo and I think it a good investment, even in the strict business sense.

(4) Here comes the real reason: I think that Cuba is the beginning of the real Latin American [LA] revolution, and think that in a very real sense it may be the LA revolution that will determine the fate of U.S. capitalism. I don't think that we (and I mean you and I as well as *MR*) can afford to stand aloof at this critical juncture. We *must* establish close ties with the LA revolution and I believe this is the time to do it. We have already established an excellent contact with Raul Roa Kouri, a Cuban delegate to the UN *and son of the present foreign minister*. I believe all doors will be open to us, and that we may be able to give as well as receive valuable educational material. In the long run, I think very seriously of you and me as going somewhere in LA and teaching Marxism where it would really count. Not now, of course — but now is the time to get to know the people who are going to play the key roles in the years ahead. And of this you may be sure: they all have their eyes completely glued to Cuba now, and many of them are in Cuba or visiting Cuba from time to time.

(4) I badly need to see and feel and be revived by a real revolution. The atmosphere of this country and its academic life is stifling me. I'm utterly

convinced that Cuba is the real thing (read the series by Tad Szulc now appearing in the *NY Times* — i.e. Dec. 17, 18, 19, 20 — for some of the indications). I realize that the U.S. may be able to overthrow the present Cuban regime, but it will be a Pyrrhic victory. Here is something really happening on our very doorstep and I want to participate in some way. I'm convinced that I'll be a better person for it and that all of us will reap great benefits in the longer run.

(5) I confess that I am dying of curiosity about how much the present Cuban regime *understands* and whether it is prepared to take the measures which may become necessary to carry through on the required socio-economic reforms and to prevent Cuba from becoming another Guatemala or Iran. From a few glimpses of what's going on, I have a strong impression that Castro is now surrounded by people who know the score and who are not going to be any pushovers for Allen Dulles & Co. But I want to confirm this impression firsthand.

(6) All of this may involve a month's delay on opus — I don't see why it should be more. But I honestly think that in this case it is worth it.

*   *   *   *

Don't imagine for a moment that I disagree with you on the importance of the opus. Quite to the contrary, a stretch in the regular season at Cornell has convinced me that our colleagues in the economics profession, clever as many of them are, simply don't see what U.S. capitalism is like, what its inner essence consists of. And though they won't let us show *them*, we have a sacred duty to show anyone who is willing to look. My trouble now is that the semester's work has produced for me quite a lot more facts and details on corporations, price policies, waste, etc. How much of all this should we try to include? Or should we try to present the bare bones of the theory — the vision without clothes, as it were? I lean to the latter view: *We should write the book with no more facts or references, but write and get it out!* But it is hard to do it that way. This, and not Cuba, is what holds me up, I am afraid.

[…]

Love,

/s Paul

PAB to PMS

Palo Alto, California

December 23, 1959

Dear Paul,

[…]

I can see and sense exactly what you say about Cuba, and I know that you have a "*Punkt*" there. It is indeed quite possible or even probable that the big shake-up here may start in Latin America which is more important to American Capitalism than China and the rest of Asia, but I wonder whether Washington won't be able to crush, bribe and destroy there for a considerable period of time. To be sure the crushing, bribing and destroying would in itself constitute a major historical force back home and would not be very easy to carry out, but the smoothness of the Guatemala operation and the zero effect of same back here are worth remembering. One thing about Cuba which is most remarkable is that the USSR is apparently destroying one of our strongest weapons: their sugar purchases may actually avert a major economic catastrophe into which we would very much like to plunge Castro. I wonder whether this will do the trick.

[…]
Love,
        s/ Paul

[…]

[1960]

PMS to PAB

[*Handwritten*]

[Hotel Nacional de Cuba]
March 7, 1960

Dear Paul,
This is a beautiful and fascinating place. There is no doubt that the revolution is genuine. The old state apparatus has been completely smashed, but completely, and replaced by Castro supporters. Armed workers' and peasants' militias are all over the place. Castro is the most genuinely popular leader I have ever had any experience of. And, last but not least, the boys around him are tough, able, *and* dedicated socialists with a very good understanding of the problems of political power and the economics of underdeveloped countries. We spent all day yesterday in continuous discussion with the planning group at the Agricultural Reform Institute (IMRA), including the No. 2 man, a former journalist who is very able and is the executive driver of the central institution of the revolution. The weakness of the setup is *not* economic. It is a rich country with so much potential surplus that they have been able to raise standards of living very considerably — especially for the landless and unemployed rural workers who are the political backbone of the revolution — even in one year. With Soviet help, and even moderately effective planning they should be able to keep the

balance-of-payments problem under control and get a workable development program under way.

The potential Achilles' heel is the lack of a real political party to educate and discipline the masses for the tough years to come when they really feel the brunt of the imperialist counter attack. Everything is in fine shape now, but if Castro should get killed and when the revolutionary enthusiasm wears off, the old divisive and corrupting power of the still largely intact bourgeoisie will begin to do its nefarious work. Whether the revolution can stand up then is a big question mark. The CP [Communist Party] of course is trying to fill the gap in the political machinery, but I doubt if it can. It has made too many mistakes and seems to have little "feel" for the special problems of this kind of underdeveloped country. Castro himself is an absolutely brilliant and highly intelligent political leader who learns fast. If he lives, maybe it will succeed. Anyway, it's a very exciting place and makes you feel wonderful to be in it. We've been given the red-carpet treatment.

I'm told that you can come down here — and Hoob and I will come back too — to help with their educational and training problems — but only after opus is finished. We *must* get that thing out of the way in the shortest possible time.

I'm to talk on planning *some time* next week for all gov't officials who want to come. Meanwhile, we're going to travel around the countryside and see some of the agricultural co-ops. Hoob joins in sending love. Write to this hotel (a lovely place)!

Yrs.,

/s P.

PAB to PMS

Palo Alto, Cal.

May 2nd, 1960

Dear Paul,

You are busy now with other things and probably do not feel like pondering the *Dreck* I am concerned with, but I want to communicate it to you anyway because (a) something may occur to you, and (b) of a need for *Selbstverstaendigung* [self-understanding]. What is at issue is the following: the *opus* hinges — in my opinion, not on statistical measurement, and not even on a big display of factual information. What it does hinge on, however, is what you have called "vision" combined with conceptual clarity. I think we have the former but I am having a dog's time now with the latter. The difficulty is essentially to define properly the notion of the economic surplus for the purposes of our discussion.

Engels remarked that Marx's greatest achievement was to uncover *"surplus value"* underneath all the different income streams that were considered more or less autonomous by Smith, Ricardo and others: interest on capital, ground rent, much of mercantile revenues and, naturally profits *sans phrase* [goes without saying]. What we are really trying to do is *precisement* the same. We want to show that the sum total of profits, interest, rents + (and this is crucial) swollen costs of distribution + advertising expenses + PR + legal depts + fins and chrome + *faux frais* of product variation and model changes + govt. exp. = *economic surplus*, which economic surplus increases both in absolute and relative terms under monopoly capital. It is important to understand that our economic surplus is not the same as surplus value of Marx's but a much more comprehensive and much more complex term.

Indeed, I am somewhat exhilarated by the thought that we may actually have in our hands something that is an important contribution to thought *beyond* Marx. For what I have been thinking about is that under competition economic surplus is essentially identical with surplus value. If you have a universe of output consisting of more or less "sensible" commodities (where need and want more or less converge) and if you have a competitive mill in which costs are being held down to socially necessary levels with what is socially necessary determined by the state of development of productive resources then surplus value is the difference between the net value of output (net that is of depreciation which is in turn sensibly calculated) and the aggregate wage bill. *NB* on the assumption of socially necessary costs being maintained with what is socially necessary determined really by the "state of the arts" it is quite permissible to deduct the entire wages + salaries bill from the aggregate value of output in order to arrive at surplus value (with due allowance for c [constant capital]). Out of that surplus value the capitalist gets his profits, the banker his %%, the landlords their rents, and the merchants (part of) their commercial gains. (The other part constituting productive services comes out of the costs proper and still another part based on milking v [wage] recipients is "profit by alienation" and constitutes a net addendum to surplus value.)[111]

So far so good for competition. But when we get to monopoly capitalism the whole thing shifts and economic surplus is no longer even approximately

---

111. The concept of "profit by alienation" or "profit from deduction," derived from Marx, was to play a key role in the argument in the unpublished chapter that Baran drafted for *Monopoly Capital*, entitled "Some Theoretical Implications," finally published in 2012 in *Monthly Review*: Paul A. Baran and Paul M. Sweezy, "Some Theoretical Implications," *Monthly Review* 64, no. 3 (July-August 2012): 24–59.

identical with surplus value but *very much larger*!!!! Simply because with
aggregate output no longer consisting of a heap of "sensible" commodities but
of an agglomeration of commodities a large part of which is *due* to the sales effort
— the notion of socially necessary cost of its production gets a new meaning. It
is no longer socially necessary in terms of prevailing productivity + technology, it
is socially necessary primarily in terms of the *modus operandi* of the Big Business
economy.

The surplus value concept would give you wrong or rather irrelevant
measurements. For if you take the value of aggregate output and deduct from
it the aggregate v [wages] (with due allowance for c [constant capital] which is
incidentally now much more difficult to make) you get surplus value alright but
this is *only a part* of the economic surplus. This would be even true if you would
draconically confine your v to those engaged in *production proper*. Since the
production process proper is under monopoly capitalism *inherently corroded by
the sales effort* the distinction between costs of production (still meaningful in
Marx's competitive universe!) becomes extremely hazy. . . . The adman is in costs
of distribution alright; what about the construction engineer who devises the
new car model for sales reason and the worker who retools the joint to produce
it? The Charlie Van Dorens are costs of distribution boys and partake of the
surplus value but what about the blue collar type who with socially necessary
skills produces the booklet conveying the message of the remedy against sour
stomachs?[112] The crux is the interpenetration of production and sales effort with
the result that in that embrace the concept of "socially necessary" gets stifled.

What does socially necessary mean now? Everything that is needed for
conduct of business under monopoly capitalism? Surely not, because the coal
miner is as necessary for that as Batten, Barton, Durstine & Osborn. Everything
that is needed to *produce* (physically) the material output of society? Certainly
not, because that output consists to a large extent of fins, chrome, remedies
against sour stomach, new models etc. with lots of engineers, foremen, workers
engaged in turning this stuff out. This, incidentally, all on the assumption that
those boys operate with maximal *technical* efficiency — the story gets even more
"mixy upy" if there is monopoly-shielded inefficiency cum waste. In other words,
without the competitive assumption, the surplus value concept is mortally ill!
[Note by PMS: Also applies to the competitive case, *mutatis mutandis*.]

---

112. The reference to Charlie Van Doren has to do with the famous Quiz Game hoax. See Leo
Huberman and Paul M. Sweezy, "The TV Scandals," *Monthly Review* 11, no. 9 (December 1959):
273–81.

(Amusingly, this is the opposite of what Schumpy, Leontief among others used to argue saying that with perfect competition there would be no surplus value because entrepreneurs would bid up wages to a point of 0 surplus value — this is because what is needed is not their crazy *perfect* competition but just Marx's free competition with all the social constraints). And if on top of all wages are not determined by the value of labor power in Marxian sense but are higher, i.e. permit reduction per alienation, and the capitalists are able of shifting their various expenses (if only partly) onto the consumer (including wage earner) then the derivative surplus value recipients (merchants, bankers, landlords but also advertisers etc.) do not only eat into surplus value but actually *increase* it per alienation.

Where does all this leave matters except with the necessity to leave this alone [Note by PMS: "No! It must be developed and explained! That is the point!"] and to define *konsequent* economic surplus with reference not to what is socially necessary *hic et nunc* but to what would be socially necessary in a rational society. I began moving in that direction in *PEoG*: "Most generally speaking the unproductive share of a nation's total economic effort consists of all labor resulting in the output of goods and services the demand for which is attributable to the specific conditions and relationships of the capitalist system, and which would be absent in a rationally ordered society." (p. 32) — By the way, Marx hints at this in discussing Smith's notion of unproductive labor. There he speaks of what is productive and unproductive under capitalism and adds "*absolut gesprochen*" [strictly speaking] all this would be different! Without the "*absolut gesprochen*" one gets stuck *now* — simply because monopoly capitalism is much more removed from that "*absolut gesprochen*" than competition ever was! — I am attaching a little translation I made of a lovely passage in Marx [attachment is missing] — the new, Moscow-Berlin *Theorien* [Marx, *Theories of Surplus Value*]— which should be appended to one of the chapters of *opus*.[113] This undoubtedly requires a full-dress discussion of what is meant by a rational social order etc. but we cannot shirk that for otherwise we hang in the air. On the other hand once this nut is properly cracked the *opus* is a cinch. Then we go ahead and give a "casually empiricist" sketch of the forms in which the *Dreck* [the garbage of economic surplus] appears, and I do not give a damn whether we have plenty

---

113. Handwritten marginal note by PMS: "Also wonderful with respect to Keynesiana." The passage from Marx's *Theories of Surplus Value* in question was quite likely the following passage used by Baran in "Some Theoretical Implications": "The industrial capitalist becomes more or less unable to fulfill his function as soon as he personifies the enjoyment of wealth, as soon as he wants the accumulation of pleasures instead of the pleasure of accumulation." Karl Marx, *Theories of Surplus Value*, Part I (Moscow: Progress Publishers, 1964), 282ff.

of statistics or none. As long as we have illustrations and as long as it is clear what we mean. I think this represents *"eine Umwaelzung der Wissenschaft"* [a transformation of the science] because it explains and systematizes what the Galbraith's of all descriptions are at best able to *describe*! The same step KM [Marx] made by comparison with Smith, Ricardo, etc.

At least, I am modest!

[...]

And cheer up; we have a *mission* Goddamit, and let us not be gotten down by anything!

Love,

/s Paul

PMS to PAB

Wilton

May 11 [1960]

Dear Paul,

We are in *medias res Cubana* (something wrong with my Latin grammar there, isn't there?) & between us have already churned up well over a hundred typed pages with no end in sight. What we will do with all this remains to be seen, but in the meantime the watchword is that of Marx's capitalist: Accumulate! Accumulate! Actually, I think we have some good stuff, including what I would call the "secret" of the Cuban revolution which is to be found in an analysis of the character and structure of the "peasant" class. Actually, it is not a peasant class at all in Marx's sense (as defined, e.g., in the text vs. Bakunin produced by Mayer) but a rural proletariat — rural wageworkers, according to the 1953 ag. census, outnumber all others in the rural labor force (owners, tenants, subtenants, sharecroppers, and squatters) by approx 3 to 1. And in addition the wage workers in the sugar industry, by far the biggest and most developed in the island, live in the countryside, near the agricultural workers. Further, the Cuban ruling class has never bothered to do anything for the rural worker — no education, not even a church (Lowry Nelson, the leading authority on the sociology of rural Cuba, reports that he was not able to find *one* chapel outside the towns and cities). Add all that up and you have the perfect formula for producing revolutionaries. *Quelle* difference between that and a European peasant country! But elaboration must await the finished product.

I like your letter re opus matters very much. We march together, to use a famous phrase, the "only" problems being matters of formulation. I am not clear that we need to define economic surplus by reference to what would exist under a rational form of society. Can't we start by defining it by reference

to the competitive model and then show how monopoly capitalism inevitably
and completely futzes the picture, *making it impossible any longer to achieve a
rational definition or measurement of what is surplus and what is not.* This is
the natural condition of the affluent society and it can be remedied only by going
over *in practice* to a rational social order. The consequences of the obscuring
of the difference between surplus and non-surplus are to be found primarily in
the cultural, moral, and ideological fields. It is here that the decay of monopoly
capitalism must be sought and analyzed, not in the economic stagnation or
Zusammenbruch [collapse] which earlier generations of Marxists thought. But all
this just suggestions. . . .

[. . .]
Love and write,
      /s Paul

PAB to PMS

                                                                    May 13, 1960
Dear Paul,
Your letter of May 11th arrived this morning. What you say about Cuba is
mucho interesante and undoubtedly correct. The rural proletariat corresponds
to Russia's "*bednyaks*": the landless peasants and agricultural workers whose
central importance for Russia and the colonial and semi-colonial countries was
repeatedly stressed by Lenin. Indeed in his strategy of the revolution the alliance
of the urban workers with the "*bednyaks*" (cum neutralization of the middle-
peasant) was a crucially important factor.[114]

It is interesting that the more intelligent Russian conservatives saw the issue
after 1905, and felt that the system could not survive unless it would find a
way of giving land to "*bednyaks*" (if ever so little) to turn them into *proprietors*,
and to imbue them with the spirit of *ownership*. The famous Stolypin reform
had something of that sort in mind and capsized essentially because of the
myopia and narrow-minded greed of the latifundia owners but also because
time was running out: the 1st WW was just around the corner — in fact it has
been conjectured whether the St. Petersburg elite did not precipitate (or help
precipitating) the war precisely in order to escape the agrarian catastrophe
which was coming one way or another. . . . The Cuban condition was aggravated

---

114. On his copy of the letter Sweezy highlights the above and adds this handwritten comment:
"Right. But there is a big difference in Cuba. The *bednyaks* there were the overwhelming *majority*
of the countryside and the regime was able to base not only its revolutionary strategy but also its
reconstruction program on them. *Quantum mutatus an ille!*" [quite a different thing].

in addition by the plantation factor: the colonial feature of the country. This is all fascinating stuff and I am looking forward to reading your story. By the way Mexico would have been precisely in the same spot if it weren't for the Mexican agrarian revolution which postponed but did not solve matters. . . .

In re: *opus*, I am depressed by what you refer to as the "only" problem: how to formulate it all. I think the trick is exactly to juxtapose monopoly capitalism with *both* competition and socialism. Focusing exclusively on the former comparison is doubly dangerous: would create the impression of idealizing competition and be a "petty bourgeois" deviation; furthermore it would be inadequate because it would necessarily sidestep the significant *advances* embodied in monopoly capitalism. It is undoubtedly true that the mere fact that the definition and measurement of economic surplus is so goddamn difficult if not impossible is an aspect of an irrational order, although also here I don't believe that one should fall into the "affluent society" trap. It is *not* the affluence that matters; it is *monopoly capital-affluence* that is at issue. For affluence in a socialist society could be twice as high and express itself altogether differently: tremendous reduction of work-weeks and work-years with corresponding extension of the education span to comprise college or university, earlier retirement, housing, travel, large-scale assistance to poorer countries and millions of things which we cannot anticipate and which will absorb affluence for as long as it is worthwhile speculating about. It is this current trick of equating affluence under monopoly capitalism with affluence *ueberhaupt* [in general] that represents the sophisticated ideological gimmick of the JKG's [Galbraith's] et al. But more on this when we meet.

[. . .]

Got a note of Marcuse's; he is coming here next week.

See you soon.

Love,

/s Paul

PAB to Stanley Moore re: Moore's paper on Das Kapital

Oregon Ave.
Palo Alto
August 5, 1960

Dear Stanley,

Thank you very much for sending me your paper and the (somewhat mystifying postcard) from Honolulu. I have perused both most carefully, and while deferring my reflections on the latter until I have the pleasure of seeing you again, I would like to submit to your attention such thoughts as occurred to me in connection with the former. In doing so I take the risk of disappointing you: what has occurred to me in connection with your article are not so much comments on your statement as some more general reflections on the matters under consideration.

The most important among them has to do with the concept "law of value." On p.26 you define the law of value as follows: "For Marx, the law of value—that is, the proposition asserting the proportionality of exchange ratios and labor costs — holds for all exchange economies without exception." (The definition that I am interested in is given in the words between the hyphens.) In defining the law in this manner (or in understanding the law of value to mean this) you undoubtedly follow the established practice among Marxists. Thus Paul in *The Theory of Capitalist Development* (pp. 52 f.) explains the meaning of this term as follows: ". . . what Marx called the 'law of value' summarizes these forces at work in a commodity producing society which regulate (a) the exchange ratios among commodities, (b) the quantity of each produced, and (c) the allocation of the labor force to the various branches of production. The basic condition for the existence of a law of value is a society of private producers who satisfy their needs by mutual exchange." I myself used to accept this interpretation of the concept equating thus the law at value with the labor theory of value.

More recently, however, — primarily in connection with trying to think out some problems related to the book which Paul and I are attempting to write — I have come to look at the thing somewhat differently: I would propose to consider the law of value as a set of propositions describing the characteristic features of the economic and social organization of a particular epoch of history called capitalism. This organization is characterized by the prevalence of the principle of *quid pro quo* in economic (and not only economic) relations among members of society; by the production (and distribution) of goods and services as commodities; by their production and distribution on the part of independent producers with the help of hired labor for an anonymous market with the view to making profit. (*NB* this definition of the law of value is adumbrated in the second sentence of Paul's statement cited above.) It is by the dominance of this law of value that the capitalist order differs from all others: from antiquity in which slavery dominated the conditions of production and distribution; from feudalism which system was based on a comprehensive network of rights, duties and traditions; from socialism in which planning becomes the overriding principle.

Now—and this is most important for what we are talking about now — the law of value so conceived implies nothing whatsoever about (a) the mechanism bringing about any given system of relative prices, (b) the mechanism responsible for the allocation of resources, (c) the mechanism accounting for the existing distribution of income. To be sure, those 3 mechanisms are interrelated and may be even considered to represent parts of one whole — all that matters to me now is to state that the law of value as just defined representing the "basic law of capitalism" (Stalin) is *not* affected let alone abolished by the three mechanisms just referred to (*not* being adequately explained by the labor theory of value). To put it differently: one could (and I believe should) insist on the validity and paramount importance of the law of value and at the same time accept a general equilibrium theory of relative prices, particularly in the form in which it is suggested by [Piero] Sraffa and the input-output analysis which he so ingeniously anticipates.[115] You may ask me: what is then the "operational" significance of the law of value as I define it if the labor theory of value is thrown out of it? Answer: very large indeed. For it is the law of value which explains the basic mechanism of capitalism, explains why it is that a general equilibrium theory of relative prices is necessary, explains why the theories of "organized capitalism" are rubbish, shows what the crucially important differences are between both pre-capitalist and socialist formations on one side and capitalism on the other. The failure to distinguish between the law of value (in my definition) and the principle of rational resource allocation accounts for a great deal of confusion in Lange and other writers who believe that the mere fact of attachment of numerical values to goods and services under socialism (so as to render their rational allocation i.e. comparability possible) is tantamount to the maintenance of the law of value. In other words: the acknowledgment of and conduct according to the principle of scarcity and rational resource husbandry is *not* equivalent to the dominance of the law of value. The arrangements under the law of value is one historical form in which scarcity and the need for resource allocation are dealt with but not the only conceivable one. Under planning they are dealt with differently.

Therefore, I believe that it would be better if you confined your strictures upon the labor theory of value to the narrower problem: does the labor theory of value provide an adequate theory of relative prices, resource allocation and income distribution? A negative answer to this question with which I would agree if the Marxian version of the labor theory of value is what is had in mind does not, however, dispose of the law of value, nor vitiate in any manner a whole set of propositions which are derived from the law of value rather than from the labor theory of value. Thus Marx's theory of commodity fetishism and all that goes with it is based on the law of value (in my sense) and suffers no harm from adopting any possible explanation of the existing structure of relative

115. Pierro Sraffa, *The Production of Commodities by Means of Commodities* (Cambridge: Cambridge University Press, 1960).

prices. Your own statement (which is accompanied obviously by a noticeable sneer): "For Marx commodity values are alienated social activity; that is, they are creations of men which appear to be independent of men. The origin of the doctrine of commodity fetishism is to be found in Marx's lifelong preoccupation with the Hegelian concept of alienation" is wholly adequate and what you say is *not* invalidated by a possible rejection of the labor theory of value. (A proposition unrelated to the main argument: you must have had a change in mind in re: alienation in Marx—I remember your telling me that the old man gave up talking and thinking about alienation after *Philosophische und Oekonomische Manuscripte* [*Economic and Philosphical Manuscripts*]; now you say — and I believe correctly — that this was a "lifelong preoccupation" of his . . .)

And in connection with all of the above I beg to dissent from your remark that the "distinction between appearance and reality which serves . . . to render certain propositions immune from either confrontation or refutation in terms of empirical evidence" is an invention of the Devil. While it may be readily granted with respect to "certain propositions" (that ain't saying much) this distinction is most relevant for other — and most important — propositions. And saying that this distinction cannot be verified straightforwardly by reference to empirical evidence misses — in my humble opinion — the entire point. It is the very nature of immediate empirical evidence — *ex definitione* — that it encompasses *appearance*. Indeed if empirical evidence would always present you what you call reality (essence, *Wesen*) life would be a picnic, one would have never anything else to do but go around photographing rather than analyzing empirical evidence. But this bone of contention we have dealt with before. More orally. Please call me as soon as you get back; I hope to see you next week.

As ever,
/s Paul

PAB to PMS

[*Handwritten from Stanford Hospital, where PAB is recovering from a heart attack. Note that PMS is about to return to Palo Alto to begin his two-quarter teaching stint at Stanford beginning in January 1961. PMS had come out in November of 1960 to make preliminary arrangements and also to visit Zirel, who was living in Berkeley at the time.*]

Stanford Medical Center
December 20, 1960

Dear Paul,
Being locked up here gets to be increasingly what the English call a "bore," and the thought of having to spend here at least another 2 weeks is causing me

another heart attack. This could develop into an infinite series if it were not for its obvious point of convergence. The only comfort is a perfectly charming Canadian nurse — unfortunately as unattainable as she is untouchable. Becomes even questionable whether under the circumstances this is a comfort or an aggravation. A genuine *crève coeur* [heartbreak] is [...] who calls, comes, delivers presents and is an embodiment of devotion. What does one do with a thing like that? I wonder what kind of unreciprocated love is worse — active or passive?

Otherwise lots of visitors; there is apparently nothing like illness to increase one's "popularity." Bowker [academic dean] comes every day. My colleagues have all paid their respects — the prospect of a possible vacancy seems to be most intriguing.

Norman Howard has taken care of the real estate problems; within the next few days all this will be signed, sealed, and delivered.

Your automobile was obviously *eine Zitrone* [a lemon]. I have authorized Mr Gunn to do $145 worth of fixing if this chariot is to be counted on for 6 months. On the other hand, with this work done, it should be a respectable means of locomotion.

Voilà, c'est tout [that is all]. Reading a bit, thinking a bit, dreaming a lot and reminiscing. Old age apparently sets in at the point at which hopes for the future recede in favor of remembrances of the past.

Am very glad you'll be back soon. But I don't want you to drink so much no more, otherwise you'll be in this goddamn position of mine. One is enough.

Love, Yours,

/s Paul

6
The Kennedy Years: Civilian Government Spending

[PMS was in Palo Alto from January until end of June 1961, teaching at Stanford. Thus, there is no extant correspondence between PMS and PAB until the end of June 1961.]

PAB to PMS
[Written from PAB's new house after selling the Oregon Ave. house at a loss.]

Laguna Oaks Place
Palo Alto
June 30, 1961

Dear Paul,

[. . .]

Had yesterday dinner with Moe [Abramovitz]. He was shown the whole mountain of correspondence that the Administration has received in re: you and me and Cuba. Apparently an impressive heap. He also saw the (more or less) standard letter which was sent to the writers by the President's office. Even he remarked that the letter was despicable. It did not point out that the University is committed to the principle of academic freedom or anything of the sort, but stressed its having the very difficult problem of my having tenure. The business of freezing my salary, far from being treated as a secret, is being widely advertised (among donors) to show that nothing would be done to "encourage me to stay here." One *should* be above all this, one *should* know that one cannot have one's cake and eat it too, one *should* realize that after all this is a class struggle and *a la guerre comme a la guerre* [in a time of crisis all means are good] — nevertheless it burns me all up, plays havoc with the nervous system and the rational comprehension does very little if anything to one's irrational sensations and emotions. There is obviously no point in resigning from this outfit *at this time*. Next year I still have the Rabinowitz fellowship which means that I'll teach only one quarter. The year thereafter (1962/63) I'll take my sabbatical leave. In other words I don't have to return to regular teaching until the fall of '63. By that time we'll see what gives. . . .

   [. . .]

So much for today.

All the best, Yours,

   /s Paul

PMS to PAB

Wilton, N. H.

Sunday July 9 [1961]

Dear Paul,

Here is a briefest outline of Ch. 6 (government) as I now see it. Comments, amendments, etc., are in order.[116]

1. According to older economic theories (classical, Marxian, neoclassical), the economy normally operated at full capacity, hence whatever went to government must be at the expense of private parties. If a fixed (conventional subsistence) real wage be assumed, then government can only take from surplus receivers. Ergo the bitter resistance of ruling classes to government spending. All this was probably reasonably realistic during most of 19th century.

2. Under monopoly capitalism, however, matters are different. Here less-than-capacity operation is normal. If government creates new effective demand, surplus can be produced which otherwise would not have been. This can take the form either of government directly purchasing goods and services, or of government handing over, via transfer payments, purchasing power to favored private parties (subsidies, pensions, interest on public debt, etc.). When these possibilities first began to be understood during the 30's (credit to Keynes & Co. here), it was thought that government could create new effective demand only by running a deficit: a balanced budget would necessarily be neutral no matter what its total magnitude.

3. This is now seen to be wrong. Exposition of the simple arithmetic of the unit multiplier. GNP equals 100 and government now decides to spend 10 more and at the same time impose additional taxes of 10. The increased spending will add 10 to total demand and (since there is idle labor and equipment) the same amount to output. The other side of the coin is an increase of private incomes by 10, the equivalent of which is drained into the treasury by the additional

---

116. Sweezy here outlined what was to be chapter 6 of *Monopoly Capital*: "The Absorption of Surplus: Civilian Government."

taxation. Net result: expansion of demand and output by the exact amount of the increased balanced budget. Next a brief exposition of how the multiplier is bigger with a deficit. General principle: demand created by government is a function of both the level of spending and the size of the deficit. However, a temporary deficit has only temporary effects; and even a continuing deficit, unless steadily growing, does not give rise to a cumulative increase of demand. (Here abstraction is made of the secondary effects of a persistent deficit via the money supply.)

4. If we assume that apart from wartime emergencies deficits are essentially cyclical phenomena and are at least partly offset by surpluses, then in the long run they cannot be a decisive factor in the amount of effective demand attributable to government that is measured by changes in the level of government spending.

5. Brief discussion of whether it is total spending or government purchases of goods and services which is the relevant magnitude. Conclusion that from our point of view it is the total, including transfer payments. The appropriate correction to make in official GNP statistics is to subtract transfer payments from private consumption and saving. In this way we get the total amount of effective demand created by government.

6. Next a brief review of the record of government spending, using the Sylos [Labini] estimates for 1900-1953 and adding latest figures.[117] Secular peacetime updrift of ratio of government spending to GNP from circa 7 percent to circa 25 percent.

7. Is all of this surplus in our sense of the term? Not all. Some government activities are properly considered socially necessary costs: provision of roads, public utility services (where publicly owned as in the case of the post office TVA, municipally-owned water and power systems, etc.). I'm not sure how far we should go in conceding this point. From a tactical point of view, it may be wise to make generous estimates of government's productive contribution. Your views on this would be appreciated — also any elaboration of the categories that may occur to you. In any case, by far the largest amount of what government absorbs is clearly surplus — all transfers, all military, all administration, all education, culture, etc. (Or do we want to include at least part of education and public health as necessary costs?) Here we make absolutely explicit that to say these things absorb surplus is in no sense minatory. They do so in any and all forms of society. And in a rationally ordered socialist society with productive potential comparable to that of the U.S., the amount and proportion of surplus

117. Sylos Labini, *Oligopoly and Technical Progress* (Cambridge, Massachusetts: Harvard University Press, 1962), 181.

absorbed by the state for such purposes as education, health, culture, etc., etc., would certainly be larger, not smaller. For the moment we want only to establish that by far the largest part of government activity does in fact absorb surplus. At the present time, well over one fifth of gross output is government absorbed surplus. This compares with something of the order of 5 percent (?) for the sales effort and R & D combined.

8. It must be emphasized here that this is *not* surplus which would otherwise have accrued to corporations and individuals for their private purposes. We have already seen that the structure of the monopoly capitalist economy is such that vast additional quantities of surplus could not be absorbed through private channels, hence it would not be produced at all. What government absorbs is additional to not subtracted from private surplus.

One can see in a general way how it works by looking at corporate profits before and after taxes. Before the 30's, corporate income taxation was rather low and as a result of increases during the depression and more especially during World War II the amount went up sharply. This did not mean any reduction in profits after taxes, however. On the contrary, the amount of corporate profits after taxes increased as the economy expanded and remained at about the same proportion of GNP during the 50's as during the late 20's. Corporate profits before taxes, on the other hand, jumped up. What the government took was additional to, not a deduction from, private surplus. And because the large-scale government absorption of surplus enabled the economy as a whole to operate much closer to capacity than would otherwise have been the case, the net effect on private surplus has actually been both positive and large. This explains a basic shift in ruling-class attitudes toward taxation and government spending. The older hostility still persists in the realm of ideology, but the really modern Big Businessman no longer takes it seriously. Government spending, to him, means more effective demand, and he knows that he can shift most of the taxes forward onto consumers or backward onto workers. In the meantime, the intricacies of the tax system, specially tailored to fit the needs of special interests, open up magnificent opportunities for speculative and windfall gains. (Cite the Harper's article on the real estate boom.)

9. Speaking of shifting raises the question whether the increased government absorbed surplus doesn't in fact come out of the hides of lower-income groups. To a certain extent, undoubtedly. Those with relatively fixed incomes do suffer as taxes rise and are shifted by business. But in general, the answer is no. The mechanism of government absorption, as already pointed out, works in such a way as to raise the operating rate of the economy, hence to expand employment and lower-class incomes. Some of this increase is taken in the form

of taxes, of course, but much less than all. Like the ruling class, the workers and lower-middle class are better off with higher government spending and higher government taxes than they would be *under conditions of monopoly capitalism* with lower. This explains why there is no really effective political opposition to a more or less steady rise in the levels of spending and taxation. Given the irrational system of monopoly capitalism — which most people living under it take for granted as natural and inevitable — it is to the interest of all classes that government should steadily increase its spending and its taxing.

10. The question therefore is not *whether* but *on what*. And here private interests come into their own. Here follows a discussion, somewhat along the lines of the *Nation* article,[118] of how the pattern of monopoly capitalist interests blocks all the good forms of government surplus absorption and favors all the bad forms. Transfer payments are mostly of two kinds: (1) direct subsidies to special interests (purchases of agricultural surpluses, stockpiling of various commodities, subsidizing banks via interest on the national debt, etc. [added in the margin: veterans' benefits]), and (2) political bribes to unemployed, old agers, etc., to keep them from becoming unduly discontented with the system (the policy initiated by Bismarck in the 1880's). Show with figures from Bator how these forms of government spending have grown absolutely and relatively since 1929.[119] Government purchases of goods and services can be either for welfare or warfare purposes. Show, again with figures, how welfare spending has scarcely held its own since 1929, while warfare spending has multiplied many times.

11. Here we relate the growth of arms and "defense" spending to the nature of imperialism and the struggle against world socialism. Such subjects as the internationalization of Big Business, the importance of sources of cheap raw materials, the tremendous profit rates in underdeveloped countries, the threat of revolutions "a la Cuba," etc., should come in for brief but pointed attention. In this connection, any ideas you may have on the content and organization of this section will be much appreciated. In passing, some misconceptions about imperialism and its relation to the functioning of the monopoly capitalist economy are to be corrected. As already indicated in the brief section on foreign investment in Chap. 4, empires are *not* absorbers of surplus but just the opposite.[120] But the tremendous and growing expense of trying to hold onto empires and to repel the advance of socialism does absorb surplus on a

---

118. Paul Sweezy, "Power Blocks to a Peace Economy," *The Nation*, March 28, 1959.
119. F.M. Bator, *The Question of Government Spending* (New York: Macmillan, 1962).
120. Sweezy is referring to his draft of Chapter 4 for *Monopoly Capital* on "The Absorption of Surplus: Capitalists' Consumption and Investment."

fantastic scale. It is this more than anything else that has become the crutch of
monopoly capitalism, the explanation of how it has been able to survive despite
its profoundly stagnationist nature.

I can't think of anything left out, but maybe you can. If so, let me know as
soon as possible so that I can make plans for incorporation before I get too far
along in the writing.

I hope that this outline leads naturally up to the next chapter, which
would be in two parts (or maybe two chapters): (1) the historical sketch of
the development of U.S. monopoly capitalism, giving due weight here to
revolutionary innovations on the one hand and wars and their aftermaths on the
other (neither has been built into the analytical model); and (2) the statistical
sketch of the irrational system (here the Joe Phillips stuff).[121]

More on other stuff soon. I want to get this into the mail as soon as possible
so as to get your ideas in good time to take account of them. Hope all goes well at
Big Sur and that you are doing what the medicos prescribe.

Love,

/s Paul

PAB to PMS

> [*PAB spent a month in Big Sur in the summer of 1961,*
> *ostensibly recuperating from his heart attack.*]

Big Sur, California

July 10th, 1961

Dear Paul,

Thanks for sending me the end of the chapter; I think this is fine, and provides
a good lead to what is to follow. For the Government chapter you must read
quickly William J. Lederer, *A Nation of Sheep* (Norton, NY 1961). Remarkable
both for the facts he puts together (nothing new but still impressive) and for
the utter helplessness in explaining them. I read it here sort of together with
Steinbeck's new novel (*The Winter of Our Discontent* — the reason for his
having chosen this particular title is somewhat obscure to me), and while
Steinbeck comes very much closer to the nub of the matter, he also — almost
consciously and purposefully — shies away from dotting the i's and crossing
the t's. It is amazing, how it has turned into something like an universal taboo
to draw conclusions from one's own material and observations. "There is no
doubt that business is a kind of war. Why not, then, make it all-out war in pursuit
of peace? Mr. Baker and his friends did not shoot my father, but they advised

---

121. Economist Joseph D. Phillips was working on a statistical appendix for *Monopoly Capital.*

him and when his structure collapsed they inherited. And isn't that a kind of murder? Have any of the great fortunes we admire been put together without ruthlessness? I can't think of any." (p. 105).

It is quite dramatic to see, how all of those people throw up their hands in despair about the rotten society this is and leave the matter right there without the slightest ray of hope. . . . They see, feel, touch starving little children, they know somewhere that milk is what is needed but they are forbidden to mention let alone to recommend milk. . . . If they do not hide themselves from themselves and from the world what should they do but commit suicide? And the extent to which the rottenness of the society has gone even into their bones is breathtaking. Mr. Hemingway has left one or two finished novels in his safe deposit box in the bank; why? Because of tax reasons. . . . Corruption has reached even the heart of the artist (he *was* a great artist) and the incapacity of experiencing genuine gratification and joy and pride of accomplishment, the alienation has gone so far that an artist does not even care to see his very child, the object of his thoughts and dreams and labors in print. . . .

He thinks like the NY real estate shyster of the . . . tax angle. Imagine Aeschylus, Goethe, Shakespeare trying to turn their "royalties" into capital gains. . . . Not that great artists were not also in earlier days corrupt and money-hungry. Balzac certainly knew about money and Daniel Defoe, and Mozart and Bach composed for hard cash, and still this today is a new *quality* for money and money is not the same, for money to pay your rent and to buy your dinner is different money from the money that is collected from Metro-Goldwyn-Mayer. Hemingway's greatest because fundamentally truest book will turn out to have been *The Old Man and the Sea.* He had the courage to announce publicly that he was through; he committed suicide in print before he committed it physically. Steinbeck does now the same, I wonder, how long he can live after this book. . . .

[. . .]
Write.
Yours,
        /s Paul

PAB to PMS

Big Sur
July 13, 1961

Dear Paul,
On the assumption that you have a carbon copy of the outline of Ch. 6, I'll write my comments with reference to your point #'s. The outline as a whole looks fine

to me; what follows are *Randglossen* [glosses in the margin] as they occur to me while I re-read your statement.

Ad 1. I think, one should avoid idealizing the 19th century. The economy was also then *not* operating at full capacity. Far from it. But what is probably decisive is that the underemployment was — to use Joan Robinson's distinction — of the Marxian rather than of the Keynesian type.[122] That is, there were lots of under - (and un-) employed men (in cities as well as in villages) but relatively little under- (and un-) employed machines. Given a subsistence level of wages (or in any case an *irreducible* level of real wages) and given competition, every increase of taxation had to come out of the surplus. Interesting to note that at that time all "progressive" economists (not only Henry George and Franz Oppenheimer but also John Stuart Mill and even Marshall) advocated (or banked upon) increased taxes on land rents. Those affected neither real wages nor the sources of capital accumulation! Under those circumstances also an increase in government spending had to lead to inflation (supply being essentially inelastic) and inflation was undesirable partly because much capital was still in its money form, partly because of fear of the inevitable increases in *money* wages (not easily reversed), partly because creditors [were] probably still more powerful than debtors (*Finanzkapital* notions reflecting that state of affairs), partly because of the difficulty of a *Flucht in die Sachwerte* [flight to commodities], partly finally because of fear of political unrest. "Cultural lag" in the ruling class undoubtedly also an element, also perhaps less important than often thought.[123]

Ad 2. Not sure whether it is right to say that it was at first thought that *only* deficits could do the trick of raising effective demand. Don't forget that under conditions of *massive unemployment* the unit multiplier device is not powerful enough. I don't know whether Keynes, RF Kahn & Co already grasped the unit multiplier principle (Keynes certainly has it more or less clearly in his *General Theory*), but it is clear that raising taxes and re-spending them under conditions of a major depression is a doubtful procedure. The demand is increased *only* by the amount of extra taxes, while that demand increase may be completely inadequate to offset the negative effect of the tax increase on (anyway) flagging investment. In a major depression all this may be for the birds and what is really needed is a *large* deficit drastically raising total demand and not interfering with

122. Baran is referring here to the fact that Cambridge School economists have traditionally used the term "Marxian unemployment" to refer to the level of unemployment that exists at Keynesian "full employment equilibrium" (or full capacity output). See Adrian Wood, *A Theory of Profits* (Cambridge: Cambridge University Press, 1975), 124–78.

123. The concept of the "cultural lag" is associated with Thorstein Veblen who made use of it in *The Theory of the Leisure Class*.

private incomes (profits). What is more: in a *major* depression a small increase of aggregate effective demand may be abortive: the most depressed industries (investment goods) wouldn't even notice it.

Ad 3. I *think* the argument is ok. The way I got to look at the unit multiplier theorem is this: since all incomes (private) reflect services rendered, their aggregate + government *services* (reckoned at cost) = Y. If you add depreciation allowances, you get GNP. A tax imposed does *not* reduce GNP. By spending the tax proceeds on previously unemployed lawyers and/or ditch diggers the government increases GNP exactly by the value of their newly rendered services. What confuses me at this point are the transfer payments (veterans' bonuses, pensions, and the like). It is my impression that they are *excluded* from GNP (as not representing payments for services rendered). Therefore strictly speaking, new tax spent on such transfer payments would do exactly the same trick as one spent on services rendered but would not result in a direct increase of the GNP — for purely statistical reasons. Should I be wrong, however, and should the transfer payments be included *qua* [as part of] government services at cost, then all is well. The other — trickier — possibility of dealing with the thing is to realize that all the tax is reducing not only private consumption but also private saving. Since the government's propensity to spend is unity, the average propensity to spend will be raised. There is a simple algebraic step which I once understood but can no longer reproduce to the result that this increase in the average propensity will lead exactly to a unit multiplier. This is explained in the Samuelson piece in the [Alvin H.] Hansen *Festschrift*.

Ad 4. This argument seems to me to be too simple, although I must hasten to add that I haven't yet discovered a really good way to put it. In terms of pure rationality, there is no reason why government deficits should not keep rising year in and year out. I entirely agree that what matters are changes (i.e. increases) of deficit spending — but why couldn't they do it? To say that deficits are cyclical phenomena does not meet this issue. They need not be *in pure reason*. It is fairly clear, I think, why successive *tax reductions* (with government spending kept constant) could not do the trick. They would lead to increased private saving and would operate like the unit multiplier in reverse. Steady increases on government spending, however, raise my old question: on what? To all the considerations which I tried to put together in "National Economic Planning" there is an additional point which looks to me quite interesting.[124] By

124. Baran is referring here to his long article "National Economic Planning," in Bernard Haley, ed., *Survey of Contemporary Economics* (Homewood, Illinois: Richard D. Irwin, Inc., 1952); reprinted in Paul A. Baran, *The Longer View* (New York, MR Press: 1969), 115–81.

its very nature, government spending is not the same as private spending, i.e. it
generates effective demand for things that are different from those which would
be demanded by the private sector. (Unless the government would simply hand
out benefits in cash or go directly into productive investment — both ruled out in
a capitalist society short of major crisis.) Therefore government demand affects
by necessity certain special areas of the economy (armaments, construction and
so forth), creates there bottlenecks, inflation etc. Something must be said about
the fear of inflation and the reasons for it. I get more and more the feeling that
the inflation bogey begins to resemble the tax bogey. Big Business does not give
a damn, the ones who yell mostest are smaller competitive business men as well
as the "general public" which does not have the possibility of shifting.... Crux of
the matter: *pure rationality* is irrelevant under monopoly capitalism (or for that
matter capitalism in general) and all the Kaldors & Co who argue that it "could
be done" "theoretically" are lousy theorists because they abstract precisely from
what matters: the difference between capitalism and socialism.

Ad 5. Fully agreed. But again aren't transfer payments subtracted already
in GNP? I have nothing here to look it up in, but it is my feeling that on the
principle of "services rendered" transfer payments are deducted. In any case, I
certainly agree that they constitute a part of the surplus.

Ad 6. Have look at Abramovitz & Elissberg (NBER) for the same story for
Great Britain.

Ad 7. En principe everything that is not socially necessary costs of production
of a socially desirable output is surplus. Roads, post offices and under capitalism
police protection of property are socially necessary costs of production. Publicly
provided education and health service for workers ditto — they represent as
it were publicly provided bonuses to business — assuring it of a literate and
minimally healthy labor force. I don't think that TVA, municipal power and
water systems and the like have anything to do with the matter. They are big
enterprises, and only to the extent to which they are not self-liquidating and
require subsidies do they enter the picture. Since on the whole they pay their
own way, I would leave them out completely. Such *investment* as goes into
them is like any other investment supported by the surplus — in their case by
government channeled surplus. I believe that one should insist on theoretical
grounds on a pure concept of surplus, stressing, as you say, that there is nothing
invidious about the term. Things supported out of surplus may be as essential
to the well-being of society (or even more so) than things that are supported
qua [as] necessary costs of production. The work of a scientist supported out
of surplus is more essential than the labors of a tailor making a new suit. In
PEoG somewhere I quote Marx on the point that "unproductive" must not be

mixed up with "unessential." And on what you say about the socialist society, I
also quote *The Critique of the Gotha Program* where Marx is explicit about all
of this. It is precisely the bloody way in which the surplus is being used (or left
unproduced) under capitalism and particularly monopoly capitalism that is the
issue. My guess would be that the 5% is ok as an estimate for the direct outlay on
advertising & R&D. If you take also costs of the "penetration effect" into account
+ maintenance of a superfluous sales force + financial institutions, insurance
companies and the rest of the Dreck [garbage] 5% is a massive understatement.
Maybe Joe Phillips will give us some rough estimate of what all this might
amount to. I wouldn't be a bit surprised if all of this came close to the 20% of gov.
[government spending]

Ad 8. Fully agreed. Your point is particularly well illustrated by WW II
experience when government spending produced (a) military hardware to
the tune of 100 billion, massive Lend-Lease, etc. + (b) significant increase in
civilian standards and on top of all of it (c) a military establishment of more
than 12 million people. As to the hostility to taxing and spending, partly it is
undoubtedly cultural lag, but partly also reflection of the general position of
small competitive business which by its nature hardly realizes the connections.
He [the small business man] pays high taxes and curses the government. His
profits based on relatively good demand he attributes to his own ingenuity
and efficiency and capacity to swindle. The big corp. knows how much those
things hang together, the small fellow in Toledo, Ohio finds it much harder to
comprehend. By the way, teaching of economics in colleges which on cultural
etc. grounds pure Dreck most useful to monopoly capital — it drums into the
heads of many future small bizmen, realtors, doctors and admen how the cookie
really crumbles and thus creates the ideological + political climate in which the
voter will vote the way he should vote. This the reason why all the Big Business
supported foundations etc. "waste" such a lot of dough on economics. It's all
good investment to attune the general public to the requirements of Big Business.

Ad 9. Fully agreed. One qualification, however. If you look at statistics — at
this moment I don't remember where I saw them, I think in one of the Annual
Reports of the CEA [Council of Economic Advisers] — you'll see how little
real consumption standards are going up (if at all!). Obviously under monopoly
capitalism without government and other surplus absorption matters would
be very much worse. But it is worth pointing out that the shifting mechanism +
all the assorted and combined tax swindles and loopholes *do* in fact enable the
ruling class to reduce the real wages below what would have been otherwise.
Clearly, some employment better than no employment. But decent arrangements
of government surplus absorption combined with proper tax laws, price controls

and so forth would result in a different distribution of income. But I am fully
d'accord that this is secondary. Most important vis a vis ossified Marxists is to
stress the point which you make that by comparison with a more rational society
the whole absorption mechanism is incredible madness, but by comparison with
what monopoly capitalism would be like otherwise it is of benefit to all classes.
Hence minimization of class struggle!

Ad 10. Fully agreed. Interesting to stress here the opposition of private
interests to all useful government spending but also the controlling power of
the *quid pro quo* principle which precludes under normal conditions "giving
something for nothing." Here capitalist law of value ideology becomes a manifest
fetter on the needs of society and even on the interests of the capitalist class itself.
Again, I think, it is worth stressing that the "on what?" question does not arise
in pure reason but that pure reason is not what is relevant. By the way, I prefer
"pure reason" or something like it to "theoretical" because a *good* theory has to
take all those things fully into account. Monopoly capitalist large scale spending
on welfare purposes is *theoretically* impossible i.e. in terms of a correct theory of
monopoly capitalism.

Ad 11. Again, entirely *d'accord.* I would stress two points most energetically.
One is that it is rubbish to argue that since revenues from foreign investments,
etc. play a minor part in the GNP they can be disregarded. No one under
capitalism cares for the GNP as such, to the corporations involved the matter is
most important. This can be readily demonstrated with figures. Incidentally, the
latest refutation of the imperialism theory "on the GNP account" can be found in
Hans Heisser's article in one of the recent issues of *Social Research* [publication
of The New School for Social Research] (I have an offprint at home). The other
thing which is now coming to the fore, and which could not have been taken into
consideration by Hobson, Lenin, and the later writers is what might be called
the "social order imperialism." The principle is that capitalism cannot live in
one country, that every bit of territory must be defended against socialism. By
trying to squeeze the latter form of imperialism into the formulae of the classic
imperialism theory one commits the usual fatuities of vulgar Marxism. I don't
know whether there is anything worth having in Laos, but clearly our attempt to
keep it in "the free world" has its roots in the latter and not in the former kind
of imperialism. What we often discussed: the relative autonomization of the
political sphere in particular under conditions when the class struggle has so
demonstrably moved on to the international arena. Room for some interesting
remarks about the shifting attitude of imperialist countries towards international
law. To be sure, imperialism II does *not* replace imperialism I — it supplements
and accentuates it but sometimes also overrides it. And needless to say, the

machinery of imperialism is much more important in terms of surplus absorption than anything else. On this major accent. "An errant stone setting into motion a mighty rock."

Some of the Joe Phillips stuff, if it works out would be useful all along in addition to possibly forming a skeleton of a quasi-independent chapter.

I hope that the above is of some minimal use. I think the chapter should complete the absorption business and thus round off the theoretical story. Again and again, my stress would be not on what could be done by a government in a rational world but on what can be done and is being done by government under capitalism in general and monopoly capitalism in particular.

If I finish now, I can still take it down to the PO and have it get out of Big Sur today. I mailed earlier a letter to which I could not attach this because I wasn't finished.

Love,
       /s Paul

[...]

PAB to PMS

Big Sur
July 15th, 1961

Dear Paul,
Working on the MS I came to think about the following side issue. Concerns the "law of value" and what you and I and Stanley and others have written about it.

Putting matters into their simplest form: prior to the advent of capitalism individual economic (and not only economic) activities were coordinated by a set of rules, customs and traditions sanctified by divine commandments and not rooted in any rational or quasi-rational considerations. A man was appropriated as a slave because he was captured as prisoner of war and therefore subject to his captors' will. A serf delivered a %-age of his crop to the lord for such was the time honored principle of life, etc. Although there was barter between individuals, this barter referred only to surpluses of one kind or another; what represented equivalents was established by haggling and bargaining and the principle of equivalence was not very important since the barter itself was a more or less marginal aspect of economic existence as a whole.

The big advance toward rationality under capitalism was the emergence of the principle of the *quid pro quo* as the governing principle of coordination of individual activities. Exchange moved from the margin of economic existence into its center. Under such circumstances *some* equivalence of exchange objects became inevitable. Without it no possible equilibrium of any kind. That labor had to be the basis for the establishment of the equivalence equally clear. If I remember correctly the argument of Adam Smith but also the argument which you developed in the beginning of TCD [*Theory of Capitalist Development*], the thing is quite obvious. Imagine shooting a deer took 1 day and consuming a deer would provide 2 units utility (whatever that may be). Shooting a hare would at the same time take 1/2 a day but furnish 4 units of utility (whatever that may be). Clearly no one would bother to go after the deers, they would all concentrate on hares. The result would be that hares would be exterminated at a rapid rate, shooting one would become increasingly time-consuming until the exchange-ratio would settle down in correspondence with the labor input — even if the "utilities" were in disequilibrium. In fact, chances are that on the principle of "judging quality by price," the "utilities" would adjust themselves appropriately.

But anyway this is not what I'm driving at. My point is that while the *form* in which the *quid pro quo* principle enforces itself is very important for the understanding of economic development and income distribution, whatever *form* prevails should *not* be confused with the principle itself. Thus under competitive capitalism the formula of the *quid pro quo* was a different one than it is under monopoly capitalism. The former was analyzed in *Capital* (adequately or inadequately is beside the point), the latter is analyzed more nearly adequately by Cournot in combination with some general equilibrium and input-output model.[125]

Under socialism in its early phases it becomes a complex of formulae with the state-operated factor operating differently from that operated by individual or cooperated producers (in agriculture). Stalin was perfectly right in stressing that as long as the *kolkhosniki* are *selling* and *buying* in the market, and as long as the workers work for wages (i.e. *sell* their labor power), the "law of value" holds; he failed only to stress that it holds only as the general principle of *quid pro quo* with the formula of exchange, the ratios in which *quo* is being exchanged for *quid* being quite different (and differently arrived at) than either under competitive capitalism or monopoly capitalism. This all not to say that those formulae and exchange ratios are unimportant or not worth studying. Quite the contrary! The exchange ratios are of paramount significance for a correct allocation of resources and all that.

But considered in this way, the "law of value" i.e. the principle of *quid pro quo* disappears only under full-fledged communism or in any case in a society in which

125. Antoine Cournot, *Recherches sur les Principes Mathematiques de la Théorie des Richesses* (1838).

the organizing principle of the activity of individuals is no longer the institution of *exchange*. If the planning authority plans aggregate output as well as its structure by some form of popular polling combined with historical recourse and combined with the knowledge of human behavior at socially owned distribution outlets, and if everyone gets supplies according with his needs (*not in exchange* for his work), and if everyone works not in order to obtain these supplies but as a civic duty, then and only then is the "law of value" (in my sense) put out of commission. Now there are obviously intermittent steps. It could be for instance decreed that a citizen in order to get supplies at the communal store must show an identification card proving that he is a worker, but would get anything he wants in any desired quantity. This would be a state in which *shades* of the *quid pro quo* are still observable — an undefined and unmeasured quantity of work would be *exchanged* for an undefined and unmeasured quantity of goods. Assume that even the identification card is dropped, that society takes it for granted that everybody makes his contribution to total output, then indeed the state of scarcity and all exchange are gone and with them the principle of *quid pro quo*. In that situation it may still continue to exist as a fossil of a much older past; individuals swapping old books or pictures or a hunter sharing his deer with the fisherman who caught a salmon. . . .

What I am after, primarily, is to stress that what matters from the Marxist standpoint is the principle of *quid pro quo*, the fact that a society is an *exchange* society. The formulae of that exchange differ from one historical period and one structure of society to the next. The further away society gets from the institution of exchange (structurally, not as an emergency measure such as in wartime) the further it is on the road to socialism (again, not in primitive terms but on the basis of ever more developed means of production). The study of the formulae of exchange must be conducted for the understanding of society in any particular period. To identify, say, the competitive formula with the law of value itself leads to the same error as the identification of competitive capitalism with capitalism itself. Monopoly capitalism is still capitalism alright; the law of value holds in it — except that the formula has changed. Socialism is still a transitional stage, where the formula is *quite* different. . . .

What do you think of that? I haven't seen this approach anywhere in print. Have you? If you haven't, I would like to publish it somewhere as a little note because it looks to me interesting. But where? I don't want to have anything to do with S&S [*Science & Society*], it's too recondite for *MR*. . . Maybe *Studies on the Left*?

* * * *

Ran here into Asher Harer [socialist and ILWU activist] from FPfCC [Fair Play for Cuba Committee] in SF. He told me that the whole bunch of students (led by [Maurice] Zeitlin and Dale Johnson) who planned a via Mexico summer expedition to Cuba were officially warned by the government that they would all [be] put into jail upon return, and that Washington means biz. — not just reprimand and possible future withdrawal of passport but outright indictment etc., etc. So they all stay at home . . .

May I have the favor of your comments. How is family life in Wilton? Bestest regards for Zirel and all the juniores.

Yours,

/s Paul

PMS to PAB

Wilton

July 19, 1961

Dear Paul,

This will be a very quick answer to yours of the 15th in re law of value et al. I won't try to reply to the comments on my Ch. 6 outline now but will make use of them in working on the chapter. There are no serious differences, and some of the points you make can be used to good advantage without any large changes in plan. Only one point now: I wasn't concerned to argue the point as to whether or not a continuing and growing deficit might become a permanent feature of the monopoly capitalist landscape. My point rather was that so far it hasn't become such and that in estimating the trend of government absorption the important thing to look at is the rising *level* of government spending rather than the deficit at any time. I think I can make this clearer and avoid an iffy discussion of what might or might not happen at some time in the future — esp. since neither of us believes it is at all likely to happen.

Your interpretation of the law of value problem is most interesting and certainly worth writing up for publication. Why not submit it to Bernard [Bernard Haley, editor of *American Economic Review* (AER)]? I'm sure most Marxist economists look at the AER, and it is good for us to publish there from time to time. If Bernard doesn't take it, then will be the time to decide what to do with it next. Maybe the *Tokyo Economic Review* would be the best idea. As to substance, I agree that your way of looking at the matter is logical and enlightening. The only thing I would insist on is that it is not the only possible way, and not the way Marx himself often (I think usually) looked at it. He explicitly identified law of value with the *automatism* of the system based on *private* exchange. In this sense it is closely related, e.g., to Smith's invisible hand on the one side and to his own doctrine of commodity fetishism on the other. It is a much more specific and at the same time more comprehensive notion than your identification of law of value with the principle of *quid pro quo*, and it does *not* apply to the effectively planned socialist society even in its early phases. In this sense of the term, law of value and planning are mutually exclusive opposites — I think I was right about this in TCD [*Theory of Capitalist Development*] — though as you rightly say they are not in the *quid pro quo* sense. *Quid pro quo* can be *included* in a planning system and indeed is so *ex definitione* as long as the principle of "from each according to his ability, to each according to his work" applies. The transition to distribution on the principle "from each according to his ability, to each according to his needs" precisely implies the abandonment of *quid pro quo'ism*. But you have all that, at least implicitly, and it only needs to be spelled out.

What you do not have, at least in the letter to me, is the distinction between law of value as an automatic mechanism (second nature in Lukács' terminology) and law of value as *quid pro quo*. If you include this distinction, and show that different authors have implicitly approached the matter from one angle or the other, you can I think put the whole story into proper perspective. That would be a real contribution. (It is also worthwhile, especially in view of Stanley's current aberration, to emphasize that in neither of these senses of the term is there implied any particular formula of equivalence.) Incidentally, there is no need to bring the utility issue into the Smithian Deer-Beaver example. If it costs one hour to kill a deer and two to kill a beaver, the only possible stable price is 2 deer for 1 beaver. At any other price it will pay hunters to go for only the "overpriced" commodity: only at the 2-to-1 rate of exchange will both commodities come to market in a continuous flow. What is decided by utility, or use value, is whether a larger part of the labor force or a small part goes into deer or beaver hunting. E.g. if deer is the staple food and beaver is used only for making ceremonial hats, then most hunters will go for deer most of the time. But that will in no way affect the exchange ratio.

And now to the RoM [Review of the Month]. More on other matters soon.

Love,

/s Paul

PMS to PAB

Larchmont
December 16, 1961

Dear Paul,

[…]

Speaking of Poland reminds me that I had a long interview with Zielinski on Friday, mostly on opus.[126] He is an intelligent fellow and I think understood what I was telling him. Where he kept asking questions was on a point that I am sure will be the sticking point for many of our professional colleagues: how do you define socially necessary costs which are to be deducted from total production in order to arrive at the amount of surplus? Is it what costs would be under a regime of competition? But how do you know what they would be, if that is your solution? And if you say that socially necessary costs are those which would obtain in a rationally planned society, that doesn't help much either because presumably the composition of output would be very different in a rationally planned economy. I'm afraid I wasn't very successful in answering him.

Maybe the best way out is to think in terms of the technologically efficient production of the *actual* output with the given organization of the economy, making allowance only for that part of production which is evidently and obviously motivated by sales considerations rather than by utility considerations. The trouble is that in a full-fledged monopoly regime, God only knows the mixture of motivations, and in any case one doesn't like to define *anything* by such shifty and shaky subjective criteria. I wish one of us could come up with an elegant solution of this problem: it is certainly the toughest theoretical nut in the whole basket.

[…]

/s Paul

P.S. […]

PAB to PMS

Palo Alto
December 19th, 1961

Dear Paul,

[…]

Of the crux nature of the Zielinski problem I am (and, as you know, I have been) fully aware. Number of things need to be remembered. First, one should

126. J. Zielinski, an economist specializing in issues of Soviet planning.

avoid mixing up definition or rather *definability* with *measurement*. I can speak *meaningfully* of suffering, joy, oppression, exploitation, domination, or even of my liking Mozart more than Irving Berlin without being able to answer the question, "how much?" and "how much more?" Secondly, the insistence on clear-cut definitions is in itself perhaps a trap barring further progress of knowledge. Because a really adequate definition presupposes your complete mastery of what is being defined. If we could fully and neatly *define* "cancer" or "mental disorder," we would *eo ipso* know all about them. The physicists still cannot really *define* the smallest particle (apart from the formal statement that it must be the smallest) or for that matter electricity — which does not prevent both the physicians and the physicists from working with heuristic hypotheses (quasi-definitions) in order to arrive at more adequate ones.

Translated into the terms of the surplus, all one can say, I think, is the following: Society has at its disposal a certain volume of potential *input*. The size of this INPUT is determined (a) by the natural wealth of the country in question; (b) its available capital stock; (those two things in the short run because in the long run they are both subject to change), and (c) x hours of labor (the latter depending on customs, mores etc. with regard to working age, length of the working day, vacations and holidays allowed and what have you). One could add (d) if one wanted to: scientific knowledge, managerial and organizational talent and so forth.

Now we have two clear-cut facts: (a) part of this potential INPUT is not being utilized although in the case of material items it *could* be utilized: and in the case of humans would *wish* to be utilized; (b) the INPUT yields a certain kind (volume & composition) of OUTPUT. Ideally, both the INPUT and OUTPUT should be expressible in physical, direct, non-market terms. This cannot be done for obvious index number reasons (attempts to do it in labor unit terms work only under most simplifying assumptions *vide* Sraffa; otherwise some unit of measurement has to be employed and it comes down to price).

Now a further difficulty of which Ricardo, Marx *et tout le monde* are aware: in order to compare INPUT and OUTPUT they have to be rendered comparable in a basic qualitative sense (for what sense is there in asking whether 5 hours of work is more or less than one salami?). Therefore labor input is simply set equal to sum total of wage goods eaten up by the laborers. With this adjustment made, a difference can be struck between society's *actual* INPUT and its *actual* OUTPUT. This difference is the actually observable SURPLUS. The POTENTIAL SURPLUS is this actually observable surplus plus such output as could be produced if the unused potential INPUT were put into operation. (Again with the provision that there are social limits to the length of working year, economic limits to the usability of some inaccessible natural resources or obsolete machines etc.)

This potential surplus is, however, only potential surplus *ceteris paribus*, i.e. within the capitalist system. The moment we move away from the capitalist system the whole thing begins to shift because both Inputs *and* Outputs change. It is therefore very hard, if not impossible, to identify the *magnitude* of the potential surplus under capitalism using criteria from outside capitalism. But do I have to, except for developmental planning under socialism within the first few years? It cannot be repeated often enough that the economic surplus as we use it is *not a positive but a critical concept*, a tool of analysis with the help of which one should be able to see clearer the fetishistic obfuscations of capitalism rather than make NBER type calculations.

It is not uninteresting in that connection that the "uninstructed man in the street" understands *this* aspect of the matter very much easier than the hairsplitting because ideologically befogged economist. The economic surplus in socialist not in capitalist terms is the sum total of *OUTPUT imputable to misused INPUT* — and by "misused" I mean here exploited in the Marxian sense, wasted in our sense, unemployed in the Keynesian sense. This share of output *is* constantly growing under monopoly capitalism. Question: *what do you mean by wasted?* This they all know perfectly well (again, nobody in his senses in a u/d c [underdeveloped country] will ask that question!) and if they ask it's only to create a diversionary movement. More specifically it is all output that is not conducive to and not required for the health, happiness and development of man. Who is to decide what *is* so conducive and so required? Man himself when society permits him to think, to choose with his head *and* with his heart rather than be chosen for by other people's neither heads nor hearts but pocketbooks.

To give a complete, statistically calculable and comprehensive *definition* would demand our knowing the structure, the tastes, the volitions of man in a socialist society. This was refused by Marx, this we still have to refuse today, although certain developments in the Soviet Union (particularly in the field of education) as well as certain aspects of the New Program permit now some concrete glimpses. Again: critically and negatively: *no* air-conditioned nightmares like Chase Manhattan Bdg's, *no* motorized monsters to the tune of 60 million, *no* rape of the country by superhighways and billboards, no...., no ...., no.... It should be all neatly figured out and aggregated with the help of nonexisting and unknown prices?

Just like asking Einstein to give an exact calculation of an A-Bomb impact at a time when he was working on his relativity theory... They want to get from the Statistical Abstract the data for the socialist economy and society — which is nothing but a negation of the *essential* novelty of that society.

Il me faut retourner a mon travail [I should get back to work]. Thought for
the week: When Reason turns into Commonsense, Commonsense turns against
Reason.

[…]

Merry Xmas and *tout a vous*

Bestest for Zirel, Jenny, Sammy; how is Erma?

Love,

/s Paul

PAB to PMS

Palo Alto, CA

January 4, 1962

[…]

Am up to my neck in education, the material is absorbing, and the real
difficulty is sorting, condensing and highlighting. I sent you a quote from
Hollingshead[127]; if you have a possibility, get hold of the book; it is absolutely
superb. He knows the *entire* score, chooses to say 75% of what he knows, but
this is enough! "If men and women of ideals who hope to make the American
dream a reality in the lives of American boys and girls think that Elmstowners
have failed in some measure to make this dream a fact, they should realize that
the society and its culture should be indicted rather than the Elmstown Board of
Education, the teachers, preachers, youth leaders, parents, or adolescents. These
people act as intelligently as they know how to; they act as good Americans
trying to respond to the needs of real life situations in terms of the definitions
they have learned in the culture. It is the culture which makes men face toward
the facts of the class system and away from the ideals of the American creed."
(*Elmstown's Youth*, p. 453) — [handwritten comment in margin: "What could be
a more eloquent indictment of the liberal eunuchs?"] And he knows that what is
at issue ain't not "culture," but the bloody system which underlies it. I wish there
would be at least 1 economist around with so much insight *and* honesty!

Started teaching today and feel worse than Bimbo dog who went to the Vet's
because of acute constipation. Except Bimbaka will be helped and I won't…The
120 [Comparative Economic Systems] course is huge (100 or so), I get spasms
when I start lecturing and the prospect of having to do this plus Economic
Development makes me miserable. *Mais rien a faire* [But nothing to do].

127. August Hollingshead, *Elmstown's Youth: The Impact of Social Classes on Adolescents* (New
York: John Wiley, 1949).

[...]
All the bestissimo, Love,
    s/ Paul

PAB to PMS

[Handwritten]

[Palo Alto]
January 9, 1962

Dear Paul,

You *must* have a good look at Kuznets, *Capital in the American Economy*,
Princeton Univ. Press, 1961 for NBER. He argues the *precise opposite* of
our thesis; continual under-generation of Surplus with ample investment
opportunities if there were only enough "savings." The whole thing looks to
me real mad in the light of unemployment and excess capacities. We *must* take
cognizance of the thing and it is my impression that the appearance of the book
is most fortunate because it lends itself particularly well to a really hard knock
which would be approved of even by the most circumspect Keynesian. I don't
think one should review it now but it is part of what is needed to give *the opus* a
valuable tonic. Write to me about it, please!

    Am going tomorrow to Santa Barbara. In haste — class at 10AM.

    Yours,

       /s Paul

PAB to PMS

[Palo Alto]
January 16th, 1962

Dear Paul,

[...]

    I have read in one evening's gulp the little book by Carr [*What Is History?*],
and the reflections which it set off intermingled with what was brewing in my
head after the two days in Santa Barbara. What I mean is that somehow or other
we fail to communicate. We speak while no one listens! In other countries and
in other days it could have been said, that addressing ourselves to the workers
(and read by them) we need not worry about the reactions of the "refined and
cultured crowd" and their niceties, but have to be certain that what we say is
right and contributes to the crystallization and clarification of proletarian self-
(class) consciousness. It certainly cannot be said that this is our function *hic
et nunc*; the only audience that exists *is* (essentially) the "refined" crowd or
those who aspire to belong to it, and that crowd just plainly and simply ignores

us. The answer is *not* more proficiency in the use of the Aesopian language, in more "*delicatesse*" and more "refinement" in the mode of expression. This does not solve the problem because calling a spade a spade has not merely an informative, communicative function but also plays a major and indeed all-important *cathartic* role. Just as in the process of psychoanalysis a coitus must be explicitly referred to as coitus and not as a "nice date," "pleasant engagement," or a "wonderfully spent evening" — so in ideological matters it is not enough to hint at the truth, to make people swallow the truth like castor oil between two strata of orange juice, it is important to raise the truth from the level of polite conversation to that of genuine realization.

The gentility of expression, the mild, ironic, subtle allusion — admirable as they are from the standpoint of craftsmanship — turn themselves into a form of "resistance," and to perpetuate it. You cannot speak of progress in psychoanalysis if the patient after god knows how many months of treatment still cannot pronounce the word "vagina" without suffering a heart attack — even if he is fully prepared to talk freely about an "embrace in which she and I became integrated into a totality." This is not the advocacy of using four-letter words but merely a statement that a *phobia* against those words is an index of a profound malaise.

And this the Cold War has apparently accomplished even among the best. You can hint, imply, allude to the necessity of a socialist solution; you can go to the limit of necking and petting — you must not even mention the "horrible" thing itself. From this operation one derives vicarious satisfaction, some listeners "in the know" smile at each other and say "how cunning" — the majority does not know what in hell it is all about and how does this philosopher differ from the other philosopher in his interpretation of the world. That same needs to be *changed* and not merely re-interpreted remains to them as unknown as it was before.

Thus Ping Ferry [W.H. Ferry] in a good and insightful paper (attached, please return!) says lots of perfectly correct things but would bathe in cold sweat if you were to suggest to him that he is "writing prose," that he is really making a case for socialist planning. Nor is this a merely expositional quibble: if we did not know the author and that he is [a] perfectly good guy, it would be *very* easy to interpret his address as a plea for fascism. "Law and order and government and planning" — a perfect formula for a fascist corporate state! By avoiding to call a spade a spade *in so many words*, by studiously eliminating all references to socialism, those *perfectly well-meaning* people pave the ideological road to something that they are far from intending. This is the danger with [W. H.] Ferry, with [Gerard] Piel, with many others.[128] They take capitalism for granted *a tout prix* but want it to perform as if it were socialism. But capitalism preserved cum planning, cum regulation on the part of the government is bound to be a system of some fascistoid nature — *ex definitione*. Need not be German, nor even Italian — although Mussolini *prior* to his marriage to Hitler comes damn close to it...

The Carr case is different. What he argues, I think, is as nearly correct as you can make it without letting the cat out of the bag. And the weakness of the thing is precisely that the cat is kept in the bag. Hence his very ambiguous treatment of what *reason* is, although it is a good thing that he is for it, hence his equally ambiguous acceptance of "progress" without saying what it is that constitutes it ... The cat out of the bag would have helped him so much to be more precise, more clear-cut, more definite. As it stands, it is brilliantly done, full of learning and reading, but still remains a contribution to the dialogue among historians, the "refined" ones, with the cathartic effect completely lacking. One should be grateful for small favors, to be sure, but intellectually it is terribly frustrating. And again, us being *sobaka's* [dogs] in the world of the "refined" ones, it is not insignificant and not merely narcissistically relevant, that our names do not appear in the index, although both of us on various occasions have expressed *precisement* what "Ted" [E.H. Carr] is saying now. . . .

I do not know what the answer is. Perhaps the only available one is to say to hell with the "refined" public, let's write for the Cubans, the Ghanan's, the peoples of the future. Still, there always remains the irrational perhaps, but nonetheless irrepressible longing for being at least listened to by one's immediate neighbors.

By the way, I ordered 40 copies of Carr in the Bookstore and assigned it as a must to the Economic Development class.

[. . .]

So much for now. Must return to my MS; a page a day keeps major depressions away

[. . .]

Write!

Con amore,

/s Paul

P.S. [. . .]

---

128. W. H. Ferry was at that time vice president of the Center for Democratic Institutions, a left think tank. Gerard Piel, a good friend of Paul Sweezy's, was the publisher of *Scientific American*.

PAB to PMS

[Palo Alto]

January 18, 1962

Dear Paul,

For the purpose of my talk at Santa Barbara, and in order to answer the
continually recurring question on the part of liberals, intellectuals, grad. students,
etc. on what they should *do*, I tried to distill the following 3 propositions in
connection with the question "Is Eco Dvpt of u/d c's possible *cum* Democracy?"
[Is Economic Development of Underdeveloped Countries possible with
Democracy?]

(1) There is no possibility of rapid and rationally organized economic growth
and development in underdeveloped countries without a social revolution
permitting the organization of comprehensive economic planning for the benefit
of society as a whole.

Comment: This is *not* a "value judgment," or "expression of preference" but
a scientific, factual statement, the validity of which is proved by (a) the historical
record, and (b) theoretical considerations of all open-minded economists
working in the field. Whether it is [Maurice] Dobb or [Hollis B.] Chenery, the
linear programming people or Joan Robinson, the consensus in general that
planning, synchronization and coordination of investment projects, maximal use
of economies of scale and external economies, strict husbandry of the available
and mobilizable (potential) surplus constitute *sine qua non's* of economic growth
which is both rapid and moving in a rational direction.

Second Comment: This proposition can only be rejected if it is questioned
that economic growth of u/d c's is *desirable*. The assertion that it is desirable is,
indeed, a "value judgment," the discussion of which can be safely eschewed.

(2) If American intellectuals, liberals, etc., wish to remain respectable in the
emerging u/d world and retain some claim to being heard with esteem, they
must disassociate themselves unequivocally and vigorously from *all defense of
private property in the means of production*. If this is not done or done with
insufficient outspokenness, they *must* remain suspect of grinding the axes of
capitalist interests and be accused of being either paid scribes of moneyed
interests (here and/or in the u/d c's) or naive dupes of capitalist ideology. This
is what differentiates Western acts and pronouncements from those of the SU —
whatever bad the latter does is *never* tainted with the possibility that it is done
in order to protect private property in the means of production. This explains
why Belgrade conference reacted as it did to the resumption of A-testing by

Moscow,[129] and this explains the difference in reaction in the u/d c's, say, toward Hungary on one side and Cuba on the other.

(3) If American intellectuals, liberals, etc. would accept (1) and (2), they could effectively work towards:

(a) the minimization of *violence* engaged in during the transition from the present to the future socio-economic order in the u/d c's, and thus fulfill a *humanitarian* principle to which they profess to be committed.

(b) preservation of as much civil liberty, freedom of the individual, of speech, discussion and press as is possible under the conditions of a revolutionary transition, and thus serve the cause of *democracy* to which they also profess to be committed.

Comment: 3(a), and 3(b) indicate the only available avenue of truly progressive action at home: i.e. exercising as much pressure as is feasible on the American authorities to refrain from supporting retrograde interests and forces in the u/d c's and from providing them with the means of violent resistance, sabotage, terror, etc.

Second Comment: herein and *not* in support and advocacy of aid to the u/d c's in their present state lies a possibility of doing something useful. Not because u/d c's could not very well use capital and consumer goods from here, but because under prevailing conditions all such aid is explicitly aimed at stabilizing reactionary regimes and strengthening the ruling classes' resistance to the inevitable and mandatory social revolution. Herein difference between a genuinely progressive and historical attitude toward aid as against do-goodism of all kinds.

All this perhaps banal and trite, but has a certain virtue of clarity and simplicity. Could be made perhaps into an article. No time at the moment, but *en principe*. What do you think of that? Show it, please, also to Huby, since he asked me about the SB speech.

[...]

Love,

/s Paul

---

129. Reference to Conference of Heads of State or Government of Non-Aligned Countries, Belgrade, 1961.

PMS to PAB

Larchmont,
January 22, 1962

Dear Paul,

Your letter [1/18/62] in re u/d c's [underdeveloped countries] rec'd this a.m. Absolutely first rate and ideal for German, French, and U.S. editions of *PEoG*. I offer only the following comments:

1. The "Second Comment" under (1) has something of the *non sequitur* about it. The "Comment" preceding holds quite regardless of whether one judges development of u/d c's to be desirable or not.

2. What needs to be established with quotes and documentation, and not merely by assertion, is the substance of (1) Comment (b). And I would not phrase it as applying to "all open-minded economists working in the field." What is at issue is not their open-mindedness but their competence and understanding. I would say something like: "It is the increasing consensus of the best authorities in the field regardless of their own political preferences. . . ." and then quote from a number at different points of the political compass.

3. To "American intellectuals, liberals, etc." under (2) and (3) should be explicitly added "western European socialists (or Social Democrats)."

[. . .]

Love,

/s Paul

PAB to PMS

[Palo Alto]
January 29, 1962

Dear Paul,

[. . .]

In talking about growth + investment in my grad. class, I speculated with them on the following: to an apple cart pusher in the XVIIth or XIX century the merchant or manufacturer who laid in an inventory, fixed up his store, put in displays etc., must have looked like a most irrational, *not profit maximizing entrepreneur*. The cart pusher maximized his returns *during the day*, and idea of having $100 tied up for a long period, or of selling today with a loss in order to build up goodwill for tomorrow appeared to him either to be entirely cockeyed or *never appeared to him at all*. Now the textbook analysis of profit maximization moves on the same ground as that of the apple cart pusher when what is confronted is the profit maximization policy of the large scale corporation. Viner had a notion of it when he introduced his envelop curve (I think, he was the first to do it), but he left that curve essentially ill-defined and therefore the whole problem up in the air [now known as the Wong-Viner Envelope Theorem on the equality of long-run and short-run marginal costs]. Let us assume, however, that the corporation of the oli/mono [oligarchic/monopolistic] type operates with what one might call (borrowing the term from development theorizing) a *planning horizon*. This planning horizon is *de rigueur* longer (and very much longer) than that of a competitive firm of old. Maximization of profits within that planning horizon becomes an altogether different proposition and may actually violate the canons of profit maximization of the competitive firm (or of the "short run" although that term ain't no good because it would call for a definition of the "short run" which should *not* be Vinerian i.e. referring to plant durability etc.) What I mean is, that such an oligopoly/monopoly firm can actually, say, disregard existing excess capacity, and keep investing in new technology, etc. because this would be rational over the planning horizon, without necessarily being rational *at this moment* or in the course of the next year. This clearly raises the question (also in development economics!) *how long is the planning horizon*? Could be the set of expectations of the present management, 25 years or God knows what.

Now with this "idea" in my head, I approached today Nerlove, and asked him what he as a *mathematicus* thought of this.[130] Two answers: One: most important and illuminating, but not original: Vernon Smith in a book on Investment Decisions published last year by Harvard U. Press has precisely formulated and explored this very hypothesis.[131] More important, two: Vernon Smith did just what I did, but KJ Arrow and he, Nerlove himself, are working on a model in which the planning horizon is assumed to be *infinite*. The corporation considers itself an eternal unity which maximizes its net worth in eternity and ever after without regard to the fleeting maximization considerations besetting the competitive firm. So I hit apparently upon a theme which is in the "main stream" of illuminated thought. There are interesting pitfalls in all of this: if in the first, *finite*, case the joker is the length of the planning horizon, in the second, *infinite*, case, the joker is the discount factor. Nerlove agreed that this indeed is so, and told me to talk to [Kenneth] Arrow who is in charge of that problem. I'll do so, and report to you, although I am not quite clear as yet on the meaning of the "infinite" horizon. But maybe Arrow will elucidate it for me. (By the way, he just was offered a distinguished professorship in Harvard and in Yale, but apparently will monetize it and stay here which is all to the best.)

130. Marc Nerlove, economics professor and specialist in econometrics.
131. Vernon Smith, *Investment and Production: A Study in the Theory of the Capital-Using Enterprise* (Cambridge: Harvard University Press,1961).

I think that you ought to get hold of the Smith book and have a look at it; if you cannot, I'll get it. What is important in all of this is that this approach to the matter enables us to state our position fully in keeping with "modern" thought (if without the math technique), to wit: the corporations are *perfectly rationally maximizing* if they introduce technology, invest, etc. even in the presence of excess capacity, etc. *** — they just maximize over the planning horizon (whatever that may be in length); they can shift taxes, etc. which would be impossible in terms of short-run textbook maximization because this is not the relevant frame of reference. By the way, one student told me that Musgrave has shown somewhere that the corp's *as a whole shift* at least 1/3 of the corp. taxes.[132] This sounds most sensible because it allows for the competitive corp's which cannot do so. He promised me to get the reference. All this is most interesting and fits beautifully with the opus main theses.

There are lots of other things to write about, but I'll break here and continue later.

Gute Besserung, which wish is, I trust, outdated.

Love,

/s Paul

***[*handwritten footnote by PAB*]
This by the way *could* account for tremendous stability *and* instability of the whole system (minus govt) because a collective (clustering) change in the planning horizons or rather their contents could bring the whole thing down simultaneously. If they *all* expect a 3% rate of growth [in] armaments assistance, the disappearance of the latter may "suddenly" make them scratch their heads and change the planning horizon to something quite different.

PMS to PAB
[*No provenance or date, assumed to be 1962; the following is pretty close to the text in* Monopoly Capital, *pp. 155–161.*]

Dear Paul,
I have run into a sort of impasse in Ch. 6 (Government absorption of surplus) and am going to stop for a moment to try to sketch out the general architecture of the thing for your comment.

132. The reference is to Richard Musgrave, author of *The Theory of Public Finance* (New York: McGraw Hill, 1959).

1. First, I try to show that the old notion that whatever the government takes must come out of private surplus (*sv* [surplus value] in the Marxian sense) no longer holds under monopoly capitalism. Where there are idle resources, additional surplus can be produced without any encroachment. The mechanism whereby this is done is simply a constantly expanding budget, with or without deficits is a secondary question.

2. This means that within the framework of monopoly capitalism most everyone gains from more spending and taxing, and this explains why there is no political opposition worth mentioning to the trend. Since its interruption would threaten the very existence of the system, it follows that whether or not there will be steadily mounting government spending is not a question. The only real question is: on what?

3. The liberal answer is on whatever "we" want to spend it on, and on this basis they argue for a welfare state, etc. But this begs the real question, which is not how "we" want to spend it but how it does and must get spent under monopoly capitalism.

4. To answer this you have to look first at the political system of monopoly capitalism, and more specifically at the political system of the American version.

5. *En generale*, the preferred political system for all kinds of capitalism is bourgeois democracy. Here votes (the people) are the nominal source of power, money the real source (since it takes money to work all the mechanisms of bourgeois democracy). There is a latent contradiction here which may become real. When it does, the moneyed oligarchy scraps the system and resorts to direct authoritarian rule. Many recent examples (Italy, Germany, Spain, Latin America, etc.)

6. The U.S. system is one of bourgeois democracy — democratic in form, plutocratic in content. But one must not get the idea from this that the machinery of government is merely a screen behind which a handful of industrialists and bankers sit making policies and giving orders. Matters are much more complex than that.

7. The Founding Fathers themselves were acutely aware of the latent contradiction in the democratic form — the possibility that the people might attempt to turn their nominal sovereignty into real power — and took great precautions to keep it under control. In addition, the system developed in a context of numerous and often bitter struggles among various sections of the moneyed classes, which moreover had never been united, as they had [been] in Europe, by a common struggle against feudal power. As a result the governmental institutions which have taken shape in the U.S. have been heavily weighted on the side of protecting the rights and privileges of minorities — of the

property-owning minority as a whole against the people and of various groups of property-owners against each other. There is no need or possibility to review the story here — how the system of checks and balances was written into the federal Constitution, how *states* rights and local autonomy became fortresses of vested interests, how political parties evolved into vote-gathering and patronage-dispensing machines without program or discipline. What interests us is the outcome, which was already largely shaped before the end of the 19th century.

The United States became a sort of utopia for the private sovereignties of property and business. The very structure of government prevented effective action in many areas of the economy or social life (e.g. city planning, to take a need which has become increasingly acute in recent years); and in most others the system of political representation combined with the absence of responsible political parties to give a veto power to temporary or permanent coalitions of vested interests. Under these circumstances, the positive role of government tended to be narrowly confined to a few functions: extending the national territory and promoting the interests of U.S. property-owners abroad (throughout the nation's history, these have been the first concerns of the federal government),[133] where the decisive nature of U.S. foreign relations from earliest times is correctly appreciated; perfecting and protecting property rights at home; carving up the public domain among the most powerful and insistent private claimants; providing a minimum infrastructure for the profitable operation of private business; passing out favors and subsidies in accordance with the *well-known* principles of the log roll and the pork barrel. Up until the New Deal period of the 1930's, there was never even any pretense that the welfare of the lower classes was a particular concern of government; on the contrary, the dominant ideology held that any reliance on government for income or services was demoralizing to the individual, contrary to the laws of nature, and ruinous to the system of private enterprise.

8. This was the situation which prevailed at the time of the collapse of the boom of the 1920's. We have already seen that only a small increase in the relative importance of government spending had taken place since the turn of the century (mostly caused by the need to build roads and highways to accommodate the rapidly growing number of automobiles), and in the next chapter we shall see why this was nevertheless on the whole a period of capitalist prosperity. But with the coming of the Great Depression, the need for government to play a larger role suddenly became acute. How was this need met in the liberal New Deal period?

---

133. Footnote by Sweezy: Cf., for example, R. W. Van Alstyne, *The Rising American Empire* (Oxford University Press, 1960).

In order to answer this question we construct Table 6-5 which is exactly like
Table 6-4 [Table 5 in Chapter 6 in the published version of *Monopoly Capital*]
except that it compares 1929 with 1939 instead of with 1957:

Table 6-5 [Table 5a in Chapter 6 of *Monopoly Capital*]
GOVERNMENT SPENDING
(Percent of GNP)

	1929	1939
Nondefense purchases	7.5	13.3
Transfer payments	1.6	4.6
Defense purchases	0.7	1.4
Total	9.8	19.3

9. The changes which took place between 1929 and 1939 are obviously
in sharp contrast to those which took place between 1929 and 1957. Even
though World War II had already begun before the end of 1939 and American
involvement was clearly a possibility, defense purchases were still of quite minor
importance. Both categories of civilian spending — nondefense purchases
and transfers — increased sharply relative to GNP. Of the total increase in
government spending relative to GNP during the decade of the 1930's, more
than 60 percent was in the area of non-defense purchases and more than 30
percent in transfers, less than 10 percent in defense purchases.

10. Here, it might seem, is proof that the problem of inadequate surplus
absorption can be solved, as the liberals claim, by increased government
spending for welfare purposes. Actually, of course, it is no such thing. Not that
we wish to call in question the welfare goals which the increases in government
spending during the New Deal period were intended to serve. It is true that a
large part of these outlays were in the nature of salvage operations for depression-
threatened property owners of various sizes and descriptions,[134] but also much of
genuine value for the non-owning classes was accomplished or at least initiated.
But all of this is essentially beside the point.

What was wrong with the government spending of the 1930's as a solution
to the surplus absorption problem was not its direction but its magnitude:
there was just not enough of it to come anywhere near offsetting the powerful
depressive forces at work in the private sector of the economy during that
decade. Measured in current dollars, government spending increased from $10.2

---

134. Footnote by Sweezy: Maybe quote something on this salvaging aspect of the New Deal from
[Alvin H.] Hansen, *Fiscal Policy & Business Cycles* (New York, 1941).

billion in 1929 to $17.5 billion in 1939, i.e. by more than 70 percent. At the
same time, however, GNP declined from $104.4 billion to $91.1 billion (12.7
percent) and unemployment as a percentage of the labor force grew more than
fivefold from 3.2 percent to 17.2 percent. (Footnote: Even measured in constant
dollars, G.N.P grew only from $193.5 in 1929 to $201.4 billion in 1939, which
was not enough to prevent real per capita GNP from slightly declining).

11. Regarded as a salvage operation *for the U.S. economy as a whole,* the New
Deal was a clear failure. Even Galbraith, the prophet of prosperity without war
orders, had to admit that the goal was not even approached during the 30's.
Quote passage from [Galbraith's] *American Capitalism* about the depression
never ending but just merging into the war boom.

12. War spending accomplished what civilian spending failed to accomplish.
From 17.2 percent of the labor force, unemployment declined steadily to a
minimum of 1.2 percent in 1944. The other side of the coin was an increase of
government spending from $17.5 billion in 1939 to $103.1 billion in 1944. We
do not suggest that in peacetime an increase in spending of this magnitude would
have been needed to produce the indicated decline in unemployment. During
the war, private spending of course had to be restrained in a variety of ways. If it
had not been, near-full employment would have been reached at a considerably
lower level of government spending. But it is quite obvious that a very large
increase over the 1939 level — probably of the order of a doubling or tripling —
would have been required. Why was such an increase not forthcoming during
the whole depressed decade? Why didn't the New Deal accomplish what the war
proved to be within easy reach?

13. The answer, we believe, is that by 1939 the increase of non-defense
spending had for all practical purposes reached its outer limits. The obstacles
and pressures obstructing further expansion were too strong to overcome.

[End of letter.]

PMS to PAB

Larchmont
February 1, 1962

Dear PAB,

[. . .] The only thing I was able to accomplish in that period [while sick with the
flu] was to peruse the Kuznets volume *Capital in the American Economy.* Apart
from the purely statistical work, which is doubtless useful and which I don't
know enough to criticize anyway, it is an incredible performance. Keynes might
just as well never have existed, and there doesn't seem to be even any awareness
that the Great Depression presents problems. The "shortage of savings"

theory of the slowdown in the rate of capital formation is adopted because
"it is difficult to assume" that there are long-run limitations on the "supply of
capital investment opportunities," and because the alternative approach, which
emphasizes the supply of savings, seems more plausible and more fruitful as
an analytical lead. (p. 398.) That is literally all the theoretical justification there
is. That population growth and technological change open up vast investment
outlets is taken for granted in the most naive possible way. Despite a few passages
which might be interpreted otherwise, the tacit assumption that Say's law
and full employment continuously prevail dominates everything. It is really
dumbfounding!

Two conclusions seem inevitable: (1) Kuznets is a fool, and (2) Kuznets
is a knave. The latter because this study and a whole set of monographs
on which it is based were, as a special note in the front matter makes clear,
"made possible by a grant from the Life Insurance Association of America."
The coincidence between the conclusions reached and those which the Life
Insurance Association would obviously like to have reached is much too close to
be accidental. I wonder if our colleagues like Tarshis and Despres, who at least
once knew something learned from Keynes and the 30's, will be able to swallow
this. Anyway, I will try to do the thing justice in the historical chapter: it is the
clearest sign yet of intellectual and moral bankruptcy in the profession. For the
rest, one of the most striking features of the volume is its incredible dullness. I
dread having to read certain chapters more carefully before writing about what's
in them.

Your letter in re "planning horizon" phenomena rec'd. I agree that this
is a useful way of putting the matter, and I will try to get hold of the Vernon
Smith book when I get onto that range of subjects again. Only I think you
have to be careful fitting things like mounting excess capacity into a schema
rationalized from the individual firm's point of view. Even in the most developed
monopoly capitalism, *no one* plans for overall results: the most irrational
aggregative outcome can be the result of the most rational possible planning by
the individual units. I don't need to stress this contradiction between partial
rationality and total irrationality to you, but it is terribly important never to forget
it even for a moment.

[...]

More soon, Love,
        /s Paul

PAB to PMS

Palo Alto, CA
Feb. 4, 1962

Dear Paul,

[...]

1) What you say about Kuznets is absolutely right; don't forget, however, that even the best (of whom K. is certainly not one) have recently been busily engaged in the "Keynesian counterrevolution." Joan Robinson with her characteristic inconsistency, Kaldor *et tutti quanti* talk about nothing else but "long run full employment equilibrium" which serves as *the* basic assumption and which gets them right back to Say's Law *cum* Tugan-Baranowski. Once they put the system into orbit, postulate that all the relevant ratios are fairly constant with consumption and investment (and capital-output ratios) changing very little if at all, there is no reason why it should not rotate like a sputnik *ad inf[initum*]. The only difference which actually exists today between the Keynesians and the non-Keynesians is what Solow referred to when he talked about the system's slipping off the razor's blade's edge path and starting to plummet down. The Keynesians would like the govt. to jump in (in a non-descript way), the non-Keynesians think that monetary policy or something like it could do the trick. I don't think that there is *any one* (except for the lunatic von Mises fringe) which believes that the system has enough built in mechanisms to restore the long-run full employment equilibrium. This is perhaps the only lesson which has still remained from the Keynesian upheaval. It is interesting to note that even the most committed Keynesians slide more and more into the non-Keynesian camp by two maneuvers: (a) they scale down what might be called full employment — 4% unemployment is now considered to be dandy; make it 15% and there ain't no problem no more — and (b) they discover the beauties and virtues of various market adjustments. Cf. Tarshis' meaningless article where he suddenly restores the rate of interest to its Marshallian status and in so doing sets up "assumptions" which negate 30 years of economic thinking: perfect competition, perfect capital markets and the devil knows what!

Entirely incidentally: did you ever give some thought to the swindle which is being perpetrated by using the %# of the *labor force* to indicate the size of unemployment? The labor force includes *all* gainfully employed: small biz men, doctors, lawyers and you and me. I figure that at least one-quarter of the entire *labor force* is not at all subject to the employment-unemployment dilemma, and probably one-quarter is an understatement. This means actually that when you talk about *industrial* manpower *sensu stricto* the ratio of unemployed is *very* much higher! It is much more meaningful at the present time to talk about

absolute numbers than about ratios! The most extraordinary and pitiful thing is
to see how the economics brethren don't even follow the price index but fall into
a serious lag behind the price index. They are *now* organizing their theories in
keeping with postwar prosperity — at a time when creeping stagnation is already
visible to anyone who cares to look. Did you notice Lampman's findings on
re-concentration of wealth &c reported in the Jan. 27th *Business Week*?[135]

2) What I wrote in re planning horizon does not refer to the system as a
whole; you must have misunderstood me. I do *not* assume or even suggest
that there is some planning effort for the whole capitalist class or anything of
the sort. All I am asking is the following question: if it is in the nature of the
vast, impersonal entity: The Corporation to plan not in terms of a year or even
5 years, but in terms of something *very* much longer (don't know *how* much
longer), does not *such* an orientation change qualitatively the profit maximization
strategy? In other words do not certain decisions become understandable which
in terms of the textbook maximization policy appear puzzling? In still other
words, could not, for instance, investment be justified in the light of the very
long run which appears nonsensical in the presence of excess capacity? Doesn't
it become sensible to talk, say, about tax shifting when you think in terms of a
long planning horizon, while it looks like a straight violation of the maximization
principle in the short run? Take the automobile case right after the war: the
Detroit companies *could* have charged a $1000 more per car in the years when
there were long queues of anxious buyers. Immediate profit maximization would
have indicated that this is what they should do. Thinking in longer terms, they
were undoubtedly wise in foregoing the super profits of the day for the sake of
continuity, stability, the customers' goodwill and what have you. I am sure, one
could find lots of examples where it is unprofitable to do something in the short
run and *very* profitable if the long run is considered.

[…]

All the best, Love,
    s/ Paul

[…]

---

135. Robert J. Lampman, *The Share of Top Wealth Holders in the National Wealth* (Princeton:
Princeton University Press, 1962), 24. See also Lampan, "Rich Get Richer — But Not for Long,"
Business Week (January 27, 1962).

PAB to PMS

[Palo Alto]
February 20, 1962

Dear Paul,

MS rec'd and perused. It is very good, and requires probably very little fixing. In the analysis of the political process (democratic mechanism and interests of the oligarchy) one could probably very effectively add a few trenchant quotations from Beard, *The Economic Interpretation*; Hofstadter, *American Political Tradition* and a few others. I have those passages marked and can supply them to you readily. A few sentences on the *ideology* formation may also be profitably added. When it comes to the discussion of education and housing, there is a little bit of an overlap with the "Quality of Society" stuff, but this can be later taken care of. Thus for instance Hollingshead's statement probably should not be quoted twice; on the other hand your — very pertinent — remarks on the reasons for discrimination in the educational system may well be transferred to the section on education with a suitable remark directing the reader to that section. But all this is a matter for final polishing which need not be bothered with at this stage. One minor point: on p.7 fn. you remark that only losses and profits of public enterprises enter government spending totals. What about the capital outlays themselves? As long as we do not have two budgets: capital and current but only one, the outlay on building the Post Office or TVA enters the current budget, doesn't it?

Last night two editors of *Stanford Daily* turned up on the premises and announced to me that they have decided to run a series of articles on academic freedom &c. as related to Stanford. For this noble purpose they resolved to take my "case" and go into it "deeper." The astounding thing is that they proceeded to see the Director of Public Relations, and this gentleman turned over to them a huge file of letters from all and sundry protesting bitterly your and mine teaching here, with all of those letters accompanied by carbons of answers emanating from Sterling and his various underlings (depending on the status of the letter writer.) They gave me that stuff to look at, and the answers were more distressing than the letters. After a few high-sounding sentences about the freedom of speech and inquiry which make up a great university, the argument becomes much more "concrete" and states that as far as you were concerned, no reason for worry: only a temp. appointment, too bad it happened; as far as I am concerned, unfortunately they are stuck with me in view of tenure and if I came up for appointment today no such error would be made. All this reduces the academic freedom claptrap to what it is: hypocritical rubbish. This by the way after some statements in some letters speaking of both us as "scholars well thought of by their peers" &c., &c. . . .

All of this hardly worth talking about, except that the publication of such a series of articles will stir up some more to-do around here, and will make my situation worse than it is already. I told them that I have no particular comments to make on all of this, that the letters speak for themselves and that they should base their argument on those letters rather than on an interview with me. They very much [don't?] want to implicate me, and the end was that they promised me to show me a draft of what they are going to publish and not publish stuff to which I would object. The whole business will come up while I am gone (in April) with the result that I won't be able to answer anything if an answer should be required. Not letting sleeping dogs sleep may easily result in their getting real mad and starting to bite, and I get more and more the impression that the time is coming very close when quitting the whole mess will become the only possible solution. But how go about that? *Erst kommt das Fressen und dann die Moral* [you need to eat before considering morals], as Bert Brecht profoundly remarked, and *mit dem Fressen* it ain't not simple at all . . . In spite of all one's rationality, it burns one up to the point of intolerability. "Although I fully share your distaste for Messrs B. and S. attitude . . ." is a characteristic beginning of the great univ's reply! But never without something comical: one Trustee answers that he would find it somewhat awkward to swing into action in the B & S matter because he has extensive economic interests in . . . Cuba and other countries of Latin America which may give people the "absurd notion" that he ain't "fully objective." Solution: the complaining alumnus should write to Mr. X who is also on the Board of Trustees but whose biz interests are strictly . . . domestic.

Are they knocking off Jagan in B.G. [British Guiana]? I cannot get the story straight.

Looking forward to hearing from you soon, I remain,

Your most obedient servant,

/s Paul

[. . .]

PAB to PMS

Palo Alto
March 13, 1962

Dear Paul,

No limits to my gratitude for your prompt (and superb) editing of the Foreword [Foreword to the 1962 printing of *PEoG*]. The MS arrived early this morning,

I worked on it most of the day, and fixed it up according to your advice. One or two pp. in the sinological part are new writing which will call once more for the red pencil, but this will be relevant only to the American edition; for the translators stylistic perfection is probably almost immaterial. In any case, when I get the stuff back from the typist, I'll send you the stuff for Huby and hold what is to go to Europe until I hear from you concerning those passages which are new and which will be appropriately designated. Again, many thanks.

The attached piece on Excess Capacity is very interesting. I saw here Garlin the other day, and he told me that it was he who worked on it together with his uncle (Gould).[136] He plans to make a dissertation out of it — I actually suggested to him that topic some time ago — and may succeed in turning out an interesting study. The article, as it stands, but even as it might be edited, seems to me hardly suitable for *MR*. Too damn technical. But what bothers me substantively about the thing is that, although it quotes with approval Steindl, it doesn't come to grips with the Steindl thesis, to wit: that the mounting excess capacity puts of necessity a brake on investment. The latter apparently does not quite happen. Question: why? Two answers would need to be examined : (1) whether technological progress so drastically reduces costs that the excess capacity is not really excess capacity in the economic meaning of the word. In other terms: is the estimate of 1% increase of capital efficiency an underestimate for the current period? And (2) whether in the general transition of the economy to ever increasing waste, investment other than in plant and equipment is not growing much more important than "good, old" productive investment? There is clearly little meaning to the whole notion of excess capacity when it comes to military-oriented investment, and the notion that investment in distribution, advertising etc. is minor is, I think, wrong. The whole suburbia apparatus with supermarkets, filling stations, etc., etc. probably eats up a hell of a lot of investment — in any case, an increasing share of the total. If you should decide to use it for *MR*, it would have to be cut in half and completely re-written. Not sure that it's worth it for *MR* readers. But we can certainly use the stuff for the opus, where it belongs.

136. The reference is to An Economic Observer, "Idle Machines," *Monthly Review* 14, no. 2 (June 1962): 84–95. Victor Garlin who was to be associated in the early years with the Union for Radical Political Economics and was a longtime professor of economics at Sonoma State University. Jay M. Gould was an economist and good friend of PMS. He wrote *The Technical Elite* (New York: Augustus M. Kelley, 1966).

Will send later the paper of [Carl] Kaysen on automobiles which I got today. Most illuminating and eminently quotable.[137]

Tomorrow last classes and then exams. . . .

More later, Love,

/s Paul

[Handwritten]

P.S. Don't quite understand how excessive depreciation allowances increase profit *after taxes* in the *long run*. Once the equipment is *written off*, it cannot be depreciated any further and profits accordingly increase. Only in the case in which the written off equipment is sold, can the gains be transformed into capital gains, and then made subject to capital gains taxes. Otherwise, it is not clear to me what happens if one should assume that tax rates do not change, no obvious advantage in quick depreciation, except for reduction of *risk*, but this is a different matter. It may promote investment in areas where *steady* demand cannot be assumed, but cannot influence profits or am I wrong?

PAB to PMS

Stanford

March 22, 1962

Dear Paul,

The death of CWM [C. Wright Mills] reported this morning in the Chronicle upset me no end. . . . He was only 48 years old, looked like a real oak tree when I last saw him, was full of strength, energy and enterprise. . . . His first attack came exactly at the same time as my [mine], and now he is gone. Since the profession will probably pay little, if any, attention to his passing away, maybe *MR* ought to publish an obituary. He was after all the best that American or, for that matter, bourgeois social science in general has to offer. It occurs to me that perhaps Hans Gerth, his teacher and collaborator for many years might want to write something about him, although, I think they were estranged in the last years of CWM's life. (Hans Gerth I used to know well, I could write to him, or you might do better as Editor; he is at the Dept. of Sociology at Wisconsin.)[138]

137. Franklin M. Fischer, Zvi Grilliches, and Carl Kaysen, "The Costs of Automobile Model Changes since 1949," *Journal of Political Economy* 70, no. 5 (October 1962): 443–51. This article was to play a large role in Baran's analysis of "Absorption of Surplus: The Sales Effort" in Chapter 5 of *Monopoly Capital*.

138. Baran had probably first become acquainted with Hans Gerth at the University of Frankfurt (Frankfurt School of Social Research) in the early 1930s when they were both students there.

[...]
All the best, Yours
     /s Paul

PAB to PMS

[Palo Alto]
March 23, 1962

Dear Paul,

[...]

Now to the substance: Where I make the observation that the competitive, welfare and Pigou-oriented economists had to balk at considering *monopoly* profits to be *costs of production*, it would be kind of "cute" to make a fn. saying that it was Schumpy [Schumpeter] who performed the theoretical *tour de force* of adjusting economic theory to the requirements of monopoly capitalism by treating even monopoly costs as necessary costs of production via the device of stressing their *dynamic* virtues as outweighing their *static* vices. Indeed, if monopoly profits are indispensable to obtain technical progress, innovations *et tout ça* [and all the rest of it], and if eventually they are washed out by the "perennial gale," then they are parts and parcels of social costs of production and growth — on the fundamental assumption that *Kapitalism ueber Alles*!

Another punkt: reading Hans Bethe's testimony in D.C. (clip. attached), I was struck by the consideration that the power of dialectic is truly stupendous: the economic requirements underlying military spending come now to interfere even with the ostensible purpose of that spending itself, namely providing a good military establishment. If in order to spend lots of $$ one does militarily something which is in conflict with something that would be militarily more effective but is much cheaper, then the triumph of dialectics is truly assured!

And a third reflection: With the "revolution of rising expectations" sweeping the underdeveloped countries, not only the *ancien regime* -advocates come into trouble but also socialists. The former because they cannot offer the masses anything but a couple of % annual growth p.a. — if so much; the latter, because [by] adopting a rational strategy of growth which involves the maximization of the rates of growth *over a fairly long planning horizon*, they are forced to permit consumption and employment to go up very slowly until the hump is reached, and to loosen up only at a very much later date. In either case, there is no milk and honey flowing in the immediate short-run. Crucial difference: in the first case sacrifices and misery without prospect and hope and for the sake of nothing; in the second case, privations *hic et nunc* [here and now] but with a mathematically predictable reward in the future.[139]

Tell me what you think about all of it.

[...]

Very much look forward to seeing you soon.

Love,

    /s Paul

P.S. [...]

---

139. Handwritten footnote by Baran: This is the *crux* of the Stalin biz.

7

Inflation, Imperialism, and the Cuban Missile Crisis

[April 4, 1962, PAB travels to New York on his way to Europe and beyond (Austria, Poland, Soviet Union, Iran, Greece, Italy, France, U.K). Handwritten letters (some of PAB's penmanship difficult to decipher) during his trip follow.]

PAB to PMS

Warsaw
April 12, 1962

Dear Paul,

The chapter Vienna went very well. Was received very cordially by the amiable, if somewhat dullish, Eduard März, and had a number of most interesting talks with [Josef] Steindl, [Kurt W.] Rothschild and others.[140] The lecture went off o.k. although *les bourgeois du parti socialiste autrichien e teint très épaté* [the bourgeoisie of the Austrian socialist party is quite complex]. They are Kennedy'ans, still believe that the New Frontier = New Deal. Interestingly enough the Commies could call me a sectarian too. The position of truth is apparently now firmly lodged between all stools. I got the megalomanic feeling that it is now upon you and me that the responsibility lies to keep up the Marxian theory *malgré tout* [above all]! The extraordinary irony of the situation is that being precluded by objective circumstances from being *in politics*, we are the only ones who are *free* to say what we think is right! I sensed that 6 years ago in

---

140. The Austrian socialist economists März, Rothschild, and Steindl were all important allies of Baran and Sweezy in economics. Steindl's *Maturity and Stagnation in American Capitalism* (New York: Monthly Review Press, 1976, first edition, 1952) and Rothschild's "A Note on Advertising," *Economic Journal* 52 (April 1942): 112–20, exercised a direct influence on Baran and Sweezy's *Monopoly Capital*. März was a longtime friend of Sweezy's and later wrote *Joseph Schumpeter: Scholar, Teacher, Politician* (New Haven: Yale University Press, 1991).

India, and now again in Vienna. Maybe truth does not matter unless translated into action; in that case I am writing not to matter and to hope that "history will absolve us."

Madame O.L [Oskar Lange's wife] met me at the airport — most touching, since I did not announce the date of arrival; she called the airlines; and tonight dinner at their house with the Kaleckis [husband and wife], Joan Robinson who is here and ____? All the economic stars assemble here in a few days for the u/d c [underdeveloped country] conference, but I won't have anything to do with that.

More later. All the best. Much love,

/s Your Paul

P.S. By the way, Steindl cum Rothschild — both *very* bright — approve 100% of the surplus theory and in particular of "interpenetration effect."[141]

PAB to PMS

Moscow
April 20th, 1962

Dear Paul,

I had a few most enjoyable days in Warsaw. The country is booming, people are most hospitable and friendly, and my conversations were interesting and useful. I wished I could have stayed a few days longer. The Moscow stay began rather inauspiciously. My father does not feel well at all and has got to be quite old; spending much time with him is rather trying. His principal theme of conversation is medical; his own health and mine, and there are few other things that tax my patience to the same degree. In addition I was assigned to a hotel which is way out in the suburbs; terribly far away from everything, and to cap it off, it seems to be impossible to get to see anybody. I would like to get out of here earlier than planned, but there is a major problem with reservations,

---

141. The "interpenetration effect" was a key conceptual category introduced in Chapter 5 of *Monopoly Capital* on "The Absorption of Surplus: The Sales Effort." It was derived from an earlier observation by Thorstein Veblen on the penetration of the sales effort into production. Under monopoly a vast and rapidly increasing share of what were considered production costs were in reality concerned with the marketing of the product. This was a key element in Baran and Sweezy's use of the economic surplus category to supplement Marx's notion of surplus value. Baran drafted the chapter "Some Theoretical Implications" (not included in the published book) to address some of the theoretical issues associated with the interpenetration effect, including its relation to the theory of wages. See Paul A. Baran and Paul M. Sweezy, *Monopoly Capital* (New York: Monthly Review Press, 1966), 131–38; Paul A. Baran and Paul M. Sweezy, "Some Theoretical Implications," *Monthly Review* 64, no. 3 (July-August 2012): 40–42.

tickets etc. We'll see; maybe matters will improve in a few days and I'll get some contacts established. Otherwise it will be a terrible waste of time. I got a very cordial invitation from Beograde [Belgrade] and am thinking seriously to change the whole plan and skipping Tehran, spend some time there. All "weighty" decisions.

I hope you have written here in the meantime and that you are all well.

Love,

/s Paul

P.S. Please tell Zirel that I saw the Walters in Warsaw and delivered her present.

PAB to PMS

[*Postcard from Moscow*]

April 26, 1962

I haven't heard from you since leaving N.Y. — how are you? The days here are quite hectic — lots of people to see and quite a few interesting conversations. Don't regret at all my last article — should have been if anything – sharper. [142] The only trouble is that the "have" is actually more of a "have-not" than one might have thought. Leaving here on May 6th

Love, /s Paul

PAB to PMS

[*Apparently he was able to move from the hotel in the suburbs.*]

Hotel Metropol

Moscow

May 1st, 1962

Dear Paul,

My fountain pen got lost in the traffic and I am confined to this pencil. Am also confined to my hotel room because the May demonstrations engulf the square and to get out is completely impossible — at least until late P.M. [143] This gives me a chance to sort out a few thoughts, notes and impressions. The general *Stimmung* [mood] around here is, if anything, somewhat melancholic. The first, great thaw is over and now people are taking for granted what only nine years ago appeared to be genuine liberation, and ask themselves where do we

142. Baran is most likely referring to his article, "The Great Debate,"(*MR*, May 1962), which discussed the outlook for the USSR.
143. The "May demonstrations" refer to May Day, the internationally celebrated day of labor, which was a major holiday in the Soviet Union.

go from here? Others remain bitter *plus ça change plus c'est la même chose* [the more things change the more they stay the same] — to certain things people get accustomed rapidly and no longer consider them worth celebrating. The question which one encounters everywhere — what is the historical perspective? — is as familiar as it is distressing. The economic situation is poor with regard to minimal basics and although this is not noticeable very much in Moscow, is serious elsewhere. All these things are not unrelated, to be sure but the relation involved is not as simple as our friend Michael [Harrington?] likes to see it. Somewhere at the bottom of all is a continuing sense of boredom; this is undoubtedly most prominent among the intellectuals, but affects strongly the "man in the street." Not by bread alone . . . even if there is plenty of same or perhaps particularly when there is approximately enough (as in Marx.) The very young and the very old are restless! As someone has explained to me, this is now *the* most literate, *the* most educated people on earth (which is probably true) and such a people asks for more than the daily editorial. It wants discussion, struggle, search for truth. And it is *the* most political people on earth! It does not discuss the merits of the Giants vs. Dodgers — it discusses everything — *tout compris* — and finds the material offered insufficient. And it finds reality *very* much worth talking about — the reality at home in every day's life — and very little encouragement for such conversation. The remarkable thing is that the condemnation of the past has been turned most skillfully into a glorification of the present! On all this there is much to be said; I'll see whether I'll have enough inspiration.

Psychically one thing is clear: one is either made to oppose, to fight, to criticize, or to be part of the Establishment. I am definitely no good for *any* Establishment. Schumpy's disturbing, restless intellectual — a nuisance everywhere. Maybe this is the eternal function of the intellectual after all — in all times and in all places.

Am leaving here on May 6th and shall write to you from Tehran.

Hope that all is well and would like to have more mail. In Stanford apparently some storm from what I hear. Cf. attached editorial from *Daily*. Could you, perhaps, drop them a note and ask them for the *preceding* issues which were not sent to me. Just for the sake of curiosity and archives.[144]

Write c/o Carocci — I'll get in touch with him.

Much love,

/s Your Paul

---

144. The *Stanford Daily* ran a series of articles about Baran and academic freedom on April 10–13, 1962.

PAB to PMS

Moscow

May 3, 1962

Dear Paul,

[…]

Had today an all-day conference at the Institute for World Economics with some interesting aspects. They are all very interested in our *opus*, although I have a strong feeling that it will be received with mixed feelings. Their understanding of mono[poly] capitalism is, to say the least, most deficient. I wouldn't be surprised if even the summer issue material should provoke some dissatisfaction, for somewhere at the bottom of it all, there is a great deal of admiration for *das Amerikanische Wirtschaftswunder* [American Economic Wonder].[145] The appraisal of the Kennedy administration is on the whole favorable and many believe the Alliance for Progress etc. represents a genuine change in policy towards a British-type colonial liberalization. The steel affair has greatly re-enforced the pro Kennedy sentiments with JFK now being more and more considered to be another FDR.[146] Kind of funny to hear here all the arguments of the Tarshis & Co. All this goes together with an extraordinary backwardness in economic reasoning which moves on the level of Marshall (at best). Old stories about the country being ruined by deficits etc. etc. — Why don't U.S. corporations produce simple, cheap cars if there is demand for them? And similar questions.

The Soviet economists, i.e. those working on domestic problems, worry endlessly about the law of value with God alone comprehending what it is all about. When I suggested that all that matters in my humble opinion are *relative* prices (at this stage of the game, in any case) — the answer is that I forget the substance of prices.

Tomorrow a second lecture at the University; this time for the assembled faculty. Wonder what this will be like.

In general not a very elevating picture and a strong impression that our function is much [unreadable: weaker?] than one tends to think at home. By the

145. The July-August 1962 issue of *Monthly Review* consisted of two preliminary chapters of Baran and Sweezy's *Monopoly Capital* plus a short introduction discussing the projected work as a whole. The first of the two was "The Giant Corporation," Chapter 2 in the published work. The other chapter was "On the Quality of Monopoly Capital Society," Chapter 10 in the published work. The second of these chapters was to be massively revised in the published version with much of the discussion of poverty removed.

146. Refers to Kennedy's crackdown on U.S. steel companies' price fixing.

way, if in Cuba, Mexico, etc. we are *somebodies*, here we are about where we are *chez nous* [at home]. The world is peculiarly round.

Leaving here on Sunday and shall send you a wire concerning my address. Meanwhile all the best. Love also for Zirel.

/s Paul

PAB to PMS

En route Tbilisi-Tehran
May 7th, 1962

Dear Paul,

How was your expedition to Mexico?

The present part of my trip is quite extraordinary. This is the first time in the relevant past that I have been outside of Moscow, and much becomes clearer when one gets to see — if ever so quickly — what goes on outside. I left Moscow on the plane for Tbilisi (2 hrs and 20′) and found myself in a southern, semi-oriental atmosphere. The climate is Californian, people are in the streets, and the whole setting is such that one hardly believes to be still in the SU. I got acquainted with a bunch of Georgian students who hang around coffee-houses and restaurants, drink wonderful local wine, chase girls and behave like Italians, French or Arabs. The most striking thing about them is the truly unimaginable nationalism. Georgia is above all, above the neighboring Armenia in particular, but also not to be compared with Russia or anything else. They despise *all* other nationalities, have until this very day an extremely hostile view of intermarriage and consider themselves to be the chosen people. They lead a very rich life; Stalin gave them all kinds of bonanza's incl tax exemptions, exceptionally high prices for their products (wine, citrus fruit) and provided for them receiving supplies of manufactured goods many times as high as other parts of the Soviet Union. Made me think that the whole problem of nationalism needs to be re-examined. Interesting that an oppressed nation is united in its hatred of the oppressing power. Then comes — after independence is won — class strife and class hatred disrupting national unity, turning nationalism into an ideology of the ruling class and greatly reducing the nationalist fervor of the ruled classes. But after a social revolution, nationalism instead of declining receives a new spurt. Now one need not identify oneself with the hated landlord and exploiter; now one can accept the responsibility for one's *entire* national community and . . . become [triply?] nationalistic. The Georgian who hates the Armenian loves now *all* Georgians; there are no more any *bad* Georgians! Although Stalin's statue was removed everywhere, it stands proudly in Tbilisi, and they were telling me that the army will have to do the removing job; no Georgian will touch it. He made errors, he loved power, he committed horrible crimes, but he was "our" man, a Georgian communist — not a prince, not a factory owner, but a son of Georgia; its greatest.

In the streets is music, clarinets, recorders and drums, the students long for jazz and everything Western is a hit. Their chief complaint — *boredom*! Nothing to do in the evenings, no place to take a girl, no night life and no . . . change. Travel, oh only if they could travel! Not that elsewhere is better, but elsewhere is *different*. They would come back from everywhere. They would return and kiss the earth of Georgia and they would not want to die anywhere but at home, but *see* what the world is like. What is the point in travelling in the SU — *c'est la meme chose* — but Champs Elysee, Broadway, Piccadilly Circle? They have read everything. Know more about everything than most people elsewhere — their expectations are not rising, they are galloping.

The voyage from Moscow to Teheran turned out to be quite different from what I was told. From Tbilisi it takes 2 full days on train! I had 4 hrs to have a look at Erivan, the capital of Soviet Armenia and to see a magnificent, flourishing countryside. People in Armenia are less affluent, but not too badly off. And an astonishing volume of building.

I wish I could spend a few months just looking around here; it is a unique part of the world.

More later, Much love,

/s Paul

PMS to PAB

Larchmont
May 6, 1962

Dear Paul,

[. . .]

I rec'd your May Day letter from Moscow this a.m. Apparently sending it registered vastly increases the speed and reliability factors. We should remember this for future reference. What you say about the "boredom of the intellectuals" rings all too true — and gives me that uncomfortable feeling I sometimes get that maybe Dostoyevsky's underground man is after all the representative human being. Maybe what we can't stand in the final reckoning is that 2 plus 2 equals 4. Not that everything is perfect there or anywhere else, far from it, but one wonders what the hell would one do if everything *were* perfect. Oh well, we needn't waste too much time on such worries, not in the USA anyways.

Did I write you that I had a wonderful four days in Mexico City? Cecena's exam was a political demonstration (I was brought down to lend glamor to the

proceedings) — more than 600 people crowded into the biggest auditorium
at the School of Economics to listen and applaud, and hundreds more were
turned away for lack of space. Silva Herzog was chairman of the committee,
and Lombardo Toledano was one of its members. Actually, Cecena's thesis
(Monopoly Capitalism and the Mexican Economy) is quite good — contains
much interesting information of the extent to which the Mexican economy is
dominated by the U.S. giants. The only weakness is that he is terribly addicted
to the spider webs which show that Morgan or Rockefeller or Mellon control just
about everything under the sun and presumably plot the downfall of decency
and morality in a plushy boardroom on Wall St. [Victor] Perlo has done much to
foster this kind of stuff, the net effect of which is to detract from the credibility of
what is otherwise excellent work.

I also had a two-hour interview with Cardenas which I have written up for
the June RoM. A really great man who, like Fidel, has come to an absolutely
solid Marxist position through his own experience and observation. He was
extremely gracious and cordial and at the end invited me to tour the country
with him for four days next time I come to Mexico. It is good for one's morale
not to be treated like a *sobaka* [dog] all the time. Other events were a long talk
with the young novelist Carlos Fuentes who knows the score very well, will write
for *MR* and advise us on literature by Latin American authors which ought to be
translated; and an hour's interview with Arevalo, former president of Guatemala
and author of *The Shark and the Sardines*. Arevalo is a confused romantic who
may turn out to be another Betancourt (though he hates Betancourt personally).

Back to work.

Love,

/s Paul

PAB to PMS

Tehran
Sepide Hotel
May 9, 1962

Dear Paul,

For nearly a day and a half looked out of the train window at the absolutely
dismal Iranian countryside. The filth, poverty and the sickness staring at me from
everywhere are indescribable. Spent an hour in a fruit-packing plant (almonds,
raisins and other stuff) — women are working at 25 c. per day and children 5
years old at 15 c. Kids who make errors are beaten by the overseers, and one
Azerbajdzanian who spoke Russian told me that some days ago an irate factory
owner has beaten a little boy to death.

Arrived this morning in Teheran, have established some contacts but shall not see anyone until this evening. Turns out that the place is full with American economists headed by Hollis Chenery surveying the aid program. Don't know whether I'll meet any of them and cannot say I am too anxious. Expect to stay here for about a week and then go to Belgrade. If you have a minute, drop me a line c/o Professor Stanovic POB 750. Around the 22nd I should be in Rome. Don't know yet the name of the hotel, but write either to Nuovi Argomenti, or better still c/o American Express, where I shall be looking for mail.

On Teheran etc later when I know more.

Very best regards for Zirel.

Much love,

      /s Paul

PAB to PMS

[*Undated, but probably May 11, 1962*]

Semiramis Hotel
Tehran

Dear Paul,

Had to transfer to another hotel, the noise in the first was absolutely unbearable. This one is "*lelegant*." Attended last night a party to which Mrs R. [Rabinowitz] took me — the entire *jeunesse doreé* [young people of wealth and fashion] of Iran — the likes of which I hardly ever saw. About 40 people, the women no less exquisite than the drinks and food, and orchestra and an infinity of butlers, waiters and bellhops lighting cigarettes. Caviar in pots, delicacies from *tout le monde* [all the world] and a house which is nothing short of a palace. The rich behave as if it were indeed "a feast at the time of a plague." *Carpe diem*! They all say that this state of affairs is only possible thanks to "*us*." By the way, the establishment of the R's cum garden and gardeners, cook, maids etc., etc. is something David Rockefeller might envy.

A few readers of Peography [*PEoG*] joked saying that after describing all of this I am coming to have a look at it. As you know, *not* to exaggerate takes a good deal of self-control in my case, in the case of Iran every exaggeration of the peographic type is an understatement. I'll have a seminar with a bunch of strictly phony economists at the Planning outfit, and then a public lecture at the University. A week later they'll hear Ed Mason who is coming here to survey the work of the Planning joint which the Ford Foundation "presents" to the Shah. It all defies words and description!! Never have perfidy, hypocrisy and mendacity reached such proportions. At least Lord Clive said clearly *qu il faut se enrichesses*. But this struggle for democracy in a Trujillo set-up is out of any

human frame of reference. Am going to spend the last 2 days just looking and on
May 16 off to Athens-Belgrade.

    Con amore,
        /s Paul

P.S. Hope to find a letter from you in Belgrade. Main disappointment:
impossibility of finding contacts with *l'autre monde.*

PAB to PMS

          [*Postcard showing Poros Monastery, Athens*]

                                        May 18, 1962

The paradox must have been observed by many; nothing drives it home as well
as experience. As one gets older, one gains the *possibility* of doing things and
loses at the same time the *capacity* for doing them. This is *Greek* tragedy in all its
aspects. Taking a trip to the islands; tomorrow off to Belgrade.

    Love,
        /s Paul

PAB to PMS

                                          Belgrade
                                    May 20, 1962

Dear Paul,

Arrived yesterday in Belgrade, was met by Stanovnik and spent the first two days
sightseeing. It is a nice city; the contrast with Athens is striking: this clearly and
obviously the city of the common man — there a playground of domestic and
foreign parasites. Whatever messiness and problems there are under socialism,
this difference is worth all the trouble that it takes to get a socialist order. The
conversations which I have here with Stanovnik and others who were showing
me the sights were most revealing. In the big merry-go-round, the Yugo's are now
moving towards Schlomo's position [Sol Adler]! The "Great Debate" analysis
is 100% correct and they are talking in exactly those terms! There *may* be a
possibility of seeing a top man on these matters; would be very interesting.

    I am going to give one lecture at the Institute of Stanovnik and another at
the University; curious how it'll work out. We are well known here, they inquire
about your welfare and say both of us should come for a longer stay. The main
question: what *is* the historical perspective for the U.S. *$64.*

    [...]

    Get a hold of the May 7th issue of *U.S. News & World Report.* There is
an "authoritative" statement by W.W. Rostow in "Whither U.S." — the most

outrageous document I have seen in a long time — eminently quotable. Even conservative Greeks were upset!

Leaving on Friday, May 25th for Rome. Temporarily c/o American Express Co., Rome.

Hope to get something from you here.

All the best,

/s Your Paul

PAB to PMS

Belgrade

May 23, 1962

Dear Paul,

Delivered myself this noon of a lecture at the Stanovnik Institute. The title was "Some Observations on the Theory of Imperialism." The reaction was most discouraging. Stony silence, not one single question, not one remark. I never experienced *this* kind of a reception before, and am puzzled: what did I say that had such a deep-freeze effect on the crowd? Maybe it will become clearer when I talk with some of the people later on. The ideological positions here are complex: a peculiar mixture of *very* primitive Marxism and very far-reaching revisionism. The former applies primarily to questions that have little practical importance; the latter to important problems in foreign and domestic policies. What they are really hipped on is decentralization of *everything* with this decentralization assuming grotesque forms. Not only is there really no central plan for the economy as a whole, but no central management of foreign trade, of investment, etc. etc. The Federation principle creates a vast multiplication of administrative and economic activities: *every* republic has not only a full-dress government of its own, but must have every plant, every type of industry of its own. No discrimination! The result is some peculiar sort of irrationality with economies of scale unrealized, with cross-handling, cross-administering everywhere. They all recognize that this is a mighty expensive way of doing business, but insist that this is the only politically feasible one.

And, indeed, this "muddling through" type of socialism seems to function in some kind of a way, and the political atmosphere as well as living conditions are as good as they are anywhere. The street gives the impression of being crowded with content people, walking about, laughing and having a good time. There is nothing of the Russian sternness about the whole thing and in some respects a flair of Cuba. There is apparently some virtue in sheer *messiness* and it is perhaps worth paying a price in terms of economic efficiency. To be sure, this price begins to strike them now as being too high and it looks as if they consider seriously to make a swing away from this NEPism [referring to the New Economic Plan period in the USSR under Lenin], and to turn to some more rigorous forms of running things.[147] This was the burden of Tito's latest speech. The feelings on all of this are mixed and so will be probably the results.

On the ideological front the mess expresses itself in the range of views: those regarding the SU as "imperialist power" all the way to those objecting to the "excessive" denigration of Stalin. I would have liked to have an opportunity of talking to some top echelon people, but I don't think it'll work out. Too bad!

Tomorrow another affair at the Economics Faculty of the University. Probably not very interesting. Am actually quite glad to go on Friday. One has to stay here either very long or after a few days one ceases to learn anything new. Terribly hard to comprehend things when there are no clear cut issues, no sharp alternatives, no definable problems. It all becomes a huge intellectual stew with description taking continuously the place of analysis, and with a cordial smile serving as an answer to questions on consistency or rationality. Mighty tough! Tonight party chez Stanovnik.

All the best.

Love,

/s Paul

PAB to PMS

Hotel-Pensione Bellavista Milton

Rome

May 26, 1962

Dear Paul,

Went today to see Carocci to pick up mail and to have a chat. I expected to meet a journalist or writer of some sort and was mamazed [another Nicky-ism] by what I encountered. A grand seigneur inhabiting a part of an absolutely princely palace, the legal counsel of IBM's only important competitor — Olivetti — surrounded by servants, butlers and bellhops! He expected me for a royal lunch and was as gracious and *distingué* as only imaginable. A communist *au fond*, he demonstrates one phenomenon which does not exist in the U.S. — a grand bourgeois who is cultivated, widely read, full of ideas and progressive leanings. Was both interesting and profitable. He was most indignant about the rank betrayal of Feltrinelli in general and in regard to *PEoG*. The s.o.b. went over to the Establishment. He published *PEoG* because of contract only and (a) omitted

147. "NEPism refers to the New Economic Policy introduced by Lenin in the Soviet Union, representing a greater turn to the market in the wake of War Communism.

the Preface for the Italian ed. (b) gave it a monstrously unattractive title and (c) priced it out of the market (L 3500 = $6, but even more expensive by Italian standards). One should concentrate on Einaudi who is a decent sort and have nothing to do with Feltrinelli.

Rome is as beautiful as ever — the city of all cities except for Peking — and the only "thing" that is missing, and around here desperately so, is a Romana, who would share and provide for one's delights. Alas, my object of admiration here apparently reciprocates my affection on a minimal scale. I was explained by one lady that in Italy life begins at 40 and replied that it apparently ends at 50. A short span indeed!

The Stanford uproar *in absentiam* is most interesting [see Footnote 144]. I am most pleased *not* to be around, and can only imagine, how pleased they would all be if one of my many planes would crash. On the other hand getting back will be anything but pleasant!

[…]

Everyone on the Left is talking here about Neo-Capitalism; this is the watchword of the day. Not too clear what it is that they consider to be *Neo*, but as near as I can figure it out, it is *dirigisme*, state capitalism and monopoly capitalism. *Opus* could not be more timely, except that it has to be given a sharp theoretical edge. What I am not certain about, is how much of all this here is simply *boom* and how much a real structural change of monopoly capital variety. I hope to find out more during the next few days. On Friday I'll give a lecture on the subject and the discussion should be interesting. What is crucially important here is that the whole business has set off a sharp turn to the right in the socialist movement with lots of talk about planned capitalism, welfare state, &c, &c. The remarkable thing is that the *actual* development of the last 5 years has apparently greatly disarmed the Left: there *is* a 9% p.a. !!! growth in industrial output, there is a rapid capitalist development in the South with great differentiation in the village + Kulakization & pauperization and so forth and so on, with the Left confused and uncertain where to go and what to say. The Christo's [Christian Democrats] are very skillful now and Fanfani's deal with Nenni [Italian Socialists] has split everything wide open. With nearly the majority of people socialist and all of the working class around the CP, the tenor of conversation is . . . American! At the same time $50-$60 a month *is* a better than typical wage! All this is mightily confusing and absolutely no theoretical work done by anybody. It certainly got to be a syncretic age of "trials and error," no one theorizes anymore and everyone seeking to make the best of a lousy situation and .... live well! The automobilitis has seized Italy, full steam and the merry Sixties are of the same quality as the Great American Celebration. I must confess that it is hard *not* to succumb and sitting in the breathtakingly beautiful Piazza Navona not to give everything up and turn to medieval history and art. What is the use?

Someone who came back from Prague tells me that there you have the combinations of two worlds: social democratic welfare state a la Sweden *cum* the dullest management of enlightened Stalinism. Surely, a hell of a cocktail!

As you see, I am not in the most ebullient of moods, but this like everything else will pass.

End of next week (around June 8th or so) I'll be in Paris (Hotel Lutetia). Write!

> /s Your Paul

P.S. JFK could win an Italian election hands down! [Shigeto] Tsuru's *Has Capitalism Changed?* has come out here and is causing lots of talk.

PAB to PMS

> Rome
> May 29, 1962

Dear Paul,

The stay in Rome thus far rather frustrating. Terribly hard to get hold of people; the office hours are short, in the evenings they are busy and so there is a lot of underutilized time. And I am no good as a tourist; if there is nothing to do I get restless and depressed. But things are beginning to move now, a number of appointments are made and the next few days ought to be more productive. Saw Corsini, tomorrow Sylos [Labini] will be here and so forth.[148] On Thursday I have a lecture on Mono. Cap.; this *is* the topic now everybody is talking about. As I wrote you, here this is called Neo Cap, and the confusion is unbelievable. What it all boils down [to] at this point is that there is a tremendous boom, the state is playing an ever increasing role in econ. affairs and the welfare state is open and officially the program of the Fanfani-Nenni coalition.

The labor movement — *very* strong, *very* militant, with magnificent traditions and full of spirit and vitality (*lots* of *young* people coming in every day) — becomes progressively disoriented. Since socialism and revolution are not on the historical agenda, what *are* or *should be* the policy demands of a *mass* movement? The old question: what does a revolutionary movement do in a counter-revolutionary situation is doubly complicated by welfare-statism on the part of

148. The Italian economist Paolo Sylos Labini's *Oligopoly and Technical Progress* (Cambridge, MA: Harvard University Press, 1962) was an important influence on Baran and Sweezy's *Monopoly Capital*.

the bourgeoisie. Thus far Keynes has won the day — in Italy more than in the U.S. — and since there are *here* still vast possibilities of capitalist development — much too early for stagnation: the automobile era e.g. is only in its beginning — what is the historical perspective! The country goes actually through the Merry Twenties with state intervention promising to prevent 1929-1933! Under such circumstances the best that can happen is the development of a large Labor Party British style, and this is clearly where the right-wingers (a la Corsini and others) want to go. Corsini is apparently the *extreme* right wing, but others differ from him more in terminology and nuances than in substance. Glorification of JFK, major reappraisal of U.S. policies, peaceful coexistence [à outrance?] etc., etc.

The left is helpless; they detest it all, speak of alienation, of cultural decay and other things not unfamiliar *to us*, but they are losing touch with *politics*. And whole mess is triply confounded by the fact that the socialist world is clearly going through a major crisis. Reports from everywhere are bad (had some talks with those following closely events over there), agriculture, food, political dissatisfaction etc., etc. — and this obviously does not help the Left. Also lots of critical remarks about the u/d c's [underdeveloped countries], where the Nkrumah's, Toure's, a.o., are looked upon as potential fascists. In a word — a depressing picture, if there ever was one, with the right wing calling for concentration on *domestic* affairs, more welfare, more social reforms &c. Some people said to me, "you are lucky, you can talk and write the way you do, because you have *no movement* to worry about!"

Sectarianism looks like a wonderful escape from this turmoil — the retreat to an ivory tower without all the responsibilities and demands of the political struggle. One *very* bright girl told me, *MR* sounds like a menage from the *old* world in which everything was simply straightforward, black and white. This is all very confusing, mightily discouraging but supplying plenty of food for thought. I have the feeling that an awful lot has to be re-thought, have even some hunches about the direction of the re-thinking process, but no idea on the shape of its outcome. The opus has obviously priority over everything else (I was teased here with remarks about the "mythical" book), and it should clear up at least some part of the Neo Capitalist muddle. Afterwards what would be needed is perhaps not so much a booklet reporting on impressions from this trip, but rather a kind of an Essay on Our Time trying to put together all these strands and give them some kind of a *theoretical* structure. Least of all is needed today — this is my profound conviction — current journalism. For this there are plenty of people. What is the bitterest outcry everywhere is the demand for elucidation, comprehension, [unreadable: "fed up?] with traditional thought. *Hic Rhodus, hic salto*! [here is Rhodes, jump here! (meaning "prove what you are made of . . .")]

[. . .]

So much for today

Love,

    /s Paul

PAB to PMS

Rome

June 1, 1962

Dear Paul,

After receiving the big batch of stuff which waited for me at Rome, I haven't heard from you at all. Is everything alright? Having taken off to a slow start, the stay in Rome has become quite hectic. Lots of appointments — most of them *extremely* interesting. The developments here are quite extraordinary; the Italian case needs to be taken account of in the treatment of monopoly capitalism. The law of uneven development operates full speed; the case of the U.S. (the *most* advanced monopoly capitalist country) differs significantly from the situation in a country in which the problem of investment opportunities does not exist and where the public sector plays a powerful role. While the U.S. situation presents the mirror of Italy's future, the future is not yet. We must bring this stuff parenthetically into our story. I have lots of confused notions on all of this, but not knowing the language it is very hard to read the available material and to get a firmer grasp of the problems involved. In the next few days I hope to get some further understanding of all this and may be try to write down at least a few principal notions.

Now I regret that I am booked to go to Paris on Friday, June 8th. But *rien a faire* [it's no use.] Hope to hear from you in any case in Paris.

Love,

    /s Paul

PAB to PMS

S. Gimigniano

June 3, 1962

Dear Paul,

Am spending the weekend in the paradisic neighborhood of Florence; the beauty of this tiny medieval town — wholly untouched, except for a few buildings in the outskirts — is something beyond description. After the hustle and bustle of "neo-capitalist" Rome, this is a monument of a distant past when men were poor and sick and hungry and created at the same time things of everlasting beauty. All this is obviously trite trash and bygones are forever bygones and the blood, sweat and tears of those who built these cathedrals and walls and towers have gone down in history unsung and unknown, and their works are recorded as those of the Medici's or those of some other Popes and Kings — and yet — will there ever be a time again when bulldozers and cranes and prefab sheetrock will result in something equally magnificent? There clearly is no way back — is there a way forward? Or is forward = TV, automobiles, washing machines = less hard labor, less privation, less <u>sickness</u> *et c'est tout* [that's all]? Socialism becomes more and more identified with welfare, with *bien etre* [well-being], with more radios, more TVs, more cars, and it surely does not behoove *us* — well fed, well clad and well housed — to sneer at all of them in the name of "cultural values," but somewhere, somehow there is a gnawing pain of the bourgeois, of the intellectual, of the upper class beneficiary of all of this who has dreamt of people participating in culture, rather than of culture being dissolved in "massified" high levels of consumption! Would Marx and Engels and the rest of them ever have thought that Vivaldi and Dante and Shakespeare and Tolstoy on the way to the masses would transform themselves into Irving Berlin, comic strips and J.D. Salinger?

On Friday, before leaving Rome, an evening at chez Carocci; some socialist economists who have taken a grim view of the Italian situation. Boom without end; early phases of capitalist industrialization and with the labor movement (Socialist Party, Communist Part, etc.) turning in[to] the government's most loyal opposition. The greatest victory capitalism has celebrated in a long, long time — as one of them put it. Talked at length with P.T. [Togliatti] — in different words, with different accents the same story. The difference of perspective between here and U.S. striking. Corsini hopes to transfer the Italian mood on to the American scene and is mad at us for not seeing the light. But the lights may be genuinely different!

Am returning to Rome today — four more days of activity and then Paris. Write.

/s Your Paul

PAB to PMS

Paris
Hotel Lutetia
June 8, 1962

Dear Paul,
Was delighted to find your letter at the hotel. The stuff for the Summer Issue is excellent. I hope the contents will be favorably rec'd. The *poverty vs. riches*

aspect of economic growth is nowhere more striking than in Italy; I imagine it is just as bad in Mexico. In Mexico profits used to be over 40% of Y [total output]; in Italy they are if anything, even higher. The *FR-AL [Allemagne]-IT* [French-German-Italian] complex becomes a most formidable bastion of capitalist strength, and bids fair to develop into another U.S.A. most interesting and, in the whole, unexpected development. Something about it will have to be stuck into the *opus*, just to point out that the whole mess is not *merely* an American phenomenon.

[...]

Best for Zirel.

Much love,

/s Your Paul

PAB to PMS

Paris

June 12, 1962

Dear Paul,

The intellectual "rage" among the French philosophers etc. is now what they call "negative dialectics." This is to say that Karl Marx has discovered that capitalism leads to an accumulation of horrors and was right in that, but that he erred in believing that the horrors produce the force which brings them to an end. He saw, in other words, one blade of the scissor but was mistaken in regard to the other. From this follows that the only possible position today is a radical "NO" with respect to *everything* — with no exception. Quite a standpoint, but it is apparently spreading like wild fire, and becomes the theoretical base for . . . doing nothing.

For obviously the all-embracing, radical "NO" is equivalent (dialectically) to equally all-embracing, radical "YES" with regard to the *status quo*. If in Carlo Levi's novel "Christ stopped at Eboli," the dialectic stops nowhere and total refusal amounts *de facto* to total acceptance. Not that this position is terribly new or original; the important thing is that it is taken by so many *now* when — one might think — socialism is winning on the global scale. "One might think" — but they do *not*, and say their NO to that socialism too. The "plague on both houses" argument which is heart breaking and desperate, and not easy to deal with. I still firmly believe that it is wrong and that its main weakness is the shortness of historical perspective — *one* postwar boom — but they talk about "neo-cap" forever, about the state *cum* Keynes, *cum* syndicalism, *cum* welfarism, solving the whole biz with the socialist camp eventually turning into welfarism too and with alienation etc remaining with us whichever way things go.

You and I are *famous* here on the Left. Everyone knows both of us and regard us to be the *only* orthodox Marxists in the Western world, i.e., those who accept still the *positive* side of the dialectic diagnosis. I was invited to give a lecture on these issues but have severe stomach aches about the whole thing. They clearly capitulate, liquidate, and desert, but the answer can only be given *sub specie aeternitatis*. We are being accused of not accusing sufficiently the other side. My answer that accusing *in the short run* should not be driven to the abandonment of socialism *in the long run* is rec'd with derisive sneers. "In the long run we'll all be dead" [famous quip by Keynes].

After *opus* is finished, we *must* write something on all of this. Let's do it together a short, concise statement of a *historic* position.

Nietzsche once said that true courage is not sticking to one's views but to be able to change them. But is there a need to change them? I must confess that I am disoriented and insecure, but I still think we *need not* change them.

Love,
/s Paul

PAB to PMS

Palo Alto
August 22, 1962

Dear Paul,
Attached hereto is the draft of Chapter 8.[149] Apart from minor points, I am wholly *d'accord* with pp. 1–39 until the beginning of the paragraph starting with the word "Liberals." I have severe doubts on the validity of what follows from then on.

As to the minor points: (p.2) Why are the "major external stimuli" only epoch-making innovations and wars, and not also "militarization of the economy" which latter you treat separately? It would seem to me that those phenomena should be on equal footing: militarization of the economy has all the "shaking up" features which the other two possess. And if you take the total outlay on militarization (probably somewhere around 1 trillion dollars since 1945) together with the resulting reallocation of economic activity etc., etc., militarization need not be ashamed of the other two major external stimuli. Including militarization would save the trouble of making somewhat doubtful distinctions such as the one on p. 29 n, for the argument that the Korean War

---

149. Baran is referring to what was to be Chapter 8 of *Monopoly Capital*, "On the History of Monopoly Capitalism," drafted by Sweezy. He is returning the chapter with some suggested changes.

may have been provoked by the U.S. is not an important distinction; in that sense one could also argue that WWII was only partly "imposed from without" — the U.S. ruling class had presumably some margin of choice about entering or not entering the war.

(p. 8) In the explanation of the development of backlog demand stress should be placed not on population but on the accumulation of liquid savings &c which permitted the buying spree. It is said on p.28 but on p.8 it looks very much like the acceptance of the population argument which had been essentially rejected in Chapter 4 ["Absorption of Surplus: Capitalist Consumption and Investment"]. In the same paragraph a minute question: what is the difference between "scrapped" and "wholly abandoned?"

(p. 16) It might be useful to point out in this connection that the large increase of the proportion of gainfully employed who are wages and salary receivers subject to short-notice firing and hiring as against those gainfully employed who are either self-employed or enjoy a high degree of "cycle immunity" (officials, etc.) tends strongly to reduce the usefulness of ratios of unemployed to the gainfully employed (or to the labor force). At the present time around 20 million members of the labor force are more or less exempt from *unemployment* (bad business conditions may affect their incomes without depriving them of jobs) — therefore the absolute # of unemployed should be related to the gainfully employed minus these 20 million rather than to the entire # of gainfully employed. The whole thing has been statistically worked out by Joe Phillips [*Review of Economics & Statistics*, May 1960] who was interested in the matter the other way round, from the standpoint of the "labor share in Y": the same share of Y accruing to a larger share of total population means smaller share of labor.

(p. 18 and 19) I have a somewhat uneasy feeling about the too "needs-oriented" treatment of the automobile. There is after all a dialectic at work: there is need (or demand) for automobiles because there are automobiles; this need and demand translate themselves into effective demand because there are income and prosperity. How does one know what would have happened with regard to the automobile by 1915 if the war had not filled the pockets of those who wanted and now were able to buy an automobile? To be sure, once the automobile boom was on its way, it developed its own momentum and continued on its own steam. Current experience in Western Europe shows this clearly: the postwar boom created the basis for the spreading of the automobile, the automobile in turn extends the boom. It is important to stress those *interactions*, for otherwise one gets too close to the "human wants" theory which forgets about effective demand and talks about the needs of the growing population &c.

(p. 27) This becomes a problem again where the statement is made that investment outlets were practically nonexistent (in 1937). Why were they nonexistent? There surely was — as we now know by hindsight — plenty of need for automobiles, housing and the like. The answer presumably is that the major external stimuli have run their course and that the Kalecki-Steindl forces governing the investment policy of monopoly capitalist enterprises have taken over. In general, I think that the entire Kalecki-Steindl argument explaining the limitations on investment under monopoly and oligopoly is somewhat played down, although Steindl is referred to a couple of times. It may be unnecessary to go into it again after all that has been said before; I think the reader would be better able to link it up with reality if he were reminded of it in this chapter on a few crucial occasions. Otherwise it remains somewhat unclear what role if any was played by *monopoly* in this development; couldn't Chapter 8 have been written without any reference to monopoly? It is my impression that it cannot be said often enough that the investment and output limiting nature of monopoly capitalism dominates unless there is a major external stimulus which changes drastically the conditions of demand.

Now (p. 39): I would prefer to finish the Chapter without going into what is advanced in the last 6 pages. One could conclude by saying that it is often held that all of this stagnation stuff is now irrelevant because the government can handle the shortage of demand by deficit spending, tax cuts &c. These possibilities have been discussed before, and this is it. The way it stands now, the argument is not very strong. Strictly arithmetically speaking, deficits (however incurred) *can* do the trick — as is said on p. 40 (1st par. top).[150] There are good and sufficient reasons why those deficits tend to create inflations (bottlenecks, inelasticity of aggregate supply, monopolistic practices, pressures on wages and so forth and so on) — this is not the same as saying that "a policy of persistent deficits large enough to maintain a high rate of economic activity is completely out of [the] question." In this connection the example of Latin America is quite *mal à propos*. There we do *not* have the problem of Keynesian unemployment but one of Marxian unemployment (to use Joan's distinction) and obviously under such circumstances deficits create inflation pure and simple. As Kalecki has put it as early as 1944: "Inflation will result only if effective demand increases so much that a general scarcity of labour or equipment (or both) arises . . . It is thus evident that a prerequisite of full employment is a proper relation between existing equipment and available labor. The volume of equipment must be adequate to employ the available labor and still allow for reserve capacities.

---

150. These page numbers refer to the draft typed manuscript.

If the maximum capacity of equipment is inadequate to absorb the available labor, as will be the case in backward countries, the immediate achievement of full employment is clearly hopeless. If the reserve capacities are non-existent or insufficient the attempt to secure full employment in the short run may easily lead to inflationary tendencies in large sections of the economy because the structure of equipment does not necessarily match the structure of demand. . . . In an economy where plant is scarce it is thus necessary to have a period of industrialization or reconstruction during which the existing equipment is expanded at a rather high rate. In this period it may be necessary to have controls not unlike those used in war-time. Only after the process of capital expansion has proceeded sufficiently far is a policy of full employment . . . possible."[151]

Although farther down he does mention the possibility that bottlenecks may arise also in developed countries and that the trade-unions' insistence on wage increases may cause inflationary pressures prior to attainment of full employment, he does not pursue this line much further. I should think that it is *this* line that needs emphasis, and that one ought to stress that the Keynesian prescription results in inflation primarily because of the fact that large demand brings to the fore all the monopolistic forces in the economy (price increases rather than output increases) rather than fall back on what looks very much like the pre-Keynesian anti-deficit position. I was guilty of this *façon de parler* [manner of speaking] too, and it would seem to me that we should avoid being attacked by the Keynesians on grounds of such a simple heresy. By the way, Kalecki upbraided me in Warsaw because the Feb. 1961 *MR* (RoM) came also very close to this kind of an error. He said: why does Sweezy have to repeat those pre-Keynesian stories? I "defended" your honor by confessing that this happens to be probably the sole RoM with which I had also something to do, and that the error was committed by us jointly. But in substance, I think, he is right, and we should avoid formulations which put us either in the *Wall St. Journal* class or into that of the Moscow economists.

As to the efficiency of tax cuts, the necessity of price controls &c, &c, I think it does not belong into this chapter but can be briefly handled under Government Absorption. There one could say something about the "shot-in-the-arm" character of tax cuts, on the inflationary effects and so forth. Also bringing in balance of payments considerations in this historical survey looks to me somewhat artificial; it can be mentioned *en passant* in the discussion of government absorption activities.

151. Michal Kalecki, *The Economics of Full Employment* (Oxford, 1944), p. 43.

The thing that really bothers me is the question how to present well and clearly the point that demand increases resulting from government deficits operate under monopoly differently than under competition. Sometimes earlier I thought that one could simply say that monopolists tend to respond to increases of demand with price rather than output increases. In this form the statement is probably untenable. The monopolists' response would depend on the shape of the demand curves, cost curves etc. What is the correct way of putting the true kernel of the proposition? Or is the truth that they do *both*: increase prices *and* increase outputs *pari passu* [at an equal rate of speed]? With labor helping along in the process?

So much for now; I have a number of other things to write about, but shall do it some other time.

Love,

/s Your Paul

PMS to PAB

Wilton

August 26 [1962]

Dear Paul,

Thanks for returning the Chapter 8 draft so promptly. I have sent it off to Jay [M. Gould] with a request to pay special attention to the statistical stuff. I don't think there are any boners to be found, but it is just as well to have the reaction of someone who is accustomed to working with the official data in a way that neither of us is.

I think you are probably right about the way to end the chapter: it isn't the right place for discussion of inflation, tax reform, etc., and I will substitute a short paragraph along the lines you suggest for the last 6 pages. On the substantive questions, however, we ought to take a stand somewhere, probably in the govt-as-absorber chapter (No. 6). As I see it, there are two distinct questions involved: the first is, would a policy of continuing deficits to maintain full employment lead to inflation? The answer, I think, is clearly *yes* because (as you say) of the nature of *monopoly* capitalism. Keynes never even approached this problem and even Kalecki seems to brush it off much too lightly. Monopoly capitalism *needs* 5 or 6 percent unemployment if it is to prevent inflation.

The second question then arises: what's so bad about continuing inflation? Many of the Keynesians, as you know, argue that if that's the price you have to pay for full employment then you ought to be glad to pay it. It is here, I think, that the *international* position of the U.S. becomes decisive. I've been reading an ms. on capitalism by Oliver Cox, which has one great merit: his insistence that capitalism is *essentially* an international system in which the various units are ranked in a hierarchy.[152] At the top is the *leader* nation, at the bottom the helplessly dependent colonies. In between there are various positions, ranging from rivals for leadership to colonies struggling for liberation. The attitudes, policies, etc., which are appropriate for any given country depend in a crucial way on its position in the hierarchy. The leader exploits in varying degree all of the others, but at the same time it has to assume certain obligations and responsibilities as the price of maintaining its leadership. (Incidentally, Cox doesn't see anywhere near all the implications of his schema, and most of what I'm saying isn't in his ms.) For example, it has certain military responsibilities *vis-a-vis* the system as a whole and now of course *vis-a-vis* the rival socialist system. It also has economic responsibilities, and perhaps the most important of these is to maintain a currency which can be the standard for the system as a whole. And this, I think, is the key to much in U.S. policy that seems so backward and irrational to the naive Keynesians (though it certainly wouldn't have seemed so to Keynes himself).

The U.S. is and wants to remain the leader nation (the historic meaning of the Common Market, I think, is that now there is for the first time since the U.S. became leader a serious challenger for the position), and in order to do so it must maintain the international position of the dollar. Hence the tears about the balance of payments, the dread of inflation, the allergy to any full-employment policy. By comparison, countries differently placed in the hierarchy can and do take a very different attitude toward inflation, and it is here that the Latin American example is à propos. It is certainly true, as you say, that their inflations are different from the one that the U.S. dreads (Marxian vs. Keynesian in Joan's [Joan Robinson's] terminology), but the character of the inflationary process does not determine its tolerability. For the Latin American countries, or rather their bourgeoisies, inflation and chronic balance-of-payments deficits are an advantage: they allow them to extract extra surplus from the underlying population and also to squeeze something that they wouldn't otherwise get from the leader and near-leaders higher up in the hierarchy. Rather than allow, say, Brazil to degenerate into chaos to be followed by revolution, the U.S. as leader feels it necessary to step in periodically with a big subsidy in one form or another — and the Brazilian bourgeoisie knows that it can count on this kind of help *in extremis*, hence why knuckle under to the IMF's austerity programs? It is only completely lackeyized governments that follow that course.

---

152. Trinidad-born sociologist and political economist; probably the manuscript of Cox's book, published by Monthly Review Press in 1964, entitled *Capitalism as a System*.

Perhaps all this belongs somewhere in the chapter on imperialism, I dunno. Anyway, I think it belongs somewhere. There are a couple of other points I'd like to save and transfer elsewhere in the last 6 pages, but I don't think it should be too difficult to find a place. E. G. I'd like to work into a footnote somewhere the Musgrave estimate that nearly 60 percent of taxes is collected from the income groups under $7,500. This, and not the tax rates (even the effective ones) on the various brackets is the key to the effect of taxation on consumption, investment, etc. I would also like to save the thrust at Gardiner Means' new rubbish,[153] and probably the place for that is in the corporation chapter [Chapter 2 on "The Giant Corporation"], perhaps in a footnote.

With regard to your "minor points":

1. I thought of putting militarization into the external stimulus category but rejected the idea for what I think are very strong architectural reasons. In Chapters 6 and 7 ["Absorption of Surplus: Civilian Government Spending" and "Absorption of Surplus: Militarism and Imperialism"] militarism and imperialism are treated as internal necessities of the system, not in any narrow economic sense to be sure but still as absolutely essential and inescapable consequences of the total *Gestalt*.[154] Chapter 7 develops this theme at length and assigns to it the major responsibility for the general character of the performance of the economy during the post-World War II period. It seems to me it would be both wrong and anti-climactic to turn around in Ch. 8 and put them into the "external" category. The fact that the Korean War was, or may have been, provoked by the U.S. is not the point of that footnote — though it is not an irrelevant "fact" — but that a war like the Korean and now the Vietnamese wars is a perfectly logical outcome of U.S. policy as developed since the Truman Doctrine. You may say that World Wars I and II were also logical outcomes of the functioning of *world* capitalism and hence could (or should) be treated as internal. But, though there is logic in this, I think it would be heuristically wrong. The two major wars are quantitatively unique phenomena and must be put into a class by themselves. Further, no theoretical schema can properly accommodate them as internal variables. Even if they are not in any causative sense external to capitalism, they have to be so treated. In addition: not to treat them that way would be to give implicit support to the view that another world war is inevitable in the same sense that Korean-type wars are inevitable. I don't want to take that

153. Gardner Means, *The Corporate Revolution in America* (1962); *Pricing Power and the Public Interest* (1962).
154. Both Chapters 6 and 7 of *Monopoly Capital* on civilian government spending and militarism and imperialism were drafted by Sweezy.

position, and in fact do not believe it. I just don't know whether a third world war is "inevitable," which means that I think it isn't inevitable, though there is a strong probability that it will occur. (Incidentally, I don't think that your point about the U.S. ruling class having an option to stay in or out of or get into WW II is valid. Its aspiration to leadership position meant that it *had* to repulse the desperate leadership bid of Germany and Japan: it knew that after the war it could handle Britain, the old and declining leader; but if the Axis had won, matters would have been far from clear.)

2. I agree about minimizing any implication of needs equaling demand wherever it may occur. Likewise, I agree about the dialectical nature of the cause and effect of automobilization. I'll try to fix these points up at the places you mention. If I don't succeed, you'll have to suggest alternative formulations in the final polishing-up process.

3. I'm not clear about the relevance of the point you make regarding unemployment as a % of the wage-working force rather than the total labor force to the matter in hand on p. 16. Or, put otherwise, I don't see how bringing it in at this point — or anywhere else in the chapter — would clarify or strengthen the argument. I don't deny that it is a valid point with much importance in any *analysis* of unemployment data. But I think that to bring it in by the heels, so to say, in this chapter would only hold up the argument. (By the way, isn't the effect of trends during the monopoly capitalism period to make the official unemployment percentage more and more indicative of the true state of affairs? In other words, aren't there *relatively* many fewer non-wage-workers, hence unlikely to be hit by unemployment, today than there used to be? If so, it might be useful to point this out in connection with interpreting the relatively lower unemployment rates in the semi-stag[nation] period of 1907–1914 as compared to the stag period of the 1930's. As a percentage of the wage-workers, the 1907–1914 figures might be considerably closer to the figures for the 30's.)

[…]

More in due course.

/s Paul

PMS to PAB

Monthly Review
New York
August 28, 1962

Dear Paul,

Here are four more retyped pages — one I forgot to send last time, a new one to begin Chapter 7 (the second half of what is now Chapter 6 in the draft you have) and two to replace respectively pages 70 and 87 of your draft. *NB* the staggering estimates of Latin American capital export from the latest Hearings by the Latin American subcommittee of the Joint Economics Committee. This is really a fantastic business which the U.S. presumably can do nothing about and therefore carefully refrains from publicizing. It makes the whole Alliance for Progress look like the sourest kind of a joke. And it also makes one wonder how much longer it can be before the next (post-Cuba) phase of the LA revolution begins in earnest.

[. . .]

I have been thinking quite a lot about how to handle the why-not-continuing-deficits problem. It really doesn't fit logically into true framework of the opus, which is concerned with why things happen the way they do, not with why they don't happen some other way. But I think that it ought to be dealt with all the same, if only to forestall Keynesian critics and to deal a blow to their nostrums. I now lean to a deliberate "excursus" to come right after the theoretical exposition of the unit multiplier, balanced budgets, deficits, etc., at the outset of Chapter 6. On p. 5, the words "put this question to one side for the present and" would be deleted. Section II, as now numbered (beginning a few lines below) would become III, and a new II opening somewhat as follows would be inserted:

"But before we examine changes in the level of government spending, it seems advisable to deal with a question which has long been in controversy among economists. It follows from what was said in the last section that a policy of continuing deficits, if they are large enough, would result in the maintenance of a high level of economic activity even if the absolute level of government spending remained stable. This suggests that the appropriate remedy for depression and/or stagnation in the monopoly capitalism economy is not necessarily steadily rising government spending, but manipulation of tax rates to produce deficits of the required magnitude. Many Keynesian economists seem to accept this view. On the other hand, it is strongly, often even emotionally, opposed by conservative economists and businessmen. Continuing deficits, they say, must inevitably result in inflation, and inflation is to be shunned as the devil shuns holy water. What are the rights and wrongs of this controversy?

"To begin with, we must distinguish two questions: Would continuing deficits inevitably result in inflation? And even if so, is inflation necessarily a bad thing? etc., etc."

What do you think?

Love,

/s Paul

PAB to PMS

Palo Alto
August 30, 1962

Dear Paul,

Rec'd your note of Aug. 28th plus pages which I put into their proper place.

1) That there has been quite a lot of capital flight from Latin America I've read before; I did not realize that it has been so large. Interesting question: how much of it is repatriation of foreign capital and how much money of frightened LA capitalists? This is a normal phenomenon for u/d c's [underdeveloped countries] and there is probably nothing that can be done about it in our age of wars and revolutions. The boys are just afraid and long-term productive investment isn't the kind of a thing you undertake if the deluge is around the corner. It is an incredible paradox of history that just at a time when monopoly capitalism needs nothing more than capital export markets, one has to be a Superman to risk going to the u/d c's while at the same time the ideology of monopoly capitalism dictates that private enterprise ought to do "it." The resulting question: won't there be more and more pressure for the government to do the capital exporting: (a) let the Treasury take the risks while BB [Big Business] will fill the orders for machinery etc.; and (b) let the State plus War Departments directly look after the investments rather than via BB lobbies... Actually the "neo-capitalism" boychiks ala Rostow are for that; they are the real ideologists of "state capitalism" *sensu stricto*. Interesting that the Chilean chap who was here told me that the American Embassy in Santiago has been distributing stuff (now also accepted by Chilean conservative bizmen) insisting on Agrarian Reform and mixed enterprises (Chilean government plus American investors plus Chilean capitalists). This is all on the line of Meiji Restoration: the u/d c's should travel the road of Japan rather than that of socialism with a bourgeois revolution from above underwritten and politically (militarily) guaranteed by the U.S. The pattern is the same everywhere: Iran, Turkey, Latin America, etc.

2) I am very much in favor of the "excursus" on Keynesian remedies. The more I think about the problem, the more I feel that one has to stress the competitive assumptions underlying the Keynesian prescription. I am also wondering whether it might not be worth while to point out that the tax reduction technique is in a number of respects a different animal from the spending increase technique. The principal difference would seem to me to lie in the divergence of the respective structures of demand. Let us assume that the aggregate demand deficiency is to be counteracted by a tax reduction. In that case (unless the tax reduction is of some very special nature) *all* segments

of demand are likely to be affected (although perhaps unevenly). There would be in other words more of the same without any major structural changes in the economy (on the demand and on the supply side). Under such circumstances the likelihood of physical or monopolistic bottlenecks are relatively small. The existing industries can increase their outputs by n% and that is that. This would seem to be the reason why "normal," not government-induced recoveries usually have led to some price increases but not to what might be called inflationary pressures.

Now if one considers not "deficit without spending," but new spending based on borrowing, the situation is quite different. There "my" law On What? becomes very relevant. If the government could simply send out checks to the indigent, the situation might come close to the one just mentioned. But if the government by the nature of the "quid pro quo" system is bound to engage in public works, construction of post offices, roads etc. or even to order more armaments, then the increased demand affects a very special kind of industries (construction primarily as well as some heavy industries) and encounters immediately physically or monopolistically caused scarcities, bottlenecks and ... inflationary forces. Whether such spending is government by some bidding principle or by cost plus — the potentialities of price increases within an oligopolistic system are clearly very large. This does not mean that arithmetically the two deficits differ or even that their multipliers have different magnitudes; what it means, I think, is that the nature of the *initial* expenditures has much to do with the unfolding of the pump priming process.

3) It should be stressed, I think, that tax reductions are of necessity "shots in the arm" — once the reduction has worked itself out, the system absorbs it and settles down back to a creep stag equilibrium. This leads not to "my" law but to "yours": the necessity for *increasing* government spending. In other words one tax reduction has to follow the other with deficits becoming a regular feature of the economy and the national debt growing *ad infinitum*. Although, again, arithmetically there is nothing to be said against it, it does raise all kinds of questions which are familiar. The accumulation of such readily monetisable debt becomes a Damocles sword hanging over the economy and creating the conditions for a sudden "run on the bank" resulting in a galloping inflation, the servicing of the debt does raise the problem of income transfers on a large scale and so forth. The *locus classicus* for all of this is A.P. Lerner's formalistic article "The Burden of the National Debt" in the *Festschrift* for Hansen [Lloyd A. Metzler et al., *Income, Employment and Public Policy*, NY, 1948] where there are also other papers (particularly by S.S. Alexander) bearing on that problem.

4) I think it is important to stress that the Keynesian nostrum has in reality never been tried. Pour quoi pas? With all the talk about insufficient growth, competition with the Reds etc., etc., *why* do the most radical Keynesians when in power turn away from deficit spending etc. like the devil turns away from incense? As long as "fools" were running the show it could be said that they don't understand modern economics. Is it now to be held that P.A. Samuelson, James Tobin *et tutti quanti* [and all the rest] also do not understand their own economics? Or is there perhaps something in the system which renders this economics inapplicable? Could it be that it ain't not stupidity but the structure of BB [Big Business] interests?

5) This raises the fundamental question to which I doesn't know no answer at all: why is the biz community so afraid of inflation? It is clear that an inflation German style is catastrophical, but what about *creeping* up prices as a mode of life? Various notions come to mind, but none of them is very illuminating. Is it the difference of interests between borrowers and lenders? Is it the steady devaluation of working capital? Is it the balance of payments problem? The best that I can think of it is that running the show on the principle of large deficits cum inflationary pressures [requires?] a highly organized well integrated machine with selective price controls, subsidies to importers, licenses to importers and so forth and so on. It is this that they are all afraid of, because such a juggernaut would either have to be fascist or it would be always in danger of being taken over by a democratic wave and God knows who gets into power in either case? Government should be big but not too big: what is more important it should be big as buyer even as taxer but not as *regulator* in the administrative sense of the word.

6) There is a good if also terribly formalistic piece on this whole biz by Michał. If I can dig it out in my comprehensive mess, I shall send it along to you (with request for return).

7) While I fully agree with you that we need not explain why things aren't different from what they are but why they are what they are, this Keynesian business does belong into the story particularly in the light of the Neo-Capitalism talk which is ubiquitous. It can always be said that we are running into open doors if we argue that the system *left to itself* is bound to lead not only to creeping stag but to a complete deadlock. On this every Keynesian will agree. It is most important to show that *their* answer to this is no better than what they are trying to answer. They ain't got the miraculous key which they pretend to have. That much must be given to Sraffa: every time I talked to him, he maintained that Keynesianism is *the* illusion of the epoch rather than Marxism. The only trouble has always been that the Marxian reply to Keynes was the wrong one, not that Keynes has produced the solution of the problem.

8) I am working like a sobaka [dog] and am making progress but desperately slowly. Big trouble is that I have bitten off too much for chewing and am having difficulties on this account. On QoS II I am now finishing books and other mass media, but have still lots of other stuff to do.[155] And this is still on the somewhat flat descriptive level. The "big bang" is to come in the final denouement to which I am looking forward when this stuff is done. Except that QoS II gets damn long. But anyway the movement is now on and nothing will stop it before the finale.

Hope that you are surviving somehow the reconstruction period. Write!

Love,

    s/ Paul

PMS to PAB

Larchmont
Sept. 19, 1962

Dear Paul,

[…]

Before settling down to serious opus labors I am trying to get at least an outline of that essay on Keynes I spoke to you about for the volume being edited by Robert Lekachman: that too I probably shouldn't have gotten into, but there it is and due by November 1.[156] My present idea is to deal with the problem along the following lines: The important thing about a great economist is his vision of the socio-economic process, and it is this we should try to identify and criticize in Keynes. In most respects his is indistinguishable from that of Marshall, etc. The individual entrepreneur is the central figure. He operates in markets which function well and impersonally, buying factors, combining them, and selling for a profit which is a combination of wage and quasi-rent of ability. Except in his own undertaking, he is powerless. There is thus no link via interests between the

---

155. Baran was responsible for drafting "Quality of Monopoly Capitalist Society II," which was intended as Chapter 11 of *Monopoly Capital*. It dealt with culture and communications, along with the growing psychological problems generated by the system. Although Baran completed an initial draft it had not been revised by the two authors at the time of his death in 1964 and was left out of the published book. It was published (minus the very rough section on the psychological consequences of the system) in 2013. See Paul A. Baran and Paul M. Sweezy, "The Quality of Monopoly Capitalist Society: Culture and Communications," *Monthly Review* 65, no. 3 (July-August 2013): 43–64.

156. This essay, entitled "Keynesian Economics: The First Quarter Century," appeared in Robert Lekachman, ed., *Keynes's General Theory: Reports on Three Decades* (New York: St. Martin's Press, revised edition, 1968); reprinted in Paul M. Sweezy, *Modern Capitalism and Other Essays* (New York: Monthly Review Press, 1972*)*, 79–91.

economic and political realms, the latter being thus the sphere of democracy, the public interest, etc. In all of this Keynes is a good neo-classicist.

But in one respect, and it is decisive for him, he departs from them. While they never worried (much) about investment opportunities because they regarded the price mechanism as quite capable of making any adjustments that might be needed whether such opportunities were numerous or few (in the ultimate adjustment you would have a stationary state), Keynes could not take this position. For him, the price mechanism could make every adjustment but one: it could not equilibrate the supply and demand of savings at full employment. (Here I would expect to digress a bit to argue a position that no one agrees with, namely, that a consistent adherence to the competitive model would leave him with no theoretical grounds for such a deficiency in the price system: I believe he surreptitiously smuggles monopoly into his model.) Hence the great importance of a plenitude of investment opportunities. But, and this is also a crucial part of his vision, be believed that investment opportunities, always and everywhere, have a tendency to lag behind. Hence stagnation is, in the final analysis, the norm toward which the system tends. This is the crux of the Keynesian vision, what made it so different from the neo-classical vision. And it explains all his characteristic attitudes: anti-saving, pro-state intervention in the investment process, etc.

Turning next to the critical side: twenty-five years after it is easy to see the glaring deficiencies of the Keynesian vision: giant corps, ubiquitous monopoly, technological change, domination of politics by capitalist interests, underdeveloped countries with totally different social structures, the existence of a *system* including both advanced monopoly capitalism and underdeveloped economies — these are some of the realities which Keynes either ignored or brought in only under the table and quite inadequately. But his one great insight, the relentless stag tendency, not always and everywhere but in the kind of economy he lived in, this remains. And ironically it is this that all the Keynesians have thrown overboard. What now needs doing is to put this back into the center of the analytical stage and to develop an adequate theoretical framework into which it can fit and which can "explain" it. And for this, of course, the explicit recognition of the decisive character of monopoly is a *sine qua non*.

[...]

More on other matters soon.

Love,

    /s Paul

PMS to PAB

Larchmont

September 22, 1962

Dear Paul,

[...]

Rec'd the carbon of your letter of August 30. I never saw this before, though your letter dated Aug. 29th addressed to Larchmont was here when we arrived on the 3lst. The original may have got lost in the confusion of activity which began on the 3rd. In any case, it is good you kept a carbon. I will have a copy made (they have copying machines at 25 cents a sheet around Grand Central Station now) and return the carbon for your file. I will get to the job of drafting the section on deficits and inflation soon. I don't want to make it technical or detailed. The main points, I think, are that *under monopoly capitalism* inflation occurs long before full employment is reached; that direct controls are anathema to the capitalists; and hence the preferred method of inflation control is to allow the necessary amount of unemployment to develop and persist. As to why inflation control is important, here I lean strongly to the view that it all depends on the country's position in the international capitalist system as a whole. For a follower nation, like the major Latin American countries for example, inflation control is evidently not an important matter. It is even probable that inflation acts as a siphon or pump, taking income out of the pockets of both rentiers and workers and putting it into the coffers of the capitalists. But the leader capitalist country *must* maintain a sound currency and a payments balance on pain of losing its leadership position. And its leadership position carries with it the right to exploit in varying degrees *all* the other members of the system, hence it will never be given up voluntarily. Compared to this consideration, it seems to me that all the other arguments against continuing inflation *for a country in the position of the United States* are of secondary importance.

In this connection, incidentally, it seems to me that almost everyone has tended to ignore or underplay the most fascinating aspect of the Common Market, namely, that it is a deadly serious effort on the part of the big capitalists of Europe to take the leadership position away from the U.S. In my opinion, the U.S. wants Britain in as a sort of agent of the United States to exercise a veto over the leadership bid of the Franco-German capitalists. The latter, in turn, are not going to let Britain in unless and until it cuts all its special ties to the U.S. and agrees to subordinate itself completely to the new power which aspires to become leader in its own right. It will be an agonizing choice for the British ruling class to make. I suspect that they will try to have it both ways and as a result will fall squarely between the two stools. Excluded from the Common

Market, they will be too weak to stand up to the U.S. and will become in effect a
U.S. satellite, with the remainder of the Empire & Commonwealth either going
over to the U.S. empire or joining the neutral bloc.

*　　*　　*　　*

Have you seen the special report on Latin America in the latest *Business Week*?
It practically admits that the jig is up there but doesn't dare do much speculating
on the implications. Latin America looks more and more like the Achilles heel
of U.S. imperialism and monopoly capitalism generally — and things may begin
to happen on a big scale much sooner than seemed at all possible until very
recently.

    Love,

       /s Paul

PAB to PMS

Palo Alto, CA
September 23, 1962

Dear Paul,

I hope your aching back is better. All this goes to prove how right Pascal was
when he wrote: "I have discovered that all the unhappiness of men arises from
one simple fact that they cannot stay quietly in their own chamber." *All* physical
activity, in particular that outdoors — I submit — is from the devil, and all that
there is to be said for it is that engaging in same provides one with the great
satisfaction of getting rid of it. But "only mediocrities learn from experience,"
and therefore I must assume that you will continue pushing furniture, engage in
physical exercise and the like and . . . suffer like a sobaka [dog]. *Jeder ist seines
Glueckes Schmied.* [Every one forges his own luck.]

    [. . .]

    I cannot entirely agree with your appraisal of Keynes, and here are my
Randglossen [comments in the margin] for what they are worth. It is not quite
correct to say that no one agrees with your view that a consistent adherence to
the competitive model is incompatible with the admission of underemployment
etc. This view has been expressed on a number of occasions, e.g. Leontief in the
piece which is reprinted in *New Economics*, later on Milton Friedman (*Essays in
Positive Economics*, 1953), a number of occasions and more could be adduced. I
would have thought that this is wrong, in other words that even without market
imperfections the system would get into troubles. All this relates to the validity
of Say's Law, and it is my impression that for instance Lange has demonstrated
convincingly that that Law gives no reason to believe that full employment
would be provided even if the most rigorous assumptions are made. Cf. his *Price*

Flexibility and Full Employment, but also the excellent article on Say's Law in *Studies in Mathematical Economics and Econometrics*, Chicago, 1947. Not only does he show that in any dynamic context Say's Law is worthless (expectations etc.!) but that even in a static context it is untenable. It would seem to me that you would get yourself out on an unnecessary and very weak limb by arguing what is an anti-Keynesian position of the "right."

My own impression is that Keynes' great "vision," and originality consists precisely in realizing that the mainstay of bourgeois economics up to his time: Say's Law is untenable and that capitalism can be only maintained if government enters centrally the stage. In this he becomes *the* economist of monopoly capitalism with his strengths the strengths of monopoly capitalism and his weaknesses the weaknesses of monopoly capitalism. Strengths: abandonment for all intents and purposes of "economics" and return to "political economy," secondly abandonment for all intents and purposes of the individual firm Dreck [garbage] and return to aggregates, thirdly "technical progress" in suggesting a more powerful technique of analysis making use of functional interrelations etc. Weaknesses: recognition of the role of the state and of the factors of *political* economy all but vacuous without an appropriate sociology *cum* theory of the state; secondly turning away from the problems of individual firms in favor of aggregates would have been dandy if it hadn't led to ignoring monopoly thus impairing the aggregates itself (elasticity of the aggregate supply function e.g.); thirdly, the better technique has pushed up the level of abstraction to a point where the essentials are abstracted from.

I do not "go for" the expression investment opportunity because it suggests something very naturalistic, "needs" oriented, and absolute. The IAA important thing to stress, I think, is rationality of investment *within a monopoly capitalism setting*. What was opportunity yesterday under a different system ain't no opportunity under oligopoly etc. Something on those lines, I would say; but natch, you can wholly disregard all of this if it strikes you to be wrong. Back to work. Tomorrow campus starts (registration) and I'll have to see all my colleagues again. And students. Can't think of a sight that appeals to me less.

Gute Besserung.

Yours,

s/ Paul

PMS to PAB

Larchmont
September 25, 1962

Dear Paul,

Thanks for yours of the 23rd in re Keynes etc. There is some difference between us here which puzzles me — because I can't really put my finger on it. So let's try again. I don't maintain for a moment, of course, that the competitive model is incapable of breaking down. The continuous operation of Say's law is rubbish. But this was really quite well known to Keynes's predecessors: after all biz cycle and crisis theory had a long and respectable history prior to 1936. What the earlier theorists maintained was that the breakdown couldn't persist indefinitely. Unemployment and unused plant would lead to price (incl. wage & interest rate) and income changes which would sooner or later (depending on reaction times, mobility of resources, etc.) set the stage for an upswing which, once under way, would carry up to full employment. Except under very special assumptions, the condition of full employment couldn't persist either, of course. It was universally recognized by the top theorists before Keynes (Pigou, Robertson, Schumpeter, etc.) that in a competitive, unplanned system, fluctuations were "natural" and inevitable. And that meant that none of them were slaves of Say's Law, whatever Keynes may have said about it.

What was new in Keynes was the assertion that, left to itself, the competitive economy could not recover — unless the marginal efficiency of capital happened to be high enough, which Keynes thought it had a deeply rooted tendency not to be. In other words, he introduced the problem of stagnation, *alias* underemployment "equilibrium." This you will not find in any of the earlier theories in the classical-neoclassical tradition — though of course many respectable thinkers such as Hobson and Veblen had recognized stag [stagnationist] tendencies in capitalist reality and had made serious attempts to explain them. It was thus Keynes's historical merit to bring the problem of stag into the orbit of orthodox, accredited economics where it occupied the center of the analytic stage for a good decade. (*NB*, however, that since the late 1940's it has been largely banished again.)

This is one aspect of the matter. Up to this point, Keynes gets full credit for an historic achievement. His vision of a stagnating economy has all sorts of ramifications and implications which were absent from the neoclassical vision. But when we come to his attempts to explain why the economy couldn't recover by itself, why the theory of his predecessors was deficient, we enter an entirely different realm. And I must say that the more I read of *The General Theory* the less convincing his arguments seem. The whole notion of an *equilibrium* with *involuntary* unemployment — which is what he wanted to explain — seems to me to be totally incompatible with the assumption of competitive markets. Wages *must* come down. And if one wants to insist that every wage cut brings prices and incomes down proportionately (I do not think this makes much sense, but that is another matter), then the process will keep going until (in Keynesian terms) the quantity of money measured in wage units has grown so enormously that the rate of interest finally does fall below the marginal efficiency of capital. Or if liquidity preference is insatiable, then the deflation can go on until wages and prices equal zero and everyone starves to death. But that *isn't* underemployment equilibrium. If we assume that somewhere short of this a lower turning point is reached and the reverse process sets in, why should it fall short of full employment or a reasonable approximation thereto? I cannot see that Keynes has any rational explanation as to why either a downswing or an upswing should halt and give way to a steady state characterized by the existence of involuntary unemployment. Still less has he got a rational explanation of the phenomenon of creeping stagnation. All his efforts to deal with these problems are vitiated by the fact that at bottom he accepts all the neoclassical assumptions but tries to squeeze different conclusions out of them. Some different conclusions — about the mechanisms of economic fluctuations — are doubtless valid and useful. But the real one, the difference between a self-adjusting system and a running-down system, simply can't be derived that way. Only the explicit introduction of monopoly into the macro picture can supply the missing key.

I have no desire whatever to idealize the competitive model. It is compatible with wild gyrations, with deep and even prolonged slumps; it may display continuing high unemployment of a "Marxian" variety; it may even generate *Verelendung* [impoverishment or immiseration] as Marx believed it would. But I do not see any reason to suppose that it would also suffer from the disease of stagnation, creeping or galloping, which in my judgment is specific to monopoly capitalism. This is what Keynes did not see and without which his theory remains a collection of brilliant insights and stupidities without any overall coherence.

Now please react to that, indicating (no need to spell out at any length) points of agreement and disagreement. This time I'm keeping a carbon.

[...]

Love,

/s Paul

P. S. Did you see the excellent piece on Cuba by Samuel Shapiro in the latest
Nation [Sept. 22, 1962]? He got in as a correspondent and spent much of the
summer there.

PAB to PMS

[Palo Alto]

September 25th, 1962

Dear Paul,

Just a few lines in response to your letter of Sept. 22nd — before running to the
Campus.

[...]

(3) In re: inflation. I would agree with you that the international setting is
an important factor in the anti-inflationary sentiment of the ruling class. At the
same it is somewhat of an *ad hoc* argument. The balance of payments business
is relatively new; the anti-inflationary attitudes could be observed for quite a
long time. This would lead me to believe that the bop [balance-of-payment]
considerations merely re-enforce an attitude which has its roots elsewhere.

(4) For u/d c's [underdeveloped countries] (or as you call them follower
nations) inflation has a different meaning. There by causing a redistribution of
lousy income it does increase the fund for accumulation (that is why [Henry]
Wallich and some others were pooh-poohing the inflationary danger in the u/d
c's) but at the same time (a) directs investment into altogether wrong channels
(real estate, speculation, &c) and creates (b) a serious danger of riot unrest
and revolution. So one cannot say it's there unimportant to control inflation.
There the trouble is that minus planning it is impossible to get any development
without inflation while inflation endangers the whole development on capitalist
lines. (Quite incidentally, even with planning it is apparently all but impossible to
avoid inflation on the process of development.)

(5) Fully d'accord on Common Market, except for the following: the
whole CM biz is definitely a formula for a big leap forward in cartelization,
monopolization and quota distribution among the WE cap's [Western European
capitalists]. U.S. BB [Big Business] looks upon it with equanimity; it goes across
the wall and takes its cut in the deal. British BB would like to sit at the table
when the cake is being sliced up. Who gets beaten is small biz there where it is
concerned with exports. In the U.S. it is not too important, but in Britain it is.
Therefore there is not too much enthusiasm for the whole thing even among
the conservative supporters of Macmillan. That the U.S. wants Britain in as a
counterweight to Bonn, no doubt, but it is my hunch that what is decisive in the

British position vs the Common Market is partly the Commonwealth but partly also the internal divergence of interests.

(6) The Latin America story is tremendous and that matters there are now moving into the very center indubitable. Question: is Washington absolutely unable to do anything about it?

On other things later. Making good progress in writing.

Love,

　　/s Paul

P.S. Re-read your piece in Harris, *New Economics*; it is *very* good, and much closer to the position which I submitted to you the other day, than your outline which I returned.[157]

PMS to PAB

Monthly Review
New York
September 29, 1962

Dear Paul,

[…]

P.P.S. I wouldn't equate "follower nations" with udc's [underdeveloped countries]. Britain is a follower nation vis-a-vis the U.S., ditto Japan, though both exploit udc's on a big scale. Maybe leader-follower terminology isn't appropriate, but it does have to be got across that there is what Cox somewhere calls a "gradient of power" and that attitudes, policies, etc., depend to no small degree on the position occupied on the gradient. Of particular importance, too, are all efforts to change the position within the system — not to be confused with attempts to escape from the system altogether.

PAB to PMS

Palo Alto
October 2, 1962

Dear Paul,

There are so many different things to write about that I don't know whether I'll be able to handle it all in one letter. The order in which matters will be taken up is more or less fortuitous.

---

157. Paul M. Sweezy, "Keynes the Economist," in Seymour E. Harris, *The New Economics* (London: Dennis Dobson, 1947), 102–09.

(1) I am making slow but steady progress in the MS ["The Quality of Monopoly Capitalist Society II"). Main trouble is that I am writing at the moment about lots of things about which I know less than usual (and this is saying a lot) and also the problem of architecture. There is such a lot of material that it bursts out of the framework of one chapter. I am attaching hereto a batch of pp for you to get an idea of what I mean. The books story is continued for another 10 pp (I haven't typed them yet); then radio, TV &c. Then comes a (II) and deals with the state of Psychic Well-Being or however you want to call it. When this is all done, the thing is plenty long for QoS II and there is still nothing about JD [juvenile delinquency], Family, Suicide rates, Alcoholism, &c. &c. Since it so happens that each of these topics requires a lot of study (for which there ain't much time), I lean now to the view that it should not be taken up *expressis verbis*, but woven into the final chapter pulling all those things together. Since the main purpose of the whole biz and in particular the final denouement chapter is to establish the fundamental *interconnection* of the whole complex of QoS with monopoly capitalist structure, the particulars will have to be omitted; let someone else fill in the blank spots.[158] Otherwise the QoS stuff gets out of hand. What do you think, both of the above and of the enclosure? I am keen on having your reaction so as to feel more secure in what follows.

(2) Rec'd yesterday a little booklet of St. Joan's *Economic Philosophy* in which she administers another *Fusstritt* for me [kick, literally "steps on me again"] which now, I am afraid, I believe to be justified.[159] Her statement is as follows: "Marxist critics have understood that Keynes' theory leads to conclusions which from their point of view are reactionary. They therefore deny the logic of his analysis and even find themselves in alliance with the protagonists of the humbug of finance which Keynes first attacked. For instance, Professor Baran is not content with showing that an economic system that can maintain prosperity only by expenditure on armaments is a menace to humanity, morally abhorrent and politically disreputable; he also has to bring in the Quantity Theory of Money to show that it cannot work because Government expenditure causes inflation." (Fn. attached: *PEoG*, p.124.)** [PAB handwritten footnote: **We have to show that it tends to cause inflation &c but not because of the Quantity Theory of Money.] Unfortunately, she is probably right in this particular instance; the *PEoG*

158. Here Baran is referring to the relation between "On the Quality of Monopoly Capitalist Society, II" the originally planned Chapter 11 of *Monopoly Capital*, and the final chapter of the book "The Irrational System," which Baran was to draft.

159. Joan Robinson, *Economic Philosophy* (London: Penguin, 1962). On Robinson's criticism of Baran on inflation and the validation of Baran's view in subsequent decades see Paul M. Sweezy, "Baran and the Danger of Inflation," *Monthly Review* 26, no. 7 (December 1974): 11–14.

formulation *was* unfortunate. It shows how a relatively minor slip-up provides the critics with an opportunity to avoid the principal issue and to harp on a technicality. This must net be permitted to happen again, I think, and that is why we have to be triply careful with the Keynesiana in opus.

(3) With reference to your letter of September 23rd [25th]. Let me try now to set out the issues as clearly as possible. If I understand your position clearly, what you are saying is this: under competition a depression leads at some point to such a decline of costs (wages) that the price/cost relation changes sufficiently to increase the profit *margins* to an extent necessary to induce a rise in investment and ergo an economic recovery. (The decline in the rate of % working in the same direction.) As against it, it is held by the Keynesians (and I think rightly) that (a) the decline of the rate of % is not sufficiently important, because new investment is governed not only by the rate but by the general expectation of adequate demand, and (b) the wage decline may well improve the profit *margins* but not *aggregate* profits (or returns on investment) in view of the fact that the decline of wages leads to a decline of incomes which in turn leads to a decline in demand.

This strikes me as sufficiently persuasive unless one accepts two (or one of them) possible counter-arguments: (a) one that could be called the Micawber [from Dickens's *David Copperfield*] effect: *something will turn up*. In other words: if the increase in profit margins should be accompanied by technical developments of some sort which would lead investors to believe that there is something very important in the offing, or if there is expectation of some new markets &c. In that case, however, the increase in the profit margins isn't even necessary. Those expectations would do the trick in any case.

Or (b) the so-called Pigou effect meaning that the decline in prices and costs would to such an extent raise the real value of existing money assets (cash and bonds) that investors would become tempted to acquire *real* assets instead. This is presupposing that at some point their expectations of further declines of prices and costs come to a reversal and furthermore that *quantitatively* the thing is sufficiently important. I remember to have read once a Cowles Com. monograph in which it was calculated that for the Pigou effect to work itself out it would take tens of years....[160] It is my impression that the "respectable" biz cycle theorists to whom you refer were more or less clearly aware of this trouble and therefore stuck in an *exogenous* force. Either they attached a magic force to the rate of interest (the only important cost factor the decline of which hardly if at all affects the income stream, at least in the short run) like Robertson, or they banked on

160. Cowles Commission for Research in Economics, now known as the Cowles Foundation.

the asset appreciation (Pigou) or they stressed technical innovations (Schumpy). Without such gimmicks, it would be hard to construct a recovery!

Now, this applies to both: competitive capitalism and monopoly capitalism. What is the difference between the two? I have tried to say something about it (probably badly) in *PEoG* pp.60 ff.(or thereabouts), and would put it in such terms: the main difference is in the nature of the investment process. Under competitive, the individual small capitalist who is confronted with increased profit *margins* does not think in terms of the *aggregate* demand related to the aggregate decline in income; he thinks in terms of his own small market which may be relatively unaffected by the developments in the economy as a whole. *He* may invest because now certain machines are cheaper or because now labor is cheaper. *He* may expand without regard to aggregate demand — because being a component part of an *anarchic* structure he neither can nor should worry about the whole picture. If lots of them do it, they will engage in self-fulfilling prophecy and bear each other out. If only a few do it, it will turn out that they engaged in what the Germans called *Fehlinvestitionen* [poor investments]. Then it'll turn out that their calculations were all wrong, that aggregate demand deficiency did them in . . .

Under monopoly capitalism they are more circumspect, they know their market, they are aware of the total picture, they are guided by all the Steindl considerations and do not rush into investment merely because profit margins may rise; they think of the *whole* business, can settle down to a low level of activity (underemployment equilibrium) unless there is an external stimulus which pushes the whole thing up. That is where I see Keynes coming in, who assigns the pushing up function to the State. Psychological side note: this, I think, is the reason why for instance Schumpy was so pissed off by Keynes: he also knew that you need an exogenous force, was thus theoretically terribly close to Keynes' position but just missed the Keynesian (more adequate) variable in favor of his own, less suitable (the innovating entrepreneur). [Handwritten footnote: "or, rather, suitable *only* under 'romanticized' competitive conditions."]

Where does Keynes go wrong? I would say in two ways: a) in failing to analyze the nature of the state, and (b) in ignoring the relation of monopoly + oligopoly to the aggregate supply function, i.e. the question whether an increase of aggregate demand produced by the state leads actually to an increase in output, or rather commensurable increase in output rather than to inflation and to the related but separate question whether increase in output leads to increase in employment (if technical change is assumed as it has to be).

To conclude: it is my feeling that in the discussion of the competitive situation (as in your letter) you do one of two things or both: exaggerate the elasticity of investment with regard to profit *margins* and rate of interest, and place too much faith in the Pigou effect. In sum: it is my view that the chief difference between competitive and monopoly capitalism in this as in most other respects is the higher degree of rationalization under the latter. This higher degree of rationalization exacerbates the contradictions of the system, brings them more sharply to the fore and produces certain qualitative changes. Just as bribery in a messy administrative system is a factor *alleviating* its rigidities, so is the anarchy of competitive capitalism in a sense a mechanism by which the faults of the system are *partly reduced* (and in *some* other respects *increased*). The individual capitalist makes errors, because he does not have the possibility of strictly adjusting his activities to the mess he's in. Those errors may cancel out and the effect on the total becomes more stochastic. By *accident* the system gets out of stagnation; also because in that early state of development there are choo-choo trains, automobiles &c. Under monopoly capitalism there is less, if any, room for accidents, the corporation calculates sharply (and more correctly) and therefore stagnation becomes less "accident-prone." Without the state *now*: *kaput*. This is probably highly inadequate, but you'll see the main line of argument.

(4) *My* Russian edition (and German edition) of Marx and Engels does not go up to 1893 yet. I'll have a look in the library. If they have the older Russ. ed., I should be able to find the thing of Engels.[161] On the merit of the story, however: Although I strongly incline towards the Chinese position, as you know, before the latter can be endorsed, there are two important questions to be answered: (1) Granted that disarmament cannot be expected under capitalism and monopoly capitalism in particular, does (a) the existence of the socialist world *significantly* change the analysis of the war/peace prospects, and (b) does technological progress in warfare (A + H bomb) *significantly* change the war/peace outlook; and (2) of paramount importance to the entire theory of the socialist movement: it was always an "ultra-left" deviation to say *Liberté, Egalité, Fraternité* are impossible under capitalism, therefore to hell with them, we'll get them only under socialism. It was always, in my opinion, the Marxian position to say, those are excellent things, let the bourgeoisie *deliver* them and not merely pay lip service to them! Under this principle one has fought *for* bourgeois democracy, for civil liberties, factory legislation and what have you. Similarly under this principle, one should be on one hand clear that disarmament and peace are not only not guaranteed but even improbable under

161. Frederick Engels, *Can Europe Disarm* (1893) in Karl Marx and Frederick Engels, *Collected Works* (New York: International Publishers, 1975), vol. 27, 367–93.

capitalism but one has to take those capitalist politicians who profess to be for them by their word and insist: *deliver*!

The Chinese position (in a few things that I have read here and there) tends too much to say, disarmament and peace are impossible under capitalism, therefore to hell with all this empty talk, let's get as strong as we can — this is the only answer to the imperialists. This would seem to me to be a wrong political *line* and undialectical. For clearly, a *strong* pressure for *delivery* makes the position of the war makers more complicated. We tend to be too much centered on the U.S. situation where talking about strong (or for that matter perhaps any) pressure is ludicrous. But on the world stage (Britain, Italy, the underdeveloped countries), the situation is somewhat different. And the war/peace issue is too important for sacrificing all tactical possibilities to the purity of the scientific analysis. As Togliatti said, *we* ain't got no movement and can simply say what we want. But when it comes to the Chinese-Soviet leaderships, it ain't so. They *must* insist on *delivery*, whatever intellectual reservations there should be on the feasibility of same. Therefore I would say, that if the USSR were to insist on delivery and *unilaterally disarm*, they would be stark insane; if they would only arm and not insist on delivery, they would throw away a political weapon of much potency. The trick is the right combination. Stalin tended towards the second variant, so do the Chinese. Some Poles and Yugo's tend towards the first variant. I think in this respect Khrushchev sails between the two — rightly so — although he tends in the process to fall over into statements which are wrong but probably inevitable in the heat of the debate to wit: that the delivery is also *possible*. But then the latter question depends again, on my question under (1) above.

[…]

Meanwhile, let me know what you think of all this.

Love,

/s Paul

[…]

PMS to PAB

Larchmont
October 4, 1962

Dear Paul,

A very quick reply to yours of the 2nd, just rec'd.

I am now convinced that it is worse than useless to argue about how the competitive system *would* or *would have* behaved. Everyone can make up his own competitive system, and it soon gets like the argument about angels dancing on the head of a pin. What we have is a monopoly system, and what we want to know is how it works. I think I'll handle the Keynes essay along the following lines: Keynes was right in his vision of the present-day economy in one essential respect — the deep-rooted tendency to stagnation. And this had far-reaching ideological and political implications, only some of which he drew. Subsequent orthodoxers have tried to shove all this under the rug, and in this respect we can speak of the Keynesian counter-revolution. In other respects, Keynes's vision was seriously deficient, viz., the economic role of ubiquitous monopoly, and the relation between state and economy. In both he showed his domination by the neoclassical background. Without an adequate handling of these problems no understanding of present-day capitalist reality is possible. And they need to be tied up with the stagnation thing. Keynes was no help here, but neither have the later ones improved upon him. In retrospect, despite all his shortcomings we can say that he stands out head and shoulders above the pigmy epigones and pigmier opponents. Maybe quote what Marx said about Hegel and the German pipsqueaks who came after him. What does you think of that?

Zweitens: I have read Mme. Joan's *Economic Philosophy* with pleasure, amusement, annoyance, disagreement, approval — in short all the emotions she usually evokes. I agree that she scores a point vis-à-vis *PEoG* (it would have been nice if she would also have quoted you favorably at one of the million places she could have, but that isn't the Cambridge way) and that we must guard against giving grounds for such thrusts again. In this connection, I have been almost literally sweating blood over the inflation insert. It just couldn't be made to fit where I had planned to put it (in Ch. 6 [on "Absorption of Surplus: Civilian Government Spending"]), and I wavered back and forth about some alternative. I am now working on a scheme which I think (hope) will work — a new Section VI (present VI to become VII) in Ch. 8 ["On the History of Monopoly Capitalism"]. The story has just been told about creeping stagnation in the 50's, and a section on the apparent paradox of coexistence of stagnation and inflation therefore arises quite naturally and logically. Here we talk not about inflation *en generale* but about inflation under monopoly capitalism. Then I would like to add a brief finale to Ch. 8 on the outlook ahead in which we point out that *any full*-employment policy will run up prices, whether it be increased spending or lower taxes or whatnot. Therefore, if we assume that the U.S. ruling class does not want a steady inflation it must go easy or accept price controls. There are reasons why it should not want a steady inflation (but we needn't be too dogmatic about it) and also reasons why they don't want price controls. So it looks like no effective action — more stagnation and drift. Only a political crisis and realignment would be likely to change it, and none now in sight. What does you think of *that*?

Must rush to the office. More on everything else soon. Haven't read new opus stuff yet, but it looks splendid for size!

/s Paul

PAB to PMS

Palo Alto
October 24, 1962

Dear Paul,

A few lines in haste, I must unfortunately meet a class within an hour. Having brooded for two days over the situation, I have come to the following conclusion. What has developed for Cuba (and for the Soviet Union) is strictly speaking a Brest-Litovsk.[162] As far as Cuba is concerned, it is obvious, as far as the Soviet Union is concerned it is veiled by *appearance* of strength which is absolute but *not* relative. (Quite apart from the consideration that whatever the relative strengths may be, a WW III would be the end of everything and for everybody). Khrushchev & al. being reasonable men will accept the Brest-Litovsk outcome, will make the most of it in propaganda terms, may even obtain somewhat better terms, but they are not going to oblige General Hofmann alias Maxwell Taylor by starting a war! As far as they are concerned, this seems to be clear, although I know nothing about the details, know nothing about what will happen to Soviet boats (not clear at the time of writing) etc., etc.

But now the question of Cuba. That their position is strictly — essence and appearance— Brest Litovsk cannot be questioned for a minute. Their sole and principal target at the moment ought to be to *survive*. There is absolutely no virtue in dramatic and heroic suicide, no virtue in becoming the martyrs of LA [Latin America]; they must do everything they can to *survive*! If they will behave like romantic revolutionaries, this *is* the end. If they are Marxists *and* Leninists they must do what Lenin did under such circumstances: sign Brest-Litovsk. I.e. admit each and any UN commission, dismantle each and any installation etc. etc. What do they have to lose? A heroic, epic defeat? Would it not be better to make the invasion which is obviously on the agenda as difficult as possible to our jingoists? What difference does it make *now*? Couldn't you get to see Garcia[163]

---

162. Baran is here referring to the Cuban missile crisis and the 1918 treaty of Brest-Litovsk.

163. Mario Garcia, Cuba's UN ambassador, who, ironically, a week after this letter was written, was recalled to Havana and removed from his post due to incendiary remarks made at the UN Security Council.

and impress upon him for further delivery this point of political dialectics? It is understandable how hard it is to take for proud and truly heroic people like Fidel and others. But their greatest contribution to Cuba and the world is to *survive*! It is a heartbreaking dilemma, but its other horn is the end of the Cuban Revolution with all the consequences thereof. It could be argued that this will revolutionize LA. I would think that this is more likely to discourage LA for many years . . .

Oh, it is horrible . . .

Yours,

/s Paul

PMS to PAB

Larchmont
October 25, 1962

Dear Paul,

[. . .]

I find it almost impossible to concentrate on anything, but continue to try to work. If Khrushchev can get the world out of this maniacal insanity of the U.S. ruling class, mankind will owe him an eternal debt of gratitude. But I cannot say that I am optimistic. The real aim of the U.S. of course is to get an excuse to invade Cuba and overthrow the revolutionary regime, and I suspect they have decided to do it no matter what concessions may be made.

Love,

/s Paul

PMS to PAB

Larchmont
October 31, 1962

Dear Paul,

I'm afraid there's going to be trouble getting agreement between Huby and me over the interpretation of the events of the last week. If it is too serious, we will have to adopt the device we used in the case of the resumption of Soviet testing, i.e. print two views each signed by one of us. But maybe it won't come to that, and in the meantime I want to be sure I know what I think.

Hence the following notes, on which I would appreciate your comments.

My first reaction to Kennedy's speech was: that it was based on faked intelligence and that the purpose was to provide a pretext for invasion. The assumption of Washington, I thought, was that the Soviet Union would back down. The combined effect of the overthrow of Castro and the humiliation of the Soviet Union would be a tremendous strengthening of the U.S.'s world

position. Admission by the Soviet Union that the bases are genuine requires a
new theory.

I dismiss the possibility that the Soviet Union thought that it could get away
with establishing the bases as, e.g., the U.S. got away with establishing them in
Turkey. Kennedy's repeated public statements on this, plus the U.S. political
situation, ruled such an outcome out from the very beginning; and I simply am
not able to swallow the notion that K and Co. are so badly informed or politically
illiterate as to be unaware of this. It is said that the Japanese made just such a
mistake when they attacked Pearl Harbor. No doubt true, but it is ridiculous
to compare, still less equate, fanatical Japanese imperialists with the Marxist-
Leninist leadership of the USSR.

We must therefore start with the premise that Khrushchev was making
a deliberate move with a view to achieving certain definite ends. Since we
assume he knew the U.S. could not just sit by and watch the bases be built, it
follows that he was deliberately provoking the crisis. He wanted the U.S. to
know the bases were being built (*NB* the complete absence of camouflage in
the face of daily reconnaissance flights — this would be utter insanity if the
intent had been to preserve secrecy) and he wanted to evoke a counteraction.
This was where the greatest danger lay. He could not know what the reaction
would be* [*(*PMS's note*): A super Machiavellian might assume that JFK and
Khrushchev had agreed in advance on the action each would take, each for his
own purposes. That's too much for me.] and he must have known that there
was a strong war party in Washington that would put all possible pressure on
for bombing the bases and invading Cuba at once. If that had happened, the fat
would have been in the fire and the alternatives would have been defeat or war.
Khrushchev must have known that, so we can assume that he figured Kennedy
for milder action which would then give room for maneuvering. He was of
course not only prepared but determined to withdraw the bases: that was
the currency with which he entered the bargaining. The question was what
quo could he get for this *quid*. My guess is that he didn't have much idea in
advance and thought merely in terms of getting whatever he could. Much, even
all, would depend on reactions around the world: Would the Latin American
countries go along with the U.S.? How about NATO? How scared would the
U.S. public be? Etc. If reactions were favorable to Khrushchev's side, he might
expect to get quite a lot; if unfavorable, very little or even nothing. In the event,
turned out to be mostly unfavorable. The OAS was immediately stampeded
into giving Washington a blank check, NATO rallied to the U.S., there was no
popular outcry for peace in the U.S. Hence K was forced to settle for a vague
statement that the U.S. would not invade — not nothing, but not much either.

Throwing the Turkish bases into the hopper was, in my opinion, a propaganda move pure and simple.

That, it seems to me, is the basic explanation of what happened during the period October 22-28. It was *not* a defeat for the Soviet Union, which was in an extremely weak position throughout and had the almost impossibly difficult task of defending the Cuban Revolution without becoming involved in a World War. In a sense, indeed, the statement by the U.S. that it would not invade is a victory. Certain it is that the U.S. would not have dreamed of making such a statement *to the UN* two weeks ago (Kennedy's statements about not invading "now" at his press conferences are quite different). We know, of course, that no binding guarantees have been made, and the *Times* has already carried several Washington stories to the effect that "high officials" interpret the no-invasion assurances as applying only to the present situation and in no way as a commitment for the future. Nevertheless, the assurance has been given and it is a political fact of no small importance. Proof of this, if any were needed, is the anguished outcry from Cuban refugee groups: you probably saw the R. Hart Phillips story from Miami in which she reports the remark: "This is another Bay of Pigs for us."

The next question is: What now? First, Khrushchev will obviously make the most out of the situation in propaganda terms, and on this level it seems to me he has been doing very well. More important is the struggle to strengthen in any and every possible way the no-invasion pledge, and here the primary responsibility would seem to be up to Fidel. He will try to use his ability to withhold permission for inspection as a bargaining counter. My own view is that it is not worth much, and if he tries too hard he may simply play into the hands of the U.S. war party. More promising, it seems to me, would be an effort to get the UN heavily involved in the pledge. If I were Fidel, I would want not only inspectors for the base-dismantling operation but a permanent UN commission to check any violations of Cuban sovereignty. And I would specially draw the big LA countries into this. It might even be wise to plunk for neutralization a la Oesterreich under UN guarantees and supervision. It seems to me crazy to argue that Cuba can't follow such lines of action for fear of being Congolized. The situation is totally different: Fidel is in thorough control with his own armed forces, where Lumumba had nothing. There would be no question of sending a UN *army* to Cuba. Unfortunately, I am not too sanguine about how skillfully the Cubans will exploit the situation, but maybe they will rise to the occasion.

As to the U.S., if there were any desire to reach a *modus vivendi* with the Cuban Revolution, this would of course be a great opportunity. I do not for a moment believe in the existence of any significant ruling-class sentiment for such

a course, however. What is more likely is a determined struggle against every
effort to give real meaning to the no-invasion pledge and an intensification of all
sorts of pressure on both Cuba and Latin America. Internally, we are told that the
crisis has waked up quite a few younger people and made them really interested
in political questions for the first time. In the long run this is all to the good and
we of the left must try to make the most of it. But I see no likelihood of short- or
medium-term political changes.

More on other matters soon.

Love,

/s Paul

PAB to PMS

Palo Alto
November 3, 1962

Dear Paul,

There are again clouds on the Stanford horizon; *Palo Alto Times* has carried
at least half a dozen letters demanding "drastic" measures against me, and
something is brewing in the HQ's. Don't know what. This time my position
is bad; the appraisal of the situation which I advanced was at least partly half-
baked, and I imagine that the KPFA transcript [164] wouldn't make very gratifying
reading. The world gets to be too complicated for anything sensible to be said
— at least as far as I am concerned. One has to control one's emotions, and this is
definitely the last time that I have yielded to the temptation . . . But who knows?

My reaction to Kennedy's first speech was exactly the same as yours. It was
re-enforced by listening to the Security Council's proceedings, Stevenson's
speech and the speech by Zorin. It all looked like a tremendously clever
operation to catch two birds with one net: to liquidate Cuba and to humiliate the
Soviet Union showing to the entire world the worthlessness of its promises of
aid and assistance. But, as you say, when it became clear that the Soviet hardware
was actually there, this interpretation collapsed.

Now as to the motivations behind the SU's sending the stuff there I must
admit to be more confused than ever before. There is one possible interpretation:
the Cubans supported by the Chinese and Moscow's own Stalinists pressed
for that. Chief arguments: it'll strengthen Cuba, it'll improve the SU's strategic
position, it'll lead to nothing serious because of the "paper tiger" nature of
imperialism. In addition, it could get things off dead center, force Washington

164. PAB was a regular speaker on KPFA radio broadcasts and had voiced some strong opinions
about the Cuban crisis.

to *negotiate* and provide the Soviet Union with a bargaining object for which something in Cuba or elsewhere might be gotten in return. Therefore the foray to be undertaken with perfect preparedness to withdraw if something should be obtainable for the withdrawal. To tell you the truth, this sounds to me to be much too clever to be true. How could they have conceivably have known what the reaction in Washington would be? How could they have been certain that the Pentagon would not immediately begin bombing Cuba plus invasion plus God knows what elsewhere? What is more, if all this was that premeditated, why what looks like a very *genuine* alarm in Moscow? Why the Khrushchev appeals which sound like perfectly genuine outcries of anguish? Nor is it clear to me what the experiment proves. Neither side within the Communist debate can be said to have demonstrated the truth of its position. The moderates around Khr. can argue that Washington's reaction was anything but paper-tigerish; the Chinese can argue that the display of Soviet aggressiveness elicited at least an assurance of no invasion. . . . On the other hand, I was told by a military expert at Stanford that an invasion would have been anyway a very hard nut to crack. Unless Cuba were to be softened up by bombing to the point of near-annihilation, 10-15 divisions might have been needed for the purpose with a great deal of casualties and a huge mess thereafter. So, maybe Khrushchev got in exchange something which the President was quite glad to give him? I don't know.

The other possibility — in no direct conflict with the first — is that the whole business relates directly to Soviet-Chinese relations. Moscow yielded to Peking very much against Khrushchev's preferences, the result confirmed Khrushchev's fears, they immediately pulled back and can now say once and for all that the Khrushchev course was right and the Chinese course leads to war. That Mikoyan was sent to Cuba would lend support to that hypothesis; Mikoyan is definitely the most outspoken "right winger" in Moscow. More importantly: the Chinese operations against India clearly indicate that China has decided to quit arguing and to enforce its view by actions. It is nullifying all Soviet efforts to build up a neutral group of countries led by India, it drives towards a clear cut polarization and elimination of the "progressive, anti-imperialist u/d c's [underdeveloped countries]" so much of which is made in Moscow and in the CPUSSR Party Program. That Fidel & Co have been very much influenced by the Chinese line stands to reason, although his *present* show of intransigence is perhaps more understandable (and justified) than the earlier one. At the moment he is out of the danger zone, and may be able to get something out of the bargaining process — either from the U.S. or from the USSR or from both. . . Although in the Cubans' case the talk about pride, humiliation etc. rings true rather than a makeshift for negotiations.

In this connection: the Chinese-Indian affair is probably in many respects more important than the whole Cuban business. Peking creates *faits accomplis* of tremendous proportions and how there is Sino-Soviet reconciliation on that basis to be had, beats me? Even in material terms: all the Soviet aid etc., etc., go down the drain in the process. If this ain't mad, then I really don't understand anything at all.

As to the future: the attached article in the [*San Francisco*] *Chronicle* which is obviously a trial balloon (the *Chronicle* was *very* critical of Kennedy during the crisis and *very* "pro-Cuba") would suggest that there is some sentiment for changing the whole course toward Cuba. As you do, I distrust this possibility — although on the other hand what other alternatives are there? And maybe Kennedy really wants to avoid showdowns and yells so loud primarily for domestic consumption. That view would find support in his most dilatory behavior during the Bay of Pigs crisis, for his readiness to give the no-invasion assurance now, for his frequently tough words accompanied by actually very little tough activity. Is Kennedy to be reappraised in some way? — That there is any change in the public sentiment, looks to me doubtful, although this is not the best observation point. Here there was an absolutely frantic burst of jingoism (certainly among the general population but also among students) with the main theme "let's *do* something about Cuba". Whether this activation is water on left mills or on right ones is uncertain. I tend to believe the latter.

It would be most deplorable if all this should lead to open disagreement between you and Huby. I see no reason for it at all. After all MR's job is not to moralize, condemn or pat on the back, but to analyze *sine ira et studio* [without anger or bias]. I am the last to advocate "value-free" attitudes towards events, but this does not mean that we in our position can set ourselves up as judges of history and issue certificates of good or bad behavior to the prime agents on the historical scene. . . . The biggest danger for us sectarians is to sink to the level of sentimental do-gooders and socialists who are always against sin and for virtue.

[. . .]

Love,

s/ Paul

PMS to PAB

Larchmont

Nov. 8, 1962

Dear Paul,

[...]

A new piece of *misere* has come up, infuriating because it so effectively interferes with serious, uninterrupted work. Huby has received a subpoena from HUAC [House Committee on Un-American Activities] for next Wednesday a.m. We are not certain yet, but it seems highly probable that a general Cuba inquisition is being mounted. Anyway, as you can imagine, it means all the old dreck of getting lawyers, talking endlessly to them, trying to anticipate lines of questioning, working out positions, etc. We have got a good lawyer named Ephraim London whose forte is censorship of press, films, etc., and who has had plenty of Committee experience right up to the Supreme Court. We will try to continue the same line taken before the McCarthy and NH affairs earlier. Natch, I will go to Washington with Huby. Whether I (or you) will be called separately is anyone's guess. London thinks the whole Committee is so stupid that rational predictions are not even worth trying to make.

I have never felt so frustrated by an international situation as now by the Sino-Indian biz. If one only knew what facts to believe! But of course the Chinese must have foreseen the profound political implications of what they are doing and must therefore have figured that something good would come out of it all. What that net benefit is supposed to be, however, eludes me. Nor can I see what they hope to accomplish by goading Fidel & Co. to the utmost intransigence. If no agreements with imperialists are to be trusted, then obviously they are not even to be sought, but that means war and not later but sooner. Or do they really believe the paper-tiger theory quite literally? If so, God knows we are in for it. This, by the way, seems to me a possibility. The present Chinese regime is really isolated from the West & esp. the U.S. and hence can generate a theory which feeds on itself without any real possibility of being checked against the facts. If the U.S. ruling class had any sense, they would be working hard and fast to get China into the UN, to get Chinese newsmen, intellectuals, etc., over here — in a word, to break down this extremely dangerous state of isolation. But the U.S. ruling class is even madder in its way. Oi, weh.

[...]

Otherwise, everything in order. More on various matters soon.

Love,

/s Paul

P.S. I opened the envelope to add that we've just heard from the lawyer that
the HUAC thing is about British Guiana, which would seem to have much less
potentiality for trouble than Cuba.

PAB to PMS

[Palo Alto]

December 3rd, 1962

Dear Paul,

The news about Juan Noyola was terribly distressing.[165] As John Donne said
"any mans *death* diminishes *me*, because I am involved in *Mankinde*," and Juan's
(nonsensical) end diminishes one even more because with all his weaknesses he
was an intelligent and honest man, such a rarity these days! I cannot help getting
morbid and thinking about the necessity of cleaning up my study, of bringing
my affairs into some minimal order, of finishing writing whatever there is to be
written — for the bell may toll any day . . .

The meeting in Santa Barbara was interesting and rather instructive. I came
to think that the opus must contain either in the Introduction or in the I.S.
[Irrational Society] Chapter something (if ever so brief) on what is obviously
becoming now the principal pillars of dominant thought:

(1) All economic matters cease to matter — the floor belongs exclusively to
science and technology; R&D is in charge regardless of whether it is socialism or
capitalism. That the whole problem is whether science & technology will destroy
the world or render it at last free of want, disease and toil falls conveniently
under the table. Science is unquestioningly equated with progress or — if not
—opposed in favor of good old horse & cabby. Another illustration of the basic
point that *within* bourgeois ideology there is never room for anything but two
lousy alternatives.

(2) The whole world (East and West, advanced and underdeveloped) is
moving towards *controls*. The invisible hand gets to be more and more replaced
by the visible, planning is taking over everywhere with the questions. Who *owns*
the joint? and Planning for What? considered to be old-maidish Victorianism's
of the mentally retarded Marxists. The understanding (nay, the mere mention)
of *interests* in the socio-economic universe is systematically obstructed; and the
interesting thing is that this is so precisely at a time when under the influence of
Freud, the existentialists, romanticists and assorted inspirationalists, all kinds
of non-rational (irrational), inexplicable and irreducible facticities are avidly

---

165. Juan Noyola Vázquez, a Mexican Marxist economist known for his contributions to Latin
American structuralism, died in a plane crash at the age of 40.

acknowledged and *advertised*. All interests (in sex, in "power," in "status," in "national glory") are *Salon-faehig* [appropriate salon conversation], can be (should be) freely discussed and stressed, but when it comes, God forbid, to saying that economic interests, interests in profits represent one of those irreducible facticities, the consternation is profound. Oh, well this is most unimportant; the managers have replaced the stockholders, the buccaneer has yielded to the bureaucrat, and now, the latest, the bureaucratic manager has been pushed aside by the R&D scientist. What more does you want to show that Marxism is *eine bornierte Marotte* [a dumb fad]? What are economic interests, the drive for profit, as compared with frustration, alienation, insecurity and early toilet training . . . ? And the funny thing about it is that even economists who are now, Friedman & Co apart, all sold on controls and planning shudder when the "facticity" of profits comes up. Oh, no, the question is whether or not "we" fully understand the possibilities of planning, whether "we" devise the right mix of centralization & decentralization, whether "we" learn how to combine fiscal policy with indirect controls &c., &c.

(3) Since controls and planning is what matters, the differences between socialist and capitalist wash out, in the long run we are all planners; all that we are fighting for is freedom. If it is remarked that freedom is increasing in the socialist world, that Poland is pretty damn free and that freedom might do even better over there if they were unthreatened by our freedom loving H bombs, and if one adds that Cuba would be a different place today had it been left alone and minus embargo, subversion and economic strangulation, the answer is a yawn. And should one commit the tactlessness of adding that maybe our hostility towards the socialist world is less related to freedom (cf. our attitude towards Franco *et tutti quanti*) and more related to private property the yawn is replaced by a growl.

By the way, all this applies to the mature, advanced and well situated leaders of thought. Some of the younger chappies smile knowingly when those points are (delicately) brought up. If it weren't for the gnawing suspicion that they too will start yawning and growling when their salaries get adjusted in keeping with advancing "status."

I did some tickling on those lines, remaining very polite, academic and suitably esoteric. The only one who reacted bitterly was Kenneth Boulding who let loose long tirades about the tragedy of Cuba, the horrors of China and the phony de-Stalinization in the USSR. By the way, it would seem that the USSR developments make the position of the *Dissent* types extremely difficult. Earlier they had to deny Soviet economic successes, now they have to deny Soviet political successes.

Another matter of importance which calls for at least minimal note-taking is the racial question. I read yesterday an article by James Baldwin in *The New Yorker* of Nov. 17th (you *must* read it!). Combined with a good deal of confusion (primarily towards the end) and with some apparent "adjustments" to being printable in this country, there is a great deal of insight and knowledge. It must get mentioned in the IS ["Irrational Society"] story . . .

[. . .]

Love,

/s Paul

PMS to PAB

Larchmont
December 5, 1962

Dear Paul,

[. . .]

In the meantime, I have been perusing the last batch of QOS (2) materials, and also going over again the "Theoretical Implications" draft (numbered VIII in my present file, but should be 9 according to the latest table of contents).[166] Here are some tentative reactions:

QOS (2), pp. 34–45

p. 34 — The transition from books to TV strikes me as infelicitous. I would prefer something like: "We have nevertheless dwelt at considerable length on book publishing because it seems to us to provide, next to the educational system, the best index of a society's cultural condition. The accuracy of the index can be checked by a briefer examination of a number of other aspects of the social superstructure. We begin with the quantitatively most important mass communication medium: television and radio broadcasting." This would replace the paragraph in the middle of the page.

p. 34 — The first sentence of the next paragraph seems to me to be either wrong or at any rate misleading. The "economic organization" of TV (by the way, why not use the abbreviation in the text as well as in quotes?) includes much (networks, forms of programming, etc.) that is irrelevant to publishing. If all you

---

166. "Some Theoretical Implications," drafted by Baran, was to be Chapter 9 of *Monopoly Capital*, according to the plan at this time. The chapter was drafted by Baran but was not included in the final publication of the book, since the authors were still working out elements of the argument at the time of Baran's death in 1964. It was finally published in *Monthly Review* in 2012. See Baran and Sweezy, "Some Theoretical Implications," 24–59.

mean is that TV has progressed further along the road to monopoly, then say that, omitting the ambiguous reference to "economic organization."

p. 35 — l. 10 from bottom — Surely the networks do not control what goes into the newspapers? So far as news is concerned, they are of course competitors of the newspapers, maintaining their own staffs of domestic and foreign correspondents, etc., and so far as I know they have no power at all over any aspect of the newspaper business. Through their large ownership of TV and radio stations, the newspapers may, on the other hand, exercise a considerable influence on the networks. I don't know about this, to be sure. This whole paragraph stressing the great power of the networks seems out of focus in the light of the statement on the next page that they are merely processors and agents. The latter is, in my view, a much more accurate assessment of their role.

p. 36 — line 2 from bottom: I don't think it is either necessary or convincing to stress the "power" of the big advertisers. It seems to suggest that there is somebody around who opposes them and over whom they find it necessary to wield their power, which of course is not the case. The important thing is not the location of power in the setup as a whole (sponsors, networks, stations) but that the whole kit and caboodle is single-mindedly devoted to making money by helping to sell stuff. It is this and not the will or power of any particular individuals or institutions which accounts for the quality of the cultural product (or perhaps it would be more accurate to say by-product). Bringing in matters like the TV cost function only confuses the issue. To put my point in different terms: there is no villain in the piece — neither the networks nor the advertisers; what is decisive is the character of the system itself. This is the position we strictly adhere to in dealing with corporations, and I think we should do so here as well.

p. 37 — last line running over to the top of p. 38: I don't see what granting this, or not granting it, has to do with the case. Probably you had something in mind that just doesn't get through to me here.

p. 40 — sentence beginning end of first line: What is quoted and what (if anything) inserted by you is not clear.

p. 40 — line 2 of first full paragraph: "imbecile vacuity" is more of an epithet than a helpful characterization. *En generale*, I think there is a tendency to rely too much on strong adjectives and adverbs: used too freely, they quickly lose their power to convey any meaning. And the material itself is so devastating that one does not need to resort to such linguistic devices. They even sometimes have the opposite effect to that intended.

p. 41 — first line: It seems to me that it is not really "lies" that you are now going to discuss, at least not lies in the same sense that the commercials are permeated with lies. What would you think of substituting "falsehood" (a more general term) for "the lie" in the second line from the bottom of p. 40 and then omitting "The lie permeates most of the balance" at the top of p. 41?

p. 43 — first paragraph: this needs to be reformulated. The "it" subject gets out of hand.

p. 44 — lines 6-8 of first full paragraph: At least as far as "honor" is concerned, it seems to be more a residue of precapitalist ideology than of competitive capitalism. If you mean "honesty," which is something quite different, then it certainly is a residue of competitive capitalism. In general, however, this seems to be one of those places where one should be careful not to over-idealize competitive capitalism. After all, it was about competitive capitalism that the Communist Manifesto was written with its eloquent denunciation of the dissolution of all ideals in favor of the naked cash nexus.

General — Somewhere in QOS (2) there should, I think, be a discussion of the "elite culture" into which our intellectuals and would-be intellectuals plunge themselves — art galleries, Japanese prints, hi-fi, foreign films (and their U.S. imitators), and all the rest. Quantitatively all this is by no means unimportant, and qualitatively some of it is no doubt good to excellent. But seen in its relation to the system as a whole (which is the way we must try to see everything), it merely emphasizes the lack of human solidarity (also reflected in the content of the elite culture), the torn-apartness, the alienation, the futility, the sickness of the society. I don't know just where this belongs, and perhaps you have plans for doing something of the sort at the end. But I think it is important that it be included, because many of our readers will be precisely those who are most addicted to the elite culture (for which one cannot blame them since one has to do something with oneself) and will accuse us of being "unfair" or presenting an "unbalanced" picture if we don't discuss it. The discussion needn't be long and certainly doesn't have to denounce or even criticize (in fact, a wonderful critique of monopoly capitalist society could be developed via a content analysis of the elite culture); the point would be simply to put the thing in its proper setting and perspective.

Theoretical Implications

I won't go into any detail at this stage, though I already have made a good many notes and will certainly make more on a further reading. Most generally: the chapter will have to be substantially revised to take account of what is said in the chapters that precede it and which hadn't been written when the draft was made. Somewhat less generally: the role of the autonomous individual and his needs in the traditional theory (indeed in bourgeois ideology generally) will have to be expanded and strengthened. This is a very important matter, and its treatment in the draft is probably the weakest part. There must be some good books on philosophic individualism which would be helpful and supply some badly needed quotes from the great philosophers and social thinkers. On the whole, I think the section dealing with Marxian theory is better than that dealing with bourgeois theory, but here again there is room for improvement. Specifically, I have made the following comment on the last page: "This last part (dealing with interpenetration, etc.) needs redoing to take account at least of the following: (1) Your own bread-loaf example (in the new introduction to *PEoG*) which clarifies the process very well; (2) such things as redundant distribution facilities because of market imperfections and price rigidities (too many gas stations, etc.); (3) the empirical study of [Carl] Kaysen et. al. of the costs of auto-model shenanigans; and (4) the analysis of earlier chapters (esp. 5) which had not been written when you drafted this chapter." In addition, I think my profits-vs.-surplus diagram could be usefully incorporated and that a rough breakdown of the labor force into surplus-producers and surplus-eaters (using actual statistics) would also be of value.

As you will gather, I think there is a lot of work to be done on this one, and the question arises as to procedure. Do you want to leave it until you finish up QOS (2) and IS and then return to this (and 5)? Or do you think it would expedite matters if I work on it after I get done with 4, 6, 7, and 8?[167] It is "your" chapter, so to speak, so you have to make the decision.

On Other Matters

I received this a.m. (my letter was started yesterday) yours of Dec. 3 with your thoughts after Santa Barbara. This is dandy material and belongs, I think, in IS, *not* in the Introduction.

Returning herewith the Clipping in re school segregation/discrimination. I am writing the Civil Rights Commission on MR stationery asking for two copies of the report referred to. If they are forthcoming, I will send one to you.

I have read the Baldwin piece already and was, like you, much impressed. It is interesting not only for what he says about race problems but also for his very perceptive insights into U.S. society in general. It is interesting (and understandable) that a Negro can see these things much more clearly than a white; the Negro doesn't have to be a (good) Marxist, while the white does. Leo and I are trying to meet Baldwin and to get him to write for us.

---

167. Sweezy was drafting three of the four chapters on the absorption of surplus (chapters 4, 6, and 7, addressing capitalist consumption and investment (4), civilian government spending (6) and militarism and imperialism, as well as the chapter on the history of monopoly capitalism (8). The question here was whether Sweezy should turn to the draft of "Some Theoretical Implications" (then slated as chapter 9), next in line, or whether it should be left until Baran finished his other remaining chapters.

Finally — If, as I calculate should happen, this reaches you Saturday, it will be just in time to wish you a most happy birthday and to welcome you to the fraternity of those who have attained the ripe old age of 53. The enclosed gift has more sentiment than beauty attached to it. Zirel joins in sending lots of love and best wishes for many happy returns.

Yours,

    /s Paul

[. . .]

PAB to PMS

Palo Alto

December 7, 1962

Dear Paul,

Your spec'y of December 5/6th arrived this PM. — Most kind of you to think of my birthday and to dispatch a "*presento.*" The time for such jubilees has passed long ago; it used to be a day for "looking forward," for dreaming about future "deeds"; now, alas! it is a rather unwelcome occasion for staring back, for taking stock and for sadly establishing for the nth time how desperately little has been accomplished. . . . To be remembered on a day like this is a source of compensating gratification. Much obliged.

1. Re-read Chapters 3 ["The Tendency for Surplus to Rise"] and 8 [On the History of Monopoly Capitalism"] with the new pp., and think that both should be on their way to Jack [Rackliffe], if — as you say and as I hope — he is willing and able to receive them.

2. I had a gnawing suspicion that Chapters 5 and 9 are in need of thorough redoing, both in the light of the material that has been written since as well as in view of various thoughts that have come up since they were done. But like an ostrich sticking its head into sand and believing that it cannot be seen, I pushed those thoughts aside and never looked at the stuff in the hope (fear) to return to it after everything else is done. I would still prefer to finish QoS II and to draft IS ["The Irrational System," the concluding chapter] before turning back to the earlier material. This obviously does not mean at all that you could not or should not do with it anything you want as soon as you get around to it. Since time is of the essence, it would certainly be excellent if you got to those chapters before I do; I will concentrate now on the job in hand and then work intensively on the preceding chapters while you go over the remainder of QoS II and IS.

3. Your comments on the QoS II pp. are very good, and I shall rework the stuff accordingly. There are no disagreements; most of what you say is an indication of my having expressed myself most inadequately. Thus for instance nothing was (and is) further from my mind than idealizing competitive capitalism. What did not become clear at all is that I meant to say that "freedom, justice and honor" were an *ideology* of competitive capitalism, not its *reality*. An ideology which was just as much *Falsches Bewusstsein* as cynicism is *Falsches Bewusstsein* [false consciousness]; it matters nevertheless what it is that constitutes an ideology even if an ideology remains in both cases a half-truth. But I'll try to fix it up, and let us then see whether it becomes any clearer.

4. I do have in mind to say something about elite culture, but haven't quite decided where and how. My first idea was to put it at the end of what you have read so far, but then I thought that this would overload the Ch., and I resolved to return to it in IS precisely because I felt that it should be dealt with in reference to the system as a whole, its consciousness. QoS I and QoS II are directed towards the "state of the people" — in IS I thought I'll talk a little about the "ideas of the age." That's why I did not refer as yet to "good" books — Hemingway, Steinbeck etc. — or "good" arts. . . . This is perhaps wrong, but it is not an omission; it is a commission.

5. I know Jim Baldwin; he is a friend (*very* close) of Mary Painter's. You may have noticed, in his article he refers to Mary as a white friend whom he could not hate. I doubt very much that he would be available to MR. He is most cautious, must make a living as a free-lance writer and won't do anything that might compromise him. It is interesting to note, how he drags in without any particular need the "plague on both your houses" sentence. It is also remarkable, how he ends up in a gibberish about love etc. which is a sheer *non sequitur* with regard to his entire story. By the way, he spends most of his time not here but in Paris.

6. Even our bestest intellectuals make me wince. Got in the mail and read a piece by [W.H.] Ping Ferry "What Price For Peace?" Here is as good a man as there is and the rubbish that he composes is unbelievable. He sees clearly how the economy is dependent on military orders, he sees clearly how the ruling class is afraid of communism, he knows full well what the conflict is all about and then he goes off on "our" lack of political imagination, on "our" inability to see the necessity of a warless world and so on and so forth. If an illustration was needed for the taboo character of economic interests here is an excellent one — because it comes from a good man, not from a swine.

[. . .]

Anyway, the next task is to finish QoS II. When do you want the reply to the Russians?

All the best, many thanks again.

Love,

s/ Paul

[. . .]

8
Here is Rhodes; Jump Here!

PAB to PMS

Palo Alto
Jan. 6th, 1963

Dear Paul,

[…]

The pp. which you sent me were placed where they belong. As to the contents of the statement concerning "*state*-mono-cap," I have slight doubts. If addressed to the general public (incl. economists), it is hardly necessary.[168] If it is meant to allay the worries of Shlomo [Sol Adler] & Co, it is hardly adequate. For their argument would be — strange as it may sound coming from them — that it does not take account at all of the income-and-employment-regulating, manipulating —"Keynesian"— function of the state. Although it is fairly certain that Lenin who coined the notion did not have *this* in mind, it is this meaning which is increasingly given to it in Soviet writings. And our own theory assigning an important role to the state as surplus-absorber suggests that the emphasis on the role of the state is not misplaced. It also surely makes sense stressing it in the development of monopoly capitalism in Italy, France, GB and elsewhere. I agree with you that there is no need to employ the word in the title, but there is no need either to stress that it would be wrong to acknowledge the particular and growing role of the state under monopoly capitalism. The alliance of Big Business, Big Brass, Big Bureaucracy; the "industrial-military complex," or whatever other terms have been used to reflect both an increasing amalgamation of BB [Big Business] and state as well as progress in the direction of some kind of "*dirigisme*" which needs to be recognized. Your principal point is undoubtedly

---

168. The discussion here relates to the explanation to be provided in the book of why the term "monopoly capitalism" or "monopoly capital" is preferred to "state monopoly capitalism" — a term originally introduced by Lenin in *State and Revolution*. Baran and Sweezy's final explanation of this is to be found on pages 66–67 of *Monopoly Capital*.

right: monopoly capitalism *is* all of this; it is unnecessary to give it any other names — no more than it would be necessary to speak of large-scale-enterprise-monopoly capitalism or corporation-monopoly capitalism. But the *substantive* element of the distinction or rather characterization would seem to me to be of some merit.

[…]

All the best,

/s Your Paul

PMS to PAB

Larchmont

January 9, 1963

Dear Paul,

Terrible rush to get things in order before departure, So this will be no more than a line.

[…]

I think you are right that the explanation of refusal to use "state monopoly capitalism" terminology is not satisfactory. But I also think such an explanation is needed — naturally for Marxists, not for bourgeois economists who won't understand anyway. Next time you write about such matters, jot down in a few sentences your version of the explanation. I will expand it and substitute it for the present version. Is the part on government regulation of utilities and other forms of monopoly promotion okay with you?

[…]

Love as ever,

/s Paul

P. S. […]

PMS to PAB

[*Handwritten*]

Hotel Grillon

Santiago de Chile

January 17, 1963

Dear Paul,

The last 2 days in Mexico we spent a total of nine hours with Chi, Deputy Chairman of the Bank of China and an old friend from prewar days, who has been to Brazil and Mexico on a trade mission — a very intelligent man who is in the higher CP [Communist Party] circles in Peking. From these talks it emerges very clearly that the Chinese position is a very straightforward revolutionary position. Their criticisms of the Soviet Union are both internal and foreign-policy — too much inequality, too much reliance on monetary incentives, too little democracy. Externally, fear of revolution, desire to make a deal with U.S. at too high a price, etc. (*footnote: Also very important: Chinese insistence on full equality for governing CP's. It was on this principle that they supported Yugo in 1948 and Poland in 1956.) One cannot but agree on most points. Their great weakness is underestimation of the U.S. readiness to fight even if means suicide — they really don't believe the U.S. will resort to nuclear war. Their curiosity about the U.S. is enormous, however. Chi would like to get our book in *draft* form *mammediately*, and I had to convince him that we won't have no drafts until it is ready for press.

The Latin American Left is much more disoriented and weak than one could have feared. We spent last evening at the house of [Salvador] Allende, pres. candidate of the Chilean Popular Front for 1964. Fine chap with a beautiful wife and daughter but unfortunately no Fidel. Both in Mexico and here, we find the left intellectuals longing for a "neutralist socialism"—they simply won't learn the Cuban lesson that the U.S. ain't not buying that commodity. So far as I've observed on this trip (maybe Argentina and Brazil will change the picture), the "imminence of revolution" in Latin America is a myth. Alas for dreams.

Also, the real understanding of the structure and dynamics of these societies is still at an elementary level. The attitude, potentialities, etc., etc., of the "masses" — 3/4ths or more of the population — are largely terra incognita, dealt with in copious clichés. I have been a sinner in this respect myself but have resolved to reform.

Will write again from Buenos Aires.

Yrs.,

/s Paul

P.S. The climate here is very close to that of Palo Alto.

PMS to PAB

Hotel Grillon
Santiago de Chile
Fri. p.m.

Dear Paul,

This is from some Socialist Party Senators with whom we just had a long tea [an enclosed pamphlet]. They think you're a great man (quite right!) And will receive you with open arms — as will many others — when you come over from

Buenos Aires to visit. It's only 2 hours across the Andes. Will send you all sorts
of addresses when we get back to N.Y.

Muy hastily,

Love,

/s Paul

P.S. We go to B.A. tomorrow

PAB to PMS

[Palo Alto]
January 23rd, 1963

Dear Paul,

Many thanks for postcard from Mexico and the two letters from Santiago. Prior
to my trip to Los Angeles I also received the material [copyedited chapters of
Monopoly Capital] from Jack [Rackliffe], whom I wrote a note of thanks and
promised to write more after going over the text with the necessary care.

What you report about your talks with Chi is of the *utmost* interest and
shows that in spite of everything it *is* possible to learn something from history.
Their attitude is understandable, predictable, but nevertheless — I am afraid —
"wrong." I put the word wrong in quotation marks because it is right by some
absolute standards and mistaken in the dialectical sense of leaving out of account
the *concrete*, specific conditions within which matters have to be dealt with. Thus
the Paper Tiger theory is fine if, but only if the tiger is made of paper; *similarly*
more equality, less monetary incentives &c. is a good principle if production
does not suffer unduly; and equal rights for all socialist countries &c is
unquestionable if, and only if, none of them can drag the entire world (and entire
socialist camp) into a thermonuclear war. And so it goes, and so it is inevitable
that principles of right, justice, morality &c get continually compromised and
violated in hustle and bustle of the dialectic. And how does one find out *at any
given moment* whether one compromises too much or too little? Accordingly,
I am not in 100% agreement with your Sino-Indian RoM. The Chinese are
undoubtedly right (a book of documents which I received from Shlomo proves
it beyond question); still the consideration which you express in a fn and kind
of reject is paramount: shouldn't they [have], *rebus sic stantibus* [things being as
they are] in the world at large, instead of shooting started yelling bloody murder,
calling on the USSR to mediate, demand a hearing before the Security Council
and so forth and so on?

No less interesting are your impressions *in re*: *Aktualitaet* in LA [reality in Latin America]. This comes as more of a surprise, because I too have been apparently over-optimistic on that account. . . .

My expedition to LA [Los Angeles] was terribly fatiguing: 7 (!!) appearances in 4 days was too much. There were big crowds (1000 in one case and 1400 in another) but still . . . Alan [Sweezy] and family were very nice to me and I saw quite a lot of them.

Must run now to the Campus: some more lecturing — it is hard to live by one's muscles, but living by one's tongue particularly when the feeding power of the brain so markedly declines is nothing to envy either . . .

Give my love to Huby, write more and have a good time.

Yours,

/s Paul

PS. Thanks for the pamphlet; it is funny to be considered a "great man" when one feels like a miserable pigmy.

PMS to PAB

[*Handwritten*]

Hotel Trocadero
Rio de Janiero
January 28, 1963

Dear Paul,

Make a note that when you come to Rio you *must* stay at an air-conditioned hotel — this one at Copacabana (much better in every way, incl. cheaper, than the Excelsior where our travel agent had booked us) or the Gloria nearer the center.

I saw Germani in Buenos Aires. As you probably know, he is a tired intellectual whose enthusiasms are all in the past, and lives in constant fear for his job. He is resigning as chairman of the dept of sociology and hopes his successor will be Torcuato Di Tella, from one of Argentina's richest families (autos and much else besides), with whom you will probably have to deal in future negotiations. Di Tella is said to be not quite bright and is undoubtedly under Germani's influence. Your appointment is in the nature of a test case. The money is from Ford, with no overt strings attached (except no appointments of socialist-bloc chaps), and Germani seems to think if the Univ. administration (now under control of the Catholics) doesn't intervene to block your coming to Buenos Aires, then they can do what they like. Meanwhile, the political situation in Argentina is so bad and so confused that almost anything might happen (except something good of course), so you probably ought to be thinking of an alternative for the Aug.–Dec. period in case of a cancellation. I don't say it's probable, but the possibility certainly can't be excluded.

Buenos Aires is a great city, much more impressive than any other we've seen — and more than twice as big. I'm sure you'll like it from that point of view. But the situation of the country is sad beyond description. Economic degeneration, speeding up, accompanied by absolute political stalemate from which no one can see any way out. The Left is falling apart, the huge middle strata are cynical and apathetic (Germani says Argentinians are like Americans, by which he means middle-class Argentinians), and the workers are under the spell of Peron. I have always tended to discount Peronism, but an evening with three of the most militant, class-conscious Peronist trade-union leaders was a real revelation. They await the second coming with all the religious fervor of millenarian Christians, and in the meantime are impervious to other ideas and programs. It is hard to imagine a country at once more in need of revolution and at the same time so far from it.

Montevideo was pleasant, a quiet backwater but a good place to observe things around the continent. *Marcha*, a left-nationalist weekly published there (and strictly banned in Argentina) is probably the best of its kind in Latin America.

We definitely succeeded in our mission to *start* a Spanish edition of *MR* in Buenos Aires. Charming young gals (2 of them) will do translating and all business end as well. Everyone tells us the potential market is excellent. Whether all obstacles can be overcome, and whether the Argentine authorities will permit it — these are questions no one can answer. We figure we can't lose by trying.

We haven't seen anyone in Rio yet. Everything points to the conclusion that Brazil is *the* key country — the only one capable of *sustaining* a revolution. But more on all that when we've had time to look around and get the feel of the place.

En generale, CP's everywhere seem to be in a sharp swing to the Right — Khrushchev line. Unless the Chinese influence asserts itself and new leadership of a Sino-Fidelista character emerges, they are going to degenerate and decline. Already, their importance is small except in Chile and (probably) Venezuela. A tremendous popular-front fiasco seems in the making in Chile. I remembered the same kind of higher hopes in Spain and France in '36. History *does* have a stubborn way of repeating itself.

Saw in Montevideo a review of Italian edition of *PEoG* in *Rinascita* (July 28, 1962). From what I could make out, it seems to be a vicious attack on both you and me — probably a foretaste of what to expect for opus from European CP'ers. The reviewer, as I recall, has some such name as Spesso.

    Love,

       /s Paul

[. . .]

PMS to PAB

                                          Larchmont

                                  February 26, 1963

Dear Paul.

I have finally got around to the new QoS [II] material (mental health), and I have to say immediately that I am not happy about it.[169] It seems to me that here you have become so absorbed in the mental health literature and so involved in the various methodologies and disputes which characterize it that you have almost forgotten what the purpose is. Our opus is surely not the place for discussions of the inadequacies of (obviously inadequate) conceptions of mental health and illness, nor for demonstrations that certain kinds of statistics (like hospital admission rates) prove little if anything. Further, I think there is much too much quotation from the specialist literature. The purpose, presumably, is to convince the reader that we have studied these matters seriously and are not talking through our hats. The effect, I am afraid, is rather to bore and sometimes even confuse him. Finally, I think there is too much emphasis on the inadequacy and inequality in the treatment of mental illness. The point of the section, if I understand the place of these chapters in the whole design correctly, is to bring home to the reader that monopoly capitalism produces a sick society. It is *also* true that it does a lousy job trying to deal with the consequences of this sickness, but that is a different point, and to play it up blurs the picture: it would be more effective to include such material in the section dealing with income inequality and poverty.

    As to positive suggestions, I would be inclined to favor something along the following lines:

---

169. Sweezy is discussing Baran's draft of what was to be Chapter 11 in the plan for the book at that time, "On the Quality of Monopoly Capitalist Society—II." The earlier parts of this dealing with culture and communications were completed and his efforts were now directed at the later parts having to do with mental health. This chapter was not included in the final book, due to its still unfinished state at the time of Baran's death.

1. I have tried my hand at tidying up p. 46 (new version included), but there is nothing essentially new in the mode of introducing the section.

2. I would begin the real changes right after the end of the paragraph which begins on line 20 of p. 46 and runs over onto 46a. Never mind the additional objections to the clinical empiricist's conception: you have already established the point that it is no good. Next you could *very quickly* — in a paragraph, no more — dispose of the idea that any good index of mental health can be got from hospital admission data. (This brings us through p. 49: in other words nearly 5 pages have been eliminated.)

3. By now you have made two points: that there is no handy definition of mental illness available, and that hospital statistics tell us nothing of interest. Still we find the 1-in-10 figure being quoted at us all the time. What does it mean? We are not told. Can it be plausibly supported by such specialized studies as have been made?

4. No. These studies suggest that a much higher ratio would be nearer the mark. Here summarize the findings of the Army and Midtown studies (I would omit the Rashi Fein thing since it is only persuasive if combined with your guess about the incidence of "more or less severe neuroses": if you want to keep it in, some of the "ample evidence" ought to be cited, but I don't think it's worth the trouble since the Army and Midtown studies are so much better for our purpose.[170]

5. These studies do not give us insight into the incidence of mental illness as between classes and races. If we take account of these differentials, the overall picture takes on a much grimmer aspect. Here summarize relevant data from Hollingshead & Redlich, etc., and present the evidence of higher incidence among Negroes. Anything to be said about differential treatment by class and race should be confined to footnotes for reasons suggested in the opening paragraph above. I would bring the mental illness section to a close right here.

Next, I think we should have an entirely separate section on Negroes in U.S. society.[171] It would come logically after the evidence that mental illness is greater among Negroes, but I think it should have a general rather than such a specialized focus. (It doesn't have to be placed here, of course, and perhaps the end of QoS II would be the best place. It certainly wouldn't be a bad climax to have the Baldwin quote now on lines 5–3, from bottom of p. 60, plus your

170. Leo Srole et. al., *Mental Health in the Metropolis: The Midtown Manhattan Study* (New York: McGraw Hill, 1962). The Army study was apparently not used.
171. This eventually became a separate chapter in *Monopoly Capital* entitled "Monopoly Capitalism and Race Relations."

comment, at the very end of the chapter. Didn't Marx say something very similar about emancipation of the Jews? Perhaps that should be quoted too, with a remark that it is much more apposite to the problem of U.S. Negroes than to any other group. Or is it? Maybe in a predominantly colored and socialist world, U.S. Negroes will be emancipated before whites?) The Negro section [of the chapter], if you agree to it, can be written later, and if you like I can try drafting it. At the moment, I am only concerned about the principle.

Let me know what you think about all this.

More on other matters soon.

Love,

/s Paul

PAB to PMS

Palo Alto, CA
March 5, 1963

Dear Paul,

In re: opus. I have gone carefully over your comments on the psycho stuff, and I think that your suggestions concerning its shortening and reorganizing are very good. I would feel somewhat uneasy about throwing out *all* of the material on methodology of measurement etc. because these matters are in the center of the pertinent literature and we should not simply wind up with the "discovery" that ours is a sick society; this is almost universally granted in one form or another with the big debate concerning primarily the question: did it get worse lately or has it always been that way since Adam. If you have noticed my reference to Goldhamer & Marshall (very respected figures in their trade), who, by the way, not accidentally, I suppose, work for the RAND Corp. — the chief contention of the *status quo* boys is precisely that all this is simply the "human condition" with nothing much to be done about it. The fact that some of this material is, as you say, plain boring (and I was not unaware of it when putting it together!) is no doubt bad, but what can one do about it. If such comparisons should not in themselves indicate a state of mental disorder (megalomania, in this case), there are quite a few pp. in *Capital* that ain't as *spannend* [exciting] as a mystery story. . . . Anyway, I'll try to re-fix it and we'll see how it comes out the next round.

The second question is not whence but whither? There are three topics which I would deal with to conclude QoS II: family, juvenile delinquency, & alcoholism. All of this will be pretty short, and should bring up the QoS II Chapter from its present ca 70 pp. (to be reduced in the process of revising) to, say 85 pp.[172] Again, the question, how to deal with all of this so as to not simply repeat the assertive statements on pp. 167-171 of the Summer MR [1962] issue?[173] It immediately involves going into the ifs and buts of the literature — some of which are worth discussing; others not. Well, I'll see, how it comes out and then we may have to do a revising job. I am sure that most of the trouble is due to my lack of ability; some of it is, however, caused by recalcitrance of the material.

In any case, I would *very* much like to get this whole stuff out of my way; it is not a very gratifying biz, and do the IS [Irrational System] Chapter where all those things should be brought together, structured and interconnected. That is the thing which I really *want* to do and, I would hope, could do a little better.

Now, concerning the Negro section. It surely would be *most important* to have such a discussion included; I only remember that either orally or per correspondence we once decided to state specifically in the Preface or in the Introduction that we are not attempting to deal with everything and therefore among other important topics omit the whole Negro complex. If you think that we have enough to go on to say something substantial on the Negro issue then let us by all means have QoS III on that which would have the clear advantage of protecting us also against a number of critics who would immediately pick on our not paying enough attention to a matter of such tremendous importance. It might call for taking out from preceding sections most references to Negroes and bring them together in that Chapter. What I am only afraid of is that there is such an awful lot of literature in that area that one could easily bog down in it. But if you think that you could compose such a story without too much trouble, you certainly have all my blessings. Attached is by the way an excellent article by Alan Dutscher (do you know who he is? I have come across his name before in connection with something he wrote on American publishing biz.) I also have

172. These plans to extend the "Quality of Monopoly Capitalist Society II" chapter to take into account the issues of family, juvenile delinquency, and alcoholism were never completed. The mental health part of the manuscript for this chapter remained incomplete. This chapter minus the mental health part was eventually published as Paul A. Baran and Paul M. Sweezy, "The Quality of Monopoly Capitalist Society: Culture and Communications," *Monthly Review* 65, no. 3 (July-August 2013): 43–64.

173. Baran is referring to pages 167–71 of the originally published version of "On the Quality of Monopoly Capital Society" in the July-August 1962 issue of *Monthly Review* where various declarative statements about mental health issues such as suicide and juvenile delinquency were made, indicating that social statistics made meaningful historical comparisons impossible, but still allowed generalizations about the growing dimensions of these problems. This brief discussion on the historical problem in dealing with issues of social deviance and mental health was mostly kept intact in the published book. See Baran and Sweezy, *Monopoly Capital*, 281–85.

the (interesting) *Fortune* article to which he refers. If you want me to, I shall send it to you (would prefer not to clip it out of *Fortune*, and sending the whole issue requires a truck).

So this is the state of matters. Before the end of this month you should have the end of QoS II; then on the agenda is IS and somewhere in between one has to do the articles for the Lange-Kalecki volumes.[174] I rec'd a letter from Italy saying that apparently our Sino-Soviet pieces have created an uproar with lots of people pro and con.[175] I would be *most* tempted to do "Some Further Thoughts on the Great Debate," but must control all such emotions and stick to the grindstone. The only joblet which I could not refuse for obvious reasons is a request from JPE to do a review of Milton Friedman's *Capitalism and Freedom*. A most exasperating book and I must do it just to appear, if only rarely, in the pro journals.[176]

All the bestest,
Con amore,
s/ Paul

[…]

PMS to PAB

Larchmont
March 7, 1963

Dear Paul,
[…]
Yours of the 5th arrived by the morning delivery while I was writing the above words of wisdom. It raises large issues which cannot be settled all at once. But I would like to set down a few reactions while they are fresh in mind.

---

174. Baran and Sweezy coauthored essays at this time for two *festschrifts*, one for Oskar Lange and one for Michał Kalecki. The Lange *festschrift* essay was entitled "The Economics of Two Worlds." Reprinted in Paul A. Baran, *The Longer View* (New York: Monthly Review Press, 1969), 68–91. The Kalecki *festschrift* essay was reprinted in *Monthly Review* on the second anniversary of Baran's death (simultaneously with the publication of *Monopoly Capital*): Paul A. Baran and Paul M. Sweezy "Notes on the Theory of Imperialism," *Monthly Review* 17, no. 10 (March 1966): 15–31.
175. Paul A. Baran, "A Few Thoughts on the Great Debate," *Monthly Review* 14, no. 1 (May 1962): 34–45; Paul M. Sweezy, "The 22nd Congress and International Socialism," *Monthly Review* 14, no. 1 (May 1962): 45–53.
176. Paul A. Baran, "On Capitalism and Freedom," *Monthly Review* 42, no. 6 (November 1990): 35–43. Review of Milton Friedman's *Capitalism and Freedom* originally published in *Journal of Political Economy* 71, no. 6 (December 1963): 591–94.

1. Of course you are right that it is of no use merely repeating that this is a sick society. But it seems to me that what is required is not so much a verbatim debate with the specialists as a brief description *in our own words* of the chief issues raised by the specialist literature together with a clear indication of where we stand and why. The opus is after all an "essay" and it is important not to let the proportions get out of whack. We deal very summarily with many of the extremely important problems in the economic and politico-economic areas, often not citing any of the relevant specialist literature, and in my judgment we have to do it that way. The alternative would be to try to write a multi-volume treatise with all the paraphernalia of scholarship trained on each and every important question. But that is not what we want to do. We want to push Marxist thought into some new channels, and that demands that we treat many, many issues within a brief compass. The comparison with *Capital*, in my humble opinion, is not very relevant. Vol. I, to which I assume you refer, deals with a remarkable narrow range of subjects but aims to do so with maximum intensity. Our whole purpose, if I understand it rightly, is a quite different one.

These are the considerations I would recommend you keep in mind in working over mental health and proceeding to family, juvenile delinquency, and alcoholism. As to the Negro problem: I certainly do not want to undertake a whole chapter. I had in mind a relatively brief section, saying the things you say in the relevant sections of the mental health section plus a number of others, mostly things that are obvious and well known to knowledgeable people so that nothing elaborate in the way of documentation would be required. Perhaps what is said elsewhere in the QoS chapters (on Negro income, housing, etc.) should all be removed from their present locations and put together in this section. But in any case, the purpose would not be to attempt anything even faintly approaching a full-dress treatment but simply to give convincing evidence that we are fully aware of the decisive importance of the question and of its relationship to the structure of monopoly capitalism.

2. I am fully *d'accord* in wishing this material completed and in looking forward to your putting the pieces together in the IS chapter. This, as you know, will be in a sense the keystone of the arch.

[…]

Love,

/s Paul

[…]

PMS to PAB

Larchmont

March 9, 1963

Dear Paul,

I've been thinking more about how to handle the Negro question in opus, and
my present tentative inclination is to proceed more or less along the following
lines:

1. Keep the Negro material in as is in the QoS chapters, only not making such
a special issue of it under mental health as is now the case. In other words, point
out under mental health, as under income, housing, etc., that the position of the
Negro is much worse than that of the white, but do not try to do anything else in
that section.

2. Introduce into The Irrational Society [eventually became "Irrational
System"] chapter a special section on the Negro question, the purpose of which
would not be to document how badly off Negroes are but rather to *explain* the
status of Negroes in terms of the central theme of the book, i.e. the increasing
difficulty of surplus absorption under monopoly capitalism.

3. The explanation, as I see it, could stress the following:

a. It is *always* in the interests of a capitalist class to have a divided working
class, since it facilitates exploitation of both (or all) segments, provides a special
"helotry" to do the dirtiest and meanest work (including domestic service),
makes more difficult the formation of serious political opposition, etc. A good
brief theoretical exposition of these matters would be a valuable contribution in
its own right.

b. Taking U.S. history as a whole, probably the chief form of division has
been between native workers and immigrants, with the latter being divided
not only from the former but also among themselves. As long as slavery lasted,
Negroes were confined to one special sector of the economy and were not
available for use in the other, much larger wage-labor sector. After emancipation,
the nature of the political compromise between Northern and Southern ruling
classes (from which both derived great benefits) was such as largely to maintain
the status quo in this regard, with the Negroes remaining a special resource of the
Southern plantation economy.

c. World War I seems to have been the turning point. Manpower needs
opened up opportunities in industry for Negroes, and the sharp curtailment of
immigration created a demand for a continuation of this "internal immigration."
In this connection it has specially to be stressed that white immigration from
abroad provides the basis for only *temporary* divisions in the working class.
The children of immigrants are natives and cannot be so easily discriminated

against, and after two or three more generations the distinctions cease to exist. Not so with Negroes: no matter how many generations pass he cannot change his skin color. From the capitalist point of view, therefore, race is the best basis for discrimination. (Bring in here Mexicans and Puerto Ricans as having similar though not so clear-cut advantages.)

d. The process of replacing the "old" immigrants (who simply evaporated into the native white population) by the "new" colored immigrants was given a big push by two factors: World War II and the agricultural revolution, esp. the cotton picker and other labor-saving devices which drastically reduced the need for Negro field hands in the South.

e. So far we have explained, theoretically and historically, the presence and growing importance of Negroes in the industrial cities. (Incidentally, it would be most interesting to put alongside the by-now well-known figures on the growing Negro populations in Northern cities other not-so-well-known—in fact not at all known to me—figures on the declining immigrant populations in the same cities. I wonder if the two together, as a share of the total, wouldn't remain fairly stable?) Next we have to inquire whether there are at work basic forces making for the improvement of the status of Negroes and the reduction in the severity of discrimination. Here it could be shown, I believe, that the only effective force operating in this way would be a persistent excess of demand for labor power over supply. And this could be empirically supported by the experience of the two war periods, which were notoriously the only periods in which the relative position of Negroes improved.

f. The central thesis of opus, however, is that it is the nature of monopoly capitalism to generate the exact opposite of an excess of demand for labor power over supply. In these circumstances, the only effective force counteracting the powerful urge of capitalists to discriminate — a shortage of labor power — not only is absent but on the contrary a progressively larger labor surplus tends to be generated. Negroes therefore become more and more exploitable, and discrimination tends to increase, not decrease. In the face of this situation, the counteracting power of legislation against discrimination, FEPC's [Fair Employment Practices Commission], etc., etc., is rather small. The net of it is that the relative position of Negroes is actually worsening. The *only* effective remedy is the overthrow of monopoly capitalism.

4. In a final "looking ahead" section, it could be brought out that Negroes, unlike whites, are likely increasingly to reject white U.S. society and to solidarize with the colored majority of the human race. As the latter goes increasingly socialist, U.S. Negroes will do likewise. They will therefore become not only strangers within the gates but also enemies. And we should of course express

100% approval: it is the natural and healthy result of the Negro's coming, in the words of the Manifesto, "to face with sober senses his real conditions of life and his relations with his kind."

I see many advantages in handling the Negro question along these lines and no disadvantages. It would explain what most Americans don't understand and therefore entertain all sorts of illusions about. And it would remedy a big gap (and fault) in the book as we have conceived it up to now and which cannot really be excused by a disclaimer in the Preface. The only thing I wonder about is whether after all this shouldn't be a chapter by itself. If so, I am inclined to think it ought to come right after the historical Chapter (No.8) and to be entitled something like "Monopoly Capitalism and the Negro Question." If you agree, I would like very much to try writing such a chapter. In any case, let me know what you think of the above outline. If it is not to be used for opus, I will some time make an RoM out of it.

[...]

I have just finished reading Zagoria, goaded on by Stanley [Moore] who seemed to think it would cure me of my Chinophilia.[177] It had exactly the opposite effect. The long series of quotations marshalled by our researcher seem to indicate that the Chinese are remarkably level-headed and understand the world situation very well indeed (the slander that they are warmongers, want war to promote socialism, etc., is thoroughly disposed of). The Russkis on the other hand evidently entertain the wildest sort of illusions about what can be got out of imperialism by sweetness and light, about the possibilities of reforms under capitalism, about the possibilities of peaceful accession to power, about the revolutionary potentials of national bourgeoisies, etc. (In Latin America, in my opinion, there is not *one* instance of a national bourgeoisie which has the slightest intention to break with U.S. imperialism.) The Chinese position is not that one should rush headlong into premature revolutions, but it is that one should face realities and cope with them as best you can, with confidence that in the long run a militant revolutionary struggle will pay off much better than finagling and maneuvering. Oh well, I guess I am temperamentally disgusted by reformism, so maybe I am unable to judge these matters on their merits.

Incidentally, the real story of the latest Iraqi coup is truly horrifying and apparently in no small part has its roots in Soviet insistence that the Iraqi CP should play the moderate game.[178] It seems to be Shanghai, 1927, all over again: a terrible bloodbath, with most of the Communists and progressives already

---

177. Donald Zagoria, *The Sino-Soviet Conflict 1956–1961* (Princeton, 1962)
178. In reference to February 1963 overthrow of Iraq's Abd al-Karim Qasim regime.

murdered. What the role of the CIA and the oil companies may have been is not clear, but one suspects the worst. And these new butchers are the bosom pal of Nasser who in turn is the recipient of one of the biggest of Soviet aid programs. Now, from the morning's news, it seems that the whole tragic business is about to be repeated in Syria. It is heartbreaking.

Love,

/s Paul

PMS to PAB

Larchmont

March 21, 1963

Dear Paul,

[…]

Finished over the week-end an RoM on "The Split in the Capitalist World" [*MR*, April 1963]. I'll be interested to know if you think I'm cockeyed. It seems to me like the rejection of the British bid for Common Market entry is the point of no return for de Gaulle and Adenauer and that their successors will not be able to reverse matters — nor will the other partners in the CM. At the bottom of it all is the inevitable drive of European monopoly capitalism to gain its independence of the U.S. yoke and to go on from there to struggle for supremacy in the "free world." I didn't put it that way, but one could easily say that it is simply another proof of the profundity and generality of Lenin's law of uneven development under capitalism. The implications are of course immense, and I don't do more than open up that aspect. Much more thought needs to be given to it, esp. from the point of view of U.S. monopoly capitalism and U.S. imperialism. By the way, do you ever see *Forbes Magazine*, a *Business Week* kind of mag for bizmen? Kenny May sends me clips from it from time to time. The publisher (I suppose), Malcolm S. Forbes, has a page called "Fact and Comment" which seems to be about the keenest stuff coming out of any ruling-class think shop these days. The two pieces of March 1 and 15 entitled respectively "Next on de Gaulle's List: NATO, U.N., U.S." and "South America: Economic Chaos" show more real insight than Walter Lippmann. If you are in the library, look them up and also please get the address and sub price of the mag for me. I have only some odd pages with no details on them. (I'd send them along, but at the moment Leo has them.)

More on other matters later.

Love,

/s Paul

P.S. Bill Wolman of *Business Week* came in last Friday with questions he wanted to clear up about our position, etc. We talked with him for 2-1/2 hours. He says if all goes well the piece should appear in *next* week's mag. i.e. March 29th.

PAB to PMS

Palo Alto, California
March 22, 1963

Dear Paul,

[…]

6. The outline of what needs to be said on the Negro question (your letter of March 9th) looks to me fine. The only thing that I would like to add to what you have there is more attention to the social psychology aspect of the matter. It is, no doubt, true that the ruling class likes to have a divided proletariat and does everything possible to promote such divisions. But as usual in such matters *"halb zog er sie, halb sank sie hin"* [half pulled in, half sunk on her own]. The proletariat is too goddam happy to be divided, in particular on racial lines! Everything that is to be said about nationalism here redoubled. A tremendous solace to people to have someone to be superior to. If I remember right, I wrote to you about this stuff last year from Europe (tidbits, obviously), and now it was interesting to see how the racial relations dominate the British Guiana situation (Vatuk's, otherwise not too good, pamphlet).[179] *En generale*, I think, one ought to stay away from the simple explanation that something is in the interest of the ruling class and therefore it happens. Something's being in the interest of the ruling class is an important but not an exclusive rationale. What is necessary is that this something should meet with some, however generated or developing, propensities of the underlying population. Even if it were *now* in the interest of the American ruling class to present to the world an American democracy completely free of racial discrimination etc., they *could* not produce it, because *by now* they have already a "human nature" to deal with which, to be sure, they themselves created in the course of history. And such deep-seated, phylogenetically analyzable phenomena as revulsion against intermarriage etc. *are made use of* by the ruling class but cannot be simply treated as having been created by it.

All this, obviously, in no contradiction to what you say but merely in supplementation. When it comes to the question of location of that Chapter, my own preference *at this moment and not too strongly* would be to make it into QoS (III) especially stressing that the *locus* of the Negro in this society is something

179. Ved Prakash Vatuk, *British Guiana* (New York: MR Press Pamphlet Series, 1963).

terribly important both for him and for this society, and therefore calls for special treatment, I think this would be more effective than sticking it in after Chapter 8 [the chapter "On the History of Monopoly Capitalism"]. But I am not dogmatic on this issue. The IS ["Irrational System"] Chapter could then also more easily refer back to it in an effort to sum up. What do you think?

[…]

Love,

   s/ Paul

PMS to PAB

                Larchmont

              March 25, 1963

Dear Paul,

[…]

D'accord on the Negro question. The socio-psychological aspect should certainly not be neglected, just as the interest-complex aspect should not be neglected. Together they make the problem the most intractable of all those faced by monopoly capitalism in this country — *absolutely* incapable of being seriously ameliorated, let alone solved, short of a thorough-going social revolution. It is precisely this most unpalatable truth that we must articulate and insist upon. I don't think the location of the chapter really makes much difference. We can judge that better after we have it written.

Have received Chapter 4 ["The Absorption of Surplus: Capitalist Consumption and Investment"] back from Jack with 20 pages of penciled notes accompanying it. No time yet to peruse same. I will be sending him Ch. 6 ["The Absorption of Surplus: Civilian Government"] this week and hope to have 7 ["The Absorption of Surplus: Militarism and Imperialism"] ready by the end of next week. I went through 6 again in the last few days, making a few changes and additions to the ms, and I was relieved to find that it stands up quite well after several months on the shelf. There is some, but really not much, repetition of material treated more fully in QoS(1), relating to education, housing, and highways, but I am now fully convinced that this is in no sense a bad thing and that it would be impossible to establish plausibly the thesis of political barriers to rational government spending if one left the whole argument on an abstract level.

Latest RoM, as I wrote, is on "The Split in the Capitalist World." For May I must grasp the nettle and do one on "The Split in the Socialist World." I'm going to avoid all trace of polemics but at the same time leave no doubt that our position is that *au fond* the Chinese are the true bearers of the Marxist

tradition, which is above all a *revolutionary* tradition and which is now more
than ever before relevant to the condition of the vast majority of mankind.
That the Soviet party has de facto abandoned the revolutionary position, a fact
which I do no think can any longer be seriously disputed, is to be explained,
however, not in terms of "errors," bad leaders, etc., but in Marxist terms. Its
inevitability is the saddest part in a way, and it certainly points to the futility
of denunciation, exhortation, and similar verbal reactions. Pressure from the
Chinese, considerations of political alignments in the world, fear of isolation —
these things may well keep the SU from abandoning the revolution in the udc's
[underdeveloped countries] (vide Cuba), but it is obviously useless to expect the
CPUSSR to be the inspirer and spiritual leader of that revolution. Nor should
the Chinese be put into that position either, though they will certainly do their
part. Fidel is neither the Russians' nor the Chinese' man, and there is no reason
to suppose that in historical terms Fidel is a unique phenomenon. But I must get
back to work on opus. . . .

    Love,
        /s Paul

[. . .]

PAB to PMS

                                        Palo Alto
                             March 26th, 1963

Dear Paul,
Thanks for your yesterday's letter. I had yesterday a talk with [Kenneth] Arrow
and told him that I ain't not going to do the Graduate Director job anymore.[180]
Apart from the misery that it involves, I can see no worldly reason why the lowest
paid member of the staff should carry the responsibility. He said that I had a
point, that on the other hand if one wants to be a revolutionary one ought to
be prepared to pay a price for it . . . I observed that if the University considers
it proper to pay me 3-4 thousand $ less than the youngest prof in our Dept.
because of political considerations, it should also not entrust me such a major
responsibility as the selection of grad students because I would pick exclusively
communists, anarchists and other revolutionaries. He agreed that I had a point
there too. So all this is being reported by him now to Moe who is in Paris and

---

180. PAB had been assigned the position of "Graduate Director," which primarily involved
reviewing the applications of prospective graduate students. I remember well sitting at my father's
dining room table helping him sort stacks of graduate student applications.

who will be our permanent chairman beginning next year. All this *mamusing*:
either I'll get rid of the job or at least they'll be "seized" with the problem.

[...]

5. Be careful with what you write in RoM about the Soviet Union; matters
there are very complicated with lots of opposing pushes and pulls (reflects itself
now in the Soviet press quite clearly). As usual in CPSU politics they are zigging
and zagging, and I would avoid statements including the word "definitely." If
after having written the RoM there is still time, and if you want to, send me the
MS for what possible suggestions I may have.

6. The Chinese take *verbally* a much better position, whether *de facto* it
comes to something much different, that is where the dog is buried. I do not
agree that the Sino-Indian dispute is *the* acid test. I think I wrote about it before,
but I would think that they may have made a *tactical* mistake. They should have
raised much more hell about it, bring the matter before the Security Council, ask
the SU for its good offices as an intermediary, etc., etc., *before* doing anything.
In my opinion, it is *strictly irrelevant* who was right and who was wrong in the
matter. On that there is no doubt. But even if the South-Koreans did actually
invade North-Korea, the thing to do was not to fall into the trap but to throw
them out and yell bloody murder! I think the Chinese did fall into a provocation
— and by doing so did lots of harm to the Indian CP &c. But this is a long topic
and I think should be treated very gingerly. There is probably nothing harder at
the moment than avoiding falling into one or the other grove [grave?]. And it is a
hell of a thing to have a correct "general line."

7. By the way, concerning the Split in the Cap World, have a look at Joe's
[Stalin's] *Economic Problems*. The sob predicted that particular development
very precisely, even if he went too far assuming that the imperialists begin
fighting each other arms in hands. That booklet of his was a brilliant job, much
as he ought to fry in hell for all he did and in particular for all he left behind.

Love,

/s Yours Paul

PMS to PAB

Larchmont
March 29, 1963

Dear Paul,

[...]

The Rostow boys [Eugene and Walt Rostow] may be succeeding in getting
some serious reform in Iran — I don't know. But they ain't not doing it in Latin
America, which is much more important. I only began to understand why no

land reforms worthy of the name get adopted down there on this last trip. The reason is that there simply isn't any separate landowning class: all the talk about feudalism is not only wrong but thoroughly misleading. The same class owns money capital, industrial capital, *and* land. The tenure systems often have more than a little of feudalism remaining, which is one reason why reforms are so much needed, but the owners are typically bourgeois. When you ask for land reform, you ask the bourgeoisie to reform itself, not to take something away from a parasitic landowning class. And needless to say, the bourgeoisie is not exactly enthusiastic. It is not, incidentally, a terribly, businesslike bourgeoisie and readily tolerates irrational practices inherited from the past, but that doesn't make it a feudal nobility. All of this needs to be documented and proved, which unfortunately I have neither the time nor the language ability to undertake. Until it is understood, all sorts of illusions about the possibility of anti-feudal reform (bourgeois revolution) are going to persist in Latin America. All that is sheer mythology manufactured out of textbooks dealing with the quite different historical problems of Europe.

On the subject of land reform, by the way, get Saul Landau to tell you about what has happened to the Laguna district in Mexico which started off in Cardenas's time as the showpiece of land reform on the basis of the *ejido* [communal land]. Saul is down there doing some sort of a movie and wrote us a bit about it. Seems the whole thing is a disastrous failure: I had heard something about the debacle but had no idea it was as bad as he describes it. The moral of the Mexican experience would seem to be that *bourgeois* land reform imposed on a *peasant* agriculture may secure important political gains for the party in power but solves absolutely nothing economically. The only successful part of the Mexican agricultural program is in the North where U.S.-style capitalist farming, producing export crops, has taken hold. But in the nature of the case this can affect only a very small part of the rural population.

[...]

I would like to send you the RoM and will do so provided it gets done in time. The trouble is that I usually don't get to it until the last minute and have to rush through with Leo and the printer breathing down my neck. Maybe I'll be able to do better this time. At bottom, my interpretation of the Soviet position is based more on what I have a strong intuitive feeling "must be so" than on any particular documents or statements. I don't see how a country that is in one sense still poor but has all the material requisites (including the appropriate social institutions) for overcoming this poverty could possibly be revolutionary in the sense that Marx and Lenin were revolutionary. The Russians' problem is not to overthrow capitalism or anything else, and they cannot be expected to put

themselves in the shoes of the peoples of the udc's [underdeveloped countries].
The Chinese are in a wholly different objective situation, and there is nothing
more natural than for them to be 100 percent revolutionary. I spent yesterday
reading the Chinese tract entitled "More on the Differences between Comrade
Togliatti and Us: Some Important Problems of Leninism in the Contemporary
World," 199 pages long and written by the editorial department of *Honggi*. It is
absolutely pure Leninism and an extremely able performance.

I don't say that Leninism solves all the problems. It didn't even in Lenin's
time: the theory of the labor aristocracy as the basis of the Social Democratic
betrayal was always very weak and is much more so now than ever before. (The
Chinese might, but do not, apply it to Togliatti and the French and Italian CP's:
it is a weakness of their position that they do not attempt to explain the roots
of "modern revisionism.") But I am convinced that *vis-a-vis the udc's* Leninism
is absolutely correct and "modern revisionism" disastrously wrong. With the
udc's being increasingly the focus and center of the international revolutionary
movement, this means that the Chinese have an unbeatable advantage. Perhaps
the Chinese challenge will push the Russians into a Leninist position themselves,
but I doubt it. "Modern revisionism" is no accident and cannot be sloughed off
with an apologetic "excuse it, please."

What the Chinese say, by the way, is unlikely to make much impression
on Togliatti who, I am sure, knows the Leninist texts as well as the Chinese
comrades. He has a mass party that ain't not interested in making no revolutions,
and he's got to figure out some way to keep the thing together. He either *has* to
be a reformist, whatever verbiage may be used to disguise the fact, or else go into
the wilderness. The Chinese have no answers for him, and their references to
new awakenings, etc., in the European and American working classes only go
to show that they don't know what's going on in these parts of the world. The
truth is that these working classes are now, for both economic and psychological
reasons, pretty solidly lined up with their bosses against the udc's. It's a lousy
spot for a Togliatti to be in.

On this subject, have you been reading *France Observateur?* Martinet and
Mallet are in the process of elaborating a "theory" which is probably intended
to give some intellectual respectability to a position not unlike Togliatti's (neo-
reformism for neo-capitalism). I wouldn't be at all surprised to see this current
take hold in the French CP, with Martinet & Co. joining up again in due course
and becoming the ideological pooh-bahs. In the meantime, Bourdet has

broken with M (all the rest of the staff is with M) and seems to be out of F-O altogether.[181]

I suppose one might (perhaps ought to) ask what kind of a line does make sense in a developed capitalist country if Leninism seems pretty irrelevant and modern revisionism is really nothing but a modern version of Kautskyism. But that's not for this letter. . . .

One final point: I am somewhat distressed about the apparently deep difference between us on the Sino-Indian dispute. The Chinese *did* yell bloody murder about what the Indians were doing from 1959 on. The trouble is that no one paid any attention. *Of course* the capitalist press distorted the whole business, but the Soviet attitude was also unfriendly. You should remember that the first border clash took place in November, 1959, and was certainly not the fault of the Chinese. Khrushchev was then at or near Camp David, apparently seriously and sincerely under the impression that he could come to an agreement with Ike for a *modus vivendi* plus disarmament. Chi, when we talked to him in Mexico, was convinced that the Soviet plague-on-both-your-houses statement which was issued at the time was a sop to Eisenhower, and it makes good sense. In any case, the Chinese felt, and I think rightly, that they were being badly let down by their ally. How could they turn around and ask the SU for its offices as intermediary? The fact is that they were alone, and there was not a damn thing they could do to bring *political* pressure on the Indians. Under the circumstances, they showed a very great deal of patience and forbearance, allowing the Indians to push them around for the next two years. I don't know whether they were right to act when they did, but it is clear to me that no self-respecting socialist nation can permit itself to be walked on and spat at indefinitely. When they finally did act, they absolutely did not commit the mistake of the North Koreans. They smacked the Indians down hard and then withdrew. This was a classic case of war as a continuation of politics: it had nothing to do with acquisition of territory or any nonsense like that. Nor am I impressed by the damage done to the Indian CP: any CP that is willing to play the rotten game of its own bourgeoisie, as the Indian apparently has been, had better have a crisis like this and find out what is deadwood and what is serious revolutionary cadres. It will be a better party in the long run. As for the udc's and neutralists, the plain fact is that they did not rally to India's support, and the Colombo plan concedes all that the Chinese have been claiming. The trouble is that the Indians absolutely will not negotiate.

---

181. Handwritten footnote by Sweezy: Needless to say, Bourdet did not break with Martinet because of a principled revolutionary position, but rather because of a muddle-loaded romantic anti-de Gaulle attitude. As between M + B, M is undoubtedly in a much stronger position.

This seems to me to be about as clear a case as any I know of where real socialists have no choice but to back the right side!

Love,

/s Paul

PAB to PMS

[*Memo precedes letter dated March 31, 1963, on one page.*]

Memo:

Sol writes from Peking that Engels wrote a series of articles in *Vorwaerts* in 1893 under the title "*Kann Europa Abruesten?*"[182] These were published, he says, in a collection of Engels' stuff called *Kapitalistisches Wettruessten*, Leipzig, 1929 [Capitalist arms race], which he has never seen (and which I never heard of). The only place it can actually be found now, he thinks, is the Russian *Sochinenya*. If you have ready access, you might look the item up. Perhaps it has more than passing interest under present conditions. (Sol surmises that Engels must have taken the position that disarmament is impossible under capitalism, but he doesn't know. Clearly that is the present Chinese position, and I'm afraid I go along with it. Interesting to know if the old boy already said it all.)

March 31, 1963

Yesterday arrived Vol. XXII of *Sochinenya* (the corresponding volume of the German *Werke* hasn't come out yet) which contains the series of articles referred to above [Engels, *Can Europe Disarm?* (1893)]. It so happens that Engels' position is *strictly the reverse* of what Adler surmises. The articles contain various interesting observations on the nature of standing armies, but their principal argument is summarized in the following paragraphs at the beginning.

(1) From the Preface: "I start in these articles from the following assumption which increasingly gains general acceptance: the system of permanent armies has been driven all over Europe to such an extreme, that either peoples will be economically ruined by it being unable to stand the burdens of military" expenditures, or it will lead inevitably to a general war of extermination — unless the permanent armies will be transformed in good time into militias based on the general armament of the people."

(2) Also from the Preface: "I shall attempt to prove that such a transformation is possible even now, even with contemporary governments and in the contemporary political situation."

---

182. Frederick Engels, *Can Europe Disarm?* (1893), Karl Marx and Frederick Engels, *Collected Works* (New York: International Publishers, 1975), vol. 27, 367–93.

(3) From Article #1 : "I assert: disarmament, and *eo ipso* a guarantee of peace, is possible; it is even comparatively easily attainable and Germany more than any other civilized state has for it the possibility and the historical opportunity." (The last two words freely translated.)

The interesting prediction which was borne out is contained in Article # 8 where Engels argues that the outcome of the next war will be decided by Britain, the fleet of which will be able to starve out Germany. But this point is not at issue here.— In this series of articles Engels' "swing to the right" towards the end of his life is probably as pronounced as anywhere, and the tone of the pieces is very . . . Khrushchovian.

The volume contains other *very* interesting material which I have never seen before — an interview of Engels given to *News Chronicle* — about which I will write at some other occasion.

/s Paul

PAB to PMS

Palo Alto
April 2, 1963

Dear Paul,
Your letter of March 29th and pp. for Chapter 7 duly arrived. First a few words about the latter. During my Los Angeles Disarmament debates (end of January) and also a few days ago from a (brilliant) lecture by our physicist Panofsky (member of the Pres. Sc. Adv. Board), it has become entirely clear to me that *no one* (some John Birchers perhaps to the contrary) believes in the danger of a *Soviet attack on the United States*. Even the principal opponent of mine in LA, a man from RAND, conceded this point right at the outset of the discussion. The argument which they all advance is now somewhat different: what is at issue, they say, is not the threat of the Soviet attack *hic and nunc*, but two other matters:

(1) *Would* there be such a danger in absence of a major military build-up on the part of the U.S., or is the absence of that danger the *result* of the U.S. overwhelming military might? The answer that it is not in the nature of socialist societies to launch aggressive war sounds not overly convincing (neither to the opponents themselves or — as I found out — to the audiences). Indeed, it presupposes their acceptance of a theory which they either do not know or explicitly reject. They immediately point at some (probably unguarded and ill-considered) remarks of Khrushchev that Stalin might have started another war, etc., etc.

(2) — And perhaps even more important — the existence of the U.S. military potential — they say — is what preserves the American Empire and prevents Soviet direct or indirect aggression in the rest of the free world. There the

position is complex, and probably not altogether meaningless. The RAND man
for instance went to some lengths arguing that Moscow's present position of not
encouraging local CP's to take power where such take-over's might be possible is
precisely due to Khruschev's et al mortal fear of an atomic holocaust (this is kind
of a modern version of *"vis pacem, para bellum"* [if you want peace prepare for
war]). Iraq is cited in that context, not unjustifiably, I think, and there are enough
passages in Sino-Soviet documents to support *this* contention. If the U.S. were
disarmed or poorly armed, they argue, all kinds of countries would "blow up,"
with or without Soviet help, and all the U.S. could do is to send notes of protest.
In this way, the U.S. armaments *are* a powerful counter-revolutionary force which
not only keeps various countries in their place in the free world, but also pushes
the Soviet Union into a less revolutionary, more rightist position.

Needless to say, this view can be amply supported by statements from all
sides, incl. those of Togliatti and others in the West. Therefore, I think, that while
the argument on the relevant pp of Chapter VII is absolutely correct (no danger
of Soviet Union attack on the United States), it amounts at this stage to not much
more than "forcing an open door." It can and should stay the way you have it,
but needs, I think, to be supplemented by a critique of the line of reasoning
referred to under (2) above. Here, it would seem to me, what I perhaps not too
felicitously called the "social order imperialism" is of the utmost relevance. In
the volume of Engels about which I reported yesterday there is a nice passage
where he says that all those standing armies are needed not so much for the
defense against an outside enemy as for the defense against the internal class
enemy. This is obviously nothing new, but what occurred to me is that we have
now a very interesting extension of that idea: as the class struggle has moved over
to the international arena, Engels' observation applies *mutatis mutandis* ["with
necessary changes" or "accounting for present circumstances"] with redoubled
force. But this *mutatis mutandis* must be brought out clearly. The internal class
enemy is no longer primarily the working class at home (although France at
the moment is not to be entirely neglected) but the recalcitrant or potentially
recalcitrant country in the free world. . . .

(2) I am completely *d'accord* with you on the *amalgamation* of the feudal
and bourgeois interests in the u/d c's [underdeveloped countries]. This
amalgamation is both economic and political with the latter cemented by
common fear of the "third force." I have been arguing this point for a long time
and I am convinced that this is the principal flaw of the Rostow-Meiji Restoration

doctrine.[183] One might say, and this links this up with the preceding page, that
the U.S. military might could possibly serve to *allay* this fear of socialism taking
advantage of any possible split within the ruling coalition. The amalgamation
has reached different degrees of "chemical intensity" in different countries.
You take Malaya, for instance, where it is complete. In Latin America there are
differences apparently from country to country. In Iran the amalgamation is
least pronounced with the landowning aristocracy and the merchants being
distinctly separate groups. The interesting question is whether there where
the amalgamation is not perfect, the Rostow line might have a chance. Where
the "Prussian Way" *is* complete, it is indeed a tough one to demand from the
bourgeoisie to overthrow itself.

[…]

(4) I don't think that there is a serious difference between us on the Sino-
Indian border problem. I am just not as familiar with the facts as you are. But I
still believe that the Chinese did not make as much use of the existing machinery
for rousing world opinion as they could have done. You say "how could they
turn around and ask the Soviet Union for its offices as intermediary?" I don't
know all the facts, but I still would say, they *could*. And if Khrushchev should
have refused, their position would be ever so stronger in the Great Debate. I
think they could have forced the appointment of some kind of an international
control commission a la Laos — and all this would have extremely strengthened
their hand as well as the hand of the Indian CP &c. What I am not impressed
by (and consider to be an "ultra-left deviation") is the argument that "no
self-respecting socialist nation can permit itself to be walked on and spat at
indefinitely." The operative word is indefinitely and the question is what and
where is the *casus belli*. This is not an issue in "dignity," and "pride," but an
issue in tactics. Lenin's willingness to "crouch on his belly through mud" is very
relevant here, and you know as well as I do that the argument concerning the
dignity of the young socialist republic played a major role in the debates around
Brest-Litovsk. Don't misunderstand me: I am not advocating this "crouching"
as a matter of principle, it depends on the [circumstances] and therefore on

---

183. Baran is referring to Walt W. Rostow's U.S. foreign policy role with respect to the 1963
coup in Iraq, as well as alluding to his famous argument in *The Stages of Economic Growth*, which
became the basis of U.S. counter-revolutionary development doctrines. Walt Rostow and his
brother Eugene were advisers in the Kennedy administration (and subsequently the Johnson
administration). Baran and Eric J. Hobsbawm wrote a critique of Rostow's *Stages of Economic
Growth* which was published under that title in *Kyklos* in 1961 and was reprinted under the title "A
Non-Communist Manifesto" (the subtitle of Rostow's book) in Baran, *The Longer View* (New York:
Monthly Review Press, 1969), 52–67.

the judgment about them. From reading the *small* version of the anti-Togliatti statement, I have among some others the impression that one of the dogs (certainly not all of them) is buried in the statement that the socialist camp has (or should attain: not quite clear to me) overwhelming nuclear superiority. What gives them that idea?

But all this is a large topic, and I'll write on it more later. The funny thing is that this is in my recollection the first case where I am apparently, if ever so slightly, to the right of you. You have once remarked that you have a social democrat and I have a Stalinist "deviation." Both our positions have shifted, I think, but your original observation certainly no longer holds: at least on this issue. I'd like to do a piece on "Some further thoughts on the great debate," and shall try it as soon as time permits. Or rather, as soon as my lousy productivity coefficient permits.

[…]
Love,
        /s Yours Paul

PMS to PAB

                                                    Larchmont
                                                    April 4, 1963
Dear Paul,
A quickie in reply to yours of the day before yesterday (1) before I settle down to the day's work, and (2) while the contents are fresh in mind.

I entirely agree with the analysis on p. 1 relative to the importance of the U.S. military establishment as a deterrent to Soviet assistance to revolutions in the empire. This point is implied if not actually spelled out on pp. 35 (beginning with the last paragraph) - 38. Have a look at that section and see if it takes care of the matter, and if not give some thought as to how to remedy the deficiency without too much recasting of the whole argument.

I'm glad we "march together" in re the feudal-bourgeois amalgamation problem. I am convinced that this is an absolutely crucial *punkt*. When we get opus out of the way, maybe we should consider doing something on (or including) the subject.

[…]

Apparently our positions on the Indo-china border problem are not so far apart as I had feared. I do not, by the way, rest any part of my argument on matters of national pride and the like. The point is that if a socialist country allows itself to be pushed around by reactionaries, it is certain to get a lot more pushing around. On this point, I think the Chinese are absolutely right. I am under the impression that you are considerably overestimating the extent to which the Chinese are in a position to reach and appeal to world opinion by diplomatic and propaganda methods. With the press of both the "free world" and the Soviet-controlled part of the socialist world against them, there is not much they can do to arouse world opinion.

I guess you are right that I have been moving steadily to the Left in recent times. The reason, I think, is that "life itself" has torn the mask off of bourgeois democracy and imperialism in a way that, for me at any rate, no amount of descriptive and theoretical literature could ever do. Cuba and Latin America, about which I think I really have some reliable knowledge now, have been a wonderful school (I include U.S. imperialism's policies towards LA among the best teachers). When I read what the Chinese have to say about imperialism, the state, revolution, etc., I find myself saying time and again: "This is the plain truth, and I know it because I've seen it with my own eyes."

[…]

Love,

    /s Paul

PAB to PMS

Palo Alto

April 13, 1963

Dear Paul,

[…]

Just as I finished typing the above sentence, the mailman came and delivered the April 13th issue of *Business Week*.[184] with the write-up on us. Much of the story is vulgarization *cum* outright distortion (that Marx did not foresee concentration of industry (!!) or that after 1900 "the big growth of consumer demands shifts from goods to services"), but on the whole it is ok. As they say on Madison Avenue: never mind what they say about you as long as they spell the

---

184. "Viewing U.S. Economy with a Marxist Glass," *Business Week*, April 13, 1963. The article featured the views of Baran, Huberman, and Sweezy (and the role of *Monthly Review*).

names right. Curious, what the effect will be: possibly a few additional sub's to MR + a new wave of mail in the President's office. So far, so good.[185]

[. . .]

As far as the April RoM is concerned, I have some reservations, primarily concerning the end of the article. Quite apart from the point which I never understood why trade *per se* should be a major boon to imperialist countries (unless it amounts to exports for gold or capital exports), I have the feeling that you underestimate the terribly important *negative* significance to the socialist camp of rearmament. In spite of all their fears with regard to Washington, I think the Russians are more (and rightly so) afraid of the German *revanchism* and figure that whatever may be the splits within the imperialist bloc, those splits would disappear when it comes to an anti-Soviet war.

Indeed, you don't believe, do you, that the collapse of the Grand Design would go so far as to lead the U.S. into neutrality if the Germans should manage to drag the Common Market countries into an atomic adventure against the Soviet Union? The difference between now and 1941 would be that the USA would be on the German side! I fully agree with your analysis of the existing split; I ain't sure whether the conclusions that you draw are equally warranted. Why should all this "lessen the purely military pressure on the socialist countries"? By the way, Moscow's obviously super-nervous reaction to a possible "atomization" of the Germans would indicate that they take a much less sanguine view of that turn of events. I think, they prefer to deal with Washington to dealing with the Bonn-Paris axis.

[. . .]

Love,

    /s Paul

185. Handwritten footnote by Baran: What comes to mind when reading the *Business Week* write-up is how even being a Marxist becomes "racketized" in this society. Together with the rest of the social critics a la [Gerald] Piel, [W.H.] Ferry, et al, we are being "incorporated" in the Establishment as living proof of its liberalism and freedom. Cf. last sentence [see below]. Gives one the creeps and a feeling that one gets paid for being the "exhibition goy" just as Ralph Bunche and Arthur Lewis serve as its exhibition negroes. There is — *ex definisme* — no exit from a circle that is vicious. [Last paragraph of *Business Week*: "Basically, though, it isn't such theoretical inconsistencies in the views of the Marxists that anger other economists. Rather, it is their willingness to praise countries that have abridged political freedom in the name of economic progress — including the freedom of the anti-Marxist counterparts of Sweezy, Baran, and Huberman."]

PMS to PAB

Larchmont
April 15, 1963

Dear Paul,

[...]

The *Business Week* thing irritates me, but, as you say, it may be better to be noticed, even if the notice is mostly distortion, than to be totally ignored. I'm not sure. At any rate the pictures are excellent..

[...]

The differences over the RoM are interesting and reflect at bottom, I think, different estimates of the relative importance of the capitalist-socialist contradiction on the one hand and the inter-imperialist contradictions on the other. You tend to think the former is overriding; I think the latter can easily come to take priority. Naturally, the Soviet Union raises bloody hell about the Germans' getting nuclear weapons, but all the same I do not believe in Bonn's "dragging the Common Market countries into an atomic venture against the Soviet Union." I don't believe any of them are going to start atomic wars, and I specially don't believe that the German Big Boys are going to commit suicide by bashing their heads against the eastern wall. There is much more profit to be had elsewhere, and for that one needs a quiet rear, which the USSR will be only too glad to provide. Did you read Acheson's speech at Berkeley a month or so ago? There speaks the true voice of U.S. imperialism: he tells De Gaulle, Adenauer, etc., to drop their foolish plans for independent policies, forces, etc., and get on with the business, *which is German unification*. If he can force them to accept that conception of their task, then they do indeed have to accept U.S. overlordship. But I don't think they will accept it — not after they have got everything they think they can out of the U.S., and that time is now fast approaching.

For the rest, increased trade will inevitably turn into capital export. Capitalists hungry for orders don't think in such terms; they take the orders where they can get them. But they find that they have to extend better and better terms, which means longer payment terms, lower prices, etc., and here capital export does enter the picture. Or they go to their govt's for export subsidies, and here again capital export enters the picture by the back door.

Incidentally, I was much interested to find that the Chinese estimate of the situation seems remarkably close to my line. *NB* the statement: "In terms of the actual interests of the imperialist powers, these contradictions and clashes (among themselves and between the metropolises and the underdeveloped countries) are more pressing, more direct, more immediate than their contradictions with the socialist countries." Etc. (*More on the Differences*, p. 50.) And see the excellent piece, "Rapid Disintegration of the Imperialist Bloc," *Peking Review*, March 1.

What has to be understood, I think, is that U.S. anti-Communism, while of course genuine enough, is first and foremost the screen behind which U.S. imperialism seeks to bring the whole "free world" under its control. Mao pointed this out in his 1946 interview with Anna Louise Strong, a brilliant insight for that time.

More on this and other matters later. Must get to work now.

Love,

/s Paul

PAB to PMS

Palo Alto
April 19, 1963

Dear Paul,

There is apparently a number of points on which we do not see eye to eye, and I think the time is ripe for a Summit Meeting at which those matters could be "ironed out."

1. I indeed do believe that the capitalist-socialist antagonism is *the* antagonism of the epoch overshadowing all conflicts and tensions that exist within the imperialist camp. This is not to deny that the U.S. ruling class has made full use of anti-Communism to carry out a comprehensive *Gleichschaltung* [bringing into line] both at home and abroad (having learned a lot from the experience of Hitler & Goebbels), but I believe that — as different from the Nazi's — the American *Gleichschaltung's* [indoctrination or accepting party line] effort was on the whole successful. By comparison with that success, frictions like those between Washington & Paris, between Paris & London, &c., &c. are minor ripples on the surface which are definitely of secondary importance and which would disappear over night if it came to a *major* confrontation between the socialist and the imperialist camps.

Where the differences, I believe, are important is the area of military strategy. There, indeed, the European imperialists have played a restraining role in Washington, simply because they sit in the very first front line and would have to pay the highest price for a possible outbreak of hostilities. Thence their traditionally moderating influence in Washington, and thence I think the desire of de Gaulle to gain some elbow room so as to gain more influence in the NATO councils and to have a voice in the overall strategy vs the socialist camp. Playing all this up into major contradictions within the imperialist camp seems to me to be factually wrong and politically unwise. The overestimation of these contradictions lends support to an underestimation of the present power of the imperialist bloc and by implication encourages the "paper tiger" attitude.

The chief difficulty as far as I can see for the socialist camp is the old problem: how much can one bend without breaking? This is not so much a question of those intra-imperialist contradictions as the question of the appraisal of the overall capacity and willingness of the imperialist coalition to take the risk of a global war (as Kennedy put it during the Cuba crisis) in connection with any one specific issue. A correct appraisal of that is as important as it is prohibitively difficult. It can be said now with 100% justification: look at what happened in Iraq as a result of the Russians' being afraid to get into a *casus belli*! What happened *is* terrible. Are you or is anyone else so 100% certain that a Communist takeover in Iraq (which I understand *was* possible) would not have led to a military intervention on the part of the imperialist coalition or that that intervention would have failed? It could be said that if such an attitude should be adopted there would be never an opportunity for a revolution. I don't think so. It all depends on the case, on the time, on the place, on the extent of imperialist interests involved, on the strength of the popular movement and so forth. Cuba is not Guatemala and Brazil certainly wouldn't be a Guatemala. On the other hand, Iraq might well have been a Korea or a Vietnam. In other words: what is involved is not a question of principle but a question of a specific judgment, and this to my mind all-important fact is somehow lost in the Chinese statements which do treat the matter as a theoretical issue rather than as an issue in immediate appraisal of the situation and of tactics appropriate there etc.

2. This brings me to the Chinese documents [articles in *Peking Review* sent by PMS] which I have read by now. Although they contain a number of propositions which I would wholly accept (in particular in the parts devoted to Togliatti's essential acceptance of Strachey'ism), I must confess to be unable to understand your characterization of that material as being of high quality and "ably" put together.[186] It strikes me rather as being scholastic, arguing matters on an abstract level where a concrete discussion would be in order, and in parts as outright nonsensical. The latter applies in particular to the chapter on War and Peace where I find their playing around with the terms "ruins" (pp.76 & 77) particularly obnoxious. They surely understand no worse than we do that the "ruins of the feudal order" or the "ruins of capitalism" about which Engels and Lenin spoke are something different from the ruins that would be produced by a thermonuclear war. Whom are they kidding?

---

186. The reference here is to John Strachey, British social democrat.

Again, this does not mean that the socialist movement has to fold up under the imperialist atomic blackmail, but it does mean that a number of things have to be thought about rather than handled by citing a few more or less fitting paragraphs from the writings of the masters. Indeed, isn't it quite obvious that when it comes to tactical problems one can prove absolutely everything by citations simply because Marx and in particular Lenin being master-tacticians shifted horses and arguments as conditions changed (rightly so, to be sure!) Depending on the time period you pick, you will find in the scriptures all the arguments that you need. The problem therefore is obviously the analysis of the time period one is in; that analysis may suggest the suitable analogy.

[...]

Love,

/s Yours Paul

PMS to PAB

Larchmont

April 22, 1963

Dear Paul,

[...]

I agree with you that the section dealing with building on the ruins of the old society is the weakest in the Chinese tract. But I do not see how one can read any great importance into it.

What they say about real, man-eating tigers; the need to take the enemy seriously tactically; the necessity of compromises which do not involve abandonment of principle — these are all indications of a perfectly sober and realistic attitude and mood, and are perfectly compatible with what you say about the necessity of judging every specific situation individually and in the light of all relevant conditions. But this kind of "tactical pragmatism" (which of course has been a quality possessed by every good Marxist) must absolutely not — in my humble opinion — become an excuse for neglecting, still less throwing overboard, basic theory. And that is precisely what Khrushchev, Togliatti et al are doing. What kind of nonsense is it to believe that imperialists are going to disarm, that fundamental "structural reforms" can be achieved under capitalism, that ruling classes are going to be cowed by constitutions and parliamentary majorities??? Again in my humble opinion, the Chinese are absolutely right to be horrified by this mishmash and to attack it with all available intellectual weapons. This is the heart and soul of the "Great Debate" and to divert attention from it by calling attention to secondary and largely irrelevant weaknesses in the Chinese case is a disservice.

On the Iraq question: let us suppose that the CPI [Communist Party of Iraq] could have seized power and actually did so and that the U.S. and Britain had marched in. Does that mean that the Russians should also have marched in? Not at all. The CPI is not, or at any rate should not be, an arm of the Soviet state. There can be no doubt, I think, that military occupation by the imperialists would have stirred up an Algerian-type resistance which would have involved the whole Arab world in a genuine anti-imperialist struggle. As it is now, the revolutionary movement in the whole region is being stamped out and a "neutralist" bourgeoisie is, objectively speaking, becoming the perfect instrument of U.S. domination.

I do not think the socialist countries ought to get militarily involved in the struggle between the imperialist countries and their victims. *NB*, for example, that the Chinese keep strictly out of South Vietnam and in fact have at no time mixed into revolutions or imperialist counter-revolutions. In the long run, I believe the imperialists are going to break their heads trying to hold the whole world down, just as the French did in Vietnam and Algeria, and I think the socialist camp must confine their aid to the underdeveloped countries to nonmilitary means. I do not hesitate to draw logical conclusions from this position, either: after the Cubans have been trained to use the weapons that have been supplied to them, the Soviet Union should withdraw *all* Soviet military personnel. It is true that the U.S. may go ahead and attack Cuba and occupy the island. It is horrible to contemplate but it would not be a world war, and in the long run I am convinced it would be the costliest pyrrhic victory in the history of the world.

[...]
Love,
/s Paul

PAB to PMS

Palo Alto
April 24, 1963

Dear Paul,
I am sorry that you do not want to come out in June although I understand your reasons.

What I understand less well is the irritated tone in which you reply to my remarks on the Sino-Soviet problem. If you have not thrown away my letter or April 19th, you can see there that I explicitly accept the Chinese strictures against what I call "Togliatti's essential acceptance of Strachey'ism." It goes without saying that what is involved is not merely Togliatti's position but also

that of Khrushchev and of the CCCPSU. But why do you drag in this issue on
which there is *no* disagreement in the discussion of the question on which there
apparently *is* disagreement? And disagreement exists — it would seem — on the
correctness of the Chinese appraisal of the United States' policy as well as on the
strategy of revolution in the u/d c's [underdeveloped countries]. There, I submit,
we apparently judge matters differently. I do not for a minute believe that in the
current stage of the world's history, the USSR could simply stand by and watch
the U.S. occupying Iraq after a social revolution has taken place there or for that
matter watch the U.S. invading Cuba without doing anything about it. Your
reference to China's "non-intervention" in South-Vietnam is completely beside
the point; there is a civil war going on and there is no danger of North Vietnam
being overrun by the Southerners or by the U.S. (at least not at the moment).
When such a danger did exist, namely in Korea, the Chinese intervened and
intervened promptly (and correctly!).

At the present time, more than ever before, the class struggle *is* an
international struggle, and I cannot understand at all your references to any
CP's being in the "arms of the Soviet state." Even this vocabulary strikes me as
extraordinary. . . . In my humble view, every revolution today necessarily involves
both camps *in toto*, to believe that every country can and will go its own way
without involving others is out-Tito-ing Tito. I am absolutely *d'accord* with
the Chinese and with you that betting on the so-called national bourgeoisie's
"neutrality" is mad, but — again — why do you bring up a point on which we
have *no* dispute when what is at issue is the foreign policy of the socialist camp
on which there *is* a dispute? At no time did I believe that the Soviet policy of
"neutralization" made much sense, while you actually held the opposite. Now,
I am afraid, you fall into the ultra-left aberration of holding that all of them,
Nasser and Toure, Nehru and Thant are "one reactionary mass" which has to
be dealt with indiscriminately. What is more, each of them should be allowed
to deal with his own revolution on his own terms. There I would say, that if and
when and where an intervention *is* possible it should be undertaken *provided*
that it should *not* lead to a world war. Your position would lead (as it has led)
to a condemnation of Hungary, as well as to a condemnation of Korea, to a
condemnation of military help to Cuba etc., etc.

Although it is obviously your undisputed privilege to consider my
observations on the Chinese position as referring to "secondary and largely
irrelevant weaknesses," and as being a "disservice," and although it is your even
less disputed privilege to run MR as you please, I do resent not being even
given an answer as to whether I could present my views on the matter in an MR
article. To be sure, silence *is* an answer, and I am not that obtuse that I could not

understand it; I still believe that it would not have imposed an undue burden on you to explain to me why an article of mine on what is at the moment *the* most important problem of the socialist movement could not find room in the June MR issue. Mind you, it could very well be that you have enough material for and no space in the June issue; this is not what I am talking about. What I am talking about is your not even bothering to tell me on what grounds you consider my suggestion of an article as not worth as much as a comment. An altogether different problem is whether I should do one at all with all the work that is on my hands, but that is not what constitutes the problem.

[...]

How was your trip to Boston? How are the kido's?

Love,

    /s Paul

PMS to PAB

Larchmont
April 26, 1963

Dear Paul,

Your special which just arrived puts me to shame. Perhaps you will find it hard to believe but I really had no idea that my letter of the 22nd would give offense. It started out to be nothing more than an acknowledgment of yours of the 19th which had just arrived—an explanation of why you wouldn't hear from me until after I got back from Boston and a means of conveying the information that the Los Angeles people had not replied at all (they still haven't). Then I got started on a line of thought relevant to the great debate and ran on for a page, more or less incoherently as I now see from re-reading, until I realized that I had to tend to certain matters before leaving for Boston, whereupon I hastily broke off. Whatever unconscious motivations may have been at work, my failure to answer about your suggestion to write a piece dealing with great-debate and related matters for the June issue was, on the conscious level, merely a reflection of a decision to wait until I got back to produce a "real" answer to your letter. I fully understand why you interpreted it differently and I can only offer my most sincere apology for inexcusable insensitivity and rudeness.

On the substance of the matter, let me say first that it is taken completely for granted by Leo and me that the pages of MR are always open to you. Whenever you have something to say via that medium we are delighted to have it. The matter of timing of course has to be decided as a question by itself, but I cannot overemphasize that it has no bearing whatever on whether we want your stuff — we do. So all that is involved in the present case is timing, and on this I was not entirely clear about what would be best when I got your letter and still am not. The main point is the following: The May ROM is entitled "The Split in the Socialist World" and is in effect a reappraisal (as compared to the December, 1961, ROM entitled "The Sino-Soviet Dispute") of the Chinese position as laid down in recent theoretical and programmatic pronouncements. When you write in MR about these matters you will obviously want to have read this and perhaps to refer to it, and some further comments by us may be in order. On Monday, when I wrote, I didn't have a copy of the May piece and I still don't. I have just talked on the phone to Leo, however, and he has proofs of it in the office. He will airmail you one set right away and it ought to reach you at about the same time as this letter, or rather in the first regular mail after this letter. In making up your mind what to do, there are a number of other things to take into account:

(1) We are planning to run your letter to Ping Ferry in June.[187] If you write something that, by the nature of its contents, ought to appear in June, we can of course postpone the reply to Ping until September.

(2) On the other hand, it might be better to schedule the great-debate piece for September, which would give us time to clarify our viewpoints through further correspondence and quite possibly to come to a meeting of minds. I would much prefer that whatever you write would be something to which we could say "amen" rather than something that seems to indicate a serious difference of opinion.

(3) In general the June issue is less good than the September issue for reaching people — colleges are breaking up for the summer, more copies go astray or are neglected, etc.

I look forward to your reactions to all this. Meanwhile, a few comments on what you say in the long paragraph on the first page of yours of the 24th. I have a feeling that we haven't yet succeeded in defining the issues we are talking about with the necessary clarity. Very tentatively,

I would propose to identify them in the following terms:

1. What is going to be the general nature, on a global scale, of the transition from capitalism to socialism from now on?

2. Given the answer to this question, what are the appropriate general lines for (a) socialists in the underdeveloped countries? (b) socialists in the advanced capitalist countries? and (c) socialists, including governments, in the socialist camp?

In most general terms, I would tend to answer (1) by saying that the chief form of transition for a long time to come (decades rather than years) will be

---

187. Paul A. Baran, "A Letter to W.H. Ferry," *Monthly Review* 15, no. 2 (June 1963): 103–07.

some variant of the Cuban model, but with the U.S. getting involved on the side of the reactionaries *before* they are overthrown. (There is no doubt in my mind, for example, that if the U.S. had known what it now knows Cuba would have been South Vietnamized in 1958 and guerilla war would still be going on there.) This state of affairs will tend to spread throughout the entire underdeveloped "free" world, with the U.S. quite literally fighting a world-wide anti-guerilla war. That can go on for a long time but not forever. At some stage, rot and breakdown will set in in the imperialist center. When that happens, a new phase in the global transition process will open. But that is still a long way off, and it is not now possible to speculate usefully on the problems that will then arise.

We must attempt to answer the questions under (2) for the first stage. As to socialists in the underdeveloped countries (2a), it seems to me that they have first of all to get rid of their illusions and then to prepare for a whole era of revolutionary struggle against their own reactionaries and the U.S. occupiers. Vietnam and Algeria provide extremely valuable lessons, and so do other areas (e.g. we have a piece on the Philippines by Bill Pomeroy for an early issue which throws extremely valuable light on why the Huk movement failed in its first try).[188] But at this stage of the game, it seems to me to be a matter of the greatest importance that the Left in the underdeveloped countries should achieve theoretical clarity, and it is in this connection that I think and hope that MR can make a modest contribution.

(2b) My own instinctive feeling is that there is really nothing socialists in the advanced capitalist countries can do except expose and denounce the in- and anti-human campaign of imperialism against all progress and decency on the one hand, and keep alive a core of revolutionary rationality against the time when the breakdown of the imperialist metropolises begins in earnest.

(2c) I assume that it is here that our differences are focused. It seems to me that Chinese behavior vis-à-vis South Vietnam is very germane and in fact provides a sort of model of what the socialist countries should do in the period ahead.

With regard to your remarks on Iraq, I think the problem was wrongly posed by me in the first place. There never was any chance of a clean-cut takeover by the CPI [Communist Party of Iraq] which would all at once have confronted the U.S. and the USSR with a *fait accompli*. As in Cuba, the revolution would have had to go through a more or less prolonged phase of civil war. The U.S. and Britain would have moved in during this phase, no doubt at the request of a

---

188. William J. Pomeroy, "Lessons of the Philippine Guerrilla War," *Monthly Review* 15, no. 5 (September 1963): 246–51.

crumbling government headed by Kassim [Qasim] or some successor general (it is always possible to get someone to invite you in, the only trick is that he must still be there to let you in as well). And I think the USSR should have acted as China and North Vietnam have been acting in South Vietnam.

Cuba is of course an entirely different problem, since it managed to make the transition against opposition that the U.S. mistakenly judged would be sufficient to denature or overthrow the revolutionary regime. Once Cuba joined the socialist camp, it certainly could not be abandoned by the USSR and the other socialist countries. I entirely agree with you there, and I can now see that what I said in my last letter about this is a combination of wrong formulation and wrong idea. I need to clarify my own thinking about this, which I don't find at all easy. At one time, I thought putting the missiles into Cuba was the right decision, but when I saw the tremendous damage that had been done in the rest of Latin America I wavered on the matter. Maybe leaving enough Soviet troops there to make sure that the U.S. knows that attacking Cuba would mean killing Russians is the best course now. But if so, one may well ask why not admit Cuba as a full member of the Warsaw Pact? I dunno. . . .

The Boston trip was good and useful. Kids are well and cheerful. Spent one evening with a group of old Cambridge friends, including a Negro instructor in the Harvard Government Department who has spent a couple of years in Sierra Leone. He says that the greed and rapacity of the new regimes in most of the new African countries (exceptions, more or less sweeping, made for Ghana, Guinea, and Mali) is simply out of this world. Those boys are made-to-order tools of imperialism. I'm afraid the struggle in Africa will be terribly bloody, long, and full of defeats and disappointments (the Congo is all too prophetic).

One final point: when I said in my last letter that to focus attention on minor weaknesses of the Chinese position is a "disservice," I didn't refer to your private letter: I meant that it would be a disservice to put the emphasis there in any public statements. And what I had in mind as a minor weakness was the discussion of building on the ruins, etc., not the question of socialist-camp foreign policy. On the latter, I continue to think the Chinese position is both circumspect and sound. My letter was, as I noted above, written very hastily and extemporaneously, and I apologize for the whole bloody thing.

Take a moment to write me a reassuring note when you get this? Or more if you have the time.

Love,

/s Paul

PAB to PMS

Palo Alto
April 27, 1963

Dear Paul,

Your spec'y of April 26th just arrived; I hasten to assure you that the "offense" given by your letter of the 22nd was wholly "survivable." I just got mad, and being the way I unfortunately am — not very deliberate — expressed that state of anger *mammediately* in a special delivery message. Now it is my turn to apologize for an outburst which I would have suppressed had I slept over the whole matter. . . .

Ad rem: It is probably just as well for me not to get involved now into writing a longish piece on the Sino-Soviet affaire; I feel as it is that I'll never accomplish what is most pressing: (a) the IS [Irrational System] chapter (of which I am in the middle), (b) the piece for Poland which is due by the end of June (I just looked up the correspondence), and (c) a longish review of Milton Friedman's *Capitalism and Freedom* which I owe *JPE* [*Journal of Political Economy*]. So I may just as well shorten my lines of communications and get over those humps before undertaking to climb over others. Under the circumstances I better plan to write on the Sino-Soviet stuff for the fall and combine that with a review of Stanley's book which I promised him I would do and which I feel I ought to write.

On the substance of the argument, it is my feeling that neither the Russians nor the Chinese are actually facing the issues. The Russians cum Togliatti *et tutti quanti* slide rapidly to the right; the Chinese maintain a left *terminology*, but when it comes down to business their solutions are purely verbal. It is the old and never ceasing perplexity: what does a revolutionary movement do when there is no "*Aktualitaet der Revolution*" [imminent prospect of revolution]? This theme has become complicated by the existence of socialist *states*, by the special *problematik* of the udc's [underdeveloped countries], by the internationalization of the class struggle; in essence it is the same issue. The Chinese try to solve it by pointing at the revolutionary elements in the picture (*Rote Fahne* in Berlin printed huge headlines in 1927 pointing at the sharpening revolutionary crisis in . . . China), Togliatti tries to solve it by unashamedly going the way of Kautsky. Lenin solved it in a very special way for Russia (a pro party of a few thousands who stuck to their guns come what may), but his solution ain't applicable to movements as in Italy or France. Stalin solved it by *declaring* the II period and announcing that there *is* a revolutionary situation in the world in 1928/29 and shooting everyone who dared to disagree with this appraisal.

But *is* there a solution for this predicament? The Chinese who are going through the Soviet period of the first couple of 5 year plans *must* (like Stalin) invoke a revolutionary world situation for without it it is very hard to keep morale up at home. Togliatti *must* orient his mass party towards day-to-day targets for without such an orientation it is impossible to keep the movement together. (His question: what do you want us to do; wait until the revolution comes? is a natural one). This is Greek tragedy and must be fully seen as such. In a sense the Russians are in Togliatti's position. After the Stalin period they are *tired*; their requirement at the moment is not more revolutionary excitement but more outlook for peace, quiet, domestic construction.

France Observateur's writer who said that this is a rupture *entre une revolution fatigué et une revolution impatiente* [between a weary revolution and an impatient revolution] is right — except for his failure to analyze clearly both positions.

The fundamental trouble is that — at least by my lights — there is no answer or solution. It may very well be that in the end Rosa was right who faced with this very dilemma threw her hands up and put all her hopes on historic spontaneity. If and when for whatever reason the capitalist *Scheisse* should begin to crack, the problem will take care of itself. But what until then? The "centrist" answer: left phrases and right deeds (and I am afraid that the Chinese position *de facto* boils down to it) is *emotionally* more satisfying, but remains, as I said, strictly verbal. When they say that Togliatti or for that matter Khrushchev should "struggle" I cannot help asking myself what does the word "struggle" *specifically* mean? I had a long talk with Togliatti on this very question. What does it specifically mean in the midst of a boom in Italy when there is no unemployment but shortage of labor, when Italy goes through an industrialization process embracing even the South?

Such and similar thoughts are the ones which I would like to present at some more length because I do not believe that people who are in the rough and tumble of practical politics can formulate them. Togliatti was right when he remarked to me that "you are lucky, you can think independently; I have a multi-million movement on my hands." And I should think that our contribution could be only not to take emotionally sides, not to pretend that we have politics "on our hands" (remember Lenin's remark that politics begin where millions come in), not to condemn and approve, but to sit back and show the socialist movement "the mirror of itself" to clarify theoretical questions which no one else can afford to do.

[...]

So much for now. I am sorry to have caused you a disturbance by my previous letter. This all comes from distance; what one writes looks much more "definitive" than what one says. So, let us forget about this "incident," and keep at it. I am afraid all those minor things reflect simply sick nerves which does not astound me: how in hell does one stay sane in the midst of all this?

    Love as ever,
        /s Paul

PMS to PAB

                                                                    Larchmont
                                                                 April 30, 1963

Dear Paul,

Thanks for your special of Sunday. When you get mad at me don't try to sleep it off. It is better for all concerned that you should get it out of your system. It clears the atmosphere.

    By now you should have received the proofs of the May RoM, and you will see that there is no real disagreement about the reasons for and meaning of the Khrush-Tog position. Where I think there probably is still some disagreement is in relation to the area of relevance of the Chinese position. I would say that, measured in historically relevant time units, the condition of *Aktualitaet* [imminent revolution] *does* exist in the underdeveloped countries [udc's] in the imperialist orbit, hence there classical Leninist doctrine is fully applicable and hence there the Chinese are both relevant and right. Left deeds can, should, and will match left words. Further, it seems clear to me that it is the revolutionary struggles of the udc's which will eventually — in a matter of decades rather than months or years — lead to what you call the cracking of the capitalist *Scheisse* (the mixing of the metaphor has a certain charm about it). If this is correct, I can see no other legitimate activity for genuine socialists in the imperialist centers than to preserve intact a set of ideas and aspirations for the time when they will once again become politically meaningful, hoping all the time that that time may be nearer than now seems likely.

    In the meantime, I believe it is of the greatest importance not to get bogged down in the reformist muck as all the Western CP's are doing. The problem of the USSR and the other more advanced socialist countries is, as we both recognize, quite different though it produces many of the same attitudes and policies as those of Togliatti et al. The function of people like us vis-a-vis the socialist countries is of course not to reject or denounce but rather to do what we can to encourage and help them to do what none of them has yet shown any signs of even trying to do, i.e., develop a genuinely Marxist critique of their own realities. Here, by the way, I would use the adjective Marxist rather than Marxist-Leninist because the latter has acquired a connotation of being concerned with the problems of imperialism on the one hand and state and revolution on the other, and these are certainly not the problems of the socialist world.

Again if this is on the right track, it has interesting implications for what kind of "movement" socialism is likely to be in the imperialist centers for the visible future. It seems to me that we are in fact entering, perhaps have already entered, a period of what might be called "socialist monasticism." Those of us who are genuine socialists are really cut off from our society and we live a life of our own even if we are not physically separated from the rest. Perhaps we should consciously accept this state of affairs end attempt to make the best of it rather than continuously deploring it. I believe that our numbers will grow in the years ahead as more and more people — perhaps specially among Negroes — find themselves completely unable to accept this lousy system. Why can't we consciously reject it and devote ourselves to building for a future which our children or grandchildren can hope to live to see? As a matter of fact, I think that's what we are doing anyway; we might find more pleasure and fulfillment in it if we frankly recognized the situation. In any event, we must be clear on one point: trying to play politics (looking for ways to acquire power) in the present situation is the sure way to intellectual and moral degeneration. I would be interested in your thoughts on these ruminations.

[…]

All for now — must get to work.

Love,

    /s Paul

[…]

PAB to PMS

Palo Alto

May 3, 1963

Dear Paul,

[…]

I do have some reservations about the May RoM, but shall not go into it now.[189] Maybe if and when the spirit moves me. Should I get around at some point to formulating my views on the whole matter in a more systematic and printable way, our difference may become clearer.

---

189. Leo Huberman and Paul M. Sweezy, "The Split in the Socialist World," *Monthly Review* 15, no. 1 (May 1963): 1–20.

You should not lump together the socialist movements in all advanced countries. As you see, the Italian CP is very much alive and kicking (in its own way to be sure, but nonetheless very importantly for the socialist movement), the condition in France is probably worse, but still, there is a *movement* too. It is primarily in this country, GB and WGermany where the bottom all but fell out . . . Our condition here is indeed *bien extraordinaire*; it is essentially pre-Marxian. All we can do is to engage in "critical critique" about which the old man makes so many jokes and revert to the position of Bruno Bauer [German philosopher, died in 1882] and Associates who remained on the ideational plane simply because there was no other plane to be on. In absence of practical critique, theoretical critique tends to become sterile and sectarian, and I for one would decide to quit it entirely and to go into history or literature were it not for the consideration that it is a wholly ridiculous parochialism to consider this country to be IT.

The law of uneven development works here too, we are now in *Hinterpommern* [Eastern Pomerania (remote part of Prussia or "in the boonies"], have to be aware of it and do what Immanuel Kant did: stay home, meditate, read, write and look at the world from afar. There was only one occasion, I have read somewhere, when he skipped his PM nap, and that was when he heard that Bastille was stormed. Our contribution to world events can be a little better than that, but the accent is on the word little. The only important consolation: in our days when the world is being pretty rapidly (by historical standards at least) *changed*, there may be room for *interpreting* it. That is why I am against journalism *today*, against trying to be au courant *today*, and for more theoretical, more *approfondir* [deepened knowledge] type of work. Not having to worry about votes, political expedience, &c. one can afford simply looking for and saying the truth. *Ad majorem Dei gloriam* and for one's own satisfaction and for the instruction of the future historian.

[. . .]

Attached an article by [Hans] Neisser; a very good take off point because he has in one place all the fallacies of imperialist refutation. Most important, I think, is to bring out clearly the "social order imperialism" (or whatever better name one could invent for it) and to stress that the dog is presently buried not so much in what the imperialist countries get out of the u/d c's [underdeveloped countries] but *in their preventing the u/d c's development* under the guise of anti-communism. And if and when the u/d c's manage to "take off" they are being strangled, obstructed and hurt wherever possible.[190]

I have just been reading Gerald Clark, *The Coming Explosion in Latin America* (David McKay Co., New York, 1962) — as far as I have gone, IAA; you should somehow advertise it in *MR* (if only by a quote or two), and particularly valuable because coming from an orthodox Canadian newspaperman.

So, I'll bring IS to a convenient intermediate point, and go to work on Lange and then write a review of Milton Friedman. The latter is exasperating; slick, clever, and really the lowest of low. Big difficulty there is that I do not want to appear as a defender of the Strachey-ites of all ilks which is very hard in this case. By comparison with him they are at least approximately human. All one could say about Friedman was what Marx said about free trade; I wish he had his way; that would make at last for some fireworks.[191]

[...]

Would appreciate your reactions to the above.

Love,

/s Paul

PAB to PMS

[Palo Alto]

May 6, 1963

Dear Paul,

[...]

A propos: I do not quite understand how you reconcile your statement in letter of April 30th that "the condition of *Aktualitaet* does exist in the udc's in the imperialist orbit" with your own somber report on Latin America published in the March MR. The existence of the "*Aktualitaet der Revolution*" does not mean after all that (a) the *Aktualitaet* prevails in the long run, *in*

---

190. Handwritten footnote by Baran: Also very important to point out that what matters *under monopoly capitalism* is not so much what might be called the Rosa L. GNP effect, but the direct and *very significant* interests in the 500 corp.'s. Shunting the discussion off on the GNP track is in our Keynesian world obviously avoiding the issue, or rather putting the discussion where the anti-imperialist theorists are stronger. There *are* other means to increase effective demand. . . .

191. Baran is referring to Marx's speech "On the Question of Foreign Trade" that ended with the statement that "In a word, the free trade system hastens the social revolution. It is in this revolutionary sense alone, gentlemen, that I vote in favour of free trade" (over-protectionism). Karl Marx, *The Poverty of Philosophy* (New York: International Publishers, 1963), 224.

the general historical perspective.[192] This is taken for granted: sooner or later
there will be revolutions and there will be transition to socialism in most if not
all countries. This is presumably what the Chinese mean by "despising the
enemy strategically." And (b) it does not mean that the *objective* conditions
are ripe for revolution, that the revolution is *desirable*. That has been true for
don't know how long, certainly for most of the current century. The entire
Aktualitaet concept refers strictly to the immediacy, to being on *today's* agenda of
revolutionary action, to its *hic et nunc* [here and now] character. It destroys the
usefulness of the notion to speak of it in "historical terms" — it is not a long run,
it is a short run notion *par excellence.*

Therefore for *today's* debates and decision the issue is: does the *Aktualitaet*
exist today or doesn't it? *Hic Rhodus, hic salta!*[193] If one says that one doesn't
know (in any and every of the LA countries there may be a Fidel somewhere
gathering strength and adherents in some unknown hills), one accepts the
Spontaneity theory of Rosa's (I am not arguing at the moment against it!)
and asserts in effect that there ain't no way of a rational policy formulation:
anything may happen incl. nothing. If one argues that the *Aktualitaet* exists,
one moves towards an activism which may easily turn into Putschism with all
the consequences thereof (drowning in blood of the revolutionary movement).
If one maintains with the Togliattis *et al* that it ain't there, then one slides into a
reformist, national-bourgeois-alliance &c.-type policy. I am not now taking sides
in that debate, I am simply trying to see the issues as clearly as I can.

And the issues cannot be solved verbally, as it is in the Chinese document
[*Peking Review* articles, not specifically referenced]; they have to be faced
squarely "contentwise." It may very well be — and I am inclined to that view —
that there is no "scientific" answer because we just do not know; but once more,
even this view is good enough only for ivory tower reflections; it is not good
enough for those who are in the middle of politics, or possibly even for one who

192. The principle of "The Actuality of Revolution," is presented in the first part of Georg
Lukács's *Lenin: A Study of the Unity of His Thought* (London: New Left Books, 1970; original
German edition, 1924).
193. "Here is Rhodes; Jump Here!" This derives from Aesop's Fables, meaning "prove your talk
by deeds!" It owes its significance here to its previous use by Hegel and Marx. See G.W.F. Hegel,
The Philosophy of Right (Oxford: Oxford University Press, 1952), 11; Karl Marx, *The Eighteenth
Brumaire of Louis Bonaparte* (New York: International Publishers, 1963), 19.

edits a journal. One still should be aware of the nature of the problem which — to repeat — has all the qualities of a Greek tragedy.

[…]

More later.

Love,

/s Yours Paul

PMS to PAB

Larchmont

May 17, 1963

Dear Paul,

[…]

You say that *Aktualitaet* refers strictly to the *immediate* relevance of revolutionary activity. And you contrast this with what prevails "in the long run, in the general historical perspective." I would say that for the advanced capitalist countries it is only the long run that counts, and that as of now revolutionary activity, or attempts at such, will condemn its practitioners to the status of an isolated sect. At the other extreme, there are at any given time at most only a very few places where revolution is on *today's* agenda. The vast majority of the countries of the world fall somewhere in between these two extremes. For my part, I think that in most of the udc's it will be on the agenda in so near a future that active preparations for it can be, and should be placed on today's agenda. Now I would like to know if you disagree with this statement of the case, find it irrelevant, or what?

To explain somewhat further: I do not think revolution is on today's agenda in any of the LA countries we visited: that was the message of the March RoM ["Notes on Latin America," *MR*, March 1963] (or at least one of its messages). But I think it is bound to be on the agenda in an historically near future (say, within ten years). I do not think such to be the case of the United States. Hence I think that the attitude of the Left toward revolutionary activity, and preparations for revolutionary activity, can and should be quite different in the two regions. I do not see any reason why a positive attitude in LA must lead to Putschism. I do believe that revolutions in udc's will *in the long run* be the undoing of the U.S. and other advanced capitalist countries and will, again in the long run, place revolution on the agenda there too.

Let us now take a specific historical comparison: Russia and Germany circa 1910. In neither country was revolution on the agenda in the *hic-et-nunc* sense, yet revolutionary politics was possible in Russia and not in Germany. When a severe shock came, the social order in Russia was overthrowable, that in Germany not.

As to the Chinese position, it seems to me to be very relevant — verbally, contentwise, and every other way — for most of the udc's. Since they make up the greater part of the "free world," and since it is here that history is made in our epoch (both the USSR and China were once udc's in the "free world"), the Chinese position seems to me to be, in a very real sense, "correct." Natch, this doesn't mean that they have all the answers — any more than Lenin did. What they say about the workers in the advanced capitalist countries is simply the familiar wishful thinking. And I have no doubt that they greatly overestimate the immediacy of the revolution in many udc's, esp. African and Latin American. All the same, what they are saying on the whole makes sense, and I think genuine leftists in the udc's can sense it because their own experience tells them so. By comparison, Khrushchev's advice to the udc's — don't rock the boat until we have had a chance to show you what socialism can really accomplish — does not make sense and indeed appears to be simply a new form of subordinating the interests of the international movement to the national needs of the SU. As for Togliatti and the other advanced capitalist countries' CP's, they quite literally seem to be oblivious to the fact that there is a crucially important udc problem, the solution of which — or lack thereof — could easily be decisive for them too.

I am less pessimistic about the role people like us can play than you seem to be, and I think maybe you will be too after you have been to South America. *We have had a lot to do with educating the best revolutionaries of Latin America.* I am proud of what we have done in this respect, and I believe we can do a lot more. But I can think this a really important contribution only because I believe, with the Chinese, that revolutionaries will be making history down there in the (historically) near future.

[…]
Love,
    /s Paul

[…]

PAB to PMS

Palo Alto
May 20, 1963

Dear Paul,
Thanks for the letter *cum/encl.* of May 17th. On its main contents — later. Meanwhile only a few lines to draw your attention to an extraordinary *opus* by Lenin written in 1893 when the boychik was 23 years old and entitled "Concerning the So-Called Question of Markets." The MS of that piece was

lost for many years and first published in 1937. It is now contained in the 1st vol. of his *Collected Works*. There among a number of interesting observations I found to be really startling that he had already at that time *in nuce* [in a nutshell] the entire theory of imperialism which was generally maintained he got only from Hobson whose relevant book was, however, not published until 1902. Consider the following: After discussing the schemes of reproduction &c., and arguing that in certain conditions capitalism creates its own market he observes: "Here it is necessary to make a qualification. All that was said above does not lead in the least to a denial of the proposition that capitalist nations cannot exist without foreign markets. Under capitalism the equilibrium between production and consumption is attained only *via* a series of fluctuations; the larger the production, the larger the circle of consumers for whom it is designed, the stronger the fluctuations. It is understandable therefore that when bourgeois production reaches a high level of development, it finds it impossible to contain itself within the framework of a nation state: competition forces the capitalists to expand production and to seek out foreign markets for massive disposal of products. . . . The cries about the breakdown of our industry in view of lacking markets are nothing else but a transparent maneuver of our capitalists who in this way exercise pressure upon politics, identifying (in a modest awareness of their 'impotence') the interests of their pockets with the interests of the 'country' and who become capable in this way to push the government on the road of colonial conquests, involve it even into a war for the sake of safeguarding such 'state' interests." If I get it correctly, all of the subsequent theorizing on imperialism has hardly added anything to what is said in these few sentences. Get hold of the volume and look at that piece; it probably could be well used in connection with the Kalecki piece [the piece that Baran and Sweezy were writing on imperialism for the Kalecki festschrift].[194]

Encl. are self-explanatory.

Love,

/s Yours Paul

194. Handwritten footnote by Baran: In National Income terms the stress may have to be placed more on *capital* exports. As far as individual corporations are concerned, what L. says is all that matters, although they too may be concerned with foreign investment of their surplus uninvestable [unreadable: inventory, products?].

PAB to PMS

Palo Alto
May 26, 1963

Dear Paul,

It was very good to talk to you last night; in spite of the sad message it has lifted
up my spirits a little bit. They are pretty damn low at the moment. I am kind of
stuck in the [Oskar] Lange [festschrift] piece and it does not seem to jell; I think
I know perfectly well what it is that I want to say, but when it gets down on paper
it looks awful. . . . I wish I had another occupation and I know I would not want
to have any other; a strange form of masochism where suffering is the only form
of enjoyment.

The Fri eve in the city was terribly depressing. Huby's old observation
that most of the attendants of those meetings are crackpots is gaining a new
dimension. Until recently they were old-timers, health-food eaters and Wobblies;
now those have died out or are too old to move about but their place is taken
by young bearded psychotics, one crazier and queerer than the other. . . . You
should have seen that crew; makes one shudder. All the oppositional energies
that have no social outlet go inside and create psychic havoc; it is horrifying.
This youth is no more likely to produce a decent movement than the old Scott
Nearings to take up arms. . . . Where is anything to come from in this desert?

The university situation while rationally understandable and obvious
contributes to the emotional misery. Both the bloody hypocrisy of those
sob's as well as the sheer *Schweinerei* [piggishness] involved. For next year
I got a teaching load that is about twice as large as that of my "peers," with
a pay of about 60% of theirs and all this with a broad grin "look at us, how
democratic and free and tolerant we are!" The Pres. observed that there are no
complaints about my teaching or "scholarship," but my utterances in public are
"irresponsible." I asked to be given samples of "irresponsible" statements. If the
word means mendacious or incoherent or outside of the realm of reasonable
discourse, I would like to see any such statements cited with chapter and verse.
If the word means "not in agreement with his views" I would appreciate having
this spelled out. . . . But all this is for the birds; he wants badly to squeeze me out
from here; I would be delighted to go because my nerves won't stand it much
longer but where go and how? And my "friend" Bowker observes, well, you have
to pay the price for being a revolutionary. This returns to him his peace of mind.
. . . If it weren't for Nicky, I would quit literally tomorrow; I would somehow eke
out $100 a week to keep body and soul together and rather do that than have to
tolerate those bastards spitting into my face all the time. But how can I leave the
little chappy, and how can I take him along into nothingness?

In re: Kalecki [festschrift] piece ["Notes on the Theory of Imperialism"].
In addition to stressing the point that the GNP approach to imperialism is a
scholastic *Marotte* [fad] and that what matters is the interest of the 500 corp's to
which foreign biz is a matter of tremendous importance and which run the joint,
important to outpoint in addition that (a) the paraphernalia of the thing are most
relevant (armaments etc.) as well as the (now) — (b) overriding significance of
the anti-socialist struggle (the social order imperialism or however it might be
called). I think one should include a swipe against the new "line" that "we" could
easily redirect those resources into aid to the u/d c's &c which simply by a slight
of hand substitutes a rational economy for capitalism. If "we" could do all of this
"we" would have nothing to talk about!

Very interesting also to point out that the technique of British imperialism (and
French and Belgian and Dutch) was making colonies, the U.S. modern variety is
making "independent states." Thus pushing out the old Europeans and taking the
thing over. Old Benjamin Disraeli, Earl of Beaconsfield — as shrewd a Hebrew as
there ever was — observed in a speech in the House of Commons on 5 February
1863: "Colonies do not cease to be colonies because they are independent."

Indeed not: although independence may create new problems . . . I would
think that independence minus socialist danger might actually give the national
bourgeoisie some courage and willingness to assert themselves *vis a vis* the
imperialists. But now, they are so afraid of the impending doom that they'll
lick the boots of any imperialist (a la Moise Tshombe [Congolese pro-Western
politician in the 1960s]) who will protect their sacred property.

Well, there are a number of other things, but I better get back to work, and
write about those later.

Love,

/s Paul

PAB to PMS

Palo Alto
June 29, 1963

Dear Paul,

"Notes on the Theory of Imperialism" [draft for Kalecki festschrift] came last
night. I find both style & content perfectly ok, and most useful. (1) *Technicality*:
If you wish to waste your time in re-typing the whole thing into clean copy after
it is done, you can obviously mail it directly (airmail registered) to: Professor
Lipinski. Otherwise send it back to me; the Secretary in the Dept. has nothing to
do in the summer and will be glad to re-type it *lelegantly*; then I would send the
whole biz in one package. *C'est comme vous voulez*!

(2) A few *general remarks*: I think it would be useful to introduce the thing by some statement to the effect that the imperialism theory was seen traditionally not only as a theory of international politics and relations between monopoly capitalist countries and u/d c's [underdeveloped countries], but also as a theory contributing to the explanation of the prevailing level of income and employment in the monopoly capitalist countries. This partly because imperialism was thought of as offering a drainage for the economic surplus thus augmenting aggregate effective demand and partly because it improved the monopoly capitalist country's terms of trade thus increasing its real income but also helping it along in international trade. It is *this* function of imperialism which needs to be rethought in the light of what follows. This links up with par. 4 where the approach to imperialism from the GNP standpoint is rejected. There, I think, necessary to stress that (a) individual corp's don't give a damn about national aggregates, and (b) that all arguments as to whether imperialism does or does not *pay*, confuse the accounts involved: the costs of imperialism are paid by the public treasuries of the imperialist countries i.e. by the general taxpayer; the profits are received by the small number of corp's. Therefore all the claptrap about U.S. not being imperialist because of magnanimous help *sub specie* Marshall Plan and similar philanthropic outlays plain rubbish based on the usual little word "we."

And this connects with another general point: an awful lot of what "we" are doing for the u/d c's (if and when we do anything worthwhile) is strictly a subsidy to our own corp's. The U.S. Treasury takes over the expensive function of providing the so-called Overhead Social Capital or the "infrastructure" because building railroads, harbors &c is too costly for the corp's; they love to see the government doing *that* job for them. An interesting illustration was provided by Model's enterprise in Brazil; he in company with Hanna bought huge iron deposits in Brazil; then they employed lobbyists of the highest caliber to obtain AID financing for the building of the *indispensable* harbor through which the stuff could be exported. Otherwise the biz would not pay. This familiar pattern also in domestic business where the government first picks up the tab for the big R&D developments, then leaves the exploitation of them to free enterprise. *Ergo*: not only the military component of foreign aid but most of the economic part straight imperialist activity wholly unrelated to the professed interest in the welfare of the u/d c's. On that a quote from the Clay report would be useful; also a quote from Lenin: "Where, except in the imagination of the sentimental reformers, are there any trusts capable of interesting themselves in the condition of the masses instead of in conquering colonies?" Since I am at it, the other quote from Lenin which is the one you probably had in mind in par. 7 is "Under the old type of capitalism, when free competition prevailed, the export of commodities was the most typical feature. Under modern capitalism, when monopolies prevail, the export of capital has become the typical feature." The former citation is from Chapter VI and the latter is from Chapter IV of *Imperialism the Highest Stage of Capitalism* (I imagine no need for pp. #'s — there are too many different editions.)

Thus the link between imperialism and the level of income & employment, economic stability &c is most tricky and perverse (as the rest of the story so well shows). By turning into net capital *importers* the corp's do not only not help to stabilize income and employment but work in the opposite direction. On the other hand, by setting into motion the whole paraphernalia of government spending on AID, defense, &c they provide the possibility of surplus absorption, that welfare projects could never dream of furnishing. The interesting distinction between the *young* imperialist countries: capital outflow larger than repatriated profits cum interest; *mature* imperialist countries where those in and outflows balance; *senile* imperialist countries where the inflows outweigh the outflows. Conventional Marxist-Leninist imperialist theory partly in view of its timing referred to the *young* case. I have the impression that for the purpose in hand some such introduction would be more indicated than what is referred to in par.2; it would also link up well with par.4. A sentence or two on the immense political power wielded by giant corp's in government and on the Eisenhower "military-industrial" complex would nicely complete that line of thought.

(3) *Specific points*: *Ad*: par.2: upsurge of neutralism a political development of uncertain kind and duration (cf. India) — wouldn't seem to be in the same class with the others. Par.5: most important; shouldn't it be stressed more as is done later on (par.5) with regard to Jersey? Par.16 magnificent! Par.21: I may be wrong, but I have an uneasy feeling about the argument that the expansion of foreign operations of the multinational corp's has constituted one of the important causes of the lagging rates of growth in the U.S. Had they *not* expanded abroad, would they have necessarily expanded at home? Or would they have repatriated more of their earnings thus reducing the U.S. *net* capital outflow and thus contributing to larger unemployment at home? It is the same kind of argument which was made about Britain: had Britain exported less capital prior to WW I and in the decades thereafter and used that capital instead for modernization of its industry at home, it wouldn't have gotten into

the technological fix in the late forties and all of the fifties. But would they have invested at home or would there have been more unemployment at home? Par.'s 22 and 23: this may be the place where it may be possible to add that in addition to the broadly political aims on which all the corporations are united, there are also varying and geographically disparate interests in the government of the U.S. as well as in the national governments of various countries taking over for them Social Overhead Capital outlays. Thence quite different attitudes within the corporate world with regard to foreign aid, *a la* Point IV programs &c. To some those mean important savings, to others nothing. It depends on the nature of biz involved. Certain corp's having nothing against *some* state capitalist enterprises if they would provide *them* with cheap electric power, properly located roads &c. Also the Meiji Restoration pattern which was very much observed in Turkey: U.S. financed (with or without the Turkish government) investment projects which are then "re-privatized" and sold to U.S. private interests.

(4) Conclusion: I should think that what you say in the first par. of your covering letter would constitute an excellent conclusion. In the light of all that was said it becomes clear that (a) in the cases of the "mature" and "senile" imperialist powers in particular the U.S. one cannot consider imperialist activities *per se* (i.e. apart from its "trimmings" to be a stabilizer of the level of income and employment; (b) it is impossible and silly to try to look under the bed for a hidden economic interest in seeking to explain any particular foreign policy move of an imperialist country in any one region of the world. The truth is here also the whole — the maximization of the capitalist sphere is what matters and not any one particular enterprise which does *not* preclude that on occasions, if the enterprise is big enough and its influence telling enough, the connection becomes very direct. But Guatemala would have been Guatemala also without Unifruitco!! The transformation of the "old" imperialism into the new "social order imperialism" is the transformation of national monopolies into multinational monopolies taking place in the age of social and national revolutions.

I think, this about covers what little I have to add. By the way, giving it the twist which I suggest under General Remarks brings the whole thing handsomely in connection with the whole area of income and employment in which the jubilee has done his principal work.

If the Lange [festschrift] thing comes out as nicely as this, our position as unorthodox, independent but, nonetheless or precisely therefore, Marxists will get an additional boost. What matters to me at least is not the personal gratification involved, but the advancement of a method and of an attitude!

Con amore,

/s Yours Paul

P.S. If you should come to think that you may need some extra quotes (Clay Report or other u/d c literature which I have and you don't) leave spaces, and I'll stick them in. If you ship the thing directement, please send me a carbon.

9
The Last Struggles

PMS to PAB

Wilton

July 16, 1963

Herewith a detailed outline, perhaps closer to a draft, of a proposed chapter on the Negro problem.[195] I labelled it Chapter 9 but later checked back on our correspondence and note that you expressed a preference for making it QoS(III), i.e. Ch 12, with IS becoming Ch. 13. This is probably the better arrangement, though it may be better to retain some such title as "Monocap and the Negro Problem" rather than call it QoS(III). If we adopt this course, the specific Negro material can be retained in QoS (I & II) and referred back to in this chapter, which would mean that par. 23 would not have to be elaborated but could consist of a brief reminder and reference to the earlier stuff.

As you will see, the possibility of expanding the thing exists at every point along the way, and in some places will be essential. However, this is true of the whole book, and I would hope that it would be possible to keep this chapter down to, say, 30 double-spaced typed pages.

Par. 5 on the Civil War was put in as a sort of rumination and is obviously much too controversial to be left in — the more so since it isn't essential to the argument of the chapter. However, I must confess that I was intrigued by the general idea that the way to approach the Civil War is via the divvying up of the booty squeezed out of the Negro slaves, and now I think that following it up can lead to a new and much improved Marxian interpretation of that important historical event. I sketched the content of par. 5 in a letter to Gene Genovese (whose specialty is the ante-bellum South) and asked him for his comments. He reacted sharply and immediately as though a sensitive nerve had

---

195. Sweezy is referring to the original outline/preliminary draft of what was to become Chapter 9 in *Monopoly Capital*: "Monopoly Capitalism and Race Relations."

been touched. The interpretation, he says, is ingenious but there are too many obstacles to be overcome to support it with facts. He then proceeds to detail some of the obstacles. What he says, if it is accurate, does indeed show the need for modifications of the hypothesis, particularly with regard to the assumed role of the Southern bourgeoisie, but on the whole it confirms my suspicion that the line of thought in question is pointing in the right direction. I'll show you all this stuff later on, but at the moment I must keep it in order to be able to reply to him before the end of the month. There are many very intriguing questions begging to be answered once one gets into this field at all, and my impression is that American Marxism in this, as in other matters, has shown itself peculiarly sterile.

The thesis of the chapter as a whole can be put in a nutshell: Negroes are the last of the immigrant groups to be ghettoized in the cities. There are no more to come so the system needs them there. Barriers to escape, therefore, far from crumbling, are getting more and more formidable. At the same time the deteriorating job situation which results from the profound stagnationist tendency of monopoly capitalism, makes it increasingly impossible for all but a tiny (and essentially parasitic) Negro bourgeoisie to even attempt to escape. Integration is therefore a utopia for the black masses. So is withdrawal (black nationalism). Negroes will therefore either have to abandon the struggle or take the revolutionary road.

                                *   *   *   *

[…]
              /s Paul

PAB to PMS

                                                        Palo Alto
                                                        July 18, 1963

Dear Paul,

Attached the outline of the Negro chapter which I carefully perused. Some of my comments — for what they are worth are marked on the margins. Summarizing the most important of those, I would think that you overstress the ghettoization aspect of the matter. To be sure, it is *very* important; I don't quite see that it is *the* most important factor in the picture. It would seem to me that in this particular instance the socio-economic approach is really only one leg on which the thing rests. The other is the entire penumbra of socio-psychological aggressiveness, frustration &c produced by the system as a whole. You note it in par. 25, but somehow it appears as an afterthought, although it should be, I think, given as much prominence as much of the rest. For example, it would be possible to explain the anti-Semitic measures of the Nazis by the hunger of German

Kleinbuerger [petty bourgeoisie] for the jobs of the Jews; this can never explain
Oswiecim [German: Auschwitz] and Maidanek [Lublin] and the gas chambers
and Frau Koch's making lampshades from the skins of Jewish prisoners. . . . Here,
I think, the accumulated hatred which finds no outlet: the massive obscurantism
which is continually nurtured, the frustrations which find no other vent and all
such come centrally into the picture. I remember a photograph of a white woman
in New Orleans hitting a Negro child — the expression of her brutish, infernal
face cannot be dealt with on the level of socio-economic analysis. That is why I
also feel somewhat less than convinced by Boggs (whose piece I only cursorily
read) that the Negro issue is strictly a social problem, that the Negroes are the
most oppressed social stratum, and therefore: that their struggle is class struggle
á outrance [to the end]. I have the feeling that while all this may be right, the
race issue has to be faced as such, as something additional, related to but also
independent from the class conflict. This is to say: the class relation of the Negro
problem is essentially that only a socialist society could and would create the
general atmosphere, the educational and "influencing" apparatus which would
in fullness of time overcome racism and all that goes with it. The mere solution
of the socio-economic problem would not do it. The uneven development works
here too; longest of all is the time needed to modify, let alone, change human
nature. And superstition which as the Chinese say is much worse than ignorance
yields very slowly to changes in the substructure.

   Without going into this a little more the proposition that only the abolition of
monopoly capitalism and its replacement by socialism sounds dogmatic and not
altogether convincing. Would be worthwhile to point at the USSR experience
where on one hand Central Asia has provided proofs of the power of socio-
economic developments, but where also a tremendous cultural effort was made
to eliminate racist "national minority" attitudes. And nevertheless: revival of anti-
Semitism at the first opportunity!

   As far as the prospects for the future are concerned, I would prefer to be less
general, and more concrete. That the Negro struggle will abate is not very likely.
The ruling class will try to buy out the leadership as they are already doing with
some success. There will be new and more intransigent movements. Whither will
they move? Towards terrorism a la Mau Mau in Kenya; towards ever growing
Birminghams, towards civilian disobedience? There is clearly no prospect at this
historical junction that there will be an alliance between the Negro movement
and the labor movement, nor is there any serious prospect that the American
liberal will be anything more than a coward and a strikebreaker. Maybe in this
area as in many others the only progressive impetus can be expected from
developments abroad. . . . All we can say at this stage is that the condition of the

Negro in this country manifests itself at its crassest the condition of the country itself. As there is nothing to be said about the other USA [South Africa] except that it is the home of apartheid, so there is nothing to be said about a society in which a Wallace can be a governor and a Thurmond or an Eastland can be a senator. We can only disclose the irrationality and show how the parts hang together; can we say how it will end?

Also when it comes to full employment being the only possible condition for an alleviation of the plight of the Negroes (par.24), I have a very uneasy feeling. Needless to say nobody can be *against* full employment, but in the U.S. context genuine full employment with every Negro young and grown-up getting a job (even if at the bottom or close to the bottom of the pyramid) would probably drastically curb the Negro movement and create Business-Negroism as it has created Business-Laborism. The true emancipationists there like the socialists here would become small minorities with tenuous ties to the rest of the Negro population. Slaves can be taught to put up with their slavery if properly fed . . . It is the confluence of discrimination and economic misery which makes the Negro an explosive force today, and a Negro sociologist who is at Berkeley and visited me the other day was perfectly right — I think — when he said that the Negro liberation is only feasible if (a) the Negro Gandhiists are driven out from the leadership and when there will be honest to goodness violence (and plenty of same) and (b) that such a development is only imaginable if and when the confluence mentioned above continues and becomes even more pronounced.

Those are general ruminations on the subject the main upshot of which is that the Negro problem must be seen as a part of the whole not in the declaratory sense, but in the sense of relating it not merely to the socioeconomic status of the Negro but to the entire cultural atmosphere which is a hotbed of irrationality and misanthropy. Kafka said some 40 years ago directing himself to a different matter and a different audience that a civilization which murders the Jew murders mankind. *Mutatis mutandis* (only a bit) the civilization which murders the Negro murders mankind. Only when the entire situation is changed *not* only because the Negro gets a job and a better one and is de-ghettoized but because society wages a concerted struggle to make good the crimes which it perpetrated with regard to the Negro, when racial equality is not decreed by the Supreme Court but needs no longer to be decreed by any Court, when a white's marrying a Negro man or woman is of no more interest to anyone than his or her having given birth to a child, only then can there be any genuine solution of the Negro problem. All this obviously for such use and attention as it may merit. . . .

[...]
Love,
        /s Yours Paul

PMS to PAB

                                                                    Wilton
                                                               July 23, 1963

Dear Paul,
[...]
    Thanks for the comments on the draft of the Negro chapter. Here, I think,
there is a real difference of views between us which will have to be ironed out.
If I am not mistaken, you tend quite strongly to think of the plight of U.S.
negroes as being basically similar to that of German Jews under the Nazis. I
would not deny that there is *some* similarity, but I think that *au fond* the two
problems are radically different and that failure to recognize this can lead to
seriously misleading conclusions. U.S. whites, even the most rabid racists in the
South, do *not* hate Negroes as such. They feel superior to them, which is a very
different thing. They even like Negroes — provided Negroes will recognize their
inferiority and "stay in their place" which is at the bottom doing the dirty work
and now, geographically speaking, quite literally in the city ghettoes. The utility
of such feelings and attitudes in preserving the status quo is evident. And they
may have certain corollaries. If the Negro tries to deny his inferiority and claim
his theoretical rights, then the white reacts furiously and with all the bitterness
and hatred the human soul is capable of. But that is by no means the same kind of
lunatic irrationality that characterized Nazi anti-Semitism (and lies at the bottom
of most anti-Semitism). That led to the literal destruction of six million Jews.
U.S. anti-Negroism, to the extent that it succeeds, has no such aim. This country
wants its niggers, as niggers. And this is why the Negro struggle is historically
so much more meaningful than the Jewish struggle for survival: it is a genuinely
revolutionary struggle, and once entered upon cannot stop short of its goal. It
may not achieve the goal, at least for a long time, but it is not going to go away
and leave U.S. society in peace and quiet ever again. Of that I am profoundly
convinced, and it means more than most of us have even begun to recognize yet.
    Don't misunderstand me: I am not for ignoring the socio-psychological
aspects of the problem. But I do feel very strongly that they should be put into
the specific historical and socio-economic context which has given them their
very special form and quality. This problem, unlike Nazism, long antedates

THE AGE OF MONOPOLY CAPITAL

monopoly capitalism [monocap] and has not changed its fundamental nature in the monocap period. But it does become worse and more insoluble under monocap. And in the long run it may prove to be U.S. monocap's Achilles Heel.

Only one other point at the moment; I did not intend for an instant to suggest that Keynesian full employment would "solve" the Negro problem. All I wanted to say is that it would only be in a context of relatively full employment that what you call "business Negroism" would be feasible. The profound stagnationist trends under monocap are therefore crucially important in ruling out that kind of a way out for the U.S.

On the difference between racism and anti-Semitism, by the way, have a look at the relevant chapters of [Oliver] Cox's *Caste, Class and Race*.[196] They are among the best in the book. Cox is very good in recognizing the profoundly exploitative character of racism; where he falls down is in not understanding that integration and assimilation are absolutely impossible under this form of society and that they are therefore *necessarily* revolutionary goals. I have corresponded with him some lately, and his failure to understand this leads him to support the kind of drivel the CP has been putting out (cf. that article by Jackson I sent you yesterday).

I hope to have some addresses from Yugo by the time we talk on the phone.

Love and hastily,

/s Paul

PMS to PAB

[*Handwritten*]

Villa Dubrovnik
Dubrovnik, Yugoslavia
Monday, Aug. 19, 1963

Dear Paul,

This is an address which will probably be okay for the next couple of weeks, but given the quality of the Yugoslav and Argentinian mails there is certainly no point in your using it. I hope to get some word from you when we reach Venice on Sept. 1.

The trip so far has been reasonably interesting. The boat crossing was dull — British food, even if presented on a fancy menu, is nothing to look forward to 3 times a day, and there isn't much else to divert one. Paris was rainy, and the only people we could find not on vacation were the Thorners. Dan is well established at the *Ecole Pratique des Hautes Etudes* but becomes more and more a narrow

196. Oliver C. Cox, *Caste, Class and Race* (New York: Monthly Review Press, 1959).

specialist with less and less interest in unrelated matters.[197] Still, he's very bright. His opinion of Bettelklop's book on India by the way, is very favorable.[198] Vienna I found disappointing, probably because my memories are unduly rosy. Ed März was most hospitable — spent an evening with him and [Kurt] Rothschild and [Josef] Steindl, and another with Ed and Steindl. Steindl had an operation for the ailment he was suffering from when you were here and now seems in reasonably good health, but he certainly is a difficult person to involve in a conversation, let alone a discussion. Personally, however, I found him quite charming. More than ever, I am for dedicating opus to him and Michał Kalecki as the 2 most important neglected economists of our time.[199]

We spent 4 days in Belgrade and were received in a very friendly fashion by a couple of the underlings of the Institute of Economic Research of which [economist Branko] Horvat is now the director. One evening spent at Horvat's with a few others. Horvat is undoubtedly bright, but I'm afraid my friend Kosta Mihailovich, whom I had lunch with, is right that the main effect of the brightness is to make him the most effective ambassador of Western ideas in Yugoslav economic circles. Kosta is much more orthodox and pretty sour about the way things are going here (his official position is chief of the *Serbian Institute of Econ Research*). Unfortunately, it is hard not to agree with him. This is socialism under the watchword of "*Enrichissez vous*," and I am afraid its human product is bound to be a new species of the genus *Spiessbuerger* [petty bourgeois]. Mihailovich, whose judgment I value, says things are going very differently in the USSR, where he recently spent a month; and I certainly hope he's right. But unfortunately there is all too good reason to believe that Poland, Czecho, Hungary *et al* are headed in the same direction as Yugo, only by slightly different routes.

The Chinese, I am sure, are wrong to call all this "capitalism" — that only confuses the issue — but their instinct is sound where they denounce it as contrary to the spirit of Marx and Lenin. And they are also right to insist that a long period of "Stalinism" is needed. (By Stalinism, needless to say, the Chinese do not mean a reign of terror, abuses of personal power, etc., phenomena they never experienced in China. They mean a system which is led by dedicated Marxists and is committed to a long struggle to remake the human material

197. Economist Daniel Thorner, specialist in agriculture and economics of India.
198. Charles Bettelheim, *India Independent*, first published in 1962 (American edition, New York: Monthly Review Press, 1968).
199. *Monopoly Capital* was dedicated instead to Che Guevara, whom Baran and Sweezy both knew. The importance of Kalecki and Steindl's thought and its influence on their own work was explained in *Monopoly Capital*, p. 56.

inherited from capitalism, feudalism, etc.). Nothing of the sort is going to happen, however. The whole E. European bloc — and here I include Yugo — is headed for "liberalization," "democracy," and all that sort of thing, naturally to a rising chorus of hosannahs from Western liberals, Social Democrats, Laborites, *et tutti quanti*. The result will be to arrest development at its present stage. After that, can retrogression and degeneration be avoided? Gloomy thoughts, I'm afraid, but what other kind can one generate in the face of the all-too obvious reality?

The other side of this coin is an utterly provincial attitude toward the world in general — and this is as true of Paris and Vienna as it is of Belgrade. The Chinese are dismissed as obvious madmen. When I tried to explain the rational core of their position, Horvat said he couldn't agree but that at any rate it was the first time he had realized there might be some sense to their position. As far as Asia, Africa, and L. America are concerned, the attitude seems not too different from what we would find in a U.S. faculty club. These countries have problems of economic development, need education, and help, etc. That they need and are headed for revolutions *a la* Cuba that will tear the guts out of imperialism and may blow up the world — this is not only not understood, it simply lies beyond the prevailing intellectual horizon. For the first time in a long while I've had a sense of relief at being an American. At least the U.S. is aware that great events and great struggles are under way — in the U.S. one witnesses and even in a small way participates in the mainstream of the history of the epoch. In Europe. . . .

Dubrovnik is really very beautiful and undoubtedly has a most interesting history — one can see that just from looking at its physical layout and its melange of architecture. I don't really like vacations, but if one has to take them this is probably as acceptable a place as any.

[. . .]

Zirel joins in send lots of love.

/s Paul

PAB to PMS

Hotel Crillon
Buenos Aires, Argentina
August 28, 1963

Dear Paul,

After such a long break in correspondence, it was a great pleasure to receive your letter from Dubrovnik of August 19th. I was unable to write to you all this time because of a lack of a suitable address. It is not enough for you to have a reasonable pleasant vacation; you should have a really "wonderful" time because only in this way could we *on the average* come out approximately all right. For my trip thus far was anything but particularly agreeable. While I have greatly enjoyed Mexico on a previous occasion, this time I had a miserable stay there because the altitude did not agree with my ticker. They were all most friendly, hospitable and attentive, but I could hardly move, and spent a good deal of my time in a horizontal position. The change-over to Chile was a major relief, and there I spent a most interesting week — talking to a lot of people and getting something of a feel for LA politics and economic problems. There are many intelligent and understanding people there, although the general atmosphere is more like that of Britain than that of a country on the eve of a major upheaval. Allende and the FRAP [*Frente de Acción Popular* (Popular Action Front)] people are good, honest chaps; I don't think that they would sell out if elected, but they are not the types to put the country upside down, even if given the chance. My guess is that Allende is more of an Arbenz than of a Fidel. . . . By the way, I strongly advised him against undertaking the planned lecture tour in the U.S. — for reasons which I shall explain to you when writing at home on a better typewriter — and I have the impression he is going to accept my advice.

But the stay *here* is pretty awful. In the first place, I don't like it here — the city, the people, etc., etc., — and secondly, the University works me to death. They have scheduled an endless series of lectures, the rooms are overcrowded with students who understand absolutely nothing, and the procedure of talking via an interpreter is most trying. The worst part of it all is that the kids don't have the slightest interest in reasoning — all they are concerned with is conclusions, and the way those conclusions are arrived at is of no interest to them. The result is that there is no intelligent dialogue; they have learned a few slogans by heart and consider that this is enough. The grown-ups are not much better, and the mental chaos is only matched by the organizational mess. The management has received me with a chilliness which makes me wonder why in hell they ever invited me; although half my stay is (fortunately) over, I have hardly seen Germani and such types. Not that I miss them, but it is a strange atmosphere all the way round.

[. . .]

The condition in the country is as confused as it is confusing; economically it is in a terrible state without the slightest prospect for improvement. It demonstrates like a textbook example that the mere existence of *capitalism* is anything but a guarantee of economic development in an underdeveloped country. Argentina had its Rostow "take-off," except it took off in the direction of stagnation and decay. Consumption per capita has declined in Argentina by over 13% since 1961!

What you write about the rise and prevalence of "welfare-ism" in all of the socialist countries (but also in Italy, France, Germany &c.) checks entirely with my impressions last year. That the Chinese are very uneasy about all of this and see at the end of the road an assortment of various Swedens is quite understandable. What is less understandable is what could be or should be done to avoid this "*neo-verbuergerlichung*" [neo-petty bourgeois-ation] which sweeps the world. Enthusiasm and revolutionary rejuvenation a la Cuba *is* an answer. Stalinism (even if purged of all its lousy elements) is probably not. As 1956 has shown, it does not work; and enthusiasm and revolutionary spirit may emerge spontaneously but cannot be manufactured to order. The tragedy of the situation is that hunger produces not a desire for socialism but for more food and more food creates also not a drive for a new society but for a refrigerator and an automobile.

I get more and more the depressing feeling that mankind had 2 buses sent for it by Providence both of which it missed. The Western World had its great chance in 1917/18 — it was mucked up by the Germans; the Eastern World had its great chance in 1949 — it was mucked up by the U.S. The Cuba impetus in Latin America — I think — is for the time being over. In fact it has now the opposite effect. If Cuba itself was largely possible because of the neutralization of the middle classes — the middle classes in LA now have been driven into the camp of reaction. And with them go the privileged strata of the working class, the intellectuals who sell out to almost any bidder thus forming together with the well-kept army a formidable reactionary bloc. This bloc operates "democratically" as long as conditions permit; it is willing to switch to dictatorship the minute there is a slightest danger. What is most interesting is that the ideology of the whole business now is no longer bourgeois rationalism + liberalism (there isn't a dog that would bark at those trees) but Catholicism viz. Christian democracy. *Revolucion con Liberdad.* . . . By the way, Marxists and socialists of all kinds have gotten so accustomed to debating the liberals of all colorations (social democrats &c.) that the Christian demo's leave them help- and speech-less. But since liberalism and bourgeois rationalism are wholly anachronistic in a mad world, irrationalism takes naturally over; and what better form of irrationalism is there than Christ's Eternal Church? Jesuit *paters* are all over the place, they have lots of $'s (by the way, not only from the U.S. but interestingly enough from Bonn) and surely plenty of experience!

These are all rather depressing thoughts, and history may still give the whole thing a different turn — except that it takes a Gargantuan optimism — which I ain't got — to earnestly believe in it. The tragedy is that Marx was more than right in his analysis and prediction of human misery and human degeneration; he was less than right in his belief that this degeneration will supply the energy to overthrow the *Scheisse* and create a different society + a different human animal. But all this is not something that you want in Venice and Rome and Florence where man can be seen in his most magnificent emanations and where one can study concretely what it is from which he has become *entfremdet* [alienated]. . . . This is timely and "placely" in Buenos Aires which is some strange way is the very opposite.

I cannot wait until I may get the hell out of here. On Friday, Sept 13th is departure for Rio where I expect to spend a week (if sufficiently interesting). Hope to stay there in the hotel you recommended: Trocadero, Copacabana. If I don't hear anything from the Brazilians, I'll just have a look at Rio and continue homewards. This Friday (Aug. 30th) I am going for a weekend to Montevideo (some more bloody lecturing). . . .

Depending on how long this letter will take to reach you, you could drop me a line either to BA or to Rio. Paradoxically, at this stage being back in Palo Alto looks most attractive, although the prospect of starting to teach a few days after returning makes me shudder. I have never felt so absolutely void of a message as I feel now; particularly *in rebus* economic development — the mere words make me sick now.

This place is full at the present time of British economists of various kinds, and it is interesting that the Ford Foundation is using the Britishers now instead of Yanqui's because the latter encounter too much antipathy among the students. I was told this in so many words by the chief manipulator here who is organizing cultural exports from the U.S.

Well, so much for now. Enjoy yourself during the remaining few days, and write. Without letters I feel terribly isolated, and the long interruption in our correspondence has been a serious deprivation.

Give my best to Zirel,
All my love,
       /s Yours Paul

PAB to PMS

Palo Alto
October 10, 1963

Dear Paul,
I was meaning to write earlier but pressures of business on and off campus + opus work greatly reduce my marginal propensity to type. As you so wisely observed, there could hardly be a greater blessing than an efficient secretary who would take care of current correspondence, filing, formalities and various details of life. . . .

1. On the Sino-Soviet complex some other time. On the whole I like very much your latest RoM on the subject; such reservations as I have, I shall communicate to you in due course.

2. In the latest issue of the *Review of Economics & Statistics* there is an article by Reder on Economics of Immigration.[200] I haven't read it yet, but someone told me that it is very informative and interesting. If I get an offprint, I'll send it along; otherwise drop in at the Public Library and have a look at it.

3. I find [Clement] Attlee's letter in part interesting and in part cockeyed. What is very important in my opinion, and needs to be borne in mind as a likely objection to the opus argument is the point that it is not correct to focus attention exclusively on BB [big business] investment in general and on investment in plant and facilities in particular. True as it is, that BB sets the tone of the whole show, there remains the statistical fact that one-half if not more of the total investment is undertaken in the unproductive sector of the economy, new office buildings for dentists and doctors, restaurants, motels and the Devil knows what. Although all of this Dreck is ultimately related to and in fact governed by BB behavior, there is an obvious time lag which creates a strong impression of a certain independence of that "service sector" from the productive sector of the economy. This time lag is by no means unimportant, in fact has done a lot to cushion recessions and perhaps contributed as much as many built-in stabilizers to preventing them from becoming much worse than they did. In all traditional models — from Marx to Kalecki and Keynes — this relative independence of the service sector has been understandably ignored and attention focused on Dept I and II.[201] In a sense, we do not follow this pattern by stressing the surplus absorption mechanism, but it may be necessary to refer to this particular business *expressis verbis* and point out that the investment theory applying to BB with Steindl &c does not apply to that other sector where all sorts of things happen independently even if this independence is only short-term with its impact also only short-term.

The stuff on finance leaves me cold; all that it really boils down to, if I am right, is that in addition to "legitimate" consumption, there is a certain "deficit-supported" consumption based on installment credit &c. That with existing indivisibilities cum "human nature" precluding people from saving ahead of time and then buying an automobile and forcing them to buy it first and save

200. Melvin W. Reder, "The Economic Consequences of Increased Immigration," *The Review of Economics and Statistics* 45, no. 3 (August 1963): 221–30.

201. Department I is means of production; Department II is consumer goods. See Paul M. Sweezy, *The Theory of Capitalist Development* (New York: Monthly Review Press, 1972), 76.

thereafter to pay it off, the absence of installment credit would be a major setback to the durables' industries goes without saying. It would hurt particularly badly the construction market where indeed private housing would be severely hit (and probably almost entirely replaced by apartment house dwelling), but to say that capitalism depends for its existence as Attlee says on installment and similar financial arrangements would strike me as "mildly" exaggerated.

4. [Roman] Rosdolsky did not send me a copy of his Lange review, if you still have it, send it to me, please. I would very much like to see it.[202]

5. Concerning the "book after this" [i.e. after *Monopoly Capital*]. In the first place, I must tell you that, I am so painfully anxious to get this one out, that I am just about incapable of thinking of anything beyond and after it. . . . I am redoing somewhat the IS chapter, and hope to finish writing the remainder no later than your arrival in California. Then I want to sit down with the whole MS and start revising what is to be revised. The whole thing should be out of our lives by Xmas; I cannot stand it much longer. . . .

As the next job which would fill the remainder of the academic year I would like to fix up the volume of essays, revising some and adding one or two which I have in more or less extensive notes, but not written out. Once this is accomplished, I would have a clean slate and be open for "new business." There statement #1: I would very much like for us to do something jointly. It would be useful, and as the kids say "funner." The only problem is what? This raises a major "philosophical" problem on which perhaps we do not entirely see eye to eye. The work on the opus and the perusal of a fair amount of "Americana" have convinced me that to add social criticism to existing social criticism is a labor of Sisyphus. To belabor the point that *Scheisse* is *Scheisse* and that what we have is nothing but *Scheisse* has become now an enterprise which is overtaken by the dialectic of history. Even the last *Dreckologist* from *Dissent* or some similar organ will agree today that what we live in is a lousy society and if you push him a little will even grant you that capitalism has something to do with it. After having nailed down this biz in opus and having shown how monocap creates the muck that surrounds us on all fronts, we will have placed this part of the story "on the record."

What is at the present time at issue and indeed most urgently so is the question whether Marxian dialectic has broken down i.e. whether it is possible for *Scheisse* to accumulate, to coagulate, to cover all of society (and a goodly part of the related world) without producing the dialectical counter-force

202. Rosdolsky's very extensive review of Oskar Lange's *Political Economy*, vol. 1, was to be published as the last part of Rosdolsky's major work. See Roman Rosdolsky, *The Making of Marx's 'Capital'* (London: Pluto Press, 1977), 551–72.

which would break through it and blow it into the air. *Hic Rhodus, hic salta*!
If the answer is affirmative then Marxism in its traditional form has become
superannuated. It has predicted the misery, it has explained full well the causes of
it becoming as comprehensive as it is; it was in error, however in its central thesis
that the misery generates itself the forces of its abolition.

I have just finished reading Marcuse's new book (in MS) [*One-Dimensional
Man*], which in a laborious kind of a way advances this very position which
is called the Great Refusal or the Absolute Negation.[203] Everything is *Dreck*:
monopoly capitalism and the Soviet Union, capitalism and socialism as we know
it; the negative part of the Marx story has come True — its positive part remained
a figment of imagination. We are back at the state of the Utopians pure and
simple; a better world there should be but there ain't no social force in sight to
bring it about. Not only is Socialism no answer, but there isn't anyone to give that
answer anyway. From the Great Refusal and the Absolute Negation to the Great
Withdrawal and the Absolute Betrayal is only a very short step. I have a very
strong feeling that this is at the moment in the center of the intellectuals' thought
(and sentiment) — not only here but also in Latin America and elsewhere, and
that it would be very much our commitment *sich damit Auseinander zu setzen*
[to confront and come to terms with this sentiment]. There is hardly anyone else
around. The official left simply yells [you have been victimized] a la *Political
Affairs*, others are bewildered.

What is required is a cool analysis of the whole situation, the restoration of
a historical perspective, a reminder of the relevant time dimensions and much
more. If we could do a good job on that — perhaps only a shortish booklet of less
than 200 pp — we would make a major contribution and perform with regard
to many a truly "liberating" act. Think about this and tell me what you think
about it. I am not arguing that something on the South should not be done. If an
analysis of the South would produce a major perspective, then it would be most
important. If it would merely add another chapter to the description and analysis
of the prevailing condition, then its contribution would be relatively small. But all
this we'll have occasion to talk and write about.

Meanwhile,

/s Paul

203. Baran and Marcuse were close friends going back to their days at the Institute for Social
Research in Frankfurt before Hitler's rise. Baran had asked to see Marcuse's book manuscript *One
Dimensional Man*, which Marcuse sent to him. Baran had his terminal heart attack with Marcuse's
just-then-published *One Dimensional Man* in his hand. See Paul A. Baran and Herbert Marcuse,
"Baran-Marcuse Correspondence," http://monthlyreview.org/commentary/baran-marcuse-
correspondence/.

PMS to PAB

Larchmont
October 16, 1963

Dear PAB,

[...]

Have a look at "Is Yugoslavia a Socialist Country?" in the Sept. 27th issue of *Peking Review*. Until now, I had been inclined to discount at something close to 100 percent the Chinese claims that Yugo has reverted to capitalism. But this article presents some very damaging evidence that makes it necessary to reconsider the whole problem. Unfortunately, their efforts to explain and interpret the material — in terms of "betrayal" by the "Tito clique" — are worse than useless. My own feeling at the moment, subject to change on a moment's notice, however, is that what you have in Yugo now is not (yet) capitalism but a degenerated form of socialism and that it results basically from the liberalizing policies which were introduced after the break with the Cominform, but that the introduction of these policies had nothing to do with the betrayal but rather represented an effort on the part of Tito and Co. to find a viable alternative to a "Stalinism" which in Yugo's domestic and international situation was on the verge of collapse — a collapse which would undoubtedly have been followed by Western-backed counter-revolution. But the human material had been changed very little by the few years of socialism, and once given some freedom it began to reproduce all the old dreck [garbage] — in part legally (the enterprises under the new dispensation seem to be run for the benefit of what is essentially a private group almost as much as U.S. corporations are, though the composition and selection of the group is not the same in the two cases), and in part illegally (the Chinese cite a good deal of evidence from Yugo sources to show that there are many capitalist millionaires operating as "craftsmen" and that concentration in the countryside has proceeded a long way by methods which are familiar enough from the experience of such countries as India and Mexico). Once this process of "recapitalization" gets under way, it is very difficult and perhaps even impossible to stop. The government and the party get thoroughly infected, and it is only Trotskyite romantics who can believe that somehow the masses are capable, or even want, to go back to the status quo ante (i.e. a Stalinist setup) with all its rigors and repressions.

If this is what has happened in Yugo in the 15 years that have elapsed since the great liberalization, is it not also inevitably happening, only still in a less developed form, in the other eastern European countries where liberalizing started only eight years later than in Yugo? And how about the Soviet Union itself? Does the fact that socialism has existed there much longer (under a

Stalinist setup) give any grounds for hope that the human material will react positively and creatively to liberalization rather than by retrogressing?

These questions are all evidently closely related to the theme of the "book after" which you propose in your letter of the 10th. It is a frighteningly big job to tackle, and I don't know whether I have anywhere near enough knowledge or courage to get into it. But all that had better wait for personal consultation. In the meanwhile, the present book [*Monopoly Capital*] has to take priority.

I have been thinking about the Negro chapter again, especially the "architectural" problem which it raises. What would you think of the following: (1) Leave the [existing] Negro material in the QoS chapters, and (2) confine the Negro chapter itself to showing what the problem is and why it has to get worse rather than better under monocap [monopoly capitalism]. Showing what the problem is in a sense is an *excursus* from the basic subject matter of the book, i.e., monocap. Monocap did *not* create the Negro problem, it inherited it. The logical question for us to ask, therefore, is: what does (and can) monocap do with and about it? The *excursus*, however, cannot be dispensed with since it is impossible to take for granted an understanding of the nature of the problem, i.e. how and why the Negro got to occupy the place in U.S. society that he occupies today. On the question of what monocap can do about it, I think we should guard against assuming that Big Biz has any special racial biases. As Virginia Durr [civil rights activist] says in a recent letter to me, "big industry with government contracts like Lockheed is perfectly willing to integrate the Negro into their labor force, they don't give a damn if the labor force is black, white, red, or pink (that is, color not ideas) so long as the union is weak and they don't cause trouble." And [James] Boggs told us that Chrysler is practically hiring only Negroes now.[204] The real point is that the kind of society monocap inevitably creates and perpetuates is necessarily divided into privileged and unprivileged, that regardless of the exact quantitative relation between the two groups at any time or even over time the contrast between the two grows (just as the contrast between the advanced and backward countries in the imperialist world grows), and that the Negro whom history put at the bottom has no way of escape and is bound to be the chief sufferer. Fundamentally, of course, it is a class question, not a race question, but there are historically conditioned racial reasons why the Negro happens to occupy the bottom compartment of the class structure.

---

204. James Boggs, author of *Monthly Review*'s 1963 July-August special issue, *The American Revolution: Pages from a Negro Worker's Notebook* — subsequently published as a book by Monthly Review Press.

I will proceed to try to draft something along the above lines. But if you have any strong dissenting feelings, or amendments or addenda, please let me know soonest.

Love,

      s/ Paul

Oct. 17 — P.S. Today is Huby's 60th birthday. Makes one think, doesn't it?

PMS to PAB

Larchmont
October 29, 1963

Dear Paul,

[…]

    I think I have solved the riddle of the change in U.S. immigration policy after WW I. The key is that up to 1910 (date chosen because it was a census year) demand for labor was expanding in *all* sectors of U.S. economy. Under the circumstances, immigration was essential. After 1910, however, employment in the agricultural sector began to decline and the U.S. became, so to speak, self-sufficient in the matter of supplying its own manpower needs. Internal migration could now take the place of immigration. From this time on, the U.S. could follow the "normal" pattern of Western European development. Further immigration of unskilled labor having become unnecessary, all the disadvantages that accompanied it could be given their full weight. Or to put it otherwise, there was no more vested interest to oppose the anti-immigration forces. The climax came right after the war when the revolutionary wave in Europe put the fear of God into the U.S. ruling class: lower-class immigrants were now seen as carriers of revolution. The inner psychological and political mechanisms were brilliantly highlighted by the Sacco-Vanzetti case which has to be seen against this background to be really understood. The transformation of Negroes from a regional peasantry into a national urban subproletariat was one aspect of the larger historical movement. World War I accelerated everything and brought matters to a head, but it wasn't the cause. One might even speculate, I suppose, that if the stagnation which set in after 1907 had not been interrupted by the war, and unemployment of 1930's-proportions had developed (as indeed it was already

doing by 1912–13), the pressure to cut off immigration would have come just
about as soon. The whole subject would be a marvelous one for a really profound
Marxist historical-analytical study. But where the people capable of such work?

More on other stuff soon,

Love,

/s Paul

PAB to PMS

Palo Alto

November 2, 1963

Dear Paul,

[…]

In your very good little thing on the economy in the latest MR you point at
automobiles *cum* housing and say that their expansion was possible with the
help of credit.[205] I think one could and should generalize this observation for
the benefit of economic theory and the opus. In the American society which
is bifurcated and in which the upper half is pretty well established, a new
phenomenon has popped up which does not vitiate the Keynesian analytic
apparatus but calls for its supplementation. Viz.: in addition to the possibility of
government deficit spending there has developed a possibility of *private* deficit
spending. The income generating impact of the two is naturally the same. The
difference between them is that the government can engage in it pretty much as it
sees fit without asking anyone any questions (except for Congress). Private deficit
spending is circumscribed by the willingness to lend on the part of financial
institutions and (to a lesser extent because of the always present opportunity
for re-financing) by the need to re-pay the loans. Still, there is the possibility of
a persistent growth of net indebtedness i.e. of net deficit expenditures on the
part of the population. Ergo the consumption function is no longer $C = f(Y)$ [in
this case, Y = income] nor even, as later corrected $C = f(Y+A)$ where A stands for
Assets, but $C = f(Y+A + Cb)$ where Cb stands for Capacity to Borrow. Therefore
the sales effort now much less directed towards switching the consumer's dollar
from commodity A to commodity B but towards inducing him (a) to abstain from
saving and (b) to engage in deficit spending (borrowing).

From this would follow an ever-growing dependence of the system on
advertising and on ingenuity in devising product differentiation &c but also
an interesting borrowing-repaying cycle. Since an average income recipient

205. Leo Huberman and Paul M. Sweezy, "Economic Fluctuations and Trends," *Monthly Review*
15 no. 7 (November 1963): 353–63.

has to maintain *some* ratio between his Y and installment payments, he will engage in new borrowing only after having repaid his previous debt unless his Y keeps increasing. There are obviously new borrowers to be still gotten into the borrowing stream. But if everyone would be "lent Up" and if Y would stay fairly stable or growing only slowly, one would get a swing of private deficit spending very similar to that of inventories accumulation and decumulation. Since all the private deficits are insured nowadays, there is no danger of their suddenly collapsing over the head of biz in case of *Kladderadatsch* [German Social Democrat term for collapse of bourgeois society]; the only danger that exists is that increments of deficit spending on the part of the private sector may decline or even turn negative in a case of a serious recession. If this is right and interesting, it ought to be worked out.

More later; now back to opus writing where I struggle like a Hercules with every page. When exactly (flight &c.) do you arrive?

A bientot.

Tout à vous,

/s Paul

[*Handwritten below.*]

Heard a new definition: Recession: if *you* lose your job; Depression: if *I* lose my job.

PMS to PAB

Larchmont

January 19, 1964

Dear Paul,

This letter will be by way of thinking on the typewriter. The problem is to re-architect chapter 7 ["The Absorption of Surplus: Militarism and Imperialism"] which I have been trying to fix up in minor ways and have finally come to the conclusion that it can't be done. Something more drastic is needed.

As it stands, the plan of the chapter is somewhat as follows: First, the question is posed as to why the oligarchy needs a large and growing military establishment in the post World War II world when no such need existed in the pre-war period. The answer is approached historically. After World War I, the chief have-not imperialist power was kayo'ed for the time; the U.S. was allied to the old imperialist powers which firmly controlled Asia and Africa; extending control in Latin America required little in the way of military force; and the Soviet Union was too weak and exhausted to constitute a threat. By the 30's, however, the situation had changed. Germany and Japan were on the

warpath, and it might seem that the old imperialist powers needed to arm heavily
to defend their positions. Instead, they followed the policy of appeasement
designed to push the Axis powers into a mutually destructive war against the
socialist USSR. This policy backfired, leading to World War II itself. The next
question is why there was no return to the status quo ante, armament-wise, after
the war. The official explanation of defense against Soviet aggression is nonsense.
The real explanation is the continued determination to contain, roll back,
eventually destroy socialism which became much more extensive and powerful as
a result of World War II. The inherently aggressive character of this policy calls
for an endless effort to gain (or maintain as the case may be) military superiority.
Since the other side cannot let the gap become too large, this assures an arms
race, in other words a need for more and more armed forces, *Q.E.D.*

However, this is not the whole story. The U.S., with a long tradition of
imperialist expansion, has used the opportunities presented by its leadership role
in world capitalism and the disintegration of the old colonial empires to build
up the biggest empire the world has ever seen. Quite apart from the struggle
against socialism, this effort would require enormous armed forces. And in fact
it is being admitted with increasing frankness that the purpose of the world-wide
system of bases is to police the empire rather than to counter the non-existent
threat of Soviet (and Chinese) aggression. The danger to the empire comes
from socialist revolutions, which are mutually reinforcing and gain impetus
and strength from the growing strength of the major socialist powers. So in the
final analysis, the two reasons for a large military establishment — to contain the
spread of socialism and to police the empire — merge into one. The rest of the
chapter on why, in spite of all, the military outlet for surplus doesn't solve the
problem doesn't concern me for the moment: it is the main part of the chapter up
to page 45, as sketched above, which I now find unsatisfactory.

I don't find it easy to put my finger on just what is wrong, but in most
general terms I think the trouble is — superficiality. Everything is made to
depend on hostility to socialism which is taken as a datum and as such can only
be considered to be a subjective factor. The objective factors which underlie
and explain this hostility are not examined — except belatedly and so to speak
incidentally when the threat of socialism to the empire is brought in near the end.
And even then nothing systematic is said about why the U.S. wants an empire
anyway. A critic could legitimately claim that the whole argument as it stands is
compatible with the assumption that U.S. policy is dominated by an irrational
dislike of socialism and an equally irrational desire for an empire. And that, leave
us not kid ourselves, ain't not no Marxism.

So the chapter needs to be redone.

[Interruption at that point. Resumed on January 22; Sweezy's own note.]

The question is how is the chapter to be *approfondi*. Let us try an approach and see if it shows any promise.

The beginning could be the same as now, and indeed more or less has to be unless the preceding chapter is also to be redone. In other words we start with the question: Why does the U.S. oligarchy need such a huge military machine nowadays when it used to get along with such a little one? From here we proceed to a theoretical treatment of the question of the role of armed force in capitalist society.

1. Capitalism has always been an international system. This was understood by Marx, but the plan of *Capital*, taken together with the fact that it was never finished, tends to obscure this. The international character of the system is crucial to an understanding of the role played by armed force in its structure and development.

2. The three major uses of armed forces: to dispossess and repress domestic labor; to subjugate and hold down colonies (using term in broad sense); to fight with other capitalist metropolises for monopolistic positions vis-à-vis colonies and to be able to exploit each other.

(That last one is not well expressed, but you can probably get the point.) Insert footnote along in here to the effect that the technology of warfare and the organization and provisioning of armed forces have always — and not only under capitalism — exercised a profound influence on economic development. This aspect, however, we omit from consideration in this essay. (See Marx to Engels, September 25, 1857.)[206]

Amendment to point 1 above: Not only has capitalism always been an international system; it has always been a hierarchical system with one or possibly two or three leaders at the top and completely dependent colonies at the bottom and many degrees of superordination-subordination in between. Each layer exploits those beneath it, while each nation attempts to monopolize as many of the units below it as possible. This schema will permit a more satisfactory formulation of the matter in point 2.

3. All nations — except the completely dependent, and defenseless ones at the bottom — have a need for armed force to maintain and if possible better their position in the exploitive hierarchy. How much a given nation needs at a given time depends on (1) its position in the hierarchy and (2) on the pattern

206. Karl Marx and Frederick Engels, *Selected Correspondence* (Moscow: Progress Publishers, 1975), 91–92.

of relations in the hierarchy as a whole at that time. Leading nations will always require relatively most, and their needs will vary according to whether there is or is not an active struggle going on among them for the top spot. Thus the 17th and 18th centuries, which saw almost continuous struggles among the Dutch, Spanish, and English and later between the English and French, were highly "militarized" centuries. After 1815, the period of Pax Britannica lasted for more than half a century, with the need for armed forces receding in importance in most countries. Bourgeois thought, incidentally, came to regard this period as the "norm" rather than as the exception determined by the fact that for the time being — and as such matters go quite a long time too — there was only one unchallenged leader nation which to one degree or another exploited the whole world and maintained its supremacy through its own armed strength and a system of alliances which suitably rewarded those who helped to maintain Britain on the top of the heap. The German challenge, beginning with the unification of the Reich under Prussian hegemony, of course upset this relative equilibrium and led to the new upsurge of militarism which culminated in World War I.

With so much by way of theoretical introduction, it should be possible to go on and give a sort of schematic sketch of the development of U.S. capitalism's need for military strength. The guiding principle of U.S. policy during the country's whole history up to World War I can be described as one of maximum aggrandizement at minimum cost. Up to the end of the Napoleonic Wars, this was pursued largely through exploiting the struggles among the contenders for leadership (French alliance during the revolution, Louisiana Purchase, etc.); after 1815 through playing ball with Britain while always extracting the maximum attainable price. In this way, the U.S. built up a large, if still secondary, empire on the cheap and by the early 20th century was about ready to start making its own bid for a leadership role. This was delayed by the need to join the other "have" powers in turning back the first German leadership bid and then the German-Japanese bid. After World War II, however, U.S. leadership of the capitalist world was established beyond any possibility of challenge, as Britain's had been after 1815. This by itself would be enough to explain why U.S. military needs never returned to the status quo ante following World War II. The undisputed leader of the system must have and maintain military supremacy directly and/or through manipulation of alliances. The U.S. used both methods, all the while gathering into its own neocolonial empire the debris of the older colonial empires. This too dictated a need for increased military strength, as the U.S. increasingly took over policing assignments formerly discharged by the older empires. But Britain had had a similar experience in the 19th century without feeling a steadily mounting need for military strength. In fact, British experience would tend to support the view that the very existence of an undisputed leader would have the effect of stabilizing the military needs of everyone, including its own even if at a relatively high level.

To explain why U.S. needs did not stabilize but instead expanded rapidly during the postwar period, we have to go beyond theory based on past capitalist experience and take account of a new historical phenomenon, the rise of a world socialist system as a rival and alternative to the world capitalist system. The question is: why should this give rise to steadily mounting military needs on the part of the capitalist leader nation?

Vulgar capitalist ideology (or perhaps it doesn't even deserve that label?) has a ready explanation: the threat of socialist (Soviet or Chinese or Sino-Soviet) aggression, or rather the determination of socialism to conquer the world by military means. This, of course, is nonsense — the reasons need not be gone into at anything like the length of the present version of chapter 7.

Vulgar socialist ideology also has a ready explanation: socialism has to be combatted and if possible destroyed because its advance means the loss of foreign trade which is crucial to the existence of capitalism. This also is nonsense, since socialist countries are perfectly willing to trade with capitalist countries. Even more: as bourgeois economists are never tired of repeating, the more developed a country is industrially the better it is as a trading partner. Since the underdeveloped countries develop under socialism and not under capitalism, the leader capitalist countries, on this argument, should welcome the spread of socialism in the underdeveloped part of the capitalist world. (*NB*: Somewhere in here, point out in footnote that Oliver Cox's theory of capitalism [in *Capitalism as a System*], while valuable and constructive in stressing the international and hierarchical character of the system, lends itself to errors of this kind because of its exclusive emphasis on trade as the form of relations among countries in the capitalist system.)

The problem is in reality more complex. What concerns capitalists is not trade but profits and the profits from exports and imports are but a part, and under present-day conditions a minor part, of the total profits of international business in the widest sense. One must look at the problem not from the standpoint of the "nation" but from the standpoint of the giant corporations which dominate the nation. Here follows the meat of the chapter contributed to the Kalecki *Festschrift* — Standard Oil as the prototype of the "multinational" corporation — the spread of this phenomenon since 1950 or so — latest figures on sales and profits of foreign subsidiaries (*Business Week*, Dec. 28). (Footnote somewhere in here pointing out that all this has very little to do with capital export and that the greatest weakness of Lenin's theory of imperialism was to confuse foreign investment with export of capital.) I don't suppose it's possible to get any overall figures on the proportion of the profits of, say, the 500 largest corporations derived from international operations, but if you have any ideas about how they might be procured or estimated, please let me know pronto. In any case, the decisive importance of international operations is not open to question. And the condition of their being carried on is that the laws and institutions of the host countries should be suitably adjusted — private property, receptivity to foreign enterprises, etc.

Against this background, one can see the real nature of the threat of socialism. When a country takes that path, it *eo ipso* excludes the multinational corporations. Case of Cuba as illustration. So the spread of socialism is a mortal danger to the dominant force in the advanced capitalist countries, and above all to the U.S. which has far outstripped the others [in] proliferating the multinationals.

But, it may be asked, why does countering the threat of socialist expansion involve a need for growing military might? I haven't worked this argument out yet, but a number of points to be dealt with are fairly obvious. For one thing, I think it is probably necessary to dispose of the notion that there's a better and cheaper way for capitalism to protect itself, i.e., by helping the underdeveloped countries to develop and hence rendering them immune to the socialist virus. They can't develop under a regime of exploitation by multinational corporations, and the whole purpose of capitalist policy is precisely to keep them under that regime. In fact, under that regime they are bound to get progressively worse, hence the threat of socialism must grow. The only possible way to meet it is through armed force. But the armed force needed can't be kept down to the low level that would be required to fight small wars of intervention against revolutionary regimes. Because there exist powerful socialist states at the heart of the world socialist system, and they are capable of assisting new arrivals in the socialist camp. Hence capitalist military policy, which means first and foremost the military policy of the capitalist leader country, must aim to build up sufficient military strength to intimidate the socialist leader countries. The latter, in turn, must seek to prevent this from happening. Hence a built-in arms race. *Q.E.D.*

Let me know whether you (1) approve *en générale* the foregoing alternative approach to the architecture of chapter 7; and (2) whether you have specific criticisms or amendments. If the answer under (1) is "no," do you have any ideas about what the architecture should be?

I'm sending you the carbon rather than the ribbon copy of this letter, since I may have to use it as working notes and the ribbon copy doesn't smear under continuous shuffling around as the carbon tends to do.

More on other things soon,

/s Paul

PAB to PMS

Palo Alto
January 25, 1964

Dear Paul,

Having re-read Chapter VII (with some minor disturbances due to the fact that my copy is not in perfectly good order), I also feel that in the present form it does not shape up too well. In parts it is longish and repetitive, and in parts it is dated and forces what are now either open or not very firmly closed doors. The new outline is very much better, although I have a slight feeling that the *auto-da-fe* [public penance] goes perhaps a little bit further than necessary. But let me try to formulate my thoughts on the matter in the order in which the story appears in your letter [January 19, 1964].

Acc't of the Old Version: P.l (last par.): Although the need of the ruling class to maintain a huge military establishment is not dictated alone by hostility to socialism, I would not say that if such were the case the explanation would be made to rest on a "subjective factor." With the manifest transition of the class struggle to the international arena, capitalism's doing all that is possible to combat the international class enemy is not a subjective whimsicality, but simply an extension of the original reason for the necessity of organized violence on the part of the state: the need to suppress the actually or potentially revolutionary classes. There is nothing irrational about it, and the impossibility of capitalism's existence in one country is a hardly disputable fact. It is not a question of "disliking" socialism, and, it would seem to me, there is nothing un-Marxian about giving this argument its due weight. Furthermore, it would be pedantic to demand that the armed forces of a bourgeois state should be kept in exact proportion to the magnitude of the threat from below. The military establishment has a momentum and technological drive of its own; its size has much to do with the weapon systems adopted, the speed of their change &c., &c. In fact, it would seem to be indubitable that every intelligent management would seek to keep the Establishment *larger* than may seem to be needed — simply as a hedge against uncertainties of all kinds.

But let me turn to the new version. P.2 (par. 2) — just a matter of terminology: It would seem to me that one should not speak in the U.S. context of the armed forces' function to "dispossess and repress domestic labor." It is precisely the characteristic of our situation that all the "dispossessing and repressing" has to be done not at home but abroad. With the rest of the p. *d'accord*.

On p.3 first par. you state that "bourgeois thought . . . came to regard this period (Pax Britannica) as the 'norm.' . . ." Schumpeter (*Capitalism, Socialism and Democracy*, p.128) could be referred to primarily with the view to bringing out one *very* significant (I think) point: within the framework of competitive capitalism *cum* implicitly assumed full employment, military spending was regarded rightly by bourgeois thinkers (all the way up to John Stuart Mill) as a highly undesirable encroachment of the state upon capital accumulation. Present-day occasional statements to that effect on the part of the *Wall Street Journal* and similar simpletons are still residues of that outlived ideology. With underemployment and its ideological reflections (Keynesiana of all shades) now prominent, it is clear to advanced bourgeois thought, that the net cost of military spending may be = 0 or even negative: it is a source of profits and higher income. What is more, under mono. cap. [monopoly capitalism] — all societal considerations apart — the individual corporation shifts the taxes and gets the war contracts; it surely has no reason to emphasize pacifism (a la Schumpeter) or the "normalcy" of the state of unarmedness.

On p. 3 second par. The *qualitative* change of colonialism, its transition from the outright military control of the dependent country by detachments from the metropolis (British, French, Portuguese &c. style) to the more subtle U.S. control of the formally independent country which may become allied with the socialist bloc requires in itself a military might vastly superior to what was necessary before. The British needed a few gunboats to deal with the insurgent colony itself. What is needed now is a vast machine to deal not so much with the colony (this would be still a cinch) but with the entire world system on which the recalcitrant colony could rely for help.

Related to it (also your p. 4, first full par.) is what I would like to stress as strongly as possible is the reliance on *atomic blackmail* to keep things under the control. Power which, one actually exercises can be *smaller* than the power which one holds up as a mortal threat to be employed if and when other means fail. It may be paradoxical but perhaps for the first time true: *via pacem para bellum*. If the *bellum* becomes a prospect as dreadful as it is now, it may not necessarily influence the revolutionaries in some Angola or Panama or Zanzibar who could rightly feel that it would be unseemly to H-bomb them, but it is bound to influence the strategy, tactics, and, indeed, mentality of the world socialist bloc.

In this context: in the old version (p.14) you refer to the Marshall Plan, as the "one really large-scale, solid foreign-policy success of the postwar period." Fully agreed, except that it would seem to me that there is another large-scale, solid foreign-policy success which can be claimed by Washington, and that is the ability to instill into Khrushchev *et tutti quanti* a holy fear of American might, thus to influence greatly the strategy and situation of the world socialist movement including splitting it and demoralizing it in many parts of the world. I do not know, how this should be best said, but it is a by no means negligible outcome of the build-up of the positions of strength, in fact, may constitute a complete vindication of that Acheson-Dulles line. Now, that I look at it again, this is presumably what is meant in the last few lines of the last par. on p.5. . . .

Absolute agreement on the unimportance of trade and capital investment from GNP standpoint, although of great importance for individual corp.'s.

How much the 500 giants get out of international biz, don't know, but shall see what I can find tomorrow. Meanwhile: The Walter Salant study on the U.S. Balance of Payments (Table 1 of the Appendix) shows that the Investment Income amounted to $4.3 billion. (1) This is presumably merely the portion taken home, as against what was re-invested in the source country; (2) It has presumably accrued to the 300 odd corp's that are prominent in that biz. Now, looking at SCB [*Survey of Current Business*], August, 1963 p.21 it would seem that the $ 4.2 *include* what is reinvested abroad. But the comments suggest strongly that this is all Big Business stuff...

Worth stressing, I should think, is the important asymmetry between building up the military Establishment and trying to cut it down again. The former is easy going, the latter becomes an economic impossibility. It was one thing right after the war when population pressures combined with a vast market for civilian goods; it is another story now, when without large scale economic planning, reduction of military spending = disaster. Thus international interests of the corp's and domestic economic policy requirements happen nicely to coincide.

And everything that you say about patriotism, chauvinism, anti-communism + Cold War is dandy. What might be a good point to put at the end is the internal limitedness of the military program. The fateful *On What?* question creeps subversively into the military establishment itself. *Business Week* remarks that since JFK and Khrushchev met in Vienna the military budget has risen by $17 billion. Even McNamara feels compelled, a technocrat that he is, to cut and trim.

What next? Is it possible to keep it raising, and if even the dumbest Congressman begins to recognize that too much is too much and that there ain't no use for all of this hardware, where do we i.e. the economy go from there?

That much for the moment.

Yours,

/s Paul

PAB to PMS

Palo Alto

February 20, 1964

Dear Paul,

Having started to work on Chapter V ["The Absorption of Surplus: The Sales Effort"], I have also re-read Chapter IV ["The Absorption of Surplus: Capitalist Consumption and Investment"] "Too Much Surplus?"— Two problems have occurred to me, and I would like to know what your view is on them.

1) I think it is necessary to introduce in Chapter IV somewhere an additional section discussing the *non-corporate* investment. It has to be pointed out that as a surplus absorber investment in housing but also in all kinds of supermarkets, hamburger joints, motels, pancake houses &c. &c. adds up to a magnitude that actually statistically *exceeds* the corporate world's investment in plant & facilities (this can be seen in Nat'l Income statistics). That the corporate world sets the tone and that the small fry follows is undoubtedly true, but does not take care of the matter. There is an interaction, but what is important is that all the small and sundry investment in the competitive underworld does effectively absorb a considerable proportion of the surplus. To be sure, a goodly part of it is waste, but how does one treat it properly? I think it needs to be taken care of in Chapter 4 rather than 5 because it is within the province of *biz* investment rather than *costs* of doing biz i.e. selling costs, costs of financial intermediaries &c.

2) A part (how large?) of *corporate investment* is not productive investment adding to capacity &c, and falling under the discussion contained in the first part of Chapter 4 but investment needed to generate waste. For just as it takes labor to produce waste, it takes capital to produce waste. *Ergo*: vast and increasingly plush office buildings *cum* swimming pools, show rooms, ostentatious buildings for distributive outlets &c., &c: (Compare old J.P.Morgan structure with the new Chase Manhattan edifice). Should all this be treated somehow within the *investment* bracket (Chapter 4) or the selling costs bracket (Chapter 5)? It is my feeling that the former is indicated because on one hand it is *investment* (goes on capital account, and has the same short-term impact on Y [gross output] as any other investment), and on the other hand it is an investment to which the logic of

productive investment does not apply: there is no built-in limit of excess capacity (no building is that luxurious that there couldn't be an even more luxurious one) and there is no relation of that investment to the stream of goods that come forth. To repeat: this is indubitably waste, but waste within the *investment* sector. And, what is most important to stress, particularly in conjunction with the current universal concern with growth, that this kind of investment has the highest conceivable capital/output ratio, i.e. the more of total investment goes into this kind of intra- and extra-corporate investment, the lower the rate of growth. . . .

Please, give it thought, and react *mammediately*, because I have to know whether you will take care of it in revising Chapter 4 (as I think it should be done) or whether you want me to stick it into 5 where it would, I think, fit less logically.

[. . .]

Love,

/s Paul

PMS to PAB

Larchmont

February 24, 1964[207]

Dear Paul,

I hasten to reply to yours of the 20th, just received.

I accept the proposal to add a section to Ch. IV dealing with the issues you pose. That they have so far been excluded stems, I think, from our having stuck rather closely to the stripped-down model of the monopoly economy, with all secondary features abstracted from. But I agree that one can go too far in this direction, and that this is a case in point. I would propose to deal with the problem rather briefly, explicitly stating that this is an area of the real-world capitalist economy which our methodology (i.e. the Marxist methodology) causes us deliberately to neglect in favor of what is really essential, but that we nevertheless devote a brief section to it so that the reader will not get the impression that abstracting from something is the same as being unaware of its existence. Does that meet with your approval?

Unfortunately, I have not yet been able to get at the re-writing of Ch. 7. We are planning to do a volume of past RoM's to be published in celebration of MR's 15th anniversary, and I am engaged in writing an introduction reviewing our 15-year record. This will also be published as the May RoM. And as soon as I get

---

207. The original of this letter was dated the 14th, but since it is replying to Baran's letter of the 20th, it is assumed that there was a typo and the letter has been dated as the 24th.

finished with that, I want to put together something on the Cuban economy, etc., which I need for the March 31st address at Whittier and which I will use for the April RoM. If I can get these done in the next week or ten days, I will then have approximately two months free of all RoM pressure to devote to opus.

In re Cuba, I have digested the [Dudley] Seers et al book quite carefully.[208] It is uninspired but very useful. In addition, Raul Maldonado, the little rotund Ecuadorean who is now Vice Minister of Foreign Commerce in Havana (you will remember him, I'm sure) was here last week in connection with preparations for the Geneva world trade conference, and Leo and I had a long, most enlightening talk with him about various Cuban economic matters. Raul was exceedingly friendly, and also full of optimism. They are going in for a sugar-first policy now with a vengeance, which may be much more feasible than one has been accustomed to assume because their market, including price, is guaranteed to the end of the decade and sugar therefore provides a stable base for planning. But I also have the impression that they may be overdoing it, as they have overdone most of their programs in the past. E.g. Raul says that they are abandoning the goal of self-sufficiency in rice and various other foods, on the ground that their resources are most efficiently utilized in sugar. Needless to say, the grandiose industrialization plans of our period in Cuba have been reduced to much more modest and realistic proportions. But the revolutionary spirit seems to be in no way dimmed by mistakes or changes.

Otras cosas in this connection: Raul says they are in desperate need of qualified economists, so if you know any who are also politically reliable who want to go (either U.S. or foreign) write a note to him and send it to me — I'll channel it through their UN mission here. When I told him that [Andre] Gunder [Frank] had been sitting in Rio for the best part of a year hoping to get a nod from Havana, he said he would immediately cable for him on getting back to Cuba. Meanwhile, Gunder has moved to Chile (address: 1937 California, Santiago). If anything comes of this, it will at least solve Gunder's immediate job problems. I suppose it also will mean that he will abandon all the work on development/underdevelopment for the foreseeable future. Raul wanted to be especially remembered to you.

I haven't been able to sit down with the full IS [Irrational Society] chapter yet but will do so in the next day or so. I have rented an office in a business building in Larchmont for $25 a month to which I can repair whenever the noise and hurly-burly here at the house get out of hand, as they tend to do after school and

---

208. Dudley Seers, ed., *Cuba: The Economic and Social Revolution* (Chapel Hill: University of North Carolina Press, 1964).

on week-ends. I think and hope this is going to be a tremendous productivity-increaser. My present intention is not even to have a phone there. The prospect of having periods up to 5 or 6 hours without any interruption is enough to turn one's head.

I didn't hear anything from Jack after sending him the Negro chapter (early January) and finally wrote him to ask if he had received it and whether he wanted to work on it. A telegram came yesterday that he had and did and was writing. But that's a relatively simple chapter, and if he can't cope with it in two months I'm, to say the least, dubious about sending him all the more difficult ones still to come.

There's much more but I must knock off now and get to work.

Love,

Paul

P.S. […]

PAB to PMS

Palo Alto
February 25, 1964[209]

Dear Paul,

A few lines in haste before dashing to the campus. (1) Muchissimas gracias for the Lekachman volume; I am looking forward to perusing your contribution tonight. (2) In the same mail arrived your letter of the 24th. I am seriously worried about IS [Chapter on Irrational Society] in its present form; although there is — I believe — nothing wrong with the thoughts that it contains, it will have to be somehow recast, almost for tactical reasons. Much of it somehow doesn't belong probably into a book by economists... But anyway, read it first and let me have your reactions; I would like to return to it after everything else is finished — if for no other reason, then simply because this provides for a "cooling off" period. (3) Meanwhile I am 2/3 done with the revision of Chapter 5 [on the sales effort] — I think, it comes out now quite well — and aim at finishing it this week, at the latest next Monday. At that time, I'll ship it to you. (4) Could you put at the top of your priorities list a careful going over the Chapter on Conceptual Implications; this is what I must turn to as soon as I am done with Chapter 5, and I would very much want to have on the desk your comments as I go at it. After that is done (no later than end of March and preferably earlier) — a

---

209. Baran and Sweezy's final correspondence beginning with this letter and ending on March 9, 1964 were previously published as "The Last Letters: Correspondence on *Some Theoretical Implications*" in the July-August 2012 issue of *Monthly Review*.

massive effort to re-vamp all of QoS [referring to the two "Quality of Monopoly
Capitalist Society" *cum* IS. April for QoS II. (QoS I requires relatively little
doing except incorporating some new data + the material on income distribution
when I get it from Aron Douglas who is now working on it), and April-May for
IS revisions and composition of the Epilogue.[210] That would be then the *finale*.
Anyway, the way I feel now is *Lieber ein Ende mit Schrecken als ein Schrecken
ohne Ende* [rather a horrible ending than horror without end].

Your having an office out of the house is a tremendous step forward.
Delighted to hear it. A further reform of some consequence would be to have
the bourbon bottle at some third place (out of the house and out of the office) —
then things would really start popping.

The Jack [Rackliffe] situation is most worrisome. *Que faire?* We *must* have a
decent copy editing job done....

More later.

Love,

    /s Paul

PMS to PAB

   [*Letter accompanying the draft manuscript of Chapter 10 (formerly chapter 9) of* Monopoly Capital, *"Some Theoretical Implications," originally
   drafted by PAB and now with penciled marginal notes by PMS. The manuscript and enclosed letter were sent by special delivery. See also Paul A.
   Baran and Paul M. Sweezy, "Some Theoretical Implications,"* Monthly
   Review *64, no. 3 (July-August 2012): 24–59.*]

                                                              Larchmont
                                                            March 2, 1964

Dear Paul,

Most of the penciled notes in the margins were written on first reading — don't
remember exactly when. All the separate notes are from over the weekend.
Dunno how much help any of them will be.

At some stage we must invite Huby [Leo Huberman] to read the whole
ms., and we could make a point to ask him to keep an eye open for obtrusive
repetitions, rasping inconsistencies of style, etc. He is of course not an economic
theorist but is often very good on matters relating to form and presentation. As
to straight copyediting — which I interpret to mean fixing up bad sentences, etc.,

---

210. Baran and Sweezy apparently intended to compose an Epilogue at this point that would
follow "The Irrational System." The Epilogue, however, was never written and there seems to be
no record as to what its contents were to be.

as well as imposing uniformity in such things as punctuation and capitalization
— we might try Vic Bernstein on one chapter and then give him the rest if we like
what he does.

Chapter 10—Theoretical Implications
[handwritten notes][211]
Section 1, paragraph that begins "Writing in 1873"
In connection with the query [on the manuscript here]: If I remember
correctly — I am writing without access to *Capital* — Marx dated the
transformation of political economy to vulgar economics from the French
overturn of 1830 and specifically emphasized Senior's doctrine of abstinence
as its earmark. Mill he conceded to be far above the level of the run of vulgar
economists, a sort of hangover of the earlier period.[212] He never really dealt with
the subjective value theorists of the '60s and '70s, but today we would have to
recognize their emergence and triumph as marking the final demise of political
economy and the enthronement of apologetics. Thus I would say that this whole
development *antedates* monopoly capital. Its explanation I would find, following
Marx, in the rise of the proletariat and of socialism which gave birth to Marxism,
which also antedates monocap. What one *can* say is that the arrival of monocap
rendered obsolete the apologetics of the subjective-value school(s) — J.B. Clark,
intellectually, was the foremost systematizer of the doctrine *qua* apologetics
— and [took on] the task of devising a new system of apologetics. What you
describe beginning with the paragraph that begins "Large and important
segments" is the way the profession reacted to this challenge.[213]

Incidentally, I have come to think (in connection with the formulation
on the imperialist stage in the "Towards the end" paragraph) that Lenin
did a serious disservice when he identified the monopoly phase of capitalist
development with imperialism. This almost inevitably gives the impression
that imperialism is *essentially* a new phenomenon dating from the last decades

211. The comments by Sweezy here were directed at the earlier, longer forty-two-page draft
manuscript ("A Conceptual Interlude"). The final, nineteen-page partial text ("Some Theoretical
Implications," covering sections 1 and the beginning of section 2) was redrafted largely in response
to these criticisms and has been used as the basis for those parts in the text of "Some Theoretical
Implications" published in the July-August 2012 issue of *Monthly Review*.
212. See Karl Marx, *Capital*, vol. 1 (London: Penguin, 1976), 95–98.
213. Baran revised the analysis here, which had previously focused on the rise of neoclassical
economics as a response to the monopoly stage, in the final, partial version. He incorporated
Sweezy's suggested discussion of the rise of bourgeois apologetics based on Marx's famous
"postface" to *Capital*, and added to that his own treatment of the further transformations in
apologetics that occur with the rise of the monopoly stage.

of the 19th century. The result is to direct attention from and play down the importance of the fateful expansion of the Spanish, Portuguese, Dutch, British, and French empires during the 16th, 17th, 18th, and also the first half of the 19th, centuries. It was during that earlier period of expansion that the patterns of rape and destruction and monstrous exploitation of race discrimination and hatred, in a world of development and underdevelopment, were worked out. The final gobbling up of the world after 1870 was a last, not a first, act. I *know* how misleading Lenin's theory can be on this matter because I was misled by it. My eyes only began to be opened when I first read (probably around 1940) Dutt's *India Today* (a real masterpiece by the way), and the opening was not completed until *PEoG* [*The Political Economy of Growth*]. *TCD* [*The Theory of Capitalist Development*] bears all too clearly the deforming effects of accepting Lenin's schema uncritically.[214]

Section 1, paragraph that begins "This can hardly be said"

I do not believe it could be shown that either Berle or Galbraith "derived their inspiration from Schumpeter." Since this point is not crucial I would cut it out.[215]

Section 1, same paragraph

I don't see why "pragmatic" should be in quote marks, nor do I understand what is "case-by-case" in either of these gentlemen's [Berle and Galbraith's] themes. Perhaps if the quotes are taken off "pragmatic" the other expression can simply be omitted. If not, you'll have to find a formulation which doesn't suggest the Biz school "case method."[216]

Section 2, opening paragraph

If you will read this exposition minus the numerous underlinings I think you will see how dispensable most of them are and how right Jack [Rackliffe] is to delete them in almost 9 cases out of 10.

Section 2, paragraph that begins "Accordingly such criticism"

You will see considerable question and even dissent in the margins of this and the next few pages. They all resulted from the first reading of this draft —

214. Baran and Sweezy debated this matter in letters over the next few days (see below). Baran subsequently rewrote the opening to "Some Theoretical Implications" to provide a much more comprehensive analysis of the significance of the transition from competitive to monopoly capitalism and of the role of colonialism and imperialism from the fifteenth and sixteenth centuries on, dropping the reference to the imperialist stage.
215. Baran removed the phrase referred to here from the nineteen-page version that constituted the final, partial version of the chapter.
216. Baran changed the disputed phrase to "pragmatic, piecemeal approach" in the final version in which the first nineteen pages were revised in relation to Sweezy's comments.

last year, or maybe even before that. I now think I can put my finger on what bothered me. The real trouble, it seems to me, with bourgeois economics is that it assumes a whole hierarchy of human wants and related behavior patterns to be inherent in, or perhaps it would be better to say to make up the essence of, human nature, which in turn is as elemental as air, water, and other components of physical nature. The difference between the savage and the rich in modern society is simply that the former has only the means to satisfy the highest-priority wants while the latter can pretty much satisfy the whole range of wants. It never occurs to the bourgeois economists that these want systems are qualitatively totally different. What has to be stressed is this underlying assumption of an elemental, unchanging human nature. As far as economists are concerned, I know of *no* effort to *justify* this assumption. For that one has to go to the philosophers and, in the past even more, to the theologians. I have no objection to quoting a few of those worthies to show what arguments are *implicit* in bourgeois social science (including economics), but I find the attempt to support this exposition by quoting such [figures] as Eisenhower, Kuznets, and Stigler to be less than persuasive.

To put my point in a somewhat different way: I don't think there is any point in making the distinctions you make between the "autonomous" individual, the god-determined individual, the biotically constant individual, and the "rational" individual. They all come to exactly the same thing, of course, and these are simply different spurious theories to justify the basic assumption involved. What really needs to be done is to press home the point that bourgeois economics *does* operate with this assumption (whatever justification may be explicitly or implicitly offered for it), that it amounts to universalizing capitalist man (*homo economicus* is really *homo capitalisticus*), and that whatever claim bourgeois economics has to provide a justification for the existing social order stands or falls with this assumption.[217]

Section 2, paragraph that begins "To be sure, the history of thought"
I think the endorsement of capitalist rationality in early capitalism goes too

---

217. Sweezy's point here was also addressed in his December 5, 1962, letter to Baran, at the time of his first reading of the "Theoretical Implications" chapter. In that letter he wrote: "The role of the autonomous individual and his needs in the traditional theory (indeed in bourgeois ideology generally) will have to be expanded and strengthened. This is a very important matter, and its treatment in the draft is probably the weakest part. There must be some good books on philosophic individualism which would be helpful and supply some badly needed quotes from the great philosophers and social thinkers." This was rectified in the final, partial draft. Baran was to substantially rewrite this part of the text, making use of C. B. Macpherson's recently published *A Theory of Possessive Individualism* (Oxford: Oxford University Press, 1962).

far. Don't forget what capitalist rationality meant for the "natives" all over the world — which includes most of the natives in the leading capitalist countries themselves. I'm not quite sure what kind of reformulation is needed, but I would like it to be such that, say, a Congolese reading it would not instantly say "shit."[218]

Section 2, paragraph that begins "Whatever validity these propositions"

I don't see why you suddenly bring in the question of the consumer's knowledge, nor do I see reason to suppose that there was ever *any* justification for assuming it to be encyclopedic, or anything faintly approaching that state. But maybe you have in mind something that doesn't come through to me.[219]

Section 2, same paragraph

I note that you quite often use the expression "revealed preferences"—with or without the quotation — as though everyone will naturally be familiar with it and understand its meaning. I *think* I probably know what it means, but I don't know where it comes from, so I would assume it would be wise to assume that it would simply baffle most readers. Can't some other reading be substituted?

Section 3, paragraph that begins "The situation"

On re-reading I can't see *any* relevance to the quotation from Kalecki. You haven't even raised the question of price flexibility.

Section 3, paragraph that begins "Nor is it possible"

In the discussion of capital, I think it would be good to introduce the question of the ambiguities which result from the tremendous uncertainties about how long a machine, e.g., will remain economically (not physically) viable in view of the enormous rates of technological and product change created by the corporations themselves. It used to be said that one of the insuperable obstacles to automating many processes is the very high cost and uncertainty about whether the automation equipment could be used long enough to get back the entire investment. Recently, however, I was told by some of the *Scientific American* chaps that the latest advances in miniaturization of computer components will result in such drastic reduction of computer costs that it may be possible fully to automate many processes with the assurance of completely recovering all outlays *in one year*. In other words, given the possibility to maintain monopoly prices, most of a plant's capital may be scrapped and replaced annually. Under such circumstances, what is capital and what is just

218. Baran altered the passages referred to here in the final text.

219. From this point on Sweezy's comments relate directly to the text as printed here, based on the original forty-two-page draft ("A Conceptual Interlude"), rather than to the shorter nineteen-page final draft of sections I and the beginning of section 2, which had been revised in relation to his comments.

junk? (I suspect, incidentally, that this sort of thing has a lot to do with the maintenance of high levels of investment, and accounts for the weak influence of what seems to be excess capacity in the last few years. Probably some emphasis should be given to this factor in chapters 4 and 8.)

Section 4, paragraph that begins "While thus most"

The opening, transitional paragraph is weak. I think that what needs saying in substance, is that while it is no part of our present purpose to review critically Marxian economic theory with a view to eliminating obsolete aspects, etc., there is one concept which is crucially important and that requires consideration here — economic surplus.

Section 4, paragraph that begins "For this to be true"

Does Marx actually use the expression "socially necessary" in connection with the notion of a historically conditioned minimum living standard? If so, I do not recall it.

Section 4, paragraph that begins "But as the price of labor power"

I don't think this is correct. Since there presumably still is some irreducible minimum, *that* would define the *value* of labor power. What you are saying, in Marxian terminology, I believe, is that in the course of capitalist development the price of labor power tends to rise, and to remain permanently above its value. This implies, does it not, that the workers themselves (through unions, political action, etc.) succeed in appropriating part of the surplus value. It also means, of course, that monopolists can (try to) steal some of this surplus value back from them.

Section 4, paragraph that begins "Marx referred to this increase as 'profits by deduction'"

With respect to "profits by deduction," I have to repeat what I said on first reading. I think Marx meant by this concept something quite different from what you mean here. He meant deduction from the *value* of labor power, and the result was a real pushing of wages below the true subsistence level and a failure to maintain the quality of the labor force. (You may well recall the passage about stunting of a whole generation of British workers.) You mean profits by deduction from a *price* of labor power which is well *above* its value.

Section 4, same paragraph

I believe it would be preferable to adhere throughout to the view expressed in the previous paragraph, and also expressed in the quotation from Sraffa, namely, that after a certain point in capitalist development the workers begin to share in the surplus. (I believe also, incidentally, that this is a proposition with very important *political* implications, providing a necessary part of the explanation of Social Democracy and other forms of reformism.)

Section 4, paragraph that begins "As can be readily seen"

I am not clear what *is* "the difference between what we call 'economic surplus' and aggregate surplus value." I would be inclined to say that we have, perhaps implicitly, defined surplus as aggregate surplus value minus the share of it which the workers are able to capture for themselves. Am I right about this?[220]

PAB to PMS

Palo Alto

March 2, 1964

Dear Paul,

I strongly feel that [economizing on] the editorial expenses associated with the publication of the opus is the "wrongest" possible place for saving a few hundred $$. We have to get the best available editor and pay what it takes to produce a decent book. To the extent that my part of the MS requires more editorial work than yours, and if you do not share my view on the urgency of having a good editor, I am perfectly willing to have all or much more than one half of the editorial expenses charged against my share in the royalties. And if it is a matter of liquidity, I do have a few thousand dollars in the saving bank, and would be prepared to advance whatever amount may be needed. There is no point in skimping where the saving involved is relatively small and the harm to the book could be considerable. — I do not know whether V. Bernstein is a good editor, but the chances are that he'd do a better job than someone wholly unfamiliar with this kind of stuff.

By the way, as far as copy editing policy is concerned, I am not entirely certain that one has to eliminate *all* italics. Certainly, too many ain't no good, but why all? Some of the finest writers are using them, and, it would seem to me at least, to good advantage.

---

220. Sweezy's note here suggests that in his view, when the letter was written, aggregate surplus value and economic surplus were equal under monopoly capitalism (as they were for competitive capitalism), except for that part of surplus embodied in wages. Sweezy here saw this mainly as surplus "captured" by workers (as in Sraffa's *Production of Commodities by Means of Commodities*). Baran appears to confirm this understanding in his March 3rd letter. But in replying Baran stressed the fact that under monopoly capitalism such surplus concealed in wages was mainly the product of unproductive expenditures embodied in wage goods, amounting to forced deductions from the wages of workers.

In re: Gunder.[221] On one hand, it is obviously a good thing that he'll be able to go where he wants to go. Whether it'll do him any good, and whether he'll do them any good, is a different question. He is not the type of economist whom they need at the present time, and being cantankerous, and "difficult to get along with," he'll find himself in troubles and cause troubles in no time. And as far as his work is concerned, what he needs is sitting in a library for a couple of years and getting his thoughts organized. . . . But anyway, one cannot "plan the unplanable."

I have read your piece in Lekachman ["Keynesian Economics: The First Quarter Century"]. It is very nice. As I was reading it, I realized that I had seen it in MS; but in print things do look much better. By the way, the immediately following article by Samuelson (the second that is) is quite instructive; his remarks on Jean Baptiste Kaldor are both amusing and perspicacious.

On some other stuff later. Must run now to the campus.

Love,

/s Yours Paul

PAB to PMS

Palo Alto

March 3, 1964

Dear Paul,

I was just settling down to work when your specy arrived containing Chapter 10.[222] I shall not discuss now all the points that are contained in your notes, but feel an urge to go into two, because they seem to be of central importance in general, and for the *opus* in particular.

---

221. In late 1963 Andre Gunder Frank, who was closely connected with Baran and Sweezy and *Monthly Review*, was eager to leave Brazil where he had been working since 1962. He had just drafted his early manuscript *On Capitalist Underdevelopment*, which he had sent to Baran and Sweezy for comments (but which was not published until 1975 by Oxford University Press in India). He had a number of options, but only limited job prospects, and the various plans he was considering involved: returning to the University of Chicago, or moving to Cuba, Mexico, Argentina, or Chile. He wrote a string of letters to both Baran and Sweezy about his various possibilities, and they discussed how to help him. In the end he went briefly to Chile and then to Mexico in 1965. Out of this period arose his classic book *Capitalism and Underdevelopment in Latin America* (New York: Monthly Review Press, 1967).

222. "Some Theoretical Implications" drafted by Baran and now edited by Sweezy. Baran is referring to the return of the manuscript with marginal notes by Sweezy as well as to the suggestions laid out in Sweezy's March 2, 1964, letter to Baran, which accompanied the edited manuscript (see above). "Some Theoretical Implications" is renumbered Chapter 10 in the new plan for the book (it was formerly Chapter 9) due to the insertion of the additional chapter on race relations.

1) *Imperialism.* I am afraid that you are too much influenced by (a) "Gunderism," and (b) the only too natural tendency to be morally revolted by the history of capitalism or for that matter by history in general. There is after all no doubt that history as long as we have known it has been an uninterrupted process of rape, exploitation and violence. To state this is not to state much. The whole contribution of Marx and the essence of dialectics is to discover where and when all this *Schweinerei* had an intrinsically progressive element in it, and where it was nothing but an effort to perpetuate a lousy *status quo*. He may have been too optimistic on that count, but in principle, I think, his position was correct. Read the *dithyramb* [ancient Greek hymn song] on the achievements of capitalism in the *Communist Manifesto*, or the magnificent finale of the "Future Results of the British Rule in India": "When a great social revolution shall have mastered the results of the bourgeois epoch, the market of the world and the modern powers of production, and subjected them to the common control of the most advanced peoples, then only will human progress cease to resemble the hideous pagan idol, who would not drink the nectar but from the skulls of the slain."[223] And somewhere — I don't have the citation off hand — Engels celebrated the U.S. conquest of California as being a great civilizing act taking away this land from the Mexican barbarians. The chief point in all this is obviously under capitalism "progress" advances only *via* evil; it advances nevertheless. As I just said, it could very well be that this advance was overestimated, that the revolutionary force of the evil was thought to lead to the great social revolution sooner — but let us not get into the position of saying all of history was bad and immoral, that capitalism was always nothing but ruination of the now colonial and dependent countries, and that we are "agin it." Lenin's approach was to see whether there has occurred a certain specific *change* in that process of colonial exploitation which alters its nature and modifies its revolutionary impact. He was not right in all he said, but, I think, he was right in pointing out that the organized, "civilized," exploitation by corporations &c. constituted a substantial departure from the practices of Lord Clive or the conquistadores of old. His theory has to be re-thought, but not rejected out of hand. The crux of the problem, as I see it, is at what point does the creation of the world markets, the "civilization" of the u/d c's [underdeveloped countries] &c. become a retrograde development and progressive only in the sense that it promotes liberation movements.... Lenin believed that that point was reached with the advent of monopoly in the advanced countries. My guess is that he was basically right. To take the position

223. This quote from Marx was subsequently used by Baran in the final nineteen-page revised version of the first part of "Some Theoretical Implications."

that it has always been the same brings one to the position that Julius Caesar's treatment of the Huns and Standard Oil's treatment of Venezuela differ from each other only in name. And, in general, whether or not a Congolese native thinks that something is shit or not, is of no relevance at all. He could apply this very designation to the *Communist Manifesto*! Either one sticks to Marxian dialectics or else I don't know what we are talking about.

(2) *Surplus vs. surplus value*. If under (1) you are a "revisionist" — under (2) you are too orthodox. The surplus we are talking about is of necessity *much larger* [than] the surplus value. In the first place, the "interpenetration effect" on which I have been now laboring for weeks, has obviously no room in a surplus value [*sv*] concept. In an *sv* concept the sales effort is a *deduction* from *sv* even as rent, interest and govt. taxes. In the surplus concept we have been trying to develop, a good deal of productive work is surplus without producing *sv*. Under the *sv* concept how could you classify the man hammering chrome on the automobile to be a surplus producer? If my bread loaves example (which you endorse), and if the Kaysen story (which you cite) make sense, then *eo ipso* one has to expand *sv* to *include* such resource utilization which within the Marxian system receives no attention and cannot even be accommodated. This, I thought, was the principal thesis of the opus. . . .[224]

(3) *Irreducible wage*. This related directly to (2). If a subsistence wage is assumed (or, for that matter, *any irreducible* wage) then clearly (a) the mass of surplus value is a datum, monopoly profits can be only the result of *its redistribution* (what the monopoly capitalists get, the competitive capitalists lose), and (b) all taxes of govt. come out necessarily out of profits (this remark, by the way, is in the [Joseph] Gillman review of [Victor] Perlo in the Winter, 1964 issue of *Science & Society*).[225] For any *reduction* of the *real* wage is *ex definitione* impossible. Again, I thought, that one of the central theses of the opus is to argue the precise opposite. Monopoly capitalists *can* increase their profits by *reducing* the real wage which contains a good deal of surplus (as Sraffa noted), the govt. *can* collect taxes not out of profits but out of the real wage (in fact most of them come from that source). In *PEoG* I made a mistake accepting Kalecki's classical view of the irreducibility of wages and talking about the profit redistribution. This is wrong, I now think. And surely, there is no

224. [Handwritten footnote by Baran]: You remember our extensive discussion of the difference between "g" [good surplus] workers and "b" [bad surplus] workers; is there any room for this distribution under the *sv* concept?

225. Joseph M. Gillman, "Disarmament and the American Economy," *Science & Society* 28, no. 1 (Winter 1964): 63–69 (a review of Victor Perlo's *Militarism and Industry* [New York: International Publishers, 1963]).

point now of talking about subsistence wage as being the *value* of labor power; I cannot attach any meaning to it. This is like Arzumanian's and Bettelheim's old argument (which the latter, by the way, gave up) that immiseration &c. consist of workers receiving higher wages alright, but those higher wages being lower than the value of labor power. . . .

But on all of this more (implicitly) when I redo Chapter 10; meanwhile, please, react to the above!

Started on another point, but decided to postpone that because of time.

Love,

/s Yours Paul

PMS to PAB

Larchmont

March 4, 1964

Dear Paul,

I don't know what I said that could have led you to think that I was worried about the expenses of editing the ms. of opus. Anyway, such was never my intention or preoccupation and I apologize. What does worry me is how to get someone who is good for the job. Vic Bernstein may be the right person, but without ever having had him work on anything I've been directly involved with I just don't know. That was the reason I suggested giving him one chapter to do first and then the rest if we like his work. But if you think this unwise I am not opposed to signing him up for the whole remaining job and turning over to him mammediately for study the chapters already edited. Let me know.

On italics, I agree that they have their place, and you will note that I didn't suggest eliminating them all from the theoretical implications chapter. The only point is that if used several times on every page, they lose their effectiveness, just as the term "fucking" loses its effectiveness when used as it is in the army. And they are more dispensable in some people's writing than in others' because the former build the emphasis into the vocabulary and sentence structure. In general, I think you belong to this category.

The enclosed is a reply by Gillman to a note congratulating him on his S&S review of Perlo. Just FYI — throw away.

Glad you thought the Lekachman piece came out better in print. I haven't yet perused it in that form.

I'm having a hard time writing the May RoM commenting on MR's first 15 years. In preparation, I have had to read over again some 230 RoM's, and I must say it is not a very agreeable experience. To be quite frank most of that stuff is not very good, and the ones that do stand up are too few and far between to redeem the whole performance. The only consolation is: by whom and where was much better current commentary being produced? Intellectually speaking, the world socialist movement ain't in too hot shape I'm afraid.

But enough such gloomy thoughts and back to turning out some more second-rate poop.

Love,

s/ Paul

P.S. The de Gaulle performance in recent weeks, with apparently more to come, really requires a deep analysis. It shows what can be done by a country with strictly limited military power in a situation in which those with much greater military power simply cannot make use of it. Atomic weapons are no good against the USSR because they will bring their own doom, and they are no good against guerrillas, period. Thus diplomacy gets its chance, and de Gaulle is showing us what a really fantastic lot of room there is to maneuver in [de Gaulle visited the Soviet Union in 1964 and initiated independent diplomatic overtures]. One would think that the British would get the point and start reasserting their own independence, but, alas, such is the lackey mentality of the British that not even the Labor Party shows any signs of wanting to do so — such at any rate is the impression one gets from recent statements of Wilson. Probably there is more chance of the Tories acting like men than of Labor anyway.

One problem is now beginning to pose itself: by making full use of strategic deals with the Chinese and the SU, can de Gaulle realistically hope to put France in a position to challenge U.S. leadership of imperialism even if Bonn should remain under Washington's thumb? It would have seemed a *wahnsinnig* [crazy] question only a few months ago, but now I'm no longer so sure.

PAB to PMS

Palo Alto

March 5, 1964

Dear Paul,

Your letter of March 4th just arrived. My impression that you were worried about the expense of editing the opus MS originated in your remark over the phone that "beggars cannot be choosers." If I misunderstood you, all is well. I fully agree with your idea to give Bernstein one chapter and to see how he handles it. If he should do a good job, we should give him more. What I would very much like to assure is that someone (he, or, if he should be found wanting, someone else) should go over the entire thing, incl. the material edited by Jack, simply to provide for continuity and uniformity of the editing job.

The attached is the new, and, I hope, not too far from the last version of Chapter V. I am only a few days off schedule, but would not complain if the chapter would now disappear from my "field of worries." Please, go over it, and if you think that it is in close-to-final shape, you could give this chapter to Bernstein and see what happens. If you want to make changes in it, *je vous en prie* [please do!]; if you think that I should do something more on it, *retournez s.v.p.*

Am turning now to Theoretical Implications. This looks like a big job but it cannot be helped. *Nur den der strebend sich bemueht, den werden sie erloesen....* (or something very similar to that effect) [only those who make a strenuous effort will be absolved].[226]

The encl. clip from NYT is very nice, I saw it myself, and used it for fn. Thanks.

On other things later. My heart bleeds about your being bogged down in *MR* work; hope you'll be able to return to opus soon.

Love

/s Paul

PMS to PAB

Larchmont

March 7, 1964

Dear Paul,

I don't know what I said that could lead you to suppose that I am in danger of falling into "the position of saying all of history was bad and immoral, that capitalism was always nothing but ruination of the now colonial and dependent countries and that we are 'agin it.'" Such is very far from the position I would wish to advocate. I am fully in agreement with the view stated in the *Manifesto* that capitalism was — and to a considerable extent still is, since the computer revolution and also atomic energy both stem directly from capitalist war efforts — the great multiplier of the productivity of human labor. I simply do not want to lose sight of or play down the other side of the coin, which is the ruination of the udc's [underdeveloped countries]. They did not at any time share in the advance, quite the contrary. And they can only share in the advance [by] overthrowing capitalist hegemony and making its achievements their own. But why should I waste time saying such things to the author of *PEoG*?

---

226. Here Baran quoted from memory in German from Goethe's *Faust*. See Johann Wolfgang von Goethe, *Faust I and II* (Cambridge, MA: Surkamp/Insel 1984), 301, lines 11,936–37. "For him whose striving never ceases / We can provide redemption."

As to Lenin's use of the term "imperialism," that is quite another matter. My main point in this connection was a semantic one and as such not terribly important. By identifying monocap [monopoly capitalism] with imperialism, by giving that name to the latest stage of capitalism, Lenin inevitably suggested that imperialism, in the usual meaning of the term, did not characterize the earlier stages of capitalism. I cited my own intellectual history to support this point. I don't suggest, or think there would be any point in, an overt criticism of his usage — at least not in the context of opus. But I do suggest that we avoid that usage and that when we want to refer to monocap we use that term.

I agree with you, of course that the "organized, 'civilized,' exploitation by corporations &c. constituted a substantial departure from the practices of Lord Clive and the conquistadores of old." But what I would not want to do is to lend any support at all to the view that this difference signalizes improvement *from the point of view of the mass of the people in the exploited countries. Ex visu* of their position in the world, capitalism was always and remains a disaster; as you say it is progressive for them "only in the sense that it promotes liberation movements" — and in the sense that it prepares the knowledge, technology, etc., which those movements need to create higher social forms. But the latter function is now becoming dispensable since it can also be discharged by the socialist countries. If this view of the matter is correct, however, I don't see how it can be maintained that *on the whole* and considering the system as of world-wide scope, capitalism becomes retrograde with the coming to dominance of monopoly in the metropoli. It is only about then that liberation movements really get under way, and surely the *technological* progressiveness of capitalism does not cease at that point. It might perhaps be argued that the turning point to overall regressiveness is reached when socialism is capable of assuring the continued development of science, technology, etc. But this question needs a lot of thought, which I haven't given to it. In the meantime, I wonder whether this was really a question Lenin had in mind when he wrote *Imperialism*. I haven't looked at that work for some time, but my recollection is that what he was primarily interested in was not the consequences for the udc's so much as the effects on the advanced countries — their desperate struggles over the spoils with the consequent militarization of their societies (and mentalities), the generation of a labor aristocracy as the basis of reformism, etc.

When I introduced the question of what a Congolese might think, I was not referring to an illiterate tribesman. *Ex definitione*, he will not be one of our readers. I am thinking of a Congolese revolutionary Marxist, and I am thinking of him merely as a representative of all the revolutionary Marxists in the udc's. I believe they are a very important part of the audience we want to reach —

perhaps they are the audience we want to reach. So I think it does matter what they think and that we should consciously try to express ourselves in a way to make them feel that we're on their side. Natch, that doesn't mean pandering to their weaknesses, but it does mean conscientious suppression of great-power or "advanced-country" chauvinism.

In re surplus value versus surplus: please don't misunderstand me: I am not in the least questioning the tremendous significance of the interpenetration effect and the damage it does to the traditional Marxian schema. My critical remarks were devoted to the other part of your presentation. Let me try to restate.

For Marx the value of labor power is determined by an historically conditioned minimum which is enough to enable the working class to live at a standard which, *inter alia, will enable it to reproduce itself in the required numbers and quality*. But this is in no sense an *irreducible* wage. It can be reduced and at certain times and places has been. The result is a deterioration in the labor force which Marx certainly thought had happened in England since the beginning of the industrial revolution. The other result is to add profits by deduction to "normal" surplus value. Though the opposite problem, i.e. the rising of wages above the minimum so defined, did not occur to him, I think there is no doubt that to be consistent he would have had to treat it as Sraffa does, i.e., as a case of workers' sharing in the surplus. I don't say that we should adopt this way of handling the problem; I am simply arguing for accuracy and consistency in presenting Marx's own position.

The question of the dividing line between necessary costs and surplus (in our sense) remains, of course. If it were only a matter of deciding what wage to treat as cost, one could perhaps devise a rational answer (though one would have to recognize that *au fond* it would be merely another form of the solution Marx provided with his concept of the value of labor power). But with interpenetration a major factor, as it undoubtedly is, I wonder if any solution is really rational?

The concept of what the same output would cost either under competitive capitalism or under planned socialism has many difficulties, not the least of which is that under neither setup would the "same" output be produced.

Sometimes I suspect that this problem may be like some in mathematics and logic, one to which there can be no solution. But how is one to get anywhere *without* the surplus concept? It is all very worrisome.

I hope the foregoing will not simply serve to muddy waters when what you need is exactly the opposite.

More on other things later.

Love,

/s Paul

PAB to PMS

[*This letter was on his desk and never mailed before his death on March 26.*]

Palo Alto

March 9, 1964

Dear Paul,

I thought about your letter of March 7th, and while I am far from having any definitive ideas on all the problems involved, it may be useful to write out a few lines for the purpose of *Selbstverstaendigung* [self-understanding].[227]

In re: Capitalism's switch-over from a progressive to a retrograde system. Fortunately, it is not mandatory for us at the present time to make a decision on that matter and to commit that decision to print. It does seem to me, however, that the timing of such a switch-over cannot be made to depend on technological progress such as the development of atomic energy, computers, &c. In other words, one cannot say, I should think, that a social order has become a fetter on the development of the forces of production only when such a development has come to an actual or virtual halt or even commenced to regress. If the occurrence of the switch-over were to be made contingent on such a condition, one would probably have a tough time finding in history a suitable example. From what little I have read about feudalism and mercantilism, there was at no time a condition reached when there was an actual cessation of the development of the forces of production. It may have been at one time slower than at another, it apparently kept creeping ahead even in the least progressive centuries. From what Christopher Hill, Hobsbawm and a number of other Britishers have written about the 17th century — a century of crisis — it would seem that even then there were more or less significant advances in both aggregate and per capita output.

The way to look at the matter, I imagine, is not to think about the *actual* rise in productivity of labor, but about the extent to which the opening up of *potentialities* for such a rise are being made use of within the existing economic and social order. Those potentialities may be a function of scientific development, of virtually accessible economies of scale, of seizable technical opportunities. They may not be translated into practice, or translated into practice only inadequately because the prevailing relations of production either block or effectively discourage such a translation. The conflict between the development of the forces of production and the existing relations of production

---

227. For Baran and Sweezy this reference to self-understanding from a theoretical standpoint resonated with Marx's famous statement in his 1859 "Preface" to *A Contribution to a Critique of Political Economy*, where he referred to self-understanding as the main product of his and Engels's work *The German Ideology*.

is thus not a conflict between the prevalent mode of production and the socioeconomic structure, but a conflict between the productive potentialities that are becoming visible, tangible, realizable and existing property relations, political institutions &c. which begin to play a role of a straitjacket in which the development of productive capacities suffocates. For this conflict to become relevant it is obviously not enough that there should be unutilized potentialities in the realm of the forces of production. There must be also visible, tangible, and realizable potentialities in the realm of the relations of production. One without the other creates no conflict. . . . What is more, the latter potentialities do not rise to the surface without the former. "Mankind always sets itself only such tasks as it can solve; since, looking at the matter more closely, it will always be found that the task itself arises only when the material conditions for its solution already exist or are at least in the process of formation. . . . The productive forces developing in the womb of bourgeois society create the material conditions for the solution of that antagonism." (Marx, "Preface to The Critique of Political Economy," *Selected Works*, I, p. 329). If there is any merit to the above, then it makes eminently good sense to say that the transition of competitive capitalism to a trustified or monopolistic capitalism which took place, broadly speaking, in the last quarter of the 19th century marks the mutation of the system from being preponderantly progressive to preponderantly retrograde.

This not because there has been no further growth of the forces of production under monopoly capitalism [mono cap], but because at that time the possibility of arriving at a social order in which the abolition of scarcity could be actually accomplished has become for the first time in history concrete and real. This possibility was created by the work of Marx, by the swelling of the socialist movement; it became sharply illuminated by the Paris Commune. From that point on, the capitalist system became a retrograde system because its sharp edge was no longer turned against an outlived feudal or mercantilist order but against the virtually possible, realizable socialist order. This is not vitiated by the fact that the forces of production continued to develop under mono. cap., although the fact that their most pronounced development under mono. cap. was bought at the cost of devastating wars should never be lost sight of.

All this would have some bearing also on the appraisal of capitalism's impact on the u/d c's. Without in the slightest embellishing the impact of capitalism (or, for that matter, pre-capitalist) penetration and "opening-up" of the now underdeveloped and dependent countries, it can well be said that mono. cap. has also with respect to the u/d c's turned into a more retrograde system than competitive capitalism [comp. cap.] because mono. cap's role in blocking, preventing, distorting the u/d c's development is particularly pronounced. It strangles the realization of their potentialities very much more than competitive capitalism did. Thus, far from saying that mono. cap. constitutes an improvement for the u/d c's, I am trying to say that regardless of whether they do or do not receive railroads or electric power stations which they may not have received (or received to a lesser extent under comp. cap.) mono. cap. constitutes also in the u/d world a more reactionary system than pre-monopolistic capitalism simply because now the problems of the u/d world could be solved within one generation given the existing technological possibilities. Stressing this aspect, I think, is at least to some extent the merit of the imperialism theory. It places the accent not so much on the "old-fashioned" despoliation of the colonies and their merciless exploitation for the benefit of the metropolitan capitalists, but the systematic prevention in the u/d c's of a progressive development *that is now possible*. What the U.S. is inflicting now upon Cuba, S. Vietnam, S. Korea, all of Latin America is in many regards worse, more outrageous than what has been done in the days of plain, undisguised robbery and plantation economy.

To come back to what is immediately relevant to the opus: it would seem to me to be justified to say that with the onset of mono. cap., economic theory which continued to justify the capitalist system began to justify the unjustifiable, turned therefore more reactionary than what it was before. To that extent, I would say, Marx's benchmark of 1830 was premature although undoubtedly Nassau Senior & Co were already visible as the harbingers of what was yet to come.[228] This reactionary character of the theory with regard to the system as a whole was combined at the same time with its making progress in *partial* comprehension of capitalist reality. This partial sharpening was going together with rising blindness to the totality of the system, to increasing

[The letter ends at this point in mid-sentence.]

228. English lawyer and economist in Marx's era, classified by Marx as a representative of vulgar political economy because of his rejection of the labor theory of value and a crude utility doctrine, which was to make him a precursor of neoclassical thought.

PAB to Beatrice (Bd) and Harry Magdoff
   [*This appears to be the last letter PAB wrote before his death four days later.*]

Palo Alto

March 22, 1964

Dear Bd. and Harry,

It was a great joy to hear your voices again — particularly in the cheerless flu-
state that I am in when all pleasures of life become suddenly wholly unattainable.
The head feels as if it were filled with lead, comprehension of what one reads is
barely possible, and one's own thoughts turn incoherent. The only saving grace
is that one *knows* that one makes no sense... It is especially annoying to have to
endure this incapacity between quarters rather than on "company's time" when
it would serve as a faultless excuse for not delivering a few lectures.

As to my plans for the coming acad. year. Right now I am revising earlier
chapters of the Mono. Cap. book. *On the whole* the MS is finished, but there is
still an awful lot of fixing to do, and I am now occupied with my own scribbling,
not yet with what my partner has done. I have set myself an irrevocable deadline
to have the whole mess out of my hands, my mind and my life by the end of July.
In that case I might go for the month of August either to Santa Barbara (Center
for the Study of Democratic Institutions) where I was invited to participate in a
4 weeks' symposium on "Freedom and the Economic Order," or to Mexico City
where the University offered me to teach a seminar on economic development.
The reason for doing one or the other is to pick up a bit of extra money of which
I shall be rather short during the sabbatical when Stanford only pays 50% of
the salary. Chances are that I'll go to S.B., — less work, and also a vacation from
economic development of which I have had now as the physicians say *quantum
satis*. Should the MS be still unfinished, I'll skip both S.B. and Mexico, and stay
here until about the middle of September when Nicky & I shall proceed to N.Y.
en route to Europe.

There the schedule got to be more complex than I originally thought. As
far as the boy is concerned, all is clear: he is enrolled in a school in Lausanne
where proceedings start October 1st, at which time he will be delivered against
receipt. I shall depart for Paris, go for a few weeks to England and to Italy, and
visit peepsquick a few times over weekends. On December 15th (the beginning
of the school's Xmas vacation) Nicky's mother will come to Lausanne, and
we shall go jointly to Moscow to see Nicky's grandfather. Early in January
Elena will take Nicky back to school and fly back home while I shall pay a 2
weeks' visit to Warsaw, Berlin, Prague and Budapest each where the respective
Institutes of Economics have invited me *cum* all expenses paid. After this tour
of People's Democracies and a short visit with Picknick I shall settle down for

3 months in Vienna where the Austrian Institute of Advanced Studies in the Social Sciences (a new, apparently heavily endowed outfit) has offered me an elegantly paid fellowship for that period. This, by the way, is what saves the whole situation, because minus those Austrian $$'s the entire project would be based on quicksand. . . . Then June, July I shall be vacationing from my hard labors (some of it, perhaps, in Dubrovnik), go for August (1965) to Mexico (they told me if this year ain't no good, I should come next year), and come back to my Stanford homestead toward the middle of September to get ready for the ensuing school year. Meanwhile Elena who wants to spend a vacation in Europe will have brought sonny boy home and stuck him into the local Junior High. So here you have the entire plan which looks to me "gorgeous," in fact too good not to produce some hitches. . . .

The key to success is the completion of the MS. Without it, I won't be able to do anything; this thing has been hanging over me so long that it ain't not funny no more. And whether it is any good, is another question, but one which I do not even wish to consider.

During the Europe year I want to do two things: (1) Go over, change and fix a bunch of different articles, reviews, &c. and make them into a book of essays. Leo has expressed his willingness to publish it, and a number of foreign publishers are willing to go along. (2) Work further on a half-done MS of "An Essay on Marx," which I would like to bestow upon an astonished and grateful humanity sometime in 1966. Thereafter I plan not to touch pen or pencil anymore, to dispose of my "tripe-writer" (this is how Nicky used to call the instrument I am using at the moment), and to conclude my days reading novels, listening to records and engaging in *dolce far niente*.

Before that blissful state is reached, however, there is still plenty to do. And one of the things about which I would like to know your opinion is the following: In Italy there is a *very* authoritative journal *Nuovi Argomenti* edited by Alberto Moravia and Alberto Carocci (the former a famous writer, the latter a highly respected lawyer). The editors of that thing asked me whether I would like to edit one special issue devoted to the Negro problem in the U.S. It would also be published as a separate little book in Italy; one could get it easily published here, and — what is most important — in Mexico. I would be most anxious to undertake this assignment because I cannot think of anything that would be more useful at the present time. I could think up an outline and even identify a number of collaborators; it is my impression, however, that unless one offers people some *honoraria* (reasonably substantial) one doesn't get any MS. I once fixed up a Disarmament issue for *The Nation*, and the secret of that deal was that I obtained here from a benevolent lady $1000 to pay the authors involved. Question: could one get from Rabinowitz or someone else a few thousand dollars for that Negro job? I would think that about $3000 would be enough; it would make it possible to pay a normal fee to an author (say $400) and permit to include 7-8 papers of pp. 25 on the average. If you think that it makes sense, I could write either to Victor Rabinowitz or to whomever; or if you feel that it might be better I could ask *Nuovi Argomenti* to write either a letter to me which I could attach or a letter to the source of money. Let me know what you think about the whole biz.

It itches me badly to do something on the Sino-Soviet dispute, but this I must postpone. I must confess that on that matter I do not see eye to eye with *MR* — not so much with regard to their substantive statements as primarily with regard to the overall position. With MR representing no one but its editors, I should have thought that it should not arbitrate and hand down judgments but thoroughly analyze and explain the differences without necessarily "coming out" on one side or the other. . . . But this is a big topic and refers to the entire *MR* recent line which does not fill me with enthusiasm. This *is entre nous*. . . .

Write; it would so good to be able to sit down for a quiet evening and have a chat *cum* cognac.

Love,
　　/s Paul

Leo Lowenthal to Nicholas Baran
　　[*Paul Baran was visiting Leo Lowenthal, the Berkeley sociologist, and longtime friend from student days in Germany, for dinner when he suffered his fatal heart attack. Leo wrote this letter to PAB's son.*]

San Francisco
March 27, 1964

Dear Nicki [*sic*],

Since my wife and I were the last people who were talking with your father, I thought you would like to hear about his last hours during which he was his usual self. But first, I should let you know how very, very sad both my wife and I feel about your father's death and we know how very painful this all must be for you. I had known your father for about 35 years, and I was very fond of him, and during the last few years considered him one of my closest friends whom I will miss terribly.

Before your father became very sick last night he was in a very good mood. He enjoyed food and drink and over the dinner table we had joked about his great love for champagne. Without his knowledge I put a bottle in the icebox, which I had hoped we would drink together before I would have taken him back to the railroad station. Most of our conversation turned around the year in Europe. We talked at great length about the school in Switzerland and he told me how much you looked forward to it and also what kind of difficulties you thought you might encounter. He told us that he would organize his own travels in such a way that he would always be close to Lausanne, and he planned to take frequent plane trips to see you during the period of your stay. He also described his own pleasures he anticipated in visiting England and France and Italy and other countries, and how he was planning to pay another visit to his father. He talked a good deal about his book manuscript. My wife and I were very moved about his great sense of responsibility for what he was doing and for the high standards he had set for himself.

In thinking about this evening, I would say that his last hours were enjoyed by him and that he felt easy and relaxed. When he finally became sick he had some pains but not very violent ones and they didn't last long because very soon he began to close his eyes and was obviously unaware of himself and the world around him. The physician did everything to make him more comfortable and the attendants who took him to the ambulance were very tender and careful with him. I rode with the ambulance and I still saw him for a little while in the hospital as the doctor started treating him. His face was quiet and peaceful and he didn't suffer.

I thought you might like to hear about it so that you know your father went peacefully. Of course this is only of small comfort to us who loved this man who was kind and generous and brilliant and a dedicated friend.

With much love,
/s Leo Lowenthal

CHRONOLOGY

BIBLIOGRAPHY

ACKNOWLEDGMENTS

GLOSSARY OF NAMES

INDEX

Chronology

[Up to Publication of *Monopoly Capital* in 1966.]

PAUL A. BARAN

December 8, 1910   Paul Alexander Baran (PAB) is born in Nikolaev, Ukraine, then part of the Tsarist Empire. On all official documents, PAB's birthdate is August 25, 1909, but he maintained that this was an error, and that his real birthday was December 8, 1910, which is the date he and his family celebrated.

1926   PAB graduates from German Gymnasium in Dresden, where he had moved with his parents in 1921. Returns to USSR, where he enrolls in the Plekhanov (Karl Marx) Institute of Economics at the University of Moscow.

1928–1932   PAB returns to Germany initially as a research assistant for S. M. Dubrovsky, director of the International Agrarian Institute in Moscow, in connection with a project with the Agricultural Academy in Berlin. He enrolls at the University of Berlin while working at the Agricultural Academy. When his research assignment expires he takes up an assistantship at the Institute for Social Research in Frankfurt. In 1929 he severs Communist Party membership in response to Third Period doctrine (which designates social democracy as "social fascism") and joins German Social Democrats as the best way of fighting fascism. Writes for Rudolf Hilferding's *Die Gesellschaft* under the pen name "Alexander Gabriel." Completes his graduate studies and earns Diploma Volkswirt (master's degree in Political Economy) and Dr. Phil. from Friedrich Wilhelm University in Berlin. Dissertation on economic planning under Emil Lederer.

1933–35   Visits Hilferding in February 1933 to discuss the rise of Hitler, a few days before Hilferding is forced to go into hiding. Flees to Paris in May 1933. In 1934 receives a visa to visit his parents in Russia, but his position is in danger as a former Communist, with his friends and associates mostly purged, including Dubrovsky, his main supporter. Departs for Vilna, Poland, where he has relatives.

1935–38   PAB works for his uncles' timber business in Vilna, and eventually
               moves to London as the company's representative.

1939   As Germany occupies Poland PAB moves to the United States
               with the intention of pursuing an academic career in economics.
               Meets Paul Sweezy at Harvard. Enrolls at Harvard as graduate
               student in economics.

1941   PAB receives an M.A. in economics from Harvard. (Although PAB
               had obtained a Ph.D. at the University of Berlin, he felt he needed
               to update and augment both his education and his credentials with
               a degree from Harvard.)

1941–42   PAB accepts research fellowship working on problems of price
               controls at the Brookings Institution.

1942–45   After working briefly at the Office of Price Administration, PAB
               joins the Office of Strategic Services (OSS), working under E. S.
               Mason, and is drafted into the U.S. Army and reassigned to the
               OSS. His final rank is Technical Sergeant.

1945   PAB works for the United States Strategic Bombing Survey
               (USSBS) under the direction of J. K. Galbraith. Following his
               discharge from the Army takes a position in September 1945
               as Deputy Chief of Economic Effects Division of Strategic
               Bombing Survey in Japan. Remains there until spring 1946. (For
               an entertaining account of PAB's stint with the USSBS while on
               assignment in Germany, see J. K. Galbraith's memoir, *A Life in
               Our Times,* 1981.)

1946–49   PAB works briefly at Department of Commerce and then about
               three years at the Federal Reserve Bank in New York. The first
               saved letters between PMS and PAB are from 1949 when PAB
               lived in New York.

1949   After having taught a seminar during summer quarter at Stanford
               as a visiting scholar in 1948, Stanford hires PAB as an associate
               professor.

1950   PAB marries Elena Djatschenko in Palo Alto, CA.

1951   Stanford promotes PAB to full professor with tenure.

1952   PAB's "National Economic Planning" published (see
               bibliography). Elena gives birth to a son, Nicholas Mark Baran, on
               April 16, 1952.

1953   PAB spends fall semester at Oxford University, where he delivered
               a series of lectures forming the basis of his book *Political Economy
               of Growth.*

1954	PAB is divorced from Elena Baran.
1955	PAB is visiting scholar at the Indian Institute of Statistics in Calcutta.
1957	*Political Economy of Growth* is published.
1960	PAB travels to Cuba with PMS and Leo Huberman. Suffers heart attack in December 1960.
1962	PAB makes major trip to Europe, the Soviet Union, and Iran. Second printing of *Political Economy of Growth* with new, extensive preface. Special July–August issue of *Monthly Review* publishes two preliminary chapters of *Monopoly Capital*.
1963	PAB travels to Latin America, with lectures in Mexico, Chile, Argentina, Uruguay, and Brazil.
March 26, 1964	PAB dies at approximately midnight of massive heart attack, which came on while he was dining with his friend Leo Lowenthal in San Francisco.
March 1966	*Monopoly Capital* is published.

PAUL M. SWEEZY

April 10, 1910	Paul Marlor Sweezy (PMS) is born in New York. Father is vice president of the First National Bank of New York, then headed by George F. Baker, a close associate of J.P. Morgan.
1927	PMS graduates from Phillips Exeter Academy.
1928–32	PMS attends Harvard, where he is editor of the *Harvard Crimson* and graduates with a B.A. in economics in 1932.
1932	PMS attends the London School of Economics and studies several months in Vienna.
1933–37	PMS completes his Master's and Ph.D. degrees at Harvard. He is a teaching assistant for Joseph Schumpeter, and his dissertation, "Monopoly and Competition in the English Coal Industry, 1550–1880," is published in 1937 by Harvard University Press and wins the prestigious David A. Wells Prize. He carries out an important study of "Interest Groups in the American Economy" for the New Deal's National Resources Committee—published two years later as appendix to NRC's *The Structure of the American Economy*. Member of League Against Fascism and various Popular Front organizations. Married Maxine Yaple in 1936; divorced during the war.

1938–1942	PMS takes a position as a member of the economics faculty at Harvard. Helps found the Harvard Teachers Union. In 1939 he publishes his seminal article "Demand Under Conditions of Oligopoly" in the *Journal of Political Economy*. Meets Paul Baran that autumn. His lecture notes for a course on the economics of socialism form the basis of his seminal work, *The Theory of Capitalist Development*.
1942–46	PMS takes a leave from his position at Harvard to join the Army as an officer candidate. He is assigned to the Office of Strategic Services. After a year in Washington working under E. S. Mason, he is assigned to the London branch as an economic analyst under Chandler Morse. Becomes editor of OSS's *European Political Report*. PMS is demobilized in 1946 and receives the Bronze Star medal.
1946–49	Receives Social Science Research Council Demobilization Grant. Marries Nancy Adams, whom he had met in Europe, where she too worked in the OSS, in 1944. They had three children, Samuel Everett, Elizabeth (Lybess) MacDougall, and Martha Adams. Despite two years remaining on his contract at Harvard, PMS decides not to return where the prospects of tenure are dimmed by the political situation, and settles in the family home in Wilton, New Hampshire, pursuing research and writing, producing magazine articles and the book *Socialism* as well as most of the essays that eventually would comprise *The Present as History*. The famous Sweezy-Schumpeter debate on economic stagnation and the prospects for socialism takes place at Harvard, March 27, 1947.
May 1949	The first issue of *Monthly Review* is published, co-edited by Leo Huberman and PMS, and includes an article titled "Why Socialism?" by Albert Einstein.
1952	Monthly Review Press founded, publishes I. F. Stone's *Hidden History of the Korean War*.
1954	PMS subpoenaed by attorney general of New Hampshire, investigating "subversive activity" and in particular a lecture delivered by PMS at University of New Hampshire. Sweezy refuses to cooperate, basing his refusal on the First Amendment, is declared in contempt of court and consigned to county jail, released on bail. Case appealed.
1957	U.S. Supreme Court reverses New Hampshire's decision to hold PMS in contempt, upholding academic freedom under the First Amendment; 354 U.S. 234 (1957), *Sweezy v. New Hampshire*.

1960	PMS travels with Leo Huberman to Cuba and makes second trip later that year with Huberman and Paul Baran. *MR*'s 1960 summer issue is entitled *Cuba: The Anatomy of a Revolution*, later published in book form. PMS is divorced from Nancy.
1961	Marries Zirel Druskin Dowd.
1962	Two preliminary chapters of *Monopoly Capital* published in July–August 1962 issue of *Monthly Review*.
March 1966	*Monopoly Capital* is published.

Bibliography

PAUL A. BARAN

I. BOOKS

The Political Economy of Growth. New York: Monthly Review Press, 1957. Third printing with a new Foreword, 1962.

_____ and Paul M. Sweezy, *Monopoly Capital*. New York: Monthly Review Press, 1966.

The Longer View: Essays Toward a Critique of Political Economy. New York: Monthly Review Press, 1969.

II. ARTICLES

"Kryptomarxismus." *Die Gesellschaft* 9 (1932): 415–28 (under pseudonym Alexander Gabriel).

"New Trends in Russian Economic Thinking?" *American Economic Review* 34 (December 1944): 862–71.

"Professor Despres on 'Effects of Strategic Bombing on the German War Economy.'" With J. K. Galbraith. *Review of Economic Statistics* 39 (May 1947): 132–34.

"National Income and Product of the USSR in 1940." *Review of Economic Statistics* 39 (November 1947): 226–34.

"Currency Reform in the USSR." *Harvard Business Review* (March 1948): 194–206.

"Economic Development of Backward Areas." *Monthly Review* 3 (August 1951): 128–32. (Reprint of a talk before American Economic Association annual meeting, 1950. "Economic Progress: General Considerations," in *Papers and Proceedings of 63rd Annual Meeting*.)

"On the Political Economy of Backwardness." *Manchester School* 20 (January 1952): 66–84. (Reprinted in *The Economics of Under-Development*. Edited by Agarwala and Singh. New York: Oxford University Press. 1963. Translated into French, Spanish, Japanese, German, and Turkish; reprinted in *The Longer View*, op. cit.)

"After Rearmament What?" *The Nation* 175 (November 29, 1952): 483–85.

"The Rich Got Richer." *The Nation* 176 (January 17, 1953): 45–47.

"Economic Progress and Economic Surplus." *Science and Society* 17 (Fall 1953): 289–317. (Reprinted in *The Longer View*, op. cit.)

"On Soviet Themes." *Monthly Review* 8 (July–August 1956): 84–91. (Reprinted in
    The Longer View, op. cit.)
"The Coming Depression." *The Nation* 185 (December 21, 1957): 467–470.
"Crisis of Marxism?" *Monthly Review* 10 (October 1958): 224–234.
"On the Nature of Marxism." *Monthly Review* 10 (November 1958): 259–268.
        (Reprinted in *The Longer View*, op. cit., and includes "Crisis of Marxism")
"On the Evolution of the Economic Surplus." *El Trimestre Economico*, (October–
    December 1958).
"The Choice Before Us." *The Nation* 188 (March 28, 1959): 265–67.
"A Reply (to Joseph R. Starobin and Stanley Moore). *Monthly Review* 11 (September
    1959): 143–48.
"Marxism and Psychoanalysis." *Monthly Review* 11 (October 1959): 186–200.
    (Reprinted in *The Longer View*, op. cit.)
"Reflections on the Cuban Revolution." *Monthly Review* 12 (January 1961): 459–70;
        and 13 (February 1961): 518–29. (Reprinted in *The Longer View*, op. cit.)
"The Commitment of the Intellectual." *Monthly Review* 13 (May 1961): 8–18.
    (Reprinted in *The Longer View*, op. cit.)
"Cuba Invaded." *Monthly Review* 13 (July–August 1961): 84–91. (Transcript of
    KPFA broadcast, April 21, 1961.)
"A Few Thoughts on the Great Debate." *Monthly Review* 14 (May 1962): 34–45.
    (Reprinted in *The Longer View*, op. cit.)
"Monopoly Capital." With Paul M. Sweezy. *Monthly Review* 14 (July-August 1962):
    131–224.
"Rejoinder" (to Anatoly Butenko). With Paul M. Sweezy. *Monthly Review* 14 (April
    1963): 669–78.
"A Letter to W. H. Ferry." *Monthly Review* 15 (June 1963): 103–7.
"Theses on Advertising." With Paul M. Sweezy. *Science and Society* 28 (Winter
    1964): 20–30. (Also in *El Trimestre Economico*, July-September 1963;
    reprinted in *The Longer View*, op. cit.)
"Some Theoretical Implications." With Paul M. Sweezy, posthumously published
    draft chapter to *Monopoly Capital*. *Monthly Review* 64 (July-August 2012):
    24–59.
"The Quality of Monopoly Capitalist Society: Culture and Communications."
    With Paul M. Sweezy, posthumously published draft chapter to *Monopoly
    Capital*. *Monthly Review* 65 (July-August 2013): 43–64.

III. ARTICLES UNDER THE PEN NAME "HISTORICUS"

"Not Propaganda or Plotting but History." *Monthly Review* (September 1949):
    149–53.
"Better Smaller but Better." *Monthly Review* 2 (July 1950): 82–86.
"Fascism in America." *Monthly Review* 4 (October 1952): 181–89.
"Rejoinder to Porter." *Monthly Review* 4 (April 1953): 502–4.
"How Shall We Vote?" *Monthly Review* 4 (November 1952): 226–29.

"Dollar Diplomacy — A New Drive." *Monthly Review* 5 (May 1953): 14–22.

IV. PAMPHLETS

Marxism and Psychoanalysis. Monthly Review Pamphlet Series, Number 14. New
  York: Monthly Review Press, 1960. (Reprinted in *The Longer View*, op.
  cit.)
Reflections on the Cuban Revolution. Monthly Review Pamphlet Series, Number 18.
  New York: Monthly Review Press, 1961. (Reprinted in *The Longer View*,
  op. cit.)

V. CONTRIBUTIONS TO COLLABORATIVE WORKS

"Cost Accounting and Price Determination in the Soviet Union." In *Cost Behavior
  and Price Policy*. New York: National Bureau of Economic Research, 1943,
  305–18.
Chapters in *The Effects of Strategic Bombing on the German War Economy*.
  Washington, D.C.: Overall Economic Effects Division of the United States
  Strategic Bombing Survey, 1945.
Chapters in *The Effects of Strategic Bombing on Japan's War Economy*. Washington,
  D.C.: Overall Economic Effects Division of the United States Strategic
  Bombing Survey, 1946.
"The USSR in the World Economy." In *Foreign Economic Policy for the United States*.
  Edited by S. E. Harris. Cambridge, MA: Harvard University Press, 1948.
"National Economic Planning." In *A Survey of Contemporary Economics*. Edited
  by B. F. Haley. Homewood, IL: Richard D. Irwin, Inc., 1952, 355–402.
  (Reprinted in *The Longer View*, op. cit.)
"Reflections on Underconsumption." In *The Allocation of Economic Resources*, by
  Moses Abramovitz and others. Stanford, CA: Stanford University Press,
  1959, 52–64. (Translated into Spanish (*El Trimestre Economico*, July–
  September 1959), and into French (*Economie Appliqué*, 1959). Reprinted
  in *Has Capitalism Changed?* Edited by Shigeto Tsuru. Tokyo: 1961.
  (Reprinted in *The Longer View*, op. cit.)

VI. REVIEWS

Domenevskaya, Olga. *Agrarsozialismus in Sowjet-Russland*. Die Gesellschaft 9
  (1932): 86–90, under the pseudonym Alexander Gabriel.
Olberg, Oda. *Der National Sozialismus*. Die Gesellschaft 9 (1932): 94–95, under the
  pseudonym Alexander Gabriel.
Rabinowitz, Raissa. *Arbeitszeit-und Arbeitslohn-politik in der Sowjetrussischen
  Industrie*. Die Gesellschaft 9 (1932): 273–74, under the pseudonym
  Alexander Gabriel.
Stolper, Gustav. "This Age of Fable: The Political and Economic World We Live In."
  American Economic Review 32 (June 1942): 374–78.

Yugow, A. *Russia's Economic Front for War and Peace: An Appraisal of the Three Five-Year Plans.* Translated by N. I. and M. Stone. *American Economic Review* 32 (June 1942): 366–68.

Baykow, Alexander M. *Soviet Foreign Trade*; Mikhail U. Condoide. *A Study of the Soviet Foreign Trade Monopoly. American Economic Review* 37 (June 1947): 470–73.

Schwartz, Harry. *Russia's Postwar Economy. American Economic Review* 38 (June 1948): 410–11.

Dobb, Maurice. *Soviet Economic Development Since 1917. Review of Economic Statistics* 32 (May 1950): 186–87.

Lyashchenko, Peter I. *History of the National Economy of Russia to the 1917 Revolution. Journal of Political Economy* 59 (February 1951): 85–86.

Taylor, J. *The Economic Development of Poland, 1919–1950. Journal of Political Economy* 60 (October 1952), 450. Also, "Reply and Rejoinder to Review." *Journal of Political Economy* 61 (October 1953): 447–48.

Rostow, W.W. *The Process of Economic Growth. American Economic Review* 42 (December 1952): 921–23.

Morf, Otto. *Das Verhaeltnis von Wirtschaftstheorie und Wirtschaftsgeschichte bei Karl Marx. Journal of Political Economy* 61 (February 1953): 81–82.

Bergson, Abram. *Soviet National Income and Product in 1937. Econometrica* 22 (April 1954): 251–52.

Veblen, Thorstein. *The Theory of the Leisure Class. Monthly Review* 9 (July-August 1957): 83–91.

Meier, Richard L. *Science and Economic Development: New Patterns of Living. American Economic Review* 47 (December 1957): 1019–21.

Gillman, Joseph M. *The Falling Rate of Profit: Marx's Law and Its Significance to Twentieth-Century Capitalism. American Economic Review* 49 (December 1959): 1082–83.

Rostow, W.W. *The Stages of Economic Growth. Kyklos* 14 (1961): 234–42. With E. J. Hobsbawm.

Robinson, Joan. *Economic Philosophy. American Economic Review* 53 (June 1963): 455–58.

Friedman, Milton. *Capitalism and Freedom. Journal of Political Economy* 71 (December 1963). Reprinted in *Monthly Review* 42/6 (November 1990).

PAUL M. SWEEZY

NOTE: This select bibliography goes up to only 1966 (the date of publication of *Monopoly Capital*), and includes only a small portion of the Reviews of the Month that Sweezy wrote with Leo Huberman for *Monthly Review* prior to that date. Many other works by him are excluded. No attempt, therefore, has been made to encompass all of Sweezy's voluminous writings. A complete bibliography of his works has yet to be compiled.

I. BOOKS

Monopoly and Competition in the English Coal Trade, 1550–1850. Cambridge, MA: Harvard University Press, 1938.

The Theory of Capitalist Development: Principles of Marxian Political Economy. New York: Oxford University Press, 1942 (repr.: New York: Monthly Review Press, 1956).

Karl Marx and the Close of His System by Eugen von Böhm-Bawerk, and *Criticism of Marx* by Rudolf Hilferding. Edited by Paul M. Sweezy. New York: Augustus M. Kelley, 1949. (Includes "On the Correction of Marx's Fundamental Theoretical Construction in the Third Volume of Capital," by Ladislaus von Bortkiewicz, translated by Paul M. Sweezy.)

Socialism. New York: McGraw-Hill, 1949.

F. O. Matthiessen (1902–1950): A Collective Portrait. Edited by Leo Huberman and Paul M. Sweezy. New York: Schuman, 1950. (This also appears as the October 1950 issue of *Monthly Review.*)

Imperialism and Social Classes by Joseph Schumpeter. Edited and with an introduction by Paul M. Sweezy. New York: Augustus M. Kelley, 1951.

Karl Marx and the Close of His System, by Eugen von Bohm-Bawerk, and *Bohm Bawerk's Criticism of Marx,* by Rudolph Hilferding. Edited and with an introduction by Paul M. Sweezy. Clifton, NJ: A. M. Kelley, 1951.

Principles of Communism by Frederick Engels. A new translation by Paul M. Sweezy. New York: Monthly Review Press, 1952.

The Present as History. New York: Monthly Review Press, 1953.

The Transition from Feudalism to Capitalism: A Symposium by Paul M. Sweezy et al. Introduction by Rodney Hilton. New York: Science and Society, 1954.

State of New Hampshire, Louis C. Wyman vs. Paul M. M. Sweezy, Bill of Expectations. Tilton, NH: Howell (1955?).

Cuba: Anatomy of a Revolution by Leo Huberman and Paul M. Sweezy. New York: Monthly Review Press, 1960.

Regis Debray and the Latin American Revolution: A Collection of Essays. Edited by Leo Huberman and Paul M. Sweezy. New York: Monthly Review Press, 1960.

Paul A. Baran: A Collective Portrait. Edited by Leo Huberman and Paul M. Sweezy. New York: Monthly Review Press, 1965.

Monopoly Capital by Paul A. Baran and Paul M. Sweezy. New York and London:
    Monthly Review Press, 1966.

II. REPORTS

Paul M. Sweezy. "Interest Groups in the American Economy." In National Resource
    Committee, *The Structure of the American Economy*, Part I, App. 13.
    Washington D.C.: 1939. Reprinted in Sweezy, *The Present as History*. New
    York: Monthly Review Press, 1953.
Franz Neumann and Paul M. Sweezy. "Speer's Appointment as Director of the
    German Economy," Report to Office of Strategic Services, September
    13, 1943. Reprinted in Franz Neumann, Herbert Marcuse, and Otto
    Kirchheimer, *Secret Reports on Nazi Germany*. Princeton: Princeton
    University Press, 2013, 48–60.
Paul M. Sweezy (published anonymously). *The Scientific-Industrial Revolution*. New
    York: Model, Roland, and Stone/Twentieth Century Press, 1957.

III. ARTICLES

"A Note on Relative Shares." *Review of Economic Studies* (October 1933).
"Economics and the Crisis of Capitalism." *Economic Forum* (1935).
"The Definition of Monopoly." *Quarterly Journal of Economics* (February 1937).
"Wage Policies: Discussion." *American Economic Review* 28 (March 1938):
    156–57.
"Wage Policies and Investment." *American Economic Review* Supplement (March
    1938).
"Expectation and the Scope of Economics." *Review of Economic Studies* (June
    1938).
"The Thinness of the Stock Market." *American Economic Review* 28 (December
    1938): 747–48.
"Demand Under Conditions of Oligopoly." *Journal of Political Economy* 47 (August
    1939) 568–73.
"A Public Investment Program." *American Planning and Civic Association* (1939).
"Government Spending: Its Tasks and Limits" (Discussion). *Social Research* (May
    1939).
"Is Further Debt Financing Sound?" (Symposium). The *Business Bulletin* (May
    1939).
"Power of the Purse." *New Republic* 98 (February 8, 1939): 7–8.
"Public Work as an Aid to Private Investment." *The American City* (July 1939).
"Marx on the Significance of the Corporation." *Science and Society* 3 (Spring 1939):
    238–41.
"The Decline of the Investment Banker." *Antioch Review* 1/1 (1941): 63–68.
"The Illusion of the Managerial Society." *Science and Society* 6 (Summer 1942):
    1–23.

"An Economist's View of India." *The Harvard Guardian* (November 1942).

"Rationing and the War Economy." *Science and" Society* 7 (Spring 1943): 64–71.

"Rationing and the War Society." *Science and Society* (Winter 1943).

"Has Colonialism a Future?" With Lewis S. Feuer. *New Republic* 115 (November 25, 1946): 687–88.

"Professor Schumpeter's Theory of Innovation." *Review of Economic Statistics* 25 (February 1946): 93–96.

"John Maynard Keynes." *Science and Society* 10 (Fall 1946): 398–405.

"Marxian and Orthodox Economics." *Science and Society* 11 (Fall 1947): 225–33.

"Origins of Present Day Socialism." In *Centenary of Marxism,* ed. Samuel Berstein (New York: Science and Society, 1948), 65–81.

"The Communist Manifesto after 100 Years." With Leo Huberman. *Monthly Review* 1/ 4 (August 1949): 102–20. This article was later published in Karl Marx and Friedrich Engels, *The Communist Manifesto* (New York: Monthly Review Press, 1964).

"The German Problem." *Monthly Review* 1/2 (June 1949): 37–43.

"The Devaluation of the Pound." *Monthly Review* 1/6 (November 1949): 198–206.

"Is the Marshall Plan an Instrument of Peace?" *Monthly Review* (July 1949).

"Recent Developments in American Capitalism." *Monthly Review* 1/1 (May 1949): 16–23.

"Where We Stand." With Leo Huberman. *Monthly Review* l/1 (May 1949): 1–2.

"The American Economy and the Threat of War." *Monthly Review* 2/6 (November 1950): 336.

"Capitalism and Race Relations." *Monthly Review* 2/2 (June 1950): 49.

"The Transition from Feudalism to Capitalism." *Science and Society* 14 (Summer 1950): 134–57.

"The Varga Controversy: A Reply to Professor Domar." *American Economic Review* 40 (December 1950): 898–99.

"Cooperation on the Left." With Leo Huberman. *Monthly Review* 1/10 (March 1950): 334–44.

"Labor and Political Activities." (On F. O. Mathiessen) *Monthly Review* 2/5 (October 1950): 229–43.

"The Varga Controversy: Comment." *American Economic Review* (June 1950): 405–6.

"Duesenberry on Economic Development." *Explorations in Economic History* 3 (February 1951): 182–84.

"Certain Aspects of American Capitalism." *Monthly Review* 3/6 (November 1951): 220–24.

"The American Ruling Class." Part I. *Monthly Review* 3/1 (May 1951): 10–17.

"Socialism and the Overpopulation Bogey." *Monthly Review* (November 1951).

"The American Ruling Class." Part II. *Monthly Review* 3/2 (June 1951): 58–64.

"Schumpeter on Imperialism and Social Classes." In *Schumpeter Social Scientist,* ed. Seymour Harris. Cambridge, MA: Harvard University Press, 1951, 119–24.

"Science, Marxism, and Democracy." In *The Present as History,* 330–37. Also
    appeared in Richard McKeon, ed. *Democracy in a World of Tensions*
    (Chicago: 1951).
"The Influence of Marxian Economics on American Thought and Practice." In
    Socialism and American Life, ed. Donald Egbert and Stow Persons.
    Princeton: Princeton University Press, 1952.
"How Shall We Vote?" Sweezy et al. *Monthly Review* 4/6 (November 1952): 231–32.
"Fascism and the United States." With Leo Huberman. *Monthly Review* 4/3 (July
    1952): 65–72.
"A Marxist View of Imperialism." *Monthly Review* 4/11 (March 1953): 414–24.
"The Fascist Danger." With Leo Huberman. *Monthly Review* 5/2 (June 1953): 49–58.
"Reflections on Japanese-American Relations." *Monthly Review* 5/5 (October 1953):
    245–50.
"Comments on Professor H. K. Takahashi's 'Transition from Feudalism to
    Capitalism.'" *Science and Society* 17 (1953): 158–64.
"The Roots and Prospects of McCarthyism." With Leo Huberman. *Monthly Review*
    5/9 (January 1954): 417–34.
"Labor and Socialism: A Revealing Incident." *Monthly Review* (May 1954).
"What Every American Should Know about Indo-China." With Leo Huberman.
    Monthly Review 6/2 (June 1954): 49–71.
"The Crisis of McCarthyism." With Leo Huberman. *Monthly Review* 6/9 (January
    1956): 305–11.
"Two Nations: White and Black." With Leo Huberman. *Monthly Review* 8/2 (June
    1956): 33–47.
"After the Twentieth Congress." With Leo Huberman. *Monthly Review* 8/3–4 (July-
    August 1956): 53–83.
"Marxian Socialism." *Monthly Review* 8/6 (November 1956): 227–41.
"What You Should Know about the Suez." With Leo Huberman. *Monthly Review*
    7/5 (October 1956): 1–11. Also published as a separate monograph by
    Monthly Review Press, 1956.
"We'll Vote Socialist." With Leo Huberman. *The Nation* 183 (October 20, 1956):
    322–23.
"Assessing the Damage." With Leo Huberman. *Monthly Review* 8/8 (December
    1956): 257–72. Includes "The Hungarian Tragedy."
"The Theory of Business Enterprise and Absentee Ownership." *Monthly Review* 9/3
    (July–August 1957): 105–11.
"One Year after the Twentieth Congress." (In Japanese) *Chuokoron* (February 1957).
"The Meaning of Little Rock." With Leo Huberman. *Monthly Review* 9/8
    (December 1957): 241–48.
"Poland a Year After." *Monthly Review* 9/8 (January 1958): 289–93.
"The Yugoslav Experiment." *Monthly Review* 9 (March 1958): 362–73.
"The FCC Scandal." With Leo Huberman. *Monthly Review* 9/12 (April 1958):
    401–11.

"Creeping Stagnation." With Leo Huberman. *Monthly Review* 10/2 (June 1958).

'The Condition of the Working Class." *Monthly Review* 10/3 (July–August 1958): 118–26.

"Socialism in Europe East and West." *Monthly Review* 9/9 (February 1958): 328–39.

"Marxism: A Talk to Students." *Monthly Review* 10/5 (October 1958): 219–23.

"Veblen on American Capitalism." In *Thorstein Veblen: A Critical Reappraisal.* Edited by Douglas Dowd. Ithaca, NY: Cornell University Press, 1958, 177–97.

"Veblen's Critique of the American Economy." *American Economic Review* 48 (May 1958): 21–29.

"What Is Socialism?" In *Toward a Socialist America.* Edited by H. Alfred. New York: Peace Publishers, 1958, 94–105.

"Power Blocks to a Peace Economy." *The Nation* 188 (March 28, 1959): 275–78.

"The Dilemma of Inflation." *The Nation* 188 (March 28, 1959): 200–204.

"*Sweezy vs. the State of New Hampshire.*" In Paul Warren, *Public Papers of Chief Justice Earl Warren.* Edited by Henry Christman. New York: Greenwood, 1959, 175–190.

"Theories of the New Capitalism." *Monthly Review* 10/3 (July-August 1959): 65–75.

"Economic Plannng." *Monthly Review* 12/1 (May 1960): 7–17.

"A Contribution to the Critique of American Society." *Monthly Review* (March 1961).

"The Resumption of Testing." *Monthly Review* 13/5 (October 1961): 244–47.

"The Frankenstein Monster." With Leo Huberman. *Monthly Review* 13/7 (November 1961): 289–98.

"The 22nd Congress and International Socialism." *Monthly Review* 14/1 (May 1962): 45–53.

"A Great American." *Monthly Review* 14/2 (June 1962): 74–80.

"Monopoly Capital: Two Chapters in the American Economic and Social Order." With Paul Baran. *Monthly Review* 14/3 (July-August 1962): entire issue.

"The Cuban Crisis in Perspective." With Leo Huberman. *Monthly Review* 14/8 (December 1962): 401–13.

"Rejoinder." (To Anatoly Butenko.) With Paul Baran. *Monthly Review* 14/11 (April 1963): 669–78.

"The Split in the Capitalist World." With Leo Huberman. *Monthly Review* 14/12 (entire issue) (April-May 1963): 641–55.

"The Split in the Socialist World." With Leo Huberman. *Monthly Review* 15/1 (May 1963): 1–20.

"Communism as an Ideal." *Monthly Review* 15/5 (October 1963): 329–40.

"Paul A. Baran." *Monthly Review* 16/1 (May 1964): 25–26.

"The Theory of U.S. Foreign Policy." With Leo Huberman. *Monthly Review* 12/4 (September 1964).

"Theses on Advertising." With Paul Baran. *Science and Society* 20 (Spring 1964): 20–30.

"Kennedy: The Man and the President." *Monthly Review* (January 1964).

"Paul A. Baran: A Personal Memoir." *Monthly Review* 16/10 (March 1965): 28–62.

"Gert and MR." *Monthly Review* 17/6 (November 1965): 54–57. (Note: "Gert" is
    Gertrude Huberman).
"Notes on the Theory of Imperialism." With Paul Baran. *Monthly Review* 17/10
    (March 1966): 15–33.

IV. REVIEWS

Mises, Ludwig von. *Socialism*. London: Jonathan Cape 1972. *Science and Society*
    (Winter 1938).
Strachey, John. *Theory and Practice of Socialism*. New York: Random House, 1936.
    The Nation, December 5, 1936.
Mitchell, Broadus. *The World's Wealth*. *The Nation*, October 30, 1937.
Crobaugh, Mervyn. *Economics for Everybody*. New Jersey: William Morrow, 1937.
    The Nation, March 26, 1938.
Scherman, Harry. *The Promises Men Live By*. New York: Random House, 1938. *The
    Nation*, March 26, 1938.
Hobson, J. A. *Confessions of an Economic Heretic*. *The Nation*, August 27, 1938.
Mason, A. T. *The Brandeis Way*. Princeton: Princeton University Press, 1938.
    Harvard Law Review,. April 1939.
Ezekiel, Mordecai. *Jobs for All*. New York: Knopf, 1939. *The New Republic,* April 19,
    1939.
Bingham, Alfred. *Man's Estate*. New York: W.W. Norton, 1939. *The Boston
    Transcript,* July 22, 1939.
Nock, Albert Jay. *Henry George*. New York: William Morrow, 1939. *The Nation,*
    October 28, 1939.
Lerner, Max. *Ideas Are Weapons*. New York: Viking Press, 1939. *The Nation,*
    December 2, 1939.
Schumpeter, J. A. *Business Cycle*. *The Nation*, February 3, 1940.
Thurman, Arnold. *The Bottlenecks of Business,* New York: Reynal & Hitchcock,
    1940. *Harvard Law Review,* December 1940.
McIver, R. M. *Leviathan and the People*. Louisiana State Univ. Press, 1939. *Harvard
    Law Review,* December 1940.
Hacker, Louis. *The Triumph of Capitalism*. New York: Simon and Schuster, 1940. "A
    Marxist on American History." *The New Republic* 103, October 21, 1941.
Holden, A. C. *Money in Motion;* and Warren B. Robert, *The Search for Financial
    Security*. New York: Harper & Bro., 1940. *The Nation,* February 15, 1941.
Myers, Margaret. *Monetary Proposals for Social Reform*. New York: Columbia
    University Press, 1940. *The Nation,* June 5, 1941.
Neumann, Franz. *Behemoth: The Structure and Practice of National Socialism*. New
    York: Oxford University Press, 1942. "National Socialism." In *The Present
    as History*, 233–41.
Lenin, V. I. *Collected Works Vol. XIX*. *American Economic Review,* September 1942.
Hayek, Fredrich August von. *The Road to Serfdom*. Chicago: University of Chicago
    Press, 1944.

"Hayek's Road to Serfdom." In *The Present as History*, 283–90. (Originally
    appeared in *Left News*, organ of the Left Book Club, September 1944).
Huberman, Leo. *The Truth About Unions*. New York: Pamphlet Press, 1946.
    "Unions Now." *The New Republic*, April 1, 1946.
Stratchey, John. *Socialism Looks Forward*. New York: Philosophical Library, 1944.
    Annals of the American Academy, March 1946.
Bach, Julian Jr. *America's Germany: An Account of the Occupation*. New York:
    Random House, 1946. *The New Republic* April 22, 1946. (This review also
    includes Padover; see below.)
Baykov, Alexander. *The Development of the Soviet Economic System*. New York:
    Macmillan, 1946. *The New Republic*, July 1, 1946.
Brinton, Crane. *The United States and Britain*. Cambridge, MA: Harvard University
    Press, 1946. *The New Republic*, July 1946.
Toynbee, Arnold Joseph. *A Study of History*. New York: Oxford University Press,
    1939. "Sign of the Times." *The Nation*, October 19, 1946.
Timasheff, Nicholas S. *The Great Retreat: The Growth and Decline of Communism
    in Russia*. New York: Dutton, 1946. "Blueprint and Reality." *The New
    Republic*, March 18, 1946.
Veblen, Thorstein. *An Inquiry into the Nature of Peace and the Terms of Its
    Perpetuation*. New York: Viking Press, 1946. "Veblen: A Cautionary View."
    The New Republic, February 25, 1946.
Padover, Saul. *Experiment in Germany: The Story of an American Intelligence
    Officer*. New York: Duell, Sloan and Pearce, 1946. *The New Republic*, April
    22, 1946. (See Bach above.)
Gray, Alexander. *The Socialist Tradition: Moses to Lenin*. London and New York:
    Longmans Green, 1947. *Journal of Political Economy* 55, October 1947.
Madison, Charles. *Critics and Crusaders: A Century of American Protest*. New York:
    Holt, 1947. *American Economic Review* 37, December 1947. (Also appears
    in *The Present as History* as "Critics and Crusaders," 197–201.)
Lurie, Samuel. *Private Investment in a Controlled Economy: Germany 1933–1939*.
    New York: Columbia University Press, 1947. *Journal of Political Economy*
    56, April 1948.
Debs, Eugene V. *Writings and Speeches of Eugene V. Debs*. With an introductory
    essay by Arthur Schlesinger Jr. New York: Hermitage Press, 1948. "Socialist
    Humanitarianism." *Journal of Political Economy* 56, December 1948.
Huberman Leo. *We The People*. New York: Harper and Bro., 1947. *Science and
    Sociology*, Fall 1948.
Bober M. M. *Karl Marx's Interpretation of History*, 2nd ed. *Journal of Political
    Economy*, June 1949.
Baykov, Alexander. *Soviet Foreign Trade;* and M. V Condoide. *Russian-American
    Trade*. *Review of Economic and Statistics*, February 1948.
Shaw, G. Bernard et al. *Famous Fabian Essays*. New York: Macmillan, 1948. *Journal
    of Political Economy* 57, June 1949.

Cox, Oliver Cromwell. *Caste Class and Race.* New York: Doubleday, 1948. *Monthly Review,* June 1950.

Luxemburg, Rosa. "Rosa Luxemburg and the Theory of Capitalism." In *The Present as History* 291–94. (Also appeared in the *New Statesman and Nation,* June 2, 1951.)

Wright, David McCord. *Capitalism.* New York: McGraw Hill, 1951. *Annals of the American Academy,* May 1951.

Bonner and Burns, eds. *Theories of Surplus Value* by Karl Marx. *New Statesman and Nation,* March 8, 1952.

Ulam, Adam. *Philosophical Foundations of English Socialism.* Cambridge, MA: Harvard University Press, 1951. *Journal of Political Economy* 60, February 1952.

Schwartz, Benjamin. *Chinese Communism and the Rise of Mao.* Cambridge, MA: Harvard University Press, 1951. *Journal of Political Economy* 60, April 1952.

Crossman, R. H. S., C. A. R. Crossland, Roy Jenkins et al. *New Fabian Essays.* New York: Praeger, 1952. *Journal of Political Economy* 61, June 1953.

Hallgarten, George. *Imperialismus vor 1914.* Munich: Verlag C. H. Beck, 1951. 2 vols. "Three Works on Imperialism." *Journal of Economic History* 13, 1953.

Pigou, A. C. *Socialism Versus Capitalism.* New York: Macmillan, 1937. "Pigou and the Case for Socialism." *The Present as History,* 263–73.

Lange, Oscar, and Fred M. Taylor. *On the Economic Theory of Socialism.* Minneapolis: University of Minnesota Press, 1938. "Strategy for Socialism." *The Present as History,* 338–40.

Luxemburg, Rosa. *The Accumulation of Capital.* New Haven: Yale University Press, 1951. *Journal of Economic History* 13, 1953. (See also Hallgarten.)

Sternberg, Fritz. *Capitalism and Socialism on Trial.* New York: John Day, 1951. *Journal of Economic History* 13, 1953. (See also Hallgarten.)

Crossman, R. H. S., ed. *New Fabian Essays.* London: Turnstile Press, 1952. *Journal of Political Economy,* June 1953.

Gay, Peter. *The Dilemma of Democratic Socialism: Eduard Bernstein's Challenge to Marx.* New York: Columbia University Press, 1952. *American Economic Review,* September 1953.

Starobin, Joseph. *From Paris to Peking.* New York: Cameron Assoc., 1955. "From Paris to Peking in New York." *Monthly Review,* March 1956.

Mills, C. Wright. *The Power Elite.* London and New York: Oxford University Press, 1956. "Power Elite or Ruling Class?" *Monthly Review,* September 1956.

Cole, G. D. H. *The History of Socialist Thought.* 3 vols. New York: St. Martin's Press, 1953. "Economic Systems." *American Economic Review* 50, December 1957.

Cole, G. D. H. *The History of Socialist Thought.* 4 vols. New York: St. Martin's Press, 1958. "Economic Systems." *American Economic Review* 50, March 1960.

Acknowledgments

We would like to thank Nick's wife, Esther Baran, for her diligent assistance in retyping many of the letters. We would also like to thank Dr. Jamil Jonna and Dr. Ryan Wishart, both then graduate students at the University of Oregon in 2012, during which time they helped scan hundreds of pages of PAB and PMS's papers into digital format. Finally, we would like to thank Martin Paddio for his tireless efforts in support of this project.

About the Editors

NICHOLAS BARAN is the son of Paul A. Baran. He is an attorney and former computer technology journalist and writer. His article, "The Privatization of Telecommunications" appeared in the July-August 1996 issue of *Monthly Review*. He is the author of *Inside the Information Superhighway* (1995).

JOHN BELLAMY FOSTER is editor of *Monthly Review* and professor of sociology at the University of Oregon. He is the author of *The Theory of Monopoly Capitalism* (New York: Monthly Review Press, 2014).

Glossary of Names

Abramovitz, Moses (1912–2000): Moses Abramovitz was an economics professor at Stanford, a good friend of PAB, and chairman of the department during PAB's travails with the Stanford administration over his political views.

Acton, H.B. (1908–1974): Harry Burrows Acton, British philosopher and critic of Marxism.

Adelman, Morris (1918–2014): professor of economics at MIT, specialized in economics of petroleum and other energy sources.

Adenauer, Konrad (1876–1967): Chancellor of West Germany 1949–1963.

Adler, Solomon (1909–1994): "Shlomo" Adler was an economist who spent the latter part of his career in China; a good friend of PAB and PMS.

Alexander, Sidney S. (1916–2005), professor of economics and management at MIT Sloan School of Management. Famous for the "pig principle": if you like something, more is better.

Allende, Salvador (1908–1973): president of Chile 1970 to 1973; died in a coup d'état in 1973. PMS met him on several occasions and was present at his inauguration.

Arevalo, Juan José (1904–1990): president of Guatemala 1944–1951 and author of *The Shark and the Sardines*.

Arrow, Kenneth (1921–2017): professor of economics and operations research at Stanford during PAB's tenure. Won the Sveriges Riksbank Prize in Economic Sciences in Memory of Alfred Nobel in 1972 (shared with John Hicks).

Arzumanian, Anushavan (years unknown): Soviet economist and close associate of Anastas Mikoyan, was appointed director of the Soviet Institute of World Economy and International Relations in 1956.

Attlee, Clement (1883–1967): British politician, prime minister of the U.K. from 1945 to 1951.

Baldwin, James (1924–1987): African-American writer and social critic, his best known books include *Go Tell It on the Mountain* and *The Fire Next Time*.

Bator, Francis M. (1925–): economist, professor emeritus at Harvard's Kennedy School of Political Economy.

Bauer, Bruno (1809–1882): German philosopher and historian.

Beard, Charles (1874–1948): American historian, author of *An Economic Interpretation of the U.S. Constitution* (1913).

Benson, Lee (1922–2012): left wing historian at Wayne State University, author of *The Concept of Jacksonian Democracy* (1961).

Berle, Adolf A. (1895–1971): lawyer/ diplomat, co-authored with Gardner Means *The Modern Corporation and Private Property* (1932).

Bernal, J.D. (1901–1971): British physicist and socialist; author of *Science in History* (1954).

Bernstein, Eduard (1850–1932): author of *The Prerequisites for Socialism* (1899).

Bethe, Hans (1906–2005): nuclear physicist at Cornell University.

Bettelheim, Charles (1913–2006): French economist and historian, author of *India Independent*, first published in 1962, American edition in 1968. He was well acquainted with PMS and PAB.

Bismarck, Otto von (1815–1898): Minister President of Prussia (1862–1890) and Chancellor of Germany (1871).

Bittelman, Alexander (1890–1982): founding member of the American Communist Party and longtime editor of the party's newspaper *The Communist*.

Blum, Léon (1872–1950): French socialist politician, three-time prime minister of France.

Blumin, I. (details unknown): Soviet economist from the late 1940s, early 1950s.

Böhm Bawerk, Eugen von (1851–1914): Austrian economist, intermittently Austrian minister of finance 1895–1904. PMS edited Eugen von Böhm Bawerk, *Karl Marx and the Close of His System/* Rudolf Hilferding, *Criticism of Marx* (Augustus M. Kelley, 1949).

Boggs, James (1919–1993): political activist and author of *MR*'s 1963 Summer issue, "The American Revolution: Pages from a Negro Worker's Notebook." *MR*, July-August 1963.

Bortkiewicz, Ladislaus von (1868– 1931): economics professor at Berlin when PAB was a student there. PMS translated Bortkiewicz's famous essay on the transformation problem into English as an appendix to the edited volume on Böhm Bawerk's and Hilferding's work (see Böhm Bawerk above).

Boulding, Kenneth (1910–1993): economics professor at Iowa State University, University of Michigan, and University of Colorado.

Bourdet, Claude (1909–1996): French politician, active in the French resistance during WWII.

Bowker, Albert (1919–2008): professor

of statistics and academic dean during PAB's tenure at Stanford, and was involved in negotiations between the university administration and PAB regarding his political views. He subsequently served as Chancellor at CUNY and at UC Berkeley.

Brailsford, H.N. (1873–1958): left–wing British journalist.

Brandler, Heinrich (1881–1967): German CP leader in the twenties.

Brecht, Bertolt (1898–1956): German playwright and poet.

Breitscheid, Rudolf (1874–1944): Member of German Social Democratic Party. Colleague of Rudolf Hilferding; died in German concentration camp.

Bridges, Harry (1901–1990): Leader of the International Longshore and Warehouse Union (ILWU).

Bronfenbrenner, Martin (1914–1997): American professor of economics at various universities, finishing his career at Duke University.

Bukharin, Nikolai (1888–1938): Bolshevik revolutionary theorist and politician, executed in Stalin's Great Purge.

Butenko, Anatoly (details unknown), Lecturer in Philosophy at Moscow University. Later became proponent of *Glasnost* under Gorbachev.

Cardenas, Lazaro (1895–1970): general in the Mexican Revolution and later president of Mexico, 1934–1940. Interviewed by Harvey O'Connor for June 1961 issue of *Monthly Review*.

Carocci, Alberto (details unknown):

Italian lawyer, counsel for Olivetti, and co-founder with Alberto Moravia of *Nuovi Argomenti*, the literary magazine, in 1953.

Carr, E.H. (1892–1982): English historian, author of *What Is History?* (1961).

Castro, Fidel (1926–2016): Leader of the Cuban Revolution. He was Prime Minister of Cuba from 1959 to 1976, and President from 1976 to 2008.

Chenery, Hollis (1918–1994): professor of economics at Stanford during PAB's tenure, specialized in international development.

Clark, John Bates (1847–1938): American economist, whose economic views gradually changed from a socialist critique to outright support of capitalism.

Cole, G.D.H. (1889–1959): English historian and economist, and author of *History of Socialist Thought* (multiple volumes).

Cournot, Antoine (1801–1877): French philosopher and mathematician, author of *Recherches sur les Principes Mathematiques de la Théorie des Richesses*, 1838.

Cox, Oliver (1901–1974): Trinidad-born economist and author of *Caste, Class, and Race* (Monthly Review Press, 1959) and *Capitalism as a System* (Monthly Review Press, 1964).

Creamer, Daniel (details unknown): researcher and author of publications at the National Bureau of Economic Research (NBER) in the 1950s and '60s. Fellow of the American Statistical Association. Known for work on capacity utilization. Wrote *Capital and Output Trends in Manufacturing Industries, 1880–1948* (NBER, 1954).

Davis, Arthur K. (1916–2001)): sociology professor and author who taught at Canadian and U.S. colleges in late 1950s and '60s. A frequent contributor to *Monthly Review* in this period, particularly known for his research on Thorstein Veblen. Davis was President of the Canadian Sociology and Anthropology Association in 1975–1976.

de Gaulle, Charles (1890–1970): French general, founder of the fifth republic and France's 18th president.

Dennis, Lawrence (1893–1977): American diplomat and author of *The Coming American Fascism* (Harper & Brothers, 1936).

Di Tella, Torcuato S. (ca. 1925–2016): son of Argentinian industrialist and philanthropist of same name, professor at University of Buenos Aires when PAB was visiting there in 1963, and was expected to replace Gino Germani as the head of the sociology department. Cofounded with his brother the Instituto Di Tella de Estudios Sociales y Artisticos (Torcuato Di Tella Research Center).

Disraeli, Benjamin (1804–1891): British conservative politician and prime minister.

Domar, Evsey (1914–1997): Russianborn economist, who spent large part of career as professor of economics at MIT; known for the Harrod-Domar model in economic growth theory.

Dorfman, Joseph (1904–1991): economics professor at Columbia University and biographer of Thorstein Veblen.

Dorfman, Robert (1916–2002): American professor of economics.

Drucker, Peter (1909–2005): Austrian-born management consultant and author; was a graduate student at University of Frankfurt at the same time as PAB attended the school (1931).

Dühring, Eugen Karl (1833–1921): German philosopher and critic of Marxism.

Dulles, Allen (1893–1969): diplomat and director of CIA under President Eisenhower.

Dulles, John Foster (1888–1959): secretary of state under President Eisenhower.

Durr, Virginia (1903–1999): civil rights activist.

Dutt, R. Palme (1896–1974): member of British Communist Party and author of *Fascism and Social Revolution* (1934).

Einstein, Albert (1879–1955): physicist and author of article "Why Socialism?" in the first issue of *Monthly Review*, May 1949.

Eisenhower, Dwight (1890–1969): 34th President of the United States.

Emerson, Thomas (1907–1991): civil rights attorney who successfully represented PMS in the U.S. Supreme Court case *Sweezy v. New Hampshire* (1957).

Engels, Friedrich (1820–1895): German philosopher and social scientist, and close collaborator of Karl Marx.

Estrin, Samuel (1893–1976): Russian social democrat and Menshevik, who emigrated to Berlin in 1923, and then to Paris in 1933, and the United States in 1939. He worked for the Jewish Labor Committee in New York beginning in 1940 and contributed to *Dissent*.

Fanfani, Amintore (1908–1999): Italian politician and prime minister of Italy.

Feder, Gottfried (1883–1941): German economist and early supporter of the Nazi party.

Feltrinelli, Giangacomo (1926–1972): Italian book publisher and left-wing political activist.

Ferry, W.H. "Ping" (1910–1995): human rights and environmental activist and philanthropist.

Feuer, Lewis (1912–2002): American sociologist.

Fourier, Charles (1772–1837): French philosopher and advocate of utopian socialism.

Frank, Andre Gunder (1929–2005): German–born economist, sociologist, professor, contributor to *Monthly Review*. Author of *Capitalism and Underdevelopment in Latin America* (Monthly Review Press, 1967).

Freud, Sigmund (1856–1939): Austrian neurologist and psychologist, "father of psychoanalysis."

Friedman, Milton (1912–2006): American conservative professor of economics. Winner of the Sveriges Riksbank Prize in Economic Sciences in Memory of Alfred Nobel in 1976.

Fromm, Erich (1900–1980): German sociologist and psychologist associated with the Frankfurt School.

Fuentes, Carlos (1928–2012): Mexican author and proponent of socialism.

Gabriel, Alexander: PAB's pen-name while a graduate student in Germany (1928–1931) and writing for socialist publications such as Rudolf Hilferding's *Die Gesellschaft*.

Galbraith, J.K. (1908–2006): economics professor at Harvard, diplomat, economic adviser to U.S. administrations, author; close friend of PMS and PAB, whom he had met at Harvard and at the U.S. Strategic Bombing Survey, respectively. Baran served under Galbraith's command in the latter.

Garcia Incháustegui, Mario (1924–1977): Cuba's UN Ambassador, who was recalled to Havana in 1962 and removed from his post due to incendiary remarks made at the UN Security Council.

Garlin, Victor (ca. 1935–?): graduate student at Stanford during PAB's tenure, later became professor of economics at Sonoma State University from 1970–2007.

Genovese, Eugene (1930–2012): professor of history, specializing in American South and slavery, with a Marxist perspective.

George, Henry (1839–1897): political economist, author of *Progress and Poverty*, 1879.

Germani, Gino (1911–1979): professor of sociology at the University of Buenos Aires, close collaborator with Torquato S. Di Tella.

Gerth, Hans (1908–1978): German-born American professor of sociology, close friend of C. Wright Mills, dating back to when they were both at the University of Frankfurt in the early 1930s.

Glazier, William (Bill) (ca. 1920–?): administrator at the ILWU and friend of *Monthly Review*.

Goebbels, Joseph (1897–1945): German Nazi Minister of Propaganda.

Gould, Jay Martin (1915–2005): economist and statistician and friend of PMS. Author of *The Technical Elite* (1966).

Guevara, Ernesto (Ché) (1928–1967): Argentinian-born physician, Marxist revolutionary, active in the Cuban Revolution and Revolutionary government. Wrote a statement commending PAB's work for *Monthly Review* at the time of Baran's death.

Haley, Bernard (1898–1993): economics professor at Stanford, department chair in earlier part of PAB's career; knew PAB at Office of Price Administration after WWII.

Hallgarten, George (1901–1975): German historian and author of *Imperialismus vor 1914* (1951). Hallgarten spent time in the U.S., and had met PAB and PMS, expressing interest in setting up a socialist research institute in the U.S. Eventually became a professor at University of North Carolina.

Hansen, Alvin (1887–1975): professor of economics at Harvard, expert in Keynesian economic theory, originator of the concept of secular stagnation.

Harer, Asher: (1913–2004): Labor union activist in San Francisco.

Harrington, Michael (1928–1989): socialist author and political activist. Author of *The Other America: Poverty in the United States* (1962).

Harrod, Roy (1900–1978): English economist and biographer of John Maynard Keynes.

Hawley, Cameron (1905–1969): American novelist who wrote about life in corporate America (e.g. *Executive Suite*, 1952; *Cash McCall*, 1955).

Hayek, Friedrich (1899–1992): Austrian-born British economist mentor of conservative economists such as Milton Friedman. Author of *The Road to Serfdom*, 1944. Winner of the Sveriges Riksbank Prize in Economic Sciences in Memory of Alfred Nobel in 1974 (shared with Gunnar Myrdal).

Hegel, Georg W.F. (1770–1831): German philosopher, whose theories on dialectics, "the truth is the whole" (one of PAB's favorite tenets) strongly influenced Marx and his followers.

Heidegger, Martin (1889–1976): German existentialist philosopher.

Heilbroner, Robert (1919–2005): economist and economic historian, professor at the New School for Social Research; author of *The Worldly Philosophers* (1953). Student of Sweezy at Harvard.

Heisser, Hans (ca. 1915–?): academic at New School of Social Research, New York.

Hemingway, Ernest (1899–1961): American novelist, author of *The Old Man and the Sea* (1952), one of PAB's favorite books.

Herzog, Jesus Silva (1892–1985): Mexican economist; invited both PAB and PMS to lectures and conferences in Mexico.

Hicks, John R. (1904–1989): British economist, winner of Sveriges Riksbank Prize in Economic Sciences in Memory of Alfred Nobel in 1972 (shared with Kenneth Arrow).

Hilferding, Rudolf (1877–1941): Austrian-German economist, editor, and politician, with whom PAB associated in Berlin in 1931–1932. Author of *Finance Capital* (1910). Finance Minister in Weimar Republic. Fled Germany after Hitler's rise. He was captured in France by Vichy police, and killed by the Gestapo.

Hill, Christopher (1912– 2003): British Marxist historian.

Hillman, Sydney (1887–1946): labor leader and key figure in the founding of the CIO.

Historicus: PAB's pen-name for articles written for *Monthly Review* in the early 1950s.

Hobsbawm, Eric (1917–2012): British historian and longtime friend of PAB.

Hobson, John A. (1858–1940): English economist, known for contributions to underconsumption theory and imperialism theory. Author of *Imperialism: A Study* (1902).

Hofstadter, Richard (1916–1970): American historian, author of *The American Political Tradition* (1948).

Hollingshead, August (1907–1990): author of *Elmstown's Youth: The Impact of Social Classes on Adolescents*, New York, 1949.

Horvat, Branko (1928–2003): Croatian economist at the Institute of Economic Sciences in Belgrade, Yugoslavia, in the late 1950s and early 1960s when both PAB and PMS lectured there.

Howard, Norman (ca. 1915–?): PAB's attorney in Palo Alto.

Huberman, Leo (1903–1968): socialist writer and co-founder with PMS of *Monthly Review*. Author of *Man's Worldly Goods* (1936).

Jagan, Cheddi (1918–1997): leader of British Guiana, proponent of Marxism-Leninism, invited PMS and PAB to become economic consultants in British Guiana, which did not materialize.

Kafka, Franz (1883–1924): Czech-born German-speaking author of works such as *The Castle* and *The Metamorphosis*.

Kahn, Richard F. (1905–1989): British economist, close collaborator of Keynes.

Kaldor, Nicholas (1908–1986): Hungarian-born University of Cambridge economist, studied in Berlin at same time as PAB. Known for contributions to economic growth theory and to post-Keynesian economics. Reviewed PAB's *The Political Economy of Growth* (for the *American Economic Review*).

Kalecki, Michał (1899–1970): influential and distinguished Polish economist and close friend of PAB and PMS, who greatly admired his work. Anticipated some of the core concepts associated with Keynes's *General Theory*. Was to introduce much of the theoretical analysis with respect to monopoly, class, and investment trends that underpinned PAB and PMS's *Monopoly Capital*.

Kautsky, Karl (1854–1938): Prague-born Marxist philosopher, editor of *Die Neue Zeit*, a left-wing monthly newspaper. Edited Marx's *Theories of Surplus Value*. Critic of the Bolshevik Revolution and Soviet path to socialism.

Kaysen, Carl (1920–2010): political economist and policy adviser, professor at MIT.

Kelley, Gus (ca. 1910–?): New York book publisher and supporter of *Monthly Review*.

Kennedy, John F. (1917–1963): 35th President of the United States.

Keynes, John Maynard (1983–1946): Leading British economist, fellow of King's College, University of Cambridge. Introduced the Keynesian Revolution in economics in the midst of the Great Depression with his publication of *The General Theory of Employment, Interest, and Money* (1936).

Khruschev, Nikita (1894–1971): Soviet premier from 1958 to 1964.

Koopmans, Tjaling (1910–1985): Mathematician and economist, specialized in econometrics, director of the Cowles Commission (later the Cowles Foundation now based at Yale). Winner of the Sveriges Riksbank Prize in Economic Sciences in Memory of

Alfred Nobel in 1975 (shared with Leonid Vitaliyevich Kantoriovich in the USSR).

Kosambi, Damodar Dharmananda (1907–1966): Indian mathematician and Marxist historian.

Kouri, Raul Roa (ca. 1930–?): Cuban delegate to U.N. in 1959 and son of Cuban foreign minister Raul Roa Garcia (1907–1982).

Kuczynski, Robert Rene (1876–1947): economist, statistician, and demographer.

Kuznets, Simon (1901–1985): economist and statistician and leading figure in the development of national income accounting. Known for "the Kuznets curve" relating income and economic growth, and "Kuznets cycles" or long swings in economic growth. Kuznets won the Sveriges Riksbank Prize in Economic Sciences in Memory of Alfred Nobel in 1971.

Lamb, Helen (1906–1965): economist and historian and a longtime friend of PMS. Her husband Bob Lamb (a *Monthly Review* author) died in 1952 and she subsequently married Sweezy's lifelong friend Corliss Lamont. Lamb's *Studies in India and Vietnam* was published posthumously by Monthly Review Press in 1976.

Lampman, Robert J. (1920–1997): professor of economics at University of Wisconsin, expert on income distribution and economics of health, education, and welfare.

Landau, Saul (1936–2013): journalist

and filmmaker, renowned for documentary films about Latin America and the Middle East.

Lange, Oskar (1904–1965): Leading Polish economist and friend and mentor to PAB. PAB brought with him a letter of introduction written by Lange to PMS on Baran's behalf when he arrived at Harvard in 1939.

LaPiere, Richard (1899–1986): professor of sociology at Stanford.

Lederer, William (1912–2009): author of *The Ugly American* (1958) and *A Nation of Sheep* (1961).

Lenin, V.I. (1870–1924): leader of the Russian Revolution and Marxist theorist. Author of *Imperialism, the Highest Stage of Capitalism* (1916).

Leontiev, W.W. (1906–1999): Russian-born economist and professor of economics at Harvard. Known for his role in developing input-output analysis. He received the Sveriges Riksbank Prize in Economic Sciences in Memory of Alfred Nobel in 1973.

Lerner, Abba P. (1903–1982): Russian-born British economist, known for the Lange-Lerner-Taylor theorem, relating to market socialism.

Levi, Carlo (1902–1975): Italian painter and political activist, author of *Christ Stopped at Eboli* (1945).

Lewis, Arthur (1915–1991): Caribbean-born (Saint Lucia) economist specializing in international development. Won the Sveriges Riksbank Prize in Economic Sciences in Memory of Alfred Nobel in 1979.

Lilienthal, David E. (1899–1981): public administrator, lawyer, and businessman, head of the Tennessee Valley Authority. Author of *Big Business: A New Era* (1953).

Lipinski, Edward (1888–1986): Polish economist and editor of the Lange-Kalecki Festschrift (Jubilee) to which PMS and PAB contributed in 1963.

Lippmann, Walter (1889–1974): American journalist and political commentator, co-founder of the *New Republic* magazine.

Lombardo Toledano, Vicente (1894–1968): Mexican labor party leader and Marxist, close associate of Lazaro Cardenas, co-founder of the Popular Socialist Party (PPS).

London, Ephraim (1912–1990): First Amendment and censorship lawyer, represented Leo Huberman in HUAC hearings in 1962.

Lowenthal, Leo (1900–1993): German-born sociologist associated with the Frankfurt School and longtime friend of PAB from the Institute for Social Research in Frankfurt in the 1930s. PAB died of a heart attack while visiting Lowenthal for dinner in San Francisco in 1964.

Lukács, Georg (1885–1971): Hungarian-born Marxist philosopher, historian, and literary critic. Author of *History and Class Consciousness* (1923).

Luxemburg, Rosa (1871–1919): Polish Marxist theorist, economist, and revolutionary, active in German socialist politics, and author of *The Accumulation of Capital* (1913).

Lynes, Russell (1910–1991): managing editor of *Harper's* magazine.

Macpherson, Crawford Brough (1911–1987): political scientist, professor at University of Toronto. Author of *The Political Theory of Possessive Individualism* (1962).

März, Eduard (1908–1987): Austrian economist and friend of both PAB and PMS.

Magdoff, Harry (1913–2006): economist, socialist intellectual, author, and commentator. Worked in the Roosevelt Administration in the Works Progress Administration, developing productivity statistics, and in the War Production Board, supervising U.S. industry in the war; later special assistant to Henry Wallace. Close friend of PAB and PMS. Became co-editor of *Monthly Review* shortly after the death of Leo Huberman in 1968. Author of *The Age of Imperialism* (Monthly Review Press, 1969).

Maldonado, Raul (ca. 1920–?): Latin American economist involved in the Cuban Revolution.

Marcuse, Herbert (1898–1979): German–born Marxist philosopher and sociologist; close friend of PAB from their days at the Institute for Social Research in Frankfurt in the early 1930s. Author of *Eros and Civilization* (1955) and *One-Dimensional Man* (1964).

Marshall, George (1880–1959): Secretary of State and Secretary of Defense under Truman, after whom the Marshall Plan was named.

Marshall, Alfred (1842–1924): British economist, author of *Principles of Economics* (1890).

Martinet, Gilles (1916–2006): French journalist and left-wing politician, co-founder of the French Unified Socialist Party (PSU).

Marty, André (1886–1956): prominent member of French CP; expelled from party in 1952.

Marx, Karl (1818–1883): German socialist philosopher and economist, author of *The Communist Manifesto* and *Das Kapital*.

Mason, Edward S. (1899–1992): Harvard economist and consultant to U.S. government specialized in international development. Chief economist of the Research and Analysis Branch of the Office of Strategic Services (OSS) in the Second World War, in which PMS served in Britain.

McCarthy, Joseph (1908–1957): U.S. senator from Wisconsin who led the anticommunist witchhunts of the 1950s.

McNamara, Robert (1916–2009): U.S. Secretary of Defense under Presidents Kennedy and Johnson.

McWilliams, Carey (1905–1980): American journalist and lawyer, longtime editor of *The Nation*.

Means, Gardner (1896–1988): Harvard economist, co-authored with Adolf Berle *The Modern Corporation and Private Property* (1932).

Metzler, Lloyd (1913–1980): professor of economics, primarily at University of Chicago.

Mihailovich, Kosta (ca. 1920–?): Serbian economist, member of Serbian Academy of Sciences.

Mikołajczyk, Stanislaw (1901–1966): Prime Minister of the Polish government in exile during World War II, and later Deputy Prime Minister in postwar Poland, before the USSR took political control of Poland.

Mikoyan, Anastas (1895–1978): Soviet statesman, deputy premier under Khruschev, briefly premier of Soviet Union in 1964–65.

Mill, John Stuart (1806–1873): British economist and philosopher, whom PAB greatly admired.

Mills, C. Wright (1916–1962): American sociologist and friend of PMS and Leo Huberman; author of *The Power Elite* (1956) and *White Collar* (1951).

Model, Roland and Stone (MRS): investment banking firm headed by Leo Model (1905–1982). PAB contributed to the firm's monthly newsletter, providing analysis of international economic developments. PMS wrote the anonymous report, *The Scientific–Industrial Revolution* (1957).

Moore, Stanley (1914–1997): Marxist professor of philosophy, close friend of PAB, contributor to *Monthly Review*.

Moravia, Alberto (1907–1990): Italian author and journalist, co-editor of *Nuovi Argomenti*, a literary journal founded in 1953.

Morse, Chandler (1906–1988): professor of economics at Cornell and friend

of PMS. Sweezy's immediate superior in the London branch of the Research and Analysis Branch of the Office of Strategic Services in London during World War II.

Nagy, Imre (1896–1958): Hungarian communist political leader, executed for treason after the Soviet invasion in 1956.

Nasser, Gamal Abdel (1928–1970): president of Egypt from 1956 until his death in 1970.

Nearing, Scott (1883–1983): socialist economist, writer, and political activist who wrote the column "World Events" and other articles in *Monthly Review* from the magazine's inception until 1972.

Neisser, Hans (1895–1975): German-born economist, worked at the Office of Price Administration, where he met PAB, and subsequently taught at The New School for Social Research.

Nenni, Pietro (1891–1980): socialist politician and secretary of the Italian Socialist Party in the 1950s and early '60s.

Nerlove, Marc (1933–): economics professor at Stanford from 1960 to 1965 and specialist in econometrics.

Neumann, Franz (1900–1954): German-Polish-born Marxist theorist and lawyer, associated with the Frankfurt School, close friend of Herbert Marcuse, and knew well PAB and PMS, until his death in an auto accident in Switzerland in 1954. Best known for his classic work *Behemoth: The Structure and Practice of National Socialism* (1942). Herbert

Marcuse subsequently married Neumann's widow, Inge Werner Neumann. Sweezy and Neumann co-authored a 1943 report for the Office of Strategic Services on "Speer's Appointment as Dictator of the German Economy."

Nietzsche, Friedrich (1844–1900): German philosopher, social critic, and prolific author.

Nkrumah, Kwame (1909–1972): leader of Ghana, winner of the Lenin Peace Prize in 1963.

Noyola, Juan (1922–1962): Mexican economist and economic adviser to the Cuban revolutionary government, associate of PMS and PAB, died in plane crash at age of 40.

Nutter, G. Warren (1923–1979): professor of economics at University of Virginia.

O'Connor, Harvey (1897–1987): left-wing newspaper editor and journalist, frequent contributor to *Monthly Review*.

Oppenheimer, Franz (1864–1943): German-Jewish sociologist, physician, author of *Der Staat* ("The State"), (1908).

Ostrovitianov, Konstantin (1892–1969): Soviet economist, prominent Communist Party figure, editor in chief of the journal "*Voprosy Ekonomiki*," (Economic Problems), in which Blumin's critique of Paul Sweezy appeared in 1952.

Owen, Robert (1771–1858): Welsh social reformer and utopian socialist.

Painter, Mary (1920–1991): economist who developed statistical techniques

used to analyze German military capabilities; worked at Federal Reserve Bank at same time as PAB, where they probably met; close friend of James Baldwin.

Panofsky, Wolfgang (1919–2007): physicist at Stanford, one of the developers of the Stanford Linear Accelerator.

Pareto, Vilfredo (1848–1923): Italian engineer, economist, and sociologist, who developed a method of statistical analysis known as a "Pareto distribution."

Patinkin, Don (1922–1995): Israeli-American monetary economist, president of Hebrew University and journalist.

Perloff, Harvey S. (1915–1983): urban planning expert, who wrote numerous books and articles about planning in underdeveloped areas such as Puerto Rico.

Phillips, Joseph D. (ca. 1920–?): economist at the University of Illinois, Urbana, who prepared the Statistical Appendix to *Monopoly Capital*. Author of *Little Business in the American Economy* (1958).

Phillips, R. Hart (1898–1985): *New York Times* correspondent in Cuba before and after the revolution.

Piel, Gerard (1915–2004): publisher of *Scientific American* and close friend of PMS and PAB.

Pigou, Arthur (1877–1959): British economist, professor at Cambridge, specialist in welfare economics and unemployment.

Pilsudski, Josef (1867–1935): Polish

statesman and Chief of State, 1918–1922, leader of Polish Socialist Party.

Pomeroy, William (1916–2009): American writer who contributed articles to *Monthly Review* on the Philippines (1963) and Southeast Asia (1964).

Popper, Karl (1902–1994): Austrian-born philosopher, spent most of his academic career in England. Wrote numerous books on the philosophy of science, political philosophy, historicism, and mathematics.

Qasim, Abd al–Karim (1914–1963): Iraqi general who assumed power in Iraq in 1958 and was overthrown in 1963.

Rabinowitz Foundation: progressive foundation managed, after the death in 1957 of its founder Louis Rabinowitz, by his son Victor Rabinowitz (1911–2007), who was a founding member of the National Lawyers Guild and a prominent civil rights lawyer and friend of *Monthly Review*. The foundation helped finance left-wing and socialist research projects. PAB was among its recipients.

Rackliffe, Jack (1912–1966): editor at the Toronto publisher McClelland and Stewart and freelance editor for *Monthly Review*. Worked on both *Political Economy of Growth* and *Monopoly Capital*. Longtime friend of Paul Sweezy's from their days at Harvard.

Ricardo, David (1772–1823): British economist, author of *On the Principles of Political Economy and Taxation* (1817).

Robinson, Joan (1903–1983): British economist and professor at Cambridge.

Central figure in imperfect competition theory, the Keynesian revolution, and the Cambridge capital debates. Knew well PMS and PAB. Author of *An Essay on Marxian Economics* (1942).

Rosdolsky, Roman (1898–1967): Ukrainian Marxist scholar and political activist, author of *The Making of Marx's Capital*, London (1977), among other works.

Rosenberg, Alfred (1893–1946): Nazi philosopher and ideologue, executed for war crimes in 1946.

Rostow, W.W. (1916–2003): economist and adviser to Lyndon Johnson, author of *The Stages of Economic Growth: A Non-Communist Manifesto* (1960).

Rothschild, Kurt (1914–2010): Austrian economist, colleague of Joseph Steindl, knew PAB and PMS.

Samuelson, Paul (1915–2009): American economist, well-known for his advocacy of the neoclassical synthesis and for his popular college textbook *Economics*; winner of Sveriges Riksbank Prize in Economic Sciences in Memory of Alfred Nobel in 1970.

Saragat, Guiseppe (1898–1988): Italian socialist politician, fifth president of the Italian republic, 1964–1971.

Sartre, Jean-Paul (1905–1980): French philosopher, author, theorist of existentialism, phenomenology, Marxism. Declined the Nobel Prize in Literature in 1964.

Say, Jean-Baptiste (1767–1832): French economist known for Say's Law.

Schlesinger, Arthur Jr. (1917–2007): prominent historian and liberal intellectual, author of *The Age of Roosevelt,* Vol. 1 (1957).

Schumpeter, Joseph (1883–1950): prominent and influential economist, former Austrian finance minister. Later professor at Harvard and PMS's mentor there. Author of *Business Cycles* (1939), *Capitalism, Socialism, and Democracy* (1942).

Scitovsky, Tibor (1910–2002): Hungarian-born professor of economics at Stanford and Berkeley, good friend of PAB. Author of *The Joyless Economy* (1976).

Seers, Dudley (1920–1983): British economist, specialized in economic development.

Senior, Nassau William (1790–1864): English liberal economist, known for developing the "abstinence theory of profit." Wrote *An Outline of the Science of Political Economy* (1836), and published a series of his lectures delivered at Oxford.

Shapiro, Samuel (ca. 1930–?): correspondent who wrote numerous articles for *The Nation* and *The New Republic* on Cuba and Latin America.

Shaw, Edward (1908–1994): economics professor at Stanford, expert in monetary policy, and a vociferous critic of PAB and his views on the Cold War and the Cuban Revolution.

Smith, Adam (1723–1790): British economist known as the "father of classical political economy," author of *The Wealth of Nations* (1776).

Smith, Vernon (1927–): economist and author of *Investment and Production: A Study in the Theory of the Capital-Using Enterprise,* Cambridge, 1961.

Solow, Robert (1924–): economist at MIT known for contributions to economic growth theory; recipient of the Sveriges Riksbank Prize in Economic Sciences in Memory of Alfred Nobel in 1987.

Spengler, Oswald (1880–1936): German historian, known for his book, *The Decline of the West* (*Der Untergang des Abendlandes*) (1918).

Sraffa, Piero (1898–1983): highly respected and influential Italian economist, taught both in Italy and at the University of Cambridge in England; friend of PMS and PAB. Author of *The Production of Commodities by Means of Commodities* (1960).

Srole, Leo (1909–1993): author (et al.) of *Mental Health in the Metropolis: The Midtown Manhattan Study,* New York, 1962.

Saint-Simon, Henri de (1760–1825): French philosopher, influential in development of utopian socialism.

Stalin, Joseph (1878–1953): Soviet general secretary of the Communist Party after the Bolshevik Revolution; consolidated power after the death of Lenin and ruled the Soviet Union until his death in 1953. Author of *Economic Problems of Socialism in the USSR* (1951).

Stanovnik, Janez (1922–): Slovenian economist at the Institute of Social Sciences in Belgrade in the 1960s when PAB and PMS lectured there. Served as

President of Socialist Republic of Slovenia 1988–1990.

Starobin, Joseph (1913–1976): socialist journalist and later professor; author of *American Communism in Crisis, 1953–1957*; *Paris to Peking*; and *Eyewitness in Indo-China*.

Steinbeck, John (1902–1968): American novelist, author of *The Grapes of Wrath* (1939) and other classics.

Steindl, Josef (1912–1993): Austrian economist, worked with Kalecki at the Oxford Institute for Statistics during the Second World War. Author of *Maturity and Stagnation in American Capitalism* (1952), which helped to inspire *Monopoly Capital*.

Sterling, J. Wallace (1906–1985): President of Stanford University during PAB's tenure.

Sternberg, Fritz (1895–1963): German economist, Marxist theorist, politician, author of numerous books.

Stevenson, Adlai (1900–1965): American politician, losing Democratic party candidate for president vs. Dwight Eisenhower in 1952 and 1956, ambassador to the UN under Kennedy.

Stigler, George (1911–1991): American conservative economist of the "Chicago School," recipient of the Sveriges Riksbank Prize in Economic Sciences in Memory of Alfred Nobel in 1982.

Strachey, John (1901–1963): British Labor Party politician and writer of numerous books, including *Contemporary Capitalism* (1956).

Sweezy, Alan (1907–1994): Paul Sweezy's brother and economics professor at Caltech. Known for his writings on secular stagnation in the tradition of Alvin Hansen.

Sylos-Labini, Paolo (1920–2005): Italian economist and friend of PMS and PAB. Author of *Oligopoly and Technical Progress* (1962).

Szulc, Tad (1926–2001): foreign correspondent for *The New York Times*.

Tarnow, Fritz (1880–1951): German Social Democratic trade unionist and member of the Reichstag during the Weimar Republic.

Tarshis, Lorie (1911–1993): economics professor at Stanford and friend of PAB during his tenure.

Thalheimer, August (1884–1948): German Marxist and Communist Party leader in the twenties.

Thorner, Daniel (1915–1974): economist who specialized in agriculture and economics of India.

Tillon, Charles (1897–1993): French politician, member of French CP expelled in 1952 (the "Marty-Tillon affair").

Tinbergen, Jan (1903–1994): Dutch economist, recipient of Sveriges Riksbank Prize in Economic Sciences in Memory of Alfred Nobel in 1969.

Tito, Josip Broz (1892–1980): prime minister and president of Yugoslavia, leader of Yugoslav communist party.

Tobin, James (1918–2002): economics

professor at Yale; served as president of Yale, recipient of Sveriges Riksbank Prize in Economic Sciences in Memory of Alfred Nobel in1981.

Togliatti, Palmiro (1893–1964): leader of Italian communist party, met with PAB and PMS on several occasions.

Trotsky, Leon (1879–1940): a leader in the Russian Revolution, rival of Joseph Stalin, assassinated while in exile in Mexico in 1940. Author of *The History of the Russian Revolution* (1930).

Tshombe, Moise (1919–1969): Congolese pro-Western politician in the 1960s.

Tsuru, Shigeto (1912–2006): Japanese economist and politician, studied at Harvard at same time as PMS, with whom he maintained a close friendship. Wrote the Appendix on Quesnay and Marx's Reproduction Schemes for Sweezy's *The Theory of Capitalist Development* (1942).

Tugan–Baranowski, Mikhail (1865–1919): Russian economist, politician, and academic in the Tsarist era; author of works on value theory, business cycles, Marxian economics.

Van Alstyne, Richard (1900–1983): historian and professor at Chico State University.

Varga, Eugen: (1879–1964): Hungarian Marxist economist. Author of *Two Systems: Socialist Economy and Capitalist Economy* (1939).

Vatuk, Ved Prakash (ca. 1920–?): author of *British Guiana*, MR Press Pamphlet Series, 1963.

Veblen, Thorstein (1857–1929): American economist and sociologist, author of *Theory of the Leisure Class* (1899), and subject of the *Monthly Review* Summer Issue, July-August 1957.

Viner, Jacob (1892–1970): Canadian economist, member of Chicago School of Economics; namesake of the "Viner-Wong Diagram."

Wallich, Henry (1914–1988): economics professor at Yale, member of Council of Economic Advisors under Eisenhower, rotated as a columnist for *Newsweek* with Paul Samuelson and Milton Friedman.

Walras, Leon (1834–1910): French mathematical economist, studied marginal theory of value, developer of general equilibrium theory.

Walsh, J. Raymond (ca. 1910–?): labor organizer and friend of *Monthly Review*.

Warren, Earl (1891–1974): Chief Justice of the U.S. Supreme Court who wrote the majority opinion in *Sweezy vs. New Hampshire*.

Watkins, Myron (1893–1979): economist and professor of economics at New York University.

Webb, Beatrice (1858–1943), and Sydney Webb (1859–1957), married couple who both were socialist economists and co-founders of the London School of Economics, and early members of the Fabian Society.

Winston, Cathy (ca. 1920–?): member of staff at *Monthly Review* in 1950s and 60s.

Wolman, Bill (1927–2011): longtime chief economist at *Business Week*; graduate student in economics at Stanford during PAB's tenure, who wrote the article in *Business Week* about Baran, Huberman, and Sweezy, "Viewing U.S. Economy through a Marxist Glass," April 13, 1963.

Wyman, Louis (1917–2002): attorney general of New Hampshire who initiated the subversion proceedings against PMS after his lecture at the University of New Hampshire in 1953.

Wyrozembski, Z.J. (1907–1979): Polish professor of economics, member of Polish School of Planning and Statistics after World War II.

Yaroshenko, L.D. (ca. 1910–?): Soviet economist who was criticized by Stalin in *Economic Problems of Socialism in the USSR* (1951).

Zagoria, Donald (ca. 1925–?): author of *The Sino-Soviet Conflict 1956–1961*, Princeton, 1962.

Zeitlin, Morris (ca. 1935–?): sociologist and graduate student at Stanford during PAB's tenure, contributor to *Monthly Review*.

Zielinski, Janusz (1931–1979): Polish economist, taught at University of Glasgow, member of editorial board of the journal *Soviet Studies*.

Zorin, Valerian Alexandrovich (1902–1986): Soviet diplomat primarily known for his confrontation with Adlai Stevenson in the UN on October 25, 1962, regarding the missile crisis.

Index